The publisher gratefully acknowledges the generous contribution to this book provided by the Classical Literature Endowment Fund of the University of California Press Foundation, which is supported by a major gift from Joan Palevsky

The University of California Press
gratefully welcomes the contribution
provided by

ENTE CASSA DI RISPARMIO DI FIRENZE

toward the publication of this book

The second volume of the California Lectura Dantis
draws on a wide range of international scholar-critics.
Each contributor presents his or her own reading, in essay form,
of a canto of the *Purgatorio*. The *Inferno* and forthcoming *Paradiso* volumes
follow the same format, providing the long-awaited companion
to the three volumes of Allen Mandelbaum's verse translations,
with facing Italian text, of *The Divine Comedy*.

Lectura Dantis

Lectura Dantis

PURGATORIO

Edited by

ALLEN MANDELBAUM

ANTHONY OLDCORN

CHARLES ROSS

UNIVERSITY OF CALIFORNIA PRESS

Berkeley   Los Angeles   London

The Mountain of Purgatory drawing, by Barry Moser, originally
appeared in the University of California Press's edition of
Allen Mandelbaum's translation of *Purgatorio,* in 1982.

University of California Press, one of the most distinguished
university presses in the United States, enriches lives around the
world by advancing scholarship in the humanities, social sciences,
and natural sciences. Its activities are supported by the UC Press
Foundation and by philanthropic contributions from individuals and
institutions. For more information, visit www.ucpress.edu.

University of California Press
Berkeley and Los Angeles, California

University of California Press, Ltd.
London, England

Library of Congress Cataloging-in-Publication Data

Lectura Dantis : Purgatorio / edited by Allen Mandelbaum, Anthony
Oldcorn, Charles Ross.
    p.   cm.
Includes bibliographical references and index.
ISBN 978-0-520-25055-0 (cloth : alk. paper)
ISBN 978-0-520-25056-7 (pbk. : alk. paper)
1. Dante Alighieri, 1265–1321. Purgatorio.   I. Mandelbaum, Allen,
1926– II. Oldcorn, Anthony.   III. Ross, Charles.
PQ4447.L43   2008
851'.1—dc22   2007033778

Manufactured in the United States of America

17 16 15 14 13 12 11 10 09 08
10 9 8 7 6 5 4 3 2 1

The paper used in this publication meets the minimum requirements
of ANSI / NISO Z39.48–1992 (R 1997) (*Permanence of Paper*).

This volume of the
California Lectura Dantis
is dedicated to our indispensable
colleague and peerless editor of the text
of Dante's
Divine Comedy,
the late

GIORGIO PETROCCHI

It is unthinkable
to read the cantos of Dante
without aiming them
in the direction of the present day.
They were made for that. . . .
They demand the commentary
of the futurum.

OSIP MANDELSTAM

CONTENTS

CANTO I
Ritual and Story

EZIO RAIMONDI

Translated by Charles Ross

The *Purgatorio* opens with a solemn exordium, rich in anticipation and tension, that develops in three stages (1–12). First we are given the graceful but exultant image, dear to the mannerist tradition, of the "waters" and the "little vessel" that will "course" even as it "lifts her sail." Next, the first-person narrator dramatically ("and what I sing") offers the firm, clear definition of the theme. Finally, there is an invocation to the Muses recalling, like some mysterious legend, a famous episode in Ovid's *Metamorphoses*.

One understands that this exordium is rhetorical, and that the principal voice is that of the poet who stands outside the story. But whoever listens closely will not miss that it anticipates the action of the canto by calling into account the persona, or protagonist, of the whole poem before he is named. And this perception of the narrative voice occurs, one notices, not so much because of the passion of the introductory tercets that glances, like a state of mind, at the Dante who has emerged from Hell, but because—with those multiple suggestive registers that make Dante's symbolism so genial and inventive—the discourse of the poem runs on two planes, one rhetorical and the other, one might say, existential. The "sea so cruel" that has been left behind is not only the sea of "harsh and scrannel rhymes," the "sea" of poetry that will be mentioned later in the *Paradiso,* but also the "dangerous waters" of Hell (*Inf.* I, 24) and what Dante in the *Convivio* calls the "ocean of our life" that every Christian must traverse to reach his final haven. It is also the same sea that the Hebrews crossed from Egypt—a symbolic sea that gets transformed into "better waters" because, by a mystery of faith, it prefigures the idea of baptism and, at the same time, the victory of Christ over death.

Only these allusions can explain the profound resonance of a line like "may this poem rise again from Hell's dead realm" (12), in which the contrast between death and resurrection surges above the rhetorical figures (among other things, we must not forget that, according to Dante, it is Easter Sunday) to remind man of the story of his sin and his redemption and thereby to touch on what it means to return to God, the fundamental theme of the *Purgatorio*. Even the reference to the competition between Calliope and the Pierides, which many critics have seen as only a learned excursus in the text, acquires a new brilliance, if we regard it as an image of a liturgical contest and recall that in Ovid, Calliope chooses as her subject the rape of Proserpina and her return to Ceres from the "forest" of "perpetual spring," a myth of lost innocence and renewed fertility. In one of those shrewd choices so frequent in the *Comedy*, Dante finds Christian rifts of gold in a classical tale just as, at the beginning of the *Paradiso*, he will resort to the myth of Glaucus and insinuate, among the lower registers of his prologue, the theme and image of the distant terrestrial Paradise. And there, not by chance, Matilda will appear as a pilgrim, like a new, supreme Proserpina.

The First Inkling of Joy

There is no doubt that when, in Canto XIII, the narrative begins and the figure of Dante the pilgrim takes over from Dante the poet, we already understand the spiritual dimension of the *Purgatorio*. It is a dialectic of death and rebirth, of sterility and blossoming, whose extended rhythm regulates the timing of the cosmos. The first sensation one has, after entering this world reborn into hope, is that of light and of the high heavens, of precious transparencies, "the gentle hue of oriental sapphire." To the eyes of medieval readers, accustomed to the allusive language of the lapidaries, the qualities associated with sapphires were liberty and purity, as Marbodo, for example, explains in his *Liber lapidum*. But what the gemologists present as abstract archetypes, Dante places into a lively narrative situation at the very moment when the pilgrim lifts his gaze to the serene skies and rediscovers the "joy" of nature and the world of things, after the "air of death" in Hell (16–17). The delight to which the soul returns is not just the joy of a man facing the light of a new day, but also the first inkling of a longer-lasting joy, which will become entirely clear later, at the top of the mountain, when Matilda will suggest, citing the psalm *Delectasti*, that her smile emanates from her knowledge of a divine presence and the joy of contemplating the works of the Most High.

In other words, the world of Purgatory assumes the character of a liturgical situation, and the adventure of the pilgrim takes place against a backdrop of mysterious correspondences, which interpret the history of humankind in the light of Christ's example and give it an order—just as occurs in the liturgy, following the hours of a day that symbolize the interconnectedness of life, a harmonious collocation of deeds, memories, and rituals. Even the apparition of Venus (19) is tied to a liturgical passage, in that it involves the star Lucifer, which appears in so many Christian hymns as an image of dawn's victory over night. Naturally, however, in the morning time of the *Purgatorio,* the theme is reprised and amplified in a descriptive-epic mode following the pattern of the *Artes poeticae.* Venus is the unnamed object of the periphrasis "the lovely planet that is patroness / of love." To tie this prologue to that of the *Inferno,* it is necessary to give a sign of the season, Pisces. But Dante does not lose the emotive value of the liturgical Lucifer, which is that of expectant grace. A series of thematic words (19–21) enriches his trembling sense of that salvation represented by the sun: the word "lovely" suggests the idea of a distant but hopeful God. "Eastern" suggests the sacred place of all rituals. "All" the heavens are "glad," and the sign of the Fish is accompanied by a "veiling," as in an infant's dream.

Only now, after having set the scene, does the pilgrim say "I" and take on the role of the subject, of the actor who begins (and not without some indirect references to a catechism) a cycle of initiatory purifications. The first action he completes is to circle around, always looking up:

> Then I turned to the right, setting my mind
> upon the other pole, and saw four stars
> not seen before except by the first people.
>
> (22–24)

The point of the sentence is to fix attention on those four stars that were seen only by the "first people," to signal, immediately after, the happiness that seems to him to radiate through the skies of Purgatory and then to turn back, finally, to a sad lament for the earth, where men must live, always deprived of such a vision.

For Dante, as poet, thought almost always precedes sensation, thereby conditioning his affective reaction. The critic who wants to retain emotion as well as meaning must therefore accept the rules of the allegorical art and establish the meaning of those four stars, going beyond the generic lament that humankind is fallen. He must try to grasp the economy of the scene in which Dante apostrophizes, "o northern hemisphere . . . you are a widower!" (26–27). The poem's organization depends on the interpretive level and not on the act that *requires* interpretation. Ideas structure the narrative; they are its thematic elements. From Enrico Proto's essay "Nuove ricerche sul Catone dantesco," which appeared in the *Giornale storico della letteratura italiana* 49 (1912), we know that these four stars are symbols of the cardinal virtues: prudence, justice, courage, and temperance, all of which informed men in the terrestrial Paradise before the first sin. But it is Charles Singleton, in his *Journey to Beatrice* (1958), who showed that since the four cardinal virtues were lost after the Fall, they may not be reacquired, and redeemed, except by individual effort. They are no longer natural, to Dante's disappointment. For Dante, all humanity is in a state of corruption, of permanent loss. It is written in the history of humankind that no one may return to the terrestrial Paradise with the same innocence and rightness that God gave, in the person of Adam, to human beings. Therefore, the widowed northern hemisphere stands as an admonishment, prefiguring the end of the *cantica*, which says that even those who are purified may not return to the uncorrupted state of the "first people." The serene sky, the smile of Venus, the advancing rays of the sun, confer on the landscape of Purgatory— as in the liturgical hymns to morning—a suspended awe, a lightness of innocence and infancy. Yet tension remains. One remembers the night and the cruel seas that accompany the expectation of light, creating an overarching rhythm of penitence and renewed purity.

A Solitary Patriarch

Certainly a sense of calm mystery suffuses the air. One may note that this mystery takes shape in front of us when, for an instant, the story stops as the pilgrim turns. And it follows him, at a deliberate pace, when Cato emerges from who knows where. Yet to say he emerges is not quite correct. In reality, it is Dante the pilgrim who takes his eyes off the four stars and then sees, beside him, the figure of the "patriarch" (31). The word is unusual, and the adjective "solitary" *(solo)* is cast into relief, in the Italian, by the rhyme. This figure of venerable isolation is the first of the great, suggestive images in the *Purgatorio*. His gravity draws Dante's astonished attention: "His aspect worthy of such reverence / that even son to father owes no more" (32–33).

Dante's *Convivio* mentions the reverence owed to a father. But this reverence takes other courses. In the first place, the atmosphere of this moment will dominate the entire canto. In the second, it gives an expansive sense of Dante's personality as a figure in the poem. Finally, in terms of the immediate story, it creates a frame around a new sense of solemnity in Cato—also "worthy of such reverence" is the sacred sign of the eagle (*Par.* VI, 34–35). We are saying nothing new in noticing that the iconography of Cato derives for the most part from Lucan's *Pharsalia*. But if the long beard, the white skin, and the divided tresses falling on his breast recall the Roman epic (34–36), the *Comedy* also modifies the portrait, substituting for the grays of the original— in which the hair is horrid, unkempt, and filthy—a physiognomy that is severe but luminous. The fact is that Cato, framed by the light of the four stars, joins the traits of the Roman hero to those of a biblical patriarch. Here I am thinking not only of the usual contamination of correlative forms that comes from Dante's knowledge of languages but also of a transfiguration that invests the figure with a more profound value.

Centuries ago the commentator Buti compared Cato to the patriarchs of the Old Testament. But what secret significance in Cato's life accounts for his election in Dante's world and for the dignity he attains in the Purgatory as, so to speak, a lay priest? Cato was a Stoic associated with liberty. Therefore, he has a symbolic relation to freedom from sin. Nonetheless, since he is a pagan, he will not be saved, making him a suitable guardian of Purgatory. It is undeniable that Cato relates not only to Dante as pilgrim but also to Dante as a writer and to his culture. The problem, of course, is that Cato was a suicide. And the answer seems to be that Dante judges him according to Cato's own moral values, those of the Romans, which differ from the ethics of Christians. Cato therefore shines with the "light" of the four cardinal virtues and receives the grace of implicit faith. He is a man who died for the benefit of human society and in a time of discord and ruin, affirming before the world, by his own sacrifice, the supreme law of liberty—not only civil but metaphysical. In his *Monarchy* (2.5), Dante refers to the sacrifice of Cato, the holy victim of the Decii. In the *Pharsalia,* Cato declares that his blood will "redeem" the Roman people and "absolve" them. For Dante, the Cato of the *Pharsalia* is therefore a man of destiny. As he says in the *Convivio,* Cato is, of all men, most fit to signify God, just as Old Testament figures foreshadow and prophetically anticipate Christ's life in the New Testament. Cato no longer plays the role of enemy of Caesar and the Empire (the *Convivio* also leaves this out) but becomes, as a providential figure, through his sacrifice, a shadow that foretells, within the limits of his imperfect action, the true liberation that is Christ. In this sense, it seems legitimate to refer to Cato as a patriarch. But there is more. If we pass from a consideration of Dante's culture to the poetic situation in the poem, where allusions and resonances gradually accumulate, Cato may be one of those figures, otherwise not well defined, who escaped from Limbo when Christ descended there to liberate the patriarchs and make them blessed. Like the patriarchs, but in a halo of glory that preserves the memory of Roman grandeur, he incarnates in the living and unrepeatable substance of his persona the idea of that reawakening from shadows, the victory over the realm of shades, that attended the historically unique resurrection of Christ and, through it, the rebirth of every human being. The first example of the process, naturally, is Dante himself, who leaves the dead air of Hell and returns, in the dawn of grace, to the "pure" skies of Purgatory. And so the theme of resurrection that we saw in the exordium expands within the story, a rich echo of a great event, lending unity to the episodes, situations, and movements of the canto.

Two Worlds Converse

We may now reduce the dialogue between Cato and Virgil, which occupies half the canto, to a common colloquy between two psychological types, two

souls whose condition must be explored, even as they are reflected by an ingenious and rather unsuitable realism. In truth, even if it is Dante's achievement to have introduced these two individual and historical personalities
into his ritual setting and to have made them dramatic and human, their
conversation cannot be understood outside a scheme of ceremonial liturgy.
Cato is the first to speak, even as he is surrounded by a prodigious "light"
from the four "holy" flames. He asks the questions, like one who has been
surprised and seeks information, but also like one who wants to provoke
someone into taking a position that, at bottom, is an abjuration or renunciation. His allusion to an "escape" from the shadows, even as he begins to
speak ("Who are you—who, against the hidden river, / were able to escape
the eternal prison?" 40–41), recalls the great ritual of the Exodus.

There follows a series of acts that marks the dynamic center of the canto.
Virgil expresses himself with faith and firmness, from narration to perora-
tion, restating some of the conversational formulas that applied to Beatrice
in the first canto of the *Inferno*. His tenacity appears in "by way of words and
hands and other signs" (50) and extends to the zeugma of "he made my
knees and brow show reverence" (51). He releases information, gradually introducing Cato to Dante: "I do not come from my / own self. There was a
lady sent from Heaven. . . . This man had yet to see his final evening; . . . I
showed him all the people of perdition" (52–64). He unveils his thoughts, in
a culminating moment, in a promise of eternity and beatitude:

> You know it—who in Utica found death
> for freedom was not bitter, where you left
> the garb that will be bright on the great day.
>
> (73–75)

Then he once more assumes a tone of prayer, re-creating by means of the
unlooked-for name of Marcia the sunset memory of old affections. Cato
speaks some words about her, but with the tenderness of one who leaves behind him a former communal existence.

Dante's genius was to create a tone that also sets up the clarity of the rest
of the dialogue. Those who are convinced that the poet weighed and calcu-
lated this transition like to scrutinize the stylistic web created by the words
dedicated to Marcia, which combine biblical phrasing ("Marcia so pleased
my eyes" [86] recalls *placuit oculis meis* of Judges 14:3) with the structure of
antithesis *(mentre ch'i' fu' di là . . . Or che di là)* that Dante found characteristic of Marcia in Lucan's *Pharsalia*, which he also imitated in the *Convivio* (IV
28, 16–17). Certainly what Cato now affirms is the opposite of what Lucan's
Marcia says, because he speaks from across an unbridgeable divide, while in
the *Convivio*, as in the Latin poem, the aging woman renews her desire for
the passion of love. But even reversed, the cadences of Marcia's ancient prayer
that shift into Cato's austere discourse retain a discreet, though hidden,

serenity, a memory of old affections that does not contradict the role of judge and patriarch assigned by Dante to the Roman hero. In fact, Cato loses himself in Virgil's overly polite "flattery" (93) that with a slightly allegorical undertone admonishes him that it is useless to compare Marcia to the "lady come from Heaven" (91). Something changes in the tone of Cato's words, something fundamental in his attitude, which becomes no longer that of an inquisitor, following the logic of a ritual, but that of a judge, a teacher, a master of what one might call a cult.

Cato's advice and precepts do not lessen the tension of the scene because, as crisp and imperious as they are ("Go then; but first / wind a smooth rush around his waist and bathe / his face," 94–96), they increase, if possible, the interest and vitality of the narrative and open the prospect of a new adventure with their allusion to the "custodian angel" of Paradise (99). As the dialogue turns to surrounding objects, the setting takes on a new dimension, which now, finally, after the tranquil but rigid and severe remarks of Cato, takes shape before the eyes of the two voyagers, who no longer contemplate the high heavens but consider the ground they must cover. Near them, the landscape seems indistinct, but comforting and familiar. And so the "solitary island" appears, and the breakers, the rushes, the soft and muddy ground, forming an existential design, safe from the faultiness of fleeting emotions. The exactness of the geographic references ("all around / its very base," 100–101) does not exclude an air of prophecy, of friendly mystery, of a supernatural and also inaccessible order. It is fitting, moreover, that Cato is the one to describe the landscape, because in a moment he will vanish, and there is a need to prepare a base for this arcane mystery. His role is to initiate Dante, by means of Virgil's intercession, into the first act of the vast ritual of purification. His words of farewell, which are both a command and an augury ("do not return by this same pass," 106) are complemented by the hopefulness of his announcement (107–108) that the "sun" is rising and that the hillside can now be climbed "more easily."

But the correlations and the symmetries that Dante has associated with the figure of Cato and his appearance on the shores of Purgatory do not stop here. There is one, especially, that no critic can ignore, and it is implicit in the ceremony of the "smooth rush" (95), the "humble plant" (134) that Virgil must gird around the pilgrim. Cato, who introduces Dante to humility, is one of the magnanimous heroes celebrated, in the eloquent pages of the *Monarchia,* for their moral grandeur, their human desire for honor and civil glory. Humility does not oppose magnanimity. Aquinas, in fact, concluded his debate between Christianity and the ethics of Aristotle and the Stoics by explaining that "magnanimitas et humilitas non sunt contraria," because magnanimity derives its dignity from the gifts of God, while humility makes a man consider his own defects (*Summa theologiae,* q. cxxix *De magnanimitate* and cclxi *De humilitate* in the *Secunda Secundae*). Did not Dante read in Lucan that Cato believed men partook of divinity and did nothing except by the will of God? In the final analysis, therefore, Cato signals the movement from a world in which magnanimity is the unique, supreme comfort for those condemned to live without hope to a cosmos where a soul, having left Hell, might move through humility to grace.

Movement

Cato disappears from the story rapidly and mysteriously ("with that, he vanished," 109), even if the landscape makes his vanishing seem natural, almost peaceful. The pilgrim, who had been kneeling, is finally ready, after Virgil has spoken, to celebrate, even in silence, the ritual of purification that awaits him. Here, in the final act of this canto, silence plays a noticeable role, as if to underline the clear, precise movement of the narrative action, hardly disturbed by the quiet tremor of a divine presence. When Dante and Virgil begin to move, time has changed, for in Purgatory time takes on a poetic truth, an enchanted mutability of atmosphere and color, and one's eye must necessarily pause once again on the countryside, which begins to fill with light and soft breezes:

> Daybreak was vanquishing the dark's last hour,
> which fled before it; in the distance, I
> could recognize the trembling of the sea.
>
> (115–117)

These are beautiful verses. The joyous force of that "vanquishing" and the chaste religious halo of "daybreak" overshadow any commentary. That "in the distance" could have been written by Leopardi.

Nonetheless, a few words on the "trembling" are warranted here, not only to signal the classical tradition that goes back to Virgil (*Aeneid* 7.9, "splendet tremulo sub lumine pontus"), as well as to Ovid (*Heroides* 11.75) and Claudian (*De raptu Proserpina* 2.2–3), but also to all the other uses of "trembling" in Dante, a word that the *Purgatorio* always associates with mysterious becoming, vital suspension, and disposition toward the sacred. One suspects that the "trembling" of Canto I is something more than a beautiful image converted by the infinitive form of the verb into a noble substantive, and that its most profound suggestive quality depends on an obscure field of sensations, present as if in a cosmic myth, where sky, water, dawn, light, and plants take root together, and nature, once more associated with humankind, seems to restore him to the suspended purity of childhood. In Dante's culture, it is a possibility that cannot be excluded.

The pilgrim who descends toward the "lowest bounds" (114) of the plain, at the break of day, truly returns to innocence, as if awakening, after the torpor of nighttime, from that sleep of which he was full, as he says at the beginning of the *Inferno*. The counterpoint that structures the whole canto

and resolves its symbolic allusions into a learned chiaroscuro of motives, recapitulates some of the motives and the tone of the prelude to the *Comedy*.
There is perhaps a secret reference, too, to the ocean voyage of Ulysses. The
memory of the "lonely slope" (*Inf.* I, 29) flowers only after the "lonely plain"
(118), rendering the joy of return more intimate and thoughtful and insinuating into Dante's stupor a serene consciousness of the weariness that a
search for order requires, even where there is grace.

> We made our way across the lonely plain,
> like one returning from a lost pathway,
> who, till he finds it, seems to move in vain.
>
> (118–120)

These verses touch on the great theme of Dante's journey and his discovery
of his goal with a cadence that the *Purgatorio* will repeat again, almost as a
motif: "We made our way until the end of vespers" (XV, 139); "Our steps
were short and slow as we moved on" (XX, 16); "Now we ascended by the sacred stairs" (XII, 115); "we now had reached the summit of the stairs" (XIII, 1).
In a landscape now familiar and friendly, even if mysterious, in which solitude leads to hope and not to fear, these movements compose a simply harmony, as if they are naturally obeying a predetermined rhythm: from the
"dew" that Virgil's hand "gently" touches in the grass, to the ritual of the
"smooth rush," to the quiet prodigy that is performed in the "wonder" of
the first light of dawn along the "deserted shore."

One knows because there are several clear linguistic indicators, including
the mystery of the golden bough, that Dante concludes the first episode of
his initiation with a reference to the sixth book of the *Aeneid,* which inspired
him. The comparison is imperfect, since the bough represents nothing less
than a fertility rite, a bivalent symbol of life itself, but Dante adapts it with
extraordinary intuition, placing it in a new spiritual world. This world does
not know the pagan experience, as Dante suggests when he writes of the

> deserted shore,
> which never yet had seen its waters coursed
> by any man who journeyed back again.
>
> (130–132)

He joins the theme of rebirth, which informs the image of the rush that
"sprang up / again, identical, immediately" (135–136) with a reference to Isaiah 35:7, in which the holy man will find the land renewed and "grass with
reeds and rushes" shall grow in the "habitation of dragons," and also to Job
14:7, where the tree that is cut down "will sprout again."

The movement from the "smooth rush" of the "deserted shore" to the
new plant of the divine forest explains the poetry of the *Purgatorio.* It is the

poetry of a man's journey along the difficult road of hope, of chance meetings, of conversations and memories, accompanied by a current of emotions, from the pale concert of the dawn to the shadows crouching in the evening, and the rustling of leaves and waters, the mysteries of life. Samuel Becket, in a famous essay on Joyce, called it an ascent from real vegetation to ideal vegetation, a concrete movement toward the Absolute.

CANTO II

The New Song and the Old

ROBERT HOLLANDER

The action of Canto II is divided into four parts: lines 1–12, Dante and Virgil at the island's shore; 13–51, the arrival of the angelic vessel; 52–117, Casella and Dante; and 118–133, Cato's rebuke and the pilgrims' departure.

The preeminent musicality of Canto II appears to continue the celebrative mood of the preceding canto, which is characterized by motifs such as rebirth, sweetness, delight, and freedom. Yet Canto II, like its number, has a double focus. Each of the three *cantiche* that comprise the *Divine Comedy* begins with a canto devoted to the presentation of a positive personage or experience (Virgil, Cato, Dante's ascent toward the light of God). Each second canto, in contrast, concerns an examination of a related but more problematical situation: Virgil's lack of eventual authority when compared to Beatrice's; Dante's flawed response to Casella's song, corrected by Cato's rebuke; Dante's misunderstanding of the dark spots on the moon, corrected by Beatrice's discourse. Each *cantica* thus begins hopefully and then moves to the experience of a troubling inadequacy of one kind or another. Then, in each case, aid or enlightenment comes from above: Virgil remembers Beatrice's descent to Limbo; the "celestial steersman" pilots the ship of saved souls to Purgatory; Beatrice explains the "forming principle" (*Par.* II, 147), which has shaped the created universe from above and now irradiates it.

In recent years a greater awareness of the tension between the values represented by Casella and those spoken for by Cato has developed. Charles Singleton, for example, suggests that Casella's song is a "temptation," while Cato's intervention arrests the "backsliding" of the pilgrims. Such a reading undoubtedly helps us to understand Cato's role, part of the "allegory of the theologians," which grants him a figural significance in Dante's poem. Recent critics have seen in Cato a combination of Christ the Redeemer (see Sanquineti 1970), Moses, and Paul. The "allegory of the poets," applied to Cato, leaves him in a poetic limbo, reducing him to an ahistorical quality of some kind, denying Dante his brilliant and troubling opening gambit, which saves the pagan for his anticipation of Christ in his self-sacrificing actions.

Virgil's Failure

Dante's arrival on the shore of Purgatory has been accomplished in a poetic mode that insists on the distance between Revelation—represented as being in accord with the transactions of this particular poem—and mere poetry. His Cato, borrowed from Lucan's *scriptura paganorum* (Epistle XIII, 63), has rebuked Virgil's attempt at flattery, which we are probably meant to perceive as being imitated by Virgil from Beatrice's *captatio* (*Inf.* II, 58–60 and 67–74). Indeed, no part of the *Comedy* is as concerned with Virgil's failure to have had faith and with his resultant limitations as guide in the territory of the blessed as the first seven cantos of the *Purgatorio:* in Canto I, Cato rebukes Virgil (85–93); in Canto II, Virgil and the newly arrived penitents are carried away listening to Casella (115–117); in Canto III, Virgil's *agenbite of inwit* is given outward expression by his undignified running (10–11); also in III, we hear Virgil condemn pagan philosophy—and himself—for placing too much trust in the capacity of human reason (34–45); in Canto IV, Virgil insists on his inadequacy as guide in this place (37–39); in Canto V, Virgil informs Dante that it is the neophyte living soul who is of interest to the penitents and not the great pagan poet (43–45); in Canto VI, the opening simile implicitly makes Virgil play the role of loser to Dante's winner, (1–12), and then he is forced to read *Aeneid* VI, 376, which would seem to deny the notion of the efficacy of prayer in a Christian light; and in Canto VII, Virgil gives his fullest and most telling account of himself as faithless (7–8, 22–36). The climactic scene of Ante-Purgatory, dominated by Sordello, finally allows Virgil a happier moment, one in which his political views are conjoined with those of his fellow Mantuan in an ecstatic condemnation of the political failure of Italy and of all Europe.

One leitmotif of the first seven cantos is thus the relative inadequacy of Virgil as poet and guide. Canto I, ending with Dante's Christian remodeling of *Aeneid* VI, 43—the plucking of the golden bough, as such early commentators as Pietro di Dante (1340), Benvenuto (1373), Landino (1481), Vellutello (1544), and Daniello (1568) all noted—indicates both allegiance to Virgilian text and an awareness of the necessary transvaluation of Virgilian values: golden bough replaced by humble plant. The gesture, carried out by Virgil himself, as though in a sort of poetic expiation, also underscores Dante's insistence that *Purgatorio,* introduced by this humble plant, is *his* poetic invention, as the underworld was Virgil's. For this reason also Virgil must now serve as a guide who can warn but cannot truly guide, giving way to such escorts as Sordello and Statius, to name the two most important surrogate Virgils who instruct Dante in his ascent of the mountain. Another sort of literary failure is examined in the second canto: the offending author in this circumstance is not the pagan Virgil but the younger Dante Alighieri.

On the Island's Shore

Canto II of the *Inferno* is the "canto of the word," carefully weighing the value of Virgilian speech and its better Christian counterpart, in the words of Beatrice. The parallel concern of the second canto of the *Purgatorio,* the "canto of two songs," is a similar weighing of counterpoised poetics, that of Psalm 113 and of Dante's own second ode of the *Convivio.* The opening circumlocutive indication of the time (it is nearly dawn) may continue the concern with Ulysses' failed voyage—his attempt to storm Christianity's Olympus—that is reflected in and behind the concluding verses of the preceding canto. Dante's placing of the sun by indicating three of its four coordinates (Jerusalem, Ganges, the shore of Purgatory) leaves us to consider the resultant necessary point of its current zenith: the Strait of Gibraltar, the situs of Ulysses' departure, "the narrows / where Hercules set up his boundary stones" (*Inf.* XXVI, 108). If Ulysses is only a subliminal presence at the beginning of the canto, his offstage activities quickly come into sharper focus as the narrative progresses.

Even before the arrival of the saved souls, Dante and Virgil create a mood of hesitancy and worldliness:

> We still were by the sea, like those who think
> about the journey they will undertake,
> who go in heart but in the body stay.
>
> (10–12)

Benvenuto's 1373 gloss ("like pilgrims who go in search of indulgence"), like his following positive reading of the valence of Mars (as Mars incites men to war, so does the angel incite the pilgrims "to make war on sin"), is probably overly optimistic about the current spiritual condition of these pilgrims. Vittorio Russo (243), who cites Hebrews 11:13–16, brings us closer to Dante's intention here. That passage, deriving from one of the most important loci in Scripture to support the notion that those born before Christ nonetheless were capable of believing in his advent, casts a more culpable light on their lingering. Their thoughts are more with Egypt than with the New Jerusalem. It is an affliction that we shall soon see shared first by Casella, who even after death was in no hurry to begin his spiritual pilgrimage toward Heaven, and then by the entire band of saved souls, who are similarly pleased to remain

where they are rather than moving forward and upward. And when Dante relates his former life in Italy to his own current situation as visitor to this brave
new world, he implicitly criticizes his own past behavior.

The Angelic Vessel

This first simile of the *Purgatorio* compares Mars, seen aglow against the
lightening sky from the western shore of Italy, to the approaching brightness of the angelic presence:

> And just as Mars, when it is overcome
> by the invading mists of dawn, glows red
> above the waters' plain, low in the west,
>   so there appeared to me—and may I see it
> again—a light that crossed the sea: so swift,
> there is no flight of bird to equal it.
>
>   (13–18)

Many commentators after Daniello have turned to *Convivio* 2, XIII, 20–24,
where Dante discusses the relation of the fifth planet to music as well as the
effect of its supposedly dry heat. In its second quality, "music draws to itself
the spirits of humankind, which are as though vapors of the heart, with the
result that they cease from nearly every function" (24). Since we shall shortly
witness the effect of Casella's song on the pilgrims—and that effect will be
nearly identical to what is here described—it is difficult not to believe that
Dante had this passage in mind when he composed the simile. Thus I would
argue that we must allow ourselves to consider that the relation of Mars to
Angel is not one of good to good, or of good to better, but one of wrong to
right. In the earthbound half of the simile, we may catch a glimpse of the
younger Dante at the seashore looking west to the lovely planet, which signifies the music of earth and, Ulysses-like, putting his back to the rising sun.
The angel, alive in the light of Grace, comes from the east like the rising sun.
He, in this reading, is a corrective object of vision to Dante's earlier gazing.

The trinitarian angel (possessing two wings and a body) grows before our
eyes (19–36). As "pilot" (*galeotto,* 27), he is reminiscent of Phlegyas ("a solitary
boatman at his helm," *Inf.* VIII, 17) and of Francesca's copy of the *Lancelot* ("A
Gallehault indeed, that book and he / who wrote it," *Inf.* V, 137–38)—a pilot
who conduces to a better place and to better affections. And he also puts us in
mind of Ulysses, whose presence is strongly felt at the end of Canto I and the
beginning of Canto II. For whereas Ulysses "made wings out of oars" (*Inf.*
XXVI, 125), this sailor of the same seas requires neither oar nor sail, possessing
angelic wings (31–33). The word for "oar" was last heard in Ulysses' speech (as
was the phrase *suol marino* of verse 15, *Inf.* XXVI, 129). The word for poop deck,
poppa, introduced in the poem to describe Ulysses' position as captain of his

ship (XXVI, 124, and repeated at verse 140), now recurs to set this celestial steersman against his less worthy counterpart. It seems clear enough that the angel comes to rebuke all Ulysses-like wandering souls, including Dante. The angel's silent beatitude counters the loquacity of the rhetorically attractive but mortally dangerous pagan. Presiding over the pilgrim's psalmody, he reenacts the role of the exodal Moses; small wonder that his very appearance conveys his blessedness. The song sung in its entirety by the saved souls ("all of those spirits sang as with one voice," 48) is entirely appropriate to their condition. This Easter Sunday rehearsal of the Exodus accomplished, the angel signs his flock with the cross and withdraws.

Casella's Song

The new pilgrims begin well. Raising their heads, they wish to know if these earlier denizens of the place know the way to the mountain (59–60). If their intellects are unenlightened, their wills are good. Virgil's response (61–66), which disclaims such knowledge, makes him and Dante fellow pilgrims of the newcomers (but with what different final destinations!). The second simile of Canto II, as Daniello was perhaps the first to suggest, is drawn from the *Aeneid* (VIII, 115–116 or XI, 100–101):

> as people crowd around a messenger
> who bears an olive branch, to hear his news,
> and no one hesitates to join that crush.
>
> (70–72)

The olive branch that he extends to Pallas and the latter's pleased stupefaction seem to be the precise poetic analogues that Dante had in mind as he constructed his simile. Yet the ominous undertones in Virgil's narrative are absent here (Aeneas will, in fact, bring war, not peace; young Pallas will become the central sacrificial presence in that war).

The penitents are fascinated by this living soul and disregard Virgil, who is a silent partner in the ensuing action. We only discover that he too is rapt by the sweetness of Casella's song at line 115 and that he and Dante depart in haste together in the final verse of Canto II. It is the voyage of the living Dante, not the guidance of his dead mentor, that attracts the attention of these saved Christians. While the irony is not voiced, Virgil's subsequent reactions (III, 25–45) show how keenly he experiences the loneliness of his lot in this Christian territory, his to traverse only for some seventy-two hours before he must return to Limbo. Yet if he is uncomfortably out of place here, neither are his fellow travelers in such spiritual condition as the angel might have hoped. Their first purgatorial action is to be inactive ("as if they had / forgotten to proceed to their perfection," 74–75). The innocent-sounding little phrase in fact prepares the reader for Cato's thunderous rebuke some fifty verses later.

The meeting with Casella is so charmingly presented that few of those who have dealt with the scene have been sensitive to its negative implications. Beginning with the failed attempt at a friendly embrace between Dante and Casella, the behavior of the protagonist, now acting on his own initiative at center stage for the first time in the *Purgatorio,* is subtly ironized by his author. The two singers are united in several respects besides their mutual gestures of affection. Each is associated with music; each is depicted (if with utterly differing purposes) as standing with his back to the east as he looks out at the Mediterranean (14–15, 100–101); each is content to linger in company rather than to proceed toward the difficult mountain ("then I knew who he was, and I beseeched / him to remain awhile and talk with me," 86–87). The Virgilian resonance of their failed embrace has been noted since the earliest commentators, most of whom are summoned by the familiar scene in *Aeneid* VI describing Aeneas's attempted embrace of Anchises. Since Dante will re-create that scene so vividly in *Paradiso* XV, 25–27 (where Cacciaguida reverses his Virgilian model, Anchises, and attempts to embrace his living son), it might have occurred to more readers how odd it was for Dante to have chosen to repeat himself. Further, it ought to have been observed that the context of that scene in the *Aeneid* does not fit the context here very well: Dante as Aeneas is not in this instance met by a paternal figure, but by a fraternal one. Since Casella's identity in the poem is that of a singer of love songs, it seems at least reasonable to believe that the Virgilian failed embrace in question is that between Aeneas and Creusa in II, 792–794—the same three lines that will reappear in the later scene. Contemporary commentators are surprisingly unmindful of this tradition. Yet Dante's context, a song sung for a former love, the *donna gentile* of the *Convivio,* surely helps to buttress the minority opinion. If it is correct, it serves to establish the gentle but firm undercutting of the portrayed action that runs through this part of the canto.

The delay in Casella's arrival in Purgatory, to which Dante alludes ("but why, / . . . were you deprived of so much time?" 93), along with the vexed questions of the identity of the historical Casella, and of the three months that he has waited for deliverance at Tiber's mouth (97–102), have sorely troubled the commentators. Since we cannot be certain who Casella was (whether Florentine, Pistoian, or of still another city) and consequently do not know his death date, all we can surmise is that his worldly and negligent habits caused him to be passed over for promotion for three months or longer, and that the Jubilee promulgated by Boniface on December 25, 1299, softened even angelic hearts so that, the least among the deserving, he was finally taken on March 25, 1300, or so his remarks would lead us to believe. If we are meant to make this inference—and counterarguments can and have been made—we do find in it a reason for Dante's having invented the curious detail. Without disturbing the vast corpus of literature engulfing the question of the "actual" date of Dante's voyage to the afterworld, I would merely propose that we are to understand that Casella and Dante both be-gan their voyages on March 25, and that Dante has constructed an ideal cal-endar for his poetic purposes, one that puts the date of the beginning of the journey into our minds as both March 25 and Good Friday (actually April 8 in 1300—but see *Inf.* XXI, 112–114: "Five hours from this hour yesterday, / one thousand and two hundred sixty-six / years passed since that roadway was shattered here"), despite the calendrical incongruence that he thereby in-curs. Further, and to make matters still more difficult, it seems likely that the star charts informing the *Comedy* are in fact those of 1301—and not 1300 (see Poulle). In sum, Dante wanted his dates to conform to the most propitious poetic pattern he could develop out of the materials he had at hand. Such voluntarism is not unfamiliar in this poet.

For all his hope that he will return to Purgatory on his way to Paradise af-ter his death ("My own Casella, to return again / to where I am, I journey thus," 91–92), Dante continues to act, as does Casella, in ways that recall his former rather than his hoped-for future life. His request, that Casella con-sole his soul with *amoroso canto,* should neither surprise the reader nor lull him into acquiescence, beguiled by the sweetness of the request and then of the song. Dante's initial concern, lest a "new law" remove Casella's memory or exercise of his old arts, has already revealed to us how deflected from his ordained purpose he is. For in Canto I, 89 ("no power to move me any longer"), he has learned (as have we) that a new law—one that came with the Harrowing—applies here. Cato now is beyond being moved by Virgil's rather embarrassing blandishments concerning Marcia, his former love. Dante, however, is quickly rapt when Casella sings of *his* former love. The parallel is striking and natural. A desire to behold this scene in a roseate hue has encumbered the commentators. Freed from such a self-imposed burden, one grasps the point easily enough. Responding to the term *nuova legge,* Daniello reveals that he understands that there *is* a new law in Purgatory, where "one does not sing vain and lascivious things, but hymns and psalms in praise of God." Few modern commentators have dealt as effectively with Dante's pointed phrase.

Cato's Rebuke

Dante's old song on Casella's lips has a wondrous effect on its listeners. And thus Cato's rebuke is a stumbling block to many a commentator. Elusiveness here frequently takes the form of attributing a neutral, even a good, nature to the singing, seen as an activity that is simply not as good as that so urgently proposed by Cato; on the other hand, there exists a vocal minority that in-sists on taking the song as utterly positive. In this canto of two songs, God's Psalm of the Exodus is to be chosen over and against Dante's own old song in praise of a lady who replaced Beatrice in his affections and who represents the wrong way toward the right destination. The rejection of *Convivio* here is both subtle and vigorous. The fault of Dante and the pilgrims is a grievous one—or else we must hold old Cato in a circumspection that may only find warrant in a modern distaste for the doctrinal core of Dante's poem. In Cato's words, the ode is no less than a "slough" that prevents God from being seen by the pilgrims ("Quick, to the mountain to cast off the slough / that will not let you see God show Himself!" 122–123). His admonition is not addressed to Virgil, supernumerary to this drama of salvation. His sin in listening to the song will be described as a "petty fault" at Canto III, 9. Cato's rebuke does not apply to him, because he is not there purging himself in order to see God.

But it applies with telling force to the vacillating pilgrims. The language of the rebuke is biblical; the slough is undoubtedly to be interpreted as the skin shed by the maturing snake. Cato would have the pilgrims put off the old man and put on the new. Old Cato stands for the New Law; the newly arrived saints-to-be backslide, led on by Dante and his *portavoce,* toward the old. And Cato's identity here is not only Pauline, for the scene recalls Moses's discovery of the falsely worshiping Hebrews before that golden calf (Exodus 32:18–19), which the text of Psalm 113 had already set before the minds of all who had listened to what their own lips were singing only moments before. Echoing God's command and Moses's compliance ("neither let the flocks nor herds feed before that mount," Exodus 34:3), Cato sends the music lovers flying. The final simile of the canto likens them to doves. Here they seem to occupy a moral position somewhere between the Virgilian and venereal birds of *Inferno* V, 82 ("as doves when summoned by desire") and the birds of the Holy Spirit, James and Peter, in *Paradiso* XXV, 19–23:

> As when a dove alights near its companion,
> and each unto the other, murmuring
> and circling, offers its affection, so
>   did I see both those great and glorious
> princes give greeting to each other.

Their saved souls hunger on high, but their appetitive natures are not yet wrung dry of earthly longing. If music be the food of love, there is also a heavenly music. We know this is true, as do the pilgrims. They have sung it themselves in this very place.

BIBLIOGRAPHY

This essay, in an expanded form, was first published in *Lectura Dantis Virginiana* VI (1990): 28–45. Perhaps the most important later discussion of the issues discussed here is found in A. A. Iannucci, "Casella's Song and the Tuning of the Soul," *Thought* 65 (1990): 27–46. The following, with the dates of composition, are the most relevant of the early commentators for this canto (most of the texts are available online at the Dartmouth Dante Project website, http://dante.dartmouth.edu): Benvenuto. (1373–1380); Pietro di Dante (1340); Serravalle (1416); Landino

(*1481); Vellutello (1544); Gelli (1553); and Daniello (1568). Other relevant studies and editions are:

Andreoli, Raffaello. *La Divina Commedia di Dante Alighieri.* Col Commento di Raffaello Andreoli. Florence: G. Barbèra, 1887.

Auerbach, Erich. *"Figura."* In *Scenes from the Drama of European Literature.* Translated by Ralph Manheim. New York: Meridian Books, 1959, 11–76.

Bennassuti, Luigi. *La Divina Commedia di Dante Alighieri.* Col commento cattolico di Luigi Bennassuti, arciprete di Cerea. Verona: G. Civelli, 1864–1868.

Biagioli, G. *La Divina Commedia di Dante Alighieri.* Col commento di G[iosafatte] Biagioli. Milan: G. Silvestri, 1820–1821.

Bisogni, Fabio. Fabio Bisogni, "Precisazioni sul Casella dantesco." In *Memorie e contributi alla musica dal medioevo all'età moderna offerti a Federico Ghisi [= Quadrivium* 12 (1971): 81–91].

Campi, Giuseppe, ed. *La Divina Commedia.* Turin: UTET, 1888–1893.

Di Siena, Gregorio. *La Commedia di Dante Alighieri.* Esposta in prosa . . . dal Prof. Luigi De Biase con note di Gregorio di Siena. Naples: Perrotti, 1868.

Elsheikh, Mahmoud Salem. "I musicisti di Dante (Casella, Lippo, Scochetto) in Nicolò de' Rossi," *Studi Danteschi* 68 (1971): esp. 156–158.

Ferrero, Augusto. "Il canto II del Purgatorio." In *Lectura Dantis in Orsanmichele.* Florence: G.C. Sansoni, n.d., read in 1908.

Freccero, John. "Casella's Song." *Studi Danteschi* 91 (1973): 73–80.

Fubini, Mario. "Catone," *Enciclopedia dantesca,* 6. vols. Rome, 1970–1978.

———. "Ulisse," *Enciclopedia dantesca,* 6. vols. *Rome,* 1970–1978.

Hazelfoot, F.K.H. *The Divina Commedia of Dante Alighieri.* With notes by Frederick K.H. Hazelfoot. London: Kegan Paul, Trench, 1887.

Hollander, Robert. *Allegory in Dante's Commedia.* Princeton: Princeton University Press, 1969.

———. "Dante's 'Book of the Dead': A Note on *Inferno* XXIX, 57." *Studi Danteschi* 54 (1983): 31–51.

———. *Il Virgilio dantesco.* Florence: L.S. Olschki, 1983, 257–282.

———. "Purgatorio II: Cato's Rebuke and Dante's scoglio." *Italica* 52 (1975): 348–363. Reprinted in his *Studies in Dante.* Ravenna: Longo, 1980, 91–105.

Jacoff, Rachel. "The Post-Palinodic Smile: Paradiso VIII and IX." *Studi Danteschi* 98 (1980): 111–122.

Kaske, Carol V. "Mount Sinai and Dante's Mount Purgatory." *Studi Danteschi* 89 (1971): 1–18.

Lombardi, Fra Baldassare. *La Divina Commedia.* Novamente corretta, spiegata e difesa da F. B. L. M. C., i.e., Fra Baldassare Lombardi, minore conventuale. Rome: A. Fulgoni, 1791–1792.

Marti, Mario. "Canto II del Purgatorio." In *Lectura Dantis Scaligera,* ed. M. Marcazzan. Florence: Le Monnier, 1967, 45–73.

Mazzeo, Joseph Anthony. *"Convivio* IV, XXI and *Paradiso* XIII: Another of Dante's Self-Corrections." *Philological Quarterly* 38 (1959): 30–36.

———. *Medieval Cultural Tradition in Dante's "Comedy."* Ithaca: Cornell University Press, 1960, 174–204.

Mazzoni, Francesco. *La Divina Commedia: Purgatorio.* Con i commenti di T. Casini/S. A. Barbi e di A. Momigliano. Introduzione e aggiornamento bibliografico-critico di Francesco Mazzoni. Florence: G.C. Sansoni, 1977.

Mazzotta, Giuseppe. *Dante, Poet of the Desert.* Princeton: Princeton University Press, 1979.

Montanari, Fausto. "Il canto secondo del Purgatorio." *Humanitas* 10, no. 4 (1955): 359–363.

Peirone, Luigi. "Casella," *Enciclopedia dantesca,* 6. vols. Rome, 1970–1978.

Petrocchi, Giorgio. *La Commedia secondo l'antica vulgata* a cura di Giorgio Petrocchi. Milan: Mondadori, 1966–1967.

Pézard, André. "Le Chant deuxième du Purgatoire." In *Letture del "Purgatorio,"* ed. V. Vettori, Lectura Dantis Internazionale. Milan: Marzorati, 1965, 36–71.

Plumptre, E.H. *The Commedia and Canzoniere of Dante* Alighieri. A New Translation with Notes, Essays and a Biographical Introduction by E.H. Plumptre, D.D., Dean of Wells. London: Wm. Isbister, 1886–1887.

Poletto, Giacomo. *La Divina Commedia di Dante Alighieri*. Col commento del Prof. Giacomo Poletto. Rome: Desclée, Lefebvre, 1894.

Poulle, Emmanuel. "Profacio." *Enciclopedia dantesca*, 6. vols. Rome, 1970–1978.

Proto, Enrico. "Nuove ricerche sul Catone dantesco." *Giornale storico della letteratura italiana* 59 (1912): 193–248.

Ransom, Daniel J. "*Panis Angelorum*: A Palinode in the *Paradiso*." *Studi Danteschi* 95 (1977): 81–84.

Russo, Vittorio. "Il canto II del Purgatorio." In *Nuove letture dantesche*, vol. 3. Florence: Le Monnier, 1969, 229–265.

Sanguineti, Edoardo. "Dante, Purgatorio I." *Letture classensi* 3 (1970): 257–282.

Sarolli, Gian Roberto. *Prolegomena alla "Divina Commedia."* Florence: L. S. Olschki, 1971.

Scarano, Nicola. "Come Dante salva Catone." In *Saggi danteschi*, ed. Isotta Scarano, n.p., n.d. 1970, 179–207.

Shoaf, R. A. "Dante's *colombi* and the Figuralism of Hope in the Divine Comedy." *Studi Danteschi* 93 (1975): 27–59.

Singleton, Charles S. *Commentary to Purgatorio*. Princeton: Princeton University Press, 1973, 40.

———. *Dante Studies*, vol. 1. Cambridge, MA: Harvard University Press, 1965, 23–29.

———. "In exitu Israel de Aegypto." *78th Annual Report of the Dante Society* (1960): 1–24.

Steiner, Carlo. *La Divina Commedia commentata da Carlo Steiner*. Turin: G. B. Paravia, 1921.

Thomas, J. W. *The Trilogy; or Dante's Three Visions*. With notes and illustrations by by J. W. Thomas. London: H. G. Bohn, 1859–1866.

Thompson, David. *Dante's Epic Journeys*. Baltimore, MD: Johns Hopkins University Press, 1974.

Tommaseo, Niccolò (1837). *La Divina Commedia*. Con le note di Niccolò Tommaseo e introduzione di Umberto Cosmo. Turin: UTET, 1927–1934. Reprint of second definitive edition, Milan: F. Pagnoni, 1865.

Venturi, Pompeo (1732). *La Divina Commedia di Dante Alighieri*. Col commento del Pompeo Venturi. Florence: L. Ciardettti, 1821.

Vitali, Guido. *La Divina Commedia con note e commento di Guido Vitali*. Milan: Garzanti, 1943.

CANTO III

The Sheepfold of the Excommunicates

ROBIN KIRKPATRICK

In the concluding moments of Canto III, a figure appears who, while initially unidentified, is described by Dante with characteristic precision: "he was fair-haired and handsome and his aspect / was noble" (107–108). With an uncanny exactitude of attention, the figure before us is said to carry still on his body the physical scars of the battle in which his time on earth was ended. His brow is cleft: "but one eyebrow had been cleft" (108); and before he names himself the penitent displays a wound "high on his chest" (111). This figure, as one learns at line 112, is Manfred, the illegitimate son of the Emperor Frederick II, who, upon the death of his father, became leader of the Ghibelline cause in Italy. He fell at the battle of Benevento in 1266 (at roughly the age of thirty-four) while commanding the forces of the Empire against an alliance of ecclesiastical, Guelf, and Angevin forces. At the time of his death Manfred had been excommunicated successively by no fewer than three popes: Innocent IV, Alexander IV, and Urban IV.

To many—including Lord Byron, in his verse-drama *Manfred,* and the composers Schumann and Tchaikovsky—the historical Manfred has always exerted a heroic, even a romantic, appeal. This fascination may explain why so many readers of Dante's text have been disposed to locating the final phase of the canto as the center of its imaginative interest. As we will see, there is good reason to correct this emphasis, since narrative action and thematic patterns are as significant in this canto as the representation of any single individual.

True Church, Just Empire

In his treatment of Manfred, Dante himself enters the propaganda war that raged in the second half of the thirteenth century between the Guelfs and the Ghibellines over the reputation of this remarkable figure. Nor can there be any doubt (as G. Leone has shown in *Un re nel Purgatorio: Manfredi di Svevia*) that Canto III of the *Purgatorio* represents, in part at least, Dante's own contribution to that controversy. To those who opposed the claims of imperial power—the Guelf city, states, and the papacy—it was convenient to represent Manfred as a fratricide, a parricide, and, equally, as guilty of incest. This, for instance, was the view adopted by Brunetto Latini (*Tresor* I, xcvii, 1–9), who, as a contemporary of Manfred, had suffered exile in the wake of Ghibelline success at the Battle of Montaperti (Latini was also, of course, however ambiguously, the model for Dante's own early devotion as a Guelf to the virtues of the civic life). As to the account that Dante himself offers, Manfred is emphatically still viewed as an excommunicate. He confesses to crimes—*orribil . . . peccata* (121)—in a phrase strong enough to be taken as a penitential recognition of his own extreme guilt. On the other hand, Dante—anticipating Byron—has chosen to emphasize the heroic aspects of Manfred's physiognomy, instigating the romantic myth by phrases that recall at the same time scriptural accounts of King David and Virgilian references to the fallen Marcellus. More potent and more problematic is the fact that Manfred, in Dante's view, is in Purgatory at all—and therefore ensured (as in line 73, "O chosen souls, you have ended well")—of ultimate beatitude. For Dante's decision to include Manfred among the penitent excommunicates not only affirms the possibility of redemption, even for the worst of sinners, but it also represents a vigorous rebuttal of the use made by politically minded popes of excommunication as an instrument of policy. This condemnation is strengthened when—relying on little-known or often suppressed accounts of Manfred's death—Dante describes how, on papal orders, the body of Manfred was moved *a lume spento*, secretly, with "tapers spent" (132), from the resting place it had been given after the battle. Manfred's enemies had themselves caused a great cairn of stones to be raised over their leader's body (possibly in honor of his military virtues, possibly to exclude him from Christian burial): the Church, fearing that a cult might develop around the *grave mora* ("great heap of stones," 129), desecrates the memorial.

Manfred is a member of the first group of sinners who appear in the Purgatory without as yet having been given any particular form of penitential exercise. Yet it will already be clear that the state of purgation is seen as one that—beyond rational understanding and yet in keeping with notions of the rational relationship between the soul and God—can deliver even the excommunicate to salvation. The surprise of Manfred's presence is an indication of this (as was the appearance of Cato in Canto I); and, if there is any doubt that Dante intended an effect of surprise, we have only to recall that the wounds borne by Manfred and the astonishment he arouses are regularly seen by modern readers as comparable to the wounds that Christ displays to the doubting St. Thomas after the Resurrection. This similarity may imply that all figures in Purgatory are there because of their assimilation with the Christ who suffers and then rises again from the dead. At the same time, such a view invokes the notion of a redeeming Providence, which calls into question the validity of merely retributive justice. Equally, it leads one to ask whether Dante himself, moving beyond the *Inferno,* has now abandoned the crude cut and thrust of the *contrapasso* (which is generally thought to be central to his ethical scheme) in favor of some subtler pursuit of mercy.

Parallel to this profound reassessment of ethical principle, Dante also conducts in Canto III a reexamination of his own political thinking about both Church and Empire. He continues to pursue the anti-Church policy, a familiar theme from cantos such as *Inferno* XIX and ultimately expressed in the Masque of the Church in the concluding cantos of the *Purgatorio* itself. There is indeed a case for saying (along with Jacques Le Goff) that the *Purgatorio,* in rewriting current conceptions of the purgatorial life, represents a sustained attack on the very aspects of ecclesiastical practice that were to contribute so greatly to the movement for Reformation. Yet Dante will never suggest that there can be no place for a Church—of some sort—to aid and cultivate the spiritual ambitions of the individual. Indeed, as will emerge in Canto III, Dante has an unfailing sense of the human need for social and ethical authority. At the same time, it is an indication of the reformation envisioned by Dante that Virgil should at times be ascribed an almost priestly function in the *Purgatorio* and that Dante, in his own view of a true Church, should insist that it include among its members Manfred as a representative of the Just Empire.

Canto III also reexamines the Empire as a political institution. Any suggestion that Dante is an imperialist must be subject to serious qualification. It is never accurate to associate him with the Ghibellinism of his contemporaries. The subtlety of his thought (along with a constant shift of emphasis) is most evident in his treatment of the Swabian dynasty itself. So Frederick II—Manfred's father—is taken to task for his definition of human nobility in the fourth book of the *Convivio* and is finally consigned to the circle of the heretics in *Inferno* X. Likewise, Canto XIII of the *Inferno* pictures, through the tragedy of Pier della Vigna, the suicidal implications of a society built solely on secular fidelity. On the other hand, Frederick's mother—mentioned in the present canto as a corroboration of her grandson Manfred's spiritual credentials—has already advanced to heavenly beatitude. Canto III, therefore, is pitched between the extremes of Heaven and Hell, between the poles of condemnation and celebration, and it allows one to inspect the minute realignments that constantly occur in Dante's political position.

It is appropriate, then, to see this canto as one in which Dante negotiates a very precise advance toward the unexpected appearance of Manfred, which rightly stands at the climax of the canto. However, we shall do no justice either to the intellectual subtlety of Canto III or to the craft and significance of its poetic and intellectual texture unless—diverting attention from Manfred toward the canto as a whole—we consider Dante's own poetic practice and ultimately the poetic theory that might be thought to have inspired the writing (or reading) of this canto.

A Poetic of the Body

If Manfred's bones are disturbed by the Church, then Virgil's are also disturbed by the Empire, but with contrary effect, for the purposes of celebration. Virgil is only temporarily out of Hell, while Manfred is only temporarily absent from salvation. In some ways, then, the canto seems to concern itself first and last with the human body and with the ways in which the body may be subject to honor and denigration, transported, transfigured, or brought to a final resting place. In relation to the theme of the body, there is another figure to consider: that is the figure of Dante, who, as poet, here meditates on his own body as protagonist in the spiritual realm of Purgatory. And it is this meditation that leads one, as John Freccero has shown in "Manfred's Wounds and the Poetics of the *Purgatorio*," to consider the poetics of this canto.

In his reading of Canto III, Freccero contemplates the curious poetry created by the image of wounds that are borne by a ghostly body. These wounds are seen as the scars of history. But words, too, may similarly be seen as scars, and Freccero is concerned with exploring the implications of this analogy. "At some level the disfiguring marks of history mark the soul as well. Like writing itself, they deface in the name of significance" (200).

The marks that Dante's writing makes are there only to be assimilated into the pages of some ultimately authoritative volume. It is here that the notion of conversion comes into play: whether as penitents or poets, we seek a wholeness of being that only comes to us when the wounds we receive or inflict in the course of our historical lives are converted to significance by our understanding of the ultimate word.

In Freccero's view, then, conversion calls us to a *via negativa*, where even our wounds and the best of our words will finally be as nothing. This is not an argument to be dismissed lightly. Yet it is possible to take a very different view of Canto III itself, and, more generally, of issues that are bound to be central in any understanding of Dante's thought and art. Mimesis and symbolism, interpretation and authority, and even the nature of conversional poetics are indeed all open to inspection in Canto III, which is very far from abandoning any concern with the (undoubtedly wounding) controversies of history or indeed with the body as the locus of historical contention.

Moreover, the conversion that Dante here envisages paradoxically requires, if its religious sense is to be fully realized, that we not seek to transcend history and writing but rather that we return precisely to action in these two spheres, wounding as they may be.

In reading this canto, we need to look not for certainties but rather at the processes that the text itself represents and enacts: through fact, fiction, and surprise; through the contingent nuances appearing in those very marks that, as Freccero would have us believe, are ultimately to be wished away. These same marks are also—and self-evidently—the only voice that remains of Dante the poet himself.

In the Hinterland

Canto III describes the first attempt that Dante makes, accompanied by Virgil, to find for himself a route by which to ascend the apparently unscaleable cliffs of Mount Purgatory. Up until now the action of the second *cantica* has been set in dawn light on the beaches surrounding the mountain. Dante will discover no point of entry until, in Canto IV, he comes to a fissure in the sheer rock face, which is bristling—as though it were a thorn hedge—with fragments of rocks. So the events of Canto III take place in a hinterland, dominated equally by the daunting vertical of the mountainside and by a vast horizontal distance (envisaged at lines 68–69 as being at least a mile long) in which Dante will meet others who, like himself, are temporarily excluded from the mountain and with whom he will negotiate his ascent. Dante needs guidance.

Both Church and Empire are institutions that purport to offer guidance to their bewildered subjects. But the narrative now reveals a psychological and ethical correlative to this thematic interest, impelled as much by doubts, interrogatives, and ironies as by the authoritative answers that institutions— whether ecclesiastical, imperial, or even philosophical—might provide. The figures who eventually meet Dante in this landscape are the excommunicates who themselves have been excluded, by divine authority, from entry onto the mountain until they have waited thirty times the length of their contumacy (137). Indeed, Dante will at two points speak emphatically not of what these figures know but rather of what they do not know ("they huddle close behind, / simple and quiet and not knowing why," 83–84, "though they did not know / why those ahead had halted," 92–93). Confusion and ignorance mark the minds of the penitents; and yet, as will be seen, confusion and ignorance themselves produce a solution that knowledge (at least in its epistemic sense) cannot. The first indication that some such conclusion may be imminent is the sustained attention that the canto pays to Virgil's role— as a guide who himself here proves incapable of offering effective guidance.

Canto III opens with Virgil in a state of some distress, having being chided, at the end of Canto I, by his fellow pagan Cato for failing in his responsibilities to his Christian pupil. As late as line 45 Virgil is shown to be *turbato* ("remaining with his sorrow") and deeply caught up in thoughts that concern the fate of the pagan in Hell rather than the advance of Christians toward their salvation. To be sure, Virgil's words will eventually make a considerable contribution to Dante's own advance. Yet one is never allowed to forget (as Virgil himself does not) that, while the excommunicates suffer temporary exclusion from the Church and while Dante is temporarily excluded from the mountain, Virgil is perpetually excluded, as a pagan, from every prospect of salvation.

In the variegated texture of Canto III, there is, then, at least one strand that is bleak, disconcertingly interrogative, and even tragic in its implications. Correspondingly, the opening movement, which runs until line 15, is agitated and unbalanced. At the end of Canto II, a comforting community of new arrivals in Purgatory had formed, focused on the singing of a Dantean song. But this community is now "dispersed" in a sudden and distracted flight. The penitents seek to submit themselves to the law embodied in the moral architecture of the mountain; Dante, for his part, turns to the peripatetic embodiment of reason, Virgil himself, seeking—on the suddenly unpeopled plain—to reestablish discourse with his erstwhile mentor. But the figure whom Dante here seeks to draw close to, his "true companion" (4), is wracked with remorse for having failed Dante and, deprived of his wonted dignity by his haste, "denies all acts their dignity" (11). It is significant, too, that this moment of consolidation and security in the narrative action is marked on the level of authorial voice by a pair of questions that themselves destabilize any easy enjoyment of poise, and that even (while focused on Virgil as authority and guide) draw attention to the highly questionable practices and procedures of Dante himself as author:

> I drew in closer to my true companion.
> For how could I have run ahead without him?
> Who could have helped me as I climbed the mountain?
>
> (4–6)

In one respect, these questions are rhetorical, drawing attention to the trust that Dante has characteristically placed in Virgil throughout the *Inferno*. Yet there is a quiet premonition here of the effects of surprise and even of scandal that will culminate (as much for the reader as for Dante the protagonist) in the coup de théâtre of Manfred's unlikely entry. For the implication of Virgil's presence must already be (as the presence of Manfred will largely confirm) that, in Dante's view, representatives of the Empire are as competent to guide the Christian pilgrim as any nominally Christian authority. At the same time, there is reason to take these questions as true inquiries, reflecting on the decisions that Dante himself has made in pursuing his own fiction: Dante has not only presumed to invent a Purgatory entirely different from any model known to the medieval Church, but he has also chosen to carry Virgil over from his native *Inferno*. In the canto ahead, he will represent this figure as *turbato* and ill at ease in the very territory to which Dante's imagination has transported him. Considering the theological implications of this move, has Dante himself authority for such a flight of narrative fancy? When Dante chooses to depict Manfred among those who, in Virgil's own words, are destined for salvation, and even as an analogy for Christ, it appears that scandals, surprises, and interrogations are themselves capable of producing a higher understanding than rationality itself can discover.

One may recall that, in the *Convivio* 3, X, Dante refers to the fact that human beings possess reason as a miracle. Equally, we may recall that parables are scandals, and it is as part of the poetics suggested by this canto that we should realize the importance of scandal, surprise, and wonder, not merely as a narrative effect but as an ethical and Christian *forma mentis*. Such an understanding makes a virtue out of the very ignorance that is in some measure possessed by all the protagonists of Canto III (including, finally, its author and its reader). But the cultivation of any such understanding depends—in a way that itself calls into question Virgil's propensity to offer trustworthy and definitive solutions—on a willingness to participate in a process of detailed exploration. And the impulse to make this inquiry is generated, in the second phase of the canto, by attention to the third figure, who, alongside Virgil and Manfred, dominates this scene: the figure of Dante himself.

For if there is something scandalous (or miraculous) on both a theological and a poetic level in finding Virgil and Manfred in Purgatory, then it is equally disconcerting to discover, as Dante now does, that the protagonist is physically present in the spirit world of Purgatory. Yet in countenancing that outrage, Canto III takes its place in a sustained sequence of considerations, involving the foundations both of Dante's Christian thinking and of his narrative invention, which runs from the *Vita nuova,* through the earliest cantos of the *Inferno,* to the heights of the *Paradiso.* Theologically Dante traces, from the moment of Beatrice's physical death to Solomon's celebration in *Paradiso* XIV, a concern with the ultimate mystery of the Resurrection ("When, glorified and sanctified, the flesh / is once again our dress," *Par.* XIV, 43). Poetically, his dependence on this doctrine is evident in innumerable moments of physical action closely observed, as Dante tests and elaborates the fictional logic of his own poem.

To Cast No Shadow

Much of the Ante-Purgatory is taken up with a meditation on this theme, as often comic as it is miraculous. In Cantos I and II, the question of why Dante should be where he is has only been broached in the delightful moment of magical realism when the bodily Dante attempts to embrace the spiritual Casella. Now, in Canto III, the notion strikes with the violence and disconcerting or divisive energy that from the first has characterized the opening phases of the canto:

> Behind my back the sun was flaming red;
> but there, ahead of me, its light was shattered
> because its rays were resting on my body.
>
> (16–18)

The sunlight, which had shone so comprehensibly, so comfortingly, in the "the gentle hue of oriental sapphire" (*Purg.* I, 13) is now rendered with violence. A sudden revelation is promised. Yet this revelation threatens to reverse, or expand, the familiar typologies of light and dark: for if there is a revelation, then it is carried not by light itself—which is here unimaginably shattered (*rotto*, 16)—but rather by the darkness of shadow and the intervention of the physical body. At such a moment, the disorientation that Dante experiences may well be shared by the reader. Is his body an impediment? Is he excluded from some purely spiritual realm by its possession? Or is it somehow an unthinkable sign of arrival—of the destination to which he is traveling—that Dante should be so disoriented?

These questions persist throughout the canto. But, of course, the immediate question in Dante's mind as protagonist is whether, after all, he is alone in Purgatory, since Virgil, having no body, casts no shadow of his own. And Virgil, it appears, *is* there, at least to the extent that words can assert a human presence; and he now proceeds to reassure Dante by offering a clarification. Or, rather, since the clarification itself, in the course of a long and shifting speech, comes to be shadowed by doubts and the effects of darkness, Virgil seeks to protect Dante from the violent moment of revelatory insight that Dante's own physical presence in the otherworld has unleashed.

Whenever Virgil speaks—at any point in the *Comedy*—one does well to recall the obvious truth that, in fact, the speaker is Dante himself, exploring by the adoption of his Virgilian persona characteristics of the pagan mind that he greatly admires and summoning up the resources of eloquence and intellectual precision, which he associates with such a mind. So, in the present passage, there is at least one verse that enunciates in firmly authoritative imperatives a lesson of central importance in Dante's characterization of the Virgilian mentality and, indeed, of Dante's own thinking. This is the demand that, in the face of certain manifestations of Divine action, we should accept the veil and limit of our unknowingness and—rather than asking *why* what we see should be there at all—be satisfied with the contemplation of *what* we see: "Confine yourselves, o humans, to the *quia*" (37).

Virgil's next speech threatens to drain its audience of any enthusiasm for the evidence of physical beauty and worth. It begins in the elegiac comforts of the shadow, enforced by adagio rhythms and long cadences, in significant contrast to the frenetic scherzo of the opening sequence:

> The body from within which I cast shadows
> is buried where it now is evening: taken
> from Brindisi, it now belongs to Naples.
>
> (25–27)

There is already a note of regret as Virgil confesses to lack the very form in which he had spent his illustrious human existence. But evening and the grave also seem to protect Virgil from the effects of light; and if here he offers similar protection to Dante against the disturbing yet conceivably triumphal implications of his own presence in Purgatory, then likewise he diminishes the glory that attached to his own bodily being. Thus he makes nothing of the significant fact that if his body was moved, it was moved out of imperial celebration of his achievements. Bodies in this canto are transported by triumph (as is Virgil's), from motives of enmity or rehabilitation (as is Manfred's), or else by assimilation to the Resurrected Christ (as Dante's body may be). But against any such violence or display, Virgil seeks stillness, calm, and dark finalities. His tendency is allied further with a subtly stated incomprehension of his own identity. So when Virgil speaks of "the body from within which I cast shadows" (25), it is by no means clear where the "I" is located and what relation it has to its place in the world: "The body . . . / is buried where it now is evening" (24–25). Is the self inside the body as if it were in some transient vehicle? No personal pronoun or adjective attaches either to body or to shadow: they are not Virgil's. Yet some self once made shadows, whether on the living ground or on the written page. It cannot be good to cast no shadow if to be a "shadow" is to lack one's humanity.

A discomfort, then, is perceptible at the very core of Dante's comfort; and this (in context) complicates even the undoubtedly valuable insistence on limit toward which Virgil is moving. This movement is itself strangely oblique and is accompanied by increasingly audible tones of incomprehension and recrimination. For Virgil has now to explain (or Dante has to explain to himself in constructing his theological fiction) why the inhabitants of Purgatory should appear embodied: and the transitions of thought here traverse and connect two particular areas in which the Virgilian mentality seems to be particularly uncomfortable. These are the ontological extremes represented by the Trinity and by the physical body:

> Thus, if no shadow falls in front of me,
> do not be more amazed than when you see
> the heavens not impede each other's rays.
> The Power has disposed such bodiless

> bodies to suffer torment, heat and cold;
> how this is done, He would not have us know.
> Foolish is he who hopes our intellect
> can reach the end of that unending road
> only one Substance in three Persons follows.
>
> (29–36)

One notes immediately a painful, formulaic blankness in Virgil's account of the Trinity, which stands revealed in its vacuity simply by a comparison between these lines and those which Dante writes with such lyrical intensity in the *Paradiso* to celebrate

> That One and Two and Three who ever lives
> and ever reigns in Three and Two and One,
> not circumscribed and circumscribing all.
>
> (*Par.* XIV, 28–30)

But bodily sensation is viewed, at line 31, with even greater dullness, as if "torment" were the only mode in which heat and cold might be experienced. Again, a comparison will establish Virgil's deficiencies, as for instance, between his words and those of his fellow Roman, Statius, who, in Canto XXV, speaks thus on the union of body and soul:

> That what I say may leave you less perplexed,
> consider the sun's heat that, when combined
> with sap that flows from vines, is then made wine.
>
> (76–78)

Then there is further discomfort—here in the form of the argumentative and narrative tactics of Dante himself in pursuing these lines of thought. For the Trinity is invoked to explain what otherwise might seem to be a glitch in the narrative logic—and in his mimetic program—of the *Comedy* itself, that Dante should be able to speak of the spirit bodies as visible beings. There is, at the very least, a certain incongruity of dignity between these two states. (Or one might say that, in Dante's poetics, mimesis requires not merely accuracy of observation but also a philosophical justification of vision.)

Foolish Hope

As if to stabilize this initial disequilibrium, Virgil—now approaching the imperative of "Confine yourselves" (37)—rallies with a vigorous condemnatory tone: "Foolish is he who hopes" (34). There is, one might feel, a certain overcompensation in this powerful utterance, leading Virgil to voice in repressive terms the Christian message of which he cannot be a part. At the same time there is also a strain of rancor when Virgil speaks of how he lives in Limbo in the company of "infant innocents" whose only sin is to have died unbaptized. The uncharacteristic abrasiveness of these lines points to a subtext; it is this subtext that moves into a dominant position in the concluding part of Virgil's speech, where he brings into the open a issue (largely of Dante's own invention) concerning the fate of the noble pagan.

It is said that Dante insists on a stricter view of Limbo than many of his contemporaries would have allowed and, simultaneously, gives more credence to the demands of pagan mentalities. A problem arises here that continues from Limbo until the *Paradiso*, where Dante states the question in its most penetrating form: "Where is this justice then that would condemn him?" (*Par.* XIX, 77). Arguably, he does not resolve it. The Ante-Purgatory, investigating the role of the body in human existence, correspondingly investigates the tragic position of Virgil, or the fate of rationality itself. And the tensions implied in this position are now revealed as Virgil's meditations on the practices of Christian Gods and Christian poets are brought into counterpoint with an awareness of those great fellow pagans, such as Aristotle, whose intellectual eminence would, in all justice, seem to qualify them for a better fate than Limbo:

> "Confine yourselves, o humans, to the *quia;*
> had you been able to see all, there would
> have been no need for Mary to give birth.
>   You saw the fruitless longing of those men
> who would—if reason could—have been content,
> those whose desire eternally laments:
>   I speak of Aristotle and of Plato—
> and many others." Here he bent his head
> and said no more, remaining with his sorrow.
>
>   (37–45)

The rhyme here leads down in a sterile descent from *tutto* and *frutto* to a plangent denial of any enjoyment of eternity in the final *lutto*. But braced against this is the uncomprehending, tight-lipped, and even rather brutal identification of a Christian myth centered on the plain word "Maria." So far from implying respect or reverence, the word—associated phonetically with *parturir*—pictures, in contrast to the self-evident dignity of noble intellects, a providential chain linked through the everyday banalities of childbirth. The voice even suggests a certain repugnance: it is as if the whole apparatus of the Christian myth, with its Gardens, Apples, Virgin Births, and miraculous Trinities, were momentarily seen as a coarse imposition on the sensibilities of the classical tradition.

This, however, is the nadir of the canto; and though the dark tonalities emanating from it do not wholly disappear, the rhythms and spatial organization of the narrative now begin to alter. A vertical axis—with all its suggestion of laborious advance, transcendence, and divine assistance—displays itself anew. During Virgil's discourse, "we had reached the mountain's base" (46): from Virgil himself, this arrival evokes only a grim spurt of humor, as he countenances the absurdity of the climb for any human being who happens to have no wings ("where even he who has no wings can climb," 54). Seeking a place where the cliff descends, Virgil now fixes his mind on the road at his own feet, as if logical minds and sequential paths were closely akin.

Dante picks up this tune: for in contrast to the downcast Virgil, he raises his eyes, gazing with wonder and good purpose at the towering rock: "I looked up around the wall of rock" (57). Dante can now anticipate a solution that his guide cannot, commenting, with a humorous chiding of his own, on the deficiencies of Virgil's momentary self-absorption ("If you can find no counsel in yourself," 63) and urging Virgil in tones of spiritual enthusiasm to raise his eyes and—as Christians frequently do—to *behold*: "here. . . ." In the distance, Dante has seen figures invisible to the introspective Virgil and perceptible only to his own penetrating and vital gaze.

For all that, the assistance now at hand will not come in the form of any celestial epiphany or even from the mouth of some apparently authoritative figure, such as the Cato of Canto I. On the contrary, the solution sought by Dante (delayed until Canto IV) will be the result of conversation and negotiations with figures who are as ignorant as Dante and Virgil are. In any case, these figures are at present still a thousand laborious paces away, huddling as if for comfort against the rock face (which undoubtedly carries symbolic suggestions of the faith that these penitents sinned against). Yet, once Dante with his living eyes has alerted Virgil to these distant presences, Virgil's mood alters again. With new animation ("less distressed," 64) and a regenerated sense of purpose ("Let us go there," 65), Virgil sets out briskly to cover the thousand paces between himself and the souls, sluggish and petrified, who shelter beneath the very rock that eventually they will have to climb. It is as if—since we are now dealing with human beings and also with the horizontal plane of human negotiation rather than the vertiginous mysteries of the Trinity—Virgil has rediscovered a role for himself.

At the Mountain's Base

To initiate the courtesies of this human encounter, Virgil begins with a gallant and encouraging *captatio benevolentiae*:

> "O chosen souls, you who have ended well,"
> Virgil began, "by virtue of that peace
> which I believe awaits you all . . ."
>
> (73–75)

We are reminded here, as we are elsewhere in the *Purgatorio,* that Virgil has been chosen by Beatrice for his "persuasive word" (*Inf.* II, 67), to inspire and foster common understanding. Correspondingly, in the following phases of Canto III, the interchange of verbal courtesies will prove to be far from a matter of trivial display or superficial grace. Whereas up to this time the canto has depicted failing, isolated, and directionless individuals plunged into their own thoughts, from now on it will be concerned with recognitions, with reciprocations of regard, and with requests for spiritual assistance. The narrative will itself represent—and enact—the processes by which new direction can be established and new communities formed. A comparable courtesy—understood as a capacity for negotiation and an animating attention to the detail of human behavior—will lie at the center of the poetics that Dante, here as elsewhere in the *Purgatorio,* pursues in the structuring of his poem.

Nonetheless, the final form of courteous "persuasive word," which Canto III itself represents, will be in the form of Christian prayer. (In the concluding lines of the canto, the penitent dead Manfred urges the pilgrim Dante to invoke the intercession of his living daughter.) Inevitably, in that perspective of Christian hope, even Virgil's new confidence carries with it a certain hidden darkness. Once again (as in the "Not man; I once was man." *Purg.* I, 67) Virgil, in encouraging others, is obliged to acknowledge his own deficiencies, evoking the faith that he cannot enjoy in order to celebrate these persons whose souls are "chosen" and elected, certain of the ultimate peace. Virgil here may adopt the rhetoric of Christian confidence and point to the ultimate goal that Providence allots to the redeemed; that same Providence in Virgil's case is the fate that relegates him to the melancholic community of Limbo, along with Aristotle and Plato. However, it is against this melancholic regression that the canto now begins to envisage another form of rhetoric—and correspondingly another form of community, humbler and yet more whole—that develops as much between the author of the canto, Dante himself, and his reader as it does between Virgil and the excommunicates.

For at lines 79–84 the epic elevation and theological niceties uttered by Virgil are displaced by a pastoral simile of Dante's own devising. In response to Virgil's words, the excommunicates shuffle with flickering diffidence towards their interlocutor:

> Even as sheep that move, first one, then two,
> then three, out of the fold—the others also
> stand, eyes and muzzles lowered, timidly;
>   and what the first sheep does, the others do,
> and if it halts, they huddle close behind,
> simple and quiet and not knowing why.
>
> (79–84)

The first courtesy extended in these lines is to translate the excommunicates from the abstract ranks of the "O chosen souls" to the Christian community established by the earthy parables of sheep lost and found. In a context that concerns the need for institutions and leaders (and that will even refer to a corrupt and inimical pope as the "pastor" at line 124), it is, of course, impossible to ignore the comparison of the Christian community to a sheepfold. Such a community is built not on the supposed rationalities favored by institutions but rather on the paradoxes demanding that we seek—against the burden of utility—for the one lost sheep. The linguistic and intellectual forms, which themselves will ensure entry to that community, are forms of paradox. So in a sequence that will shortly reveal the piratical Manfred as a member of this particular flock, the sheep themselves are comically led by a leader who is himself lost. More strikingly still, this community is not—as it would have been in Limbo—formed around those who, like Aristotle, are masters of knowledge but rather around those who do not know: "not knowing why" (84). With the impetus of these light (indeed delightful) contradictions, the simile, so far from offering emollient persuasions or final certitudes, initiates—as do parables and courtesy alike—a true attention to detail and process. Here the unexpectedness of the simile draws attention to the hesitant motion of a flock of sheep—"first one, then two / then three"—and captures mimetically in its own stuttering alliterations their forward movement. Likewise, one is invited to linger not only on the eye of the sheep but also on the "muzzles," exposed to comic effect in the rhyme position, and finally to see, even feel, the undulation of backs rubbing one against the other. We are invited to view these details as miraculously fresh. The human eye need not seek only an ultimate or transcendent destiny: the things of the world—in their ever-new and ever-shifting relationships—are themselves objects of regard, even of courteous attention.

If this, however, is courtesy, then it is not merely the courtesy that a superior might show to an inferior. For the reader too is caught in processes—initiated by the change of stylistic level and carried through in the sequential movement of the written text—which at line 87 produce their own moment of surprised attention. Here, as we move from vehicle to tenor, we realize that we have been deceived: these are not sheep after all but human beings with faces worthy of regard, and their pace, so fretful up till now, is now described with the adjective *onesta* ("modest"), which Dante had once used of the great spirits of Limbo:

> So, then, I saw those spirits in the front
> of that flock favored by good fortune move—
> their looks were modest; seemly, slow, their walk.
>
> (85–87)

The simile, concluding in this way, provides not a frame but rather a mode of engagement in which our sense of what *is* comes out enlivened and enriched precisely through its encounter with the unexpected. Through the prism of Christian imagery and a renewed attention to what lies before our eyes—which is to say, the presence of human persons—a varied spectrum of human possibilities is disclosed, and our reading of the simile invites us, as readers, into the community that carries forward these possibilities. This is a working community, *in fieri*, which reads (as though by braille) the character of human worth by touching the marks we leave on the matter of the world.

In a number of ways, the shift of level and tonality that occurs at this point in the canto could well be described not only as courteous but also as comic; and such a suggestion is sanctioned by the fact that henceforth the canto is dominated, not by Virgil, "remaining with his sorrow" (45), but rather by the figure of Manfred, who at line 112 appears smiling to Dante, because he is sure of salvation.

Virgil displays a slightly comic embarrassment as he characteristically attempts to explain away the marvel of Dante's bodily presence in Purgatory to the bewildered excommunicates ("Don't be astonished," 97), and speaks with equally characteristic negative structures of Dante's providential destiny:

> "rest assured that he
> would not attempt to cross this wall without
> a force that Heaven sent him as support."
>
> (98–99)

But the canto will henceforth be dominated by a fictively wounded renegade and an exile wonderfully out of place in his possession of bodily form: even as imperial representative Virgil has, one might think, now been replaced by Manfred, a lost sheep who is simultaneously a redeemed soul.

Manfred

The wounds displayed by Manfred are better understood not as authoritative symbols of some ultimate truth but rather as signs of identification, distinguishing marks, and details. If these wounds recall the wounds that Christ displays to the doubting St. Thomas, then this in itself will suggest that the doubts arising from the pursuit of plausibly rational solutions must ultimately yield before that miraculous conviction of a truth that only the presence of a particular human person can communicate. People carry the truth of other people in the stories of their own existences; and prayer marks the way in which such stories may intersect not in some sentence out of the divine law but rather in the providential will of God as it continues to display itself in creation.

With Manfred's plea for the prayers of his daughter, a final feature of the canto reveals itself: the history of warring institutions, Church and Empire, here viewed in a light that reveals the feminine presence of Costanza, the grandmother, and Costanza, the daughter, of Manfred. Similarly, far from adopting military or public attitudes, the tonalities of the canto for the first time reflect the responsive idiom of the intimate life. To be sure, Manfred will speak here of horrible sins, of wounds, and above all of the subjection of his body to the watery grave—ever moving and shifting—which now contains his corpse. But where Virgil's voice was skeined with the heavy rhythms of his "sorrow," Manfred's rhythms possess a light and varying texture of their own, in which metaphors personify the open arms of mercy: "Goodness has arms so wide that It accepts / who ever would return, imploring It" (122–123).

From this perspective it is fitting that the canto should end with a reference to the Church, now seen for what it truly should be: not a political institution but rather the living body of those who seek prayers and seek to pray. That this is the nature of the Church will be revealed in the final cantos of the *Purgatorio* with the advent of Beatrice. But an anticipation of that is here carried in the father's dependence on the good will of his own daughter:

> Now see if you, by making known to my
> kind Constance where you saw my soul and why
> delay's decreed for me, can make me happy;
> those here—through those beyond—advance more quickly.
>
> (142–145)

Manfred's pride in a child that he has fathered is also humility revealing the generative possibilities that lie in the courteous and attentive considerations of the living Church. But Dante himself has his place in this progressive relationship. As protagonist he is called on to mediate between father and child. And whether or not the unlikely meeting between exile and imperial princess ever took place, Dante's poem serves the same turn. Rediscovering and redefining the role of the true Church, Dante creates a text that is to be read in creative detail as a place of inclusion rather than of excommunication. And if Virgil remains excluded and yet present in the nuances of the words he speaks, then this itself indicates that the interpretative act, which is also in its confession of unknowingness an act of courtesy, of prayer and of penitence, will continue wherever there are people to read and people to be read.

The meeting between Manfred and Dante does not conclude until the beginning of Canto IV, where Dante describes how, although his mind is absolutely absorbed in its attention to Manfred, his body keeps time and, despite its apparent insentience, nevertheless conveys Dante to the point at which he may begin to climb the mountain. The picture that emerges from the sequence we have been considering disallows the suggestion that human beings are in any way designed to advance through purely intellectual intelligence (even though they are capable of that) or that we should ever seek, in any simple sense, to transcend the particularities that mark and identify our historical being. On the contrary, we advance by participating in an action (abrasive or enlivening as this might be) that is impelled by our engagement in a historical attention to other beings. To climb is itself an action in which we realize anew the paradoxical unity of our physical and spiritual gravitations. So in Canto IV—which concludes with one of the subtlest pieces of comedy in the whole *Commedia*—Dante constructs a scene in which, in complete contrast to his meeting with the heroic Manfred, he encounters and recognizes a figure from his own past, the indolent Belacqua, who is suddenly and very corporeally present to him. And it is Belacqua who asserts—in an exchange suffused with smiles of recognition—that Dante will "perhaps" (significantly) have to rest before he arrives at the summit of his intellectual aspirations: "Perhaps you will / have need to sit before you reach that point!" (*Purg.* IV, 98–99).

Our conclusion, developed in the course of Canto III, is that truth resides not in any well-finished utterance but rather in practice and in regenerative process. Canto III (in common with every other canto of the *Comedy*) may be seen as a series of thought experiments, conducted on our conception of figures such as Manfred, Virgil, and Dante himself and ultimately on our conception of the human person. But these experiments are very different from those conducted by philosophers since the time of that other great dualist, Descartes. Our concern in reading Dante is not to command humanity but to re-create ourselves as human beings in the company of others. The courtesy required for this act is, simultaneously, an act of interpretation. The true community lies neither in Limbo nor in the sheepfold of the excommunicates but rather in our continued desire to understand others.

BIBLIOGRAPHY

Boyle, Nicolas. *Who Are We Now?: Christian Humanism and the Global Market from Hegel to Heaney.* Notre Dame, IN: University of Notre Dame Press, 1998.

Brieger, Peter, Millard Meiss, and Charles S. Singleton. *Illuminated Manuscripts of the "Divine Comedy."* Princeton: Princeton University Press, 1969.

Foster, Kenelm. *The Two Dantes, and Other Studies.* London: Darton, Longman and Todd, 1977.

Freccero, John. *Dante: The Poetics of Conversion.* Edited and with an introduction by Rachel Jacoff. Cambridge, MA: Harvard University Press, 1986.

Kerr, Fergus. *Immortal Longings: Versions of Transcending Humanity,* Notre Dame, IN: University of Notre Dame Press, 1997.

Kirkpatrick, Robin. *Dante's Inferno: Difficulty and Dead Poetry.* New York: Cambridge University Press, 1987.

———. *Framing Medieval Bodies.* Edited by Sarah Kay and Miri Rubin. New York: Manchester University Press, 1994.

Le Goff, Jacques. *La Naissance du Purgatoire.* Paris: Gallimard, 1981.

Milbank, John. *The Word Made Strange: Theology, Language, Culture.* Cambridge, MA: Blackwell, 1997.

Nussbaum, Martha Craven. *The Fragility of Goodness: Luck and Ethics in Greek Tragedy and Philoso-phy,* Cambridge: Cambridge University Press, 1986.

Pite, Ralph. *The Circle of Our Vision: Dante's Presence in English Romantic Poetry.* Oxford: Clarendon Press, 1944.

Scott, John Alfred. *Dante's Political Purgatory.* Philadelphia: University of Pennsylvania Press, 1996.

CANTO IV

The Lute Maker

ENZO QUAGLIO

Translated by Charles Ross

It would perhaps seem a little superfluous to pause long over a figure as much discussed as Belacqua or to try to offer a new reading of the forty verses at the end of Canto IV where he appears, given the attention that has been paid to him by such luminaries as Bosco, Petrocchi, Fallani, Romagnoli, and Chiari. An anecdote by the Anonymous Florentine is the archetype behind all the variations that appear throughout the fourteenth century and after, even into our own time:

> This Belacqua was a citizen of Florence, an artisan, and he fashioned mountains of lutes and guitars, even though he was the laziest man who ever lived. They say of him that he arrived in the morning at his workshop, sat down, and never rose except to eat or sleep. One of his relatives is reported to have upbraided him for his negligence, until one day, when he was being upbraided, Belacqua responded with the words of Aristotle: the mind that sits quietly gains knowledge. To which his relative responded, "Certainly, if one can become wise by sitting, no one was ever wiser than you."

In the writings of scholars from Boccaccio to Politian, Belacqua became the universal figure of laziness, a figure who existed outside the context of the canto: facetious, ironic, impertinent, clever, malicious, sarcastic, skeptical, aloof, and wise—in short, the portrait of a Florentine.

Eventually, however, critics reconsidered Belacqua not as Dante's antagonist or as the practical voice of a citizen who redirects the heroic enthusiasm of an overly zealous neophyte, but as a companion of Dante's lost Florentine youth whose exchange of courtesies makes him the pilgrim's instructor. Belacqua's experience corrects Dante's enthusiasms. He condemns himself and his delayed repentance that prevents him from initiating the true cathartic process. Many critics have analyzed the minute psychology of this character, his movements, ironies, gestures, and words to reaffirm his place in the only text that matters—that of Dante. Perhaps the critics have gone too far. At any rate, it is time to attempt another path.

Commencing the True Ascent

It has been observed that the first twelve lines, or the prelude to the canto, unfold in one of those temporal indications so common in the "incipits" (first lines of cantos) in the *Purgatorio* (a full fifteen out of thirty-three cantos). Moreover, there is a turn toward terrestrial time that is unknown in the other canticles. One might add that the same adverb, "when," is called on to begin Canto VI ("When dicing's done and players separate") and XXX ("When the first heaven's Seven-Stars had halted"). But the reader is more struck that "when" returns at lines 7 ("and thus, when something seen / or heard"), 43 ("I was exhausted when I made this plea"), and 91 ("Therefore, when this slope seems to you so gentle"), marking the movement of the pilgrim through the cantos. In fact, the repetition of this common adverb marks the commencement of the true ascent in Purgatory, the ascent, up to the Earthly Paradise, of the mountain of expiation, Dante's preparation for the final flight to Paradise. Dante's meditation on the movement of time sets up the climate for the canto and repeats the Thomistic battle against the Platonic error of multiple souls that had taken place a short time before at the Council of Constantinople (1311–1312). That this debate is one of the sources of the opening discourse on how humans perceive time is proved by the rational causality of lines 10 through 12:

> The power that perceives the course of time
> is not the power that captures all the mind;
> the former has no force—the latter binds.

Dante shows no grammatical fear of reiterating, even in the restricted circle of a tercet, adjectives (*altra . . . altra*), pronouns (*quella . . . quella . . . quella*), and verbs (*è . . . è . . . è*); moreover, he creates verbal patterns of great complexity. He takes a formal risk that poets of the next generation, like Petrarch, will not dare to try (to say nothing of Bembo), because he is willing to emphasize the way his own thought turns to syllogisms, as well as his inimitable style of poetical philosophy. What is more, his doctrinal purpose focuses the very center of these opening dozen lines, which he anticipates with the proverbial "time moves and yet we do not notice it" (9), by highlighting the existential situation of the pilgrim ("And I confirmed this by experience," 13), which is all but the same in substance as the narrative itself ("hearing that spirit in my wonderment," 14). The reference is to the missing close of Canto III (it ends with the words of Manfred), which Dante delays, so as not to disturb with any external considerations the dolorous story of the famous Swabian knight illustrating the human and heavenly misfortunes of a blessed and attractive heroic spirit. Similar considerations do not, however, prevent Dante from establishing his temporal coordinates ("for though the sun had fully climbed fifty / degrees," 15–16), giving us the exact time—three hours have passed, and it is 9:30—in which he begins his ascent.

There follows another, differently formulated, comparison:

> The farmer, when the grape is darkening,
> will often stuff a wider opening
> with just a little forkful of his thorns.
>
> (19–21)

Most commentators refer us to *Inferno* XV, 96, and to XXVI, 25, where we previously saw the peasant farmer. My mind, however, returns to the opening of Canto XXIV in the same canticle, to the "farmer who is short of fodder" (*Inf.* XXIV, 7). Note that the passage is parallel, but that the correspondence, in different scenes, between the two diminutives—"forkful" *(forcatella)* and "farmer" *(vilanello)*—and their similar lightness of touch, lend the two autonomous rural scenes an agricultural and festive flavor that seems to derive from the same inclination to portray farm life realistically ("when the grape is darkening").

The Topography of Purgatory

Dante's focus on the terrestrial world, on agriculture and the countryside, is evident once again when Dante describes the steep slopes of the Apennines (San Leo, Noli, Bismantova, Cacume), conjuring up the Italian mountains in order to represent his rocky, arduous climb. More so than in the other canticles, here Dante ties his description of the terrestrial dimension to topography and geography through the verbs that run through the *terzina* ("can be climbed," "one can descend," "ascend"), to end suddenly on a last line ("but here / I had to fly") that re-creates the rapidity and means of ascent.

The grand theme of the pilgrimage renews itself with an energetic fervor and a marked lack of hesitation. The climbers face difficulties ("along each side the edges pressed on us; / the ground beneath required feet and hands," 32–33), and the difficulty of the undertaking ("The summit was so high, my sight fell short," 40) takes on the sense of moral duty ("with rapid wings / and pinions of immense desire," 28–29) in the exchange between Dante and Virgil (35–39 and 43–52). In truth, the relationship between the two that has been established since the first canto of the *Inferno*—that of a guide and his disciple—continues here. And so the teacher gives paternal advice and encouragement to help Dante complete the arduous climb, while the alpine landscape clarifies, but does not insist on, a moral allegory whose tenor is intellectual attainment (52–57). It is during their rest period, when they look down from their mountain height and Dante is stupefied by all that is new and by the precision of his teacher, that a romantic moment is created in which their words fit their actions and the stages of the voyage on the sacred mountain conform to the information imparted to the pilgrim:

> he said to me: "Suppose Castor and Pollux
> were in conjunction with that mirror there,
> which takes the light and guides it north and south,
>   then you would see the reddish zodiac
> still closer to the Bears as it revolves—
> unless it has abandoned its old track.
>
>   (61–66)

This is Virgil's first genuinely scientific lecture, the first of many that will mark the journey of the voyagers in the second *cantica,* occurring often in dialogue with Dante. Here, for example, the zealous scholar not only understands and accepts the master's explanation, but he develops and reinforces it. After having indirectly and tacitly solicited this information, Dante now ably gives it shape, almost physically, by asking a question motivated by his concrete situation (85–87) and directing it toward more general questions of ethics and psychology, as shown by Virgil's answer, which definitively finishes the debate (88–95).

The purpose is obvious but not banal. The poet owes the reader some explanation of the topography of Purgatory, including the exact collocation of the mountain in relation to the hemisphere occupied by the *Inferno.* Virgil explains how Jerusalem and the holy mountain are in opposite hemispheres, north and south. Dante, calculating the angle of the sun's rays, determines that the distance from the equator to the mountain is the same as it is to the city of the Hebrews. We learn why, then, as they go around the mountain, the sun strikes them first on one side, then the other. This information moves toward the allegorical and symbolic; the ascent represents the psychology of penitence, with all its urgency and rationality. Moreover, the contrast between the anxiety of the student and the knowledge of the expert creates a scientific plane for the external speaking voices, including that of Belacqua, who will turn a new page in the actors' script.

Dante's use of the hypothetical ("Suppose Castor and Pollux / were in conjunction with that mirror there," 61–62; "If you would realize how," 67) signals a scientific demonstration, as in a medieval mathematical theorem. But in the context of this syllogistic logic, one also notices a sense of connectedness, symmetry, consequences, and unshakeable certainty with regard to knowledge that contrasts with the uncertainty of the undertaking ("as clearly as I now can comprehend," 78). The earliest commentators nonetheless regarded Dante's work, including its mythological references, as a summa of medieval learning; and Boccaccio, Dante's most enthusiastic scholar, told the world first that Dante was self-taught but also an expert. The result was a belief, in Italian culture, that a didactic poem could only be written by another Dante.

Bellacqua Intervenes

Many commentators linger over the moment that separates Virgil's words from Belacqua's voice (97). The purpose of Virgil's discourse, which is implicit in his abrupt conclusion ("I say no more, and this I know as truth," 96), signals the difficulty of the ascent and invites us to recognize that the climb requires a conscious act. Others, by contrast, believe that Virgil is signaling the limits of his knowledge, of reason without grace, and that Belacqua's intervention is a providential means to lessen the tension that has mounted as a result of recognizing reason's—and therefore Virgil's—ancillary role. It may be that we are not meant to choose between the two positions. At any rate, Virgil will not speak again until the end of the canto, while for most of the remainder of it the two Florentines talk together. Belacqua's appearance slows down the impetus to ascend, and the mental and intellectual force required, by giving a horizontal movement to their circuit ("We made our way toward it . . . and the distress . . . did not prevent my going to him," 103–117).

I have already noted that Belacqua's reputation has changed from that of a clever cartoon character to that of a complex personality who has almost set aside his worldly personality as he waits for his destiny in Purgatory. During the twentieth century, his conversation was read less for its sarcasm, parody, and irony and more for its ability to edify and extend charity, as Belacqua is transferred from Florence to the sacred mountain, from his workshop to the station where he waits. Belacqua's first word, forse, has been interpreted as a sort of dig at Dante. It has been thought to mean "probably," but also "certainly." It corresponds to the pilgrim's ambivalence, as he exchanges his sense of expectancy for his old sense of friendship, which becomes clear in Dante's smile ("The slowness of his movements, his brief words / had stirred my lips a little toward a smile," 121–122) and the questions that follow ("but tell me, why / do you sit here? do you expect a guide?" 124–125).

At this point the lazy man teaches the enthusiastic pupil a moral lesson about the true condition of one who stands and waits. His speech is affectionate, fraternal, and thoughtful. Gradually he sets aside his earthly amiability, saying, "O brother, what's the use of climbing?" (127). Dante is relieved to find his old friend safe ("From this time on, Belacqua, / I need not grieve for you," 123–124). Dante is not pardoning his friend indulgently but listening to his explication of the laws of this new world and learning a lesson in punishment.

It is worth noting that the three figures of the Ante-Purgatory whom Dante meets form a triptych, with two Florentines—Casella and Belacqua—flanking the Swabian prince Manfred, whom Dante does not at first recognize. Yet though the earliest exegetes strove mightily to identify Dante's friends, no one can say with certainty that Casella was even Florentine or that the lute maker Duccio di Buonavia, who was alive in 1299, was really the model for Dante's figure. Yet the two are connected, one as a singer of songs, the other as a maker of instruments, and both are therefore connected with poetry. And both are said to have been friends of Dante.

A Friend in the Place of Expiation

Dante lived seven centuries ago; I do not think we need to struggle to make him our contemporary. It is up to us, as readers, if we wish to interpret his message, to approach his world, not vice versa. We cannot forget that Dante lived in a different world, and this accounts for the exile's silence on the subject of his wife and family, which would be unthinkable in a writer today. The same must be said about the theme of friendship. Dante's encounters in the *Purgatorio* with his former friends are not private encounters and are not explained by chroniclers who evoke these characters. Their interest lies in the one who organized them on the page and in the verse, from Casella to Nino Visconti, from Oderisi to Forese. Friendship, for Dante, ever since his *Vita nuova,* is literary, philosophical, and lyrical in theme, explicitly connected to the departure of Beatrice, to Dante's salvational reading of the *Laelius* of Cicero, and to the friends and poets (Oderisi, Guinizzelli, Bonagiunta) with whom he discusses art in the *Purgatorio.*

My preference is to regard the relationship between the landscape, and its verbal expression, with the two conversations of the cantos, that between Dante and Virgil and between Dante and Belacqua. A series of adverbs of place begins with "nearby" (98) and continues with "toward" (*là* and *ivi,* 103), "here" (*quiritto,* 125), and repetitions of *giù* (down) and *sù* (up) in several places, framing the intense location of line 101: "and to the left we saw a massive boulder." The phrase "to the left" (*a mancina*) is quite rare (in fact, it is unique to the *Comedy* and to Dante). The usual phrase is *dal lato mancino,* as in *Inferno* XXVI, 126 ("and always gained upon our left-hand side"). It is followed by a figurative contrast between the "massive boulder" (*gran petrone,* 102, in a line containing an assonance with *-ina* and *-one*) and the simple "boulder" (*sasso,* 104). The effect is to create an accurate and realistic landscape, almost as in a novel. At the same time the unidentified voice has several unusual inflections. The verb *sonò* ("was heard to say") is not a neutral equivalent for a speaking verb. And then there is the music of Belacqua's first words, created by the initial *forse,* an enjambment, and the closure on *distretta:* "Forse / che di sedere in pria avrai distretta" ("Perhaps you will / have need to sit before you reach that point!" 98–99). The penitents use the archaic word *negghienza* ("listlessness," 105) and a pseudo comparison ("as men beset"), prefiguring the following word "laziness" (110) and recalling the "negligence" of which Cato complained (*Inf.* II, 121). The spiritual tension of the allegorical discourse that follows requires adverbials, sound effects, occasional odd words—the whole arsenal of Dante's verbal art.

A full examination of Dante's linguistic dexterity would suggest that the colloquium between the pilgrim and Belacqua relies on a delicate varnish of uniform, comic artistry to establish not the laughter but the smile of amiability and allusive irony. These are not the heavy hits of Hell, but quotidian exchanges, casual words between friends, old customs. Belacqua belongs to a world of letters, not to life. He is a product of vocabulary, not psychology. At the same time, it is legitimate, I believe, to look at the scene from his point of view. At first Belacqua is only a voice, a breath that whispers with an ironic cadence. Then he materializes, the shadow of a lazy man among the lazy. As he speaks to the pilgrim and his guide, his appearance takes shape in a way that creates a psychological profile. Finally, his natural inclination finds expression in another outburst that recalls his first words. At this point, in a certain sense the climax, the pilgrim regards him again ("Then I knew who he was," 115) or at least believes that he has understood, from Belacqua's slow movements, who it is that addresses him. Once they see each other face-to-face Dante lets fly a third verbal arrow, a question that will rebound like a boomerang:

> "From this time on, Belacqua,
> I need not grieve for you; but tell me, why
> do you sit here? Do you expect a guide?
> Or have you fallen into your old ways?"
>
> (123–126)

On the slopes of the sacred mountain of Purgatory, Dante no longer worries, as he once did in Florence, about Belacqua's quips. He has found a friend in the place of expiation, a friend in pain. It is true that his initial request for information ("why / do you sit here") is followed by an alternative (*o pur*), that posits, first, a celestial possibility ("Do you expect a guide?") and second—more subordinate and conditional, less precise—a terrestrial uncertainty ("your old ways?"). Belacqua's response is more affectionate than friendly ("O brother"). His words are edifying, unequivocal. Until now Dante has thought that his Florentine friend would continue to play the part of the lazy man, the prankster. But instead Belacqua denounces the vanity of any solitary effort and signals both his resignation and that of his penitential companion to the divine will, even as he is shedding his earthly vices.

The courtesy of his words and the deliberateness of his actions no longer result from his congenital tardiness; rather, they exist as a *contrapasso* to the negligent way he has led his life. Only the intervention of mortals on earth can shorten his punishment. Belacqua, finally, represents Dante's farewell to comedy.

BIBLIOGRAPHICAL NOTES

See Umberto Bosco, *Tre letture dantesche* (Rome, 1942) and "Il canto di Belacqua," in *Dante vicino* (Caltanisetta-Roma, 1966), 122–134; Giorgio Petrocchi, *L'attesa di Belacqua,* in *Lettere italiane* 4 (1954): 221–234, and "Il canto IV del *Purgatorio*" (Alcama, 1955) and "Il canto IV del *Purgatorio,*" in *Nuove letture dantesche,* 3 (Florence, 1969), 291–310, also in *Itinerari danteschi* (Bari, 1969): 311–332; G. Fallani, "Il Canto IV del *Purgatorio*" (Turin, 1961); S. Romagnoli, "Il canto IV del *Purgatorio,*" in *Letture dantesche,* ed. Giovanni Getto (Florence: Sansoni, 1964), 747–763; A. Chiari, "Il Canto di Belacqua," in *Nove canti danteschi* (Varese, 1966), 99–132.

CANTO V

The Keys to Purgatory

ALDO SCAGLIONE

In Canto V there appears none of those cruxes on which contemporary criticism often fastens as a basis for understanding the poem's deeper meaning. Nevertheless, this canto contains some of the most vivid episodes of the journey, especially in its second part, which involves the stories of three memorable characters. As is typical of the whole *cantica,* and especially evident in the first cantos, we find that the three souls we meet here are, by the very definition of their realm, in a liminal state between two forms of existence, the earthly and the celestial. They are gradually shedding the prejudices and passions that had made them cling to their illusory earthly existence and are getting ready, through their painful purgation, for the bliss to come. We shall see how, by the very progression that distinguishes them one from another, the three main characters grow increasingly detached from worldly values and more prepared to take the final step.

Dialectic Composition: Sudden Discovery, Insistent Request

Giambattista Salinari (1969) finds this canto to be marked by a high degree of lyricism, considering the progression of the three generic ingredients of the entire poem, namely the descriptive (or epic), the dramatic, and the lyric. He also stresses the particularly conspicuous presence of what he calls the three types of *contrappunto* in which Dante excels, namely the "horizontal" (when contrasting episodes are juxtaposed for the sake of variation and emphasis), the "vertical" (when the same situation or theme is developed in several characters through rising tonalities), and finally the "stylistic" (when in the same episode the epic or narrative element is expressed through elegiac description, the dramatic through dialogue, and the lyric through monologue). This is, in short exposition, an interesting analytic point that concerns a striking yet little noticed feature of Dante's method of composition and that I have attempted to define and analyze by use of the term "dialectic composition."

The structure of Canto v leans, as it were, backward and forward, tying in with the conclusion of the episode of the lazy in the preceding canto and then concluding the episode of the violently slain, who properly occupy this canto. In the following canto, the same group continues to crowd around Dante to secure prayers on their behalf from the living. This flowing of cantos one into another, though not exceptional, is particularly typical of this canto as well as of Cantos II–VIII of *Purgatorio*, namely that of the Ante-Purgatory, which the poet seems to have conceived as a rather tight subunit. In turn, this tying in with contiguous portions of the poem is achieved in a way that heightens the logical coherence of the narrative. For example, at the beginning of the canto one of the souls discovers that Dante is alive:

> one
> shade shouted: "See the second climber climb:
> the sun seems not to shine on his left side,
> and when he walks, he walks like one alive!"
>
> (4–6)

His realization gives the others a chance to obtain, through Dante's intercession when he returns to the earthly realm, the prayers that can shorten their stay in Purgatory.

Dante had been recognized, with surprise, as being alive before, even in the preceding canto, but also in the *Inferno* (e.g., VIII, 84–85: "Who is this who, *without death,* / can journey through the kingdom of the dead?"; then by Farinata: "O Tuscan, you who pass alive across / the fiery city" X, 22–23; and again by Chiron among the Centaurs: "Have you noticed / how he who walks behind moves what he touches," XII, 80–81), and this occurrence is a most efficient way to achieve that effect of realism so uniquely produced by Dante's narrative method. Indeed, the theme of this discovery and that of the subsequent request for prayers, both of which have been brought into focus by critics, especially Hatzfeld, are not unique to this canto. They are here more insistently repeated, so that they become, as is usual in Dante, one of several themes giving each section of his poem a close inner consistency, rich in motivations and in tightly interlaced threads, narrative, and argument. This recognition of Dante as a creature still of the earthly world goes together with the most pervasive feature of the whole canto, namely,

Dante's interlocutors' insistent begging of him to obtain prayers for their souls once he has returned to earth.

Canto V contains two major parts of almost equal length. The first (1–63) begins with a preamble, occupied by the twice-repeated, surprised discovery of a living wayfarer in their midst (4–6 and 25–27), together with Virgil's admonition to Dante not to let himself be distracted and slowed down by such incidents. Virgil's rebuke of Dante for being so ready to listen to the souls' entreaties that he delays his journey upward to Grace (10–18) has been much discussed by critics. The incident is perhaps to be understood as a moral lesson of a general nature that Virgil, solicitous but stern fatherly guide, chooses to enter at this precise point, after the repeated interruptions caused mainly by Casella, Manfred, and Belacqua, the first of which had already given occasion to Cato's rebuke. We have then the major portion (64–136), itself in turn subdivided into the three discretely juxtaposed personal episodes of Jacopo del Cassero, Buonconte da Montefeltro, and Pia.

Requisite Forgiveness

Dante's attitude toward the souls in Purgatory contrasts sharply with his attitude in Hell. Whereas in Hell his treatment of the damned had become less and less empathetic and compassionate (as it has been, for example, with Francesca and Brunetto) and more and more in harmony with the severity of the divine judgment, here we go from a degree of human sympathy, even with faults of character (as is still the case with Belacqua), to the higher degree of admiration and reverence that we shall witness at the end of the purgatorial journey. In the particular case of Buonconte, Dante's compassionate interest in the fate of a former enemy marks his own moral and psychological progress toward the blessed forgiveness of Paradise.

As to the souls' attributes, we notice that they distinguish themselves from those we had encountered in Hell: instead of being frozen in their sinful features, they display an increasing propensity to divest themselves of their more mortal characteristics, which they are in the gradual process of transcending until they are completely purified and cleansed of their mortal dregs. In this process of purification they are still subjected to a certain form of *contrapasso*. Whereas Belacqua is still the lazy character he had been throughout his life, the violently slain of Canto V show from the beginning an unusual degree of speed, which reminds us of their active lives. Characteristically, the messengers sent "running" to inquire about Dante return, with the surprising news of his being alive, "with the speed of lightning" (17–40), whereupon the whole group rushes toward Dante and Virgil ("without a rein," 42).

The souls of the new group, those dead by violence who repented only on point of death and who therefore died without last rites, appropriately go around the terrace singing the Miserere, the canonical prayer for God's mercy and the cleansing of guilt. A key word pertaining to their state and specifically to their moral condition at the point of death is the *perdonando* of line 55 *(pentendo e perdonando)*. They ended their lives repenting of their life-long sins and pardoning their enemies—the latter being a necessary condition of true repentance. We shall have to keep this forgiveness in mind, for it will affect the tone and substance of their narratives, in explicit and implied details.

Jacopo: The Motif of Blood

The first character we now meet is Jacopo del Cassero (ca. 1260), member of an ancient noble family from Fano and a one-time Florentine ally who had been *podestà* of Rimini in 1294 and of Bologna in 1296–1297. He had vigorously defended Bologna's independence from the machinations of the ambitious marquis of Ferrara, Azzo VIII of Este (1293–1308), even to the point of spreading defamatory rumors about the latter's personal life. The marquis vowed revenge and had Jacopo murdered by his henchmen in 1298 while Jacopo was journeying just outside the Este territory, on his way to taking on his new role as *podestà* of Milan.

The motif of blood in Jacopo's story is heightened almost to the status of a leitmotif by a repetition that frames the whole episode, since it appears both in the initial lines ("but the piercing wounds / from which there poured the blood where my life lived," 73–74) and as a closing brushstroke ("I saw / a pool, poured from my veins, form on the ground," 83–84), thus becoming a sort of obsessive accompaniment of Jacopo's recollection of the facts. Several critics, Grabher and Puppo among them, have underlined this sense of surprise at the separation of the soul from the body, at this pervasive sense of the actual occurrence of death that is typical of the present group of souls, as expressed here, first by the visual separation of the soul and the vital spirits in which it was supposed to reside—typically, and traditionally, the blood—from the remainder of the body. The most striking detail here is precisely the closing image of Jacopo watching his life element, his blood, leaving his body and forming a red pool around him. This plastic image expresses all the surprise and horror that is one of the pervasive themes of the whole canto. Buonconte will also linger, in his own story, on the moment of dying, and Pia, in a uniquely personal reference, will refer to her end as an "unmaking" of her body *(disfecemi Maremma)*.

Yet the deep meaning of the episode, which corresponds to that of the other episodes in this canto, is one of meek acceptance or at least forgiveness of the perpetrator of the violence suffered. Even while Jacopo does not refrain from the just charge that his murderer, Azzo VIII, exceeded all bounds in his revenge, he does recognize that he had provoked his enemy to anger with his own "heavy sins" (72, presumably referring to his vicious rumors against the lord of Ferrara). Perhaps the reference to Azzo as simply *quel da Esti* betrays Dante's own irritation at the behavior of the lord, who as Florence's ally had helped to persecute the Guelf exiles. Likewise, his calling the Paduans "Antenori" (75, from the archtraitor Antenor, Padua's mythic founder) may contain an implication of treacherous attitudes, since he had called the infernal region of political betrayers of country or party "Antenora."

Buonconte and the Devil

The next character is Buonconte da Montefeltro (ca. 1250/1255–1289), son of that famous condottiere Guido whom we remember from *Inferno* XXVII and himself, as an active military man, deeply involved in the strife between Guelfs and Ghibellines within the commune of Arezzo. He then participated in the military encounters between Ghibelline Arezzo and first the Sienese and, later, the Florentines. He was also a Ghibelline participant in the battle fought at Campaldino on June 11, 1289, by the Aretines against Guelf Florence, in which Dante himself participated as a horseman.

Dante asks Buonconte to disclose how his body had mysteriously disappeared from the battlefield. In the way he tells his story Buonconte, too, shows a detachment from the emotional involvement of the battle, but his narrative marks a poetic step forward. It is more vivid and dramatic than Jacopo's, not because of greater personal attachment to the affairs of the world, but on account of a factor that intervenes at this point and that invests Buonconte's end with cosmic and theological meanings of the highest order. He will recount how the devil, angry at having lost a soul that he had taken for granted, took revenge on his body by causing a storm that swept it into the Arno and covered it with debris. (Dante's own recollection of the weather conditions on the day of the battle is confirmed in Dino Compagni's *Cronica* I, 10.)

The motif of the blood, a plastic visualization of the violent end of these characters, ties Buonconte's story to Jacopo's. Buonconte staggers away from the battlefield mortally wounded in his throat; fleeing on foot, he leaves a long trail of blood on the ground until he reaches the point where the Archiano Torrent joins the Arno:

> There, at the place where that stream's name is lost,
> I came—my throat was pierced—fleeing on foot
> and bloodying the plane.
>
> (97–99)

Incidentally, we observe that, unlike in Hell, where the souls were "deprived of the present," being without knowledge of present events on earth, here in Purgatory Buonconte knows that his family has forgotten him (89). At the same time, the living are placed by divine will in an inherent bond with the souls of the dead in that, with their prayers, they can shorten the sufferings of those in Purgatory.

It is worth noting that such a perceptive and penetrating reader of Dante as John Ruskin (*Modern Painters* III, 1856, 252, also quoted by Longfellow in his translation of the *Comedy*) referred admiringly to the Buonconte episode: "There is, I feel assured, nothing else like it in all the range of poetry; a faint and harsh echo of it, only, exists in one Scottish ballad, 'The twa corbies'" (also well-known in the English version "The Three Ravens"). Ruskin held up Dante as a supreme example of one who is able to describe the inner and outer world in the manner of poets "of the first order," those, that is, who are capable of strong feelings and passions but can master them in their objective representation, in contrast to the poets "of the second order," who are subjectively swayed by their imaginations into quasi-literal renditions of poetic metaphors (cf. "The Pathetic Fallacy," *ibid*, iv).

The cosmic principle and romantic drama of Buonconte's end contrast with the preceding visually constrained static quality of Jacopo's narrative and the ensuing peacefulness of Pia's psychological state, the whole sequence being marked by an admirable climax. I would not hesitate to suggest that there is no more eloquent precedent to the natural romantic furies to which such nineteenth-century fiction as *Wuthering Heights* has accustomed us. The devil's power to trigger such natural phenomena as storms was sanctioned by St. Thomas's *Summa* (I, *quaestio* CXII, *art*. 2). It is also noteworthy that as part of Buonconte's detached, objective attitude toward his end, his dramatic telling of that supernaturally determined event is prefaced by an Aristotelian explanation of the origin of rain (109–111).

The devil's refusal to accept the divine verdict underlines the seeming theological paradox of God's infinite mercy and his willingness to save a soul even if only for one final little tear, *una lagrimetta* (107). This contrasts with the fate of Buonconte's father, Guido da Montefeltro, who, as shown in *Inferno* XXVII, lost his soul after a similar battle between St. Francis and the "black cherub" because of one last unrepented sin, even years after he had converted and become a Franciscan friar. Dante also stresses this theological principle in the episode of Manfred (*Purg.* III), with a particular twist of warning against hasty judgment even in the face of a formal verdict of excommunication by the Church. In these three cases Dante's message is that human actions can only be judged by God, in spite of all appearances and against all human judgments, even when those actions appear to be sanctioned by the loftiest institutions.

Critics have speculated about the possible sources of this powerful scene, and without detracting from Dante's originality one can think of many medieval battles over the soul of a deceased, battles that often hark back to the struggle between Michael the archangel and the devil over the body of Moses in Jude's Epistle IX. But even the theological texts often mentioned this common belief that angels and devils would come for the soul at death and fight for possession of it. St. Bonaventura, an authority well-known to Dante, stresses this belief (both in his *Comm. in Sent. Petri Lombardi*, IV, xx, i; a, I, q, 5, and in his *Sermones de Sanctis*, cf. Singleton's commentary, 103ff). Furthermore, the struggle between the good and the bad angel over the soul at the point of death can be likened not only to the fate of Buonconte's father, Guido (with opposite outcome), but also to Manfred's episode.

Pia's Story

The narrative proceeds in extremely realistic details: Jacopo had referred to the topographic site of his murder and to his *profondi fori*, Buonconte to his being *forato ne la gola* and, more important, to the precise details of the battle's location and of his supernatural burial. By sharp contrast, Pia's story, which follows the epic tone of Jacopo's and the dramatic tone of Buonconte's with a new tone of elegy in a pianissimo timbre (the word is Bosco's), is intentionally sparing in concrete details about her final outcome, leaving it to the reader (and a host of critics) to guess exactly how her life came to an end. Murdered she was, but the only one who knows how, she strongly hints, is her husband. This is a remarkable case of functionally poetic silence that expresses a clear indictment but without anger or resentment. Her pianissimo is thrown all the more into relief by its following, in another most effective dialectic contrast, so suddenly the violent and noisy storm of Buonconte's end. Another contrasting feature is Pia's uniquely different way of asking for prayers, which is also a constant of this canto from beginning to end. After the "petulant" (Bosco) insistence of the crowding souls in the first part of the canto, after the courteous but explicit directness of Jacopo's and Buonconte's requests, Pia, alone among all the souls of Purgatory, subordinates her timid request to the expressed hope that Dante may get the rest he will deserve and need at the end of such a strenuous journey. She asks him to remember her "after returning to the world / when, after your long journeying, you've rested" (130–131).

Pia tells her story by making the Maremma the grammatical subject of her murder, not the culprit who committed it, her husband: "Siena made—Maremma unmade—me" (134). Nor does she describe the manner of her violent death, in sharp contrast to the two preceding victims, even though the verb she uses, *disfecemi,* implies well enough the violence that had occurred. Hatzfeld is one of the many critics who have insisted on Pia's *grazia femminile,* claiming that she is a shining example of the *eterno femminino,* owing to her aptitude for forgiveness, an aptitude that stands out in relative dramatic contrast to the preceding bloody descriptions of the manner of her death, thus ending the whole canto on a high note of catharsis (786). The conclusive gentleness, generosity, and serene acceptance of her fate close the canto in a way that echoes the other episodes as well. Her words are enclosed in a sad sense of loneliness: she does not even hope for anyone in particular to pray for her and only wishes that Dante himself will remember her. It is relevant to keep in mind that the image we have of her personality effectively neutralizes and all but obliterates, by poetic means, our eventual afterthoughts concerning her possible culpability: she is, after all, in Purgatory as a sinner, perhaps because of her very relationship with her husband (the legend did speculate on possible adultery).

The commentators have always commonly surmised, without clear evidence, that Pia was from the Sienese Tolomei family, married to Nello della Pietra dei Pannocchieschi, *podestà* of Volterra and Lucca, who had her murdered either out of jealousy over her behavior or because he wanted to marry one Margherita Aldobrandeschi. Despite the absence of any records of a Pia either in Nello's well-documented family history or in the history of the Tolomei family, the fact remains that Dante never gratuitously invents characters but draws them from history, chronicle, or at least myth. One rather sophisticated hypothesis (cf. Varanini in *Enciclopedia dantesca*) has it that Pia was not a Tolomei but a Sienese Malavolti, married to a Tollo da Prata in Maremma, and that Nello, whom she never married, ordered the widowed Pia murdered, for unknown reasons. The legend of their marriage would have been formed later. In any event, since the traditional genealogy originates with the earliest commentators, it seems fair to assume that it was what Dante, correctly or not, believed to have happened.

Pia's position in the topography of the *Comedy* gives us reason to assume a significant parallelism with the somewhat analogous female characters who appear toward the beginning of each *cantica*, namely Francesca (*Inf.* V) and Piccarda (*Par.* III). All three are unusually gentle toward Dante, and all three had been the victims of their husbands. Yet, when seen in succession, they mark an interesting and telling progression from Francesca's complete, tragically lasting involvement in human passion to Pia's transcending her private affairs in a willful state of preparation for the final, total salvation of her soul, and finally to Piccarda's having reached the complete identification with divine will, as expressed in the memorable line, "And in His will there is our peace" (*Par.* III, 85; cf. Ephesians II: 14, "ipse enim est pax nostra").

As frail as Pia is, or at least appears to be, as impotent as she is in relation to her lordly husband, she triumphs in the end through the force of her love, which transcends even the murderous cruelty of a husband who perhaps did not deserve her but whom she vanquishes by continuing to love him. In her supreme charity of forgiveness, poetically heightened by the juxtaposition of the differently slanted contiguous stories of Jacopo and Buonconte, Pia marks a climax: she comes last because she is the closest to God, being the most prepared for total love. The dialectical contrast between this abruptly peaceful ending and the fury of the highly emotional, bloody, and tempestuous stories that immediately precede (64–129) is another example of Dante's unprecedented and uniquely effective method of arranging the parts of his poem using frequent variations in mood in the form of dialectically contrasting episodes, somewhat like the movement of a sonata. This discreet, subdued ending suggestively closes a canto that had been so full of dramatic action.

BIBLIOGRAPHICAL NOTES

The most significant *lecturae* of this canto are Umberto Bosco, "Iacopo del Cassero—Bonconte—Pia" (1953), in *Dante vicino* (Caltanissetta: Sciascia, 1966), 139–150; Carlo Grabher, "Il canto V del *Purgatorio*" (Florence: Sansoni, 1942), reprinted as "Iacopo del Cassero, Buonconte da Montefeltro e Pia de' Tolomei," in *La Divina Commedia nella critica*, II: *Il Purgatorio*, ed. Antonino Pagliare (Messina-Florence: D'Anna, 1965), 142–153; Helmut A. Hatzfeld, "Il canto V del *Purgatorio*," in *Letture dantesche*, vol. 2, ed. Giovanni Getto (Florence: Sansoni, 1962); Angelo Jacomuzzi, "Il canto V del *Purgatorio*," *Lettere Italiane* 28 (1976): 3–17; *Nuove letture dantesche (Casa di Dante in Roma)*, vol. 3 (Florence: Le Monnier, 1969), 311–331 (by Giambattista Salinari); Mario Puppo "Canto V," in *Lectura Dantis Scaligera: Purgatorio* (Florence: Le Monnier, 1963), reprinted in *Aggiornamenti di critica dantesca*, ed. Silvio Pasquazi (Florence: Le Monnier, 1972), 439–445; Corrado Ricci, "Jacopo del Cassero, Buonconte e la Pia," in *Ore ed ombre dantesche* (Florence: Le Monnier, 1921), 249–283; Pasquale Vannucci, *Il canto V del* Purgatorio: *Lectura Dantis Romana* (Turin: SEI, 1961); William Warren Vernon, *Readings on the* Purgatorio *of Dante, chiefly based on the* Commentary *of Benvenuto da Imola*, I, 3d ed. (1889; repr., London: Methuen, 1907), 149–184.

Further analyses of the canto can be found in the following: Vittorio Ugo Capone, "La nostalgia della Pia," in *Civiltà teologica e civiltà cortese* (Rome: Istituto Editoriale del Mediterraneo, 1974); Francesco D'Ovidio, *Studii sulla* Divina Commedia (Milan-Palermo: Sandron, 1901), 59–61; Dante Alighieri, *The Divine Comedy*, trans. with a commentary by Charles S. Singleton, *Purgatorio*, vol. 2 (Princeton: Princeton University Press, 1973); Dante Alighieri, *La Divina Commedia*, ed. U. Bosco and G. Reggio (Florence: Le Monnier, 1982); Isidoro Del Lungo, "Dante e gli Estensi," *Nuova Antologia* 16 (1887): 549–577; *Enciclopedia dantesca*, 6 vols. (Rome, 1970–1978), ss. vv. "Del Cassero (Iacopo)" by Giovanni Fallani, "Montefeltro (Bonconte da)" by Giorgio Petrocchi, "Pia" by Giorgio Varnini, etc.; Aldo Scaglione, "Sonata Form and Structural Strategy in the *Divina Commedia*," in *Studies in the Italian Renaissance: Essays in Memory of A. B. Ferruolo*, ed. G. P. Biasin, A. N. Mancini, and N. J. Perella (Naples: Società Editrice Napoletana, 1985), 13–26; Francesco Tateo, "Senso morale . . . ," in *Studi di letteratura italiana in onore di Calogero Colicchio*, ed. V. Paladino (Messina: EDAS, 1983), 35–61; Gianluigi Toja, "Buonconte da Montefeltro," in *Studi in onore di Alberto Chiari* (Brescia: Paideia, 1973); William Warren Vernon, *The Contrasts in Dante: A Lecture delivered at the University on 24th October 1906* (Manchester: UP, 1906).

CANTO VI

Abject Italy

MARIA PICCHIO SIMONELLI

Translated by Charles Ross

By the middle of the twentieth century, the critical question concerning Canto VI was no longer one of historical identification or aesthetic appreciation, but of whether the canto was substantially unified or, instead, contained a series of poetically unresolved issues. Aurelio Roncaglia, in his "Lectura Dantis" of 1955, showed that the repetition of disjunctive verbs such as *si parte* ("is done," 1), *disgiunto* ("without a passageway," 42), *non m'accompagne* ("not at my side," 114), and *scisso* ("dissevered," 123) creates a "convulsive marker" connecting the various parts of the canto. Twenty-five years later, in a completely different cultural climate, one no longer characterized by patriotic rhetoric or the passions of the Italian Risorgimento (the nineteenth-century movement for national unity), Alberto Varvaro objected that it was better not to speak of the unity of the canto, or of the equivocal words of Dante's "polysemous" style, but rather to ask if the canto possessed any internally coherent organization.

To me it seems clear that Dante gave each of his cantos a particular function. In his *Epistle* 13.9, he explains that "the work is divided into three canticles . . . and each canticle is divided into cantos . . . and each canto into tercet rhymes." These tercets indicate the logic of the various arguments; rarely in the *Comedy* is the rhythm broken by a hiatus in thought. It therefore follows that Dante wanted to structure each canto as a coherent whole. Sometimes the coherence is easy to discern; sometimes it is hidden, and the apparent fragmentation disguises the effort Dante made to organize his work.

The sixth canto is clearly segmented. Its 151 lines are divided into two distinct parts of almost equal length: a narrative section (75 lines) and the famous digressive invective that begins "Ah, abject Italy" (76 lines). Each section contains a striking simile.

The initial figure of the winning gambler, who retires surrounded by a crowd of people petitioning him for a little gift or a word, resembles Dante's own search to liberate himself from those who died by violence, who flock around him asking for a pious memory or a prayer. The simile that concludes the second section compares Florence to

> that sick woman
> who finds no rest upon her feather-bed,
> but, turning, tossing, tries to ease her pain.
>
> (149–151)

This closing figure recalls the gambling scene, because before describing the winner, to whom he compares himself, Dante pauses over the loser ("left alone, disconsolate— / rehearsing what he'd thrown," 2–3). But this dolorous and abandoned man finds no comparison to anyone in the poem, unless it is to the image of sick Florence, who tosses and turns and can find no ease for her pain. Florence is said to change often:

> How often, in the time you can remember,
> have you changed laws and coinage, offices
> and customs, and revised your citizens!
>
> (145–147)

And every change is for the worse.

Both the narrative first half and the concluding digression divide into three sections. In the narrative portion we have 1) a continuation of the pilgrim's various encounters with those who died by violence, 2) Dante's query about the efficacy of prayers for the dead, 3) his encounter with Sordello. In the digression we find 1) an invective lamentation over the fate of Italy, 2) a prayer to God, 3) a ferocious invective against Florence. Each part is organized by a discontinuous crescendo, in which the center portion unwinds before an explosion in the final section. The query about the efficacy of prayer, along with the inspirational memory of Beatrice and the prayer to "highest Jove" (118), who was "crucified / for us" (119–120), signal, each in its respective section, a pause, almost a moment in which to breathe, to isolate the culmination to which each section tends: the encounter with Sordello and the bitter sarcasm of the invective against Florence.

Death by Violence

After the simile of the gambler, to which I shall return, we are given a list of those who died by violence (13–24). These are not separate personalities but members of a chorus. For us, distant in time, they are six mere names, although they spurred Italian scholars to archival research, with varying degrees of success. But Dante's point lies elsewhere. For the poet and his contemporaries, each name was attached to a scandal of blood and politics. Four were assassinated (Guccio dei Tarlati, Federigo Novello, Gano Scornigiani, and Orso degli Alberti), preceded and followed by two murdered without justice. The judge Benincasa da Laterina, in effect the mayor of Siena in which role he condemned to death two close relatives of Ghino di Tacco for having seized one of the city's castles, was himself murdered by Ghino while a judge in Rome. The scandal revealed the impotency of the law in the face of evil intentions combined with power. The last name is that of Pier de la Brosse, chamberlain of Philip III of France, who was murdered "out of spite and envy" (20), falsely accused by the queen, Marie of Brabant. If justice is not respected in the free communes, how much less is it in the courts, where intrigues and the meanest of passions rule? Dante's examples give us a glimpse of profound corruption and social disorder.

Canto VI, in each of Dante's canticles, is devoted to politics. I believe this choice may be traced to two small treatises *de numeris* (on numbers), composed in the twelfth century by Geoffroy d'Auxerre and Thibaut de Langres, claiming that the number six signifies *operum prima perfectio* (the first perfection of a work). Genesis is obviously the source, since God made man on the sixth day. For Dante, the restoration of civil justice would be such a "first perfection."

The second part of this first section of seventy-five lines contains a dialogue between Virgil and Dante concerning the efficacy of prayers for the dead. This discourse justifies the opening simile of the gambler, because Dante's mind is burdened by doubt. As soon as he releases himself from those who died violently, his words explode at Virgil:

> I started: "O my light, it seems to me
> that in one passage you deny expressly
> that prayer can bend the rule of Heaven, yet
>   these people pray precisely for that end.
> Is their hope, therefore, only emptiness,
> or have I not read clearly what you said?"
>
> (28–33)

The passage in question occurs in Virgil's *Aeneid* when the Sibyl tells Palinurus to "leave any hope that prayer can turn aside / the gods' decrees" (VI, 373). What the Sibyl says, if true, would nullify the insistence of the souls

Dante meets that the prayers of the living might accelerate their ascent. Their illusion, then, would be like that of the gambler throwing dice. Dante the pilgrim is privileged to be fully aware of the guidance he receives from Virgil and the virtue that descends from above. But why do the souls make their requests? Are they lost in illusion, like gamblers? Dante's question is worrying, and Virgil's response is not fully satisfying: at the time of the false and lying gods, "prayers" did not provide a "passageway to God" (42). Now, however,

> the peak of justice is not lowered when
> the fire of love accomplishes in one
> instant the expiation owed by all
> who dwell here
>
> (37–39)

Dante the poet does not wish to give an exhaustive response. Virgil's role does not permit it. The explanation will come much later, in the sphere of Jupiter, from the chorus of the blessed who form the Eagle:

> Regnum celorum suffers violence
> from ardent love and living hope, for these
> can be the conquerors of Heaven's Will;
>   yet not as man defeats another man:
> the Will of God is won because It would
> be won and, won, wins through benevolence.
>
> (Par. xx, 94–99)

Hurrying On

From a purely narrative point of view, Dante needs to divert the reader's attention not only from the flock of souls but also from this discussion of the efficacy of prayer. So Virgil names Beatrice, the only one who can answer every question, since she is the "light between your mind and truth" whom Dante will see "smiling joyously" when he reaches "this mountain's peak" (45–48). Mention of Beatrice's name banishes Dante's weariness. The pilgrim wants to move "more quickly" (49). The reader is caught up in Dante's desire, distracted from the preceding philosophical problems, and amazed at how love continually incites his movement.

The shift to another tonality is marked by Dante's rush to travel and the calming words of Virgil, who muffles his enthusiasm: "our climb won't be as rapid as you thought" (54). Two days will have to pass before Dante can see Beatrice, and the road is long. This calming voice prepares for the solemn crescendo of the final segment of this first part: the encounter with Sordello.

"I Am Sordello"

This encounter, at the center of the canto, is carefully prepared. Virgil shows Dante "a soul who is completely apart" (58–59), one who can teach him the most direct way to ascend. Because of his solitude he stands in contrast to the banks of spirits, a difference that strikes the pilgrim and, then, the reader. The exceptionality of the encounter is underlined by Dante's commentary and recall:

> O Lombard soul, what pride
> and what disdain were in your stance! Your eyes
> moved with such dignity, such gravity!
>
> (61–63)

Mention of Mantua breaks into the rarefied atmosphere of the figure's solitude. The figure gains impetus, passion, and movement as it shouts, "O Mantuan, I am Sordello, / from your own land!" (74–75). Whoever he is, this Sordello regards himself as Virgil's neighbor and friend because he has breathed the same air and contemplated the same vistas. He overcomes the "pride" and "disdain" (61–62) with which he stands and rises "from his position" (73) to embrace Virgil. Only later will he learn that he embraces one who was the "glory of the Latins" (*Purg.* VII, 16).

Here Dante interrupts his story to include a digressive invective on the evils of Italy, attacking the Church and the Empire, which both fail in their providential duty. This embrace, then, opens the second half of the canto.

The rank of souls to which Sordello belongs and the reasons that moved Dante to single him out remain problems, for the most part unresolved and difficult to penetrate. One can only guess. It is not the first time that Dante leaves his readers to reflect on their own. One thinks of the splendid tenth canto of the *Inferno*, dominated by the figure of Farinata and the appearance of the disconsolate Cavalcante de' Cavalcanti. What we do know is that these figures find themselves inside the city of Dis, entombed among the heretics, in a cemetery along the walls of the city. But although Virgil will explain, in the next canto, the moral ordering of Hell, he will make no mention of heretics. Virgil explains the condition of the incontinent, who are punished outside the city, but his explanation starts with the violent and includes only the first souls who sinned by malice. One must assume that the heretics were also guilty of malice, but Dante blurs anything that might clarify their position.

Sordello presents us with a similar situation. He is not one of those who died by violence (despite the efforts of some critics to prove otherwise), nor is he a negligent prince who might be found in the valley of the princes. Rather, he is a servant of princes, and he assumes the role as guide to point out others in the valley, stigmatizing their defects and those of their descendants.

Sordello was a poet—a troubadour who wrote in Provençal—but also a Mantuan, two good reasons that Dante chose him as a character. If we read the poetry of Sordello that has reached us, we detect a moralistic poet who may well have appealed to Dante's imagination. In a poem on nobility, "Lai a n Peire Guillem man ses bistensa," he insists that wealth is not important: "Valer pot ben qi de valor a cura / Paupres o ricx, sol quel cors sia protz" (41–42). In his poem "Qui be's membre del segle qu'es passatz," he shows the destructive effect of greed on the hearts of evildoers ("Tant los destren non fes e cobeitatz, / C'onor e pretz en meton en soan," 19–20), a theme that could arouse a profound feeling of appreciation in Dante. Greed, which subverts the order of the world, and nobility, a matter of the heart and not of worldly goods, are exquisitely Dantesque themes that make him the poet of rectitude and justice. If we regard Sordello as a Mantuan and as a poet of right rectitude, we can begin to understand his presence in the *Purgatorio*.

The second part of the canto—the digression—is entirely entrusted to the narrative voice. The fact is that Dante the man always exists on two levels with different functions: that of the activities contingent on the journey and that of memory, which follows the journey. The fiction concerns not only the travels through the three realms but also the active agent who has the capacity to record and narrate what happened. The pilgrim Dante, who reprises his own journey in the book of memory, becomes the narrative voice. And so the *Comedy* becomes an autobiographical fiction in which the two aspects of the first-person narrator alternate, controlled by the author of the story. As we read the *Comedy* we must keep this complex narrative structure in mind. The digression belongs not to Dante the author, but to the character who remembers and comments. Obviously the political ideas expressed are those of Dante the author; nonetheless, if we want to truly understand the logical structure of the canto we must bear in mind the two levels of Dante's poetic persona.

The invective does not come from nowhere. In Dante's work any interruption is only seemingly disjunctive. In reality, everything is carefully prepared to allow the reader to follow the narration adequately. This observation holds for philosophical, theological, and historical discussions.

The pilgrim who returns from his voyage and, sitting at his desk, recounts what he has seen, is a character always clearly present in the mind of the author. Even in this canto, before the outburst prompted by his memory, Dante anticipates the commotion of that recollection in the terzina that begins "O Lombard soul!" (61–63), which we have already noticed. The two functions of the first-person narrator—the composer of the fable and he who remembers and narrates—have been clear.

The second terzina of the invective serves to coordinate the digression with the narrator's voice, that is, the Dante who remembers and relates what he remembers:

> That noble soul had such enthusiasm:
> his city's sweet name was enough for him
> to welcome—there—his fellow citizen.
>
> (79–81)

The structural connection between the two parts is thereby assured.

The first segment of this second half of the canto subdivides into three parts: 1) a general lament on the condition of Italy (76–90), in which Dante proclaims that Italy is "abject" and an "inn of sorrows," because the law, which Justinian had restored, is no longer respected, nor does anyone bridle arbitrary justice; 2) an invective against the Church (91–96); and 3) an invective against the emperor (97–117). For Dante Italy does not exist as a nation, but as the "garden of the Empire" (105), the "queen of provinces" (78). It is an extension of Rome and therefore participates in Rome's dignity and supremacy. It is the Italy of Virgil, not of the Risorgimento.

Dante's Invective

After lamentation, accusations. The first one attacks the Church:

> Ah you—who if you understood what God
> ordained, would then attend to things devout
> and in the saddle surely would allow
>   Caesar to sit—see how this beast turns fierce
> because there are no spurs that would correct it,
> since you have laid your hands upon the bit!
>
> (91–96)

The first phrase, an anaphora of "Ah, abject Italy," reinforces the tone of lamentation. If Italy is not "queen of the provinces but of bordellos," it is because those who do not "understand what God/ordained" (the Roman curia) no longer listen to God's commands but strain to usurp a temporal power that does not belong to them. The anaphora beginning in line 106—"Come . . . come"—creates a transition from lamentation to a sad appeal. The two types of anaphora underline two aspects of the invective: first, the injustice that prevails in every city in Italy, provoked by the Church's greed for power and, second, the shame of the inept emperor, who does not know how to "ride astride its saddlebows" (99) to tame Italy, which becomes a "recalcitrant and savage" beast.

Dante's polemic against ecclesiastical corruption is a theme that runs throughout the *Comedy*. The accusation is always the same: greed for gold and power upsets and sidetracks the hierarchies of the Church and the religious orders. There is no salvation. The Church is the prime cause of moral, and therefore political, decline; but the emperor, weak and distracted by local factions, is no less guilty: "O German Albert . . . may / shame for your own repute move you to act" (97–117). More violence—which recalls those souls who died by violent means—and other deaths will increase the infamy of one whose duty it was to restore law and order. Rome is the most abandoned city in Italy, and it is the natural seat of the emperor. Now it is "widowed and alone" and "weeps bitterly" (112–113). Dante's appeal for the emperor to witness firsthand the wounds and sufferings of Italy is long and heartfelt.

The prayer to God, which follows and signals a pause between the first and final parts of the invective, arises from the same cause as the dolorous appeal, but it is no longer addressed to the terrestrial ruler but to the source of his imperial authority:

> And if I am allowed, o highest Jove,
> to ask: You who on earth were crucified
> for us—have You turned elsewhere Your just eyes?
>   Or are You, in Your judgment's depth, devising
> a good that we cannot foresee, completely
> dissevered from our way of understanding?
>
> (118–123)

A dramatic closing resolves this invocation: To what inscrutable end of goodness can so much evil be directed? Civil corruption has reached such a point that all of Italy knows tyranny, and every petty villain desires, like some new Claudius Marcellus, to oppose the authority of Caesar and proclaim himself prince of the people.

"Oh, my wretched, wretched country! What pity pierces me for you, how often I read, how often I write about our commonwealth"—so Dante writes in his *Convivio* (IV, 27.11). The passage is often cited in commentaries on the final section of this invective. But verses 127–151 are written in a very different spirit. Here there is no pity, only denunciation. Dante's words are biting, violent. Love of country has been transformed into disdain and hatred. We might call it a holy disdain, in that love of the good provokes a holy hate of evil, and Florence collects all that is bad. Nonetheless, sometimes this holy hatred finds just the right, efficacious tone, as in the close of this canto. Only the tercet that opens *Inferno* XXVI matches it in ferocity.

It is true that here in the *Purgatorio* Dante's sarcasm does not strike at Florence so much as at her people, her citizens. The good are exiled; only the bad remain. When Dante wrote the *Convivio,* he hoped not only to reenter the city but to work actively for the common good of his homeland. But when he wrote this portion of the *Purgatorio,* all his illusions had been shattered.

The people of Florence had no more sense of justice. Justice had become an empty word, coming from the mouth and not the heart. Everyone was ready to grab power by any means necessary. Florence was a sick woman who found no "rest upon her feather-bed": laws, coinage, offices, and customs changed every two months.

Dante understood that the internal politics of his city were no more than a con game played by individuals looking for illicit gains. A new breed had won, destroying the luxurious citizen life of former days, when life in Florence was "sober and chaste, lived in tranquillity" (*Par.* xv, 99). That Florence exists only as the memory of Cacciaguida. For Dante nothing remains but the bitter sarcasm of an exile, an unrequited lover, driven off and humiliated. No trace remains of the spirit in which Dante composed the *Convivio*.

BIBLIOGRAPHY

Boni, M., ed. *Sordello: Le poesie. Nuova edizione critica.* Bologna: Biblioteca degli Studi mediolatini e volgari, 1964.

Bowra, C. M. "Dante and Sordello." *Comparative Literature* 5 (1953): 1–15.

De Lollis, C. *Vita e Poesie di Sordello di Goito.* In *Romanische bibliothek,* vol. 9. Halle, 1896.

Lange, Hanne. *Traités du XIIe siècle sur la Symbolique des nombres: Geoffrey d'Auxerre at Thibault de Langres.* Edition critique par H. L. Cahiers de l'Institut du Moyen-âge grec et latin. Copenhagen: University of Copenhagen, 1978.

Roncaglia, Aurelio. "Il Canto vi del *Purgatorio.*" *Rassegna della Letteratura Italiana* 60 (1956): 409–426. Contains an extensive bibliography.

Varvaro, Alberto. "Il Canto vi del *Purgatorio.*" In *Purgatorio: Letture degli anni 1976–1979.* Rome: Casa di Dante in Rome, 1980, 123–133.

CANTO VII

Sordello and the Catalog of Princes

MAURIZIO PERUGI

In the preceding canto, however willing he may be to answer Sordello's rapid-fire questions, Virgil is allowed to utter "Mantua" and nothing more. No doubt he would have gone on reciting "me genuit" and the rest of the epitaph ascribed to him by Donatus and St. Jerome, but his reply is cut short by Sordello who, after revealing himself as a native of Mantua too, enfolds him in a most emotional hug.

Now, at the beginning of Canto VII, Dante is obviously expected to pick up the thread of the story at precisely the point where it had been cut off. Sordello repeats his former question ("But who are you?" 3), and Virgil is given the opportunity to round out his own epitaph in a version that is a somewhat more indirect, paraphrastic version than the primitive Latin text. Only at this point does Sordello grasp the identity of the prominent figure he is speaking to: that is why, when he embraces him once again, he shows much greater deference than previously. But critics have been at pains to suggest any adequate motivation behind the words of praise that now spring to Sordello's lips:

> He said: "O glory of the Latins, you
> through whom our tongue revealed its power, you,
> eternal honor of my native city."
>
> (16–18)

We are confronted with a puzzling problem: How does such a literary valuation of Virgil's language and poetry concern Sordello? His loud, boasting claims of fellow citizenship seem to provide no sufficient grounds for justifying the role in which he's been cast: Dante's spokesman who stresses Virgil's central significance in the prehistory of Italian literature. Sordello's poetic work, as far as it has been preserved, consists of forty-three chansons in Provençal. There is no reason to presume that Sordello ever wrote a single line in his mother tongue—especially since this term is to be taken in its loftiest expression, as the *volgare illustre*. And we should really expect this to be the case. The documentary evidence supporting our assertion can be substantiated throughout Dante's *De vulgari eloquentia* I, xv, 2—provided that this much quoted and much disputed passage has been correctly interpreted. As far as Dante's analysis is concerned, the Mantuan dialect violates Dante's grammatical standard. On the one hand, *garrulitas* and *acerbitas* are taken as an inheritance from Lombard superstratum; on the other, *yspidum*, *rudis asperitas,* and a tendency to *barbarismus* are recorded as distinctive features of the variety peculiar to Marca Trevigiana. Neither Sordello nor anyone else would have been able to turn to poetic advantage such a queer and incongruous mixture of local dialects.

It should be further recalled that in *Inferno* XXVII, 21, Virgil is referred to as having used his own native dialect when addressing Ulysses: "Istra ten va, più non t'adizzo" ("Now you may leave—I'll not provoke more speech"), might be rightfully set alongside the vernacular specimens recorded in *De vulgari eloquentia* for the purpose of making a critical parody of each of the various Italian dialects. One should hardly be amazed at Virgil's untimely vernacular performance: what would offend today's reader as a brutal anachronism is instead to be considered as being in full agreement with the comparative lack of chronology peculiar to Dante's underworld, as well as to the medieval mind, as regards the quite different mode of relating oneself to the classical past.

Sins of the Tongue

If, as we may surmise, no gap is assumed to open up between Virgil and Sordello with special reference to the evolution of their mother tongue, it seems legitimate to conclude that both Mantuan poets were faced, in Dante's view, with the same cumbersome linguistic handicap with which they had been born. That's precisely what Sordello means by *lingua nostra*—that it is not, therefore, to be identified either with Italian or with Latin as the common source of the *ydioma trifarium*. So what marks the difference between the two poets are the exactly antithetical ways they found to get out of the same impasse. Virgil's handling of Latin is taken as the maximum adherence to Dante's ideal of grammar. Indeed, Sordello's appraisal sets up Virgil's style as the most prominent pattern to be strictly followed with a view to building up the *volgare illustre*. Both Virgil and Sordello have succeeded in overstepping the narrow bounds of vernacular municipalism. Virgil resolved to display his own superior craftsmanship by having recourse to the language of the Holy Roman Empire, whereas Sordello's first-rank poetic activity implies a factual, self-evident getaway from the urgent task of securing the complete supremacy of *volgare*. In Dante's outlook the *volgare illustre* was finally to take the place of Latin in Italy as the only undisputed literary language in accordance with the rules of an ideal, never-changing grammar. Sordello, on the contrary, chose to unfold his own outstanding talent for poetry by turning to the most refined and glamorous language in the medieval Western civilization: notably, the langue d'oc.

There's little doubt, according to Dante's implicit view, that Sordello's option is to be judged as a proper sin. In *De vulgari eloquentia* we are told that in order to build up the *volgare illustre, discretio* is first required, that is, a preliminary process of chiefly lexical selection intended to purify one's native dialect from any sort of dross, alloy, or sediment. That's precisely the duty Sordello has evaded by resorting to a ready-made, faultless, but taken-from-abroad language—a language, moreover, that, having reached its full maturity, was likely, through its intrinsic prestige, to become the most serious obstacle to the *volgare illustre*'s ability to fully develop and to become more widespread. As a consequence of having eluded the responsibility involved with the task of *discretio*, Sordello is found guilty of negligence, in the full etymological sense implied by the term *nec-legere,* or "not to choose." That is why he is placed among the negligent spirits. Virgil himself, while making his identity and position known, seems to suggest a specular analogy between his own lack of faith and Sordello's evasion of literary duty. A sentence such as "Non per far, ma per non fare" ("Not for the having—but for the not having—done," 25), when read between the lines, might easily refer to Sordello's fault as well.

Sordello, moreover, in giving up the task both of using and refining his mother tongue, can be said in some degree to have misapplied his own talent: indeed, his poetic work might be regarded as a necessarily unfaithful self-translation. That is why, in the preceding canto, Sordello, making amends for his own fault, shows himself so eager: "sol per lo dolce suon de la sua terra, / di fare al cittadin suo quivi festa" ("his city's sweet name was enough for him / to welcome—there—his fellow-citizen," VI, 80–81). As we are told in *Convivio* I, xii, 3–6, devotion to one's native language is nothing but a natural consequence of the devotion one is expected to feel for one's country and fellow citizens. So the mere literary task is subordinated by Dante to a major civil and political plan to be set in close relation to the providential function performed by the Holy Empire. It's worth recalling that in *Convivio*'s book IV Dante had just been stressing the weight of Virgil's work, along with his own freshly restored valuation of the spirit of ancient Rome. In contrast, as far as our relatively copious documentary evidence allows us to know, both Sordello's literary and his political performances chiefly took place outside Italy. So by stressing some points and at the same time leaving much to be understood, Dante works Sordello's exemplary characterization skillfully into this crucial episode of the *Comedy*. That is to say, Dante selects those aspects of Sordello's historical identity that are most central to his specific purpose of linking his own political vision with the linguistic and literary issues at stake. Dante will continue with his literary gallery in Canto XXVI, where it looks as if Sordello's distinctive features would be overshadowed through the selection of two further prominent figures: he's neither such a forerunner as Guido Guinizzelli, though endowed perhaps with better qualifications in the building up of *volgare illustre,* nor is he such a paragon of excellence as Arnaut Daniel, because he chose to write poetry in a language other than his native one.

Impending Darkness

The sun is sinking now: "But see now how the day declines" (43) provides a variant on the previous line in Canto VI: "And—you can see—the slope now casts a shadow" (51). As the canto progresses, Dante keeps working out further variations on this basic theme: "While the horizon has enclosed / the day" (60–61) and "Before the meager sun seeks out its nest" (85). It cannot escape the reader's attention that such a step-by-step creeping sundown conveys a symbolic meaning, with the specific purpose of preparing the way for something essential to follow. Virgil's surmise, that darkness is to obstruct their way, is confirmed by Sordello's gesture—once more, an exemplary one:

> And good Sordello, as his finger traced
> along the ground, said: "Once the sun has set,
> then—look—even this line cannot be crossed."
>
> (52–54)

Once Dante has come into the princes' valley, the allegorical theme of impending darkness—obviously meant to herald the devilish snake's next coming in—is led on through the mention of the *Salve Regina* (82). It should be recalled that in thirteenth- and fourteenth-century liturgy this antiphon had been turned into the prayer of compline; in the times of the First Crusade, however, it was a song of pilgrims and soldiers and was believed to have been composed by, among others, Adhémar, bishop of Le Puy, who was first given the crusaders' cross by Pope Urban II. The leading theme moves toward a final climax through the *Te lucis ante* in Canto VIII (13), a hymn by Ambrose that was intended to exorcise nightmares, ghosts, and whatever devilish temptations were expected to occur in the night.

This faint, yet cunning, hint at the crusading spirit becomes more significant when it is connected back to Canto VI's invective—a tirade stuffed with a number of formulae borrowed from Middle Latin hymnology and traditionally employed to complain of Jerusalem's lamentable doom. Much the same can be said of the catalog of princes, which Dante has placed as a proper counterpart to the previous invective. The princes' dwelling place is described after the Middle Latin technique called *topographia*.

Dante is drawing on handbooks of rhetoric to quite an extraordinary extent in this passage of the *Comedy*. He makes the reader aware of this trend by scattering all over this episode a series of metalinguistic markers: "would you point out" (38); "just as the lesser gives way to the greater" (78); "you'll be better able to / make out the acts and features of them all" (88–89), each of them implying a straightforward relation to a well-known topic of rhetorical art—that is, *argumenta, enthymema,* and *descriptio* respectively. On the other hand, the twice-repeated key word *diletto* ("delight," 48 and 63) is possibly intended to hint at the *solatz* or, *deport,* which in troubadours' chansons usually occurs in close connection both with conventional opening descriptions of a springtime landscape and with customary descriptions of courtly life. When confronted with such a plurality of closely interwoven and often overlapping literary codes, one cannot help but appreciate how much headway Dante has made since the years of his apprenticeship. Take, for instance, the famous sonnet "Guido, i' vorrei." While taking over the style he and his schoolmates have been brought up on, he strips it of any tendency toward what today's reader might mistake for a kind of escapism or disengagement. Dante, as we have seen, sets up an imposing rhetorical apparatus with the special purpose of coding a transcendent message. Within a wide-ranging frame, Dante draws a sheer veil of melancholy over his idealized landscape and court.

The Cataloger

There is some ground for presuming that Virgil, while recollecting his fellow spirits' dwelling place (28–36), provides at the same time a kind of rehearsal for both the *topographia* and the catalog to come later. Evidence can be drawn from a few passages: "Luogo è là giù" ("There is a place below," 28), borrowed from Virgil's "Est locus," is Dante's usual formula for any reference to topographical details; and the pair of synonyms "guai . . . sospiri" ("outcry . . . sigh," 30) possibly implies an indirect suggestion of the partial analogy between princes and lofty spirits (Sordello himself might be thought of to some extent as a lofty spirit manqué). As for Dante's conscious strategy, to be discerned in the background, it's worth pointing out the wide-apart splitting of the two immediate constituents—the literary and the political one—conveyed by Sordello up to now. The *topographia* may be taken as a high-concentration mixture of rhetorical and literary patterns going back to Virgil's Elysium, and through Middle Latin and Provençal tradition, down to *l'uno e l'altro Guido;* the catalog of princes, on the opposite side, is primarily intended to serve Dante's political and religious purpose.

As for the antecedents of the catalog, it is commonly acknowledged that Dante used two different sources and combined them into a single episode. One is Anchises' enumeration in *Aeneid*'s Canto VI: to mention but one detail, Dante takes up the couple Caesar-Pompeius, "concordes animae nunc" (*Aen.* VI, 827), as a starting point for arranging his list by correlative pairs. The other source was identified long ago as the most famous among Sordello's poems, notably the *plant*, composed about 1237, on the death of Blacatz, a vassal (and a somewhat unreliable one) of Raimon Berenguer IV, at whose court Sordello dwelled until Raimon's death. As D'Ovidio says, Dante's catalog arises from a double Mantuan source and, while appearing to reflect the previous embracing between the two Mantuan poets, may be regarded as a further illustration of Dante's skillful mingling of ingredients from the medieval and the classical traditions. In his *plant* Sordello dresses up a list of eight, each of whom is summoned to eat a bit of dead Blacatz's heart in order to recover some of his own failing courage (this theme was widespread throughout medieval literature, down to *Decameron*'s thirty-ninth novella). In Dante's catalog the number of princes (most of whom are the heirs of the mighty ones enumerated by Sordello) and their strictly hierarchical arrangement are similar—except that they are drawn up by twos, and in Dante's underworld their struggles for power obviously turn into displays of mutual friendship. Both lists (which include Henry III of England as the only personage in common) start from an emperor and break off at the point where an aphorism is made to fit into the whole.

The only open reference in Dante's catalog to Italy's lamentable state is found in connection with the head of the list, Rudolph of Austria (91–93). Nonetheless, Dante directs our attention to the eschatological consequences of the decline affecting Italy's and Europe's rulers. In comparison to the previous invective, in which Dante deals only with Italy's state of affairs, things have now moved onto a wider stage: the snake's arrival in Canto VIII is intended to remind the princes of the devil's unceasing attempt to overthrow civil order and to replace the Holy Roman Empire with the domination of the Antichrist, whose task is made easier because of the European rulers' anarchy.

A More Sensible Invective

It is self-evident that in point of style the invective retains a more sensible echo of Sordello's powerful enumeration. The stormy, picturesque spirits of the *plant* get watered down in Dante's catalog. One may posit several reasons for such a change of mood. First of all, the catalog's general outline harks back unquestionably to Anchises' enumeration, which may be taken as the actual negative of Dante's catalog. While conforming very closely to Virgil's episode, which serves as the primary model, Dante is tracing an irretrievably slumping curve, to be thought of as symmetrically the opposite of the ascending scale suggested by Anchises: in such an imaginary diagram both lines originate on opposing sides of a peak to be placed in the age of August.

To emphasize his own cynical survey of historical events, Dante draws a careful distinction between the rhetorical devices he uses to describe the princes, on the one hand, and their degenerative offspring on the other. With the exception of Rudolph of Austria, princes are afforded a chiefly superficial description: drawing on current judgments of contemporary sovereigns, as can be read in full in Giovanni Villani's chronicle, Dante stresses in each of the princes a single physiognomic feature. Descendants, on the contrary, are directly blamed for their moral habits; so, for instance, the phrase "la vita sua viziata e lorda" ("his life—its filth, its vice," 110, relating to Philip the Handsome) conforms to an epideictic formula that finds several parallels in Matthieu de Vendôme's pattern descriptions. The *proverbium* woven into the catalog (121–122) comes also from the vast repertory of ready-made Middle Latin stock phrases.

Likewise, the multifarious literary reminiscences, as displayed in the catalog of princes, is further illustrated in a couple of passages in which Dante sums up biblical quotations and includes additional echoes drawn from Sordello's poems: the phrase "d'ogne valor portò cinta la corda" ("wore the cord of every virtue," 114), in which Peter III of Aragon is the grammatical subject, may be traced back to Isaiah 11:5 ("Et erit iustitia cingulum lumborum eius, et fides cinctorium renum eius," as well as Sordello's *Ensenham* 1007–1010 ("per qu'es morta onors / e pretz e donars e valors; / qu'aissi son quais en una corda / tug, que no s'en descorda").

Links to a Cryptic Prophecy

Verse 96 is to be ranked among the most prophetical, that is, puzzling lines Dante has scattered all over his *Comedy*. Strict adherence to standard literary patterns might be produced as indirect evidence to support Sapegno's opinion, which warns scholars away from drawing any chronological conclusions from such a hint. It is clear, however, that the mention of Rudolph of Austria, while unquestionably out of place in the catalog, should rather be connected back to Canto VI, 97–105, with the purpose of revealing the full purport of what might be read there as an obscure, cryptic prophecy. Because he had become entirely taken up—just as his father had—with his reign in Germany, Albert I of Hapsburg, Rudolph's son and the emperor from 1298 to 1308, gave up any assertion of his rights over Italy against the papacy's increasing usurpations. That is why Dante calls on Heaven for an exemplary punishment to be inflicted on his offspring, so that dread of divine retribution might prevent his successor from incurring the same fault.

The link between these two passages provides Georgio Petrocchi with the opportunity to infer that Canto VII would have been retouched soon after Arrigo VII's death. It is a highly attractive hypothesis, yet not essential to our thesis. Dante would have assembled the diptych by stages, having readjusted it again and again, influenced by the rush of events. That is the reason one may also give for the comparatively high number of anomalous features to be found all over the episode: take, for instance, the twofold Sordello-Virgil embrace, as well as the *praecisio*—a device used as a boundary marker—or Sordello's double-faced, somewhat inconsistent character. While carrying on *Convivio*'s chiefly linguistic controversy, Sordello is charged with reflecting Dante's spirit and ideals; the purpose of securing the prevalence of *volgare illustre* lies in the background as a crucially important aspect of the poet's main design: to restore Italy to its former condition of *giardin de lo 'mperio*. Bursting into his famous invective, Dante boldly takes the stage and plays Sordello off. In fact, Sordello is displayed from the position most proper for him along the vertical line corresponding to each of the sixth cantos: he is made to shift to the following canto, where, in a way consistent with his own life story, he is appointed as fault-finder of the mighty ones' negligence.

Invective and catalog may indeed be thought of as two sides of the same coin, that is, as two opposing sides of the one and only *sirventes*. It is worth recalling that the *sirventes* is closely related to the *planctus*, both in current Middle Latin handbooks and in the literary practice of the troubadours. One is reminded of the quite similar interrelation between Anchises' enumeration and Dante's catalog. So, from the evidence so far collected, it is tempting to conclude that Dante's whole diptych should be read *post eventum* as an implicit lament on Arrigo VII's untimely death—a singsong and pathetical dirge on Dante's hope that he, too, may be buried by the young emperor's side.

BIBLIOGRAPHICAL NOTES

For a full bibliography on the Sordello cantos (*Purg.* VI–VIII), the reader should refer to my study "Il Sordello di Dante e la tradizione mediolatina dell'invetiva," (*Studi danteschi* 55 [1983]: 23–135), from which the present reading is partially derived. Accordingly, just a few items in close relation to the main theses supported above are recorded here: G. Contini, *Un'idea di Dante* (Turin: Einaudi, 1976), 143–157; M. Corti, *Dante a un nuovo crocevia* (Florence: 1982); F. D'Ovidio, *Studii sulla Divina Commedia* (Milan-Palermo: Sandron, 1901), 1–13, and *Nuovi studii danteschi* (Milan: Hoopli, 1906), 392– 420; P. V. Mengaldo, "oc," in *Enciclopedia dantesca*, 6 vols. (Rome, 1970–1978); S. Pasquazi, "Antipurgatorio," in *Enciclopedia dantesca*; G. Petrocchi, *Itinerari danteschi* (Bari: Adriatica, 1969), 83–118.

Provençal texts are quoted from Sordello, *Le poesie*. Nuova edizione eriditica . . . a cura di M. Boni (Bologna: Biblioteca degli Studi mediolatini e volgari, 1954), I; C. de Lollis, "Ballata alla Vergine di Giacomo II d'Aragona, *Revue de langues romanes* XXXI (1887): 289–295; *Sämtliche Lieder des Trobadors Giraut de Bornelh . . .* kritisch hggb. von A. Kolsen (Halle: Niemeyer, 1910). Quotations from Middle Latin *Artes* are drawn from E. Faral, *Les arts poétiques du XIIᵉ et du XIIIᵉ siècle* (Paris: Champion, 1924), except for Matthieu de Vendôme's epistles, which are quoted from the critical edition by Franco Munari, *Mathei Vindocinensis Opera*, vol. II (*Piramus et Tisbe—Milo—Epistule—Tobias*) (Rome: Edizioni di Storia e Letteratura, 1982).

CANTO VIII

In the Valley of the Rulers

RICARDO J. QUINONES

The *Purgatorio* was one of the great discoveries of the twentieth century. The post-Napoleonic nineteenth century not only was preoccupied with but also identified with the overwhelming, larger-than-life personalities that impose themselves on us from within the pages of the *Inferno*. Twentieth-century readers, traumatized and chastened by two world wars, were not in a position to gain much pleasure from doomed, heroic personalities, but they did find much to identify with in the *Purgatorio*, particularly in its mixed condition of sadness and of hope, its remarkable elegiac lyricism and strong personal conviction, its structural polyphonism, and its delicate interweaving of many strands—episodes of personal encounter with liturgy, ritual, and myth—all suffused with a unifying, subdued tone.

While readings of the *Inferno* have in the past generated great ideological dispute, the *Purgatorio* was not so much debated as devalued. The late Charles Singleton and Erich Auerbach were mainly responsible for allowing us to appreciate better its allegorical-liturgical nature. Operating within a more generalized atmosphere of mythic receptivity (this was, after all, the century of Frazer, Eliot, Joyce, and Mann, one that, going beyond the nineteenth-century preoccupations with plot and character, also permitted the reclamation of Shakespeare's final romances), Singleton explained the lively and intricate theological resonances of what might have appeared to be cold formalism. Auerbach, on the other hand, with his concept of the *figura* (certainly not his alone), showed the way for appreciating the larger poetic possibilities of Christian eschatology.

These two methods of understanding, the one of poetic polyphonism and structural integration and the other of increased liturgical and mythic comprehension, have been of the greatest assistance in recuperating the *Purgatorio*. And each has aided our understanding and appreciation of Canto VIII, perhaps the most representative of the purgatorial cantos (rivaled for this position only by Cantos XXIII–XXIV, with which it in many instances compares). This representative nature is enhanced by its being the last of the cantos in the Ante-Purgatorio and hence by its serving somewhat as a summary. Canto VIII opens with a valedictory image of remarkable lyrical sadness and closes with firm pronouncements of future hope. In the midst of examples of decline, dispersion, and disintegration, it shows the emergence of strong personal conviction.

While Canto VIII could well be thought of as a compact unit, it obviously benefits from a consideration of its placement in the overall structure of the canticle as well as of its relationship to the preceding cantos. Indeed, these cantos seem to possess an overarching political theme, political in the larger sense of establishing ways not only of good government but also of good conduct. If Canto VI terminates with the great political invective, Canto VII shows the European rulers of the preceding generation in a tableau of quiet recollection, reflecting on their ambitions and their failed dynastic hopes. No longer focused on the goals of lineal historic succession, they have instead been moved to contemplate the mystery of God's ways. The larger public vision becomes more personal in Canto VIII, when the moment of recollection becomes elegiac, the *pianger* of the concluding line of Canto VII linguistically resumed in the celebrated opening tercets of Canto VIII. As we come to the close of the first day, it now seems that universal nature is joining the lamentation: it is the dying day that is weeping. Lingering earthly attachments in the midst of the dawning spiritualness provoke the mood of remarkable lyricism. But also in Canto VII, the *Salve Regina* enters as much into the human meaning of the canto as does the *Te lucis ante* sung in VIII.

Following the scene-setting introduction (1–18), Canto VIII consists of two personal encounters (with Nino Visconti, 43–84 and Corrado Malaspina, 109–39, who are still public figures) interspersed by two symbolic moments (19–42 and 85–108). Dramatically, of course, these moments are intertwined: the center of the canto, the narration of Visconti, is a vividly human realization of the sacred drama of the angels and the serpent, which both the *Salve Regina* and the *Te lucis ante* illuminate. In turn, the repulsion of the serpent makes possible the vision of hope with which the Malaspina leaves Dante at the canto's close.

A Quiet Longing

Canto VIII precisely marks the close of the first day in the second realm: it is the canonical hour of compline *(dies completa)*, thus concluding the day that began in Canto I, 115: "Daybreak was vanquishing the dark's last hour." And as was the case in the first canto, the announcement of the hour is associated with the loneliness of the journey. At the dying of the day, the natural movement of the human heart is a longing for the home and the human society left behind. The opening lines expressing the nostalgia of the seafarer and the pilgrim reveal the full lyric expressiveness of the Ante-Purgatorio, with its strong residue of human attachment in the midst of a world of disintegration. With all the tremulous beauty of the lines, it should also be pointed out that if the overwhelming human impression is one of the dying of the day, the death of friends, the decline of social life, and the decay of the human body itself, the *Purgatorio* is also the realm of the dawning spiritual conquest of moral energy, firm conviction, and hope. In this sense, of course, the nostalgia for home is transcended and translated into the greater yearning for the spiritual home (Cecchetti).

These contrary tendencies, so representative of the mixed condition of the *Purgatorio* itself, explain why, while the day is dying in the West, indicating the inevitable downward trend of Nature itself, one of the souls raises his palms toward the East. The resurgent nature of the *Purgatorio* works to establish a community that runs counter to the tendencies of physical nature. One is indeed reminded of John Donne's "Good Friday, 1613: Riding Westward": the later English poet regrets, in an elaborate conceit typical of English metaphysical poetry, that worldly affairs are directing him westward, while his true attention ought to be oriented toward the site of Christ's crucifixion. In the *Purgatorio,* however, the exemplary soul is turned properly toward the East, as if deriving his strength from a religious structuring of experience that is theocentric: "I care for nothing else" (12).

Te lucis ante, the hymn sung by the particular soul and in which he is then joined by the rest of the souls (13–18), is of extraordinary relevance in this canto's depiction of the generalized sense of separation and yearning, even the vulnerabilities of the flesh and the spirit. In this, of course, it is joined by the *Salve Regina* of Canto VII, in which Mary is supplicated by the exiled children of Eve. We are once again witness to the remarkable poetic correspondences afforded by the Christian mythology, one that Dante exploited as imaginatively as anyone. The first woman is redeemed by the second, and here in Canto VIII, if the angels come from "Mary's bosom" (37), the serpent is perhaps the very one that offered the "bitter food" (99) to Eve. The drama of womanhood is established here: just as Mary redeemed Eve, so, too, does Nino Visconti, who feels betrayed by his wife, Beatrice, still entertain a hope that the prayerful remembrance of his daughter, Giovanna, may redeem him. Mythic informing travels in two directions: if Mary and Eve are brought home in Giovanna and Beatrice, through the latter two we understand that Eve's character cannot overcome the normal dispersion of nature, the condition of exile, while Mary's attributes are precisely reintegrative.

The *Te lucis ante* expresses the need for external support in fellowship, prayer, and divine grace. In its fullness it explains the nature of the threat posed by the serpent and connects the yearning vulnerability of the opening lines of the canto with the drama of Nino's widow:

> Procul recedant somnia
> Et noctium phantasmata
> Hostem nostrum comprime
> Ne polluantur corpora.

(Keep far from us the phantasms and evil dreams of the night; tread under foot our mortal enemy, nor let our bodies be corrupted.)

This hymn sung at compline addresses the kind of quiet longing, set out in the opening lines of the canto, that is also of great relevance to Nino's widow. While not directly referring to her, it is about her as well as about the drama of womanhood central to the canto. *Hostem nostrum comprime*: this has been the function of Mary. The hymn's effect on Dante further calls to mind his reaction to Casella's song in Canto II: so ravished were Dante and the other souls that they stood transfixed. But if the first ravishment indicates a lack of direct concentration on the primary matters of salvation (it is a detour, a vicarious aesthetic pleasure), the second shows the improved direction of his spiritual journey.

Angels Descend

The next section of the poem begins with Dante's alerting the reader to its allegorical dimensions. While we are surprised that Dante should have felt the need to do so, if we recall the elementary explanations in the *Vita nuova,* as well as those of the *Convivio* and the *De vulgari eloquentia,* we sense how new Dante felt his own poetic endeavors to be, and how much rudimentary assistance he felt his novice readership required. Dante's warning signal, "Here, reader, let your eyes look sharp at truth" (19), underlines the importance of the pending allegorical drama for the canto.

If the action that follows is allegorical, it is dramatically so, more in the nature of a *sacra rappresentazione.* Indeed, the angels that descend occupy positions at opposite sides of the valley, forming between them a dramatic center stage, of which the purgatorial souls are both spectators and battleground. This is not a novel experience; it is ritualistic and perennial. As if in anticipation, the souls grow "pale and humble" (23). The ritualistic reenactment of the serpent's expulsion could in a modern sense be called mythic. "Now as at all times," wrote William Butler Yeats, in his poem "The Magi," which helped determine the mythic method for Modernist writers. Yeats can see the coming of the holy men, and in *The Waste Land,* T. S. Eliot can emphasize the contemporaneity in the rape of Philomel: "Still she cried, and still the world pursues." Similar to these twentieth-century expressions, the drama of the serpent, emphasized in the liturgy and borne out in the story of Nino's widow, is a repeated occurrence, a re-creation of an ongoing struggle. And although the two angels assume positions of protective custody (in apparent answer to the imploring hymn, *Sis praesul et custodia*), there is some terror in their coming: while their arrival is expected, they still inspire fear and trembling. And well they should, for the drama they portend is one that reaches far back into the mythic memory, the moment of the expulsion from the Garden, the story of the first fall. The angels come bearing *due spade affocate,* the flaming swords that will forever exclude humankind from the original Garden of Paradise and serve as dread reminders of its fallen condition. The element of terror is never lost in the purgatorial struggle. But these same swords also have their points broken off. That this would seem to indicate a defensive purpose is made clear by future action, when the angels repulse but do not defeat the intruding serpent. This is, of course, another cause for humility: the struggle never ceases, the trial is never terminated.

But these suggestions, both terrible and humbling, are a prelude to hope. The innocence of the founder of Eden may have been irretrievably lost, but the future is still open to a Paradise Regained. Consequently, the angels communicate hope as well (and thus conform to the dramatic pattern of the canto as a whole): the garments and wings of the guardian angels are green (28–29). If the terror and humiliation are perennial, so too is hope literally newborn every day. The *Purgatorio* is the place of bodily and social death and decay, but it is also the place of renewal and revival, albeit a renewal and a revival that are not part of the scheme of natural generation. Rather, these are experiences born out of defeat, humility, the charted discipline of the Church, and the mysteries of divine grace. If the angels' hair is blond, nevertheless their true natures are elusive to human perception: "my sight was dazzled by their faces" (35). In the first canto Dante's sight is dazzled by the transfiguration of the four classical virtues in the face of Cato. Here, in the presence of the agency of divine grace, human reason experiences its own limitation, just as it will later in the canto when Dante admits that he did not see, and hence cannot explain, how the angels moved, except to say that they were moved (presumably he could tell that the places they had occupied were vacant). Sordello explains that the angels come from the lap of Mary, and Dante, making a gesture out of habit (a habit that will be transcended in the course of this canto), takes refuge behind Virgil to protect himself from the fear that freezes him.

A Daughter's Prayers

In the next episode Dante meets his old friend Nino (Ugolino) Visconti, who, through his mother, was the grandson of the famous Count Ugolino della Gherardesca. Nino and his grandfather shared power in Pisa for a term, but the grandson, sensing betrayal on the part of Ugolino, fled his city and became part of the Guelf league allied against Pisa. In turn, of course, Ugolino was betrayed by Archbishop Ruggieri, leading to Villani's apotheg-matic conclusion in his history of these goings-on, "E così fu il traditore dal traditore tradito." Taking refuge in Florence, Nino became a leader in the Guelf cause and had opportunity to befriend Dante, testimony of which is so warmly presented in Canto VIII.

The *Purgatorio* is Dante's grand meeting place with friends, Casella, Nino, Forese. These encounters are joyous, most unlike those in the *Inferno,* which are hedged by irony and restraint, marred by sudden rancor (Ciacco) and by hidden agenda (Brunetto Latini). The *Inferno* is about identification and su-persession: despite external obligingness, it is clear that Dante is leaving be-hind former friends and mentors. The *Purgatorio,* in contrast, is about identification and independence. Each of the friends has come to see and to follow his own way; there is no rancor at parting because each seems secure.

Several elements link this encounter with Nino and the later one with Forese. Both men died in 1296; in each encounter Dante himself intervenes in a pseudonaive manner to express his pleasure and joy at seeing old friends again; and in each an essential part of the discourse is directed against women, although in each, one woman seems to escape overwhelming con-demnation. Forese's account takes exception to the stylish Florentine women's modish décolletage (a feature of the dress that alluringly reveals the nipples); against this degenerative practice Forese raises the model of his wife, Nella, by whose faithful prayers Forese's own purgatorial progress has been advanced. In Nino's account it is his daughter who stands out. And in each episode, expressing the resurgence of the spirit in the midst of bodily decay and decline, recognition occurs despite physical obstacles:

> The hour had now arrived when air grows dark,
> but not so dark that it deprived my eyes
> and his of what—before—they were denied.
>
> (49–51)

Despite the darkness (another indication of natural limitation), they were able to make one another out; the spiritual quality of their friendship pre-vailed, as it does in Canto XXIII, when Dante is able to detect by the timbre of his voice the character of Forese, despite Forese's decayed body.

The personal apostrophe, "Giudice Nin gentil" ("Noble Judge Nino," 53), emphasizes, as will other references, that this is, as Vallone has suggested, "il canto cavallaresco," the canto of nobility. However, we should resist any at-tempts to ennoble it falsely. Charles Singleton dismisses some evident con-clusions. Just as he denied the obvious and multiple anthropophagous references in *Inferno* XXXIII, so does he here, in his systematic commentary, dismiss the notion that Dante's exclamation might be intended to refute any commonly held notion that Nino was not among the saved. Yet it is hard to resist the inference that for Dante to repudiate the notion so explicitly might indicate that there was some currency to the concern; otherwise, why raise the issue at all?

Just as the overarching myth presents the conflicting qualities of Mary and Eve, so too does this central episode present two different portrayals of women. The part of Mary is played by Nino's daughter, Giovanna. Although she would have been only nine years old at the fictional date of the telling, Dante expresses in anticipation what he knows to be true in fact: Giovanna has remembered her father in her prayers. This is another crucial difference between the *Inferno* and the *Purgatorio*. The one dominating yet fragile ethic of the first canticle is the humanistic notion of fame, so eloquently espoused and requested by such figures as Pier della Vigne and Brunetto Latini. But the consolation of fame turns out to be a debility when it exists in obvious compensation for a flawed life (hence Cato's stern rebuke of the dawdling souls in *Purgatorio* II). Fame is all too obviously a consolatory writ—the last infirmity of the noble mind—and its humanistic dimension is further undermined by the lower *Inferno*, where being named is too opprobrious, and where the true and ultimate wish is for silence, the utter denial of the original trumpeting powers of Creation. In the *Purgatorio* the positive powers of intercession, based on faithful remembrance, replace the vicariousness of fame. Just as the nature of pilgrimage blurs the distinctions between the living and the dead—one feels a greater spiritual rapport with the departed than with the dissolving social order—so does the faith of the prayerful establish a spiritual communion with the dead. That Giovanna remembers is an indication of her character. Dante entertains what Paul Reyher has called, in reference to Shakespeare, "le culte de la mémoire des morts" (the cult of the memory of the dead). And oddly enough, this cult is most acutely developed in regard to another forgetful wife, Gertrude in *Hamlet*. Remarkably, the locus of Shakespeare's play is also purgatory (where Hamlet's father is placed for the purging of his sins). Unfortunately, in both misogyny looms large. Hamlet carries on against women, "Frailty, thy name is woman," and while Nino first laments his wife's dereliction, he then launches into a general condemnation. At risk in both works is a concept of human dignity that is allied with nobility of soul.

Nino's first complaint is one of injury as well as concern:

> "I do not think her mother
> still loves me: she gave up her white veils—surely,
> poor woman, she will wish them back again."
>
> (73–75)

He cannot refer to Beatrice, his wife, in terms of their voluntary, contractual relationship ("wife"), a product of her deliberate will, but only in terms of her biological role as Giovanna's mother. This attention to nomenclature persists when he proceeds to a more universal condemnation. Nino, as will Hamlet, is ready to generalize about womanhood; he does so by way of the Eve-Beatrice mythology:

> "Through her, one understands so easily
> how brief, in woman, is love's fire—when not
> rekindled frequently by eye or touch."
>
> (76–78)

Beatrice is no longer a lady; that is, she has abandoned the nobility of her feminine nature and has succumbed to the pressures of existence (the very pressures that the circumstances of the canto, particularly the opening lines, make clear). The point of the word choice is clarified in the fourth book of the *Convivio*, devoted to *gentilezza*, as well as the description of another Beatrice, as *donna della cortesia*, in the *Vita nuova*. This is another indication that Canto VIII is the canto of nobility, its virtues being the obvious link between the two personal encounters, the one private and confirmed by its absence, and the other public and exemplary in the house of the Malaspina.

Canto VIII exists in an atmosphere of historical decline (carried over from Canto VII) and social disintegration. It opens with images of departure and deals with breakup and exile. But while overwhelming, this portrayal of degeneration must not give the impression of natural necessity, which doctrine would contravene the firmly held sense of human freedom. While *most* of the world is suffering from general decline, not *all* the world is. Hence we see emerge in Dante a notion dear to John Milton, as presented in the remarkable last two books of *Paradise Lost*, that of the "single just man," the person who throws up resistance to the general tendency of decline. The impression is that of a superendowed personal nature that stands out against a widespread tendency. In Dante, of course, the single just man may be a woman. Giovanna plays the part of Mary to her mother's Eve. It is interesting to note that despite the overdose on misogyny, it is the Christian dialectic (Eve-Mary) that restores the balance. Moreover, despite Nino's righteous zeal, the very dimensions and ethos of the canto lend some understanding to his widow's actions: to fall is sadly all too human; one needs extraordinary grace to transcend the natural human tendency to decline.

Typical of the canto and of the *Purgatorio* as a whole, this section ends with an expression of firm conviction, which in some ways counters the proemial expression of extraordinary natural sadness. Using the heraldic signs of the different houses (thus keeping within the noble dimensions of the canto), Nino denounces his widow's untimely and unfortunate remarriage. The cock of Gallura (the region of Sardinia for which Nino was *giudice*, or governor) would have provided a more suitable tomb sculpture than the viper of Milan (the sign of the Visconti of Milan). This might seem (and does) to us a kind of excessive gloating, so much so that Dante feels obliged to justify his comments as tempered. Nino's bearing bore the stamp of that "unswerving zeal which, though it flames / within the heart, maintains a sense of measure" (82–84); Dante, whose moral severity is allied with his sharp sense of righteousness, can find justification in Nino's hard words. They are said with measure and describe the realities of the situation. There is nobility in the rectitude of Judge Nino, and indeed this is not a defeated person whom Dante leaves. He possesses integrity and a sense of self (despite his pain), and thus he and Dante can part as equals.

This encounter is followed by the expected arrival of the serpent and the enemy's repulsion. Typically it is Virgil who responds to Dante's implied questioning about the appearance of the three stars, representing Christian virtues, where the four had been in the morning. But it is Sordello who directs Virgil's attention to the arrival of the serpent and the sacred drama about to be reenacted. Given the *Purgatorio*'s atmosphere of human yearning, and the implications of sexual vulnerability in the account of Nino's widow, we understand why the serpent should be described in strongly erotic terms. This serpent might well be the very one that tempted Eve. Accordingly he makes his way through "grass and flower," suggesting the unsuspecting natural innocence of pleasure and delight that was so abruptly given over to abomination (the recovery of a different kind of garden will be the ultimate reward of the purgatorial ascent):

> Through grass and flowers the evil streak advanced;
> from time to time it turned its head and licked
> its back, like any beast that preens and sleeks.
>
> (100–102)

Innocence is violated not only by means of the obviously luxurious nature of the serpent but also, and more important, through the preening quality of its sexual consciousness. Showing a thoroughly sensuous nature, the serpent flees at the mere sound of the wings of the angels of grace, as if he too knows his accustomed role in the drama.

The Malaspina

The temporary defeat of the serpent prepares us for a new installment of hope, one most pertinent to Dante's own fortunes as an exile. It was with the Malaspina in Lunigiana that Dante took refuge in 1306; there he was able to perform valuable diplomatic services on their behalf. His host at the time was Franceschino, the grandson of the original Currado (*l'antico*), to whom Currado II, who died in 1294 and who is Dante's interlocutor here, refers. This concluding section permits a splendid and gracious means of acknowledging the patronage and support of a particular house, the Malaspina, and in so doing, to complete the picture of nobility. If Giovanna was the single just woman, the Malaspina represents a noble house that stands out against the common practices of a degenerate nobility. It still exemplifies the antique virtues of generosity and valor (*la borsa* and *la spada*):

> Custom and nature privilege it so
> that, though the evil head contorts the world,
> your kin alone walk straight and shun the path
> of wickedness.
>
> (130–133)

While God-given nature is crucial, one other element enters into the continuing virtue of a house, and that is *uso*, "custom" or "habit," which is based on good education. The concepts anticipate those of Marco Lombardo, who makes a place for free will, while rejecting the concepts of necessity. The decline of the world is historically and causally attributable to the *capo reo*, who permits bad examples to proliferate. Interpretations may vary as to the identity of this "evil head," which could be referring either to the negligence of the emperors or to the intervention of the papacy, or to both (although the passive indifference of the imperial power would not seem to suit fully the designation of *capo reo*). Marco Lombardo later attributed the degeneration of the Romagnuola to that time when the papacy began to cause trouble for Frederick II. But the main point is that if the evidence of decline is historically induced, it thus has causes, and if prevalent is still not necessary. The single just house stands out as a testimony on behalf of human freedom and as a rejection of any arguments of insurmountable decline.

Typically, when Corrado Malaspina initially addresses Dante, in a language of courtly elegance, he refers to Dante's own free will:

> "So may the lantern that leads you on high
> discover in your will the wax one needs—
> enough for reaching the enameled peak."
>
> (112–114)

This prelude to Corrado's request for news emphasizes the waxing of Dante's own will, the essential cooperating agent if the lantern of divine direction is to lead to its proper destination. Throughout this canto, dramatic and philosophical dimensions of the Fall and of recovery are played and played again (Cervigni).

We find another association with Forese Donati in this section, and that is the word *sfregiarsi*, which means to "disornament" oneself, to divest oneself. Dante attests that the house of the Malaspina does not divest itself ("non si sfregia," 128) of the glory of the purse and of the sword. If Dante in his time was witness to such general disintegration as the cantos of the *Antepurgatorio* evidence, then such verbs of undoing correspond to his experience. Life was once a compact whole, a firm unity, the Dantean myth seems to hold, but the very processes of existence break apart that unity, not only physically but morally. Thus Forese's gaunt death-mask face has been victimized by processes of *sfogliarsi*, or unleaving. And morally Florence, day by day, *si spolpa* of decency. *Spolparsi* could be rendered neologistically as "to depith oneself," to rob oneself of a fundamental integrity. "Unleaving" is a purgatorial process against which the resurgent spiritual resists, but it is also a process of moral decline with which humankind's free will can contend.

Thus in several ways the progress of the canto represents something of a rejection of the nostalgic indulgence—powerful and comprehensible though it may be—of its opening lines. Dante's own spirits revive when the praise he bestows on the house of Malaspina returns to him in a dramatic prophecy of future hope. Throughout the *Inferno,* in fact, constituting the line along which many of the cantos may be strung, dire prophecies of Dante's future exile accumulate. In Cantos VI, X, XV, and XXIV Dante is warned about the blow coming toward him. Here in Canto VIII, for the first time, offsetting the bleak news from the *Inferno* and anticipating the clear and final blessing of Cacciaguida in *Paradiso* XV–XVII, Dante hears more hopeful words about what is in store for him. It is part of the specific dynamics of the poem that the last prophecy made by the abhorred Vanni Fucci in *Inferno* XXIV should have alluded, however cryptically, to the pending defeat of the last hopes of the exiled Florentine Whites (of which Dante was one) by Moroello Malaspina, who was much admired for his military skills. Dante underlines the dimensions of hope by having his last defeat and his first recovery administered by different branches of the Malaspina. One understands how the *Purgatorio* is the poem of second chances, bringing together in small and in large, in contemporary matters and in mythic, the tremendous sense of fundamental loss along with the means, the possibilities, and the realities of recuperation and return.

If the proemial nostalgia is somewhat denied by the spiritual energies of the canto, it is even more undone by the lexical force. Dante had good reason to identify his nature so thoroughly with the bluntness of Marco Lombardo and with the no-nonsense gruffness of the old campaigner Cacciaguida. The ethical strength of the poem is strongly rooted in convincing personal experience. And it is through these means, and not through others' words, that Dante will appropriate the full meaning of the Malaspina beneficence. Once full of courtly elegance, the language now becomes forceful, direct, and practical. Not seven years will go by, Currado informs Dante, before this gracious report will be

> squarely nailed into your mind
> with stouter nails than others' talk provides—
>
> (137–138)

Lexically, the canto ends with a firmer hold on experience and a better appreciation of some of the true possibilities contained in the bitter fate of exile. Here we come to what might be Benedetto Croce's most enduring contribution to our understanding of Dante's qualities as a poet. If the liminal lines of the canto are pre- or proto-Romantic, Croce seems to understand Dante's own self-comprehension when he reminds us that we are considering a poet of faith, judgment, and will. Dante, after all, referred to himself as a "poet of righteousness," thus forging another link of identification with the *dritto zelo* of his old friend Nino Visconti.

BIBLIOGRAPHICAL NOTES

In addition to the indispensable commentaries by Charles S. Singelton, Natalino Sapegno, and John D. Sinclair, see Singleton, "'In Exitu Israel de Aegypto'" in *Dante, Twentieth Century Views,* ed. John Freccero (Englewood Cliffs, NJ: Prentice-Hall, 1967), 102, and more specifically on Canto VIII, Giovanni Fallani, *Studi danteschi* 55 (1983): 137; Dino S. Cervigni, "Antitype of the Adamic Fall and the type of the Redemption in Purgatorio VIII," *Esperienze Letterarie* 7 (1982): 5; Gaetano Ragonese, "Motivi umani e religiosi nel canto VIII del *Purgatorio,*" in *Due Letture Dantesche* (Palermo: Manfredi, 1970); Giuseppe Petronio, "Canto VIII," in *Lectura Dantis Scaligera* (Florence: Le Monnier, 1967); Giovanni Cecchetti, "Il Peregrin e i navicanti di *Purgatorio,* VIII, 1–6: Saggio di lettura Dantesca," in *A Dante Symposium,* University of North Carolina Studies in the Romance Languages and Literatures, vol. 58 (Chapel Hill: University of North Carolina Press, 1965), 159; Aleardo Sacchetto, "Canto VIII," in Casa di Dante in Roma (Rome: Societa Editrice Internazionale, 1961); Guido di Pino "Il canto ottavo del *Purgatorio,*" in *Stile e umanità* (Messina: G. d'Anna, 1957); Aldo Vallone, "Canto VIII," in *Casa di Dante in Roma* (Rome: Conte, 1953); Eugenio Donadoni, *Lectura Dantis* (Florence: Sansoni, 1919), frequently reprinted, most recently in *Letture dantesche,* ed. Giovanni Getto (Florence: Sansoni, 1962).

CANTO IX

The Ritual Keys

CHARLES ROSS

In the third hour of the night following his three days in Hell and a day in Ante-Purgatory, Dante sleeps in a flowering meadow. He feels mournful, like the swallow, which according to myth was once a ravished maiden. Probably at dawn, although the text allows the possibility that his vision lasts all night, he dreams that an eagle carries him up to the circle of fire. He compares himself to Ganymede, whom Jove, metamorphosed into an eagle, carried to the heavens, and then to Achilles, whom bright light awoke when he was carried to Sciros. When Dante revives he finds himself with Virgil before the gate of Purgatory and learns that Lucia carried him there in her arms while he slept.

The gate to the holy kingdom is preceded by three steps, some of the most discussed images in the *Divine Comedy*. The first step is polished white marble, like a mirror. The second is rugged stone with a fissure along its length. The third is made of flaming porphyry, a kind of marble, whose color Dante compares to blood. The threshold is made of diamond, and on it sits an angel dressed in ash-colored robes. His face is luminous, and he holds a naked sword. Dante kneels, strikes himself three times, and asks the porter to open the gate. The angel cuts seven *P*s on Dante's forehead with the point of his sword, and then with his two keys, one of gold and one of silver, he unlocks the gate and introduces the two pilgrims to the world of penitence.

The portals open with a great sound that, in yet another simile drawn from the classics, Dante compares to the sound of the Roman treasury opening, as described in Lucan's epic the *Pharsalia*. Then Dante hears from within the singing of *Te Deum* mixed with music, as in a church where hymns merge with the playing of an organ. It is not completely clear that there is no organ music: the simile merges with and confuses reality, like the description of dawn that begins the canto. The hymn rising from a background of sound seems to befit a canto in which Dante makes one of his periodic appeals to the reader to attend carefully to what he is saying:

> Reader, you can see clearly how I lift
> my matter; do not wonder, therefore, if
> I have to call on more art to sustain it.
>
> (70–72)

Despite the difficulty of several passages, both ancient and modern commentators agree that Dante symbolically renders the sacrament of penitence through what Natalino Sapegno, whose commentary has been the basis of my own, calls a series of ritual representations. The angel represents a priest. The three steps, despite some caviling on the part of critics, represent contrition of the heart, the confession of sins, and expiation by works. The two keys represent the authority conferred by God on his ministers to remit sins and to absolve those who are penitent and who confess. But Dante's narrative, says Sapegno, is far from a cold allegory. The tercets unfold a rhythmic narrative rich in events and surprises, from the description of the dream and Dante's awakening and wonder to the representation of the particulars of the liturgical ceremony and Dante's anxious, surprised, and contrite reaction.

Canto IX forms part of a larger symbolism wherein Purgatory is an image of the process of the soul's purification as it overcomes temptation and turns toward God. But it is also part of a concrete event that draws on art, knowledge, and the customs of a living liturgy. It is a true ritual that the pilgrim undergoes to make himself worthy of entrance into the world of penitence and expiation, a fitting conclusion to the experience of Ante-Purgatory, and a solemn prelude to the various religious and moral sentiments of Purgatory proper.

Ritual and Ceremony

In his 1988 Newberry Library seminar on ritual and ceremony, Thomas Greene, who was following Sapegno's commentary, as I have been, asked whether Dante's improvisation of a ritual in Canto IX is slender and precarious or strongly grounded. This is a true ritual that the pilgrim undergoes, says Sapegno, yet as Greene pointed out, Dante made it up. The explanation for this paradox is that Dante lived in a world where ritual and ceremony were strongly felt. The Christian sacraments and such ceremonial gestures as the crowning of a king retained the kind of power observed by cultural anthropologists like Arnold van Gennep in *The Rites of Passage,* Victor Turner in *Ritual Process,* Clifford Geertz in *The Interpretation of Culture,* O. B. Hardison in *Christian Rite and Christian Drama,* Roy Rappaport in *Ecology, Meaning, and Religion,* and S. F. Moore in *Secular Ritual.* Based on their work, Greene attempted a definition of ritual and ceremony. Although they are not mutually exclusive, a ritual is a symbolic performance that is *transformative* and more solemn than ceremony. A ceremony, by contrast, is a performance that *confirms* values and patterns that are already present. When Dante hears Virgil say, as the two part company, "I crown and miter you over yourself" (*Purg.* XXVII, 142), he knows Virgil is validating what Dante has already experienced in the passage from Hell to the Earthly Paradise. Virgil's last words to Dante are a ceremonial farewell. But when, in Canto IX, Dante ascends the three steps to the gate of Purgatory, beats his breast, and asks the guardian angel for admittance, he is participating in what Ezio Raimondi called a "liturgical universe," where not just words but things signify: *non solum voces: sed et res significativae sunt.*

This shift from a verbal representation to the description of a rite or an object is signaled by Dante's address to the reader. The gate, the three steps, their colors, the silent porter, his shining face and naked sword are more than poetical discourse; they represent truth. Since Homer's *Iliad* a door has signaled a rite of initiation, a passage from shadow to light. Psalm 99:4 ("introite portas eius in confessione") connects that initiation, as Raimondi points out, to the mystery of penitence that begins when the angel speaks to Virgil in words similar to those of Cato, while Dante remains silent as he pauses before beginning his necessary ascent through Purgatory. The rite raises questions, and its symbolism is not altogether clear, as Raimondi says, although the normal reading of the steps seems correct: that they represent the contrition of the heart, the confession of the mouth, and expiation through works. Dante uses his memory of the ecclesiastical life and its ceremonies to create a narrative situation out of the language of the liturgy. Dante's ritual entrance is deeply felt, formal, symbolic, and efficacious, even though its images derive from his imagination. In Greene's terms, Dante's world is still that of the Middle Ages, before the waning of ceremonial power that characterized the Renaissance.

This combination of symbolic uncertainty and generally perceived meaning characterizes the canto from its first lines, starting with Dante's odd use of the word *concubina* (usually "concubine" but here "bedfellow") for the wife of old Tithonus. (Tithonus was the son of Laomedon and the brother of Priam. He made Aurora fall in love with him, carried her away, and married her. Jupiter made him immortal, like a god, but did not give him eternal youth, which is why Dante calls him "old.") At the same time that the theme of penance ties together various images in the canto, so does a set of familiar numbers. A dream features Lucia, a symbol of light or God. Two keys represent the power of the Church and its representatives. Penance has three steps. Finally, Dante must erase the seven *Ps* from his forehead during the course of his progress through Purgatory. The numbers 1, 2, 3, and 7 seem odd but also familiar, like the image of dawn with which the canto opens.

Lucia and Light

The canto starts with an image of light, but Dante forces his readers to think allegorically by telling the time in Purgatory, which lies on the opposite side of the world from Jerusalem, in terms of a dawn that takes place in Italy. According to Sapegno, an interpretation must begin with the least problematical part, the indication of time in lines 7–9. Dante says the night had created two steps by which it ascended and almost completed a third. During a night of twelve hours' length at the equator, the first six hours before midnight are ascendant, and the remainder are descendent. Dante, therefore, means that almost three hours of the night had passed. This indication makes sense if we recall that at sunset the two pilgrims found themselves with Sordello on the edge of the valley (*Purg.* VIII, 1–9) and that about an hour later, when evening was darkening, they descended into the valley. There they spoke with Nino Visconti and Currado Malaspina and watched the angel chase away the serpent. It is therefore almost 9:00 P.M. in Purgatory. Here, as in *Purgatorio* III, 25–27, and IV, 137–140, Dante gives a double indication of time, juxtaposing the hour of Purgatory with the corresponding time in the opposite hemisphere, and more exactly, with the time in Italy, where he is writing. He gives this indication by calling attention to "the valley where we were" (7), which would only need mentioning if his astronomical signs referred to somewhere else. Half a world away in Jerusalem the sun has been up for three hours, while in Italy, which is 45 longitudinal degrees west of Jerusalem, Aurora is whitening on the eastern balcony (like a woman putting on makeup or powder). In other words, it is dawn. This explanation serves better than the lunar dawn proposed by ancient commentators, a phenomenon, Benvenuto said, that no other poet ever imagined.

The early exegetes were confused not only by the double indication of time but also because Scorpio ("the chill / animal that strikes men with its tail," 5–6) is on the western horizon, opposite from the dawn. Pisces is in the east, but that constellation is too faint to be compared to the jewels on a lady's forehead ("di gemme la sua fronte era lucente," 4). Francesco Torraca solved the problem by having the stars reflected on the lady's brow, while Manfredi Porena, whom Mandelbaum follows, reads *la sua fronte* as meaning not forehead but "the heavens facing her" (4).

There is further confusion because despite Sapegno's certainty, we do not really know for sure what the "steps" (8) are. They might be thirds or quarters instead of hours of the night. If we follow our own first reading and not that of the commentators, we might suppose that the image of the dawn refers to Dante's own position and that he has been up all night watching the guardian angels fend off the serpent of Canto VIII before he finally falls asleep and dreams in the early hours of the morning. Either that or Dante sleeps all night, without comment, in the short span between lines 12 and 13.

By insisting on telling the evening time in terms of a sunrise, Dante foregrounds the image of light inherent in the name Lucia. In his dream Dante is carried by an eagle to the fiery "orbit" (30), and he wakes as he is catching fire ("and there it seemed that he and I were burning," 31). In reality Lucia is carrying him up the mountain. Dante dreams, then, of what is actually going on. The sensation of fire can be explained by the heat he must feel from the sun, which is two hours high when he wakes. The Bosco-Reggio commentary hesitates to follow all the ancient commentators in identifying Lucia with divine grace. If we follow her image as it develops in the poem, however, we can see that Virgil pairs her with sleep in line 63 ("then she and sleep together took their leave"). We know it is she who prompted Beatrice to help Dante at the beginning of the poem. Virgil saw her. Her name means light. She carries the sleeping Dante out of darkness, whether the dark woods of *Inferno* I or the night of *Purgatory* IX, into the daylight. She must, then, be the light of truth or revelation (or grace) that Dante cannot see awake but that comes to him in sleep as well as in his moment of moral darkness.

The idea that material lights are images of the outpouring of an immaterial gift of light, probably inherent in the gospel according to John, derives in Western thought from Christian readings of Plato. Plotinus was the first to formulate the One as infinite and beyond being, beyond the world of finite forms. It is an elevated, radiating Source, but also, in contrast to Plato, spiritually accessible. The world is no longer a cave where we inhabitants see only shadows of the truth but a receptacle and reflection of the light and good of the One. Because light is partly spiritual and partly material, we see not shadows but radiating light. Images are not a step removed from the truth but indicators of it. Ann Meyer has noted that the sun receives special status in Plotinus's theory of emanation, since it is the most appropriate physical receptacle for the incorporeal "light above light" (*Enneads* V. 3.12, 15). By affirming the material world's spiritual potential, the Plotinian tradition that passed through Augustine, Dionysius, Boethius, Eriugena, and Hugh of St. Victor allowed Dante great images that coalesce the infinite and unknowable with the created cosmos. It is the same process that made the soaring arches and rose windows of Gothic cathedrals symbols of divinity or that invested the liturgy with an inner beauty that goes beyond virtuous words and acts.

Dante's dream may be a prevision. The fire represents the purging he will ritually accomplish in the next seven levels of Purgatory, or perhaps the brightness of the fire prefigures the vision of God for which souls who pass through Purgatory are eligible. To emphasize the latter possibility Dante compares his fear on waking, which leaves him cold, to that of Statius's Achilles, who was snatched sleeping as a boy by his mother and taken to Sciros, where the Greeks later found him, just as Lucia carries Dante. Moreover, like Achilles, Dante looks toward the sea when he wakes. That is, a destined hero recognizes his upcoming tests, with a hint, perhaps of his doom. But if we look at Statius we see that Achilles is snatched from all he knows. He does not dream but wakes up with the sun in his eyes ("oculique patentes / infusum sensere diem," *Achilleid* I. 248–249) and asks where he is. It is possible that Dante, who makes Statius a Christian in Canto XXII, reads the light that strikes Achilles allegorically, as a Christian light. Achilles' mother soothes her son but also informs him that he is only half mortal, on her side; moreover, the times are to be feared ("quin et metuenda propinquant / tempora," 257–258). Unlike the classical hero, however, Dante is not doomed. He may seize his chance at repentance.

Before Virgil and Dante resume their journey, Virgil points out that Dante has left the political rulers behind him, in the valley, indicating that he has separated himself from them. This theme ties into Dante's lament in Canto VI for those who did not serve the function of emperor to pacify Italy. In that canto Dante moved around the mountain away from the sun. Here he again feels its light. At this point Virgil sees that Dante's confidence has increased, and off they go up the slope (69), just before Dante asks the reader to see how he has increased his art. In his previous address to the reader, in Canto VIII, Dante pointed out how easy it was to see through the veil of allegory, which barely disguises the meaning of the serpent threatening the Valley of the Rulers. Here the poet who rises above the politicians moves from the easy images of Ante-Purgatory to the more difficult *contrapassi* of Purgatory proper as well as to the ritual of penitence figured by the three steps, the two keys, and the seven *P*s.

The Three Steps

Dante's elevated art adds complexity to the steps of penitence. The first step, according to the Anonymous Florentine and others who follow Aquinas, is *contritio cordis*, the contrite heart that every penitent must have before coming to confession. Those who have recalled all their sins and feel contrite have hearts that are white and pure, without spot or the stain of sin. Some commentators, like Edward Moore, make the first step oral confession and the second one contrition. But the Anonymous sees the second as *confessio oris*. The step's color is that of shame, and the crack indicates that one must feel shame within as well as show it without. Another interpretation, summarized by J. A. Symonds, is that the crack indicates the roughness of the road of repentance. Moore, who believed that the second step represents contrition, compared the cracked stone to a broken heart. In either case the stair illustrates Dante's use of a material metaphor to signify the qualities of immaterial existence. The third step is *satisfactio operis,* and its red color may indicate the ardor of charity and love that makes men penitent.

Whatever the stairs mean exactly, the penitent climbs them to meet the guardian angel. In Sapegno's mid-twentieth-century summary of learned opinion, the diamond threshold shows the discretion, constancy, and firmness of the priest who must not be moved from right justice for love or money. Once the guardian, whose gray color indicates humility, learns that Lucia has led Virgil and Dante to his doorway, he permits entrance onto his three steps. His naked sword that flashes reflected rays and that both cuts and illuminates is yet another image of light, whether God's grace or a more general metaphor of illumination. Virgil has Dante ask the angel to unlock the gate, and Dante does so while beating his breast three times. The angel inscribes seven *P*s on his forehead and tells him to wash them away once he is in Purgatory. Then he takes out two keys. These images of seven and two are less difficult to understand than the single Lucia or the triple stairs, but no less imaginative.

The Two Keys

Whatever the meaning of the one, or of Lucia, there is little dispute, at least among the commentators, about the meaning of the two keys held by the guardian angel. They identify him as an image of the priests delegated by the Church to hear confession. In the sacrament of penance, the priest must first use his wisdom to judge sins (the silver key) and then use his power to absolve (the golden key). For Dante the virtue and sacrament of penance were based on the words of Christ "Paenitentiam agite" (Matthew 4:17). The *Enciclopedia dantesca* ("penitenza") records that Christ gave the apostles the power to absolve sins in John 20:23, and that the acts and letters of St. Paul insist on the necessity of a change of life, of desiring only what God wants. Whereas the *virtue* of penitence has three parts, the *form* of the sacrament is absolution, executed by the keys of the Church (Aquinas, *S. Theol.* III, supp., xvii, 3). Therefore the two keys that Jesus gave to Peter and that pass from pope to pope are symbolically entrusted to the angel who guards the entrance to Purgatory. (Elsewhere in the *Comedy* they represent not the sacrament of confession but the power of a priest with regard to the *matter* of a vow; see *Inf.* XIII, 59, and *Par.* V, 2, or to pontifical succession itself, as in *Inf.* XIX, 101).

Although the meaning of the two keys seems reasonably stable in Dante and the commentators, the ritual unlocking they superintend lost its power to persuade during the Renaissance. Matteo Boiardo's Fata Morgana, a figure of Fortune, carries only a silver key, which she can use to unlock the gates of her underworld and release her prisoners. She tells Orlando that the point of her key is knowing how to use it—that is, knowing how to manage

Fortune (*Orlando innamorato* 2.9.24). Her lesson mimics the moral of Dante's silver key, which needs "much art and skill before it will unlock" (125). Dante retains the key that symbolizes the authority of the Church, despite his deep suspicions of the men who govern that institution. Boiardo, on the other hand, offers no golden key to his hero Orlando. Whether he was already feeling the decline in the meaningful power of ritual, ceremony, and the sacraments, or whether, like Machiavelli, he felt intensely his frequent warnings against trusting in Fortune is almost impossible to decide, given the famous *sorriso*, or sly smile, of the Italian Renaissance epic. But Boiardo's ironic tone, his muddling of earnest and game, stands in stark contrast to Dante's seriousness.

Both Dante's allegory of the authority (the golden key) and the science (the silver) of confession and absolution, like Boiardo's allegory of Fortune, condense complex thought into subtle and magnificent visual images. Both form part of a narrative as well. In Boiardo's story Orlando is eventually forced to return to Morgana's underworld to make her swear not to bother him again. The point is that a man of moral strength must avoid situations, such as war, where Fortune rules. In the *Comedy* Dante is commanded not to look back, meaning that he or anyone must remain penitent and not return to sin, or the absolution will be in vain. Both poets draw on classical images to form their allegories. Orlando's adventure mimics Odysseus's tryst with Circe, when he makes her swear an oath not to enchant him before he makes love to her. Orlando makes Morgana swear by Demogorgone, the ruler of fairies (*Innamorato* 2.13.27), whose name derives from a commentary on the unnamed power Tiresias invokes in the fourth book of Statius's *Thebaid*. Demogorgone is also said to whip witches, shades, and fays with live snakes, like Erichtho, who lashes corpses with live serpents in Lucan's *Pharsalia* (6.725). Boiardo would have learned some of his allegorical technique from Dante, who himself collected fragments from earlier writers to construct his tale. The prohibition against looking back echoes the story of Lot in the Bible as well as that of Orpheus in Ovid's *Metamorphoses*. Boiardo resumes his narrative at the start of 2.13, after the Morgana episode, by imitating the passage in *Paradiso* XI where Dante hymns the various vocations men choose. Compare the lines "Each to his own, his own to each: Some like to soldier, some tend sheep" (Boiardo 2.13.1) to Dante's "One meant to plunder, one to politick; / one labored"). He signals his homage to Dante and confirms his appreciation for Dante's elevated art, despite his own different sensibility.

The Sounds of Purgatory

The concluding image of Dante's canto is as odd and resourceful as anything that precedes it, although once again the narrative action advances unhindered. When the angel opens the gate to Purgatory, Dante compares the screeching of the great portals to an episode in Roman history mentioned by Lucan. To reach the Tarpeian Rock where Rome's treasury was located, Caesar has to have Metellus removed by force (*Pharsalia* 3.154–155). The treasury remains *macra*, spoiled of its treasure, and Tarpeia was *acra*, resistant to opening. If Dante, who puts Brutus in Hell and has dreams of empire, may be thought of as pro-Caesar, why, then, is Metellus said to be "good" (136)? He may have been good because it was his job, like the angel's, to guard the door, but there came a time when he had to open it. At some point the image contrasts with Dante's gate, since unlike Metellus, the angel porter does not leave. The point of the comparison is not limited to the sound the doors make, but it is not a perfect fit either. It is strange that the Tarpeian Rock is said to be "barren" without the "good" Metellus and that Caesar is said to have spoiled it. The image is as odd as the description of dawn opening the canto.

And even the image of sound that concludes the canto is difficult to unpack. Dante is attentive to the sounds of Purgatory, says Cristoforo Landino, and pays close attention to see and learn what is there. The words "gentle music" (141) do not necessarily refer to the sound of the portals already described but to the first hymnlike sounds Dante hears on entering. The sound gives the same impression of intermittence that one gets from voice and organ. That is, Dante hears singing from inside the portal and compares how it mingles with instrumental music to the mixed sound of an organ and chanting. He is not saying that he hears organ music, but that the sounds are sometimes audible and other times inaccessible: "And now the words are clear and now are lost" (145)—like the imperfect fit of the images in this canto.

However difficult the images in this canto, they all seem tied to the theme of penitence. Conte argues that Canto IX starts with the dawn of man, his humanity, his dreams, his hopes, his new loves, labors, and history. There is danger, but it is in Florence, under the Scorpion, where it is now dawn. The passage underscores Dante's insistence on his humanity as he enters Purgatory. There are more hints of danger in the song of the swallow (13), which is not joyful but mournful in recollecting the story of Philomel. But as Raimondi points out, the swallow is a reference to the soul of a penitent in medieval commentators. And the eagle that seizes Dante in his dream is a figure of the renewal of the soul in Psalm 102: "renovabitur ut aquilae iuventus."

The canto provides a crescendo to the rituals of Purgatory that start with the pliant rush that Dante binds around his waist after washing away the stains of Hell in Canto I. As Mandelbaum's introduction to his translation of *Purgatory* points out, the marveling of the shades that Dante has a body takes on a ritual rhythm. So does the sequence of dreams each evening that he passes in Purgatory. Drawing on his belief that dreams indicate our divinity and immortality (*Convivio* II, viii, 13), Dante describes the three dreams, at the beginning, middle, and end of Purgatory proper, nine cantos apart.

His pilgrim dreams when he enters Purgatory in Canto IX. He dreams again of the Siren and nameless woman in Cantos XVIII–XIX on the fourth terrace, that of sloth. And last, he dreams of Leah, who represents the active life, and Rachel, the contemplative life, in Canto XXVII.

The ritual element of which Canto IX forms a part also includes Dante's frequent intervals of solitude or shared solitude, the monastic quality of the terraces with their hymns and psalms, and the liturgical Latin inserts that occur frequently in the canticle. Another ritual occurs when Dante sinks in Lethe, the river of forgetting, and then drinks from Eunoe, which he invented, to restore his memory of good deeds. These patterns and repetitions help construct the mosaic of memory, both as Dante remembers his pilgrimage and as his pilgrimage recalls and reorganizes, with hierarchical and numerical symmetry, the world of Florence and books that informed and grounded Dante's imagination with ritual and feeling.

BIBLIOGRAPHICAL NOTES

In addition to the *Enciclopedia dantesca*, 6 vols. (Rome: 1970–1978) and the edition of Bosco-Reggio, I have benefited most from the annotations of *La Divina Commedia*, ed. Natalino Sapegno (Florence: "La Nuova Italia" Editrice, 1956) and Ezio Raimondi, "Analisi strutturale e semantica del Canto IX del 'Purgatorio,'" in *Studi danteschi* 45 (1968): 121–146. Material on Plotinus comes from Ann Meyer's *Medieval Allegory and the Building of the New Jerusalem* (Rochester, NY: Boydell & Brewer, 2003). For comparative purposes two works remain useful for English readers: Edward Moore's *Studies in Dante* (Oxford: Clarendon, 1899) and John Addington Symonds, *Study of Dante* (1873; 4th ed., 1899; repr., Brooklyn, NY: AMS Press, 1968). See also Jeffrey T. Schnapp, "Introduction to *Purgatorio*," in *The Cambridge Companion to Dante*, ed. Rachel Jacoff (New York: Oxford University Press, 1993), 192–207; Pietro Conte, "Il Canto IX del *Purgatorio*," in *Lectura Dantis Romana* (Turin: Società Editrice Internazionale, 1965); and William Franke, *Dante's Interpretive Journey* (Chicago: University of Chicago Press, 1996) for comments on Dante's apostrophe to the reader, and Peter Armour, *Door of Purgatory* (Oxford: Clarendon Press, 1983), which raises the old theological question of at what stage, exactly, absolution occurs. I have also drawn extensively on the commentaries available from the Dartmouth Dante Project.

CANTO X
The Art of God

HERMANN GMELIN

Translated by Charles Ross

Canto X begins the great cycle of penitence and education that characterizes Purgatory proper. The souls in Purgatory follow the order of the
seven mortal sins as defined by Christian doctrine. They traverse the seven
circles of the mountain, pausing in each circle, for a time, according to
their inclination toward each sin that has remained in them after their life
on earth. They are not punished for any specific crimes they may have
committed, as happens in Dante's Hell. Instead, at each stage of Purgatory, penitence regularly consists of a meditation and a *contrapasso* (a punishment suited to the sin). The normal object of the meditation is this:
three examples of the opposing virtue and three examples of the punished
sin. These examples are always chosen first from classical antiquity, second
from the Old Testament, and third from the New Testament life of the
Virgin Mary. In this way Dante creates an amazing symmetry that is not at
all monotonous, because Dante has learned from his master the art of
variation. The examples sometimes strike the eye, like sculptures, or they
strike our interior eye, like visions. In the course of the canto, Dante's individual encounters with the penitent souls he finds himself among separate these examples.

The tenth canto, along with the eleventh and twelfth, contains the circle
of the prideful. Pride is the first of the seven deadly sins because it forms the
foundation of all the others: its ultimate source is the soul's rebellion against
God; for this reason Pride has no place to itself in Hell but is intermingled
among all the other sins.

By contrast to that of the Inferno, the system of Purgatory makes this sin more serious than any other. Here the souls do not languish eternally in the punishment their sins provoke. Instead, they follow a continual progression until they are liberated from the weight of their predisposition to any particular fault. Dante himself is especially interested in the circle of Pride, because he knows that his own character tends toward a noble disdain for baseness. Moreover, as he admits in Canto XIII, his defining sin is Pride itself:

> I fear much more the punishment below;
> my soul is anxious, in suspense; already
> I feel the heavy weights of the first terrace.
>
> (136–138)

In what follows I will show that Dante's exquisite art allows him to create inventive examples of his being educated about Pride and, moreover, to feel enormous sympathy for the prideful as he contemplates the punishment that suits them so well.

This canto does not narrate individual encounters with proud souls. It merely describes: first the ascent to the circle of Pride; second, some exemplary bas-reliefs; and third, the general punishment for the proud, who march under the weight of massive stones.

The landscape of the proud is a naked, deserted terrace, completely ascetic, adapted—we would like to say—to concentrate the eye and the mind on images of humility sculpted into the surrounding walls. Dante created these images in the name of God, the highest artist, as he once pronounced his judgment in the name of the high judge of the world. In so doing, he has proposed, by his descriptions, the highest goal of the plastic arts, the ideal of a profoundly realistic and at the same time animated sculpture. The examples of humility, the annunciation to the Virgin, the dance of David in front of the holy arc, and the judgment of Trajan in favor of the widow form a marvelous gradation of technical and psychological complications. Moreover, they form only a subset of the series of images offered for the consideration of the proud as they circle the mountain of Purgatory. The gaze of the voyagers becomes drawn by the slow procession of the penitents. Even this vision, however, is interrupted and animated by a double exchange between subjective and visual contemplation, an apostrophe and a moral exclamation by the poet, which is succeeded by a final image, the sculpture of the living caryatids.

Landscape

Having surmounted the gate of Purgatory, the voyagers are not lovingly welcomed as they might have hoped, based on hearing the hymn *Te Deum laudamus*. To the contrary, they experience all the bitterness of penitence through the arduous crevice by which they ascend; nor are they any more welcomed on the next level. Nonetheless, they have no time to worry about it, since their gazes fall on the bas-reliefs chiseled into the marble facade found at the foot of the cliff, which rises toward the second terrace. This facade inclines less than the cliff's face, so that the prideful souls can contemplate it as they travel, bent under the weight of their burdens. This is the meaning of the line that has given commentators so much trouble: "less sheer than banks of other terraces" (30).

The object of meditation for the prideful is a series of sculptures that represent examples of humility, just as the sculptures of Canto XII represent pride punished. Some commentators have wanted to see in their descriptions an imitation of the descriptions in epic poetry, such as those occurring in the temple of Dido or on the shield of Aeneas in Virgil, or the description of Arachne's weaving in the *Metamorphoses* of Ovid, or the royalty of Argos in the *Thebaid* of Statius. But really there are only traces of epic precursors. Dante's great models are, rather, contemporary sculptures found on the portals of churches, on altars, and on pulpits, which recount the biblical stories in order to edify and teach the principles of Christianity.

Just as Dante competed against Ovid and Lucan for primacy in the description of metamorphoses in the *Inferno,* in the canto of thieves, now here, as he describes the bas-reliefs of Purgatory, he competes, in words, against contemporary sculptors. Precisely during Dante's time Italian sculpture reached an extraordinary level of maturity. One thinks of the Pisano brothers, for example, who were influenced in their work by ancient sarcophagi.

Dante supposes that the author of his sculptures is God himself, who also created the edifice of Hell and imagined all the pains and punishments of the otherworld. He recognizes this agency when he comes to the embankments along the Phlegethon (*Inf.* XIV and XV), and he repeats it with regard to the imperial eagle:

> He who paints there has no one as His guide:
> He guides Himself; in Him we recognize
> the shaping force that flows from nest to nest.
>
> (*Par.* XVIII, 109–111)

Dante alludes three times, once in each canticle, to the art of God. In Canto X the effigies of humility are said to be "dear, too, to see because He was their Maker" (99). Supposing that God were the direct creator of these sculptures, Dante would be attributing a superhuman quality of expression to them, a "speech made visible" (94) that surpasses the faculties of human artisans and that Dante now seeks to express in words. Human powers can never achieve this extreme ideal after which it strives. According to scholastic doctrine, however, nature imitates the mind of God, and the artist imitates nature. Therefore Dante praises the artwork of God by comparing it to that of "not only Polycletus / but even Nature" (32–33).

The Angel and the Madonna

The first of these images—"these effigies of true humility" (98), as Dante calls them—represents the annunciation of the Archangel Gabriel to the Virgin Mary. Thus he begins a series of mediations on the seven virtues. Each virtue is opposed to a deadly sin. All find exemplification in the life of the Virgin, an idea that derives from the *Speculum beatae Mariae Virginis* of Saint Bonaventure, who presents an entire system of opposing correspondences. For example, Mary's humility contrasts with pride, her charity with envy, her mildness with anger, her plainness with avarice, her sobriety with gluttony, and her virginity with lechery. Bonaventure's amplification of these virtues suggests to Dante, at least in part, the very episodes depicted by the sculptures; for example, the manger stands in for poverty, the visit to Saint Elizabeth for caring, and, naturally, the annunciation for humility. As for physical models for his subjects, Dante could have contemplated numerous examples during his lifetime. One thinks especially of Nicola Pisano's pulpit in Pisa (ca. 1260).

Of the three key moments of the annunciation—Mary's fear and surprise, her wonder, and her acceptance—Dante, like most artists, preferred the third. By attributing superhuman art to the craftsman, he can even suggest to our imaginations the dialogue *Ave Maria—Ecce Ancilla Dei,* which was often represented in words in a picture or on a sculpture:

> [there] appeared before us,
> his gracious action, carved with such precision—
> he did not seem to be a silent image.
>
> (37–39)

Dante underlines the potential for psychologically realistic expression by making a comparison to a seal impressed on wax, an image dear to him, which derived from Aristotle and classical poetry and which appears many times in Dante's Latin works and seven times in the *Comedy.* Since Dante's words often contain one or two hidden, allusive, or allegorical meanings in addition to the literal, here the verse "precisely like a figure stamped in wax" (45) condenses a whole series of artistic modes and medieval anagogical levels that elude a modern reader. In the Middle Ages, the word "figure" meant "saying," "word," or "sentence." An artist might write, on a right-handed banner in a picture, inverted letters, to be read from right to left, as if sealed in wax or viewed in a mirror. A left-handed banner would contain normal writing. If the viewer read either banner from right to left, he would see *Eva* instead of *Ave.* This reversal would reveal the anagogic sin of Eve that was erased by the *Ave Maria,* that is, by the birth of the Redeemer, a thought that directs this meditation on humility toward one of the central tenets of Christianity.

David and Michal

The second example of humility occurs in a scene from the Old Testament, the dance of David in front of the holy ark, an act that the medieval period considered an example of great humility. Dante allowed himself, as did other artists of his time, to conflate two biblical stories. The first occurs in II Samuel 6, where the ark is carried on a wagon drawn by oxen. When Uzzah, one of the drivers, puts out his hand to steady the ark, the Lord smites him dead. When men move the ark a second time, David dances. Dante enriches the scene with two details. Following the reading of the Vulgate, which mentions seven choruses accompanying David, Dante makes them sing, and he adds the smoke of incense hanging over the sacrifice mentioned in the Bible. He also introduces, in the right corner of the scene, on a palace balcony, the figure of Michal (68), following the biblical text: "Michal Saul's daughter looked through a window, and saw king David leaping and dancing before the Lord; and she despised him in her heart" (II Samuel 6:16); in Dante's words, "Michal watched as would / a woman full of scorn and suffering" (68–69). And for good reason, since the dialogue between Michal and David defines the form of the dance—"lifting up / his robe" (65–66)—from which David won his fame for humility. Michal says to David: "How glorious was the King of Israel today, who uncovered himself today in the eyes of the handmaids of his servants, as one of the vain fellows shamelessly uncovereth himself." But David answers, "And I will be yet more vile than thus, and will be base in mine own sight: and of the handmaidens which thou hast spoken of, of them I shall be had in honor" (II Samuel 6:22).

One might see God's judgment in the punishment that follows: "Therefore Michal the daughter of Saul had no child unto the day of her death." And so the figure of Michal prefigures the punishments of the proud in the twelfth canto. At the same time, this scene of David's humility, like that of the Virgin, evokes a series of religious perspectives, since David is an anagogic replica of Adam and of Christ, who have their definitive places in Paradise, where the humble psalmist of the Purgatorial sculptures reappears as the singer of the Holy Spirit.

The Emperor and the Widow

The third example of humility, the scene from the life of the emperor Trajan, who halts to render justice to a poor widow, is taken from the tradition of classical antiquity but is transformed by Christian legend. Dante knew the story according to which Trajan (d. 117 A.D.), moved by the prayers of

Saint Gregory the Great (ca. 600 A.D.), was resurrected from the dead and became a Christian before being elevated to Heaven. It is not by accident that Trajan will appear in Dante's Paradise, in the sphere of Jupiter, as one of the lights of the imperial eagle next to David and other good princes. The episode of Trajan and the widow probably owes its origin to the presence of numerous Roman arches, still existing in the Middle Ages, which displayed the triumphant emperor with a female figure (which originally represented a conquered province). The scene was explained, however, as a widow's appealing to the emperor to render justice for the assassination of her son. As a result the medieval guides to Rome *(the Mirabilia Romae)* called these structures the Arches of Mercy *(Arcus Pietatis)*. The most famous one could be seen in Trajan's Forum, and it is possible that Dante saw it and that it inspired this scene of humility.

Moreover, the encounter between the widow and the emperor occurs in the "Life of Gregory the Great" and in other contemporary writings, such as the *Novellino,* which presents a story very similar to Dante's. Dante probably knew the *Polycraticus* of John of Salisbury, which recounts this exemplary episode for the instruction of princes. It appears that this text inspired Dante's moral explanation of the deed, when he makes Trajan explain the cause of his imperial humility: "so justice asks, so mercy makes me stay" (93), which echoes the *Polycraticus:* "sometimes a prince must show justice, sometimes mercy" ("Alterum namque justitiae, alterum pietatis est; quae adeo principi necessaria sunt"). Also in this scene, Dante makes a comparison with the other two bas-reliefs; to the left is the figure of a man; to the right, the figure of a woman: the angel and the Madonna, David and Michal, Trajan and the widow. Again, Dante enriches the scene with sumptuous details: the emperor on his horse, his departure for the wars, the surrounding knights, and the forest of fluttering banners (pennants bearing the eagle on a field of gold, in the manner of the medieval emperors, not the triumphant eagles of the ancient Romans).

If the scene of David, which suggests sounds and songs and the smoke of incense—so much so that "my nose / and eyes contended, too, with *yes* and *no*" (62–63)—offers itself as a miracle of realistic artistry and surpasses the "speech made visible" (94) of the scene of the annunciation, Dante in this case strives to increase still further the sense of admirable artifice. Keeping in mind the superhuman power of the artist (that is, of Dante himself), he presumes that viewers might fill in the characters' dialogue from their expressions and gestures. That is, the figures represent not only the specific moment of the episode, such as the annunciation itself, but also the ensuing changes of mood and spirit: the hurry of the emperor, the joy of the widow.

Naturally this Dantesque scene cannot be considered a sculpture in any strict sense, but neither is it merely an epic description. Rather, it is an attempt by Dante to present, in words, the miracle of a divine art, one that concentrates on a given moment even while, within the unity of a work of plastic art, suggesting psychological states that precede and follow:

> This was the speech made visible by One
> within whose sight no thing is new—but we,
> who lack its likeness here, find novelty.
>
> (94–96)

Contemplation

With his innate desire constantly to discern what is new—not out of curiosity, but out of yearning to create the experience of a transcendent world—Dante turns his gaze, at the suggestion of his guide, toward the procession of the proud. It is not by accident that here in the region of the sculptures he affirms the importance of the visible world in aiding our understanding of theological ideas, as he will declare with so much force in Paradise:

> Such signs are suited to your mind, since from
> the senses only can it apprehend
> what then becomes fit for the intellect.
>
> (Par. IV, 40–42)

As he does in so many other cases, Dante knows how to impart a dramatic note to this encounter with these penitent souls. The pilgrim discusses them with Virgil and watches them slowly come forward under their heavy burdens until, as they approach, he discerns their conditions: "you can / already see what penalty strikes each" (119–120).

Dante's contemplation of the proud becomes a source of meditation and warning. The poet spontaneously breaks out in one of his seven apostrophes to the reader that in every canticle intervene to emphasize moments of particular importance, passages of special difficulty and depth. Here, in particular, the mood is one of consolation, and the subject matter is the limits and boundaries of penitence. Dante interrupts his descriptions with an apostrophe addressed to all Christians, an exhortation against human pride. His dominant image is that of a butterfly, the timeless symbol of the soul, which emerges from its worldly habitation to rise to the heights of celestial beauty. At the same time, this apostrophe evokes the lowliest worm, that symbol of all that is imperfect in terrestrial life. The worm is the sign of original sin: "like the imperfect grub, the worm / before it has attained its final form" (128–129).

But Dante does not conclude the canto on this admonitory note. Instead he introduces a feeling of profound empathy as he contemplates the prideful. And still in a sense imitating the art of the sculptor, he expresses this sympathy by recalling those statues that act "as corbel for / support of ceiling or of roof" (130–131), whose mute but almost vocal expressions arouse pity in onlookers.

And so in this tenth canto, in the circle of the proud, where he feels profoundly affected because of the nature of his own prideful character, Dante still employs the plastic arts to produce a highly objective representation of his thoughts on penitence. He creates exemplary sculptures of humility, and with the utmost poetic skill he dares to imitate God and seeks to attain a realistic and psychological expressiveness beyond the capacity of humans. Nor is he diminished by this visible exaltation of the virtue of humility and the resulting admonitions. Dante knew how to sympathize with those penitents who were particularly close to his own sensibility. And he found his solution in the figures of the caryatids, those sculptures that evoke the beautiful simplicity of the final line of the canto: "in tears, [they] appeared to say, "I can no more."

CANTO XI

Gone with the Wind

ANTHONY OLDCORN

> Whose flowring Pride, so fading and so fickle,
> Short *Time* shall soon cut down with his consuming sickle.
>> Edmund Spenser, *Two Cantos of Mutabilitie* VIII, I, 8–9.

> CRY what shall I cry?
> All flesh is grass.
>> T. S. Eliot, *Coriolan* II: *Difficulties of a Statesman*
>> (with apologies to the Prophet Isaiah)

> Pull down thy vanity, I say pull down.
> Learn of the green world what can be thy place
> In scaled invention or true artistry,
> Pull down thy vanity,
> Paquin pull down!
>> Ezra Pound, *Canto* LXXXI

Sandwiched between two descriptive cantos, in which there are remarkably few lines of actual dialogue and in which the foregrounded speech is the increasingly complex virtual (or visual) discourse ("speech made visible," X, 94) evoked by the attitudes of the figures in relief (in the most complex of these trompe l'oeil—or is it *trompe l'oreille?*—dialogues, the sculpted stances of the emperor Trajan and the supplicant widow are read as an extended exchange in which each of the two participants speaks no less than three times), Canto XI, the second of the three cantos dedicated to the sin of pride, is also the most dramatic. Half the lines contain direct discourse. As Nino Borsellino recently pointed out, this sudden loquacity is all the more striking, even disconcerting, when we recall the crushing physical burdens that all but gagged the prideful in the final lines of Canto X. Bent double beneath the weight of enormous rocks, their chests literally resting on their knees, "in tears, [they] appeared to say: 'I can no more'" (X, 139). It is "appeared to say," not "said," because even this minimal protestation of impotence, for all its laconism, was a reading not of their lips but of their contorted corbel-like postures, reminiscent of those of the pillar-bearing telamones outside the entrance to the cathedral in Ferrara. Just as the Sublime Artificer had, through their body language, put words into the mouths of these performers of exemplary acts of humility carved on the admonitory marble frieze, so Dante, interpreting his ambulant caryatids' imagined speech, had brought Canto X to a resounding conclusion with the alliterated protestation of powerlessness that formed the last four syllables of the Italian canto: "Più non posso." Nothing has prepared us for the lengthy prayer that opens Canto XI or for the speech making that follows.

The canto is dramatic, too, because of the author's personal involvement in the sin of pride ("my overswollen pride," 120), confirmed two cantos later in his dialogue with the envious Sapia (XIII, 136–138), but already apparent in the pilgrim's sympathetic stooping under an invisible burden, which mirrors the stooping of the penitents beneath their own weights. It has been suggested, in fact, that after Omberto, Oderisi, and Provenzano Dante is the fourth penitent. Moreover, this failing seems to run in the Alighieri family. Although the poet does not meet his great-grandfather Alighiero I on the terrace of pride, we learn from Alighiero's father, Cacciaguida, that his son has been toiling there for over a century waiting for Dante to free him through his good works (*Par.* XV, 91–96). Furthermore, commentators since the fourteenth century have assumed that Dante is alluding to his own poetic achievement in lines 98–99, when he speaks cryptically of someone perhaps already born who will chase both Guidos (poets of the recent past) from the nest. The dramatic tension will reach its climax in the final lines of the canto with the account of Provenzan Salvani's heroic act of self-abasement and its prophetic relevance to the imminent banishment from Florence and consequent humiliation of Dante himself, still struggling as he writes about shame and dishonor, injustice and wounded pride (in its less reprehensible sense).

The Seven Deadly Sins temporarily atoned for in Purgatory are different in kind from the mortal sins eternally punished in Hell: they are not individual, unrepented offenses but, rather, sinful dispositions, habits of the soul, torsions of the will that call for reeducation—vices more than sins. Moreover, unlike the retributive *contrapasso* of Hell, the penances of Purgatory are corrective. On this first terrace what is corrected is not legitimate pride in the merits of one's family or in one's own artistic or political prowess— sentiments that Dante does not necessarily condemn—but an unjustified excess of such pride. And not a moment's excess, but a habit of pride so inured as to have become a defining trait of character. Latin and Italian have a specific negatively connoted noun, *superbia* (adj.: *superbo*), for the sin of overweening pride. The English "pride" is not a perfect match, since it covers a moral spectrum ranging from self-respect on the plus side to arrogance on the minus. True, the noun "superbness" once had this meaning, but it has lost it, and the resonant Latinisms "superbious," "superbous," or "superbient," available to sixteenth- and seventeenth-century writers, no longer appear in the modern dictionary.

There is no one place set aside in Hell for the prideful. Nevertheless, we met a number of sinners there—from Filippo Argenti to Capaneus to Vanni Fucci to the giant Ephialtes and Lucifer himself—who, though punished for other transgressions, were presented as paragons of pride. It could, in fact, be argued that, since pride is the fundamental sin leading us to prize our own wills above the will of God, everyone in Hell is guilty of it. The Aristotelian theory of ethical motivation expounded by Virgil in the second half of Canto XVII (91–139) defines pride as misdirected "mental love" (amore . . . d'animo) obsessed with excelling at the expense of one's neighbor. From the narrative point of view, the self-presentations of the souls in Purgatory are considerably attenuated in their anecdotal content, and they typically have less memorable tales to tell than did those in Hell. They are not interested in defending their reputations on earth and have more to say (remorsefully) about how they lived than about how they died. The exception is Canto V, though in that case the recital of their violent deaths provides the shades with an occasion to celebrate God's merciful forgiveness. The discourse of the souls in Purgatory is a mixture of regret and hope, morally reflective, admonitory, and homiletic. This movement toward the eclipse of the narrative dramatic monologue will be still more pronounced in *Paradiso*.

Canto XI may be divided into three parts, corresponding to its three major discourses, one choral and two individual, with a bare minimum of authorial gloss and almost no narrative or descriptive interpolations. As noted, the canto opens *ex abrupto* with the previously unannounced prayer of the penitents, followed by the author's comment on the prayer (1–36). Next (37–72) comes Virgil's request for directions—his only appearance in a canto in which his role is mostly that of a mere spectator—and Tuscan feudal overlord Omberto Aldobrandesco's reply and self-presentation. The remainder of the canto (73–142) is occupied by another of Dante's meetings with a previous acquaintance—a meeting that recalls those with Casella in Canto II and Belacqua in Canto IV—this time with manuscript illuminator Oderisi da Gubbio, whom Dante may have known in Bologna. Oderisi will deliver a lengthy homily on the vanity of earthly glory, replete with biblical, classical, and patristic citations, and, as a corollary to a thumbnail sketch of Sienese Ghibelline leader Provenzan Salvani, he will add one more obscure but ominous prophecy regarding Dante's earthly destiny for the poet to set down in his tablets for future elucidation. Dante's son Pietro seems to have been the first commentator to suggest that the three penitents who appear in the canto represent three different kinds of pride: the *arrogance* or disdain of caste (what Hamlet called "the proud man's contumely"), the *vainglory* of the individual talent, and the *presumption* of entrenched power (Hamlet's "insolence of office"), though Pietro stopped short of suggesting that his father could be accused of all three.

The Paternoster of the Prideful

Dante could count on his liturgically sophisticated Christian audience knowing their prayers, and knowing them in Latin. In fact, he usually does count on it, citing only the first few words of a prayer, psalm, anthem, or hymn and taking the rest for granted. He takes it so much for granted that when, in Canto XXX, 83–84, for example, the angels intone the psalm *In te, Domine, speravi,* the poet can state that they stopped at the words *pedes meos,* confident in his readers' ability to bracket off the relevant segment in their memories. Purgatory already aspires to a paradisiacal condition of music, and the ritual punctuation of the hopeful ascent from terrace to terrace with sacred song and recitation is as characteristic of the new realm as the cacophonous clamor of despair was of Hell. Here, in Purgatory "it is with song one enters; / down there, it is with savage lamentations" (XII, 112–113).

The great nineteenth-century Romantic critic Francesco De Sanctis saw in *Purgatorio*'s liturgical citations a failure of originality on the poet's part, a bow to the conventions of the medieval Church. But despite Dante's denunciation, say, of the corruption of the monastic orders or of the conduct of individual popes and clerics, the poet never repudiates the notion of the Church as Christ's mystical body, the transcendent facilitating structure necessary to individual salvation. Furthermore, like Blaise Pascal, Dante believed in the efficacy of religious practice, habit, ritual, order, rule, and discipline. Interestingly, De Sanctis's reservations did not extend to Dante's Italian version of the Paternoster, which the critic rightly saw as being in some degree autonomous, part and parcel of the poet's narrative invention. To treat it simply as a gratuitous tour de force, an exercise in rhymed translation or in paraphrase, or, heaven forbid, as a variation on a theme inviting comparison with the original, as some commentators have, is to miss the point. The point is the appropriateness of the prayer's wording in the present context. If Dante had been content to have his penitents recite the traditional Our Father, all he had to do was to cite the prayer's incipit, as he does with the other prayers cited.

The poet Guido Guinizzelli will, in fact, refer to the standard version of the prayer in this allusive manner when the pilgrim meets him on the terrace of the Lustful, asking Dante to say the prayer on his behalf when he is finally in the presence of God: "pray say, for me, to Him, a Paternoster" (XXVI, 130). Instead, the prayer placed in the mouths of the recovering sinners of the first terrace is subtly recrafted to be spoken by them at this precise juncture, reinforcing the themes of humility and selflessness introduced by the sculptured bas-reliefs of the previous canto and setting the contrite, submissive, and fraternal tone, not just for the Prideful, but for the seven-step program of Purgatory as a whole. Dante's subtext is, of course, the prayer par excellence, the *oratio Dominica,* or Lord's Prayer, the prayer taught by Jesus Christ to his disciples in response to their request, "Lord, teach us to pray," (Luke 11:2–4, Matt., 6:9–13), the prayer that was for the second-century Roman convert Tertullian "a brief compendium of the entire gospel" (*breviarium totius evangelii*—for Nazi-persecuted German theologian Ernst Lohmeyer, the opening words by which the prayer is known, "Our Father," are a compendium of the compendium, *breviarium breviarii*). The Lord's Prayer is Aquinas's "perfect prayer," the prayer about of which Augustine declared to the Lady Proba: "Whatever other words we may prefer to say . . . we say nothing that is not contained in the Lord's Prayer."

Since pride is the one vice that Dante explicitly accuses himself of in Purgatory, we may presume that the poet's ad hoc adjustment of the prayer's emphasis owes not a little to his personal meditation on the dangers of excessive and exclusive self-love. Of course, though he may give the liturgical prayer a purgatorial spin, the poet cannot stray far from its canonical formulation. The invocation to our Father in Heaven, the three "thou-petitions" and the three "we-petitions" are each expanded to fill a three-line metrical unit. The formerly proud souls propose a series of theological glosses on the evangelical text in harmony with their newfound conviction of their lowly and subservient place in the universe, their impotence, and their comparative worthlessness. The latter part of the prayer is prayed for the living. Commentators are divided over exactly how much: only the last petition (for deliverance from evil and temptation—which these saved souls no longer need) or all the we-petitions. The members of the Church Suffering in Purgatory express their Christian solidarity with the members of the Church Militant on earth by including them in their prayers (22–24), an act of charity that Dante exhorts the living to reciprocate (31–36). Thomas Aquinas, incidentally, denied that the souls in Purgatory pray for the living, stating that there were not in a position to do so. Dante omits the final doxology ("For *Thine* is the kingdom, the power, and the glory"), present in the Didache but not in Matthew or in Luke, and most likely an interpolation from traditional Jewish prayer practice, though it would have perfectly served as a reminder of our total dependence on God and hence as an antidote to pride.

Umberto A.

Omberto (a Tuscan variant of Umberto) Aldobrandesco, count of Soana, or Sovana, in the Tuscan Maremma, southwest of Siena, died in 1259. The circumstances of his death are elided in his confession here, just as those of Provenzan Salvani's death will be elided in Oderisi's account later in the canto. Two early Sienese chronicles present two conflicting versions: in one he is reported to have been smothered in his sleep by assassins paid by the commune of Siena, and in the other he is said to have been killed on horseback in the public square of the fortified village of Campagnatico in a skirmish with Sienese soldiers who had come to take him prisoner. Ironically, his sway had been of short duration, a mere five years, since his father, Guiglielmo, had died in 1254. The branch of the family represented by Guiglielmo and Omberto were Guelf in their loyalties (one of the Aldobrandeschi was elected pope in 1073), allies of Florence, and hostile to Ghibelline Siena. A sensitive critic, like Attilio Momigliano, finds traces of unresolved pride in Omberto's response to Virgil's inquiry, but properly read, the text does not lend itself to such an interpretation. What may have led to that impression is Dante's own sympathy, not, of course, with the immoderate pride for which Omberto is making expiation, but with the aristocratic and chivalrous values he stands for. Omberto's first words, however, retain the anonymous choral quality of the preceding prayer. Moreover, they are not *his*, but *"their words" (le lor parole)*. They proceed from the crowd. The individual speaker is still unidentified when he invites his unknown questioner and his questioner's unnamed but alive companion to "come with *us*" (49). Only then does he switch to the first-person singular, explaining who he is (and was) in order to provoke the living man's compassion and, consequently, his prayers. It is significant that he does not ask Dante for his name and pedigree. It is enough for Omberto that the visitor be a man—a son of Adam (44) and of "our common mother" (63)—who is not yet dead and therefore in a position to pray for the liberation of Omberto's soul. The name of Omberto's father, a formidable name in Dante's Tuscany, occupies most of a line; so too would Omberto's if he were to put his first name and his family name together. Instead, he implicitly repudiates his former family arrogance, modestly calling himself only by his nonancestral Christian name.

The Oderisi Smile (Or, What's in a Name?)

Nomina sunt consequentia rerum: names are the consequence of things. No essay on Dante is complete until it pays at least token homage to this deterministic medieval Latin tag. In the case of Oderisi and his rival Franco, however, modern critics have succeeded in turning the realist axiom on its nominalist head—and the irony is all the more scandalous because the theme of Canto XI is precisely the *vanity* of names—*res sunt consequentia nominum*, things are the consequence of names. When addressed as the "glory of Gubbio" ("onor d'Agobbio," 80) and "the glory of that art / they call illumination now in Paris" ("l'onor di quell'arte / ch'alluminar chiamata è in Parisi," 80–81), Oderisi, bent double beneath his burden, turns aside the similarly bent pilgrim's ingratiating compliment (much as Guido Guinizzelli will defer to Arnaut Daniel in Canto XXVI), and although, with occasional prompting, he will hold forth for the remainder of the canto (and introduce a number of names, including that of Guinizzelli), he will say nothing about himself or his achievements. To set the stage for Dante's encounter with Oderisi, modern editors identify the latter as a celebrated illuminator of manuscripts or as a famous miniaturist. (The Italian equivalent of French *enluminer,* rendered with the verb *alluminar* by Dante, is *miniare*—in which the element *mini-,* also present in the English "miniature," has nothing to do with smallness but comes from the Italian noun *minio* [Latin *minium*], the name of the red lead oxide paint that was the *miniatore's* stock-in-trade). They fail to point out, however, that the miniaturist owes his enduring fame not to anything the historical Oderisi actually did but exclusively to his appearance in Dante's poem, where his function was supposed to be that of instilling humility in the pilgrim by reminding him that our earthly name, however worthily won, is passing and cannot endure.

Some commentators have interpreted the passing of the honor to Franco as an allusion to a revolution in style. And the fact that we cannot point with certainty to a single page illuminated by either of the two *miniatori* has not deterred these would-be connoisseurs from seeking to distinguish the old style from the new. Like a character in Pirandello or Borges, Cardinal Giovanni Fallani made more than an avocation out of identifying the two illuminators' respective hands, while many twentieth-century art historians describe in some detail the works they have never seen. A case in point, though he is not alone in his reading, is Stefano Bòttari who, after having qualified previous attempts at defining the accomplishments of Oderisi and Franco and the relationship between them as "a curious seeking after phantasms" (54), two pages later finds himself declaring,

> The smile in Dante is an inner quality of the light, a luminous splendor of colors. . . . [The use of the verb *ridon* in line 82] implies that Oderisi's coloring, however brilliant or heightened, was still tied to the tradition, indeed to the Byzantine tradition, while Franco's miniatures shone with the magic of their golds, with the happy and untrammeled prestige of their colors. But Dante goes one step further and makes another very subtle observation. Oderisi does not 'paint with the brush' [*pennelleggia,* 83], while Franco 'paints with the brush,' which presupposes in Oderisi a commitment to the tradition of line drawing, and in Franco a more freestyle approach, independent in a sense of that tradition. (56)

The distinction Bòttari is making here, incidentally, seems to owe something to that between the "master of the brush or of the stylus" made in the next canto (*Purg.* XII, 64), though there the two techniques seem to be associated rather than contrasted. Admittedly, Dante, in the *Convivio,* exclaims memorably: "What is a smile *(ridere)* but a coruscation of the delight of the soul, a light that appears on the outside indicative of the state of things within?" (*Conv.* III, viii, 11). Furthermore, the radiance of the smiles of the blessed is one of the great conceits of the *Paradiso.* But surely Professor Bòttari is burdening these two words, as Oderisi and the rest of the prideful are burdened, with more weight than they can reasonably bear. Particularly since, as Guglielmo Gorni has pointed out, the verb *ridon,* used in the present tense to metaphorically describe Franco's pages, is a play on words that picks up on the final two syllables of the rhyme words *Oderisi* and *Parisi* (*Purg.* XX, 52—an unusual form of the toponym, elsewhere spelled *Parigi*). Oderisi, in other words, in a self-effacing pun, invites the reader to isolate and interpret these last two syllables as *risi,* the first-person singular of the preterit of the verb *ridere,* meaning "I smiled" or, in terms of the metaphor, "my pages smiled." Oderisi's pages once smiled too, but now the once proud limner is dead, and Franco has already taken his place. Now it is Franco they acclaim; Franco has chased Oderisi from the nest.

More than artists, in the context of Canto XI, Oderisi and Franco, Cimabue and Giotto, are essentially *names* (first names at that, and, in the case of Cimabue, a derogatory nickname). While they are hallowed names for Longhi, for Dante (in Herbert Marks's apt phrase) they are "hollowed names." It is Roberto Longhi and the other heirs of Renaissance mythographers Lorenzo Ghiberti and GeorgioVasari who fetishize the names and for whom the names mobilize the myths.

It was not ever so. The earliest commentators tend, if anything, to be nonplussed by Oderisi's appearance. They seem never to have heard of him, although at least two of them (Iacopo della Lana and Benvenuto da Imola) came from somewhere near Bologna or from Bologna itself, where twentieth-century archival research has uncovered references in legal documents, dated 1268 and 1269 respectively, to an *Hodericus miniator* and an *Odorisius Guidonis miniator* (Oderisi, son of Guido, illuminator)—documents that, if nothing else, attest to his historical existence. Dante didn't make up Oderisi. Iacopo (implicitly) and Benvenuto (explicitly), however, read Dante's fulsome praise of Oderisi as a tongue-in-cheek put-on. Lana paraphrases the pilgrim's flattering hyperbole: "No one of renown ever came out of that city [Gubbio] except you!" ("de quella terra no ne insì mai persona nomada, for che tue"); while Benvenuto uses his imagination to fill in the backstory: "Dante, who was well aware of [Oderisi's] avidity for praise and glory, deliberately praises him to see if he has rid himself yet of the wind that used to inflate him."

Why, asks Benvenuto, would Dante have introduced, on the terrace of pride, alongside the great and magnificent Count Omberto, such a mean and plebeian spirit as Oderisi? Why should he introduce two such anonymous and rude mechanics? He concludes that Dante's point is to demonstrate that pride is not the prerogative of the high and mighty but rears its stiff-necked head in the most unexpected of places. And here he is echoing the Ottimo, who also finds it necessary to point out that a man can be proud "even for excellence in a manual art" ("eziandio per eccellenza d'arte manuale"). For the most part in Dante, *artista* is a synonym of tradesman or craftsman. True, times were changing: Burckhardt's Renaissance was just around the corner. For the moment, Benvenuto cites the fact that painters had begun signing their works as an indication, not of any sociological revolution afoot, but of their fatuousness.

Mr. Perhaps and the Empty Nest

In addition to this art history conundrum, Dante left another puzzle for the literary historians. Who are the two Guidos of line 97? There is consensus among Dante scholars that one of the two Guidos is the Bolognese judge and poet Guido Guinizzelli; but there is some disagreement about which one. It has been customary for commentators to identify Guinizzelli as the first Guido, assigning the second place to the Florentine Guido Cavalcanti, Dante's somewhat older contemporary, already an affirmed poet when Dante first appeared on the literary scene. The candidates for the third slot include Dante himself, Cino da Pistoia, Guido Cavalcanti (if he is out of the running for the second), Petrarch (yes, Francis Petrarch!) and—my personal favorite—Mr. X. Dante himself is statistically the major contender, from the earliest commentators down to those of the present day. My reasons for excluding Dante have nothing to do with the incongruity (for some, the reprehensibleness) of the poet's insinuating pride in his own achievement into a context in which pride is supposedly being rebuffed. Even if Dante does have himself in mind, his accomplishment is placed in a context so transcendent that his fame will stain the white radiance of eternity only for the blink of an eye. Guglielmo Gorni's commandeering of the author of the letter prefatory to the fifteenth-century Raccolta Aragonese (1477)—in all probability Medici poet-philologist Angelo Poliziano (or Politian)—as one of the first to oppose the inertia of the exegetical tradition is perhaps high-handed and at best circumstantial. Nevertheless, a goodly company of respected scholars has opted for Guittone d'Arezzo as the first Guido ever since poet Ugo Foscolo rejected Pietro Ferroni's nomination of the hermetic Aretine in 1814. Guittone is the only Italian predecessor who can rival Dante for sustained rhetorical argumentation and seriousness of moral purpose, to say nothing of the sheer volume of his literary production. Dante's debt to him is considerable and unacknowledged. What is at stake is not an endorsement by Dante of Guittone's excellence, however indirect and grudging, but once more the voice of fickle opinion, in this case that of the "the champions of ignorance" ("ignorantie sectatores," DVE, II, vi, 7–8) who had hailed Guittone (wrongly, in Dante's view) in his heyday. For these reasons, and for the sake of what I see as the internal consistency of the canticle—the parallel, in other words, between the present lines and the literary bookkeeping of Canto XXVI, in which Cavalcanti is not mentioned, any more than he is elsewhere in the Comedy, apart from Inferno X, where his shade is conjured in extraliterary terms by his dead father—I am inclined to believe that the two Guidos are Guittone and Guinizzelli.

Another verbal crux concerns the chasing from the nest. A cognate of the French chasser (to hunt, to drive out), and hence of English "chase," the verb used in the Italian text, cacciare (from a hypothetical Vulgar Latin *captiare, which eventually took the place of the Classical deponent verb venari), is also a vigorous colloquialism meaning "to toss, dash, hurl, pitch, fling, sling, chuck, etc." The metaphorical locution *cacciare del* (or *dal*) *nido,* created to fit the present context by Dante, has entered the Italian dictionary as an out-of-use metaphor that calls for and receives no explanation.

So out of use is it, in fact, that it is listed among the idioms involving the verb *cacciare* in De Mauro's *Grande dizionario italiano dell'uso*—where it is glossed as *scalzare da una posizione preminente* (to oust from a preeminent position)—without quotation marks and without attribution. It should come as no surprise, then, that commentators on this passage do not seem overly curious about its possible origins. At most they elaborate on the word *nido,* as if the metaphor were confined to that word alone. Francesco Torraca in particular dwells on the affective connotations of the word "nest": "it evokes the idea of a dwelling of one's own, tranquil and beloved, which one does not give up without sorrow." But in that touching simile with which *Paradiso* XXIII opens, do we not have Dante's own pathetically fallacious celebration of the affectionate domesticity of the family nest and the welcome labor of feeding one's own brood?

> as does the bird, among beloved branches,
> when, through the night that hides things from us, she
> has rested near the nest of her sweet fledglings
> and [. . .] anticipates
> the time when she can see their longed-for faces
> and find the food with which to feed them—chore
> that pleases her, however hard her labors.
>
> (*Par.* XXIII, 1–6)

Such, then, is the idyll that the predicted ousting from the nest threatens to destroy. A weighty burden of responsibility indeed for the one doing the ousting!

But who is this heartless evictor, this destroyer of families and nests? I am convinced that Dante, with his unrivalled grasp of nature lore, exhibited for the most part in his always apposite and personally observed similes (Benvenuto da Imola called them his *comparationes domesticae*), is here referring to the disconcerting behavior of the European cuckoo, first reported as a local legend in the pseudo-Aristotelian *De mirabilibus auscultationibus* (*On Marvellous Things Heard*): "The cuckoos of Helice when the young bird is born and has grown big, it casts out of the nest [the Italian here would be *caccia dal nido*] those with whom it has so far lived." Aristotle himself, Dante's "master of the men that know" (*Inf.* IV, 131), repeats the allegation, with a distancing "so they say," in his *Historia animalium* (trans. D. M. Balme [Cambridge, MA: Harvard University Press, 1991], VIII (IX), xxix, 291–292). Several centuries would pass before eighteenth-century British physician and naturalist Edward Jenner would lay to rest the philosopher's skepticism and confirm this item of venerable popular lore by personal observation.

The common European cuckoo *(Cuculus canorus)* is in fact a brood parasite. The hen cuckoo builds no nest (the point of the nursery-rhyme paradox, "One flew over the cuckoo's nest") but lays her eggs singly in the nests of other much smaller insectivorous birds (the willow or sedge warbler, the pipit, the pied wagtail, the titlark and—axiomatically for Shakespeare—the hedge sparrow). At the same time she removes one of the eggs from the host's clutch, which, by a remarkable phenomenon of egg mimicry, the cuckoo's egg matches in size and color. The gestation of the cuckoo egg is more rapid than that of the other eggs in the nest, so that the fledgling cuckoo is usually the first to be born. And the changeling does not wait to be grown before dispatching his fellow nestlings. Blind, featherless, and feeble though he may be, the newborn cuckoo is able to wriggle under and shoulder out of the nest all the remaining eggs or newly hatched chicks, whereupon the usurper proceeds to protest obstreperously and to consume voraciously all the food his harried and unsuspecting foster parents labor to carry to the nest.

Shakespeare himself, Eliot's divider of the world with Dante, had little time for the "hateful cuckoos [who] hatch in sparrow's nests" (*Lucrece*, 849; see also *Antony and Cleopatra* II, vi, 28). In the face of Goneril's rejection of her father, Lear's "all-licens'd Fool" quotes what commentators assume to be a contemporary proverb: "The hedge-sparrow fed the cuckoo so long, / That it's had it head bit off by it young" (*Lear* I, iv, 224–225). In *Henry IV*, the rebel Worcester accuses the king of supplanting him and his allies in similar terms:

> And, being fed by us, you us'd us so
> As that ungentle gull, the cuckoo's bird,
> Useth the sparrow—did oppress our nest;
> Grow by our feeding to so great a bulk
> That even our love durst not come near your sight
> For fear of swallowing."
>
> (V, I, 59–64)

The source of this climactically gruesome worst-case scenario—a mini Senecan tragedy—in which the fully fledged cuckoo, by now three times as big as the sparrow, bites off, ogrelike, not the hand, but the head of his hapless benefactor, is the account given by the credulous Pliny: "[The foster mother] delights in [the changeling's] beauty and admires herself for having borne such a child, while in comparison with it she convicts her own chicks of not belonging to her, and lets them be eaten up under her own eyes, until finally the cuckoo, now able to fly, seizes the mother bird herself as well" (*Naturalis Historia*, trans. Henry Rackham [Cambridge, MA: Harvard University Press, 1940], Book X, xi, 310–311).

My point is that much of this classical lore—as well as, presumably, the popular oral tradition that the written authorities record—was potentially available to Dante. Aristotle and Pliny were the sources critically examined, for example, by Albertus Magnus in the entry on the *Cugulus* in his *De animalibus* (Albert the Great, *Man and the Beasts,* trans. James J. Scanlon, MD [Binghamton, NY: MRTS, 1987], 216). If Dante had the cuckoo's behavior in mind when he used the metaphor of chasing or chucking one's rivals from the nest, it is unlikely, first, that he would fail to register its monstrously negative connotations, and second, *à plus forte raison,* that he would be thinking of himself in the role of pitiless usurper.

But there is also a further consideration, which depends on one's reading of the previous crux regarding the two Guidos, on whether, that is, one admits Guittone and excludes Cavalcanti altogether or whether one opts, as most do, for Cavalcanti as the second Guido. Cortelazzo and Zolli's *Dizionario etimologico della lingua italiana* records an instance of the noun *cacciata* from Dino Compagni's *Cronica* (1310–1312), more or less contemporary with the composition of the *Purgatory.* They gloss the usage as synonymous with *espulsione, bando* ([political] expulsion, banishment)—the fate that lay in store for Dante himself in 1302, two years after the date of the fictive journey described in the *Comedy,* as we will be reminded in the closing lines of this canto. But later in 1300, as one of the priors wielding political power in Florence, Dante, among other factional leaders, would be responsible for the *cacciata* of his "first friend" Guido Cavalcanti, an exile that would lead directly to Guido's death from malaria within the year. A bitter exchange in *Inferno* X, between White Guelf pilgrim Dante and prideful Ghibelline leader Farinata degli Uberti brackets the pathetic apparition of Guido's father, Cavalcante de' Cavalcanti, condemned to spend eternity in the same fiery tomb. There too we find the verb *cacciare* used by the pilgrim in this political sense: "S'ei fur cacciati, ei tornar d'ogne parte" / [. . .] "l'una e l'altra fiata" ("If they were driven out, . . . / they still returned, both times, from every quarter," *Inf.* X, 48–49) is his reply to Farinata's boast that he had twice scattered his personal, familial, and political enemies, Dante's forebears. The fact that the Guelfs returned to power a second time (and that the Ghibellines would never do so again) is the news that Dante brings to exacerbate Farinata's punishment, just as he brings to Cavalcante the false conviction that his son is dead. His son's death was imminent, however, and the harsh measures that Dante took against him—chasing him quite literally from the Florentine nest (for Florence as nest, albeit of wickedness, see *Inf.* XV, 78)—would prove, however unintentionally, responsible. Apart from considerations of fair play or loyalty, no doubt anachronistic and naive, for Dante to proclaim, however tenuously, his literary eclipsing of his early poetic sponsor Cavalcanti with so violent a metaphor that it cannot fail to recall the tragic outcome of Guido's political expulsion would seem uncharacteristically indelicate, not to say gloating; unless, that is, we are prepared to seek a subconscious motivation. Dante's relationship with Guido, indeed, was notoriously complex, and already John Freccero (1988 and 1989) has drawn our attention to the cruelty of putting the rhymes of *Donna me prega* (*nome, come, lome / lume*) into the mouth of Guido's grief-stricken father (*Inf.* X, 65–69). Dante, as Curtius famously remarked to Contini, was a great mystificator.

Stooping to Conquer

The pilgrim's third and last encounter in this canto, with Provenzan (a truncated form of Provenzano) Salvani, is an oblique or indirect one, mediated through Oderisi's ongoing discourse. The stooped figure of the once proudly strutting Salvani, now creeping beneath his massive penitential burden, is pointed out as yet another example of the fickleness of earthly fame. This time, however, rather than a mere name, as were the painters Cimabue and Giotto or the two poets who answered to the name of Guido, the once famous man, now almost forgotten, is actually present, one of Oderisi's fellow shades. Salvani, a contemporary of Dante's father, died in 1269, when Dante was barely four years old, at the age of about fifty, thirty-one years before the turn of the century. As a Florentine and a Guelf, Dante had good reason to feel animosity toward Salvani, the leading Ghibelline in Siena, the city that was Florence's greatest rival for political hegemony in Tuscany. And, because Salvani was a native of Siena, his vanity certainly fit the mold. "Was there ever so vain a people as the Sienese?" the pilgrim had questioned rhetorically among the alchemists in Malebolge (*Inf.* XXIX, 121). What's more, Salvani was quite prepared to raze Florence after the crushing Ghibelline victory at Montaperti in 1260, when the city was only saved from destruction by the impassioned patriotism of his Florentine comrade in arms Farinata degli Uberti (see *Inf.* X, 91–93).

If Salvani persisted in his prideful ways until the eleventh hour, as Dante silently assumes he did (he also assumes that he left no one to pray for him), then according to the parity rule set forth by Belacqua (IV, 130–134), he ought still to be in Ante-Purgatory with the other late-repentant shades who died violent deaths. Instead, in 1300 (the date of Dante's imagined journey), here he is making progress in Purgatory, a good nineteen years before his time. The reason for this remission, one more testimony to the infinite goodness and mercy of God and the outreach of his welcoming arms (III, 121–123), was a single gesture—the heroic act of self-mortification that Oderisi presents in a rapidly delineated *tableau vivant* reminiscent of the "effigies of true humility" contemplated in the previous canto (X, 98). Salvani's eventful life is reduced to a single pivotal moment, the moment that—after the point-of-death repentance and the "little tear" (V, 107) that the reader can supply from Buonconte da Montefeltro's account of his own battlefield conversion—sped him on his purgatorial way. The exemplary moment, in which the long arrogance and violence of a successful political and military career are weighed against the single selfless act of friendship by which it was redeemed, is evoked with great economy of means: six lines (133–138), without a word too few or too many; although there are certain historical facts, well-known to his contemporaries, that the narrator takes for granted and that need to be explained.

The episode narrated by Oderisi occurred, we are told, when Provenzano was at the height of his power, "when he was living in his greatest glory" (133). But the unnamed friend for whom he made his heroic moral sacrifice, motivated by a charity up until then foreign to his nature, had in fact been taken prisoner in the famously bloody battle of Tagliacozzo (see *Inf.* XXVIII, 17) by Charles of Anjou, the brother of the Capetian king of France, and Charles was demanding an extortionate ransom. This places the incident sometime after August 23, 1268, the date of the Guelf victory at Tagliacozzo. Only ten months later, in June 1269, Salvani would himself die in the battle of Colle di Val d'Elsa. His personal power and glory, then, however great they may have been in late 1268, could hardly in retrospect have been more precarious. *How are the mighty fallen!* Furthermore, coming on the heels of the death of Hohenstaufen emperor Frederick II in 1250, and that of his illegitimate son, Manfred, at the battle of Benevento in 1266, Charles's victory at Tagliacozzo, followed by his execution of the sixteen-year-old Conradin, last in the Hohenstaufen line, left the Ghibelline supporters of the imperial cause without a rallying point. Benevento and Tagliacozzo were fought in southern Italy. Colle di Val d'Elsa, the clash in which Salvani—who led the Sienese forces alongside Count Guido Novello—lost his life, was the Tuscan showdown. It would prove to be the definitive victory of Guelf Florence over Ghibelline Siena. Not only did Provenzano have only a few months to live then, but the Ghibelline cause, to which he was no less committed than Farinata showed himself to be in *Inferno* X, was about to die with him.

The significance of Provenzano's figure becomes clearer, in fact, if we set him, as Dante must have intended us to, beside the complementary and contrasting figure of Farinata, if we set the damned Farinata's resonant and peremptory voice against the redeemed Provenzano's silence and Farinata's unflinchingly erect, disdainful, and defiant posture against Provenzano's awkward but eager shuffle beneath his saving burden ("eager" because all of Purgatory's penitents share Forese Donati's willing embrace of his suffering: "I speak of pain but I should speak of solace" XXIII, 71). Farinata was a staunch Ghibelline and a loser, Provenzano a staunch Ghibelline and a winner. Politics neither damns nor saves.

The presumptuous Salvani's wordless self-installation "of his own free will" in the vast public space of Siena's oval Campo—we must imagine the urgent whispers and the crowd of gawkers flocking from all over town to witness the extraordinary spectacle—in order to beg the ransom for his friend's release is recounted by Oderisi with remarkable reticence. The dynamic heart of his account lies in the extreme compression of the climactic line 135 of the Italian text, "ogne vergogna diposta, s'affisse," whose ablative absolute construction and strong perfect bring over into Italian the pith and vigor of Latin syntax. Critics since Tommaso Casini are quick to point out that Dante borrows the ablative absolute construction verbatim from Saint Bonaventure's *Latin life of Saint Francis of Assisi* ("deposita omni verecundia," *Legenda maior* II, 7—the *Legenda* is Dante's chief authority for the laudation of Francis as ascetic hero in *Paradiso* XI); and the hagiographical source is certainly an important key to the interpretation of this passage. What the same critics have neglected to explore, however, are the fruitful psychological ambiguities evoked by the apparently lapidary wording of Dante's text. For the two syntactic elements of the line quoted above imply both what they say and the opposite of what they say. The first element, the ablative absolute "ogne vergogna diposta" ("setting down all shame"), it would be permissible to translate, switching metaphors, as "swallowing all pride."

The original metaphor, however, with its reference to an act of *deposition,* is crucial to the text's punning wordplay. At this turning point in his spiritual life, the life, that is, of his soul, the life that extends beyond his physical death into the afterlife (where Dante finds him)—at the moment, in other words, of his ideal moral conversion—in *setting down* the burden of *false* shame or fear of losing face, an aspect of his pride, Provenzano was actually *taking up* the burden of *true* shame or humility, the burden he now gladly shoulders in Purgatory. The second element, the sibilant reflexive verb s'affisse (literally, "he fixed or installed himself"), coupled as it is with the notion of the removal of a burden, suggests a rigidity of bearing, a tense uprightness, which is a far cry from the encumbered stoop of the purgatorial figure. A rigidity and a tension reminiscent, if anything, of the defiantly reared-up stance of the impassive and "great-hearted" Farinata (*Inf.* X, 73), but which, in Provenzano's case, are the outward signs of an intensely concentrated inward effort at self-domination. It is the final line of the six that takes us beneath the inscrutable surface of the Sienese tyrant's constrained composure, stripping away the skin to reveal the pulsing and trembling veins—seat and theater, for Dante, of the emotions—that proclaim the proud man's inner turmoil and the psychosomatic cost of this supreme struggle to conquer his own worse nature.

What Oderisi fears will be obscure to the Dante of the fiction—Provenzano's "trembling in each vein" for the abasement of his pride—will, he prophesies, become all too clear to the exiled Dante two years hence. The full extent of the misery of Dante's proscription will be spelled out memorably by Cacciaguida in *Paradiso* XVII: "You shall leave everything you love most dearly" (55). The author of the fiction is well acquainted with the grief and bewilderment of banishment and the shame of begging. It is this acquaintance that gives Dante the empathy to penetrate the secret precincts of Provenzano's soul.

BIBLIOGRAPHICAL NOTES

This reading, like the others in this volume, presuppposes eight centuries of Dante exegesis. A detailed bibliography of my sources, almost all in Italian, may be found in the considerably longer and more closely argued version of the text published in the 2005 *Festschrift* celebrating the seventieth birthday of University of Bologna professor Emilio Pasquini, *Da Dante a Montale. Studi di filologia e critica letteraria in onore di Emilio Pasquini,* edited by Gian Mario Anselmi et al. The articles by Nino Borsellino, Stefano Bòttari, and Guglielmo Gorni cited above can be found, respectively, in the periodical *La parola del testo* 4 (2000): 253–261; in the miscellaneous volume *Dante e Bologna nei tempi di Dante* (Bologna: Commissione per i testi di lingua, 1967), 53–59; and in Gorni's *Dante prima della Commedia* (Florence: Cadmo, 2001), 15–42.

The most remarkable treatment of Canto XI in English—a veritable tour de force—is Herbert Marks's "Hollowed Names: *Vox* and *Vanitas* in the *Purgatorio,*" *Dante Studies* 110 (1992): 135–178. One can only regret that the author's *Languages of Adam: Biblical Naming and Poetic Etymology,* scheduled for publication by the Harvard University Press in 1992, has not yet, to the best of my knowledge, seen the light of day. Teodolinda Barolini's "Re-presenting What God Presented: The Arachnean Art of Dante's Terrace of Pride," *Dante Studies,* 105 (1987): 43–62, also included as a chapter in the author's *The Undivine Comedy: Detheologizing Dante* (Princeton: Princeton University Press, 1992), 122–142) deals with Canto XII. The Guittone-Guinizzelli camp includes, in chronological order, Gioacchino Maruffi (1901), Salvatore Santangelo (1921), H.D. Austin (1926), Guido Di Pino (1968), Michelangelo Picone (1979 and 2001), Marcello Ciccuto (1982), Enzo Noè Girardi (1984), Guglielmo Gorni (1994), and Ruggero Stefanini (1995). Among the many useful Italian commentaries, the reading by Antonio Enzo Quaglio in Dante Alighieri, *Commedia. Purgatorio,* a cura di Emilio Pasquini e A. E. Quaglio (Milan: Garzanti, 1982), sticks in my mind as among the most elegant, dramatic, and memorable. I remain unconvinced by Karlheinz Stierle's ingenious argument—in Georges Güntert and Michelangelo Picone, eds., *Lectura Dantis Turicensis: Purgatorio* (Florence: Franco Cesati, 2001)—that Provenzano's act of self-abasement is actually a paradoxical assertion of his pride (and, indirectly, of Dante's own pride) and a substantial repudiation of the whole of Oderisi's foregoing ascetic discourse. For one thing, I believe, as does Amilcare Iannucci, that Canto XI offers not a confirmation but a correction of the false notion of self-eternalization proposed by Brunetto Latini in *Inferno* XV. Stierle's citation of Nietzsche is also revealing: the oxymora "humble pride" and "prideful humility" appear more appropriate to a fin de siècle decadent like D'Annunzio than they do to Dante.

CANTO XII

Eyes Down

JÁNOS KELEMEN

In terms of its narrative, Canto XII is tightly connected to the previous three cantos, which describe the entry of the poet and his leader into the genuine Purgatory, along with their experiences in the first circle. We cannot even locate a dividing line between Cantos XI and XII (from the perspective of the narrative, at least); the borderline appears instead to be within the new canto, since the episode of the previous canto is yet to be completed. The poet is still accompanied by Oderisi da Gubbio, the miniaturist punished for his pride, with his back bent almost to the ground from the weight around his neck. Only Virgil's customary urging prompts the poet to move on. Dante is also forced to assume a slouched posture, a "bow" in a physical, intellectual, and moral sense (the two walked "as oxen, yoked, proceed abreast," 1), with this bow becoming the canto's chief motif.

Of course, Oderisi has been silent, having ended his speech about the poet's imminent exile with a prophecy. In the *Purgatorio,* this is the second prophecy—following the one spoken by Currado Malaspina (VII, 133–139)—which, like its predecessor, appears in a prominent spot: at the very end of the canto. This is precisely the reason why the episode describing the encounter with Oderisi extends into the next canto, thus making for distinct borderlines required within the intellectual, moral, and narrative structure. Just as in other cases, the text calls for different divisions in terms of narrative, doctrine, semantic units, and motifs. As a result, the relationship of the text to the structure of the poem as a whole also varies, depending on the reader's perspective.

After the travelers part with Oderisi, they do not encounter further penitents on the way to the stairs leading to the next circle. The sources of their
edification are the images on the marble pavement at the edge of the cliff
wall. Something similar already appeared in Canto X, in which the travelers
who have just passed through the gate of Purgatory are greeted by sculptures
along the cliff, live caryatids, which, in the meditation, serve as positive examples of souls rewarded for their virtue (that is, humility). Thus the journey
through the first circle of Purgatory divides into the following sections: entry
into Purgatory (IX, 73–145); "effigies of true humility" on the cliff wall (X,
I–139); encounters with souls repenting for their pride, Oderisi among them
(XI, I; XII, 91); and images on the marble pavement (10–76). In accordance with
Purgatory's laws of purification, the latter two sections serve as counter-
points to the positive examples, displaying instances of pride punished.

The narrative structure of Canto XII itself can be divided as follows: the
travelers' farewell to Oderisi (1–9), the description of the images on the marble pavement (10–78), and the arrival of the angel who erases the first P from
Dante's forehead (79–136). Based on all this, we could say, using Croce's
words, that Canto XII of the *Purgatorio* has a "structural" nature, unlike several other cantos of *The Divine Comedy* that create powerful dramatic effects
through encounters with penitent, repentant, or saved souls. The structural
nature of this canto (and by this I do not mean to contrast "poetry" with
"nonpoetry") consists in its being the first canto of the *Purgatorio* in which a
full cycle of repentance is completed—illuminating the general rule of repentance, absolution, and moving to the next circle. The punishment, in accordance with *contrapasso*, is supplemented by meditation on the punished
crime and the opposite virtue relative to the crime, providing either three
examples of each or three types of the examples illustrating them.

Farewell to Oderisi

Dante keeps up with Oderisi (bending low next to the figure bent under his
weight) until Virgil calls on him. Rather than suggesting that time is short,
however, this time he explains that in Purgatory everyone has to move forward out of his own strength, advising that "each urge his boat along with
all his force" (6). That is to say, everyone has to repent for his own crimes,
although—as becomes apparent numerous times—the amount of time the
penitents spend in the fire of Purgatory also depends on how eagerly those
alive are praying for them. Virgil's mention of the "sail" and "oar" in his
warning brings the text closer to one of the overarching semantic dimensions, dominated by images of the sea, ship, and sailing (*Inf.* II, 106–108; *Inf.*
XXVI, 91–142; *Par.* II, 1–16ff). The significance of this goes beyond the poet's
fondness for using a metaphor that has already been introduced. The con-
notation of danger is always present in images of the sea and sailing, and
this danger is not absent in *Purgatorio* either, even though here we are sailing

on calmer seas: "To course across more kindly waters now / my talent's little vessel lifts her sails" (*Purg.* I, 1–2).

On his leader's urging, Dante parts with Oderisi and presses on, straightening his back. But we should note that he straightens up in a physical sense only:

> I drew my body up again, erect—
> the stance most suitable to man—and yet
> the thoughts I thought were still submissive, bent.
>
> (7–9)

It is easy to recognize the metaphoric meaning of this elaboration filled with moral and psychological implications. But on a narrative plane, we should consider the literal meaning of the quoted lines: Dante is still bowed in thought, just as the souls repenting in the first circle are. After all, he too is guilty; he too has to rid himself of pride. The weight on him presses down on his soul just like the rock forcing Oderisi into a bow; he finds it difficult to walk, just as Oderisi did. This difficulty is affirmed by the physical relief he experiences when the angel erases the first *P* from his forehead:

> "your feet will be so mastered by good will
> that they not only will not feel travail
> but will delight when they are urged uphill."
>
> (124–126)

Ekphrases

Before the angel arrives, Dante has to examine the didactic images under his feet. We have arrived at a section (13–75) in which the poet directly formulates his aesthetic conception, along with his overall view of the visual arts and the nature of visual images in general. But let us first stay on the narrative plane, where the episode builds up as follows: Virgil calls his protégé's attention to the images under his feet (16–18); this is followed by a detailed description of the physical placement of the images (16–24), a description of the images themselves (25–63), and an aesthetic and moral evaluation of them (64–72).

At the beginning of the episode, the chief motif of the canto resurfaces. To examine the images, Dante has to look down on the ground again, as urged by Virgil:

> "Look downward, for the way
> will offer you some solace if you pay
> attention to the pavement at your feet."
>
> (13–15)

Therefore, he has to cast down his eyes again, to take a look at the images on the marble pavement. He lifts his head only after he has finished looking at the images and Virgil urges him to rise ("Lift up your eyes; / it's time to set these images aside," 77–78) as the angel approaches. Thus those roaming the first circle of Purgatory are forced into a bow not just because of heaviness of the physical and spiritual weight upon them, but also because of the place-ment of the images. The situation is characteristic of Dante's irony: the im-ages, which can be viewed only with downcast eyes, in the posture of humility, portray famous instances of pride punished.

Dante employs an often-used tool of his by taking as a starting point ob-servable features of his environment, rather than *inventing* the situation. Us-ing the kind of elaborate simile, stretching across several triplets, to which we have grown accustomed, Dante gives a detailed description of the slice of reality that inspired his imagination:

> As, on the lids of pavement tombs, there are
> stone effigies of what the buried were,
> before, so that the dead may be remembered;
>
> . . . .
>
> so did I see, but carved more skillfully,
> with greater sense of likeness, effigies
> on all the path protruding from the mountain.
>
> (16–24)

Dante displays thirteen pictures, devoting a tercet to each. The images are divided into three series, based on the three distinct categories of pride (the one punished illustrated the crime by three types of examples), each of which consists of four cases. The thirteenth tercet should be read as a sum-mary of the previous ones. Each series displays in turn biblical and mytho-logical heroes who were already punished in their lifetimes.

The heroes in the first group (Lucifer, Briareus, the giants, and Nimrod) had been driven by their haughty pride to revolt against God (or the gods) and are punished by the deities; those in the second group (Niobe, Saul, Arachne, and Rehoboam) are punished by their own conscience, while the members of the third group (Alcmaeon / Eriphyle, Sennacherib, Cyrus, and Holofernes) are punished by one of their enemies or victims. The thirteenth example, summarizing the preceding twelve, is about Troy, whose punish-ment came from a combined effort on behalf of divine will, human beings, and the city itself.

The unity of the examples in each group is reinforced by external, formal marks: the triplets of the first series start with the letter V (= U), while the triplets of the second and third series start with O and M, respectively. The initial letters of the lines in the thirteenth tercet repeat the same formula. It is easy to notice the acrostic (VOM = UOM, that is, *uomo*, or man) obviously suggesting that "man" is the root of sin. The sequence of examples reads the word OMO as it is written across the human face:

> Their eyes seemed like a ring that's lost its gems;
> and he who, in the face of man, would read
> would here have recognized the M.
>
> (*Purg.* XXIII, 31–33)

The images are morally instructive, but some of their themes are additionally interesting because they play a role in establishing the poem's overall architectonics. For example, the figures of Lucifer, Briareus, and Nimrod—in accordance with the symmetries among individual parts of *The Divine Comedy*—recall the last cantos of the *Inferno*. In Hell, Dante had already encountered or seen these sinners, depicted here with their characteristic gestures. Their figures thus appear to us from a double angle: verbally and visually. The image in Purgatory depicts the moment of Lucifer's downfall:

> I saw, to one side of the path, one who
> had been created nobler than all other
> beings, falling lightning-like from Heaven.
>
> (25–27)

The image of Lucifer falling down like lightning recalls, among other things, the words of Christ in Luke 10:18: "Videbam Satanam sicut fulgur de caelo cadentem" (I beheld Satan as lightning fall from heaven). In the corresponding place in the *Inferno,* the lightning simile is missing, but Dante refers to it in his description of Lucifer's downfall, embedded in a longer story, in part with the same wording ("giú dal cielo"): "This was the side on which he fell from Heaven" (*Inf.* XXXIV, 121).

Briareus and Nimrod are first mentioned in Canto XXXI of the *Inferno*. As for the former, one of the giants revolting against Zeus, Dante *would have liked to have seen him* ("If it is possible, / I'd like my eyes to have experience / of the enormous one, Briareus," *Inf.* XXXI, 98–99), but Virgil showed him Antaeus instead. Now, to make up for the missed opportunity, we see an image of the fearful giant, depicted in his death throes. The poet discussed Nimrod at greater length in the *Inferno* (*Inf.* XXXI, 46–81), this giant whose chief sin was to bring about the confusion of tongues in Babel ("He is his own accuser; / for this is Nimrod, through whose wicked thought / one single language cannot serve the world," *Inf.* XXXI, 77–78). He is characterized there as a "stupid soul" (*Inf.* XXXI, 70), and his punishment is to lose his ability to speak and therefore to think. The figure of Nimrod carries an important allegorical meaning with respect to the poem as a whole, expressing the opposition of language and lack of language, the relationship between his crime and his punishment, and the degradation of human into beast. It is the relation between crime, punishment, linguistic deprivation, and beastly confusion that the image in *Purgatorio* succinctly summarizes:

> I saw bewildered Nimrod at the foot
> of his great labor; watching him were those
> of Shinar who had shared his arrogance.
>
> (34–36)

"Bewilderment" is the state that Dante himself is in, while roaming in the dark forest—the first tercet of the entire poem tells us about this. It is well to note that in characterizing Nimrod, the poet uses the term *smarrito* ("Vedea Nembrót [. . .] quasi smarrito")—the same word he uses to speaks of his own straying ("ché la diritta via era smarrita," *Inf.* I, 3). If the shipwreck of Odysseus, the poet's alter ego, expresses the fate that would have been Dante's if it were not for Beatrice's intervention, then the figure of Nimrod gives a warning: the giant signals the danger of becoming brutish, which could befall the conceited, sinful humankind.

The Angel

Immediately after Dante has viewed the images, the angel arrives. Many readers think he is the most beautiful angel in *The Divine Comedy:* he is a "handsome creature" dressed in white, "and in his aspect he seemed like / the trembling star that rises in the morning" (88–90). The angel's narrative function is to absolve the poet of his pride, his greatest sin, by erasing the first *P* and making it possible for him to continue his journey. But first he meditates over the examples, drawing some moral lessons from what he had seen:

> "Approach: the steps are close at hand;
> from this point on one can climb easily.
> This invitation's answered by so few:
> o humankind, born for the upward flight,
> why are you driven back by wind so slight?"
>
> (92–96)

Here we should note that it is unclear whether the above warning should be attributed to the angel or to the narrator. But let us assume that it is the angel speaking; after all—as others have pointed out—coming from Dante, this would seem like a somewhat redundant repetition of the moral admonition in Canto X ("O Christians, arrogant, exhausted, wretched," 121–129).

Immediately after the angel has erased the *P* from Dante's forehead, the road leading to the next circle becomes more placid, and the choir's song

rises ("Spiritu pauperes beati"), completing (as always, at the end of each circle) the passage of repentance and praising the happiness that succeeds the
absolved crime (this time, spiritual humbleness). At this point, Dante shifts
his tone, describing the tamed landscape through another lengthy simile:

> As on the right, where one ascends the hill
> where—over Rubaconte's bridge—there stands
> the church that dominates the well-ruled city,
>   the daring slope of the ascent is broken
> by steps that were constructed in an age
> when record books and measures could be trusted,
>   so was the slope that plummets there so steeply
> down from the other ring made easier;
> but on this side and that, high rock encroaches.
>
> (100–108)

   As on countless other occasions, here we find a splendid example of poetic realism in one of the two compared terms in a precisely structured simile, encompassing a wide segment of natural, political, and historical reality.
Emblems of the old, happy times free of corruption are listed: Florence, the
"well-guided" city; the church above the Rubaconte Bridge, San Miniato; the
record and the stave ("il quaderno a la doga"). (There is no need to add that
Dante is referring to specific events and individuals.)
   The canto's closing section provides a similarly chiseled image, providing
a vivid description of the poet's gesture, a gesture that makes Virgil smile:

> Then I behaved like those who make their way
> with something on their head of which they're not
> aware, till others' signs make them suspicious,
>   at which, the hand helps them to ascertain;
> it seeks and finds and touches and provides
> the services that sight cannot supply;
>   so, with my right hand's outspread fingers, I
> found just six of the letters once inscribed
> by him who holds the keys, upon my forehead;
> and as he watched me do this, my guide smiled.
>
> (127–136)

The description of this gesture is another fine example of the way in which
Dante's poetic realism always takes over, even when, as here, his voice perhaps sounds tired and overly moralizing.
   Two factors determine the moral significance of this canto, along with its
place in the moral structure of the poem as a whole: on the one hand, of
course, the canto is about the worst crime and the punishments for it, and

on the other, significantly, this crime is the one that the protagonist takes on himself. Two places explicitly bear witness to these factors. The references to the penitence of the proud are quite clear in the subsequent canto:

> I fear much more the punishment below;
> my soul is anxious, in suspense; already
> I feel the heavy weights of the first terrace.
>
> (*Purg.* XIII, 136–138)

But Dante's words in the previous canto are no less clear:

> "Your truthful speech has filled
> my soul with sound humility, abating
> my overswollen pride."
>
> (*Purg.* XI, 118–119)

This is Dante's reply to Oderisi's speech chastising human pride. He employs the biblical metaphor of being "overswollen," that is, puffed up, to describe this sin (Esther 16:12). In fact, the severe accusations that Beatrice will level at him when they meet (*Purg.* XXX–XXXI) are explained by the fact that "Dante's sin" calls for the most severe punishment, according to the moral order of Hell and Purgatory. Absolution for this sin through heavenly help requires the most sincere remorse. Owing to his pride, Dante chose the wrong path on leaving Beatrice after her death.

Art and Nature

Meanwhile, pride is a characteristic sin committed by artists. In the first circle of Purgatory depicted by three consecutive cantos (X, XI, XII), Dante encounters only three souls who once lived (XI) and has a real conversation with only two of them. Of the two, Oderisi is without a doubt the main character. He embodies artistic vanity and contemplates at length the relationship between Cimabue and Giotto, on the one hand, and between Guido Guinizzelli and Guido Cavalcanti on the other (XI, 91–99), as well as the ephemeral nature of earthly fame (XI, 91–108). It is no accident that the great artists of the era come up in the context of a general discussion of fame, although the relevant passages can also be read as a critical study, or as an independent summary of the history of art and literature.

Beyond this, significance should obviously be attributed to the fact that the theme of art—which has such a strong presence throughout *Purgatorio*—dominates in each of the three cantos devoted to pride. This is not to imply that Dante's negative moral judgment about artists should be extended to art as well. After all, the poet—in the spirit of the principle that "your art is almost God's grandchild" (*Inf.* XI, 105)—distinguishes between the fallible, vain, sinful artists and eternal art, whose final cause is God. The problem of art occupies center stage in these cantos because the relationship between art and pride is indeed different from the relationship between the individual artist and his vanity. While the Oderisi episode displays artistic vanity as a typical instance of pride, the drawings on the cliff wall and the marble pavement illustrate the high moral function that Dante ascribes to art.

Dante describes nonexistent works of art, or rather, "creates" them through verbal means. The visual effect created by Dante's poetry bears witness to his extraordinary power of evocation. Naturally, his accomplishment would be unimaginable without the Italian sculpture of his time: the bases for his descriptions were stone-carved biblical scenes on church gates, pulpits, and altars and among them, as many suspect, perhaps a sculpture by Nicola Pisano depicting damned souls who, while turning toward God, are being pushed into an abyss by devils.

While attempting to preserve the unique features of visual language, Dante cannot help but use narration as his descriptive method. He presents the statues and pictures to us by telling the story either through a detailed description (in the case of the statues carved in the cliff) or, in a more condensed way, through a single, characteristic, dramatic scene (in the case of drawings on the marble pavement). This method reflects his conception of visual art as, in a sense, narrative art. After all, along with his contemporaries, Dante learned this from the pictures of didactic scenes that served to edify churchgoers. Telling evidence of such a narrative, historic conception of image-based depiction is the verb *storiare,* used in reference to the carving about Trajan and the widow: "And there the noble action [storïata] of a Roman / prince was presented" (*Purg.* x, 73–74). But there is more. Dante may well have been aware of the intrinsic linguistic nature of the images; that this is so is supported by his calling the carving of Trajan "speech made visible" ("visibile parlare," *Purg.* x, 95). This view is by no means inconsistent with the suggestion in other commentaries that the "visible speech" terminology refers to the idea that the relief is a wonder from God: created by God, it does not just seize the moment (as images created by humans inevitably do) but displays the successive moments of the dialogue between the emperor and the widow.

God is a realist, according to the lesson of the artwork in *Purgatorio.* We see maximally faithful depictions of reality as the aesthetic ideal suggested by the live caryatids and each of the images on the ground. In terms of this criterion, God surpasses earthly artists: on seeing his creations "not only Polycletus / but even Nature, there, would feel defeated" (*Purg.* x, 32–33).

The mimetic nature of art is perfectly realized in the context of fine art, for the visual depictions nature can re-create the impressions of the other senses as well (at least in the case of God's perfect creations): the relief depicting a chorus really seems to be singing, and the smoke from the incense is real to the eye, if not to the nose (*Purg.* x, 58–63). In the ideal case, artistic representation is no longer just imitation, secondary to reality, but an indiscernible likeness of it:

> What master of the brush or of the stylus
> had there portrayed such masses, such outlines
> as would astonish all discerning minds?
>   The dead seemed dead and the alive, alive:
> I saw, head bent, treading those effigies,
> as well as those who'd seen those scenes directly.
>
> (64–69)

It is worth noting that the just-described aesthetic ideal goes beyond the problem of judging the nature of artwork, constituting part of the thoughts that serve as basis for the entire poem. The poet describes Beatrice's beauty in exactly those terms ("nature and art") that he had previously used to characterize his aesthetic conception:

> "Nature or art had never showed you any
> beauty that matched the lovely limbs in which
> I was enclosed."
>
> (*Purg.* XXXI, 49–51)

The statues and drawings in Purgatory serve as examples in two ways. Their referents, at the level of the stories they recall, are examples that help purify the soul. At the level of self-reference (regarded as self-referring signs or texts) they are examples that justify a conception of an artwork as something that serves to teach and display the truth. The examples thus belong to the sequence that includes *The Divine Comedy*, which realizes the task Beatrice has set:

> "and thus, to profit that world which
> lives badly, watch the chariot steadfastly
> and, when you have returned beyond, transcribe
> what you have seen."
>
> (*Purg.* XXXII, 104–105)

CANTO XIII

Among the Envious

ALBERT WINGELL

Of the various text divisions that have been suggested for Canto XIII, the best is perhaps Benvenuto's three-part reading: the description of the place with its voices (1–42), the description of penance and purgation (43–72), and the conversation with "a modern spirit" (73–154). Like all the others, however, this division submerges the brief but eerie episode of Virgil's prayer to the sun (10–23), which demands and will receive special treatment here.

Critics often remark on the stark contrast with the cornice below that Dante rapidly creates on reaching this second level. A dry, geometrical account of the narrowing mountain (4–6) is followed by word repetitions (7–8) that give a feeling of monotony and emptiness. The rock is featureless and livid (9), a color that in Latin and Italian is connected with envy *(livore)*; it is the bluish-gray pallor of ashes or lead and not simply "green," as in English. This monotony is maintained, since later the sedentary penitents wear cloaks of lowly haircloth of the same color as the rock (48, 58), blending the medieval hair shirt with the sackcloth and ashes of biblical penances. Here there is nothing like the sensory overload of the previous cornice and no movement, not even the slow progress of the proud.

The moral significance of this contrast has become a commonplace since Benvenuto first expounded it. Pride is ostentatious and manifests itself in a multitude of words and deeds, while envy is secret, hidden, and inactive, a vice of meanness rather than of superfluity that makes itself known only by the change in a person's complexion. Buti adds that coldness produces the same complexion and that the envious are lacking in charity; Ciardi thinks of bruises (a related word in Italian). But there is also a dramatic point not to be missed, in that the silence and solitude force the two pilgrims to fall back on their own resources. Dante has provided another opportunity to reveal just what Virgil's resources are. The strangeness of the landscape is conveyed partly by the vocabulary: five words in the first twenty lines appear nowhere else in the *Comedy* (Accordo). Confronted with this landscape, Virgil engages in behavior that is equally strange, or, more exactly (as we shall see), alien.

Virgil's Prayer to the Sun

Up to this point in Purgatory, one could say of Virgil what St. Augustine said of the Platonists in his *Confessions* (VII.xx.26), that they knew the goal but not the way. Virgil has displayed from the start remarkable theoretical knowledge of the scheme of this new realm (I, 82). He continues to demonstrate that here (37–42), along with considerable witlessness about how to proceed. We need only recall that the first time the two were left alone like this, it was the pilgrim Dante who found the way by catching sight of souls who could give them directions, souls whom Virgil failed to notice because he was walking with his eyes to the ground in a fruitless effort to find the road by thought alone (III, 52–66). Virgil learned from Cato's rebuke (II, 121) that time cannot be wasted on the mountain (XIII, 12), and Dante has come close to complaining of the regularity with which his companion repeats that lesson (XII, 85–87). Virgil also learned quickly to keep his eyes up (IV, 39), but the narrative suggests that at this point he proceeds to abuse his eyes (XIII, 13). From what Dante says elsewhere about staring at the sun (*Purg.* XXXII, 10–12; *Par.* I, 46–57), it would follow that Virgil will be blinded, especially since it is just after noon (XII, 81). That is not explicitly stated, nor do the commentators offer anything on the point, but the puzzle is echoed in Virgil's later instruction to his charge to look more closely at the mountainside (43), an odd line of assonance, homonymy, and disyllables broken into anapests. The instruction sounds superfluous in full daylight (Conte), though it might be provoked by the uniformity of color that makes the penitents difficult to see. Blinded or not, Virgil then undertakes the movements that are so minutely described (14–15) that modern critics have suggested a sense of the military or the gymnastic. Critics should suggest the "priestly" air (Biondollilo) more often, since Virgil's movements here seem ritualistic. Swinging around and away from the mountain to face the visible sun, Virgil has planted himself to deliver to it an apostrophe in two spare and balanced tercets (16–21).

The commentaries are in tangles over this episode. Almost unanimously, the early commentators explain it by interpreting the sun allegorically as divine grace or as divine justice or as God himself. Lana, the Ottimo, the Anonimo Fiorentino, and Benvenuto all invoke "the true light that lighteth every man that cometh into the world" (John 1:9). Since Benvenuto also cites *Inferno* I, 18 (like many after him), and though that line echoes the Book of Proverbs, a better referent might be Divine Wisdom, particularly in proximity to Sapia's pun on her own name ("I was not sapient, though I was called Sapia," 109). In any case, most modern critics take this same approach, not without some expressions of unease that betray a concern with literal sense: "wonderful interference of the pagan and the Christian" (Santini); "not a prayer but an invocation, of exquisitely pagan flavor" (Musumarra). Since Zenatti, commentators often refer to the Franciscan hymn to the sun (Santini, Cassell).

On the literal level, in fact, Virgil's prayer contains no trace of such an allegory. Its conclusion, "unless a higher Power urge us elsewhere, / your rays must always be the guides that lead" (20–21), would suggest rather that the sun is quite a secular sort of authority, fallible and subject to correction. As Ciardi put it, "how could the Sun as Divine Illumination fail to lead men right?" Considerations of this sort led Sapegno to recommend the minority opinion of Tommaseo and Andreoli, that the sun here represents human reason, the light of the mind, which can be transcended. But that view brings with it the difficulty that Virgil himself is a regular vehicle for the same signification; it is not clear why human powers should be such an object of veneration, and the *Comedy* suggests an arrangement in which the moon is rather to be linked with unaided human reason (*Inf.* XXI, 127; *Purg.* XVIII, 76).

Finally, there is Momigliano's deviant opinion that the whole episode is just filler, since Dante has not yet been inspired to come to the point of the canto. Critics horrified by this heretic accuse him of denying the validity of the allegorical sense, but, on the other hand, if we apply Momigliano's scheme here, it is true that little of what Virgil says is necessary.

Dramatically, this performance belongs to the character of Virgil alone, as shown by the first-person pronoun (16). Buti may be uncomfortable that the pilgrim Dante is thereby excluded from so pious a prayer, but the central question is how it emerges from Virgil's consciousness. How much of his knowledge is theoretical, and how much of it is much practical, in the sense of effectively influencing his conduct? In other words, though he may know that the Christian God exists, is he capable of Christian prayer? Among modern critics, only Zenatti makes exactly that claim, but the result is a syncretism that is internally self-contradictory: the Roman poet prays as he did under Augustus and as primitive mankind did, and yet he is not involved in the ancient error, since he knows the sun is a sign of divine grace. The Franciscan *laude* that Zenatti quotes makes unimpeachable distinctions between the Lord and his creatures, among whom "Brother Sun" especially carries the signification of the Most High. No trace of this finesse appears in Virgil's prayer, in which Christian theology functions only as a hypothesis that might well contradict or condemn his own loyalties: "Unless a higher Power urge us elsewhere, / your rays must always be the guides that lead" (20–21). He feels obliged to provide a naturalistic justification for his veneration: "You warm the world and you illumine it" (19) is an unsophisticated echo of Aristotle's awestruck rhapsody over the ecliptic that allows the sun to renew perpetually the cycle of life on this earth (*On Generation and Corruption*, I. 10). Instead of the virtue of faith, which Virgil explicitly denies possessing (VII, 7; XVIII, 47), he confesses to his "trust" (16; the words are cognates in Italian) in a superior natural power that could well be grounded on his science.

Correspondences

The complexity of Virgil's thoughts and the basis of his prayer can be garnered from two earlier cantos of the same number. To answer Sordello's question about his ultimate fate, Virgil replies:

> Not for the having—but not having—done,
> I lost the sight that you desire, the Sun—
> that high Sun I was late in recognizing.
>
> (VII, 25–27)

This is the language of Christian allegory, implying at least theoretical knowledge (again) of a Sun beyond the visible sun. (That Virgil should stumble on the word is an effect of translation not present in the original but entirely appropriate.) Since he gained this knowledge after his death, however, and therefore too late for his salvation (Singleton), it is reasonable for us also to gloss "late" as meaning too late to have any practical effect on his outlook and beliefs.

The clearest representation offered by Dante of Virgil's actual beliefs are to be found in the famous lecture on the goddess Fortune (*Inf.* VII, 72–87). While Virgil stresses in his lecture the supreme wisdom of the one who makes both the heavens and the entities that serve as their guides, he does not name him or call him God. Instead, he refers to all the guides of the heavens themselves as gods. The three words that rhyme in alternate lines at the start of his lecture on Fortune (*Inf.* VII, 74, 76, 78, *conduce/luce/duce*) are the same three rhyme words that in Canto XIII frame his prayer to the sun (17, 19, 21, *conduci/luci/duci*). Indirectly, these two cantos are also linked by a thematic thread, since, as the opening words of Sapia's confession make clear (109–111), envy and its opposite qualities derive from the way we respond to the good and bad fortune of ourselves and of others.

About *Inferno* VII, 87, Singleton cites Dante's remarks in the *Convivio* II.iv.2–6, to the effect that the celestial Intelligences popularly called angels are called gods and goddesses by the pagans. Whatever he thought when writing those remarks, in the *Comedy* Dante has not attributed to Virgil a mere manner of speaking but, rather, a doctrine held with so much conviction that it results in an act of religion. The Roman poet is fixed in a kind of philosophic polytheism. Like Augustine's Platonists (*Conf.* VII.ix.15), he has lapsed into idolatry, though of a rather sophisticated sort; unlike them, he enjoys an uneasy awareness of the inappropriateness of his deed. His prayer to the sun is spoken at the same hour of the day at which he first appeared in the action of the poem, according to one school of thought: the hour at which Christ was crucified, according to St. Luke 23:44, and the hour at which Adam fell (*Par.* XXVI, 142). It is even spoken in a kind of desert:

> On that peak rising highest from the sea,
> my life—first pure, then tainted—lasted from
> the first hour to the hour that follows on
> the sixth, when the sun shifts to a new quadrant.
>
> (*Par.* XXVI, 139–142)

The whole episode passes without explicit comment either from Dante the pilgrim, for whom anything but silence might be both disrespectful and premature, or from Dante the poet, who recorded Virgil's troubled silence about his eternal state some time before (III, 45). Dante does attach to his later stage directions an apparently gratuitous remark about the danger of falling off the mountain (80–81). Singleton interprets Virgil's position to the pilgrim's right, on the outside of this terrace, as a gesture of protection on the part of the character, though Benvenuto and Serravale have it that human reason guards us from a fall. Whether its meaning is literal or allegorical, Virgil has been standing on that side of Dante for some time. On the previous cornice, he was on Dante's left (X, 47–48: "he had me on / the side of him where people have their heart"); it is the ritual movements preparatory to his prayer that have brought him toward the edge of this terrace. Dante's remark is a muted anticipation of an actual fall from the mountain, namely, Virgil's eventual disappearance when Beatrice appears (XXX, 49–51, where he is called "father" as he is called "father" here, 34). On the other hand, a positive comment, equally muted, is contained in the fact that his prayer is successful. To walk westward, following the course of the sun, turns out to be the right direction to go in. The pagan poets and philosophers accomplished the best they could with an "eager will" (24), but without the higher reason of Revelation (20).

Eyes Sewn Shut

A certain musicality has been discerned in the passage describing the flying voices (25–36), with counterpoint in the overlapping words and crescendo in the content. Some hear onomatopoeia in the rustling of wings. The brevity of the texts pronounced corresponds to the poverty of the visual scene (Cassell). The divine economy also renders the spirits who speak invisible, a fact that provokes wonder, since we only learn later that the penitents here cannot see. The early commentators glossed Orestes as an example of murderous envy (since he murdered Pyrrhus) until Benvenuto intervened with a eulogy of his charity toward Agamemnon, Hermione, and Pylades alike. Most critics retain only Cicero's story of his generous refusal to accept Pylades' equally generous sacrifice of his own life in his friend's place. Virgil's explanation (37–42) requires that he be an example of charity.

We should note that this is the first and only occasion on which the expressions "lash," or "whip," and "curb," or "bit," are used for the counterposed sets of examples at the start and finish of the pilgrims' passage along each cornice (cf. XIV, 143–147: "That is the sturdy bit / that should hold every man within his limits."). Commentaries often extend that vocabulary to every terrace. The equestrian language has its most remote source in Plato's *Phaedrus*, where the passions of the soul are as horses that must be dominated by the charioteer, an image beloved of Neoplatonists both pagan and Christian.

Dante opens his description of the penitents' piteous condition with an explicit appeal to compassion (52–54), repeated in the simile comparing them to the blind beggars that huddle against the wall near the doorways of a church (64–66). Pietro di Dante cites St. Paul's precept of charity: "Rejoice with them that do rejoice, and weep with them that weep" (Rom. 12:15; also quoted by Cassell). The pilgrim is being drawn into a literal observance of the second half of this precept, which the theologians identified with the virtue of mercy or "grief over the misery of another" (St. Thomas, *ST* II–II. 30.3). Mercy is an offshoot of charity, and Dante chooses the beatitude pronounced on this cornice so as to bring out these connections: "Blessed are the merciful" (XV, 38). It will later appear that the opposite of either member of Paul's precept constitutes one form of envy, so that the vice actually has two contrary forms.

To good dramatic effect, the most horrible feature of the penance is saved for last (70–72); we only learn that these souls are actually blind after the long simile. Needless to say, it was thread that was used to stitch together the eyelids of young falcons, and not iron wire. In this description and in the pilgrim's address to the penitents, their loss of the sun's light is stressed (67–69, 86, 87):

> And just as, to the blind, no sun appears,
> so to the shades—of whom I now speak—here,
> the light of heaven would not give itself.

> that high light
> which is the only object of your longing.

In one of his rare allegorical expositions of Genesis, albeit in a book widely read, St. Augustine decided that the divine gift of wisdom in the "new creation" was prefigured by the visible sun that God made on the fourth day

(*Conf.* XIII.xviii.23). St. Thomas associated that same gift of wisdom with charity, to which envy is opposed (*ST* II–II. 36.3, 45.2). We are reminded again of Sapia's pun on her own name.

The early commentators often rested content with justifying the appropriateness of this penance by invoking Seneca's etymology for *invidia* (envy) as coming from *in-videre*, "not being able to see," that is, not being able to bear the sight of the good fortune of others. Certainly the vice originates in the observation of others, but the penitents' condition also represents their former moral state. There is an apostolic warrant for representing the absence of charity as blindness in the first letter of St. John:

> He that loveth his brother abideth in the light, and there is none occasion of stumbling in him. But he that hateth his brother is in darkness and walketh in darkness, and knoweth not wither he goeth, because that darkness hath blinded his eyes.
>
> (1 John 2:10–11)

Dante's Address

It adds to the irony that the penitents are not only blind but also at first invisible, because of the uniformity of color here. The symbolism is bivalent; conveyed here is not only the monotony of resentment but also an obliteration of the inequality of worldly goods that so tortured these souls in this life. Everyone is on the same miserable level here; the souls lean against each other for mutual support (59), and they pray, with effort, a fragmented version of the Litany of the Saints (50–51). The point of their prayer is no doubt the doctrine of the communion of saints, which implies the mutual sharing of benefits between Church triumphant, Church suffering, and Church militant, with the ultimate goal of eternal life for all. Modern critics call attention to Dante's powers of observation, which make him adept at describing in posture and gesture the body language of the blind.

The pilgrim is sensitive to the fact that because he can see the penitents while remaining unseen, he enjoys a status superior to theirs (73–75). To prolong this situation would be discourteous and a violation of charity (cf. 27). Speech can bring him to their level, but it is interesting that language is all he can share with them. On the cornice of the proud, talking to the penitents forces him to bend over, thereby sharing their penance somewhat for a space of time (XI, 73; XII, 7), though without the weight on his back that he mentions here (138). But it is impossible for him to participate in the penance of the envious to any degree; a kind of alienation still clings to the penitents. Only at the exit from this cornice, when the penitents are far behind, is the pilgrim himself—apparently—blinded by the sun (XV, 7–15).

Virgil's granting of permission to speak (78) includes two canons of classical rhetoric (brevity and consequence), but it also reminds modern critics of a similar instruction that opened Dante's conversation with Farinata (*Inf.* x, 39). The comparison establishes links in the cast of characters. In the Battle of Montaperti won by the Ghibellines in 1260, Farinata, from Florence, would have been the ally of Provenzan Salvani, leader of the Sienese forces. Contemporary documents make Sapia a Salvani, an aunt of Provenzan, and the wife of Ghinibaldo di Saracino, lord of a castle near Montereggione. To close the circle, Provenzan, who lost his life directing the fateful battle of Colle nine years later (115), is doing penance for pride on the terrace below (XI, 121–123), where internal opposition to his dominant position in Siena is suggested. The two Sienese whom Dante encounters on these first two cornices exemplify the complementary vices that can arise from worldly power and worldly weakness, respectively. They also represent how even the bonds of family could be broken by the civic hostility produced by factionalism in the Italian city-states.

Dante's elegant address to the penitents is almost a schoolbook exercise in the rhetorical art of *captatio benevolentiae* (capturing the audience's goodwill from the start). He ends by pointing out a benefit of the communion of saints that he could provide for any member of his own language community (91–93). With her first words Sapia declares that all such earthly communities are transcended here in the common citizenship of the heavenly city (94–96). St. Augustine marshaled a number of biblical texts to back up that notion in *The City of God*, XI. I, a work that speaks from start to finish of the "pilgrim city" and the "pilgrim church" on this earth. As Buti first noted, the word "pilgrim" recaptures St. Paul's "We have here no lasting city" (Heb. 13:14). For those who know the poet's biography, this spiritual interpretation of membership in any Italian community has a particular twist, since to be a "pilgrim in Italy" was literally Dante's condition after his exile.

Sapia's Definition of Envy

In expounding Sapia's tale of herself, the commentators often fall back on the historical details. That the loser of the battle of Colle was Sapia's nephew would make her sin even worse, since it was a violation of family ties. A grisly item from the chronicles is often mentioned, that after Provenzan's defeat, his head was carried about on a pike by the victorious enemies. Although Sapia and her husband were Guelfs, it is suggested that she felt Provenzan had been wrongly promoted to certain dignities that her husband deserved. Lana first reported as hearsay the story that she watched the battle from a castle window, leading Zenatti to remember Michal (x, 68), though the two women are practically of opposite character. Much ink was wasted trying to find that castle, since her husband's was quite far from Colle, until Santini finally pointed out that Dante says only that she saw the chase (120–121). Few of these particulars have any relevance to the text. It is noteworthy that Sapia speaks in the plural, saying "fellow citizens" (115), and never mentions her nephew; her remorse is for her violation of those very civic ties that she has just declared dissolved in the afterlife. She is conscious that her sin was darkened, but precisely because it resulted in a blasphemy. Sapia commemorates her mockery of God with a self-mocking simile. The point of the folktale about the blackbird's premature exultation was the bird's stupidity (the tale can be found in modern collections of Italian folklore), and she seems to suggest her own hastiness in line 117.

Among all the penitents in Purgatory, Sapia is the only woman to speak besides Pia dei Tolomei, also of Siena, whose words only occupy two tercets plus a line (V, 130–136). It is unfortunate that Sapia has been so roughly handled by a few commentators. Benvenuto trucks out the medieval stereotype and catalogs all the feminine vices she still manifests, starting with loquacity. Although Momigliano grants that her sinfulness appears only through the transparency of repentance, he believes that, incompletely purged, she reverts to her old ways at the end of the canto. Biondolillo accuses her, among other things, of envying Dante the privilege by which he is there in the flesh (145–147). But surely her first thought on learning that Dante is alive is of God's love, which she does not lack, and the good the pilgrim can do for her, which is also beneficial to him. As many maintain, Sapia is really one of the most admirable and adroit characters we meet in the *Comedy* and is portrayed with considerable complexity. The vivacity of her feelings in this life (118–120) and her aggressive directness reappear in the tone of her questions to Dante (130, 139) and her response to his answers. In some respects, such as her capacity for self-measurement, verbal wit, precision with language, and a tendency to sarcasm, she is not unlike Dante himself.

> There they were routed, beaten; they were reeling
> along the bitter paths of flight; and seeing
> that chase, I felt incomparable joy,
> so that I lifted up my daring face
> and cried to God: "Now I fear you no more."
>
> (118–122)

Their similarity may be what accounts for the astonishing honesty of the pilgrim's reply, a confession of his own vices (133–138), which hardly seems called for. Perhaps confession invites confession, since language is all Dante can share with these penitents. He differentiates himself from his interlocutor by acknowledging a far greater sense of guilt with regard to pride, and it is easy to see that a person so conscious of his own talent would seldom have occasion to be envious (cf. *Inf.* XXV, 100). On the other hand, Dante never answers Sapia's questions about his identity and that of his guide—despite her gracious and fulsome satisfaction of his desire to know her by place and name (105)—and she makes no protest (149). It is not clear whether this is humility on his part or an effect of her lesson about the transitoriness of earthly communities. When two souls farther on put the question to him again, he does identify his birthplace but suppresses his name with a modest commonplace that nevertheless suggests his eventual fame (XIV, 10–21).

Some find a fracture in tone between the second and third sections of this canto, since the lively figure of Sapia hardly seems to need our sympathy and generally inspires a kind of awe. Certainly a stark literary contrast is evident here, but there are at least two reasons for this shift in gear. One is that envy takes more than one form. We commonly think of it as a sadness both mordant and sterile, a fairly passive disposition. Following Gregory the Great, however, St. Thomas admitted that envy could also express itself as the opposite passion, exultation over the adversities of others (ST II–II.1.4. and 3m). The vice is symmetrical with the virtue, since St. Paul's precept of charity also produces either weeping or joy. The second expression of envy is the sort we might expect from a more active personality, or better, from a sanguine type, and that is what Sapia confesses (110–111). Thus Dante has deliberately prepared a surprise, instantiating the familiar with the unfamiliar and playing, as usual, with his knowledge of paradoxes, using the logic of morals. (Compare the mirroring of avarice and prodigality in the case of Statius, XXII, 22–26.)

In this light, since Sapia is among the saved (142: "I am alive; and therefore, chosen spirit"), we must certainly see in her outburst of wonder at Dante's presence there (145–146) an expression of joy at the good fortune of another. She is true to character, but the same passion that served her vice, when redirected in its object, can be a vehicle of charity. This is the more general point that Dante makes with his stylistic contrast: that the penance, no matter how impressive the horror of its oppression, does not obliterate the character traits of the penitents but disciplines the penitents (103). In another metaphor, these persons are still what they were but are being cleansed. "The stream of memory" (89–90) suggests that their past personalities persist, each individual with his or her particular resources.

Many of Sapia's character traits, and certainly her verbal skills, qualify her admirably for the task of "fraternal correction," classified as an act of charity by St. Thomas (ST II–II.33.1). Fraternal correction is literally the note on which she opened with Dante (94), and it is also the note on which she ends (151–154). Her mockery of the futile ambitions of the Sienese (their projected seaport will turn out to be costlier than the elusive underground river, and for some in particular) is hardly just a reflection of Florentine stereotypes of the Sienese that Dante is putting in her mouth. In light of the religious practice of fraternal correction, it is clearly his dramatic intention to have a Sienese lady criticize Siena (as the Florentine poet so often inveighs against Florence). The mockery is gentle: her motive is no longer the hatred that gave her joy at their military defeat but the wish that they were not so vain. Even with her lesson about the impermanence of earthly communities, an undertone suggests that the cities of this world are the arena for the practice of charity in preparation for the world to come. Their true end is frustrated by political factionalism, party hatred, commercial factionalism, and material competition.

Envy and the sun were both mentioned at the start of the *Comedy* in a complex context that, whatever else, sets the two in opposition (*Inf.* I, 60, III; notice that Sapia completes her definition of envy in line III). Singleton called Canto XIII the canto of "seeing" and "not seeing." It is a brilliant strategy of narrative economy that Dante has taken a framework in which the sun is necessarily prominent, and in which the effects of sight serve as the central moral question, to illustrate in action just what Virgil sees and does not see. And there is irony in the fact that the poet who represented the journey of Aeneas as guided, not always too clearly, by the sun god Apollo, should exhibit such ambiguity as a guide here.

BIBLIOGRAPHICAL NOTES

Readings of the canto (all entitled "Il canto XIII del *Purgatorio*") include those by Albino Zenatti, "Letto nella sala di Dante Orsanmichele, 1909," in *Lectura Dantis* (Florence: Sansoni, n.d.); Francesco Biondolillo, *Letterature Moderne* 5 (1954): 513–522; Carmelo Musumarra, in *Lectura Dantis Scaligera*, vol. 2, 442–471 (Florence: Le Monnier, 1967) (reprinted in his *Saggi Danteschi*, 63–93, Firenze, Gionnotta, 1979); Paolo Conte, in *Nuove letture dantesche*, vol. 4, 129–148 (Florence: Le Monnier, 1970); Emilio Santini, in *Letture dantesche*, a cura di Giovanni Getto, vol. 2, 255–272 (Florence: Sansoni, 1971); and Salvatore Accordo, in *Purgatorio*, Letture degli Anni 1976–1979, Casa di Dante in Roma, 263–281 (Rome: Bonacci editore, 1981). Neither these critics nor any of the commentators has recognized the quality of Sapia's long discourse as an exercise in fraternal correction, from start to finish (with self-correction framed in the center). The principles of Aristotelian ethics that Dante is using seem to be neglected: namely, that virtue is multiform and not restricted to stereotypes of passive piety and that any human temperament, even the harshest and most acerbic, is ripe for the development of virtue as well as vice.

The study by Anthony K. Cassell, "The Letter of Envy: *Purgatorio* XIII–XIV," *Stanford Italian Review* 4 (1984): 5–21 (reprinted in translation as "Il sapore dell' amore: i canti dell' invidia," in *Studi americani su Dante*, a cura di Gian Carlo Alessio e Robert Hollander [Milan: Franco Angeli, 1989], 165–183) focuses on the biblical and theological sources of the severity with which envy was condemned, and thereby for the horrors of the penance that Dante has created for the envious.

As one of the motives projected for Satan's fall, envy took on a radical association with the very essence of sin. The conceptual move involved resembles the transmutation of vainglory, avarice, and sloth into more general denominations (pride, cupidity, and acedia, respectively) to express fundamental facets of the will to evil.

In approximate chronological order by date of first appearance, the following is a sample of the early commentaries available in printed editions: Jacopo della Lana, *Commedia di Dante degli Alaghieri* (Bologna: Tipografia Regia, 1866–1867); L'Ottimo, *Commento della Divina Commedia* (Pisa: N. Capurro, 1829); Petri Allegherii super Dantis ipsius genitoris Comoediam Commentarium, nunc primum in luce editum, ed. Vincenzo Nannucci (Florence: G. Piatti, 1845); Benvenuto de Imola, *Comentum super Dantis Aldigherij Comoediam* (Florence: G. Barbera, 1887); Francesco da Buti, *Commento*, vol. 2l, *Purgatorio* (Pisa: Fratelli Nistri, 1860); Anonimo Fiorentino, *Commento alla Divina Commedia* (Bologna: G. Romanogli, 1866–1874); and *Comentum totius libri Dantis* (Prati: Giachetti, 1891). An almost universal but unseemly haste to Christianize Virgil characterizes this early tradition and its modern followers. Only Buti seems to sense something wrong; he remarks that the literal and the allegorical interpretations of Virgil's prayer are in flagrant contradiction with each other.

Recent Dante scholarship has opened up a far wider and deeper perception of the ambiguity of Virgil's moral position in the *Comedy,* the narrative indications of his limits as a guide, and even the incredibility of his texts. This work includes Robert Hollander, "The Tragedy of Divination in *Inferno* xx" in his *Studies in Dante* (Ravenna: Longo, 1980), 131–218, *Il Virgilio Dantesco: Tragedia nella Commedia* (Florence: Olschki, 1983), and "Dante's 'Georgic': *Inferno* xxiv, 1–18," *Dante Studies* 102 (1984): 111–121; as well as C. J. Ryan, "*Inferno* xxi: Virgil and Dante, A Study in Contrasts" and Margherita De Bonfils Templer, "Il Virgilio dantesco e il secondo sogno del *Purgatorio,*" both in *Italica* 54 (1982): 16–31 and 41–53; Teodolinda Barolini, *Dante's Poets: Textuality and Truth in the Comedy* (Princeton: Princeton University Press, 1984), esp. 201–256; and Margherita Frankel, "Dante's Anti-Virgilian *Villanello* (*Inf.* xxiv, 1–21)," *Dante Studies* 102 (1984): 81–109, and "La similitudine della zara (*Purgatorio,* vi, 1–12) e il rapporto fra Dante e Virgilio nell' antipurgatorio," in *Studi americani su Dante* (cited above), 113–143. In this last piece, Frankel offers an excellent in-depth review of "i vari piccoli contrattempi" (140) that precede Virgil's desperate measure on the cornice of envy.

The following are the modern commentaries referred to in the reading: Gabriele Rossetti, *Comento analitico al Purgatorio* (Florence: Olschki, 1967); *La Divina Commedia,* con le note di Niccolò Tommaseo e introduzione di Umberto Cosmo (Turin: U.T.E.T., 1927–1934 [reprint of the Milano ed., F. Pagnoni, 1865]); *La Divina Commedia* di Dante Alighieri, col commento di Raffaello Andreoli (Florence: G. Barbera, 1887); *La Divina Commedia* di Dante Alighieri commentata da Attilio Momigliano, 3 vols., (Florence: Sansoni, 1946–1951, 1969–1971); *La Divina Commedia,* ed. Natalino Sapegno (Milan and Naples: R. Ricciardi, 1957); *The Divine Comedy,* translated, with a commentary, by Charles S. Singleton, *Inferno 2: Commentary* and *Purgatorio 2: Commentary* (Princeton: Princeton University Press, 1970), 1973. Momigliano's originality includes a fine sense of literary qualities; in the same vein, Singleton has also written "Campi semantici dei canti xii dell' *Inferno* e xiii del *Purgatorio,*" in *Miscellanea di studi danteschi,* Istituto di letteratura italiana (Genoa: Mario Bozzi, 1966), 11–22. Ciardi's intelligent question comes from his translation, *The Divine Comedy* (New York: Norton, 1977), 260.

CANTO XIV

The Rhetoric of Envy

MASSIMO VERDICCHIO

In the previous canto, Dante and Virgil have arrived at the Second Terrace, where the envious are punished. In Canto XIV, they meet two souls, Guido del Duca and Rinieri da Calboli, who denounce the sin of envy. However, the actual invective against envy will spill over and conclude in the following canto (XV).

Canto XIV has often been viewed as a political canto. "It would be difficult," writes John A. Scott, in *Dante's Political Purgatory*, "to find more striking proof that the poet is concerned above all with the message he must impart 'for the sake of the world that lives wickedly'" (*Purg.* XXXII, 103). It would be a mistake, however, to view Guido del Duca's invective as political thought. The implications, to be sure, are political to some extent. But to focus on the political or on some other apparent meaning of the canto is to be blind to its central focus on envy. As many critics have indicated, Dante associates envy with bad decisions: "Envy causes bad judgment, as it does not allow reason to argue for the thing envied" (*Conv.* I, iv, 6–7; my translation). In the *Comedy*, envy is said to be the root of all evil, since it is responsible for the presence of the evil she wolf in the poem: "From which she [the she wolf] was first sent above by envy" (*Inf.* I, III). Canto XIV has to be read in terms of this definition of envy, and what is said by the envious souls, as well as by Dante himself, is related to envy and is the result of envy. We should not assume, as many commentators do, that because these souls seem to denounce their sin they are now free from it. The reader should not interpret the words of Dante the pilgrim to mean that he is well disposed toward these sinners in this and in other related cantos. The opposite is the case, in my opinion.

Once we realize that those who speak are blind and that their eyes are sewn up with steel wire in penance for their sin, we see that the first lines of the canto are already expressions of envy. Envy is a sin of the eyes, and the etymology of the word "invidia" is sometimes given as "non video" ("I do not see"), which in this canto refers not only to the present state of the envious but also to their inability to see and judge correctly.

Dante among the Envious

In contrast, not only is Dante able to move his eyes as he pleases, "at will" (3), but he is also a living being, until death "grant[s] him flight" (2). This initial situation, of apparent equality between Dante and the envious—they are all men—and also of difference—they are dead and he is alive, they are blind and he can see—is sufficient to generate envy in the envious, who are confronted with someone more privileged than they. "Equality," Dante writes in the *Convivio*, "is cause for envy in the corrupt" (I, iv, 6–7). Thus Canto XIV establishes the theme of envy, as it should, and also the theme of slander. The topic of the canto, having been introduced in *Purgatorio* XIII, continues in Canto XIV with one difficulty: the souls do not know who the object of their envy is and therefore cannot slander him. At the sight of a living Dante, the envious souls want to know who he is, and why he is so privileged, and not just out of normal curiosity. Rather, we have to suppose that they also want to know who he is in order to slander him:

> "O soul who—still enclosed
> within the body—make your way toward Heaven,
> may you, through love, console us; tell us who
>   you are, from where you come; the grace that you've
> received—a thing that's never come to pass
> before—has caused us much astonishment."
>
> (10–15)

Instead of "astonishment" one might read here "envy." Therefore, it is no surprise that Dante refuses to tell them: "To tell you who I am would be to speak / in vain—my name has not yet gained much fame" (20–21). Although Dante replies that his name has not "yet" acquired enough fame to be defamed, the mere fact that he is able to see and is a living man moving through Purgatory is sufficient to qualify him as an object of envy. Dante's reply is vague, alluding indirectly to his birthplace, Florence, and to the Arno River, which crosses it:

> And I: "Through central Tuscany there spreads
> a little stream first born in Falterona;

one hundred miles can't fill the course it needs.
I bring this body from that river's banks."

(16–19)

When one of the spirits replies, correctly identifying the river in question as
the Arno (24), the other spirit understands—or, better, misunderstands—the
allusion and Dante's circumlocution as a reference to a horrible crime that
Dante wants to hide:

The other said to him: "Why did he hide
that river's name, even as one would do
in hiding something horrible from view?"

(25–27)

Yet Dante is being as vague as possible, not to hide something, but to avoid
becoming the object of envy. The envious spirit's reasoning is guided by his
misunderstanding. But the envious do not miss their mark. Since they
know that Dante was born in the valley crossed by the Arno River, they deduce that the region is Tuscany, and they slander him, indirectly, along with
all the people of Tuscany. In the *Convivio*, Dante already alluded to how the
envious behave in this way: "The envious argues, not by blaming him who
claims to be incapable of speaking, but blames the matter of his work, and
in so scorning that part of his work, he takes away from his honor and
fame. Just as he who blames the blade of a sword, does not blame the blade
but the craftsman's entire work" (I, xi, 17–18). In Canto XIV, we have not
only a similar situation, in which a person is blamed by association, but also
an instance of the circumspect and indirect way in which the envious are
given to slander, hiding their envious venom behind falsely benign words.
It is for this reason, too, that we must not read Guido del Duca's invective
against Tuscany and Dante as one of Dante's many diatribes against Florence and the people of Tuscany. Even though they may have the same
views, here the two envious souls are not only slandering Dante, but, as
Romagnoles, they are also slandering Tuscany. Yet the reader does not
know at first that the two envious souls are indeed Romagnoles. It is only
later, when Fulcieri is mentioned, that we understand the true measure of
the envy, if not the hatred, that the Romagnoles have for the Florentines
and the Tuscans. The second soul, Rinieri da Calboli, ignorant of the reasons for Dante's reserve, is certain that he must be hiding something horrible, "as one would do / in hiding something horrible from view" (26–27).
The other envious spirit, Guido del Duca, corroborates his opinion. Whatever Dante is hiding, it must be something horrible because we are dealing
here with Tuscany and its people, and it is right that their name should perish: "I do not know; but *it / is right* for such a valley's name to perish" (29–30,
my italics).

Guido's Attack on Tuscany

Guido del Duca's diatribe against the Tuscans is, first of all, then, an instance of envy on the part of a Romagnole. His speech is patterned on the movement of the Arno that widens as it flows through the valley "from its source . . . until its end point" (31 and 34), covering all Tuscany. Along with a description of the river's flow, Guido del Duca gives examples of the corrupt nature of the people of the region, who, in this view, hold virtue as an enemy—"Virtue is seen as serpent, and all flee / from it as if it were an enemy" (37–38)—either because the land itself is corrupt or because of the Tuscans' evil customs (39–40). Guido's envious attack on the inhabitants of the "squalid valley" transforms them from human beings into animals as a way to signal their lowly and corrupt natures: "The nature of that squalid valley's people / has changed, as if they were in Circe's pasture" (41–42). As the river flows, the speech moves downward from the "foul hogs" of the Casentino to snapping and snarling dogs, an allusion to the people of Arezzo. As the river widens, the dogs become ferocious wolves, that is, Florentines:

> And, downward, it flows on; and when that ditch,
> ill-fated and accursed, grows wider, it
> finds, more and more, the dogs becoming wolves.
>
> (49–51)

In a movement reminiscent of Dante's own descent to Hell, the river flows downward through "many dark ravines" (52), to find even shadier and darker transformations among the people of Pisa, who are called foxes, owing to their deceit:

> Descending then through many dark ravines,
> it comes on foxes so full of deceit—
> there is no trap that they cannot defeat.
>
> (52–54)

Yet the worst transformation is reserved for the Romagnoles. At this point in Guido del Duca's speech, a shift takes place in the discourse. Now it takes the form of a prophecy but is really a condemnation of Fulcieri da Calboli, the barbarous and sanguinary *podestà* of Florence in 1303, Dante's time. Rinieri da Calboli, we discover, is Fulcieri's grandfather:

> I see your grandson: he's become a hunter
> of wolves along the banks of the fierce river,
> and he strikes every one of them with terror.
> He sells their flesh while they are still alive;

then, like an ancient beast, he turns to slaughter,
depriving many of life, himself of honor.

(58–63)

This mention of Fulcieri da Calboli not only emphasizes—to an extreme—the hatred of the Romagnoles for the Florentines and for the Tuscans in general but also marks the people of Romagna as even more despicable and ferocious than those of Tuscany. Fulcieri is not even seen as an animal. This transformation is denied him. Rather, he is a "hunter" (58) who kills in a way that no animal ever would. He is a monster who sold his victims' flesh when they were still alive and then butchered them. Fulcieri's crime is so abominable and bloody, and of such magnitude, that it will have an impact on future generations for centuries to come:

Bloody, he comes out from the wood he's plundered,
leaving it such that in a thousand years
it will not be the forest that it was.

(64–67)

His crime is not only against man but also against nature, which he has desecrated and perverted with his bloody actions. Fulcieri's hatred of the Florentines, however, is not unlike the hatred demonstrated in Guido's speech, and it reinforces that the names of Florence and Tuscany should perish.

Romagna's Former Glory

The second part of the canto begins with Dante asking the envious spirits his usual questions about their identities and origins. This time, however, the question is even more poignant because earlier Dante had refused to tell them who he was. In fact, Guido del Duca's reply reminds him precisely of this fact: "You would have me do / for you that which, to me, you have refused" (76–77). Perhaps Guido del Duca hesitates to mention his name because doing so might make him the target of Dante's envy. But in Dante's case, we know from the previous canto that he hardly suffers from envy. Referring to his eyes he says: "The offense of envy / was not committed often by their gaze" (XIII, 134–135). His sin is, rather, that of pride (XIII, 136–138).

When Guido introduces himself, he is forthcoming about the sin of envy he is expiating:

"My blood was so afire with envy that,
when I had seen a man becoming happy,
the lividness in me was plain to see."

(82–84)

But the topic of Guido's speech is the moral decline of the ancient Romagnoles' nobility:

> The ladies and the knights, labors and leisure
> to which we once were urged by courtesy
> and love, where hearts now host perversity.
>
> (109–111)

Where once the illustrious people of Romagna inspired courtesy and love, in the new generation of Romagnoles there is only wickedness. Commentators have rightly pointed to the *ubi sunt* motif in Guido's address, which laments the passing of a generation of illustrious and noble figures known in Romagna for their graciousness and their affability. "Where is good Lizio? Arrigo Mainardi? / Pier Traversaro? Guido di Carpigna?" (97–98). Or, "When will a Fabbro flourish in Bologna? / When in Faenza, a Bernardin di Fosco?" (100–101). This noble generation of courteous men is gone now, and the current generation has betrayed its ideals and perverted its good name and good deeds. In their hearts reign only wickedness and evil.

Included in this list of illustrious people is Rinieri, who was said to be "the glory, / the honor of the house of Calboli" (88–89). In Rinieri's case, too, no one has followed in his footsteps, as "no one has inherited his worth" (90). Similarly, the whole of Romagna, the territory bound to the north by the Po, to the south by the Apennines, to the east by the Adriatic, and to the west by the Reno (91–92), has lost the well-being and the virtue it once possessed and that was reflected in its everyday business as well as in its noble customs and arts: They have "lost the truth's grave good and lost the good / of gentle living, too" (93–94). Now in its place there is only a wasteland where nothing good and virtuous grows, or will ever be able to grow: "By now, however much / one were to cultivate, it is too late" (95–96). The new generation has abandoned the traditional and noble ways of their fathers: "O Romagnoles returned to bastardy!" (99).

The second half of Guido's speech, narrated in tears ("Don't wonder, Tuscan, if I weep when / I remember," 103–104), not only recollects the times that once were but also becomes an exhortation to these noble men to have no more children:

> O Bretinoro, why do you not flee—
> when you've already lost your family
> and many men who've fled iniquity?
>   Bagnacaval does well: it breeds no more—
> and Castrocaro ill, and Canio worse,
> for it insists on breeding counts so cursed.
>   Once freed of their own demon, the Pagani

will do quite well, but not so well that any
will testify that they are pure and worthy.
   Your name, o Ugoli de' Fantolini,
is safe, since one no longer waits for heirs
to blacken it with their degeneracy.

(112–123)

Guido's tearful plea seems to be a last attempt at remedying a situation that in Romagna has reached catastrophic proportions, with the perversion of all the values and virtues the region was traditionally known for. Guido's speech ends in a similar vein. His heartbreak over the present conditions of his land interrupts his speech:

"But, Tuscan go your way; I am more pleased
to weep now than to speak: for that which we
have spoken presses heavily on me!"

(124–126)

There are reasons why some might not take Guido's speech literally. We have already alluded to Guido's duplicitous role in the previous speech, and in this speech there is no reason to believe his tears or that he is a changed man or, which is stating the same thing, that Dante has granted him space to praise Romagna as it once was and to commiserate over its present wicked state. In fact, this speech is not unlike the previous one. In this second speech Guido wants us to believe that only the new generation is responsible for present-day perversity and evil, of which Fulceri da Calboli is the prime example. But as he did in the previous speech, Guido is again shifting attention away from where the real problem lies. One need only look at the passage a little closer, that is, open one's eyes wide, as Virgil advises Dante to do in the previous canto, to differentiate between the rhetoric of the envious who conceals his own guilt, while attributing the cause of his misgivings to others, and the situation that Dante the poet wants to portray, the dissimulation of the envious. The critical strategy that one has to adopt is that of carefully distinguishing between the contours of the envious and the background with which it tries to blend. As we know from the previous canto, this is a physical condition of the envious soul whose cloak blends in with the color of the rock against which he leans. When Dante and Virgil arrive on the Second Terrace they cannot see anyone, and everything is the livid color of the rock:

No effigy is there and no outline:
the bank is visible, the naked path—
only the livid color of raw rock."

(*Purg.* XIII, 7–9)

The souls are there but cannot be seen. But when Dante follows Virgil's advice to open his eyes wide, he can suddenly see figures:

> I opened—wider than before—my eyes;
> I looked ahead of me, and I saw shades
> with cloaks that shared their color with the rocks.

(XIII, 46–48)

Guido's speech is structured in very much the same way, making it difficult to tell the difference between his rhetoric and the message that Dante means to convey, between the speech that condemns the future generation of Romagnoles and the guilt that their fathers share and that Guido attempts to conceal.

A closer look, in fact, reveals that the reasons for present-day evil and perversity, as in the previous case, do not lie solely with the new generation but principally with their fathers, from whom the new generations have sprung forth. It is by taking literally the metaphors of plants, seeds, and stumps that we can discern Dante's condemnation of Romagna's ancient nobility as those responsible for the present state of affairs and for having poisoned and perverted their offspring for generations to come.

When Guido del Duca says, "My blood was so afire with envy," the word "blood" may also refer to his children, who are contaminated with envy through his envious blood. The line "from what I've sown, this is the straw I reap" (85) is usually interpreted to mean that Guido now reaps in Purgatory the just punishment of the envy he has sown. But the line also indicates that he has sown envy for which he has only gathered straw. In the case of Rinieri da Calboli, who is said to be "the glory, / the honor of the house of Calboli"— with an emphasis on the fact that none has inherited "his worth"—the issue is a lot clearer. We know from Guido's previous speech that Fulcieri has inherited "his worth"—and how! The line, read this way, becomes an even greater condemnation of Rinieri, who is not only responsible for his grandson's horrible accomplishments but who is also as depraved as, if not more so, than Fulcieri. We should recall that Fulcieri was called an "ancient beast" (62), a strange characterization, unless we see in it Fulcieri's indebtedness to his noble ancestry and to Rinieiri. The line pairs very well the old and the new beast.

The same can be said of those ancient Romagnole families in the area that is now Romagna, to which Dante refers as a territory full of "poisoned stumps" (95), where it is impossible for anyone of virtue and courtesy ever to grow: "However much / one were to cultivate, it is too late" (95–96). Similar images are used to characterize the forest where Fulcieri's butchery will take place, which will be similarly desecrated for centuries to come:

> Bloody, he comes out from the wood he's plundered,
> leaving it such that in a thousand years
> it will not be the forest that it was.

(64–66)

The image of the poisonous stump becomes even clearer with the example of Bernardin di Fosco, who is called "the noble offshoot of a humble plant" (102). The phrase that Mandelbaum translates as "humble plant" is *picciola gramigna.* The word *gramigna,* even in the language of Dante, means "weed," the bad grass that wreaks havoc in gardens. *Gramigna* describes perfectly the devastation created by the offspring of the ancient noble Romagnoles, who destroy everything in their path. Mandelbaum translates *picciola* as "humble," referring to the noble fathers, as they were once thought to be. The term *picciola* may also mean, simply, "small." Therefore, line 102, "verga gentil di picciola gramigana," can be translated as the "gentle rod of a small weed." This line characterizes Bernardin di Fosco as the gentle or noble rod of small (future) bad weeds—that is, as the procreator of future destruction. This reading places the blame and responsibility directly on Bernadin di Fosco, as it does on all the other noble and courteous casts of ladies and knights. The word *gramigna,* in fact, implies an origin, and Bernardin is precisely that origin, which Guido's speech conceals.

In my reading, then, the remainder of Guido del Duca's list of names emphasizes not so much that the noble Romagnoles should not have any offspring because their children will turn out to be bastards, but that they themselves are the root of the problem, since they are the corrupt plant from which only weeds can flourish. We have mentioned Bagnacaval, Castrocaro, and Conio. Guido also mentions Pagani, stating that there is none who will claim to be "pure and worthy" (120). They are not, literally. And, finally, he mentions Ugolin de' Fantolin, whose name is safe, because no heirs are expected. However, this is not because the family name will degenerate but because they will not transfer their degeneracy to their lineage, "blacken[ing] it with their degeneracy" (123). In other words, Guido's second speech, if not the canto as a whole, is a condemnation of Romagna's nobility, from its ancestry to future generations, owing to their envy and hatred of the Florentines and of Tuscany in general.

Detecting Envy

The canto concludes with what is traditionally thought as examples of punished envy. The first, piercing the air like lightning, is the speech of Cain after killing Abel: "Whoever captures me will slaughter me" (133). The second is the speech of Auglaros, daughter of Cecropes, the king of Athens, who envied Mercury's love for her sister Herse, opposed their union, and was turned to stone: "I am Auglaros, who was turned to stone" (139). The two examples, however, are quite different. Cain's cry, "whoever captures me will slaughter me" (133), is not an example of punished envy, since Cain is not punished at that point. Cain will be captured and vanquished only when he is found out. The reader will discover the dissimulation that hides the envy in Guido del Duca's speech. Only then will envy and Cain be punished.

Canto XIV concludes with a final invective when Virgil, after the voices of Cain and Aglauros are heard, tells his readers to heed these examples and to keep envy in check, within the bounds allowed by the law, by human decency, and by morality. "That is the sturdy bit / that should hold every man within his limits" (143–144). But as soon as he gives this warning, he also makes clear the impossibility of heeding and following these examples. The desire for earthly possessions is so overwhelming that examples are of little use:

> "But you would take the bait, so that the hook
> of the old adversary draws you to him;
> thus, neither spur nor curb can serve to save you."
>
> (145–147)

Not only do the examples of Cain and Aglauros fall on deaf ears, but the envious are also blind to the beauties of Heaven and the love of God:

> "Heaven would call—and it encircles—you;
> it lets you see its never-ending beauties;
> and yet your eyes would only see the ground."
>
> (148–150)

Like the envious in this canto, man is blind to the beauty of creation and to God, and his glance is turned toward the earth.

CANTO XV

Virtual Reality

ARIELLE SAIBER

Three hours before sunset in Purgatory we find Virgil and Dante in an open space somewhere between the Terrace of Envy and that of Anger, climbing a slight incline, toward the northwest. The solar light, which seems to be hitting the Pilgrim straight in the face, is so intense that he cannot help but shade his eyes. The Pilgrim forms a visor by putting his hand over his brow, but it is ineffectual, and he has to turn away from what he now likens to light reflected from a mirror or a mirrorlike surface. Soon he learns from Virgil that the source of this dazzling light is not the sun, but the Angel of Charity, who has come to direct them to the next terrace. From behind them they hear *Beati misericordes* and "Rejoice, you who have overcome" (39). Dante is left wondering about something said by the penitent of envy, Guido del Duca (*Purg.* XIV, 85–87), regarding the phenomenon of charity in Paradise. With the help of Virgil's surprising theological knowledge, Dante begins to understand. The two travelers then walk together in silence. During this transitional period, Dante has three inner visions of gentleness. Disoriented and wobbly yet again, the Pilgrim is sharply spoken to by Virgil, who claims to know what Dante has seen. Virgil spurs him on, and the two solemnly move into the smoke that purges the vice of wrath.

By entering the zone between two terraces in which souls endure blindness as penitence for their earthly flaws—the covetous vision of envy and the blindness of rage—Virgil and the Pilgrim enter a realm of optical and catoptric illusions. These illusions demonstrate temporal, spatial, and kinetic inversions and repetitions; they instruct in counterintuitive thinking and acting. In fact, Canto XV contains more occurrences of "appearing" (in both senses of the word) than any other canto in the *Comedy*. A thing can "appear" (like the sun through the clouds), or it can appear to you (like something that "seems"). In numerous instances throughout the *Comedy*, and especially throughout this canto, *parere* and *apparire* take on a double meaning. The Pilgrim encounters phenomena that simultaneously *are* and *seem*, the real and the virtual. As he did when he first encountered Beatrice, Dante both marvels at a divine appearance and is baffled by what this vision seems to be (*VN* II). It becomes clear as Dante ascends to the seat of God that the *truly* real is the virtual:

> As many as the hours in which the sphere
> that's always playing like a child appears
> from daybreak to the end of the third hour,
>   so many were the hours of light still left
> before the course of the day had reached sunset;
> vespers was there; and where we are, midnight.
>
> (1–6)

This opening astronomical exordium—a truly circuitous periphrasis—forces us to count backward to figure out the time of day in Purgatory. Dante inverts chronological order in a sort of hysteron proteron by speaking first of the *ultimar de l'ora terza* (9 A.M.) and then of the *principio del dì* (6 A.M.). In doing so, he invites us to hold up a sundial to a mirror to see that the time in Purgatory—the number of hours left before the end of vespers (6 P.M.)—is the flip of 9 A.M. on a sundial: 3 P.M. It is a perfect operation of reflective symmetry.

Symmetries

As we shall see, many forms of symmetry fill this canto. Four fundamental graphic operations generate all two-dimensional symmetrical patterns: a *translation*, which is a repetition of an image along a line, as in a wallpaper border (**bb**); a *reflection*, which is a flip of an image, as in a mirror (**b | d**); a *rotation*, which is a movement a certain number of degrees around a central point (**b_q**); and a *glide reflection*, which is a combined reflection and rotation (**b_p**). A translation is actually a special case of rotation—it is a rotation around an infinitely small angle or around a center lying infinitely far away (an excellent description of Dante's vision of God lying at the center of the universe and surrounding it). From these four basic operations arise the strictly limited seven linear and seventeen planar patterns possible in two dimensions (there are quite a few more in higher dimensions). Any linear or planar symmetrical pattern—whether engraved, printed, painted, or sewn—follows one or a variety of these operations. While the number of "dimensions" contained within a work of literature could be debated, the four basic symmetry operations for two-dimensional patterning are useful tools for analyzing a repeating literary motif, theme, structure, or rhetorical figure. Like any graphic symmetrical pattern, repeating motifs in literary texts directly echo one another, invert one another, twist and turn one another to fit into new sets of circumstances. Here in Canto XV, as in many other points along the journey and in the architecture of the journey itself, Dante makes ample use of these symmetrical devices. Of primary relevance to the study of this canto are the means by which Dante uses catoptrics (the study of mirror reflections) to echo the central lesson of the first half of the canto: how by giving love and goods in Paradise, the giver increases the amount of love and goods he or she has. Of secondary interest are the further optical illusions and various symmetries the Pilgrim experiences before arriving at what is, effectively, the middle point of *this* journey through the three worlds: the first step away from the mirror's boundary and into the land of increasing wonder and "virtue-ality."

Jumping back to the opening astronomical periphrasis of this canto, we learn that it was midnight in Italy, where the Poet and his contemporary readers were. Purgatory was thought to be the antipode to Jerusalem, and Jerusalem was thought (incorrectly) to be three hours ahead and 45 longitudinal degrees away from Italy. Thus, when it was 3 P.M. in Purgatory, it would have been 3 A.M. in Jerusalem, and subsequently midnight in Italy. The word that begins the canto, *quanto* ("as many as"), could equally refer to "how much time" and "how much space" has been traveled by the sun, since the reference to the number of hours left in a day depends on the degrees the sun has left to sweep in its setting arc. Measuring time by the location of the sun, or vice versa, will always reveal a commutative relationship, a kind of translatory symmetry (**bb**). Theodore Cachey has noted that this opening periphrasis uses rhetorical strategies that defamiliarize and disorient the reader, sharing with him or her the Pilgrim and the Poet's almost comic, parodic sense of limitation. The Poet orients through disorientation. What at first glance may seem asymmetric on the literal level, or between vehicle and tenor, turns out to be "supersymmetric."

Of even further symmetrical and optical interest in these first two tercets is the curious motion Dante attributes to the *spera* that is "always playing like a child" (2), curious especially because of Virgil's recent praise of the sun (if that is what Dante meant by *spera*) as their guide on their journey up the Mountain (*Purg.* XIII, 16–21). In Eudoxus' model of celestial motion, the sun is attached to three spheres: one rotates with the sphere of the fixed stars, one along the zodiac (the ecliptic), and one along an angle to the zodiac (the meridian). It is the combined motion of these spheres, as Bruno Nardi and others have noted, that accounts for its apparent spiral or helical motion (the *giratio laulabina*) across the sky over the course of year, a kind of rotational symmetry (**b_q**). The sun seems to "play," moving forward in a symmetrical, helical path through the constellations: never rising in the same place, never making the same arc, never staying still. It is, of course, our perception while standing on earth that would give the sun's path this appearance. Perhaps it is not by chance that *pare* (2) can mean "to appear" as in "coming into view" and "to appear" as in "to seem." After all, much of the childlike, spiral or helical motion of the sun we observe is with respect to the backdrop of stars, which cannot, in fact, be seen when the sun is shining.

After many centuries of scholarly debate as to whether by *spera* Dante meant the sun (Benvenuto da Imola, Pietrobuono, Porena, Sapegno, Chimenz, Singleton, Bosco and Reggio, Musa, Nardi, Mandelbaum), the celestial sphere of the sun (Jacopo della Lana, L'Ottimo, Buti, Vellutello, Scartazzini, Vallone, Gallardo), light (Pietro di Dante, Anonimo Fiorentino, Tommaseo, Marti, Soprano), or even the moon (Pézard), the term still has not received an universally accepted interpretation. *Spera* has also been shown to refer to a "mirror" in Tuscan dialect, and Dante will not only call the sun (*Purg.* IV, 62) and individual spheres mirrors (*Par.* IX, 61), but he will call the entirety of Paradise (*Par.* XIX, 29 and XXI, 18) a mirror as well. Michio Fujitani, in a detailed study of the optical references in Canto XV, wonders why scholars have not explored this fact further, since doing so may offer a way to help gloss these initial verses. The notion of celestial mirrors is certainly important to this canto of symmetry, counterintuition, and illusive imagery. Another potential reading of the term *spera* can be found in its etymological link to the Greek word for "spiral" or "twist" *(speira)*. Yet another meaning of *spera* can be found in *Inferno* VII. This is the first occasion in the *Comedy* on which a canto straddles two penitentiary places (that of avarice and anger—ones quite similar to those straddled by *Purgatorio* XV), and one of the other few cantos without a particular interlocutor for Dante. Here, the term *spera* means "wheel," in reference to the object turned by Fortune's hand (*Inf.* VII, 96).

Wheel, spiral, mirror, globe, celestial sphere, light, sun: *spera* is all these (although arguably not Pézard's "moon"). A number of recent studies have asserted that by choosing the term *spera,* Dante wished us to think in terms of its multiple meanings. The term's polysemy does, in fact, lend itself well to a description of what seems to be the peculiar heliokinetic journey we observe from the earth; a journey that is, following Giuseppe Mazzotta's discussion of *theologia ludens,* indeed a play.

Reflected Light?

Another significant quandary that emerges both for the Pilgrim and for readers of this canto is why it is that the light of the sun, which is now setting and about 45 degrees from the horizon, has become so bright that covering one's brow to shield one's eyes does not suffice. The Poet accounts for the "unaccounted things" (12) that leave the Pilgrim, and us, confused. We are left to guess, along with the Pilgrim, about the nature and source of this light:

> As when a ray of light, from water or
> a mirror, leaps in the opposed direction
> and rises at an angle equal to
>   its angle of descent, and to each side
> the distance from the vertical is equal,
> as science and experiment have shown;
>   so did it seem to me that I had been
> struck there by light reflected, facing me,
> at which my eyes turned elsewhere rapidly.
>
> (16–24)

The vehicle of this extended metaphor is an intense light that *seemed* (and "seemed" is key here) to be reflecting off something mirrorlike and into his eyes, much like the stunning reflection of light from the sword of the Angel at the gate of Purgatory (*Purg.* IX, 82). The Pilgrim, however, does not know if this is what was actually happening; nor do we. The light is virtual in more ways than one. It is not until line 28 that Virgil, whose eyes are apparently unaffected by the brightness, explains that the source of bedazzlement is an angel sent from heaven to guide them up to the Third Terrace. The metaphor of angelic light as reflected light primes the reader, as we shall soon see, to think about the various symmetries implicit specifically in divine charity and generally in all virtue.

This passage has rarely been discussed in terms of its reflection of virtue. Instead, it has inspired extensive debate as to the source of the light, and the nature and placement of the reflective surface. Some postulate that it is the sun's light (the incident beam) that reflects off the Angel and into Dante's eyes (Pietrobono, Zingarelli). Others have concluded that the beam being reflected into Dante's eyes is coming from below, where the light of the Angel bounces off the blue-black or pale stone (the *livida petraia, Purg.* XIII, 9) of the mountain's surface (Tommaseo, Scartazzini, Vandelli, Vernon, Porena, Maier, Casini-Barbi, Nardi, Boyde, Chiavacci Leonardi, Gilson). Yet another large camp argues that the Angel functions as a mirror reflecting God's light into Dante's eyes (Buti, Landino, Pietrobono, Casini-Barbi, Momigliano, Sapegno, Bosco and Reggio, Esposito, Figurelli, Picone).

It *seems* that the Angel stands (or perhaps hovers) in front of, or near, the sun. And it *seems* that the light moves toward the travelers (26). In the first scenario—the one in which the Angel reflects the light of the sun into Dante's eyes—there is a problem. Even this diaphanous, luminous creature could not have reflected light radiating from behind it into something that was evidently in front of it. This would go against the laws of catoptrics. The sun's light could, however, be "refracted" if it traveled *through* the

Angel, and thereby bent into Dante's eyes. Interestingly, Dante uses the verb *rifratta* (refract) to describe the light that found its way into his eyes, instead of *reflettere* (to reflect), which is what light actually does on a mirror. Simon Gilson has shown that although a group of medieval writers on optics and catoptrics—the "perspectivists," as he calls them (Bacon, Pecham, Witelo, Grosseteste)—knew the details of the difference between reflection *(reflexio, reflectio, reflectere, reflettere)* and refraction *(refractio, refrattere, rifrattere, rifrangere)*, many others, including Dante, Aquinas, and Albertus Magnus, apparently did not differentiate between the terms and used all interchangeably to mean "reflection." As scholars have noted, most considered the deviation of light that occurs when it travels through a substance or object a breaking apart, not a refraction. Dante used both words to refer to an act of reflection, or to an analogous act of bouncing off, or pushing back. In the simile Dante gives us in this instance, it is indubitably reflection, not refraction, that takes place when light hits a mirror. He did not intend the light entering his eyes to have traveled through the angel and to be bent by refraction. Furthermore, the balanced property of reflective symmetry (**b**|**d**) serves to enhance the recurring pattern of symmetries articulated by this canto.

The reflection of light off a flat mirror is a simple law of the science of catoptrics: the angle of the incoming light (angle of incidence) will be the same as the angle of the deflected light (angle of reflection) with respect to the mirror and an imaginary line, the cathetus (the *cader de la pietra* [20]), drawn perpendicular to it. The earliest articulations of this law can be found in such works as Euclid's *Catoptrics,* Alhazen's *De aspectibus,* Hero of Alexander's *Catoptrica,* and Ptolemy's *Optica*—works Dante did not know firsthand. Contrary to the previously accepted position of Nardi, Simon Gilson shows that it is also unlikely that Dante knew the optical writings of the perspectivists. He believes, instead, that Dante gained his knowledge of optics and catoptrics from Albertus Magnus, Averroës, Aquinas, Pseudo-Aquinas, Vincent of Beauvais, and Bonaventure (Gilson, 112–116). But even if Dante did not fully comprehend the physics of reflection (or its distinction from refraction), he most certainly would have observed the two phenomena through his own "experience" or "experiment" (*esperïenza* [21]). Dante's scientific interest in geometric optics, eye anatomy, perspective, light, and mirrors is articulated most explicitly in books II and III of the *Convivio* but is also present in his erotics of vision and in his metaphysics of divine light.

The second interpretation—that of the Angel's light reflecting off the ground into Dante's eyes—although the most to the letter of the interpretations, does not explain why the surface of Mount Purgatory is *not* reflective. The *livida petraia* of the mountain, although of an ashen color that might remind one of the thin film of lead applied to glass to make a mirror, is not described anywhere in the text as highly polished and reflective. Nor does Dante mention any body of water on this Terrace that could function as a reflective mirror. Advocates of this interpretation hinge their argument on

the verbs *salta* (leaps, 17) and *salendo* (rising, 18)—verbs that indicate an upward motion of reflected light from a surface that was below Dante, that is,
the ground, and forced him to turn away (toward Virgil). Furthermore, it is
probable that the Poet experienced the effect of light striking a shiny surface
that is not a perfect mirror—the incident light gets absorbed to a certain degree, and the reflected light is consequently weaker. If the Pilgrim assessed
the "reflected" light as intensifying, then it is unlikely it could have come
from a surface such as stone, or even, for that matter, from a mirror: only if
the angel were approaching would this make sense. For a stationary light to
intensify, it would have to be focused by a lens that concentrates the rays.

The third interpretation of the "apparent" reflected light is the most figurative. Here the Angel functions as a mirror, as an intermediary, reflecting
the light of God from above into Dante's eyes. Dante and many medieval
theologians (Pseudo-Dionysius, Aquinas, Vincent of Beauvais, Bonaventure) believed that although angels possess their own light, they also reflect
God's light (see *Par.* XXIX, 144). Scholars who object to this reading, however,
ask why the Pilgrim would say that the light only "seemed" (22) to be approaching and "seem[ed]" (27) to be reflecting into his eyes? Why would he
not confirm, in fact, that the Angel *did* reflect God's light at him? Why
would he not confirm that the Angel is a moveable mirror? A possible response to these objections is that the Pilgrim did not yet know the catoptrics
of Heaven, nor had he himself experienced what it means to be a true, pure
mirror.

One way scholars have resolved this debate is to ask the more fundamental question of whether or not any reflecting was actually taking place
(Benvenuto, Torraca, Del Lungo, Fallani, Pézard, Singleton, Vallone, and
Cachey). If one answers, "No, the Pilgrim only *thought* that was what happened," then one might recall the numerous other occasions on which the
Poet sacrifices scientific accuracy to metaphoric meaning. The light of the
approaching Angel was so vast and so bright that it eclipsed the sun, and a
simple *solecchio* (shield) could not deflect it. If the Angel stood on the
ground slightly above the travelers, or even hovered close to them, and we
submit that the Angel radiated light (whether only its own or also that of
God), then some of that light, inevitably, would sneak in below the shield
the Pilgrim made on his brow. The angelic light only *seems* as if it were a reflected beam directed precisely at the onlooker. What is actually happening
is that the Angel is translating light (**bb**).

The Pilgrim, however, is not certain how the Angel's light is being trans-
mitted to him. It *appears* as both a revealed, translatory symmetry (**bb**) and
as a concealed, "virtue-al" reflective symmetry (**b | d**). In essence, what the
Poet is expressing here is the notion that Angelic light is both kinds of symmetry: part the Angel's own, part reflected from God. Furthermore, if
God's essence is light, and He exists both at the center of the universe and
surrounding it, as *Paradiso* will explain, then angelic light also contains

symmetry that is rotational (**b_q**) and gliding (**b_p**). God is perfectly symmetrical in all ways, in all directions. The Angel's light "appears," and in appearing it *seems* (reflects) and *is* (translates). Part of what the Pilgrim must learn is that virtue needs to be translated by the individual in order to reflect supreme virtue. This two-step process, which Dante portrays in the baffling origin of the Angel's light, is the paradox of "virtue-ality" and is an anticipation of the canto's primary teaching: that true charity is a kind of giving in which the giver receives. It is a translation and a reflection.

Dante is stunned by the Angel's light, and he will be stunned in other instances in this canto as well. All is not what it seems. It is not that the noblest of the senses is playing tricks on Dante, but rather that his perceptive abilities are not yet what they could be. Virgil tells the Pilgrim that "soon, in the sight of such things, there will be / no difficulty for you, but delight" (31–32); eventually there will be no illusions. Francis Fergusson draws an analogy between the development of Dante's perception as he ascends the mountain and Saint Bonaventure's three kinds of progressive spiritual motion: *extra nos, intra nos, and super nos* (Fergusson, 1966, 134). In Ante-Purgatory on the first day, Dante remains in a stance of observing that which is external to him. Slowly, as he travels through the seven terraces, Dante's experiences become more intimate and internal, and by the time he reaches the Earthly Paradise, his vision is set "above" himself. Walking between the Terraces of Envy and Wrath, Dante is solidly in the *intra nos* stage, and as we shall see, he will soon have a series of inner visions. These visions he will call "not false errors" (117), thereby involving his readers in a paradox—having us experience the stunned state that both proceeds and follows an ecstasy.

Sharing

The radiant Angel of Charity guides the travelers to the next terrace and silently, invisibly, erases the second *P* from Dante's forehead. There is no mention of its removal. When did it happen? We and the Pilgrim are not sure, but we know that it did, since now Dante and Virgil have climbed onto the Terrace of Wrath and hear *Beati misericordes* and "Rejoice, you who have overcome" (Matt. 5:12) from behind them. The vice of envy has been transcended, almost. In their solitary walk together (one of the few times the Poet mentions the two together alone; see also *Inf.* XI and XXII), Dante begins to "look" backward, to *reflect* on something he had heard on the Terrace of Envy but did not understand. "What did the spirit of Romagna mean / when he said, 'Sharing cannot have a part'?" (44–45), Dante asks Virgil. The spirit of Romagna, Guido del Duca, a penitent of envy, had cryptically spoken to Dante of the nature of charity in Heaven. Now Virgil becomes, as many critics have pointed out, an uncharacteristically adept theologian, echoing commentaries by Gregory the Great, Augustine, Aquinas, and Fra Giordano da Pisa on the paradoxical multiplication of love shared in Heaven.

To understand "sharing cannot have a part," the Pilgrim must once again turn his sight and understanding to a mirror image (**b** | **d**), to a counterintuitive logic. True giving is that in which the giver of a good does not have less of the good given, but more, since by giving, one shares, and by sharing, assures that the goods augment for all. Of course, a mundane understanding, like that currently held by the confused Pilgrim, holds that you cannot increase a good by giving it away. The envious are people who desire those things that others have and they do not, things that cannot be shared, but are made into "parts." Dante is still baffled by this necessary flip, or inversion, of his habitual reasoning. Virgil must further explain:

> "That Good, ineffable and infinite,
> which is above, directs Itself toward love
> as light directs itself to polished bodies.
>   Where ardor is, that Good gives of Itself;
> and where more love is, there that Good confers
> a greater measure of eternal worth.
>   And when there are more souls above who love,
> there's more to love well there, and they love more,
> and mirror-like, each soul reflects the other."
>
> (67–75)

In the first two tercets Virgil explains how God's love is attracted to those who love. God gives His love to those "polished bodies" and simultaneously augments the worth of the lover and the amount of love there is to give. If we become highly polished (full of love for God and for all), then like a mirror we will easily receive God's light (love) and be able to reflect love back to Him and to those around us:

> "Who made the heavens and who gave them guides
> was He whose wisdom transcends everything;
> that every part may shine unto the other."
>
> (*Inf.* VII, 73–75; see also *Par.* XIII, 55–60)

Heaven is like a hologram (which is made, not incidentally, by light and mirrors) in which every piece (if broken into pieces) contains the entire image. As Beatrice explains,

> "By now you see the height, you see the breadth,
> of the Eternal goodness: It has made
> so many mirrors, which divide Its light,
>   but, as before, Its own Self still is One."
>
> (*Par.* XXIX, 142–145)

Shared love in Heaven augments exponentially. The souls, "mirror-like," give and receive love in such a way that it becomes impossible to tell whose is whose. In this sense, Heaven is like a hall of mirrors—Beatrice's eyes being two of the countless mirrors—reflecting (**b | d**) and translating (**bb**) infinite "virtue-al" images, or as Dante calls them, *second[i] aspett[i]*, secondary images (*Par.* XVIII, 19) in all directions. A single mirror will reflect an object only once. If you join two mirrors together at an angle and place an object in the middle, you will get, perhaps surprisingly, three images. If, however, you place two mirrors facing each other and an object in between them, you will get an infinite repetition of images "inside" each mirror. If you place even more mirrors at different angles to one another, the actual location of the object becomes more and more difficult to determine. It could be anywhere and seems as if it is everywhere. In Heaven, however, love is, simply, everywhere, reflected in all directions. Beatrice explains this in her description of an experiment with three mirrors in *Paradiso* II (see also *Par.* XXVIII, 4–9).

At this point Virgil admits his exegetical limitations and tells Dante that Beatrice will further illuminate him on this and other subjects (76–78). What is curious in Virgil's prediction here is that it is not entirely accurate. It will be Piccarda (*Par.* III, 43–45; 70–87) who will expound on the nature of charity in Heaven, although Beatrice will, in fact, aid Dante in further understanding this phenomenon (*Par.* XIV, 40–60). Is this an oversight on the Poet's part (a skipping over of Piccarda)? Or is it an example of Virgil's visual limitations?

At line 83, Canto XV takes a turn. Dante feels "appeased" (82) now that his queries have been answered and is suddenly aware that he and Virgil have reached the next circle (83). He becomes quiet. His *luci vaghe,* his "desiring eyes" (84), wandering like the stars and the *spera,* are absorbed by new sites. That the anatomical eye was considered a *luce* in and of itself, that is, able to send out light to perceive images, derives from theories of extramission, reasoned as early as Alcmaeon and Plato and carried through Grosseteste, Pecham, Bacon, and the early Italian lyric poets. The opposing theory of intromission, in which the eye was thought of as a receptor of light and images, was held by Aristotle, Galen, the Scholastics, the Atomists, and the Epicureans. While Dante generally accepted Aristotle's notion of intromission (see *Conv.* II, ix; III, ix; *Par.* XXVI, 71–73), his notions of the physics of vision change with respect to love and divinity. They include the Platonic and Neoplatonic theories of extramission (see, for example, *Par.* XXVI, 74–79). The Pilgrim's *luci vaghe* foreshadow the *novella vista* (*Par.* XXX, 58): the healing eye beams of the angelic Beatrice and the luminous souls and angels in heaven, who desire only to sing their love and praise of God, reciprocating their love through both extramission and intromission. Here in Purgatory the Pilgrim's *luci* are still imperfect, since they have not yet undergone the laser surgery that would allow them to receive or emit such radiance, nor have they become the *spegli* (mirrors) that they will become as they approach the Light (*Par.* XXX, 85). What ignites Dante's eyes and quiets him is a series of visions, examples of gentleness. Using the word *parve* again, as he did when describing the light of the Angle of Charity (22), Dante says that he *seemed* to be caught up in a vision. He is not sure of the reality of what he is seeing. This uncertainty is a translational symmetry (**bb**) of the canto's motif of illusion: the sun/celestial sphere *seems* to move as a playful child does; the light from which Dante cannot shield his eyes *seems* to derive from a reflection; the Angel of Charity *seems* to move toward him; giving something away does not *seem* to be able to increase one's propriety of that thing; and now Dante is uncertain of the reality of what *seem* to be visions.

"Virtue-al" Visions

The visions begin with Mary, as the first of all the examples of virtue do in the *Purgatorio*. Mary gently explains to the eleven-year-old Jesus, whom she finds discoursing with rabbis in the temple, that she and his father had spent days searching for him (88–93; from Luke 2:48). Another scene then overlays the first. This time an enraged mother—in rotational (**b_q**) contrast to Mary—demands that a man who embraced her daughter in public be executed. Her flustered, hyperbolic speech includes yet another reference to science and light—so central to this canto—when she uses metonymy to indicate Athens, the city in which *ogne scïenza disfavilla*, "every science had its source of light" (99). Her husband, the tyrant Pisistratus, calms his wife and pardons the young man, saying, "[W]hat shall we do to one who'd injure us/if one who loves us earns our condemnation?" (104–105; from Valerius Massimus, *Memorable Deeds and Sayings* V, i, 2). A gentle tyrant: an oxymoron and a reflective symmetry (**b|d**). In the final vision, Dante sees Saint Stephen being stoned to death for heresy by a crowd screaming, "Martyr, martyr!" (106–114; from Acts 7:54–59). Dante depicts Stephen as a *giovinetto*, a youth, but in reality (as we will soon discuss), Stephen was not young at the time of his stoning. His eyes are turned toward the sky, his voice only asking God to bless and forgive his persecutors.

Besides the virtue of being gentle at moments when anger would be the expected response, what connects these three visions is, as Cachey has noted in detail, the theme of youth, the theme of progressing age, and the theme of the education of a young mind. We see Jesus as a child, a young embracing couple, and Saint Stephen portrayed as a young man. The motif of youth also translates outward into other parts of the canto: the playful *spera*; the Pilgrim's youthlike dim-wittedness with respect to the mystery of heavenly sharing; and Virgil's prodding Dante as a parent would a child (133–138). The visions of gentleness and the motifs of youth have a double connection: on the one hand, youth can be playful, gentle, and innocent; on the other, it can be impulsive, thoughtless, and ignorant—in need of gentle instruction or pardon. The symmetrical motif of youth in this canto thus translates (**bb**) by repeating itself, and rotates (**b_q**) by changing its orientation from high-lighting certain positive characteristics of youth to highlighting certain neg-ative ones.

Of the three visions, the one that elicits most discussion is that of Saint Stephen. Many have asserted that the reason Dante portrayed him as a youth was to "unlock" (114) more compassion in his readers, a technique he used when making Ugolino's children younger than they actually were at the time of his imprisonment. Others have pointed out that Dante considers a "youth" anyone between the ages of twenty-five and forty-five, as demon-strated in his calling Scipione and Saint Francis "young" (*giovanetti*) (*Par.* VI, 52 and XI, 58). Still others have wondered if Dante was fusing or confusing Saint Stephen with Saul, who was, in fact, a young man when he witnessed Stephen's martyrdom and later became Saint Paul (see Acts 7:58). It is also possible that the Poet, exiled in his thirty-sixth year, might be revealing a per-sonal sympathy for the martyr. Michelangelo Picone notes that Dante uses the rhyme *terra, guerra, serra* in describing Stephen's martyrdom, echoing the Poet's verses on exile in "Amore, da che convien," and "Tre donne in-torno al cor" (Picone, 234). As such, perhaps yet another mirroring is taking place. Enzo Esposito and Bruno Nardi have observed that the medieval iconography predating the *Purgatorio* does not show Saint Stephen either as a youth or in a reclined position on the ground, as Dante does. Only after Dante's dramatic depiction do representations of Stephen take on these characteristics. Anna Maria Chiavacci Leonardi, on the other hand, cites the tradition of seeing Stephen as young at the time of his lapidation: his face is described as "angelic" in Acts 6:15. What is most striking about Dante's de-piction of Saint Stephen, however, is that his eyes are turned upward, an im-age that certainly fits in a canto in which the direction of one's vision (one's line of sight) is an important marker of one's ability to understand.

When the Pilgrim "awakes" from his ecstasy, when his "soul returned outside itself/ and met the things outside it that are real" (115–166), he ac-knowledges what he calls his *non falsi errori* (117). "Not false," as a double negative, gives us "true," and "true errors" gives us a sort of oxymoron, de-pending on how we interpret the term *errore*. If by *errore* Dante meant a "fal-sity," then the "true falsities" of the visions would mean, essentially, that from one perspective the visions were true, and from another they were false. It depends on which side of the mirror you are. What you see in the mirror when you look at yourself is both truly you and not you. Your mir-rored image, which looks back at you, is looking at the truly you, but it is not actually truly looking. The visions were true in that they spoke of events that were true (and offered examples of "true" gentleness); they were false in that they were only visions—illusions that appeared (or one might say, "seemed") and then faded away. The visions were "virtue-al," simultane-ously revealing true virtue and a mere virtual reflection of the truth. Some scholars have pointed out that Dante's reaction to the visions as "not false errors" could be considered his claim to the truth value of his journey as a whole (Barolini). The Pilgrim is beginning to distinguish between truth and images of truth, but it will take more time for him to be able to perceive the Ultimate Truth that creates all reflections.

Virgil speaks brusquely to the dazed Dante, asking him,

> "What is wrong with you? You can't walk straight;
> for more than half a league now you have moved
> with clouded eyes and lurching legs, as if
> you were a man whom wine or sleep has gripped!"
>
> (120–123)

Again, the Pilgrim is caught stumbling. Dante begins to explain to Virgil that he has experienced a series of visions, but Virgil stops him and says that even *cento larve,* a "hundred masks" (127), or as Musa has noted, "apparitions" (again we encounter a term referring to "appearing"), on his face could not have concealed his slightest thought. Here, as often before, Virgil demonstrates quite excellent vision, as he did when the Angel approached and when he "saw" what Guido del Duca meant by "sharing has no part." This is a clear echo of his reply to a frightened Dante, pursued by demons: "Were I a leaded mirror / I could not gather in your outer image / more quickly than I have received your inner" (*Inf.* XXIII, 25–27), a metaphor that is recalled again in the speed with which a mirror "captures" an image (*Purg.* XXV, 26). Just how far Virgil can see will soon be revealed, but until then, it is not surprising that this poet-guide, who can see in the dark and through smoke (*Purg.* XVI), who holds a lantern behind him (*Purg.* XXII, 67–69), who "foresaw" the coming of Christ, and who might even be at fault for being a "seer" (*Inf.* XX) is so able to see into the Pilgrim's mind. Virgil sees with an inner vision, not with "earthly eyes, which—once / the body, stripped of soul, lies dead—can't see" (134–135). He knows Dante is not sleepwalking, drunk, or ill. He is able to perceive the truth (albeit a limited amount of it) that corporeal eyes—such as the ones the Pilgrim is still using—cannot. At this point in the journey it is time for Dante to change the placement of his lens; he must now be able to see through his heart, opening it to "the waters of peace that pour from the eternal fountain" (130–132). That in medieval psychology and theories of love the eyes are connected to the heart is worth remembering here. When we keep this in mind, the debated meaning of the verb *s'intende* (73), which Dante uses in reference to what the souls in Heaven feel and share, makes even more sense as "love" from the Provençal, *s'entendre.* Seeing through the lens of love, one comes to understand.

It is also through the lens of love that Virgil asks, "What is wrong with you?" (133). He does this to spur on his stumbling charge. It is not unreasonable to think that Virgil was also *seeming* particularly impatient to test Dante on what he learned in viewing examples of gentleness. Can he respond to

curt words without getting angry? Yes, he can. But it is perhaps more relevant to our discussion of Canto XV as a whole to think about the veiling and
unveiling of illusion and knowledge by the words *apparve, larve, parve* (appeared, masks, appeared) and *chiuse, scuse, diffuse* (conceal, refuse, diffuse)
display (125–132). Like the on-off lights of the days and nights in Purgatory,
the truth flickers for the Pilgrim at this intermediary stage of the journey.
He is experiencing the *via negativa*, a literal cloud of unknowing, as he balances on the precipice of the cathetus, glimpsing into the Truth via its illusion and reflection.

The reflecting-rotating-translating-gliding, the *appearing* and *appearing to*
of Canto XV, are all performed quietly, even silently. The canto feels like a
deep sigh, a contemplation, a meditation. At this point in the journey, Dante
is in the last place of the first half of the journey. It is a good moment for
him to introspect, to turn within to "see" teachings (the visions), and to
"spec-ulate" on what will come in the second half of the journey. *Intra nos*
before *super nos*. At this stage the Pilgrim is partially in the real and partially
in the virtual, hence the confusions, the paradoxes, the veiling and unveiling, the double appearing (coming into sight and seeming), the stunning
brightness of the canto's opening and the dark smoke of its ending. He is on
the edge, about to be himself a reflected beam, "as a second ray will issue
from / the first and reascend, much like a pilgrim / who seeks his home
again" (*Par.* I, 49–51). "Home" is Paradise, the focal point and the vertex. This
second half of the journey is the return, the reflection into what is paradoxically both the "virtual" world and the *real* world. Paradise is the *verace
speglio*, the Truthful Mirror "that perfectly reflects all else, while no / thing
can reflect that Mirror perfectly" (*Par.* XXVI, 106–108). It is the singular "light-
ray reflected from the summit of / the Primum Mobile" (*Par.* XXX, 106–107).

A virtual image reflected in a mirror; the unseen rays of light that radiate
or reflect off of objects and into our eyes; the path of the sun over the
course of a year; the paradox of divine charity: the imagery and language
Dante uses in this canto portray the *errori* of perception. Perception becomes an epistemological problem. This canto of appearances *seems* to be
one of optical allusions to optical illusions.

While nearly every canto of the *Comedy* has been christened by scholars,
naming Canto XV has proved to be a challenge; the canto is elusive, quite like
the "secondary" image in a mirror. The Pilgrim encounters no salient figure
here, nor does he endure any particular drama. It is, in many readers' eyes, a
minor canto. As Tibor Wlassics noted, critics speak about its importance un-
certainly or defensively with "buts" (161–162). At worst, it has been considered an infelicitous canto—especially with regard to the opening verses
(1–24)—in terms of its poetics (Momigliano), a tedious and somewhat self-
congratulatory display of optical theory and didacticism. More neutrally, it
has been called a transitional, or connecting, canto. More benevolently and
more recently it has come to be thought of as a canto with important

themes of light; of youth; of ironic, metaliterary playfulness; of truth progression; and of mirrors, as well as an unusually prescient anticipation of
Paradiso (Salsano, Wlassics, Picone). Canto XV is, without doubt, a canto of
many possible identities, and no single fixed one. Edoardo Sanguineti, while
hesitatingly dubbing it the *divieto consorte,* wondered if, instead, it should be
known as the "unnamable" canto (Sanguineti, 171 and 175).

For a canto to remain simultaneously unnamed and so variously named
after all this time is a sort of triumph. It has managed to evade a buzzword,
a sound bite, a metonymy. It practices what it preaches and stands as a virtual image "behind" the mirror, ungraspable. It reflects the lights and
virtues of Paradise and is a luminous peek into the paradoxes of Paradise
itself. It is the point of departure for the reflected ray's return Home.

BIBLIOGRAPHICAL NOTES

For the most comprehensive study and most complete bibliography to date, see Simon A.
Gilson, *Medieval Optics and Theories of Light in the Works of Dante,* (Lewiston, NY: 2000). David C.
Lindberg's many works on medieval optics are also invaluable. See also Dana Stewart, *The Arrow
of Love: Optics, Gender, and Subjectivity in Medieval Love Poetry* (Lewisburg, PA: Bucknell University
Press, 2003); and Robert Podgurski, "Where Optics and Visionary Metaphysics Converge in
Dante's 'Novella Vista,'" *Italian Quarterly* 35 (1998): 29–38.

BIBLIOGRAPHY

Bonaventura, Arnaldo. *Il canto XV del "Purgatorio."* Florence, 1902, 7–33.

Boyde, Patrick. *Dante, Philomythes and Philosopher: Man in the Cosmos.* Cambridge, 1981.

Cachey, Theodore J. Jr. "Purgatorio XV." *Lectura Dantis* 12 (1993): 212–234.

Calenda, Corrado. "*Purgatorio* XV." *MLN* 108 (1993): 15–30.

Chiavacci Leonardi, Anna Maria, ed. "Introduzione a *Purgatorio* XV." In *Dante Alighieri: Commedia.* Milan, 1994.

Di Somma, Paolo. "Canto decimoquinto." In *Attualità di Dante. Rileggendo la "Divina Commedia"
nell'anno del Giubileo del* 2000. Napoli, 2000, 234–237.

Esposito, Enzo. "*Purgatorio* XV." *Nuove letture dantesche* 4 (1970): 167–192.

Fergusson, Francis. "Canto XV: The Light of the Mind." In *Dante's Drama of the Mind: A Modern
Reading of the "Purgatorio."* Westport, CT, 1953, 63–68.

———. *Dante.* New York, 1966.

Figurelli, Fernando. "Il canto XV del *Purgatorio.*" 1973. In *Studi danteschi.* Naples, 1983, 254–280.

Floro di Zenzo, Salvatore. "Canto XV." In *Lectura Dantis neapolitana: Purgatorio,* ed. Pompeo
Giannantonio. Naples, 1989, 317–336.

Fujitani, Michio. "Dalla legge ottica alla poesia: La metamorfosi di *Purgatorio* XV 1–27." *Studi
danteschi* 61 (1989): 153–185.

Maier, Bruno. "*Purgatorio* XV." In *Problemi ed esperienze di critica letteraria.* Siena, 1950.

Marti, Mario. "Canto XV." In *Questioni di critica dantesca,* ed. Giorgio Petrocchi and Pompeo
Giannantonio. Naples, 1969.

———. "Il canto XV del Purgatorio." In *Letture dantesche,* ed. Giovanni Getto. Florence, 1962,
953–968.

Mazzotta, Giuseppe. *Dante's Vision and the Circle of Knowledge.* Princeton, 1993.

Nardi, Bruno. "Il canto XV del *Purgatorio.*" 1953. In *"Lecturae" e altri studi danteschi,* ed. Rudy
Abardo, 127–138. Florence, 1990.

Pedrazzoli, Ugo. *La sfortuna di un bel verso della "Divina Commedia."* Rome, 1904.

Picone, Michelangelo. "Canto XV." In *Purgatorio,* ed. George Güntert and Michelangelo Picone. Florence, 2001, 225–237.

Porena, Manfredi. "*Purgatorio* XV." In *La mia lectura Dantis.* Naples, 1932.

Salsano, Fernando. "Dialoghi meditativi nel centro del Purgatorio." In *La coda di Minosse e altri saggi danteschi.* Milan, 1968.

Sanguineti, Edoardo. "*Purgatorio* XV." In *Dante reazionario.* Rome, 1992.

Sermonti, Vittorio. *Il "Purgatorio" di Dante.* Milan, 1990, 231–239.

Soprano, Edoardo. *Il canto XV del "Purgatorio."* Turin, 1962.

Tartaro, Achille. "Il canto XV del *Purgatorio.*" In *"Purgatorio": Letture degli anni 1976–79,* Rome, 1981, 315–343.

Vallone, Aldo. "*Spera* in Dante." *Giornale italiano di filologia* 14 (1961): 355–358.

Vernon, William Warren. *Readings on the "Purgatorio" of Dante.* New York, 1907.

Wlassics, Tibor. "Il canto XV del *Purgatorio.*" In *Filologia e critica dantesca: Studi offerti a Aldo Vallone,* Florence, 1988, 161–174.

CANTO XVI

A World of Darkness and Disorder

JOHN SCOTT

The opening words of Canto XVI, *Buio d'Inferno* (Darkness of Hell), challenge the reader's attention with the plosive force of the initial *B* and the unexpected backward glance to the *tenebrae* of Hell. In contrast to the beauty of the seascape on the shores of Mount Purgatory, illuminated by Venus, "the lovely planet that is patroness / of love," and the four stars seen only by Adam and Eve (*Purg.* I, 13–25), the terrace of Wrath plunges us into Erebus, its smoke thicker than any "Darkness of Hell" and darker than "night deprived / of every planet" (1–2). The pilgrim is so blinded that Virgil draws even closer to him, offering his shoulder as support in navigating this third terrace. In line 24, Dante learns that the penitent's spirits are untying the "knot of anger,"[1] unlearning their reactions to "injury / received" that led them to "seek out another's harm" (*Purg.* XVII, 121–123). We note that Dante, who has already confessed to harboring great pride (*Purg.* XIII, 136–138), is here obliged to undergo the blindness inflicted on the formerly wrathful (a telling participation in the *contrapasso* that will be repeated when he has to pass through the wall of fire on the terrace of lust: *Purg.* XXVII, 10–57).

The Folly of Wrath

In this central episode, the poet illustrates the consequences of "blind anger." Those who had given way to this sin on earth are enveloped in dense smoke that reflects the way in which wrath had overcome their rational faculties in their earthly lives, thus destroying the "light of reason"

(*Monarchia* III, iii, 4). Anger had been condemned by classical writers (Cicero, Seneca) as well as by Christian moralists. Among the latter, Gregory the Great wrote in *Moralia,* book 5: "When anger covers the mind with the darkness of confusion . . . the splendor of the Holy Spirit is cast aside . . . the mind is empty and soon driven to madness." However, the Christian tradition made a fundamental distinction between wrath—a capital vice giving rise to twenty-four sinful offspring (pseudo-Bonaventure, *Speculum conscientiae*)—and righteous anger *(ira per zelum)* such as that displayed by Christ when he evicted the merchants from God's Temple (Matt. 21:12–13). God's righteous anger is, in fact, an essential part of his Justice, and its full force will be felt by the wicked at the Last Judgment (*Dies irae,* "Day of anger"). Wrath, on the other hand, is opposed to justice and to the concord that should reign in civil society. Natural in animals, in people wrath is a sin committed against human nature, which should be guided at all times by reason and the injunction to love one's neighbor, even one's enemies.

Penitent souls recite the Gregorian prayer that beseeches the Lamb of God (*Agnus Dei,* a symbol of Christ's absolute humility) to grant them mercy and peace. Unlike the disruption and enmity caused by their anger on earth, now they are united in "fullest concord" (21). A voice from the darkness asks the pilgrim who he is, for he sounds like "a man who uses months to measure time" (27). Commentators have questioned the spirit's ability to discern that the pilgrim is still alive, pointing out that the dense, black fog would make his physical body invisible: we may simply note that, along with the fact that his body "pierces through" the smoke (25), the doubt evident in Dante's question—"Master, are those whom I hear, spirits?" (21)—distinguishes him from disembodied souls undergoing purgation. Instead of revealing his identity, Dante highlights that God has bestowed on him the grace of seeing the Court of Heaven in a way quite unknown to modern custom—thus preparing the way for his ancestor's question phrased in Latin (*Par.* XV, 28–30: "unto whom / as unto you was Heaven's gate twice opened?") and setting the record straight after the pilgrim's initial denial ("For I am not Aeneas, am not Paul; / nor I nor others think myself so worthy" *Inf.* II, 32–33). Dante is the new Saint Paul (II Cor. 12:2–4).

Before this affirmation, the pilgrim's *captatio benevolentiae* refers to the soul's desire to return "fair" to its Creator (31–33). After Marco promises to accompany Virgil and his charge, Dante explains that God's grace has made it possible for him to undertake this journey "in a manner most / unusual . . . [to] see His court" (41–42). We may note that the early commentators (the Ottimo, Lana, and Benvenuto) merely identify this Marco as a well-known and upstanding courtier. As such, he would have immediately contrasted the heavenly court, characterized by mutual love and harmony, with the earthly courts he had known and which Pier della Vigna stigmatizes as whorehouses of envy (*Inf.* XIII, 64–66).

O Evil, Where Is Thy Abode?

Marco tells the pilgrim that he was a "Lombard" (46). In Dante's time, "Lombardy" could signify a region covering not only present-day Lombardy but also large tracts of the Veneto and Emilia. Marco may have been active at the court of Gherardo da Camino, the de facto ruler of Treviso from 1283 to 1306. Marco claims that during his life on earth he cherished the ideals of virtuous living that are now utterly neglected. His reply to Dante's second question indicates that, whereas motion in Hell is circular, here the way up is straight. Penitent souls have requested prayers from relatives on earth; Marco is the first soul to ask the pilgrim to pray for him when he reaches his heavenly goal. After promising to do so, Dante says that he is literally bursting (*scoppio*, 53) with a doubt—first sparked by Guido del Duca's words in *Purgatorio* XIV, 22–126, describing the corruption rampant in the entire Arno Valley and in Romagna—now made doubly acute by Marco's extension of this evil to the whole world. The pilgrim assures Marco that he is well aware that the contemporary world is devoid of all virtue and full of every kind of evildoing. But what is the cause? Some say that the fault is in the stars; others, that it lies within human nature itself.[2]

Marco's explanation is given in thirteen *terzine* (67–105), followed by a corollary of eight *terzine* (106–129). His analysis has been dismissed by some as that of a radical Ghibelline. Nicolae Iliescu (1988, 14) went so far as to accuse him of "garrulity." This accusation is quickly dismissed, for in fewer than three hundred and fifty words (67–114), Dante's Marco cover the main themes of the whole poem: the importance of free will; God's justice in rewarding and punishing humankind; the creation of the human soul and its attraction to everything that reminds it of its origin in the source of all happiness and good; the need for laws and a supreme temporal guide; the complementary roles of Church and Empire; the catastrophe that has ensued since "each has eclipsed the other" (109) by combining temporal power with spiritual authority. At the very center of his poem (in its fiftieth canto), the poet expressed this urgent message, one intended "to profit the world which / lives badly" that has gone astray (*Purg.* XXXII, 103–104) Critics who assert that in *Purgatorio* Dante set intellectual traps for his readers by making penitent souls express falsehood or half-truths should take into account that such a game would violate an essential law of Purgatory—the souls are no longer capable of sinning (*Purg.* XI, 19–24, XXVI, 131–132)—while it would defeat the very purpose expressed in the pilgrim's entreaty to Marco: "But I beseech you to define the cause, / *that seeing it, I may show it to others*" (62–63; my emphasis).

The hapax "Oh!" (*Uhi* [64]; with its long drawn-out closed vowel *u*, possibly echoing the first wail of the infant, latinized as *heu* in *DVE* I, iv, 4) introduces the (temporarily) blind Marco's aphorism that the world is blind and that the pilgrim must come from this blind world. The first falsehood he demolishes is astral determinism: the idea that all human actions are conditioned by the heavens (one of the thirteen propositions condemned by the bishop of Paris on December 10, 1270). This idea would destroy free will and the justice inherent in rewarding good and punishing evil (70–72). It is true that the heavens do exert an influence on human beings and their inclinations (cf. *S. Th.* II. II. 95.5)—a belief perhaps not unlike the concepts of heredity and DNA in modern science. Nevertheless, we are endowed with the light of reason, which can distinguish between good and evil, as well as free will, which is capable of overcoming all negative influences and circumstances. Two references to free will (*libero arbitrio,* 70 and *libero voler,* 76) in the space of six verses indicate its importance as God's "greatest gift" to both angelic and human beings:

> The greatest gift the magnanimity
> of God, as He created, gave, the gift
> most suited to His goodness, gift that He
> most prizes, was the freedom of will.
>
> (*Par.* V, 19–24)

Such repetition also points to an essential palinode on Dante's part. In a sonnet addressed to Cino da Pistoia, "Io sono stato con Amore insieme," possibly written around 1305, the poet asserts that the will and human reason are never free in love's arena (9–11). Only a few years later, he rejected the concept of love's omnipotence in his condemnation of Francesca da Rimini (*Inf.* V, 73–142). Critics who are fond of highlighting episodes in the *Comedy* where its author recants his former beliefs rarely pinpoint this radical volte-face in the *Comedy*'s central canto, soon to be reinforced in *Purgatorio* XVIII, 55–75, and whose importance in the entire structure of the sacred poem could hardly be exaggerated.

With the oxymoron "On greater power and a better nature / you, who are *free, depend*" (79–80, italics mine), Marco expresses the Christian paradox that human beings are in fact most free when they are subject to God, who directly creates the human soul (cf. *Purg.* XXV, 67–75). Thus, the cause of the world's evil state lies "in you . . . , in you it's to be sought" (83). The repetition "*in voi* è la cagione, *in voi* si cheggia" hammers home the essential truth that men and women are responsible for the corruption of a world gone astray. Marco describes the human soul as issuing straight from the hand of God, who loves it even before it comes into being. Created as a tabula rasa, the soul—laughing and weeping like a little girl—knows nothing, except that, having its origin in the source of all happiness, it instinctively turns to whatever seems to offer pleasure and joy (cf. T. S. Eliot's poem, "Animula"). From this theological disquisition (amplified in *Purg.* XXV, 37–78), the poet makes an astonishing conceptual leap to the consequences of the soul's attraction to false or secondary goods, where it will remain entangled "unless there's guide or bridle to rule its love" (93).

Unbridled Immorality

No better example of the indissoluble link between Dante's theology and his political thought could be found than in this passage. The metaphor of the "bridle," signifying the laws that must be applied by the emperor, has already appeared in *Purgatorio* VI, 88, and it will return at the end of *Monarchia*, where Dante reiterates his belief that greed for earthly things would destroy humanity, if they "like horses, carried away by their bestiality, were not held in check and guided 'by bit and bridle'" (*Mon.* III, xv, 9; cf. Ps. XXXI, 9). The laws exist, thanks to Justinian's divinely inspired work on the *Corpus iuris civilis* (*Purg.* VI, 88–9; *Par.* VI, 22–4); but there is no one to apply them, since the shepherd of Christ's flock has usurped the emperor's role. As the divinely appointed executor of the law *(executor legis),* the emperor is the ruler who can "discern at least the tower of the true city" (95–96). Some commentators insist that "the true city" is the ideal city on earth. This is unlikely for two reasons. The first is that the emperor's mission is to guide humanity to a state of earthly happiness, symbolized by the Earthly Paradise (*Mon.* III, xv, 7)—which is precisely Virgil's role as herald of the Empire in the *Comedy.* If the "true city" were this goal, then it would be insufficient for the ideal emperor to discern only its loftiest feature from a distance. The medieval reader inevitably associated the phrase *la vera cittade* with Augustine's City of God: that city was partly found on earth but not in any civic state. Dante's readers have, moreover, been given an essential clue as recently as in Canto XIII, 94–96, when Sapia answers the pilgrim's question with a salutary reminder:

> "My brother, each of us is citizen
> of one true city: what you meant to say
> was one who lived in Italy as pilgrim."

"Pilgrim" is the Augustinian term for one who belongs to the City of God during his or her time on earth; but Sapia's statement that "each of us is citizen of one true city" reminds Dante that the penitent souls are no longer members of an earthly commonwealth but are citizens of the true city, "that Rome in which Christ is / Roman" (*Purg.* XXXII, 102–103). It is the tower of this city (perhaps symbolizing Divine Justice) that the emperor must keep in his sights in order to fulfill his mission on earth. Merely to discern the tower of the ideal community to be established on earth would not enable him to guide humanity to terrestrial happiness. Rather, the verb *discernere* implies understanding as well as vision (cf. 131: *e or discerno,* "I understand"); it points to the fact that the emperor must bear in mind that "earthly happiness is in some measure *[quodammodo]* directed to immortal happiness" (*Mon.* III, xv, 17).

The divine formula of two guides and two complementary but distinct goals has been obliterated. There is no one to execute justice in the temporal sphere—or, as Beatrice will tell the pilgrim in the heaven of the fixed stars (*Par.* XXVII, 139), everything on earth is in confusion and error because no one governs the world: "therefore, the family of humans strays." Here, in 98–99, the message is conveyed by reference to the law that allowed the Jews to eat the flesh only of ruminants with a cloven hoof (Lev. 11:3–8, Deut. 14:7–8). Scholastic theologians offered various allegorical interpretations of this non-Christian precept. Dante's son Pietro asserted that the cloven hoof (which the pope does not possess) must be interpreted as indicating the ability to distinguish between temporal and spiritual matters. Benvenuto stated that the pope in 1300, Boniface VIII, although an expert in canon law, confounded the spiritual and temporal realms. As a consequence, everyone follows the terrible example set by their spiritual leader: seeing him lust after temporal power and wealth, they naturally give way to their greed "and seek no further" (102).

The conclusion is evident: it is the bad example set and that evil way that "have made the world wicked and not nature that is corrupt in you" (103–104, *my own literal translation*). Mario Agrimi (1966, 22) claims that Dante emphasizes free will and human choice so much that he "does not seem to take account of original sin"; his analysis contrasts with the "Christian pessimism" of medieval thinkers, who for the most part accepted Augustine's view of human nature. Such an approach is misleading. Augustine did not view human nature as totally corrupt. Rather, he referred to original sin as a malady (*In Psalmos* 118, sermon 3: "Unde peccatum originale languor naturae dicitur"), even as Aquinas referred to it as a deep wound *(vulneratio)* inflicted on human nature. Here, at the heart of his poem, Dante expresses his conviction that the world has gone astray because it is no longer guided by the two supreme authorities specifically designed by God to counteract the effects of original sin *(Mon.* III, iv, 15: "remedia contra infirmitatem peccati"). To point out that the poet does not have Marco Lombardo refer to Grace would be equally beside the point. It is interesting to note that in his Latin treatise, when Dante refers to the effects of original sin, he not only describes human nature as "corrupt" (*natura . . . depravata, Mon.* II, xi, 2), but he states that, if Christ had not made satisfaction for that sin, we should all be the "children of wrath" (cf. Ephesians 2:3).

A Two-sun Eclipse

The chapter from the third book of *Monarchia* quoted above refutes the hierocratic interpretation of God's creation of the two great luminaries (Gen. 1:16–18) by denying that the sun was intended to symbolize the papacy or that the moon was meant to indicate the Empire (as the hierocrats claimed). Such a "lie" (*mendacium: Mon.* III, iv, 17) had overturned the traditional Gelasian principle of coexistence between the two supreme powers. The struggle between the papacy and Frederick II was followed by ideological warfare between Boniface VIII and the king of France. It was claimed that the pope possessed "a plenitude of power" and was thus "lord of all things temporal and spiritual." It was his privilege to ratify or depose any king or emperor, and he could transfer the imperial authority to whomever he chose (translatio imperii). In lines 106–108, Dante reaffirms the dualist principle with a scientific absurdity (decried in Ep. VI, ii, 8): "Rome, which made the world good, used to have two suns" that illuminated both the world's path and the one leading to God. Here, as Francesco da Buti was the first to point out, the poet (who referred to Henry VII as "our sun" in Ep. VII, ii, 7) "said 'suns,' in order not to make one lesser than the other." It is perhaps idle to speculate on the golden age envisaged by Dante. In Convivio IV, v, 8, he asserted that at the time of the Incarnation the world had reached a state of perfection in universal peace that had never been—and could never again be—equaled. In the Comedy, a moment of ideal cooperation between the two supreme authorities was enjoyed when Justinian was converted to orthodoxy by Pope Agapetus I (Par. VI, 13–24).

What is certain is that one sun has extinguished the other (109–114). The "crook" symbolizing the spiritual authority is now joined to the "sword." As a result, the supreme powers no longer respect each other's jurisdiction, and the results are obvious for all to see, "for every plant is known by what it seeds" (114; Matt. 7:16 and 20). Just as in Inferno XVI, 67–75, Dante bewails the absence of all virtue and nobility in Florence (and its idealized golden age will be celebrated in Par. XVI), so here (115–120) Marco laments the disappearance in the whole of northern and northeastern Italy of valore e cortesia,[3] courtly qualities and virtues that flourished until Frederick II's authority was undermined by the papacy. Nowadays, the region is a haven for criminals and evildoers. Just as the fate of Sodom (Gen. 18:23–32) lies behind Ciacco's claim that there are only two just citizens left in Florence (Inf. VI, 73), so too does Marco declare that in this region there are now only three good men who decry the present and who long to pass on to a better life (121–123). Dante probably set his eyes on Currado da Palazzo (a native of Brescia) when the latter was podestà of Florence in 1276. "The good Gherardo" (124), lord of Treviso from 1283 until his death in 1306, was celebrated for his hospitality to poets. In Convivio IV, xiv, 12, Dante asserted that Gherardo da Camino's exemplary virtues and nobility of spirit would have been universally recognized, even if he was the grandson of the "basest peasant." Guido da Castello (praised in Conv. IV, xvi, 6) was expelled from Reggio Emilia; Dante may well have encountered him at the court of Cangrande della Scala during his stay in Verona. We are told that Guido is better described as "the candid [or more literally, 'simple'] Lombard" (126), provided we understand the epithet "simple" (semplice) to indicate (as in French: francescamente) his honesty and probity—a true oxymoron, since the French attributed duplicity to all Lombarts (Italian bankers or moneylenders).

Into the Smoke

The fact that all three were leading Guelfs (although some doubt remains about Guido's political allegiance) is further proof that the rabid Ghibellinism attributed to Marco is the result of prejudice in scholars who object to his denunciation of the papacy's political interference and its hostility toward emperors. Despite the uncertainties surrounding the *Comedy*'s chronology, it is most likely that *Purgatorio* was composed during at least part of the fateful period (1310–1313) that witnessed Henry's descent into Italy and the failure of his imperial mission. Whatever the chronology may be, it is indisputable that the description of the Church as *la Chiesa di Roma* (127) is unique in Dante's writings. It is a forceful reminder that the papal seat was no longer in Rome but in shameful exile at Avignon (cf. *Purg.* XXIII, 148–160). The evil tree of the French monarchy that casts its shadow over the whole of Christendom (*Purg.* XX, 43–4) has deprived Rome of both her lights (cf. *Ep.* XI, x, 20: "Romam urbem, nunc utroque lumine destitutam"). In 1300, however, and under Boniface VIII, the Church had already seized "two powers" and "into the filth *(nel fango)* / it falls and fouls itself and its burden *(la soma)* (129)"—imagery that will be used again by the poet when he makes Pope Adrian V declare (*Purg.* XIX, 103–105) that he had quickly learned how difficult it was to keep "the great mantle" (a metonymy for the papal office) "from the mire" *(dal fango),* so that all other burdens *(tutte l'altre some)* seemed mere feathers.

Dante declares that he is convinced by Marco's sound reasoning, that he now understands why the priestly functions of Levi's sons precluded them from any right to inherit land (Num. 18:20–32). However, he asks about the identity of this Gherardo, praised for his nobility in such "savage" times (135). Marco, recognizing by his speech that the pilgrim is a Tuscan, reacts sharply: "Either your speech deceives me or would tempt me [to anger]" 136), for Gherardo da Camino was well-known in Tuscany (and specifically in Florence for his connections with the Donati family). Marco adds for good measure that Gherardo was the father of Gaia. We know almost nothing about her, except that she married a relative, Tolberto da Camino, and died in August 1311. The Ottimo, Lana, and Benvenuto state that Gaia was notorious for her love affairs; others claim that she was virtuous. It seems likely that the poet is bent on illustrating the world's degradation by citing the example of a daughter whose life stands in utter contrast to her father's nobility. The canto is brought to an end by the reappearance of rays of light that begin to penetrate the smoke, as well as the angel guarding the exit of the terrace, who will greet the formerly wrathful with a reference to Matthew 5:9 "Blessed are the peacemakers," adapted by the qualification "those who are free of evil anger" (*Purg.* XVII, 69). Marco turns back into the smoke, putting an end to this crucial encounter.

Postscript

The centrality of this episode in the economy and structure of the *Comedy* has been stressed. Charles Singleton pointed to a pattern of seven cantos ("the poet's number") extending from *Purgatorio* XIV to XX, with Virgil's discourse on love in *Purgatorio* XVII at its center. This was extended by Joan Ferrante to include cantos XII to XXII. Moreover, Singleton's significant line numbers (139, 145 = 10, 151 = 7) also "occur in a similar pattern in the Ante-Purgatory, centered on the political Canto VI and its fierce attack on Italy and Florence" (Ferrante 1993, 154). An interest in numerology was evident in certain areas of medieval literature, and the diligent reader may delve into its mysteries even in translations. Readers will also notice the frequency of the verbs "to see" and "to discern" on the terrace of the blind. Imagery, too, is accessible in any faithful translation. What cannot be appreciated is the rhythm and verbal music of the original. That is why it is so important to read the Italian text, once translation has provided a necessary understanding of the narrative. Dante, supreme craftsman that he was, had to accept the exigencies of the triune form—*terza rima*—that he invented and exploited to the full and that cannot be satisfactorily reproduced in English translations. The rhyme sequence used only once in the *Comedy* *scoppio-doppio-accoppio* (53, 55 57), introduced with "I explode" *(scoppio)*, surprises the reader with the sound of rhymes produced by a particular combination of velar and double plosive consonants, rhymes that are exceptional in the second *cantica* (cf. *Inf.* XXIII, 8, 10, 12: *accoppia-scoppia-doppia*). Even more surprising is the "infernal" trio *cozzo-sozzo-mozzo* (11, 13, 15). Words placed in the rhyming position are always given prominence: thus, *pargoleggia* (87: the simple soul "sporting" playfully like a young girl) resounds with the echo of God's love that leads to its creation (85: *vagheggia*), while the rhyme *fanciulla-trastulla* (86, 90) reinforces the ingenuous nature of the newly created soul. As a craftsman, the poet makes discreet but effective use of chiasmus: for example, *Lombardo fui, a fu' chiamato Marco* (46), and *ché nel ciel uno, e un qua giù la pone* (63). Strong caesura sets off and highlights the importance of free will in *lume v'e dato a bene e a malizia, / e libero voler* (75–76). Enjambment gives added emphasis to the concept of free will in *Se così fosse, in voi fora distrutto / libero arbitrio* (70–71). Alliteration and assonance abound: *fummo fendi* (25); *se mi secondi* (33); *vuol ch'i' veggia* (41); *ti prego / che per me prieghi* (50–51); *non natura* (105); *vegno vosco* (141). We find repetition (more specifically, polyptoton), for example, in Marco's entreaty, set out in courtly style: *I' ti prego / che per me prieghi quando sù sarai"* (50–51). The pilgrim's answer is equally "courteous": *Per fede mi ti lego / di far ciò che mi chiedi* (52–53). Other examples of *repetitio* are *fora . . . non fora"* (70–71); *in voi . . . in voi* (83); *convene . . . convene* (94–95); *L'un l'altro . . . l'un con l'altro . . . l'un l'altro* (109, 110, 112). Finally, we should note that an Italian ear will be jolted by the "unnatural" stress on *rimprovèro* in 135, required by its placement as the fourth syllable of an *a minore* hendecasyllabic line—and put to good effect by the poet in stressing that the *rimpróvero* ("reproach") of an age of darkness and corruption is true *(vero)* and just.

To conclude, readers will surely concur with Edward Peters's judgment (1961, 64) of this central episode in Dante's "sacred poem": "The topic of earthly beatitude is now linked to the problem of human individuation and freedom in a remarkable discourse on political anthropology that has no equal anywhere else in medieval political thought."

NOTES

1. The polyvalence of the word *nodo* is characteristic of Dante's language in the *Commedia*. Of the ten occurrences, the one that has sparked most debate is in *Purgatorio* XXIV, 55, while its most dramatic use is found in the description of the climactic moment of the pilgrim's vision of God's creation: *Paradiso* XXXIII, 91. In the context of *Purgatorio* XVI, it may echo Isaiah 5:18 (and cf. *Purg.* IX, 126).

2. The meaning of line 63 ("ché nel cielo uno, e un qua giù la pone") is deduced from Marco's reply; however, no commentator—to my knowledge—has noted the strange deictic *qua giù* ("below"). Certainly, the Mountain of Purgatory is still on earth (cf. the Hollanders' translation "the earth"), but "down here" is hardly a straightforward pointer to "la volontà degli uomini" (Sapegno, Bosco-Reggio, Chiavacci Lenodardi, et al.). Cf. Hugh Capet's "Carlo *venne* in Italia" (*Purg.* XX, 67), which implies a strange perspective for a soul high up on the Mountain in the southern hemisphere. As Lino Pertile observes, "[S]olo il soggetto parlante sa con precisione a che cosa si vuol riferire quando dice 'qui'" ("Only the speaker in the text knows precisely what is being referred to when he says 'here'"). "*Qui in Inferno:* deittici e cultura popolare," *Italian Quarterly* 37 (2000): 57–67.

3. The theme of degeneracy is already present in *Convivio* II, x, 8, where Dante observes that "'Courtesy' and honesty are one and the same and because in courts in former times the virtues and fine customs were practiced—just as today the opposite is done—that word was derived from the courts, and 'courtesy' was equivalent to courtly behavior. If that word were to be derived from courts nowadays, it would signify nothing but turpitude."

BIBLIOGRAPHY

Agrumi, Mario. "Il canto XVI del *Purgatorio*." In *Lectura Dantis Romana*. Turin: SEI, 1966, 5–47.

Boitani, Piero. "From Darkness to Light: Governance and Government in *Purgatorio* XVI." In *Dante and Governance*, ed. J. R. Woodhouse. Oxford: Clarendon Press, 1997, 12–26.

Bosco, Umberto. "Il canto XVI del *Purgatorio*." In *Purgatorio: letture degli anni 1976–79*. Rome: Bonacci, 1981, 345–361.

Cioffari Vincenzo. "Canto XVI." In *Lectura Dantis Neapolitana: Purgatorio*. Naples: Loffredo, 1989, 337–347.

Cipollone, Annalisa. "Canto XV." In *Lectura Dantis Turicensis: Purgatorio*, ed. G. Güntert and M. Picone. Florence: Cesati, 2001, 239–259.

De Rosa, Mario. "Prima che Federigo avesse briga (*Purg.* XVI, 117)." *Esperienze Letterarie* 13, no. 2 (1988): 79–88.

Ferrante, Joan. "A Poetics of Chaos and Harmony." In *The Cambridge Companion to Dante*, ed. R. Jacoff. Cambridge, NY: Cambridge University Press, 1993, 153–71.

Girardi, Enzo Noè. "Al centro del *Purgatorio*: il tema del libero arbitrio." In *Il pensiero filosofico e teologico di Dante Alighieri*, ed. A. Ghisalberti. Milan: Vita a Pensiero, 2001, 21–38.

Grassi, Giacinto. "Il canto XVI." In *Letture del "Purgatorio,"* ed. Vittorio Vettori. Milan: Marzorati, 1965, 197–216.

Iliescu, Nicolae. "The Roman Emperors in the *Divine Comedy.*" In *Lectura Dantis Newberryana,* ed. P. Cherchi and A. Mastrobuono. Evanston, IL: Northwestern University Press, 1988, 1:3–18.

Kantorowicz, Ernst H. "Dante's 'Two Suns.'" In *Selected Studies.* Locust Valley, NY: J. J. Augustin, 1965, 325–338.

Maccarrone, Michele. "Le teoria ierocratica a il canto XVI del *Purgatorio.*" *Rivista di storia della Chiesa in Italia* 4 (1950): 359–398.

Malato, Enrico. "'Sì come cieco va dietro a sua guida / per non smarrirsi (. . .).' Lettura del canto XVI del *Purgatorio.*" *Rivista di Studi Danteschi* 2 (2002): 225–261.

Mazzamuto, Pietro. "Canto XVI." In *Lectura Dantis Scaligera.* Florence: Le Monnier, 1967, 2: 579–608.

———. "Marco Lombardo." In *Enciclopedia dantesca,* 6 vols. Rome, 1970–1978.

Muresu, Gabriele. "La *sentenza* di Marco Lombardo (Purgatorio XVI)." In *I ladri di Malebolge. Saggi di semantica dantesca.* Rome: Bulzoni, 1990, 83–121.

Peters, Edward. "Human diversity and Civil Society in *Paradiso* VIII." *Dante Studies* 109, no. 991: 51–70. (Reprinted in E. Peters, *Limits of Thought and Power in Medieval Europe.* Burlington, VT: Ashgate Variorum, 2001.)

Scott, John A. "The Poem's Center." In *Dante's Political Purgatory.* Philadelphia: University of Pennsylvania Press, 1996, 144–157.

Scotti, Mario. "Il canto XVI del *Purgatorio*" In *Nuove Letture dantesche, Casa di Dante in Roma.* Florence: Le Monnier, 1970, 4: 193–219.

Scrivano, Riccardo. "Il discorso di Marco Lombardo (*Purg.* XVI)." In *Studi filologici, letterari e storici in memoria di Guido Favati.* Padua: Antenore, 1977, 539–558.

Singleton, Charles S. "The Poet's Number at the Center" *Modern Language Notes* 80, no. 1 (1965): 1–10.

Trovato, Mario. "*Purgatorio* XVI." *Lectura Dantis Virginiana* 2, no. 12 (1993): 234–247.

Vallone, Aldo. "Marco Lombardo (*Purg.* XVI)." In *L'uomo di Dante a Dante uomo. Lectura Dantis Pompeiana,* ed. Pasquale Sabbatino. Pompei: Biblioteca "L. Pepe." 1985, 13–33.

CANTO XVII

On Revenge

JO ANN CAVALLO

Dante Alighieri would have known a thing or two about anger. While he was representing the White Guelfs in a diplomatic mission to Pope Boniface VIII, the Black Guelfs seized control of Florence with the pope's support and set in motion a campaign of revenge against the Whites, who had participated in the previous government. In January 1302 Dante was sentenced in absentia by the Florentine *podestà* for "graft, embezzlement, opposition to the pope and Charles of Valois, disturbance of the peace of Florence, and turning over control of Pistoia to the Whites with the resultant expulsion of the Blacks"; as a result he was barred from ever again holding public office in Florence, fined 5,000 florins, and banished from the city for two years (Barbi, 16).[1] When he failed to appear in person and pay the fine within three days— he had not yet returned from Rome—his property was confiscated. The sentence was extended two months later to banishment in perpetuity, on penalty of death by burning. Several White supporters were banished along with Dante, and a subsequent sentence of June 1302 extended the expulsion to the wives, sons, and all male descendents of the condemned men. Although the sentence, imposed without due process, was evidently also without foundation, the matter was not resolved during Dante's lifetime. Following Durling and Martinez's insight that "the writing of the *Commedia* is, as a political act, in large measure the expression of Dante's despair at the political realities and the normal avenues of political action" (51), this *lectura* pursues the question of how Dante's life circumstances could have shaped his representation of *ira* in Canto XVII.[2]

Images of *Ira*

As the canto opens, Dante calls on the reader to enlist his or her memory and imagination in envisioning the poet's experience of leaving behind the Terrace of the Wrathful. To participate in the pilgrim's move from the total blackness of dense smoke to pale sunlight, the reader needs to *remember* what it feels like to emerge from mists in the mountains and to *imagine* how moles peer through the membranes covering their eyes (1–8). As the emerging sunlight wanes, soon to give way to a more natural darkness (9–12), Dante goes on to attribute an even greater role to the imagination, no longer in alliance with sense perception of the natural world, but an instrument of divine illumination (13–18). Directly addressing Fantasy itself, he explains that the imagination is capable of overpowering and completely blocking out sensorial impressions when it is "moved" by a light coming down from Heaven.[3] This statement on the power and origin of this higher form of imagination is not simply theoretical musing, but an anticipation of the three vivid images that a divine source is about to pour into the pilgrim's mind. A succession of images illustrating the consequences of sinful anger suddenly appears to him with explosive force. Italo Calvino likened these images to cinematic projections on a screen separated from the "reality" of Dante's otherworldly journey (82).

The reader is now required to use memory and some degree of imagination to recall and unpack the classical and biblical episodes alluded to in these scenes:

> Within my fantasy I saw impressed
> the savagery of one who then, transformed,
> became the bird that most delights in song.
>
> (19–21)

> Then into my deep fantasy there rained
> one who was crucified; and as he died,
> he showed his savagery and his disdain.
> Around him were great Ahasuerus and
> Esther his wife, and the just Mordecai,
> whose saying and whose doing were so upright.
>
> (25–30)

> then there rose up
> in my envisioning a girl who wept
> most bitterly and said: "O queen, why did
> you, in your wrath, desire to be no more?
> So as to keep Lavinia, you killed
> yourself; now you have lost me! I am she,
> mother, who mourns your fall before another's."
>
> (33–39)

The first scene recalls one of the most horrific episodes in Ovid's *Metamorphoses*. Tereus, charged with protecting his sister-in-law, Philomena, instead drags her off to a hut and rapes her. When she threatens to reveal his evil deed, Tereus, in a fit of anger (*ira; Met.* VI, 549) brutally cuts out her tongue. Then he rapes her repeatedly before returning to his wife, Procne. When the violated and maimed Philomena finally manages to communicate with her sister by means of a tapestry, Procne's pain (*dolor*) and indignation (*indignantia*) are beyond words, and she seeks punishment (*poena*) without distinguishing right from wrong (*Met.* VI, 585–6). Both sisters have a share in the gruesome revenge: in her anger (*ira, Met.* vi, 623, 627), Procne murders her son Itys, Philomena cuts up the boy's corpse, Procne serves the cooked flesh to Tereus, and then Philomena flings the severed head at his face. As Tereus chases both women with a sword, all three are transformed into birds.

The second vision refers to an Old Testament episode set in motion when Mordecai refuses to bow before Haman, the chief minister of the Persian king, Ahasuerus. When Mordecai justifies this apparent lack of reverence by explaining that he is a Jew, in retaliation Haman wants to kill not only Mordecai but all the Jews in the Persian Empire. Haman tells Ahasuerus that the Jews are hostile to the laws of other nations, and the king initially approves his official's murderous plan in the interest of national stability. Mordecai entreats his relative and foster daughter, Esther, who also happens to be the Queen of Persia, to intercede with the king. Esther reveals to Ahasuerus that she is also Jewish and asks him to save Mordecai and all her people from destruction by Haman. In response, the king has Haman hanged on the scaffold originally prepared for his intended victim, then awards Haman's possessions to Esther and his position of vizier to Mordecai himself.

The motif of vengeful anger is perhaps more obvious in the third vision, taken from the *Aeneid,* in which Dante imagines that a tearful Lavinia reproachs her mother, Amata, for her suicide (33–39). Virgil had written that Amata fell into a state of heartache and anger (*curaeque iraeque, Aen.* VII, 345) when she learned that the foreign intruder Aeneas aimed to replace the noble Turnus as her son-in-law and heir to the throne. The fury Alecto, sent by Juno, subsequently incited her to even greater rage. When Amata could not convince her husband, Latinus, to honor his promise to Turnus, she raced through the streets in a frenzy and carried her daughter off to a hiding place in the mountains. She later told Turnus that her fate was bound with his and that she would die before submitting herself as a captive to the Trojan invader (*Aen.* XII, 60–63). When she erroneously believes that Turnus has been killed by Aeneas, she is led to suicide by feelings of desperation, grief, sorrow, and a deep sense of guilt: "her mind distraught by sudden anguish, [she] cries out that she is the guilty source and spring of sorrows, and uttering many a wild word in the frenzy of grief, resolved to die, rends her purple robes, and from a lofty beam fastens the noose of a hideous death" (*Aen.* XII, 598–603).

Definitions of *Ira*

In what way do these vivid revenge scenarios exemplify the sin of *ira?* Before examining more closely the nature of the anger depicted in these divinely inspired images, let us turn to the characteristics of *ira* outlined in the subsequent narrative. As Dante comes out of the trance induced by the visions, he is struck by an even brighter light, one that temporarily blinds him. He has thus taken us from the black smoke of wrath, to the pale light of a setting sun, to intense visions sent down by a divine source, and finally to the overpowering light of an angel (40–54). The angel of gentleness, the only character Dante actually meets in this canto, erases the third *P* from his forehead and seems to rule out the legitimacy of anger in any form as he praises the *Beati / Pacifici,* echoing the Seventh Beatitude from the Sermon on the Mount (66–69). This celebration of the peacemakers, who stand in contrast to the wrathful, reminds us of the visions illustrating meekness in Canto XV. (Indeed, in the third vision Saint Stephen was depicted praying for his persecutors as they stoned him to death.) The pilgrim and his guide ascend to the top of the Terrace, but they can go no further because a divine law prohibits forward movement after dark (70–78). As Dante asks about the upcoming Terrace, Virgil takes the opportunity to expound on the arrangement of Purgatory according to the Seven Deadly Sins (82–139). In this exposition, *ira* is included, along with pride and envy, and is depicted as the love of harm for one's neighbor. It is specifically described as a desire for revenge: "there is he who, over injury / received, resentful, for revenge grows greedy / and, angrily, seeks out another's harm" (121–123). Revenge, it would appear, is unacceptable, since the only appropriate Christian response is meekness. This view seems to concur with the teaching of Jesus in the Sermon on the Mount (e.g., "Do not resist one who is evil. But if any one strikes you on the right cheek, turn to him the other also"; "Love your enemies and pray for those who persecute you"; Matt. 5:39, 44) and the admonitions of St. Paul (e.g., "Bless those who persecute you"; "Repay no one evil for evil"; "never avenge yourselves" (Rom. 12:14, 17, and 19).

At the same time, whereas Jesus had simply said "Blessed are the peacemakers" (Matt. 5:9), the angel's Benediction qualifies peacemakers as "those free of evil anger" (69), leaving open the possibility of an anger that is not evil. Dante, in fact, had before him the authoritative precedents of Aristotle and Aquinas in distinguishing between legitimate and illegitimate forms of anger. Aristotle considered anger to be a natural and appropriate sentiment when exercised within reason: "It is the man who is angry on the right occasions and with the right people and at the right moment and for the right length of time who wins our commendation." Conversely, one errs through excess if one is angry "with the wrong persons, or for the wrong reasons, or too violently, or too quickly, or too long" (*Ethics*, IV, 5). The contrasting virtue would not consist in a complete lack of anger, which for Aristotle signaled a deficiency, but in a "good temper," which, although tending more toward the deficiency, was the mean state between the two extremes. St. Thomas Aquinas likewise condemned both the excess and the deficiency of anger, stating that anger was sinful only when it was against reason and not accompanied by a sense of justice (*ST* I.ii.46–48, 74; II.ii.157–158).

Aligning himself more closely with Aristotle's writings than with Jesus' Sermon on the Mount, Dante explains in the *Convivio* that the virtue opposing *ira* (i.e., *mansuetudine*) is not outright meekness but, rather, the mean between the extremes of excessive anger and excessive patience ("gentleness . . . regulates our wrath and our excessive patience with regard to evils that confront us," *Conv.* IV, xvii, 5). And in the *Comedy* itself he maintains the distinction between sinful wrath and righteous anger, using the terms *ira folle* ("insane anger," *Inf.* XII, 49) and *ira mala* ("evil anger," *Purg.* XVII, 68–69) to refer to the former and the terms *dritto zelo* ("unswerving zeal," *Purg.* VIII, 83) and *buon zelo* ("righteous zeal," *Par.* XXII, 9) for the latter.

Keeping in mind Dante's distinction between two kinds of anger, let us return to the exemplary images described at the outset of the canto.

The Displacement of Blame

In searching for examples of "evil" and "insane" anger, Dante had a myriad of episodes to choose from, since revenge was a predominant theme in both the Old Testament and in classical literature. In asking what makes these three scenes exemplary in illustrating what sins to avoid, I shall consider them in relationship to each other as well as to Dante's real-life drama. In the first example, Procne and Philomena are in a position of utter powerlessness. Philomena is helpless against Tereus's force, and during the rape she calls out in vain to her family and the gods (*Met.* VI, 525–526). Ovid heightens the wretchedness of the violation by comparing Philomena first to a frightened lamb that has been ripped apart by a wolf and cast away and then to a dove that still fears the claws that pierced it and stained its feathers with blood. Ovid thus arouses a sense of outrage in the reader and a desire to see Tereus punished. Yet when Procne becomes so enraged that she loses control and murders her innocent son, she commits an additional injustice instead of punishing the evildoer.

This tendency toward displacement in revenge was recognized as a problem in Dante's day, and it was addressed through penalties regulating vendetta in the Florentine statutes:

> It is established and ordained that, if any assault is made against anyone's
> person . . . , and he on whom such assault is made, or someone else of his family,

while the original attacker is alive, takes revenge for the assault against someone else, not the one who made the manifest and public assault, then the podestà is to convict such an avenger in the following way: if, from the vendetta, death follows, the avenger is to be beheaded and all his property to be given or adjudicated to the sons or heirs of the dead man.

(Dean, 188)

According to this statute, taking private revenge on the person who assaulted you was considered legitimate in itself, so much so that if the original attacker was dead, then the injured party had the right to substitution in avenging himself. The unjustified circumstance was that of *unwarranted* displacement.

This same tendency toward displacement is at work in an anecdote recounted by Boccaccio that conveys the extent of Dante's enduring rage as an exile:

Seeing that he could not return [to Florence], he so changed his mind, that there was never any Ghibelline and enemy of the Guelphs fiercer than he, and that which causes me the most shame in the service of his memory is that it is very publicly known in Romagna that every young lady, every little boy, taking sides politically and damning the Ghibellines, would move him to such insane fury that he was given to throwing stones if they did not become silent. And with this animosity he lived until his death.

(Boccaccio, 90–91)

In Boccaccio's story, Dante's rock throwing involves displacement, lack of proportionality, and relentlessness. His direct adversaries are not the Guelfs themselves, who are out of reach, but "every young lady" and "every little boy" who takes a Guelf position. While the repetition of the adjective "every" stresses the enduring nature of Dante's rage, the identification of his opponents as young ladies and little boys denotes the patently uneven nature of the confrontations. Moreover, Dante responds to their words with deeds—stone throwing. His anger at the Black Guelfs, who unjustly condemned him to exile, and also apparently at his fellow White Guelfs, who blamed him for their failure to regain power, is displaced onto the innocent young women and children he encounters during his exile. Of course, it is somewhat incongruous to imagine the scholar and citizen Dante beleaguered by women and children wanting to argue politics, and I do not mean to take Boccaccio's scenario as a reliable biographical note. Indeed, Mazzotta refers to Boccaccio's *Vita di Dante* as "a self-conscious fictional work" that gives "the novelistic sense of Dante's life" ("Life of Dante," 3). Yet precisely because of the exemplary quality of the anecdote, Boccaccio's depiction of Dante manifesting displaced anger in this relentless and excessive way renders him the very personification of wrath.

In the other example of *ira* drawn from secular Latin literature, Queen Amata, despite her high rank, is as powerless as Procne. When she suddenly finds that her world has fallen apart, she too responds with unthinking violence. Her fatal error involves a particular form of displacement, since the target becomes her own self. While Virgil's Lavinia simply tore at her hair and face (*Aen.* XII, 605), Dante's Lavinia explains that her mother's anger led to self-destruction ("why did / you, in your wrath, desire to be no more?" 35–36). And whereas Virgil had focused on Amata's guilt and self-recrimination, Dante singles out anger as the sole motivation for the suicide. From the perspective of Dante's vision, Amata's anger against Aeneas was turned inward, and such a displacement led her to go against the most basic of loves, that of self. Dante's Virgil states later in the same canto that the love of self is, like the love of God, the most basic of all loves:

> "since love never turns aside its eyes
> from the well-being of its subject, things
> are surely free from hatred of themselves."
>
> (106–108)

Reflecting on the events that led to the Black takeover of Florence, Dante was perhaps not immune to the impulse toward self-recrimination and in his grief may have been tempted at times to blame himself for the "death" of the White Guelfs. María Rosa Menocal writes that during his first years of exile Dante was "often a fugitive and a beggar and in despair—conspiring, contemplating suicide" (96). Yet Lavinia's words to her mother—and we remember that Dante too had children to think of—show how tragically unproductive it is to let anger turn into guilt-based self-destruction.

But what would a valid response to injury be? In light of the distinction between evil and just anger established later in the canto, can there be a just revenge? The question was clearly of pressing urgency in Dante's day, even beyond his own personal circumstances. After the pro-papal Guelfs had prevailed over the enemy Ghibellines, the Guelfs divided and began a series of reciprocal acts of revenge on the part of the rival factions. The situation was no better beyond the local politics of Florence. As Michele Barbi aptly put it, "Wherever his harsh exile drove him throughout Italy, Dante found other unhappy persons who had been cast out of their cities; nowhere did he find orderly, peaceful government; quarrels, oppression, and the despotism of factions or usurpers raged on all sides; there were conflicts and wars between neighboring cities" (21).

A Constructive Model

I would like to argue that in his central vision of Haman punished, Dante offers a constructive model for responding to injury. This vision runs counter to the pattern of the two classical episodes. Procne and Amata lost control of their reason and unthinkingly misdirected their violent impulses against the innocent; Haman uses (or rather, misuses) reason to defame Mordecai and to convince the State to take action against him and against those connected with him (in this case, the Jews). Procne and Amata are subject to a state of explosive fury; Haman secretly harbors wrath as he engineers a plan for unmeasured requital. Procne and Amata act outside the law; Haman aims to manipulate the law to serve a personal vendetta. Finally, whereas the reader can understand that rape and mutilation in one instance and death in the other can provoke a desperate response, the enormous lack of proportion between Mordecai's refusal to bow and Haman's subsequent desire to annihilate Mordecai, along with all the Jews, greatly magnifies the fault. Essentially a figure of malice and fraud, Haman is moreover an example of the abuse of political power.

If the first and third examples show only what to avoid, this central biblical example not only depicts illegitimate revenge punished but also includes a successful response to a wrong done and thus offers an illustration of just revenge. Unlike Procne and Amata, who take matters into their own hands, Mordecai works within the system available to him so that the retribution is not a frenzied act of personal revenge, but the punishment of the guilty party ordered by the State.

Mordecai's initial predicament offers a suggestive parallel to Dante's circumstances. Just as Haman had convinced the Persian king to destroy Mordecai and his fellow Jews without due process, the Black Guelfs had won over Pope Boniface VIII in their campaign against Dante and the White Guelfs. Like Mordecai, Dante was one of the intended victims of revenge masquerading as law.[4] In the biblical episode, Mordecai seeks help from his relative, Esther, and Ahasuerus punishes Haman for his abuse of power. Dante also sought help as he attempted repeatedly to restore justice. During his early years of exile, he planned with his fellow Whites to seize Florence from the Blacks. He wrote to members of the government and to the people of Florence, recalling his previous service to the city and the injustice of his exile (Barbi, 19). He also entreated a foreign power, Emperor Henry VII, to oust the Blacks from Florence and to reinstate the exiles. Yet despite all Dante's best efforts, neither Boniface nor Henry VII assumed the role of the just Ahasuerus. An occasion eventually presented itself for Dante to return to his native city in 1315, when his sentence could have been repealed through an acknowledgment of error on his part; however, as Barbi notes, "Dante, the disdainful exile and the friend of justice, refused to return to Florence by any such means" (27). Upon Dante's death in 1321, after he had been in exile for twenty years, the Black Guelfs were still in control of Florence, and the judicial sentence against him was still in effect.

Indeed, in light of Dante's own vicissitudes, the vision of Haman crucified looks very much like a wish-fulfillment fantasy. Dante's vision even goes

beyond the biblical text; he imagines that Ahasuerus, Esther, and Mordecai are all looking on a savage and disdainful Haman at the moment of his
death (which in the Book of Esther was by hanging, and in Dante's vision
by crucifixion). He thus gives the intended victim the pleasure of witnessing firsthand the destruction of his false accuser, a pleasure that Dante
himself was never to experience. Moreover, Dante chose a biblical story
that conspicuously celebrates the revenge of an intended victim over his
false accuser. With the king's approval, Mordecai and Esther order the
Jews throughout the kingdom to act as they please against their enemies
on the day that Haman had planned their destruction. Even though out of
fear the enemies of the Jews do not fight them, the Jews kill five hundred
people in the capital city of Susa, including Haman's ten sons. Seconding
the wishes of Esther, whose desire for revenge is not yet sated, the king
gives the Jews free rein on the following day, and they kill three hundred
more people in Susa and thousands more throughout the realm. Such far-
reaching revenge is celebrated as a day of rejoicing for the Jews. In this
context, Dante's implicit identification with Mordecai would perhaps explain the extended depiction of him as "the just Mordecai, / whose saying
and whose doing were so upright" (29–30), a description that otherwise
risks diverting the reader's attention needlessly away from the example of
Haman's wrath punished.

It may be argued that wish fulfillment underlies Dante's earlier encounter with Filippo Argenti as well. In the fifth circle of Hell, where the
wrathful are immersed in a bog as they beat one another and tear at each
other with their teeth, the Florentine Filippo Argenti reaches out to pull
the pilgrim from the boat or perhaps to capsize it into the marsh of Styx in
revenge for Dante's insulting words. In retaliation Dante wants to see him
"soused within this broth / before we've made our way across the lake"
(*Inf.* VIII, 53–54). While many readers have debated whether the pilgrim
Dante was contaminated by his wrathful surroundings or whether he was
displaying righteous anger (see Cioffi, 112–122), the author Dante justifies
his fictional persona first by having Virgil praise his expression of vindictiveness as a fine wish and then by turning the wish into reality: other
angry souls dismember Filippo, who in his anger bites himself. Even as
Dante writes he is still praising and thanking God for the scene he has witnessed. Early commentators explain that Argenti, a member of the Black
party, had apparently struck Dante in a fight, that his brother had obtained
Dante's confiscated possessions, and that the family subsequently opposed the idea of Dante's return. In his imagination, then, Dante settles
the score. The pilgrim's joyful witnessing of Filippo Argenti's suffering
provides an apt analogy to the scene of Mordecai observing the crucifixion of Haman. Dante the pilgrim rejoices in God's divine retribution, just
as we are to imagine that Mordecai rejoiced in Ahasuerus's imperial punishment.

Writing as Revenge

Dante's revenge is not limited to this wish-fulfillment fantasy, however; he achieves revenge through the act of writing itself. Dante knew full well the potency of the pen in the absence of a sword. If in Boccaccio's saucy novella Alibech enjoyed "putting the devil back in hell" (*Dec.* III.10), it may be that Dante derived no less satisfaction from placing his enemies there. "Vengeance is mine; I will repay, says the Lord" (Rom. 12:19), and Dante, in fact, leaves vengeance to God, albeit a God of his own imagination. As Joan Ferrante and others have noted, the road through Hell is lined with Florentines, whether the Ghibellines and Guelfs of the mid-1200s or the Black and White Guelfs of Dante's day. And while Dante the writer plays God, Dante the character, like Mordecai and Esther at the crucifixion of Haman, has the pleasure of seeing those hateful souls suffer the most horrific punishments.

A potential glitch in Dante's vast imaginary revenge scenario was that those responsible for his exile were still alive at the fictional date of the poem. Dante gets around this technical difficulty in a most ingenious—albeit unorthodox—way by condemning them in advance. Dante guarantees Pope Boniface's damnation in Hell by showing Pope Nicholas III awaiting his arrival among the Simonists, who are plunged upside down into the rock with their protruding feet on fire (*Inf.* xix, 52). Boniface continues to arouse Dante's vindictive impulses in the course of the poem, even in *Paradiso*. Not only is Boniface shown to be on the mind of St. Peter, who condemns him as a usurper, but Beatrice's final words to Dante refer to Boniface's hellish torments: she announces that when Pope Clemente V arrives in Hell (he dies in 1314), he will push Boniface lower down into the rock (*Par.* XXX, 148). Such condemnation in advance is not just reserved for popes. In the *bolgia* that punishes those who have deceived their own relatives, country, or party (populated, not surprisingly, with Florentines), one of the souls is awaiting his relative, Carlino de' Pazzi (*Inf.* XXXII, 52–69). Carlino had betrayed the exiled Whites in 1302 by handing over a fortified town to the Blacks in exchange for money.

Dante also expresses his anger in a more orthodox manner—by asserting his innocence and vituperating his enemies. Charles de Valois, sent by Boniface as "peacemaker" but actually given the task of facilitating the Blacks' takeover of the city, is said to have come into Italy armed with "the lance that Judas tilted" (*Purg.* XX, 74). From the perspective of Paradise, his ancestor Cacciaguida, comparing Dante's situation to that of the unjustly accused Hippolytus, gives him hope for "just vengeance":

> "The blame, as usual, will be cried out
> against the injured party; but just vengeance
> will serve as witness to the truth that wields it."
>
> (*Par.* XVII, 52–54).

Dante uses the occasion to target his fellow exiled Whites: Cacciaguida first condemns "the scheming, senseless company" who "against you . . . will be insane, completely / ungrateful and profane" and then gives Dante the satisfaction of hearing of their demise: "not you but they will have their brows bloodred" (Par. XVII, 62–66).

In Dante's otherworld, not only does God exact His own revenge (in this case, as it is in Scripture, it is divine retribution), but He is not beyond allowing for some meaty revenge, even on the part of the damned. In Inferno XXXII–XXXIII, Count Ugolino feeds his anger by perpetually gnawing the brain of the Archbishop Ruggieri for having starved him and his young sons and nephews to death in a prison tower. The pilgrim Dante desires revenge at various moments during his otherworldly journey. In addition to his outburst against Filippo Argenti in Inferno VIII, Dante expresses a desire for revenge in his verbal exchange with the Ghibelline Farinata (Inf. X, 40–51, 73–84; see Durling, 140) and in his attack on Bocca degli Abati, a betrayer of the Guelfs (Inf. XXXII, 85–105; see Ahern, 419).

A Fellowship of the Angry

The one soul Dante encounters on the Terrace of Wrath is Marco Lombardo, his contemporary (Purg. XVI). When the angry Lombardo attributes the evils of his day to the usurpation of secular power by the papacy in the hands of Boniface ("the Church of Rome confounds / two powers in itself; into the filth, / it falls and fouls itself and its new burden" Purg. XVI, 127–129), Dante agrees wholeheartedly with the reasoning of "good Marco" (130). Some scholars have seen a resemblance between the two men. Giorgio Siebzehner-Vivanti writes that "Marco Lombardo is Dante himself," and his description of the historical Marco Lombardo could easily fit the poet, whom he describes as "among the wisest but least fortunate men of his age, gifted with moral, chivalric, and intellectual virtues, an expert of the world [who] wandered from court to court . . . , living a bitter life, despised for his poverty, but always correct and magnanimous" (354–355). Even if Dante did not intentionally depict himself in the character of Marco, one gets the feeling that if he were to return to this Terrace in the afterlife, he would be in good company with such a kindred spirit. This sense of worthy company is extended to the reader who, through memory and imagination, is drawn to participate not only in Dante's otherworldly voyage but in his anger as well, condemning his enemies and applauding their (actual and anticipated) eternal punishments.

Returning to Boccaccio's judgment of Dante, we can note that although the biographer declared himself ashamed of Dante's angry rock throwing, he expresses his own righteous indignation (giusta indegnazion, 60) over Dante's unfair treatment by joining in the vituperation of those responsible for his suffering: he composes invectives against the enemies of Dante following the account of the poet's exile and against the Florentines as a whole following the account of his death. Boccaccio's verbal artillery, following the example Dante had set forth in the *Comedy*, demonstrates a belief in the efficacy of words to cut down one's enemies.

Just as the cantos on anger are central to the structure of the poem and to its otherwordly realms (falling at the midpoint of both the text and the journey), the emotion of anger can be seen as central to Dante's mission as a writer. In this context, the three visions in Canto XVII, which offer models of both negative and positive forms of revenge, can be considered in relation to Dante's personal circumstances. Unjustly deprived of his rightful place in Florentine society, Dante did not think of turning the other cheek. Nor did he give in to the temptation of self-destruction. Rather, thanks to the power of his memory and imagination, he channeled his anger into a poem that would condemn his enemies to Hell for eternity and turn his exile from Florence into a journey to Paradise.

NOTES

1. Barbi's *Life of Dante* (first published in 1933) is the classic account of the poet's life; for more recent biographies, see Bemrose and Mazzotta, "Life of Dante." See also Boccaccio's early *Vita di Dante,* which conveys a clear sense of Dante's rage over the injustice of his sentencing and exile.

2. Finding that Dante's political circumstances shaped his other works of exile as well, Durling and Martinez see the *Convivio* as "stemming in large part . . . from the new exile's sense of intense wrong and from his desire to testify explicitly before men both his innocence and the sense of his earlier work" (3). Menocal has compellingly argued that a treatise as seemingly academic as the *De vulgare eloquentia,* concerned as it is with language, was in fact "a dramatically and openly political text" (97) and as such "one of his various answers to the impardonable pains of his exile" (see 92–106). For the effects of political exile on Dante's *Comedy,* see especially Mazzotta, *Dante, Poet of the Desert* and "Theology and Exile," in *Dante's Vision.*

3. Mazzotta notes that this is "the only time that the 'imaginativa' is invested with the attribute of autonomy from the world of the senses" (*Dante's Vision,* 118).

4. Referring to these circumstances, Bemrose writes, "The revenge of the victorious Blacks was wide ranging" (63).

BIBLIOGRAPHY

Ahern, John. "Amphion and the Poetics of Retaliation." In *California Lectura Dantis: Inferno,* ed. Allen Mandelbaum, Anthony Oldcorn, and Charles Ross. Berkeley and Los Angeles: University of California Press, 1998, 413–423.

Aristotle. *The Nicomachean Ethics.* Trans. J. A. K. Thomson. 1953. Reprint, Great Britain: Penguin, 1959.

Barbi, Michele. *Life of Dante.* Berkeley and Los Angeles: University of California Press, 1954.

Bemrose, Stephen. *A New Life of Dante.* Great Britain: University of Exeter Press, 2000.

Boccaccio, Giovanni. *Vita di Dante.* Ed. Paolo Baldan. Bergamo: Moretti & Vitali, 1991.

Calvino, Italo. *Lezioni americane. Sei proposte per il prossimo millennio.* Milan: Garzanti, 1988.

Cavallo, Jo Ann. "Wrath," "Wrathful, The." In *The Dante Encyclopedia.* Ed. Richard Lansing. New York: Garland, 2000, 890–893.

Cioffi, Caron Ann. "Fifth Circle: Wrathful and Sullen." *California Lectura Dantis: Inferno.* Ed. Allen Mandelbaum, Anthony Oldcorn, and Charles Ross. Berkeley: University of California Press, 1998, 111–122.

Dante. *Il Convivio (The Banquet)*. Trans. Richard Lansing. New York: Garland, 1990.

Dean, Trevor. *The Towns of Italy in the Later Middle Ages*. Selected sources translated and annotated. Manchester, England: Manchester University Press, 2000.

Durling, Robert. "Farinata and Cavalcante." *California Lectura Dantis: Inferno*. Ed. Allen Mandelbaum, Anthony Oldcorn, and Charles Ross. Berkeley and Los Angeles: University of California Press, 1998, 136–149.

Durling, Robert, and Ronald L. Martinez. *Time and the Crystal: Studies in Dante's Rime Petrose*. Berkeley and Los Angeles: University of California Press, 1990.

Ferrante, Joan. *The Political Vision of the* Divine Comedy. Princeton: Princeton University Press, 1984.

Mazzotta, Giuseppe. *Dante, Poet of the Desert: History and Allegory in the* Divine Comedy. Princeton: Princeton University Press, 1979.

———. *Dante's Vision and the Circle of Knowledge*. Princeton: Princeton University Press, 1993. See 116–134 for a discussion of knowledge that refers extensively to *Purgatorio* XVII.

———. "Life of Dante." *The Cambridge Companion to Dante*. Ed. Rachel Jacoff. Cambridge, NY: Cambridge University Press, 1993, 1–13.

Menocal, María Rosa. *Shards of Love: Exile and the Origins of the Lyric*. Durham: Duke University Press, 1994.

Ovidius Naso, Publius. *Metamorphoses*. Trans. Frank Justus Miller. 2 vols. Loeb Classical Library. 1916. Reprint, Cambridge, MA: Harvard University Press, 1994.

Siebzehner-Vivanti, Giorgio. *Dizionario della* Divina Commedia. Ed. Michele Messina. Ca. 1954. Reprint, Milan: Feltrinelli, 1965.

Virgil. *Aeneid*. Trans. H. Rushton Fairclough. 2 vols. Loeb Classical Library. 1918. Reprint, Cambridge, MA: Harvard University Press, 1998.

On anger and revenge:

Averill, James R. *Anger and Aggression: An Essay on Emotion*. New York: Springer-Verlag, 1982. For a succinct overview of historical teachings on anger from Plato to Descartes, see 73–101.

Elster, Joan. "Norms of Revenge." *Ethics* (July 1990): 862–885.

Jacoby, Susan. *Wild Justice*. New York: Harper and Row, 1983.

Kerrigan, John. *Revenge Tragedy: Aeschylus to Armaegeddon*. Oxford: Clarendon Press, 1996.

Keyishian, Harry. *The Shapes of Revenge: Victimization, Vengeance, and Vindictiveness in Shakespeare*. Atlantic Highlands, NJ: Humanities Press, 1995.

Marongiu, Pierre, and Graeme Newman. *Vengeance*. Totowa, NJ: Rowman and Littlefield, 1987.

Tavris, Carol. *Anger: The Misunderstood Emotion*. New York: Simon and Schuster, 1983.

Wilker, Josh. *Revenge and Retribution*. Philadelphia: Chelsea House, 1999.

CANTO XVIII
Love, Free Will, and Sloth

MARILYN MIGIEL

Many readers have been inclined to pass quickly over Canto XVIII, thinking its philosophical discussion of love and free will to be of little importance and finding no particularly significant character or event. To such readers, the philosophical discussion may appear repetitive of Marco Lombardo's statements on free will and the soul in Canto XVI; moreover, there is nothing in Canto XVIII to match Marco's engaging image of the *anima semplicetta* ("soul is simple," *Purg.* XVI, 88), with her delight in all that is pleasurable, or Marco's political fervor and spleen. Even the pilgrim's attention wanes in the second part of the canto. But this idle moment is interrupted by the penitents' expiating sloth in the Fourth Terrace, the penitents rushing by so quickly that it seems we arrive at the beginning of Canto XIX and Dante's fascinating dream of the siren almost before we know it.

In recent years, the Italian scholars Giorgio Padoan and Pier Giorgio Ricci have attempted to rescue this canto from critical oblivion. The discussion of love and free will has also drawn the attention of readers such as Christopher Ryan and Lloyd Howard, because they see in it the potential to shed light on Dante's judgment of other characters in the *Divine Comedy*. A reading of this individual canto, such as the one presented here, inevitably addresses the import of the philosophical discussions on love and free will in the center of the *Purgatorio* and in the center of the *Divine Comedy* itself, as well as the choices Dante makes in his representation of the slothful and of their penance.

Nightfall

At the beginning of Canto XVIII, Dante and Virgil are already on the Fourth Terrace, and Virgil has just finished his account of the division of the purgatorial terraces and the role love plays in determining this division. Virgil's explanation, a counterpart to his explanation of the ordering of Hell in *Inferno* XI, was initiated in the previous canto, when the pilgrim found that his legs failed him as he arrived at the Fourth Terrace. It is almost nightfall, and as Sordello has already explained in Canto VII (43ff.), no one in Purgatory is physically able to move when darkness descends on the mountain. To use the time fruitfully while they are forced to wait, Virgil explains that Purgatory is ordered on the principle of love: love of an evil object is corrected on terraces one to three, insufficient love on terrace four, and excessive love on terraces five to seven.

Reviewing the penances found on the first three terraces, we find that there was a taking account of the self and a progression toward vision that partakes of the divine. The penitents gazed on divine art; their eyes were sewn shut, thus forcing them to rely on a vision not purely physical; then they experienced inner visions. But accompanying this increased inner vision is a decreased mobility. The movement of the proud is impeded by the stones they carry; the envious cannot move because they cannot see; and, on the Third Terrace, the souls momentarily give up the use of their limbs when the visions appear to them. If this progression is to continue, the souls should lack the ability to move by the time they reach the Fourth Terrace; and, indeed, we find that Virgil and the pilgrim are unable to move by the time they reach the top of the stairs.

Dante and Virgil's immobility, the natural outcome of the lessons of the previous terraces, will seem strange later in the canto when the penitent slothful speed by them. This contradiction in the law of Purgatory may be attributed to the fact that the Fourth Terrace serves as a kind of pivot in the purification process. In Canto XVIII, as the pilgrim moves from the correction of misdirected desire on the terraces below to the correction of love defective on the terraces above, he sees dramatized the dialectical resolution of desire necessary in achieving purification. Decreased mobility is thus seen both as a sign of increased love (because movement is reduced as hatred falls away) and as a sign of insufficient love (because lack of movement bespeaks slowness in love). The dialectic of desire is expressed throughout these middle cantos of the *Purgatorio* not only in terms of mobility and immobility but also in terms of movement away from the ground and toward the ground, love of earthly glory and love of spiritual goods, natural love and free will.

The Impulse to Love

Dante requests that Virgil explain what love is, since Virgil has argued that it is the foundation of all good and bad actions. Virgil's psychology of love has an explicitly Aristotelian character: the intellectual soul, like Marco Lombardo's *anima semplicetta,* feels a natural love for all that appears to promise happiness ("The soul, which is created quick to love, / responds to everything that pleases, just / as soon as beauty wakens it to act," 20–21). The apprehending faculty perceives the object, which exists outside the mind—in the philosophical terminology of Dante's time, this object was called the *appetibile* or "appetible" object; the apprehending faculty derives an image from that object ("Your apprehension draws an image from / a real object" 22–23); the intellectual soul turns toward that image ("expands upon / that object until soul has turned toward it," 24), though Virgil neglects to point out that it does so in order to judge the object; if the intellectual soul further inclines toward the appetible object, this is called love ("And if so turned, the soul tends steadfastly, / then that propensity is love " 25–26). The movement of the intellectual soul toward the object is a second stage, desire ("so does the soul, when seized, move into longing / a motion of the spirit," 31–32). The third and final stage, one of repose in the beloved object, is joy ("the soul . . . / . . . never resting / till the beloved thing has made it joyous," 31–33). Virgil concludes that not all loves can be sanctioned, even though the initial movement of love, being natural, is always good (34–39).

The pilgrim's response to Virgil's explanation suggests that he has a somewhat different conception of what is going on:

> "Your speech and my own wit that followed it,"
> I answered him, "have shown me what love is;
> but that has filled me with still greater doubt;
> for if love's offered to us from without
> and is the only foot with which soul walks,
> soul—going straight or crooked—has no merit."
>
> (40–45)

Some critics would be inclined to interpret this difference of opinion between the pilgrim and Virgil as yet another sign of the poet's ironic perspective on Virgil's Aristotelianism and paganism. Bernard Stambler, for example, says: "The pilgrim, asking 'if love is offered to us from without,' is altering and extending his teacher's statement. We must notice that in what follows, Virgil makes no clear effort to deal with the situation in which 'love is offered to us from without'—for example, in the form of 'divine grace'" (180). However, it seems evident from the pilgrim's question that he is *not* referring to cases such as that presented by divine grace. Most critics, in fact, see Virgil as repeating ideas about love that were current in the Scholastic discussions of Dante's time; one reader goes so far as to attribute Virgil's statements to the poet Dante (Padoan, 666). The pilgrim's question is thus taken to be a technical device designed to provoke the discussion, in Canto

XVIII, 46–72, of the individual's responsibility for his actions (Ricci, 257). The question, which raises a possible objection to Virgil's account of love, reveals a serious flaw in the pilgrim's conception of love, for it describes love in passive terms.

According to Virgil's understanding of it, love begins when the soul leans toward an object it finds pleasurable. The pilgrim outlines a situation in which love can be offered from without (43), so that the soul makes no move of its own and can therefore not be considered responsible for its action. Though the pilgrim's argument partakes of a certain brand of fatalism to be found especially in thirteenth- and fourteenth-century discussions of love, there are two points in his favor. First, his statement is hypothetical. Second, he reintroduces the metaphor of the soul's feet, a metaphor that, as John Freccero has argued in his essay on the "firm foot," had been used to represent the soul's faculties of intelligence and will. The pilgrim is therefore at least partially aware that the soul relies on intelligence and will when it defines its relationship to the appetible object. Virgil had been silent on this point, since he eliminated the feet from the intellectual soul by comparing its movement toward the beloved thing to fire that flies upward naturally (28–33).

In response to the pilgrim's question, Virgil promises the fullest explanation reason can offer, even as he indicates his limited authority and points beyond to Beatrice, who will provide further enlightenment (46–48, 73–75). He goes on to demonstrate that natural loves or first passions are not judged good or bad in themselves, for they exist in man "sì come studio in ape / di far lo mele ("as in bees there is / the honey-making urge," 58–59). Man is judged only for the way in which he responds to these passions and maintains them in conformity with the first will (61–72).

The Slothful Race By

When Virgil finishes his discourse on free will, Dante does not respond immediately. Rather, the scene changes, and the pilgrim becomes aware of the time and of the surrounding landscape:

> The moon, with midnight now behind us, made
> the stars seem scarcer to us; it was shaped
> just like a copper basin, gleaming, new;
>   and countercourse, it crossed those paths the sun
> ignites when those in Rome can see it set
> between the Corsicans and the Sardinians.
>
> (76–81)

The heavens reveal the tension at the heart of this canto between productive activity and apparently productive activity. The moon, though it often connotes somnolence and passivity, appears brighter and more active than usual. It outshines the stars; it is compared to a basin or bucket *(secchion),* which gleams new but can also be said to burn *(ardere);* its journey across the heavens is depicted by means of the verb *correre* (to cross, to run), a key term in this canto. Furthermore, the sun appears to take second place to the moon. Though the poet speaks of the moon moving countercourse on the path ignited by the sun, suggesting that these are equally active entities, he chooses to speak of the sun when it sets—or literally, falls *(cade,* 81)—between Sardi and Corsi, names that echo the moon's two principal activities in these lines: burning *(ardere)* and running *(correre).* The pilgrim now indicates his satisfaction with Virgil's response (82–86); sleep appears to weigh heavily on him: "So that I... / ... stood / like one who, nearing sleep, has random visions" (87). The pilgrim's wandering in thought is not the result of a physical weariness, which brings on a momentary and necessary interruption of one's life and work, even though he implies that his is a kind of somnolence. Appropriately enough, he is stunned out of his stupor by the arrival of the souls who run in expiation of their sin of sloth.

As the penitents race by, they call out the examples of zeal, Mary and Caesar, both of whom are recalled as running:

> In her journey, Mary
> made haste to reach the mountain, and, in order
> to conquer Lérida, first Caesar thrust
> against Marseilles, and then to Spain he rushed.
>
> (99–102)

The counterexempla recall those persons who delayed or wandered on their journeys to promised lands:

> The ones for whom
> the sea parted were dead before the Jordan
> saw those who had inherited its lands;
> and those who did not suffer trials until
> the end together with Anchises' son
> gave themselves up to life without renown.
>
> (133–138)

Love of good is expressed as movement and the lack thereof as sloth, an unwillingness to suffer hardship to attain one's goal. Furthermore, the exempla the poet chooses carry a burden of secular signification that is incorporated into the purification process and that brings a new meaning to this process. The inclusion of extrabiblical examples suggests, as has often been noted, Dante's commitment to the earthly empire and his attempt to validate the political enterprise (Padoan, 677). Manfredi Porena has pointed out that even the example of Mary going to visit her cousin Elizabeth suggests care for temporal rather than spiritual relations; but he reminds the reader that Mary undertakes her journey at the prompting of the archangel Gabriel (Porena, 174). We are reminded that there is no progress toward Divine Good in the *Comedy* if purification means complete exorcism of the earthly and of the political. The question, "Is man motivated exclusively by love of God or also by love of the earthly?" becomes, in a certain sense, irrelevant.

In keeping with this attention to the secular and the earthly, the exempla of zeal focus on the relationship between historical characters or peoples and formations of the earth: between Mary and the mountain (not between Mary and her cousin Elizabeth, who presumably lived there), and between Caesar and Marseilles and Lérida. In the first exemplum of sloth, the drama of the Israelites is played out by the Red Sea and the Jordan. Only in the final example of sloth do we see the abstract ideal *(gloria)* that the slothful do not pursue with sufficient love ("and those . . . / gave themselves up to life without renown," 136–138). In the exempla of zeal, Mary and Caesar run to and act on formations of the earth and cities, while in the exempla of sloth, land and waters play a more active role than the people do.

An Abbot Apologizes

The one penitent with whom the pilgrim speaks in this canto is the former abbot of San Zeno (113–129), who seems to have been Gherardo II. No amount of historical research has brought to light any other information about this character, to whom critics accord a singular colorlessness. Almost every commentary notes that he may appear here because sloth was considered the vice of the ecclesiastical orders par excellence; the suggestion that Dante kept the abbot anonymous because the abbot led a life without renown has been largely discredited (cf. Porena, 178). The abbot's words here have come to be more important than the question of his identity.

The abbot's presentation of himself begins when, in response to a request for information from Virgil, he invites the travelers to follow the penitent slothful on their way to the Fifth Terrace. He then excuses his own brevity by commenting on the nature of the penance:

> We are so fully anxious to advance—
> we cannot halt; and do forgive us, should
> you take our penance for discourtesy.
>
> (115–117)

Fully aware that their penance can be construed as rudeness, the abbot argues against such an interpretation by simply stating that the pilgrim should be inclined to read *in bono*. Indeed, only an awareness of the penitents' good intentions and their intense commitment to the Divine Good assures that their penance will be accepted as productive activity rather than as the movement of persons whose energy was not harnessed and employed toward a definite goal. (Aquinas, for example, in discussing the daughters of sloth, commented on the "tendency to wander" which manifests itself variously as "uneasiness of the mind," "curiosity," "loquacity," "restlessness of the body," and "instability" (*Summa Theologiae* II–II, Q.35, A.4). Especially given the fact that Dante and Virgil do not move in Canto XVIII, one might momentarily suspect the penitents to be guilty of restlessness of the body—"we cannot halt" (116). The word the abbot uses to describe discourtesy, *villania,* is derived from the word *villano* (a peasant, one who works with and is close to the earth), so as to acknowledge the interrelation between the material and the spiritual, which the pilgrim may not yet entirely understand.

The abbot then introduces himself with a reference to Frederick Barbarossa's domination of that legendarily proud city, Milan:

> I was St. Zeno's abbot in Verona
> under the rule of valiant Barbarossa,
> of whom Milan still speaks with so much sorrow.
>
> (118–120)

The reference to Frederick Barbarossa celebrates a virtuous authority. As the abbot proceeds to point out, God's children are sometimes interested in their own power and material welfare, to the detriment of spiritual values:

> And there is one with one foot in the grave,
> who soon will weep over that monastery,
> lamenting that he once had power there,
>   because, in place of its true shepherd, he
> put one who was unsound of body and,
> still more, of mind, and born in sin—his son.
>
> (121–126)

The people referred to here are Alberto della Scala and his illegitimate son, Giuseppe, who was abbot of San Zeno from 1292 to 1313. Alberto della Scala also had three legitimate sons, one of whom was Cangrande della Scala. The abbot's criticism of his successor's behavior, following on his praise of Frederick Barbarossa, is an attempt to put temporal power and politics into perspective: Frederick, known as a handsome man of fine character, razed Milan to the ground; Alberto della Scala, described here as practically underground himself, exalted his physically and mentally infirm, and illegitimate, son in a way that makes a travesty out of authority and power. Politics, the abbot emphasizes, is a crucial force in the striving for spiritual good and ought to remain in the service of God and of virtue.

Sleep

The pilgrim's encounter with the penitents on the Fourth Terrace appears, however, to prompt no significant change in him. Once the slothful are out of sight, their lesson is out of mind, and the pilgrim retreats once again into his own wandering thoughts:

> Then, when those shades were so far off from us
> that seeing them became impossible,
> a new thought rose inside of me and, from
>   that thought, still others—many and diverse—
> were born: I was so drawn from random thought
> to thought that, wandering in mind, I shut
>   my eyes, transforming thought on thought to dream.
>
> (139–145)

The pilgrim closes his eyes not because he is weary at the end of his second day in Purgatory, but because he is almost hypnotically fixated on his thoughts. His dream—which, as we shall see in the next canto, is the dream of the siren—leaves us with a final doubt. In which of the three categories of dreams outlined by Alanus de Insulis in his *Contra Acediam* (*Summa de Arte Praedicatoria,* cap. VII) would we place this dream: that of contemplation *(contemplationis)*, imagination *(imaginationis)*, or idleness *(pigritiae)*?

BIBLIOGRAPHICAL NOTES

The following are relevant articles and books, some of which are cited in the above text: Francis Fergusson, "Canto XVIII: The Fruit of Philosophy," in *Dante's Drama of the Mind: A Modern Reading of the "Purgatorio"* (Princeton: Princeton University Press, 1953), 88–98; John Freccero, "The Firm Foot on a Journey without a Guide," in *Dante: The Poetics of Conversion,* ed. Rachel Jacoff (Cambridge, MA.: Harvard University Press, 1986), 29–54; Lloyd Howard, "Virgil's Discourse on Love in *Purgatorio* XVIII and Guido Cavalcanti," *Quaderni d'italianistica* 6, no. 2 (1985): 167–177; Giorgio Padoan, "Il canto XVIII del *Purgatorio,*" in *Lectura Dantis Scaligera* (Florence: Le Monnier, 1967), 2:657–688; Pier Giorgio Ricci, "Il canto XVIII del *Purgatorio,*" in *Nuove letture dantesche,* Casa di Dante in Roma (Florence: Le Monnier, 1970), 4: 251–265; Christopher J. Ryan, "Free Will in Theory and Practice: *Purgatorio* XVIII and Two Characters in the *Inferno,*" in *Dante Soundings: Eight Literary and Historical Essays,* ed. David Nolan (Totowa, NJ: Rowman and Littlefield, 1981), 100–112; Fernando Salsano, "Dialoghi meditativi nel centro del *Purgatorio,*" in *La coda di Minosse e altri saggi danteschi* (Milan: Marzorati, 1968), 109–155; Dorothy L. Sayers, "The Cornice of Sloth," in *Further Papers on Dante* (New York: Harper & Brothers, 1957), 119–147; Bernard Stambler, *Dante's Other World: The "Purgatorio" as Guide to the "Divine Comedy"* (New York: New York University Press, 1957), 178–183; Giuseppe Tarozzi, "Il canto XVIII del *Purgatorio,*" in *Letture dantesche,* ed. Giovanni Getto (Florence: Sansoni, 1958), 2: 349–372; Siegfried Wenzel, *The Sin of Sloth: Acedia in Medieval Thought and Literature* (Chapel Hill: University of North Carolina Press, 1967).

Also invaluable are the commentaries on the *Purgatorio* by Manfredi Porena (Bologna: Zanichelli, 1965), Natalino Sapegno (Milan-Naples: Ricciardi, 1957), and Charles Singleton (Princeton, NJ: Princeton University Press, 1973).

Theological writings referred to here are Thomas Aquinas, *Summa Theologica*, trans. Fathers of the English Dominican Province, 3 vols. (New York: Benziger Brothers, 1947–1948); and Alanus de Insulis, *Summa de Arte Praedicatoria*, cap. VII, "Contra Acediam," in *PL* 210, col. 126.

CANTO XIX

Vectors of Human Love

SARA STURM-MADDOX

Canto XIX of the *Purgatorio* has not been among the most favored in terms of its readers' attention. A survey of its critical history reveals, moreover, that readers have been attracted largely by one element, that of the dream of the siren with which the canto begins. The account of the pilgrim's dream, however, occupies only nine tercets, or twenty-seven verses out of a total of 145. Even if we include in the episode the two introductory tercets that afford a temporal orientation, as well as the dreamer's awakening to Virgil's call and the latter's explanation of the dream experience, we account for no more than some forty-two verses, rather less than one-third of the canto. In fact, Virgil's very brief explanation is followed by an uncharacteristically abrupt admonition to get on with the business at hand, the ascent of the mountain: "Let that suffice, and hurry on your way" (61). Assuming that Dante's disposition of his narrative *materia* within the controlled confines of the numbered canto structure is seldom arbitrary, we may, with some profit, consider the various elements of Canto XIX not only individually but as parts of a significant whole.

The Prelude

For the prelude to the pilgrim's dream we must return to the end of the preceding canto. It is after nightfall: following the rapid departure of the souls of the penitent slothful, Dante and Virgil find themselves unable to continue their progress toward the passage that leads from the Fourth to the Fifth Terrace. Obedient to the "rule of the mountain" that active advancement can be made only by day, the pilgrim remains immobile. During his first night on the mountain, in the Valley of the Princes, where the penitent kept prayerful vigil, his somnolent state served as a reminder that he alone of the company was a living man:

> when I, who bore something of Adam with me,
> feeling the need for sleep, lay down upon
> the grass.
>
> (IX, 10–12)

Dante had described his falling asleep on that occasion. In contrast to this discontinuity, this rupture between the waking and sleeping states, the passage between those states, is now represented as one of continuity, a gradual shading in which thought becomes dream:

> A new thought rose inside of me and, from
> that thought, still others—many and diverse—
> were born: I was so drawn from random thought
> to thought that, wandering in mind, I shut
> my eyes, transforming thought on thought to dream.
>
> (XVIII, 141–145)

This description, soporific in its own meandering, closes the canto in effective anticipation of the dream to follow.

The air of expectancy with which Canto XVIII closes is heightened by the opening verses of Canto XIX, as Dante briefly delays the account of the dream to set the stage for its occurrence: it is that coldest hour before dawn,

> In that hour when the heat of day, defeated
> by Earth and, sometimes, Saturn, can no longer
> warm up the moon-sent cold.
>
> (1–3)

This is, then, the hour when the sun's warming effect is least felt on the inhabited planet; within the pervasive sun symbolism of the *Comedy*, it suggests a time of alienation, reinforced by the verb *vinto*, "defeated," which suggests the cosmic struggle between light and darkness. But by the same token, it is the hour that precedes the sun's return, as Dante immediately reminds us in the following tercet. The *Fortuna Major* to which he refers is a configuration of stars divided between the constellations of Aquarius and

Pisces, so called because in divination it was read as a sign of good fortune. In the simplest sense, the allusion functions as a temporal indicator: if Pisces is rising, the sun—known at this date in the *Comedy* to be in Aries—is soon to follow. It is predawn, then; yet as a purely temporal marker the mention is superfluous, for Dante immediately adds that this configuration is seen in the east, before dawn.

The reader's attention is drawn, then, not to these stars but rather to those who concern themselves with this sign in the heavens, the geomancers. By noting that the *Fortuna Major* pertains to the geomancers—it is identified as "their" sign—Dante reminds us that our astrological reference, unlike the many others found throughout the *Comedy*, is not to the great heavenly signs that will reappear in the *Paradiso*, majestically circling in the heavens, but rather to a sign contrived by men in an attempt to read the future. But Dante's reader has already encountered soothsayers in the otherworld of the poem: in retribution for the willed distortion of their sight as they attempted to look ahead, they are condemned to the fourth pouch of *Inferno*'s Eighth Circle, where they pace eternally with their heads twisted to the rear. In light of this rejection of human attempts to read God's design and thus to influence events, we cannot validate the reference to the *Fortuna Major* as a positive omen for the pilgrim. The activity of the geomancers prepares us, however, for the magical atmosphere of the dream to follow.

The Dream

That dream, in fact, has a particularly hallucinatory quality. A hideous woman appears to the dreamer, the degree and detail of her deformity immediately marking her for a symbolic role. Under his steady gaze she is transformed into a beautiful creature who begins a seductive song, the theme of which is her own irresistibility. It is she who leads mariners astray, she who had enticed Ulysses from his course, she who can fulfill all the desires of those who succumb to her spell. Because Ulysses' voyage is a major subtext of the pilgrim's journey in the *Comedy*, readers have frequently sought for the siren's meaning in Dante's presumed sources. Her boastful claim concerning Ulysses in particular has prompted a wealth of commentary, precisely because it does not conform to the role of the sirens in that epic voyage: forewarned by Circe and bound securely to the mast, Ulysses was piloted safely past the sirens' rocks by a crew whose ears were literally sealed. It is generally conceded that Dante, who had not read the *Odyssey*, knew the episode instead from a passage of Cicero's *De Finibus*; some readers conclude that he misread his secondary source, others that he conflated the sirens and the enchantress Circe. Most important, however, is the recontextualization of the siren in Dante's own poem. Whether or not she is to be understood as lying in her claim, whether or not Dante deliberately altered his sources, it is clear that the effect of which she boasts is produced in the pilgrim himself, since he is mesmerized by her song:

> then she
> began to sing so, that it would have been
> most difficult for me to turn aside."
>
> (16–18)

While the dreamer listens, enthralled and apparently helpless, a lady suddenly appears at his side. To Virgil, whose presence has not previously been noted within the dream, she addresses a scornful demand: "O Virgil, Virgil, tell me: who is this?" (28). The question is apparently rhetorical, because it calls forth not words, but violent action: Virgil comes forward, the siren is seized, her clothes are torn away, her exposed belly is shown to the pilgrim, and from it comes a stench so powerful that it brings the dream to a precipitous end.

A Question of Identity

Thus the lady's question concerning the siren is answered, not with a name, but with a demonstration. But who indeed is this, she who presides over the siren's unmasking? The question has been much disputed, with proposals ranging from abstractions such as Reason or the active life personified to personages already known in the poem: an angelic messenger similar to the one who had opened the gates of Dis for the pilgrim and Virgil, or Lucia, or even Beatrice herself. It is neither necessary nor appropriate, however, to insist on such a precise identification, not only because Dante does not suggest it, but also because the lady, like the siren, is a figure exclusively of the pilgrim's dream. What is evident is that the *femmina*, or siren, and the lady are set in opposition: the lady is not only quick to act but *santa*, "saintly" or "holy," and the stench that issues from the siren's belly upon this lady's intervention suggests the presence of corruption.

The dream of the siren serves a particular structural function, linking the central doctrine of the *Purgatorio*, the lesson in human love pronounced by Virgil in the preceding canto, with the final terraces of the mountain that lie above. By God man is "created quick to love" (XVIII, 19), Virgil had told Dante, and innate in man is the response to pleasing stimuli. But not all loves are praiseworthy: free will, Virgil explains, is also innate and given to man as "keeper of the threshold / of . . . assent" (XVIII, 63–64), so that he may order the response to the myriad potential objects of love. These two principles are the basis of the small drama staged in the pilgrim's dream; his spellbound reaction to the siren's song illustrates the instinctive response to the stimulus of pleasure, while the lady who appears to confound the siren dramatizes the intervention of that "power that counsels" (XVIII, 63) to abort the seductive

program. Resuming the ascent with his now pensive charge, Virgil will identify the siren as she for whom atonement must be made on the terraces
above, and this too is consonant with the master's earlier discourse: the pilgrim is about to enter that tripartite region already described to him (XVII,
138) where he will encounter penitents who sinned through excessive love of
secondary objects of desire.

That the dream of the siren should prefigure an experience yet to come
is fully in keeping with medieval dream psychology, in which dreams are assumed to reveal something not about, but to, the dreamer. The interpretation of dreams, and of predawn dreams in particular, as warnings and
premonitions had its roots deep in antiquity: medieval theologians acknowledged dreams as a channel for divine revelation. Yet the dream in
Canto XIX is not fully explained by the anticipatory and didactic functions
attributed to it by Virgil. In fact, the dream of the siren marks one of the
points of closest convergence between the allegorical and personal levels of
the Dante-pilgrim's story. The conflict between the siren and the saintly
lady in the dream is simultaneously the sign of an inner tension that has
from the beginning marked the story of the protagonist of the *Commedia*: a
certain Dante who recently found himself lost in a dark wood. Dante's
dreams in *Purgatorio,* of course, are not part of the divinely ordained pattern of purgation on the mountain. The penitent souls on the terraces,
who have no living bodies, do not sleep, nor do they dream; thus the
dreaming function can be attributed to Dante alone, and it may be expected to be highly personal, personally and individually relevant to this
unique pilgrim caught up not just in the struggle of Everyman but in one
that is peculiarly his own.

The World's Enticements

On this personal level the dream of the siren suggests two things. First, the
fact that Dante remains apparently spellbound until the intervention of the
saintly lady demonstrates that divine assistance is still necessary to this
particular pilgrim's progress. In this, her role recalls that of the angel who
opened the gates of Dis when the Furies threatened to block the pilgrim's
passage, as well as Lucia who had carried him upward to the gate of Purgatory. It also points backward to the Beatrice who had first sought out Virgil
to help the errant Dante, and forward to the Beatrice who will come to
meet him in the Earthly Paradise, to whom in the *Paradiso* he will gratefully exclaim:

> "You drew me out from slavery to freedom
> by all those paths, by all those means that were
> within your power."

> (*Par.* XXXI, 85–87)

Second, the fact that the obstacle to his progress is now figured by the siren suggests a particular vulnerability on the part of the pilgrim. The siren's lure not only anticipates those sins to be purged above: traditionally, she bears strong associations with a particular form of concupiscence, that of lust. In Dante's dream, in which his rapt gaze colors and transforms her "as love prefers" (14), it is evident that her attraction is specifically feminine. Virgil observes that the pilgrim has learned from his dream how to free himself from the siren. He refers to that alert and unbewitched moral vision that sees the world's enticements for what they are, while at the same time refusing to be specific about the sin of lust. The point is more general, that the saintly lady and the siren (opposite in the nature of their attempt to influence his journey) are dramatic rivals for this dreamer's allegiance.

That the temptations represented by the siren, and in particular by the pilgrim's pliant yielding to their spell, carry a special autobiographical weight in the poem will receive confirmation in Dante's reunion with Beatrice in the Earthly Paradise. There, after evoking his promising *vita nova* in which she had sustained him, she will sternly rebuke him for his straying after her death, framing her reproach in terms of a "green young girl or other novelty" offering "brief delight." At that time, she will add, her own attempts to call him back "in dreams and otherwise" were unsuccessful because he was intent on "things deceptive." The siren in the dream on Mt. Purgatory, from her initial hideous appearance to the stench accompanying her eventual unmasking, is a "thing deceptive" who in this sense figures as Beatrice's rival: she has been termed both a "false Beatrice," offering promises of eternal happiness that she cannot fulfill, and an "anti-Beatrice." Beatrice will again retrospectively confirm this reading: she insists in her approach, she will tell Dante,

> "that you may feel more shame
> for your mistake, and that—in time to come—
> hearing the Sirens, you may be more strong."
>
> (XXXI, 43–45)

Look Up Instead

Virgil's presence relates the dreamworld to the waking one. Roused to action within the dream by the saintly lady's exclamation, he now wakes the pilgrim by calling him to resume the ascent in the sunlight of a new day. Yet despite its abrupt ending, in which the stench of the siren's opened belly conjoins with Virgil's insistent call, the dream that has its origin in Dante's wandering thought is retransformed into thought, no longer wandering, but fixed and intent. Now it is a burden, one physically apparent in Dante's bearing as he follows in Virgil's footsteps "like one / whose thoughts have weighed him down" (40–41). Thus the beatitude of this terrace pronounced by the angel (from Matthew 5:4), *Qui lugent,* applies to the pilgrim personally as well as to the penitent slothful, whose frenzied running exemplifies their mourning for their past error. "Surgi e vieni," Virgil urges him, "Rise and come" (35)—yet Dante's preoccupation continues even through the ritual encounter with the angel, with the pronunciation of the beatitude and the removal of yet another *P* from his forehead.

Thus it is that we find the pilgrim still bent by his dream, and to break its lingering spell Virgil exhorts him to look up instead, toward the lure of the firmament as it is whirled by God. This image, briefly conveyed in two verses and ignored in many readings of the canto, is one of the most dramatic of the *Purgatorio* and among the most daring in its anthropomorphic suggestiveness. Dorothy Sayers's response captures its evocative power: "Of all the images of Deity with which religious literature has supplied us," she writes, "I know nothing . . . which can compare for boldness, for gaiety, for sheer, breathtaking excitement, with this picture of God the Falconer, riding out, hawking for souls, whirling the whole glitter of the immeasurable heavens about His head like a lure" (147). The image certainly has its effect on the pilgrim, for it functions like the falconer's cry of the hawking simile that now follows: alerted to his desire for this heavenly reward, the pilgrim, like the falcon when it soars after its prey, speeds upward through the passage in the rock to the terrace above.

Proceeding through a cleft in the rock, Dante and Virgil emerge into the fifth of Mt. Purgatory's circles and find at their feet souls prostrate on the ground, bound hand and foot. Immobilized with their faces to the earth, they repeat with tears and sighing a verse from Psalm 19, *Adhaesit pavimento anima mea.* This, we will discover, is a purgatorial instance of the *contrapasso:* just as their souls in life had clung to the earth, so now their purgatorial bodies are bound closely to it. These are the avaricious, and as one of them will explain to Dante, their state now makes visible the work of avarice, "quel ch'avarizia fa" ("what avarice enacts," 115). Just as their avarice had precluded all good works in life, so now their hands and feet are literally bound; they are unable to avert their eyes from the ground because in life their eyes, fixed on earthly things, had not turned toward Heaven.

The Informant

Dante's informant, while his face cannot be seen, does not seek to protect his anonymity. Rather, in answer to Dante's questioning, he reveals in solemn Latin that he had been a pope, successor to Peter. Finding a pope here among the avaricious does not seem to surprise the pilgrim, and the reader too is well prepared. Already in the Fourth Circle of the *Inferno,* discoursing on various forms of excessive preoccupation with worldly goods, Virgil had identified avarice as a characteristic fault of the clergy, pointing out "clergymen, and popes and cardinals, / within whom avarice works its excess" (*Inf.* VII, 47–48). The worst form of avarice, according to St. Bonaventure and others, is simony, the particularly clerical offense of selling spiritual goods or ecclesiastical office, and this too receives its just retribution in the *Comedy:* simoniac popes are immobilized in flaming holes in the rock of the Eighth Circle. Dante's indignation there is not nuanced by respect for the papal office; learning the identity of the cupidinous Nicolas III, he bursts into a lengthy and vehement condemnation of papal avarice "that afflicts the world" (see *Inf.* XIX, 90–117).

While this pope does not give his name, he offers enough biographical clues to assume the pilgrim recognizes him. The family crest to which he alludes enables us to identify him as Pope Adrian V (Ottobuono de' Fieschi of Genova), nephew of Innocent IV; he assumed the papal mantle in 1276, to rule "for one month and a little more"—historically, for some thirty-eight days. In response to Dante's question eliciting the names of any still on earth who might be asked to speed his progress in Purgatory with their prayers, he mentions only one, his niece Alagia. There is some debate over the identity of this virtuous lady; it is likely that she was the wife of Moroella Malaspina, a member of the noble family who had hosted Dante, and that she figures here as one of the compliments offered by Dante in the *Commedia* to the patrons of his exile years.

Historically there is little confirmation of the characterization of Adrian V as avaricious. It has been proposed that Dante may have confused him with Pope Adrian IV, cited as avaricious in the *Policraticus* of John of Salisbury. Tonelli has suggested instead that the conversion to which Adrian refers, turning him at once from avidity for riches and power to love of Heaven, accompanied his ascension to the papacy. In either case, its point is unmistakable: he was to discover, with Augustine, that only in God can the heart find peace.

In opening his self-identification with a Latin phrase, Adrian has been accused by some readers of haughtiness, of an obdurate pride. Yet his use of Latin here, like his later citation of Scripture, is in keeping with the solemnity of his office, and it is precisely the juxtaposition between his former eminence as pope and his present position as penitent that reminds us of the biblical admonition against pride: that he who is most exalted in worldly terms shall be cast most low. Adrian himself seems intent on pointing out that lesson to the pilgrim. When he senses that Dante has assumed a kneeling posture beside his supine figure and hears the pilgrim defer to the dignity of the papal office, he responds quickly and sharply: "Rise up!... / Don't be mistaken!" (133–134). The Scriptural phrase, *Neque nubent,* to which he calls Dante's attention, drawn from a parable in which Jesus proclaims the nonperseverance of matrimonial bonds in Heaven, here also evokes all other symbolic marriages, including that which weds popes to their office. With death the latter bond, like all others, is dissolved: Adrian remains no more and no less than "a fellow-servant of one

Power" (135)—presently, a penitent among penitents. In any case, it is in his solitude that we will remember Dante's Pope Adrian. Even his recall of his papal service suggests the solitary burden of he who assumes that charge, in his evocation of "how the great mantle weighs on him who'd keep it/out of the mire" (104–105). Now he dispatches Dante so that he may continue his own lamentations, and the canto closes with his saying that of all his household, inclined to wickedness, only the good Alagia "is left to me beyond" (145).

Earthbound or Soaring

A sober canto, then, and an admonitory one. For free will to serve its function, it must be alerted; one must be able to read the signs. We recall that it is the astrological configuration of the *Fortuna Major* that presides over the encounter with the siren. To God's signs, the immutable constellations fixed in the heavens, the geomancers oppose a sign of their own contriving; likewise the siren, who will be identified by Virgil as "that ancient witch" (58), proposes her own magic: she predicts not good fortune but total satisfaction of desire. It is for yielding to the desire for worldly possessions that the avaricious now lie bound, and these possessions too can be seductive. In Book IV of his *Convivio*, Dante characterizes riches as deceiving harlots, "false *meritrici*," in that they promise all satisfaction, *ogni appagamento*—we recall Dante's siren's claim, "I satisfy him so" (24)—but deliver instead the contrary. In the account of Pope Adrian, no holy lady is credited with the unmasking of the siren; rather, Adrian bears personal witness that worldly riches and power cannot quiet the heart and still its restless desire.

The two episodes are bound together by the postures of the two men, the pilgrim bending to his dream, Adrian bent to the earth. They are punctuated by an image that further unites them, with the reminder that the soul has an alternative: looking above, it will find a different powerful attraction for its affection, in the heavenly lure whirled by God as the great falconer.

Binding and rising, earthbound and soaring: spiritual vectors, then, are repeatedly underscored in both segments of the canto. The pilgrim, bound by the recollection of his dream, prompts Virgil's demand: "What makes you keep your eyes upon the ground?" (52). Attentive then to the heavenly lure, he speeds upward like the falcon craving the food that draws him. Pope Adrian, though now prostrate, is also intent on Heaven, describing his conversion in terms of the kindling of his desire for the celestial prize: "Nor could I, in that life, ascend more high;/so that, in me, love for this life was kindled" (110–111). Two narrow escapes, we might say: the pilgrim's dream experience of escape from the spell of the siren is confirmed in the pope's story of his late conversion. For both, in their different ways, the path of ascent remains open, and the ultimate goal still lies ahead.

BIBLIOGRAPHICAL NOTES

Most of the general studies of the *Purgatorio* devote some attention to the dream of the siren in this canto. Among the readings of Canto XIX, the reader may consult Dorothy Sayers, "The Cornice of Sloth," in *Further Papers on Dante* (London, 1957), 119–147, and in Italian the following: Mario Marti, "Il canto XIX del *Purgatorio*" (Turin: 1962), 5–28; G. Paparelli, "Il canto XIX del *Purgatorio*," in *Nuove letture dantesche* (Florence, 1970), 267–306; L. Tonelli, "Il canto XIX del *Purgatorio*," in *Letture dantesche,* ed. G. Getto (Florence, 1962), 375–394. For the dream of the siren see Robert Hollander, *Allegory in Dante's Commedia* (Princeton, 1969), 136–144; Glyn P. Norton, "Retrospection and Prefiguration in the Dreams of *Purgatorio*," *Italica* 47 (1970): 351–365; and Charles Speroni, "Dante's Prophetic Morning Dreams," *Studies in Philology* 45 (1948): 50–59.

CANTO XX

Hugh Capet and the Avarice of Kings

VINCENT MOLETA

The subject of Canto XX is avarice, for Dante the most detestable of vices. Avarice—in this case the collective avarice of the kings of France, who in the poet's lifetime thwarted the election of an emperor and effectively subjugated the papacy—destroys the ordered fabric of life, and the canto is notable for an impassioned speech delivered by a shade, Hugh Capet, who is a mouthpiece for the poet's anti-gallicism. Canto XX is virtually devoid of lyricism, as befits the gravity of the vice, and it can be seen to fall into three parts, with a sustained central speech flanked by two outer narrative members. There is a broadly descriptive opening, up to line 33, a long declamatory stasis in direct speech, in lines 34 to 123, and a provisional narrative close from line 124 to the end of the canto. The passion of the central speech is tempered by the narrative recorded in the outer members of the canto, while the first and last *terzine*, which describe interior states in the pilgrim-poet, ensure continuity from Cantos XIX to XX and from XX to XXI. Besides harnessing a specific polemical motif to the scheme of the cornice, Canto XX demonstrates well the simple elements of Dante's dramatic style, for the tentative mobility and relative silence of the travelers highlight the voluntary immobility of the souls on this ledge and the splendid assurance with which Hugh Capet speaks.

The Descriptive Opening

1–3: the double chiasmus in the first two lines, "miglior voler voler mal.../...'l piacer mio, per piacerli" ("Against a better will, the will fights . . . / . . . to please him, though against my pleasure"), ensures a tight interlace between the preceding canto and this one, and through a conceptualized expression of mental conflict the poet eases the way for his own imminent response to the vice of avarice, as it was described by Hadrian in Canto XIX. If the pilgrim overcomes his reluctance to obey the pope's injunction, "Drizza le gambe, lèvati sù, frate! . . . Vattene omai" ("Brother, straighten your legs; rise up! . . . Now go your way," XIX, 133, 139), he shows how far he still is from the "religïone / de la montagna" ("the sanctity / of these slopes," XXI, 40–41) which, as Statius will explain, lies in perfect conformity with the divine will. In the apt third line, the colorful metaphor, the first in a string of familiar images that confer an air of popular eloquence on the central harangue, is governed by the precise verb used by the poet to convey physical proximity to the chosen souls in this cornice: "trassi de l'acqua" ("I drew . . . out of the water") as he straightens up beside Hadrian. It had been "trassimi sovra quella creatura" ("I moved ahead and bent over that soul," XIX, 89) when he first bent over Hadrian. He will later say "io mi trassi oltre" ("I / moved forward," 28–29) as he draws alongside Hugh Capet. That is, a narrative hint, given in the metaphor, leads to the explicit forward movement recorded in the next two *terzine*.

4–9: the two descriptive lines, 4 and 5, are clarified by an incisive comparative term, line 6, which brings this ledge to life by recalling, for a city-state audience, the common experience of citizen volunteers keeping watch. Apart from the equally terse lines 21 and 81, there will be no further simile until the closing section of the canto. The next line ostensibly completes this firm topographical incipit by explaining why the travelers must keep to the rock face at the inside of the ledge as they pick their way past the prostrate bodies; but in the dense double relative clause defining these souls as repentant, *avari* (7–8), the poet asserts, as if it were narrative fact, the relentless and minutely measured purgation, "a goccia a goccia" ("drop by drop," 7), that awaits a vice that is on earth rampant and apparently irresistible. In the long, serrated line 8 (of fifteen syllables if unelided), we sense the poet's dismay at the hopeless impracticability of his own frugal ideal: "per li occhi il mal che tutto 'l mondo occupa" ("the evil that possesses all the world," 8). It is this sentiment that prompts the seemingly abrupt exclamation and rhetorical question in the next two *terzine*.

10–15: as if preempting the pilgrim's response to the discourse of Hugh Capet, the poet drops his narrative guise to recover an emblematic image he had introduced in the first canto of the *Comedy*. There, at the very start of his journey, in an uneasy blend of narrative and allegory, the pilgrim had been blocked and forced back by a ravenous she wolf, evidently a symbol of cupidity; but in the same canto, Virgil had reassured him that the *lupa* ("wolf," *Inf.* I, 49) would eventually be driven off and killed by the *veltro* ("greyhound," *Inf.* I, 101), probably a symbol of a Holy Roman Emperor. Thus the pervasive evil of avarice as a socially destructive force was identified in traditional animal form at the beginning of the poem; in the course of the journey, it has taken recognizable contemporary shape in Florentine mercantile activity and social mobility, in the Italian disunity procured by politically ambitious popes, and in the disarray of an *imperium* without an effective head, all of which the poet berates throughout the poem. By now the image of the *lupa* needs no gloss, and it can be restored directly to its proper proverbial and non-narrative context, reinforced by a single epithet to convey its ageless voracity: *antica lupa* ("ancient wolf," 10). Yet the memory of Virgil's initial promise now prompts the poet to cry out for an earthly savior to come in his turn, and the rhetorical question draws on the lesson of Fortune handed down by Virgil in *Inferno* VII, the canto of the damned avaricious. If earthly affairs mutate in a way that matches the ineluctable circling of the heavens, surely avarice will eventually be toppled from its present supremacy in human affairs. In these two imprecatory *terzine*, inserted seemingly against the grain of the narrative, the poet conflates the allegory for avarice in *Inferno* I with the sublime lesson of indifference to Fortune in *Inferno* VII, and he shows how the pilgrim's separate acquisitions in earlier steps of the journey can be fused and distilled in a later passage, thus ensuring for the poem, across the intervals between the periods of its composition, a unity of vision that resides in the identity of the poet with his pilgrim person. Thus the next line, 16, and the set of examples it introduces, need not be seen as a glaring suture; rather, the economy of the cornice scheme and the preamble required for the next encounter reassert themselves, and the poet can slip back to his narrative with two verbs in the imperfect tense, "noi andavam . . . / i' sentia" ("as we moved on . . . / I heard," 16–17), which close any gap opened up by the preceding two *terzine* and refresh our sympathy for the victims of avarice strewn along the rock ledge, where they were when we first met them in the previous canto (XIX, 70–75).

16–33: the examples of virtue contrary to avarice had been withheld since the travelers entered this cornice midway through the previous canto and had been preceded, unusually, by an encounter with one of the repentant *avari*, Pope Hadrian V, so as to align his disposition with that of Pope Nicholas III in *Inferno* XIX and to place an exemplary statement of the *contrapasso* for avarice in the mouth of a recent pope. The narrative of each cornice is framed as a rule by the counterbalancing examples of whip (virtue) and bridle (vice), disposed on either side of a central meeting with souls representative of that cornice. In Canto XX, the whip examples precede Hugh Capet's denunciation of avarice, and the bridle examples follow it; and since the canto begins and ends with narrative movement along the ledge and contains all the *exempla*, plus a major statement by a representative shade, we have here the essentials of the cornice of avarice condensed into one canto. All that is lacking are the concluding rites, the beatitude and the erasure of the *P*, held over until the start of Canto XXII. From this we can see that of the four cantos over which this cornice is spread (XIX, 70–XXII, 117), the specific attack on avarice is concentrated in Canto XX: hence the stylistic tension and the unusual and harsh rhymes present throughout. Hugh Capet's violent denunciation of his own offspring is carefully contained within a framework of formal exemplification, its rhetorical excess thus being curbed in the process.

Although Hugh will assure the pilgrim, at the end of his speech (121–123), that he was not alone in reciting the examples of virtue, the single voice that the pilgrim hears is that of Hugh Capet (35–36), and it is he who makes these examples appropriate to his own case. In the first exemplum, 19–24, the opening phrase, *Dolce Maria!* (19), expresses the positive fruitfulness of the soul's purgation and announces the theme of the Nativity, for the voice sounds like that of a woman in labor. Yet the lines introduce no mere note of sweetness into the canto. The self-spoliation of the King of Kings was a favorite theme of Mendicant piety, and since this supreme example of voluntary poverty is couched here as the *mother's* choice (24), Hugh Capet, the butcher's son who planted his own son on the throne of France, this overweening king maker (52–60), invokes the example of a parent who chose to despoil, from birth, the earthly trappings of her divine son.

The second example (25–27) is also tuned to the political diatribe about to follow, and the name, once again in the strong, rhyming position, now determines a syntactic inversion by which the contrasting motifs of *povertà* ("indigence") and *ricchezza* ("wealth"), *virtute* ("virtue") and *vizio* ("vice") are visually matched in each line and with insistent alliteration (26, 27), leaving the key element of choice and rejection to be brought out by the verb, straight after the *caesura* in both lines. Fabricius had already entered the canon of Dante's Roman heroes in the *Convivio,* in a list of *magnanimi* whose selfless patriotic virtue had confirmed the providential mission of Rome well before the Incarnation (*Conv.* IV, v, 13). This echo, conflated with two passages in the *Monarchia* (II, v, 11; x, 7), suggests that the poet, in his generic praise of Fabricius in our canto, had in mind two famous refusals by the Roman consul, one of tribute money offered by the Samnites after a peace treaty, the other of a bribe offered him by Pyrrhus over an exchange of prisoners. At the center of Hugh Capet's speech, 61–93, the butt of his tirade is the cupidity behind the political and military activity of the Anjou and the Valois. Against that ongoing history of tribal greed, the ancient republican figure of Fabricius is invoked as an enduring model of political rectitude, defined by the one epithet that declares his simple honesty: *O buon Fabrizio* (25).

Now, in lines 28–30, at the point of transition from exempla to dialogue with one of the souls, the poet sacrifices to narrative function any direct speech in the mandatory third example; yet he is careful to include an example of unostentatious liberality that also bears on the subsequent tirade. Lines 32–33 recall an incident in the early life of St. Nicholas of Myra, when the young nobleman, hearing that a neighbor, unable to afford dowries, was about to sell his three virgin daughters into prostitution, secretly entered the house on three occasions to leave a bag of gold as ample dowry for each of the girls. In Dante's shorthand, this legend is turned into an example of exquisite paternal delicacy, and it establishes a precise measure of the depravity of the Anjou prince, Charles I (61), who married by force the heiress already betrothed to the duchy of Provence, and of that of his son, Charles II (79), who sold his daughter into the d'Este family to gain control through her of Modena and Reggio Emilia.

This brings us to the oration at the center of the canto, ninety lines of direct speech unbroken by any narrative description. In the fourth circle of Hell (*Inf.* VII) the pilgrim meets no single *avarus* or prodigal, thus no character portrayal detracts from the punishment of the vice. On the Fifth Terrace of Purgatory, the souls are represented by three individuals—Pope Adrian, Hugh Capet, and Statius—who impersonate the poet's mature understanding of the nature and effects of avarice, and of the working of justice on the mountain. Through Hugh Capet, founder of the Capetian dynasty, the poet pronounces his solemn judgment on the French dissolution of the Roman institutions of empire and papacy.

Hugh Capet's Declaration

34–42: in the pilgrim's address the exempla are grafted to the dialogue (34) as if he were interrupting the last exemplum ("esso parlava ancor," "he kept on speaking," 31), and he uses a variant of the *captatio benevolentiae* that is standard in the *Purgatorio* (37–39). In earlier cantos this bait was taken instantly because it presupposed a living bond between those on earth, who pray for the dead, and the shades in Purgatory, whose suffering is alleviated by those prayers; this is the secret of that tenderness that suffuses so many encounters on the mountain face. But here the unexpected reply anticipates the speaker's blanket rejection of his latest offspring, and, as a formal opening (40–42), it mirrors the separate conditions of the two speakers: the pilgrim, alive but more than ever aware of his mortality and of the need to rectify his life before death; the shade, bodily dead but saved and repossessed of his human faculties as he suffers in preparation for beatitude, aware as no living person could be of the miraculous privilege that the pilgrim has been given "nel mezzo del cammin" ("half of our life's way," *Inf.* I, I).

43–48: the shade begins to answer the first question, "dimmi chi fosti" ("do tell me who you were," 35), not yet with his name but with a figure of speech that acknowledges grievous responsibility and with a cry for vengeance on what he himself has sired. These two *terzine* contain the main elements of the following discourse—its pungent metaphor, its historical extremism, and its manipulation of the time sequence for prophecy of an apocalyptic judgment. They do so with an intensification of the harsh rhymes (*-anta*, *-uggia*, *-etta*) which, since the mid-1290s, when the poet entered political life and at the same time brought stylistic asperity into his repertoire, had signaled his adoption of the mantle of *cantor rectitudinis*. The speaker was, he says, the hidden taproot of that poisonous tree that now blocks out the light from all Christendom, which is what makes the *terra cristiana* godless, if the sun is an image of its maker. But Dante has something more specific in mind when he floats the idea of an all-enveloping shadow *(aduggia)* cast by the infected tree. In *Purgatorio* XVI he had called emperor and pope the "two suns" that illuminate separately the natural and the spiritual paths of a man's life, twin luminaries ordained by Providence to guide the destiny of the human race. The light blocked out by the *mala pianta* ("obnoxious plant," 43) is that of both suns, and hence the essence of the poet's lament lies already in the unpretentious metaphor at the start of Hugh Capet's story (43–44). As so often happens in the *Comedy,* a prevailing sentiment or leitmotif is released through a simple figure of speech by which the poet's singular vision displays at the outset the conviction of a proverbial dictum. Now it is not the imperial dream that is uppermost in the poet's mind, but the double demise of Roman *imperium* and Roman papacy, brought about by the House of France; and the next *terzina*, 46–48, introduces the visionary and imprecatory element informing the latter half of Hugh Capet's biography. This too hinges on the present time of the pilgrim's journey, spring 1300. We need to know that between 1297 and 1299, Philippe le Bel and his brother, Charles of Valois, annexed Flanders, but that in 1302, a Flemish league inflicted a heavy defeat on the French at Courtrai. The prophecy (46–47) is phrased *per impossibilia* as an unrealizable hypothesis; the cry for revenge (48) can be seen to have been answered in the event. Now we pass to the biography proper, through a patent gallicism, *giuggia* ("judges," 48), which is proper for the Frenchman whose name the pilgrim now learns.

49–69: Hugh Capet's private history extends over four *terzine,* and here, too, the chronicle turns on its extreme points and on the rhetoric of heightened contrast, beginning with the humble origins of the founder (52) and ending with the hallowed succession he set in motion (60). The chiaroscuro is made plain in the verbs and names in the first *terzina* of the group, 49–51: "chiamato fui . . . *di me* son nati . . . novellamente è Francia retta" ("the name I bore . . . /of me were born . . . /by whom France has been ruled most recently"); Ugo Ciappetta, too remote to be recalled without his nickname; and i *Filippi e i Luigi,* a succession of recent French kings too well-known to require further identification. Whatever the current dominance of the Anjou, Hugh Capet's story shows the rise of the Capetian dynasty to be a classic case of gross social climbing and therefore to be predictably corrupt or at least infected from the start. Again and again Dante inveighs against the vulgarity of the nouveaux riches and the wholly bad effect, in his Florentine experience, of fortunes quickly gained. Commenting on line 52, critics usually explain that Hugh Capet was the son, not of a butcher, but of a duke, and that he himself was king of France for nine years. This is not relevant to the passage in question. The legend of Hugh's lowly origins suited a deeper purpose: one closer to Dante's sensibilities as a member of a minor noble family displaced by the rise of the Florentine *borghesia* and as an individual casualty of the political upheaval following Charles Valois's entry into Florence in November 1301. Of necessity Hugh Capet's story is an ironically crude and brutally frank confession of opportunism (53–59), and it mocks the solemnity of that line of *sacrate ossa* ("the consecrated bones," 60) descending from his son. A graceless start, but for the next two centuries not shameless, and we might see the intervening period, alluded to in 61–63, as the trunk of the *mala pianta* ("obnoxious plant"), as yet unmarred by maleficent foliage.

61–69: three *terzine* are devoted to the history of Capetian avarice, lines that cover in some disorder notorious events from the 1240s to the 1290s, with the dense succession punctuated by the sarcastic refrain, *per ammenda* ("make amends," 65). Once again the poet isolates salient features to prove his case. He gives a thumbnail sketch of key Anjou depredations in France (66); after that French frontier line comes the fatal step into Italy; and suddenly, against the scattering of French provinces the peninsula is seen, as it was in Dante's Romanizing eyes, as a geographical and cultural unity, "Carlo venne in Italia" ("Charles came to Italy," 67). The tragic catalog ends with the decapitation of the last Hohenstaufen pretender to the imperial throne (68) and with the reputed poisoning of Thomas Aquinas at Fossanova (69). The name Tommaso, which comes after the royal names, brings the assorted string of conquests to a wryly improbable climax, as if Charles of Anjou, in eliminating an unlikely troublemaker, did so to ensure the angelic doctor of his heavenly reward. Angevin activity in Italy before 1300 is compressed into one cutting *terzina*, beginning with Charles of Anjou's descent into Italy in the year of Dante's birth, 1265, and ending on an apparently random date, nine years later, to prove the indiscriminate and sweeping nature of the French incursion into the Italian and imperial stronghold. It was a campaign that in one decade put an end to the Hohenstaufens and crushed the Ghibelline revival. The notional term for this historic reversal is set at 1274, the year in which, as the poet records solemnly in *Vita Nuova* II, the nearly nine-year-old Dante first saw the eight-year-old Beatrice.

70–96: we now come to the heart of Hugh's speech, where sarcasm gives way to fierce indignation, released through a tissue of metaphors. The nine *terzine* fall into two groups, each culminating in an exclamation (82, 94). Once again the rhetorical order of the salient features predominates over the chronology. From the first line, with a verb of actual vision that recurs at every step in this passage, Hugh Capet looks from the journey time of Easter 1300 across the coming decade, not to foretell but to *see* the terrible proof of the corruption that had beset the House of France during the 1200s. In these nine *terzine* the poet alludes to four events, grouped in two pairs, the first in each pair being more amply treated than the other. This carefully irregular arrangement, seemingly the natural unrehearsed shape of prophetic utterance, is enhanced by the metaphors, which match up in the first and in the second events in each part: in 1a and 2a, the Passion of Christ; in 1b and 2b, a maritime image. All this helps to control otherwise explosive material.

The first event that will certainly occur, and soon (70), etched in three lapidary sentences of one *terzina* each, is the descent of Charles Valois, brother of Philippe le Bel, in the autumn of 1301; his entry into Florence on November 1, 1301, as the *paciere* ("peacemaker") of Pope Boniface VIII, ostensibly to reconcilè Black and White Guelfs; and his hasty return to France in the spring of 1302, when he took with him the scornful Florentine nickname *Sanzaterra*, after his failure to oust the Aragonese from Sicily. It is characteristic of the poet's formal sense that the political event that triggered his own exile should lie embedded in the physical center of the canto, yet he tries to elevate his personal bitterness by producing a strong mixture of sarcasm (72), plebeian language (75), and moral logic (76–78). The most biting detail, however, is the metaphor "la lancia / con la qual giostrò Giuda" ("the lance that Judas tilted," 74). Among the other characters soon to emerge from the Passion sequence, Boniface will play, by virtue of his office, the Man of Sorrows; however, in lines 73–74 we may glimpse him in his role as High Priest in the transaction by which Charles of Valois was sent as his emissary to give up to him the city of Florence.

The third of these Carlos was Charles II of Anjou, the Lame, identified maliciously (79) by his naval defeat at the hands of the Aragonese in 1284, and who, in 1305, gave his daughter Beatrice as a child bride to Azzo d'Este in exchange for money and two cities. Here the only suitable analogue the poet can find, in the more studied form of the simile (80–81), is the notorious female slave trade and auctions conducted by Muslim pirates. This simile, the first since line 21, shows how hard it was to find an accurate parallel. Yet this incident shows that for more than sixty years father and son had established a pattern of behavior that amounted to genetic transfer. For the decline of the Capetians began, as Hugh notes at line 61, when Charles I of Anjou, father of Charles the Lame, forced another Beatrice, heiress to the Duchy of Provence, to marry him. At line 61, the greedy pursuit of the Provençal dowry had removed any sense of shame from Capetian blood; at line 80 an Anjou could now prostitute his own daughter, which means that Capetian blood had become completely absorbed by avarice. Hence the exclamation "O avarizia" ("O avarice," 82). For the first and only time in the canto the underlying vice is given its proper name, apostrophized by the founder of a dynasty who sees inexorably—"veggio . . . veggio"—that his own descendants will in their greed exploit their own flesh and blood. What greater power can avarice display than this? In answer to that rhetorical question, Hugh predicts the crime against which all other crimes pale, Philippe le Bel's attempted deposition of the reigning pope. The poet, in interpreting the sense of public outrage that followed the assault on Pope Boniface in his summer house at Anagni on September 7, 1303, condenses into five lines the story of Christ's passion and death, here introduced as the only fit analogue for an attack on the person of Christ's vicar. The verb *veggio* now intensifies into a crescendo, as if the Passion were unfolding again, step by step, before Hugh Capet's unbelieving eyes. The whole episode is couched, every line of it, in the passive, to present Boniface as *victim;* and the last *successor Petri* before the Babylonian captivity is recognized for the dignified and tragic figure he proved to be in that crisis that marked, for the next seventy-five years, the end of the papacy in Rome. This heroic treatment of Boniface VIII need not surprise us if we recall, from the previous canto, the self-abnegation of Pope Adrian V. His sense of the obligations of the papal office and his humility suffuse this canto, redeeming the part played by his successors during the French incursions into Italy; and it is his tardy example of Petrine evangelical poverty that allows Boniface to be cast, in his final act, merely according to his office.

In the last of the prophetic *terzine* (91–93), Dante accurately singles out the final blow under which the papacy submitted to the French monarchy: tolerating and even abetting the suppression of the wealthy Templars in 1307, in exchange for a lifting of the posthumous trial of Boniface VIII threatened by Philippe le Bel. The last image (93)—*Pilato* a pun here on *pilota*—takes up the image of the corsairs (87), converting that simile into an instinctive metaphor; and, like the corsair image, it is followed by an apostrophe, this time addressed to Christ as universal judge. It is the most anguished, the most desperate, of the three rhetorical questions in the canto, for it is directed to some future working of Providence which, unlike the tragic events just foreseen, lies beyond the vision of Hugh Capet and beyond the experience of the poet.

97–123: with no apparent break Hugh now takes up the pilgrim's second question, put at lines 35–36, "e perché sola / tu queste degne lode rinovelle" ("and why / just you alone renew these seemly praises"). The absence of any signpost for this obvious change of subject and tone is itself important because it allows the diatribe to pass as an unremarkable insertion or as a mere extended answer to the first question, "dimmi chi fosti" ("do tell me who you were," 35). Hugh's speech continues unbroken, as if the speaker were as alert as ever to a question, put some sixty lines earlier, that could have sunk beneath the intervening flood of words, or as if the new topic were as pressing as the one he has just covered. The two *terzine* that precede the list of exempla (97–102) serve to tie Hugh Capet's singular lament back into the daily and nightly round of choral repentance in which his voice is indistinguishable from that of the others. The exempla of avarice punished cover nine *terzine* (97–123), as did the passage of prophecy (70–96), and they thus counterbalance, with an incontestable and paratactically straightforward series of ancient examples, the rhetorically heightened chronicle of current events foreseen by Hugh Capet as the ultimate degradation of his line. Drawn from mythology, ancient history, and the Bible, the seven summary examples of avarice demonstrate once again the ethical ground common to pagan and Christian experience, while the apparently banal note on which Hugh's speech ends (118–123) completes the integration of his private lament into the scheme of the cornice, for his voice is but one of many. It is the renewed sense of choral unanimity and collective submission to justice that brings his speech full circle (121–123) and that allows the travelers to resume their journey without the formality of leave-taking.

A Provisional Narrative Close

124–151: coming nine *terzine* before the end of the canto, the strong narrative resumption may seem needlessly disruptive to the unity of the canto if we forget the four-canto span devoted to the terrace of avarice. It includes a remarkable invention, that of the release of a soul from Purgatory, that the poet will work organically into the canto structure for the terrace. After the long pause occasioned by Hugh Capet's speech, during which Dante silently shared the immobility of the repentant soul, the story now moves rapidly to establish a fresh mood of expectancy designed to keep the reader, along with the pilgrim, in suspense across the canto break. Virgil and Dante press on together until an earthquake, accompanied by a cry from all the souls on the terrace, stops them in their tracks. Virgil encourages his terrified companion, and they cautiously proceed with Dante now tagging dutifully behind his guide, perplexed but unable to bring himself to seek an explanation for what they have just experienced. This narrative, however, is interwoven with the pilgrim's inner response to what he perceives, and here, because the event is extraordinary, the poet takes unusual pains to evoke credible reactions of fear and stupor. Elsewhere in this canto, the figured language is primarily metaphorical, that is, it springs from within the discourse as an already assimilated verbal correlative, the only exceptions being the short similes at lines 6, 21, and 81. In this closing segment, however, similes abound, for in this way an external event can be shown to impinge on the pilgrim's consciousness; the similes save the narrative from slumping into a series of flat diary entries while effectively creating that air of tension the end of the canto is meant to convey.

"Come cosa che cada" ("like / a falling thing," 127–128): the comparison, of like to like, is more description than plausible physical explanation; 128–129: the term of comparison, more distinct than the previous one, conveys the pilgrim's mortal dread, after two days and nights on these vast, intractable slopes, that the mountain may collapse before he completes his journey; 130–132: this is the most elaborate simile member in the canto, a negative term, matching the muted simile in 127–128. "Li due occhi del cielo" ("the sky's two eyes," 132), Apollo and Diana, may suggest the *due soli* ("two suns") that Rome used to have (*Purg.* XVI, 106–107), whose light has been blotted out by the *mala pianta* ("obnoxious plant") of the Capetians (43). This bookish comparison introduces the idea of the birth of luminaries in a pagan context and thus adumbrates the release of Statius; but it is difficult not to recall, in the repeated infinitive *parturir,* the first example of voluntary poverty in this terrace, that of the Virgin at the birth of her son (19–24). As if consciously extending that example, the next simile (139–140) provides a corrective to the monstrous parturition recounted in the myth of Latona, with a gloss on the cry *Gloria in excelsis Deo,* which the shades have just raised. In this final image, of innocent wonder and expectation before the Nativity, the idea of birth and new life is clothed in sacred garb to herald a marvelous act of divine power and condescension, matching the Incarnation itself. Even Virgil, pagan prophet of the Incarnation, seems to pay unwitting tribute to this mystery, by speaking, at line 135, his only words in the entire canto, words that convey his archetypal role as guide to and precursor of faith.

In lines 142–151, the travelers resume their journey, just as the souls resume the chant that Dante had heard on first entering the cornice, *Adhaesit pavimento anima mea* (XIX, 73). The poet can find no comparison for the mental conflict that the pilgrim now undergoes, and his reductive admission, "Nulla ignoranza mai . . . né per la fretta . . . né per me" ("My ignorance has never . . . nor did I dare to ask . . . nor, by myself," 145–150), prepares the pilgrim for a revelation by stripping him of all pretense to knowledge, while at the same time declaring his thirst for knowledge. In the last line, the reflexive verb and the two adjectives expose the pilgrim in all his fragility and loneliness. A state more pathetic than his inner conflict at the start of the canto and one in sharp contrast to the righteous anger that animates the central speech, it is a note crying out for resolution.

BIBLIOGRAPHICAL NOTES

For general background see R. Fawtier, *Les Capétiens et la France* (Paris, 1942); G. Mollat, *The Popes at Avignon, 1305–1378,* trans. from 9th French edition (London-Edinburgh, 1949); G. Walter and E. Pognon, *Hugues Capet roi de France* (Paris, 1966); W. Ullmann, *A Short History of the Papacy in the Middle Ages* (London, 1972); J. Favier, *Philippe le Bel* (Paris, 1978). Among "Letture Dantesche" see P. Rajna, "Ugo Ciappetta nella *Divina Commedia,*" *Studi danteschi* 37 (1960): 5–20; E. Bonora, "Il canto XX del *Purgatorio,*" in *Letture dantesche,* ed. G. Getto (Florence, 1964), 1071–1091; R. Manselli, "Il canto XX del *Purgatorio,*" in *Nuove letture dantesche* (Florence, 1970), 4: 307–325; R. Scrivano, "L'orazione politica di Ugo Capeto: morale, politica e retorica in Dante," *L'Alighieri* 12 (1971): 13–34; R. Giacone, "Ugo Capeto e Dante," *Aevum* 49 (1975): 437–473.

Recommended for their comprehensive commentaries on the text of Canto XX are the editions of the *Comedy* by N. Sapegno (Milan-Naples, 1957); N. Mattalia (Milan, 1960); C. Singleton, *Purgatory. Commentary* (Princeton, 1973); and U. Bosco and G. Reggio (Florence, 1979). For points of detail and "cruces," see the *"chiose e luoghi puntuali"* in *La Divina Commedia: Purgatorio,* with commentaries by T. Casini, S. A. Barbi, and A. Momigliano, edited by F. Mazzoni, 1973, 463–468, which are here abridged: 19–123; for the historical setting of Hugh Capet see, in the *Enciclopedia dantesca,* vols. 1–6, Rome, 1970–1978 *(ED),* the following *voci:* "Ugo Capeto (Ciappetta)" (C. Varese, V, 791–792); "Capetingi" (G. Arnaldi, I, 815–817).

Is Hugh an "avarus," along with Pope Adrian V, or a prodigal, along with Statius? P. Rajna (cit., 13–17) argues that he was a prodigal, which would give more point to his denunciation of his avaricious descendants. 19–33, 103–117: on Dante's use of exemplification see C. Delcorno, "Dante e l'*Exemplum* medievale," *Lettere italiane* 35 (1983): 3–28. 43–45: for the metaphor of the "mala pianta" see F. Maggini, "Associazioni etimologiche nelle immagini di Dante," *Lingua Nostra* 6 (1944–45): 25–28.

Controversy has arisen over whether to read "per ammenda" or "per vicenda" in line 67. The latter, a "lectio difficilior," upheld by M. Barbi, *La nuova filologia e l'edizione dei nostri scrittori da Dante al Manzoni* (Florence, 1938), 13–16, and by A. Pagliaro, *Ulisse: Ricerche semantiche sulla Divina Commedia* (Messina-Florence, 1966), as being more ironic. For G. Petrocchi, *D.A. La Commedia secondo l'antica vulgata* (Milan. 1966–67), *Purgatorio*, 338, "semanticamente entrambe le lezioni sono pienamente soddisfacenti," but he settles for the "lezione più diffusamente e autorevolmente tràdita, per ammenda," which fits a rhetorical pattern of triple repetition.

Lines 67–69, 79–84: for Dante's attitude toward the Anjou, see *ED*, "Angiò" (E. Petrucci, I, 272–273); "Carlo I d'Angiò" and "Carlo II d'Angiò" (R. Manselli, I, 834–838). Lines 71–78, 85–93: for Charles Valois and Philippe le Bel, see *ED*, "Carlo di Valois" (R. Manselli, I, 838–840); "Filippo IV di Francia" (S. Saffiotti Bernardi, II, 876–879). For Pope Boniface VIII and the episode at Anagni, see A. De Lévis Mirepoix, *L'Attentat d'Anagni* (Paris, 1969); R. Manselli (cit.), 317–319; *ED*, "Bonifazio VIII" (E. Sestan, I, 675–679). Line 93: *portar* or *porta*? Petrocchi, *Introduzione*, 201–202, prefers the former on grounds of syntax, as an example of the infinitive dependent on *vedere: Veggio . . . portar*. It maintains a symmetry in the three *terzine*, 86–93, governed by the verb *veggio* with the infinitive. Line 93: for the Knights Templar, see *ED*, "Templari" (A. Frugoni, V, 546). Line 100: *risposto* or *risposta*, *riposto* or *riposta*? Petrocchi, *Purgatorio*, 342–343, clarifies *risposto* as a noun. The souls recite Psalm 118 (*Purg*. XIX, 73) alternately with the examples, and the examples are a responsory *(risposto)* to the psalm, as in the recitation of the Office. Line 119: *ad ir* or *a dir*? For Petrocchi, *Purgatorio*, 345–346, the former confirms the metaphor for speech (120); to step more quickly or more slowly is to speak the examples louder or more softly.

CANTO XXI

Greeting Statius

JANET LEVARIE SMARR

Canto XXI is in many ways a canto of thresholds and surprises or, as William Stephany has emphasized, of conversions. These threshold crossings involve both poetic and religious issues, nor can the two ever be far apart for Dante. The canto, which introduces a major classical poet and discusses the influence of Virgil's poetry, is also the first in which we meet a soul fully cleansed of sin and ready to ascend to Paradise. Beginning with the appearance of Statius and ending with his recognition of Virgil, this canto offers the last concentration on classical poetry before the series of encounters with vernacular poets. Statius, as both classical poet and Christian, is in himself one of the many thresholds in this canto, a point of crossing over between the classical Virgil and the Christian Dante.

A Natural Desire to Know

The canto opens with a thicket of scriptural allusions. Dante has just felt the mountain tremble, as at Christ's death, and heard the tremendous shout of *Gloria,* as at Christ's birth. His intense desire to understand what is happening is described in the canto's first lines as a thirst like that of the Samaritan woman's. Immediately afterward, another simile describes the appearance of a shade as being like that of the resurrected Christ to the two disciples on their way to Emmaus. Thus, within a short span, we have allusions to the major moments of Christ's life: his birth, his recognition as prophet and savior, his death, and his resurrection. The Christian context of the opening lines provides another threshold, for in these lines Dante is correcting his own former opinions and demonstrating the shift of his hopes from philosophy to theology.

Aristotle began his *Metaphysics* by declaring that all beings naturally desire to know; and Dante began his philosophical *Convivio* by explicitly quoting this declaration. Dante went on to explain that each creature is providentially designed to seek its own perfection, and that "knowledge [*scienza*] is the ultimate perfection of our soul, in which is our supreme felicity." He explained further, in the final chapter of section 3, that nature itself would be frustrating if it made men desire what is beyond their ability to fulfill. Thus the rational human nature seeks only what it can understand in this life through reason, and further desire is unnatural. Knowledge of God is beyond our ability and hence not naturally desired. By the twenty-second chapter of section 4, however, as Dante drew close to the moment when he left the work unfinished and turned to the *Comedy,* he began to revise his thinking and to acknowledge that the intellect could not find its perfect use in this life but only in the next life, when it will rest "in God who is the supreme intelligible." Here on earth we can think of God only indirectly through his effects, but direct knowledge will be ours in heaven. Dante embellished his point by citing the scriptural episode in which the three Maries went to Christ's tomb, only to find a figure in white who said, "You seek the Savior, and I tell you that he is not here; do not therefore be afraid, but go and tell his disciples and Peter that he will precede them into Galilee; and there you will see him, as he said to you." And he interpreted the three Maries as the three major branches of moral philosophy that seek for beatitude in this life in vain. Yet he interpreted Galilee, meaning "whiteness," as the white light of spiritual contemplation and continued to claim that the beatitude, impossible to attain through the active life (including the moral virtues), is possible to achieve through the intellectual or contemplative life. Nonetheless, he repeated immediately that supreme beatitude cannot be ours on earth. Thus we can see him wavering in his sense of the power or limitation of the intellect as the path to felicity. In the first lines of Canto XXI, Dante took the idea of man's natural thirst out of its philosophical context of the thirst for knowledge and inserted it into the religious context of the Samaritan woman's thirst for the water of life or the thirst for God's grace. The climax of that story, from John 4:7–15, is the woman's recognition of Jesus as the Savior. Dante identifies himself with this woman, whose thirst cannot be satisfied except by the saving grace of God. He will return to the image from this episode in *Paradiso* II, 19–20, to speak of man's "thirst that is innate and everlasting—/thirst for the godly realm" and in *Paradiso* XXX, 73–74, where he is told that he must drink from the river of Grace in the Empyrean before he can satisfy such thirst.

The Sacred Slopes

The rebuttal of his previously held Aristotelian notion is reinforced by a second rebuttal of Aristotle's philosophy on behalf of Christian religion. When Statius, as yet unidentified, is asked by Virgil to explain the earthquake they have just felt, he replies that it was not caused by wind trapped in the earth; that was the commonly held scientific explanation based on Aristotle's *Meteorologica*. It may still be true of normal mountains, and even of the lower portion of Mt. Purgatory, says Statius, but above the three steps that divide Ante-Purgatory from Purgatory proper, no such physical alterations occur.

Rather, the quake was caused only by what heaven receives "from itself and in itself" (44). This mysterious phrase has generally been understood to mean the soul, which comes from heaven and, when saved, returns to heaven, as Statius's soul is doing. Thus the return of his now-purified soul to Paradise has caused the earthquake. We are dealing with phenomena that are beyond rational or human capacity and yet that a human mind keenly thirsts to understand; only revelation can supply satisfactory answers. The passage implies that man cannot indeed attain satisfaction by himself; his providential thirst compels him, beyond his own abilities, to God.

Another mysterious phrase supports the shift from philosophical to Christian answers. "The sanctity/of these slopes," says Statius, "does not suffer anything/that's without order" (40–42). *Religione* ("sanctity") has sometimes been taken to mean the rules of a religious order and thus simply the rules governing the mountain; but the phrase also invokes a passage from the *Aeneid* 8.349–50, at the climax of Aeneas's tour of the area that will be Rome. He comes at last to the Capitoline Hill, "golden now, but once rough with woodland brambles. Already then the fearsome religion of the place terrified the trembling rustics; already then the forest and rock would tremble. 'This grove,' [Evander] said, "this hill with leafy summit a god inhabits (which god is uncertain); the Arcadians believe they have seen Jove himself. . . . '" Like the Capitoline, Mt. Purgatorio trembles and has felt the divine presence in the Eden at its leafy summit. Jove is, of course, the classical god most readily equated with the Christian one. Rome, moreover, is a recurring image for paradise, since Dante's otherworld journey is likened to an earthly pilgrimage. A double replacement is occurring here. Philosophy is pushed aside to make room not only for religion but also for poetry. Virgil was closer to the truth than Aristotle. In Limbo Aristotle may be "the master of the men who know" (*Inf.* IV, 131) and Dante may see him "seated in philosophical family. / There all look up to him, all do him honor" (*Inf.* IV, 132–133). But Aristotle is stuck in Hell forever, whereas Virgil is allowed to ascend the holy mountain and to glimpse the original paradise lost by Adam and Eve, a paradise of which "those ancients . . . in poetry presented/. . . perhaps, . . . dreamt this place" (*Purg.* XXVIII, 139–141) in his own description of Elysium. Even more important, Virgil, as this canto will reveal, has been able to bring about the salvation of souls. The list of wise men in Limbo is framed by Aristotle and his follower Averroes "of the great commentary" (*Inf.* IV, 144). Statius, in his discussion of human generation in Canto XXV, 61–66, will refer indirectly to Averroes as one who, though "wiser" than Dante, was led astray by error in regard to the human soul. Again we will see a poet correcting a philosopher, because, unlike the philosopher, the poet does not depend on his own rational faculties but on divine inspiration. In sum, we can see in this canto Dante's declaration of transition from the philosophical prose and argumentation of the *Convivio* to the religious poetry of the *Comedy*, from his role as a teacher through his own intellectual superiority to one as a divinely inspired scribe of revealed knowledge. This is one of the major thresholds of the canto.

Greeting Statius

As Paolo Padoan points out, the theme of human wisdom and its limitations in confrontation with religious mysteries is central to the meeting of Virgil and Statius. For that meeting emphasizes Virgil's own limitations, even though he may have been the wisest of human beings lacking revelation. The limitation of human knowledge and experience is discovered through the travelers' sense of surprise at things they cannot foresee or understand. The sudden tremor and shout was one such surprise. The appearance of Statius is another; he speaks to the two wayfarers before they are aware of his approach. Since his appearance is identified with the sudden appearance of the risen Christ, the surprise is made to contribute to a sense of the miraculous and supernatural rather than to the merely fortuitous. Statius's soul is equally surprised at its own sudden liberation. The penance of this circle, while particularly applicable to the specific sins of avarice and prodigality, is also a sign of the general nature of sin, reflecting the comment in Canto XIV, 148–150:

> "Heaven would call—and it encircles—you;
> it lets you see its never-ending beauties;
> and yet your eyes would see only the ground."

Just as Christ appeared risen from the sepulchral hole, so too has Statius's soul risen surprisingly from a deathlike condition of immobility with face to the ground, indeed from the death of sin, to an erect ascent into beatitude. What could be more surprising to reason or human experience than this rising from death into new life? This rebirth of the soul is marked by the cry of *Gloria*, which accompanied the birth of Christ. There is an emphasis here on the moment of birth, another important threshold. Even the earthquake, such as that which accompanied Christ's death, was compared in the previous canto to the tremors of Delos at the birth of Apollo and Diana. The image of parturition signifies the mystery by which Christ's death makes possible the rebirth of all men into eternal life. Appropriately, in this regard, the newly reborn Statius will discourse at length, in Canto XXV, 67–75, about the conception and generation of each new human. As we will observe later, the image of birth has implications for Dante's poetic enterprise as well. For now we may simply note that Dante's crossing the threshold from philosophy to religious poetry is a moment of birth related to his own salvation.

Dante has chosen a poet to lead the pilgrim from the dark wood toward the lost paradise of man's divinely given felicity, and he has chosen another poet to explain how the soul can be freed to return to its blessed home. Statius's explanation follows the teachings of Thomas Aquinas in dividing the absolute will *(volontà)* from the relative or conditioned will *(talento)*. The former can desire only God, but the latter turns toward other things that seem falsely good. Thus sin is the will dividing against itself. Justly then, while the absolute will of those in Purgatory continues to desire ascending to God, the relative will once more opposes that desire with another, this time the desire to do penance for its previous sin. The pains of Purgatory are thus in some sense voluntary. They are desired not in and of themselves, however, but as a means to restore the soul to God. The moment of total purification is a moment of reunification of the will, which now seeks God without distraction. The notion of sin as division and of blessedness as unification can be traced back through Augustine to Platonic ideas of the One and the Many. Similarly, when Dante reaches the end of his purgatorial ascent, Virgil crowns and miters him, thus unifying in Dante the two great powers that were so fiercely divided on earth. It is appropriate, too, that after the struggle that Dante's ignorance was causing in him at the end of Canto XX, Statius's first words of salutation should offer the wish for divinely granted "peace."

The Gulf of Faith

The joyful liberation of Statius is contrasted from the start with the melancholy state of the unsaved Virgil. When Statius greets the others, "God give / you . . . peace" (13–14), Virgil immediately rejects the possibility for himself:

> "And may that just tribunal
> which has consigned me to eternal exile
> place you in peace within the blessed assembly!"
>
> (16–18)

Virgil's metaphor of exile not only carries the emotional weight of Dante's physical exile but also alludes to the soul's exile from God, as in the phrase

Statius uses to describe his own liberation: "mio uscir di bando," "my exile's end" (102). Perhaps unwittingly Virgil is echoing the sharp contrasts of Psalm 1:5: "Therefore the wicked shall not rise again in judgment, nor sinners in the council of the just." Virgil explains to Statius that he has been drawn out of Hell to show Dante the way "as far as where I teach can reach" (33). Then he immediately asks Statius for an explanation of the tremor and shout, thus emphasizing the limitations of his *scola*. Statius's answer mentions twice the three steps at the beginning of *Purgatorio* proper, marking the threshold beyond which human wisdom and experience can no longer explain events, the threshold where natural causes yield to supernatural ones.

Parallels between the scene of Statius's appearance and the scene in *Inferno* 1 where Virgil appears to Dante produce further contrasts between these two classical poets separated by the gulf of faith. If Statius is initially presented as an image of Christ, Dante addresses Virgil with a phrase echoing the *Aeneid* 1.328: "Whoever you may be, whether a shade or a human for certain"; so did Aeneas address the sudden apparition of his disguised mother Venus, uncertain whether she was human or divine. (Dante's *od omo certo* [*Inf.* 1, 66] picks up Aeneas's *o dea certe*.) As goddess of love, Venus may be the closest thing to Christ in pagan terms, but she is still one of the "false and lying gods" (*Inf.* 1, 72) that Virgil mentions to define the era when he lived. If Virgil lived in the pagan times of "good Augustus" (*Inf.* 1, 71), then Statius lived in the early Christian times of "worthy Titus" (82), whose conquest of the Jews is described (through a pun on Jews and Judas) as the providential vengeance for Christ's death. Thus the two poets present not only two historical moments but two views of history: as human and as providential. Between these two historical moments occurred the great divide of history between the pagan and the Christian eras. That historical shift parallels the individual conversion as well as the conversion of poetry from classical tragedy to Christian comedy. If Virgil, furthermore, is the "famous sage" (*Inf.* 1, 89), Statius describes himself in life as one who "had sufficient fame beyond . . . / I bore the name that lasts the longest / and honors most—but faith was not yet mine" (85–87), thus rendering perspicuous both the absence of that term from Virgil's life and the difference between earthly fame and heavenly immortality. Virgil appears as one who is faint from long silence, and Hollander's essay on this one line has noted how the word "silence" refers to the realms of death and hell; it is Dante who first speaks to Virgil with a plea for help. But Statius speaks before Dante has even seen him coming, calling out a greeting that echoes the words of Christ bringing peace to humankind.

The emphases on Virgil's limitations have led some readers to argue that Virgil now yields his authority as Dante's guide to Statius, who functions as an intermediate between Virgil and Beatrice. It has been suggested that Statius represents something like Reason illumined by Revelation, thus providing a pivot between Virgilian Reason and Beatrician Revelation.

These abstractions, however, are much too simplifying and restrictive; they tend to move us away from confronting the significance of these poets as real, historical people. Moreover, Virgil remains Dante's guide until his disappearance at the arrival of Beatrice. Statius is never shown mediating between Virgil and Beatrice. He does, however, as a poet both classical and Christian, mediate in important ways between Virgil and Dante.

Dante's "Autobiography"

Indeed, his entire scene with Virgil has been seen as a disguised autobiography of Dante. The clear parallel between the episode in *Inferno* I, where Virgil suddenly appears and is identified and highly praised by Dante as the source of Dante's own poetry, and the similar scene here, where Statius suddenly appears and Virgil is again identified and praised, this time as the source of Statius's poetry, reinforces the identification of Statius with Dante. Furthermore, the shared Christianity of Statius and Dante unite them, in contrast to the pagan Virgil. Statius indeed represents, like Dante, the poet who owes his poetic abilities to the schooling of Virgil but who can surpass his master through the acquisition of Christian knowledge and faith. The Christian poets are united, moreover, by the structure of their praises of Virgil; for it has been well observed that Canto XXI, although in some sense the "Statius canto," is really focused less on Statius and more on the celebration of Virgil's art. In *Inferno*, Dante calls Virgil first, in two lines, the source of a wide river of speech, and then, more briefly, "my master and my author" (*Inf*, I, 85)—one of the *Comedy*'s very rare uses of this word (the other refers to God). Finally Dante says that Virgil is "the only one from whom my writing drew / the noble style for which I have been honored" (*Inf*. I, 86–87). Similarly Statius, in three lines, first calls the *Aeneid* a flame whose sparks have kindled a thousand others; then, more briefly, he calls Virgil as "mother to me, . . . was nurse" (98); and finally he asserts that without Virgil he would have been worth nothing. The word "mother" is also rare in the *Comedy* and will be repeated by Dante himself at the moment of Virgil's disappearance, along with Dante's assertion to him: "I gave my self for my salvation" (*Purg.* XXX, 51). The final lines of Statius's speech, in which he says that to have lived in Virgil's time he would gladly spend another year in Purgatory, have been viewed by some readers as blasphemy but seem, rather, a hyperbolic statement of what Statius assumes is impossible. In any case, that final "exile's end" (102), by which Statius refers to his liberation from Purgatory and his meeting with Virgil at that very moment of liberation, remind us not only that Virgil is suffering "eternal exile" but also that Dante began his own process of liberation when he encountered Virgil in the dark woods. In effect, Dante had said in *Inferno* I that he was lost until Virgil saved him. In Canto XXII Statius will inform us that he, too, was spiritually saved by Virgil's poetry. This is the most important link between Statius and Dante, and it reinforces the notion, suggested by Ulrich Leo and Robert Hollander, that *Inferno* I describes a turning point—both poetic and spiritual—in Dante's life, brought about by a reencounter with Virgil's poetry.

A Gesture of Adoration

The celebration of Virgil here is part of a series of praises to him, beginning in *Inferno* I and including the Sordello episode in *Purgatorio* VI–VII and the farewell to Virgil in *Purgatorio* XXX. The Sordello episode too shows a number of parallels to Canto XXI: Sordello's astonishment at hearing who Virgil is, and his immediate bending to embrace Virgil "where the lesser presence clasps" (VII, 15), raise the famous perplexing problem of why Statius cannot or may not similarly embrace Virgil. The answer is not one of physical impossibility—if we may use the word "physical" for these spirits of the other world—for Sordello had embraced Virgil without any problem. Nor is any distinction made between the physicality of souls in Ante-Purgatory and that of those in Purgatory proper, for high on the mountain the souls of the lustful embrace each other continually with charitable salutations. Denise Heilbronn, furthermore, has suggested that the "appropriate gesture" for Virgil to respond with to Statius's initial greeting would be the kiss or embrace of peace. Thus, just as Sordello had first embraced Virgil as a fellow Mantuan and then, discovering his identity, stooped to clasp him more humbly, so, too, Statius stoops to kiss Virgil's feet (130). Virgil's bidding, "Brother, there's no need—" (131), implies not the impossibility but the inappropriateness of Statius's humble gesture. But why should it be less appropriate for Statius than it is for Sordello?

There is a further perplexing aspect to this problem. Just as Statius's expressed willingness to delay his reunion with God in order to meet Virgil has struck some readers as blasphemous, so in a similar manner his kneeling to Virgil seems like a strange idolatry to be committed by someone purged of all sin, and his seeming confession of wrongdoing in the last lines of the canto adds to this puzzling impression. The sense of wrongness in Statius's action is reinforced by the parallel with a similar scene in Canto XIX, where Dante bends to do homage to the soul of Pope Adrian, only to be admonished in words strikingly like Virgil's:

> "Brother, straighten your legs; rise up!" he answered.
> "Don't be mistaken; I, with you and others,
> am but a fellow-servant of one Power."
>
> (133–135)

Both scenes echo that of John and the angel in Apocalypse 19:10: "And I fell before his feet to adore him. But he said to me: 'Do not so. I am a fellow servant with you and your brothers.'" If, as Bosco and others suggest, Virgil is warning Statius against adoring human beings in a way appropriate only to adoring God, how could Virgil know better than Statius the truth of this matter? After all, Virgil is damned as a pagan, while Statius is presumably ready for Paradise.

A number of explanations have been attempted. One possible answer is that, like the wish of lines 100–102, the gesture of adoration is simply a hyperbolic expression of intense admiration without any blasphemous intention. Certainly Statius's gesture and his reference to the *Aeneid* as "holy fire" (*divina fiamma,* 95) both draw from the ending of Statius's own *Thebaid* (12.816–17), in which Statius says to his book: "Nor try to equal the divine *Aeneid,* / but follow it at a distance and always adore its footsteps." Yet the climactic positioning of Statius's gesture in the canto bids one not to dismiss its significance too quickly.

William Stephany has come the closest, I think, to offering a satisfactory account of the incident. At issue is the role Statius plays in relation to Virgil, not simply as a poetic imitator to his source but as a Christian to the one who has initiated his conversion. Virgil's response, argues Stephany, fits the pattern of scriptural allusions to conversion connecting the beginning and end of this canto. It evokes the scene in which the risen Christ appeared to Mary Magdalene and said, "Do not touch me, for I have not yet risen to the Father." On the one hand, this may imply Virgil's own unrisen and unworthy condition; on the other, however, it shifts the image of risen Christ from Statius to Virgil and implies that Virgil brings about salvation for Statius just as Christ did for Magdalene. Now, obviously, Virgil could not effect Statius's salvation by himself, but he could do it by unintentionally turning Statius toward acceptance of the Christian teachings, as Statius will explain in the following canto. Virgil sees Statius's gesture only as an acknowledgment of Virgil's poetic importance and influence; thus, given the disparity in their spiritual status, he finds it inappropriate. Statius, however, is acknowledging not only the poetic but also the spiritual and salvific influence of Virgil and is, therefore, appropriately recognizing the providential cause of his own salvation. Thus, too, Statius can refer to the *Aeneid* as "divine" not simply for the beauty of its poetry but for its providential role in his life. Dante, through Statius, acknowledges here the importance of Virgil to his own salvation as well (124).

Certainly the four major celebrations of Virgil noted above proceed from the praise of his "noble style" (*Inf.* I, 87) and his demonstration of the power of "our tongue" (*Purg.* VII, 17) to Statius's and Dante's assertions (*Purg.* XXII and XXX) that Virgil has been the cause of their salvation. The effect of Virgil's poetry on Dante therefore must be seen in relation to the beginning of Canto XXI, where Aristotle's science or philosophy is repeatedly corrected by a combination of poetry and revelation, and the desire for knowledge by the desire for God.

Confessions of Error

The last line in Canto XXI, in which Statius confesses to "treating the shades as one treats solid things" (136), bears a striking resemblance to Dante's own sin as defined by Beatrice in Canto XXX and as confessed by Dante in Canto XXXI. Dante's problem has been precisely that he treated as solid, valuable, and enduring things that are only deceitful images or shadows of the true Good. The religious paradox is that what is physically solid is spiritually empty and unreliable, while what is invisible proves spiritually solid and reliable. As in Canto XXI, so in Canto XXX, the phrases defining this error follow an intensely emotional honoring of Virgil. But what can the similarity between Statius's and Dante's phrases mean? For Dante is confessing and cleansing himself of sin, whereas Statius is already completely purged and ready for Paradise. Therefore Statius's seeming confession of error must somehow not be the error it seems.

Indeed, just as Virgil mistook Statius's gesture of homage for something narrower than it was, that is, as an acknowledgment of Virgil's human poetic powers rather than of Virgil's providential agency in Statius's salvation, so, too, there may be several ways to understand Statius's final line. Most literally, it means that otherworld shades are not real, physical people. Not only Statius's embrace but also Dante's whole poem so far, which has been treating the souls of the dead as if they were material human beings, is implicated in this loving error. But *ombra* has other resonances as well. It is one of Virgil's favorite words, one on which he ended his first and final eclogue and the entire *Aeneid*, thus surrounding his own poetry with the dark and melancholy shadows that surround him still in the *Comedy*. Statius will note that both these works of Virgil helped to save him. *Ombra* is also a Platonic and Neoplatonic concept, according to which the things that we can physically perceive are merely shadows or representations (images) of the true and perfect Ideas. Statius would not be capable, in his purified state, of mistaking God's providential power for Virgil's. But he does see that Virgil, while surrounding himself with shadows, can illuminate the way for others, that he can unwittingly offer or represent an image of the true Good. Thus we can read Statius's line *in bono* as indicating that Statius has treated the unillumined Virgil's poetry as a source divinely offered for his own illumination; that he has treated this pagan poetry as a shadowy representation of Christian doctrine; that he has treated Virgil himself, though he is wrapped in shadows, as an unwitting prophet of Christian truth. This salvific misreading is better than the more proper pagan reading. Thus Statius confesses to error without sin.

Dante's sin, which includes his infidelity to Beatrice when he was lead astray by a mysterious *pargoletta* (*Purg.* XXXI, 58–59), has been related to his dalliance with philosophy and intellectual achievement before returning through a sense of human limits to the love of Divine Grace. But for Dante as for Statius, God's blessing has been enacted through Virgil's poetry. It is the voice of Virgil that had called Dante to turn from the briars and dark woods where his efforts only entangled him further to the eternal realms of the soul and humble faith. Dante identifies Virgil to Statius as "he . . . who leads my eyes on high" (124) and who leads Dante's vision to things heavenly. The surprise of Virgil's first appearance, like the surprising encounter with Statius and the surprising liberation of the soul, demonstrates the suddenness and mysteriousness of grace, the unpredictable moment of spiritual birth.

Virgil and the Use of the Vernacular

Virgil as the source of poetic style is not forgotten when the focus of gratitude shifts to his spiritual influence. Statius calls Virgil his *mamma* in specific connection with writing poetry ("when I wrote / verse," 97–98), while his image of Virgil as nurse relates to Dante's earlier image of Virgil as the source of a stream ("Virgil, you the fountain / that freely pours so rich a stream of speech" [*Inf.* I, 79–80]). Both images imply a special moment of birth for poetry. Hollander has noted further that the very word *mamma* is significant in Dante's poetic enterprise. Its conjunction with *fummi* calls attention to its sound, just as the cluster of *v* and *vi* sounds emphasize Statius's naming of *Virgilio* in the following *terzina*. Although baby talk had been explicitly rejected earlier in the *Comedy*, with Dante asserting that his poem is not for those who can speak only in this way, Cantos XXI and XXX both use the word *mamma* positively in praise of Virgil. Hollander suggests that Dante linked the notion of baby talk to his own use of the vernacular, while simultaneously exalting the vernacular in general as "the universal and natural speech" (*De vulgari eloquentia* I, chaps. 4–6), analogous to the original language of unfallen man.

How could Dante have identified Virgil's Latin as the source of his own use of the vernacular? Two passages help to explain this. One is Sordello's praise of Virgil as the one "through whom our tongue revealed its power" (*Purg.* VII, 17). The line is certainly applicable to Dante's own purposeful demonstration of the capacities of Italian. Having greeted Virgil as a fellow Mantuan and addressing him in Italian, Sordello suggests that Virgil's language enjoys the same status as Dante's Italian by being "our tongue," or a language whose potential can be best discovered and fulfilled by a great poet. This view of Latin is strengthened by a passage from the *Convivio* (1.11.14) referring to the beginning of Cicero's *De finibus* and the contempt expressed there for Romans who preferred Greek to Latin. Dante wrote, "In his time they scorned the Roman Latin and praised the Greek grammar [*la gramatica greca*], for similar reasons as those of people who consider the Italian speech lowly and the Provençal of great value." Here Latin is not only equated with Italian as one's own language in opposition to a foreign tongue, but it is even contrasted to "Greek grammar," a term used for the languages learned in school instead of from one's mother. Usually "grammar" by itself meant Latin; but here Dante has shifted it to mean Greek to signify the relation between any mother tongue and any studied language. Adam's discussion of original natural language and its history since the fall (*Par.* XXVI) is linked to Canto XXI by the recurrence of the set of rhymes "*Virgilio-concilio-essilio*"; and it is in this context that Virgil is named, by Adam, for the last time (*Par.* XXVI, 120):

> The tongue I spoke was all extinct before
> the men of Nimrod set their minds upon
> the unaccomplishable task; for never
>   has any thing produced by human reason
> been everlasting—following the heavens,
> men seek the new, they shift their predilections.
>   That man should speak at all is nature's act,
> but how you speak—in this tongue or in that—
> she leaves to you and to your preference.
>
> (Par. XXVI, 124–132)

Thus Dante's meditations on the nature of languages, Latin and Romance, seem to have led him to view Virgil's poetry, written in Virgil's own language, as a model for Dante's use of the vernacular. The word *mamma* with regard to Virgil's style expresses this recognition. Nor are stylistic issues ever separable from religious ones, for great poetry's enhancement of the beauty and signifying power of any language brings human language closer to what its original unfallen nature must have been.

From Struggle to Vision

Scholars have divided Canto XXI in various ways. Aristide Marigo separates the drier explanatory discourse of the first half from the lively emotional drama of the second. Benvenuto da Imola distinguishes four roughly equal pieces: the introduction of a spirit, the explanation of the quake and shout, the historical identification of Statius, and, finally, the identification of Virgil. Fergusson breaks the canto into similar pieces, framed by the recurring references to Dante's thirst, but substituting for Benvenuto's second category the identification of the three souls in general spiritual terms (as saved, damned, and still alive). Nonetheless, it is important to realize also how tightly knit the canto is. It begins and ends with allusions to three scriptural episodes: the woman at the well, Christ's appearance to the two disciples on the way to Emmaus, and Christ's appearance to Mary Magdalene. The latter two concern Christ's resurrection from the dead, which is mirrored in the canto's major theme: the liberation of the soul from sin. The first allusion, to the thirst of the woman at the well, also echoes throughout the canto:

Dante's thirst for understanding is alleviated by Statius's explanations, and Statius's thirst for the seemingly impossible chance to demonstrate his grateful love to Virgil is satisfied by Dante's revelation of Virgil's identity. We realize that Statius has come not only like the risen Christ to the two disciples but also like one of those disciples, who did not recognize their master as they walked with him. Thus, after the clear references to Christ at the canto's beginning, we are asked at the end of Canto XXI, especially by the final implicit image of Christ with Mary Magdalene, to return to the image of the mysteriously appearing Christ and to see that role fulfilled by Virgil as well as by Statius. The turning of Dante's poetic and moral efforts from dark struggle to enlightened vision has been, it seems, brought about by providence through the poetry of Virgil. This canto, which celebrates the soul's liberation, makes an offering of intensely loving gratitude to the unintended, unexpected, providential power of Virgil's poetry.

BIBLIOGRAPHICAL NOTES

There is no lack of scholarship on this canto, though much of it deals with Cantos XXI and XXII together. One of the best readings of Canto XXI is by Giorgio Padoan, *Nuove Letture Dantesche*, vol. 4, Casa di Dante in Roma (Florence: Le Monnier, 1970). It focuses especially on the theme of thirst and its bearing on the problem of the possible human knowledge of truth, which Padoan considers central to the Canto. Another helpful reading is the introductory essay to Cantos XXI and XXII (taken together) by Umberto Bosco in the *Divina Commedia,* ed. Umberto Bosco and Giovanni Reggio (Florence: Le Monnier, 1979), 351–371, which traces developments from the preceding cantos and allusions to Scripture and to Statius's poetry, calling attention to the encounter of classical and Christian poetry.

Recent critical attention in America has focused chiefly on the problematic nature of Statius's gesture and remarks to Virgil. Contributing to this topic are Nicolae Iliescu, "Gli episodi degli abbracci nelle strutture del *Purgatorio,*" *Yearbook of Italian Studies* I (1971): 53–63; Denise Heilbronn, "'Io pur sorrisi': Dante's Lesson on the Passions" (*Purg.* XXI, 94–136), *Dante Studies* 96 (1978): 67–72 (which argues against Iliescu), and "The Prophetic Role of Statius in Dante's *Purgatorio,*" *Dante Studies* 95 (1977): 53–67; and William Stephany, "Biblical Allusions to Conversion in *Purgatorio* XXI," *Stanford Italian Review* 3, no. 2 (1983): 141–162. The last two writers are especially interested in the Christian allegory presented through Scriptural allusions. Robert Hollander, *Allegory in Dante's Commedia* (Princeton: Princeton University Press, 1969), 68–69, contributes briefly to this discussion. John Sinclair's brief but effective comment on the canto in his edition of *Purgatorio* (1939; repr., New York: Oxford University Press, 1975), 279–281, emphasizes the sense of surprise and mystery attending the first encounter with a soul just resurrected from sin. Teodolinda Barolini, noting parallels between the appearance of Virgil in *Inferno* I and of Statius in *Purgatorio* XXI, discusses the two poets in relation to each other. A similar interest is presented in J.H. Whitfield, "Dante and Statius: *Purgatorio* XXI– XXII," in *Dante Soundings,* ed. David Nolan (Totowa, NJ: Rowman and Littlefield, 1981), 113–129. Francesco d'Ovidio, *Nuovi Studi Danteschi III: Il Purgatorio* (Naples: Alfredo Guida, n.d.), 342–353, argues against seeing Statius as a guide on the level with Virgil and Beatrice, a view proposed by John Mahoney, "The Role of Statius and the Structure of *Purgatorio,*" in *The 79th Annual Report of the Dante Society* (1961): 11–38.

A cluster of Italian articles deals with the celebration through Virgil and Statius of poetry's powers. Mario Sansone, "Il canto XXI del *Purgatorio,*" *Lectura Dantis Scaligera* (Florence: Le Monnier, 1966), and Sansone's *Letture e Studi Danteschi* (Bari: De Donato, 1975) 135–164 focus on the human, emotional relations among Dante, Statius, and Virgil, and on the celebration of poetry in the context of salvation and the way to God. Sansone drew in part on the work of Fausto Montanari,

"L'incontro con Virgilio," *L'esperienza poetica di Dante* (Florence: Le Monnier, 1959), 117–133, for poetry as offering a wisdom beyond that of rational philosophy; M. Porena, "Il canto XXI del *Purgatorio*," *Giornale dantesco* 26 (1920): 192–202, for the treatment of Statius as a representation of Dante himself and for the idea of a progressive series of lessons derived from Virgil: of style, of moral philosophy, and of faith; and N. Zingarelli, "L'incontro con Stazio nel Canto XXI del *Purgatorio* e il concetto dantesco della poesia," *Cultura moderna* 23 (1923): 31–41, for the glorification of Virgil as a symbol of the combination of poetry, wisdom, and religion. Giovanni Cecchetti, "'Per te poeta fui, per te cristiano'" (*Purg.* XXII, 73), *Pacific Coast Philology* 16, no. 2 (1981): 25–32, similarly focuses on the celebration of poetry. There is some debate about the mood of the canto's second half. Mario Bontempelli, "Il canto XXI del *Purgatorio*," in *Lectura Dantis* (Florence: Sansoni, 1910) sees humor in the final scene; Aristide Marigo, "Incontro di Stazio e Virgilio," in *La Divina Commedia nella critica: II. Purgatorio*, ed. Antonino Pagliaro (Florence: G. D'Anna, 1966), 317–323, disagrees with such a reading, seeing anxious embarrassment rather than humor. Francesco Gabrieli, *Letture e divagazioni dantesche.* Quaderni di cultura II: Letteratura Italiana, 2 (Bari: Centro Librario, 1965), gives solemn and almost tragic weight to this same scene, emphasizing the damnation of Virgil but also relating the smile's expression of the interior soul with the ability of shadows, including Dante's whole poem, to express solid truth.

Last but not least, Robert Hollander, in two articles, investigates the relation of Dante's literary project to his understanding of Virgil's accomplishment; specifically they deal with the notion of writing theologians' rather than poets' allegory, and with using the vernacular as an approach to Adamic speech. Both essays, "Dante Theologus-Poeta" and "Babytalk in Dante's *Commedia*" can be found in his *Studies in Dante* (Ravenna: Longo, 1980), 39–89 and 115–129.

CANTO XXII

Virgil and Statius Discourse

CHRISTOPHER KLEINHENZ

The various themes and narrative threads that constitute Canto XXI all come together in Canto XXII: the interrelated notions of thresholds and conversion; the shift from philosophy to theology and from philosophical prose to religious poetry; the confrontation of human reason and its limitations with profound religious mysteries; and the bittersweet celebration of the ancient world, of Virgil for the excellence of his poetic model, and of Virgil's works for the moral and spiritual influence they reputedly exerted. This combination of elements forms what could rightly be called the triumph of Virgil and of his poetry as they were perceived and interpreted by medieval Christian exegetes. The celebration of Virgil, however, yields to the celebration of Statius, which might be considered, by extension, to be that of Dante himself, for the figure of Statius is a carefully crafted alter ego of the Florentine poet. Canto XXII is, properly speaking, an extended meditation on poetry—on the interpretation of poetry and on the power of poetry to transform both individuals and society as a whole.

The meeting between these two classical Latin poets, Virgil and Statius, foreshadows Dante's encounters with several medieval vernacular poets in the next few cantos: Forese Donati (XXIII), Bonagiunta Orbicciani da Lucca (XXIV), Guido Guinizzelli and Arnaut Daniel (XXVI). It is perhaps fittingly ironic that in this canto, where the interpretation of poetic texts is of foremost concern, we find three of the most formidable cruxes in the entire *Divine Comedy*, the resolution of which has bedeviled commentators from the fourteenth century to the present day. They are: 1) the proper meaning of Virgil's verses ("Quid non mortalia pectora cogis, / auri sacra fames!" *Aeneid* III, 56–57) in their new context and in Italian paraphrase, 2) the "historicity" of Statius's conversion to Christianity, and 3) the apparent contradiction in Dante's placement of Tiresias's daughter, Manto—is she to be found among the diviners in the fourth *bolgia* of the eighth circle (*Inf.* XX) or among the virtuous pagans in Limbo (*Inf.* IV)? Each of these matters will be covered in this discussion of the canto.

The action of Canto XXII is elegantly framed, first by the backward look (1–9) at the angel who has removed the fifth *P* inscribed on Dante the Pilgrim's brow, and last by the forward look (130–154) toward the next terrace—that of the gluttons—with its unnaturally formed but morally instructive tree that preaches examples of temperance. Between these two poles the action of the canto takes place, but "action" is perhaps the wrong term, for most of the canto—some 120 verses—is given over to the conversation between Statius and Virgil, who move upward toward the sixth terrace with the Pilgrim in tow. Canto XXII is concerned not so much with actions as with words—with the power of the written word to influence and guide, to inspire and motivate, and to shape and, ultimately, determine the destiny of others. It is concerned with the polysemous nature of poetry and its awesome power to transform individuals and, through interpretation, to transcend its own age and speak with authority to subsequent eras. It is concerned with texts—biblical and pagan—and how they are read and interpreted.

Thrust Backward

The unusual opening of Canto XXII, with its retrospective reference to the cleansing rite of the angel—an act that up to now has always been described in its proper place in the sequential narration of events in Purgatory—may perhaps be explained by the Poet's desire to maintain the unity of the entire episode. The highly charged drama of the recognition scene at the close of Canto XXI is suspended by the interval between cantos. To move ahead to the questions and conversation that such a moment generates without taking the time to relate extraneous events in a prosaic fashion, the Poet reviews them, quickly and efficiently in six verses:

> The angel now was left behind us, he
> who had directed us to the sixth terrace,
> having erased one *P* that scarred my face;
>   he had declared that those who longed for justice
> are blessed, and his voice concluded that
> message with *"sitiunt,"* without the rest.
>
> (1–6)

The abrupt opening of the canto with the adverb *già* thrusts the reader back in time and makes both movement (past the angel toward the next terrace) and action (the erasing of the *P* and the recitation of the beatitude) part of a defined past. The broken rhythm of these verses, established syntactically and grammatically (through apposition, verbal inversions, participial phrases), contributes to the sense of haste the Poet wishes to convey. All the essential elements are present but arranged so as to suggest the rush of disparate events in memory.

Recognition

The scene of Statius's recognition of and homage to Virgil at the end of Canto XXI establishes both the context and the pretext for Virgil's response, which initiates the dialogue in Canto XXII. Against the background of his younger colleague's praise of him and his works (XXI, 94–102), Virgil graciously reciprocates by referring to his conversations in Limbo with Juvenal, who told him about Statius's affection for him (*tua affezion,* "[your] fondness," 15). The younger poet's admiration for Virgil and the *Aeneid* is an historical fact, for in the twelfth book of the *Thebaid* he addresses his work with the verses: "Vive, precor; nec tu divinam Aeneida tempta, / sed longe sequere et vestigia semper adora" ("O live, I pray! nor rival the divine *Aeneid,* but follow after and ever venerate its footsteps," 816–817).

   Virgil describes their mutual affection and literary association across the ages in words that, as many critics have noted, recall *mutatis mutandis* those of Francesca da Rimini in the fifth canto of the *Inferno.* Virgil's words— "Amore / acceso di virtú, sempre altro accese, / pur che la fiamma sua paresse fore" ("Love that is kindled by / virtue, will, in another, find reply, / as long as that love's flame appears without," 10–12)—stand in sharp contrast to Francesca's—"Amor, ch'a nullo amato amar perdona" ("Love, that releases no beloved from loving," *Inf.* V, 103). Through the evocative power of certain words and phrases *(amore, accese, strinse)* Dante suggests that these two episodes should be read as mutually glossing parallel texts, or, better perhaps, that the passage in *Purgatorio* should be read palinodically as the correct statement on the proper nature of *amore.* In *Inferno* V Francesca describes how, overcome by *Amore,* she and Paolo were swept away by their passion, which was kindled by the reading of a book, the Old French prose romance of Lancelot. As critics have noted, in Canto V the act of reading, which should be used to reap moral and spiritual benefits, led those protagonists to a terrible end—to death and damnation—through misreading and misunderstanding. Conversely, Statius's reading and understanding of Virgil's poetry guided him to moral and spiritual conversion—to salvation and eternal life. The so-called tragedy of Virgil is evoked for yet another time in the poem, and here the poignancy is even more acute because of the contrast developed between Virgil and Statius, the former damned and the latter saved precisely through the works, the literary "intercession," as it were, of the former.

The First Question

Virgil poses two questions to Statius—the first on the nature of his sin and the second on the reasons motivating his conversion—and these are carefully arranged in order of importance, the lesser preceding the greater. Moreover, these questions, although innocently posed, serve to focus on Virgil, on Virgil's texts, and on their moral and allegorical interpretation. Noting that Statius has just been liberated from the terrace of avarice, the Mantuan poet wonders how in all his wisdom he could have allowed avarice to rule in him:

> "how was it that you found within your breast
> a place for avarice, when you possessed
> the wisdom you had nurtured with such care?"
>
> 22–24

The atmosphere in Purgatory is suffused with gentle humor. Here, before responding to Virgil's questions, Statius flashes a quick smile, demonstrating both his affection for his poetic master and his slight amusement over his misconception concerning the nature of his sin. This knowing smile mirrors that exchanged by Virgil and Dante in Canto XXI (103–111), where they were similarly amused by the effusive praise of Virgil, which Statius innocently offers, unaware of his identity, and these two complementary moments serve to enhance the unity of the entire episode. Before disclosing the true reason for his presence on the fifth purgatorial terrace, Statius calls attention to the deceptive nature of appearances:

> "Indeed, because true causes are concealed,
> we often face deceptive reasoning
> and things provoke perplexity in us."
>
> 28–30

In addition to its immediate reference to Virgil's misperception, this tercet alludes more generally to the nature of allegory and the proper way to read and interpret pagan literature, that is, morally and allegorically. Indeed, it is precisely this application of Christian hermeneutics to Virgil's text that eventually showed Statius the error of his ways. Hardly avaricious, he had abandoned all sense of measure *(dismisura)*, becoming guilty therefore of prodigality, for which he spent *migliaia di lunari* ("thousands of months," 36)—more than six thousand months—on the fifth terrace. Statius was, however, saved from the irrevocable *giostre grame* ("sorry jousts," 42) of Hell (Canto VII)—the eternal clashes between the avaricious and prodigal souls who push *pesi per forza di poppa* ("Wheeling weights, they used their chests to push," *Inf.* VII, 27) in a semicircular collision course—through his reading and enlightened understanding of two verses from Virgil's *Aeneid:* "Quid non mortalia pectora cogis, / auri sacra fames!" ("To what do you not drive the hearts of men, o accursed hunger for gold!" III, 56–57).

Statius came to understand the true meaning of these words in a sudden moment of inspiration, captured so well with the preterit *intesi* ("understanding," 38), and he repeats here for Virgil's (and our) benefit his translation or paraphrase—in Italian—of these verses: "Perché non reggi tu, o sacra fame / de l'oro, l'appetito de' mortali?" ("Why cannot you, o holy hunger / for gold, restrain the appetite of mortals?" 40–41). For centuries commentators have engaged in vigorous debate in their attempt to determine the precise meaning of these lines. In their original context in the *Aeneid* these verses comment on an atrocity—Polymestor's murder of Polydorus—committed for gold and obviously express Virgil's reprobation of the power of avarice. Furthermore, two cantos earlier (XX, 115) Dante used Polymestor as one of the *exempla* of avarice on the fifth terrace. The interpretation depends ultimately on whether we believe Dante wanted us to understand Virgil's verses *in* their original context or *out* of it. Did Dante intend for his character Statius 1) to read and understand Virgil's text on its own merits or 2) to "misread" the passage creatively?

The question of interpretation in or out of context—right or wrong—is a thorny one. In support of the out-of-context position is the practice generally followed by Christian exegetes who, on the authority of Augustine (*De doctrina christiana* II, 40–42), searched for and found "Egyptian gold and silver" in pagan writings. This plundering of ancient texts for their "true" meaning is, as Richard Shoaf indicates, not rendered invalid if the original context is not respected, and, given the sort of exegesis that Statius applies to the *Fourth Eclogue,* an out-of-context, transformative reading of this passage would be very much in character. Moreover, Statius clearly indicates that he interpreted these verses as a warning against prodigality:

> "Then I became aware that hands might open
> too wide, like wings, in spending; and of this,
> As of my other sins, I did repent."
>
> 43–45

Finally, the fact that Statius describes Virgil's impassioned invective as directed toward all humankind—*a l'umana natura*—seems to remove the verses from their original context and make them more general in their application, as a moral injunction should be.

The Second Question

The story of Statius's moral conversion from his prodigal ways through the intercession of Virgil's text is an appropriate prelude to the more important account of his spiritual conversion to Christianity. Obviously motivated by a heightened awareness of his own tragic position in contrast to Statius's happy lot in Purgatory, Virgil, who is here significantly identified as the author of the *Eclogues* ("il cantor de' bucolici carmi," "the singer/of the bucolic poems," 57), addresses him in his role as epic poet—"Or quando tu cantasti le crude armi/de la doppia trestizia di Giocasta" ("Now, when you sang the savage wars of those/twin sorrows of Jocasta," 55–56)—and wonders out loud about the chronology of his conversion to the true faith:

> "It does not seem
> from those notes struck by you and Clio there—
> that you had yet turned faithful to the faith
> without which righteous works do not suffice."
>
> 57–60

Referring to Clio, the pagan muse of history who inspired Statius in writing his epic poem, Virgil sadly reiterates his complaint that in the absence of faith *(fede)*, good works in the world are not sufficient to win salvation (cf. *Purg.* VII, 25–36). Quickly moving beyond self-pity, however, he signals his resigned acceptance of his situation with the phrase *se così è* ("If that is so," 61), which sounds a note of fatalistic finality, and proceeds to ask Statius who revealed the Christian message to him:

> "then what sun or what candles
> drew you from darkness so that, in their wake,
> you set your sails behind the fisherman?"
>
> 61–63

The question is couched in richly allusive language. The metaphorical agents of Statius's illumination are either candles *(candele)* or the sun *(sole)*, the former denoting human agency and the latter divine, and the dramatic dispelling of his state of darkness *(stenebraron)* is expressed in terms that recall a traditional way of referring to pagan times—the *tenebrae* that enshrouded the earth prior to the coming of Christ's light. The nautical imagery aptly describes Statius's new Christian life as a follower of Peter, a fisherman by profession—he and Andrew were dubbed "fishers of men" by Jesus (Mark 1:17). In addition to its being a traditional way to speak of the course of life, the image of the sea journey helps to align Statius, as a poet, with Dante, since both use similar metaphors to describe their literary activity (*Thebaid* 12:809; *Purg.* I, 1–3; *Par.* II, 1–15). Statius's description of his conversion is a wonderful paean to Virgil's doubly efficacious power as a poet and as a prophet:

> "You were the first to send me
> to drink within Parnassus' caves and you,
> the first who, after God, enlightened me.
> You did as he who goes by night and carries

the lamp behind him—he is of no help
to his own self but teaches those who follow—
    when you declared: 'The ages are renewed;
justice and man's first time on earth return;
from Heaven a new progeny descends.'
    Through you I was a poet and, through you,
a Christian."

                                        (64–73)

It was Virgil's great poetic example that Statius first followed in his literary activity, the composition of his epic poem—in drinking from the grottos of Parnassus. He acknowledges this debt in the *Thebaid* by employing the image of his poem that follows in the footsteps of Virgil's *Aeneid*. More important, it was Statius's discovery of the "true" meaning concealed in the verses of Virgil's *Fourth Eclogue* that first enlightened him on the Christian faith. The "tragedy" of Virgil is again evoked by his description as one who carries a lantern, the light of which benefits those who follow but not himself. Statius's imagery responds directly to that in Virgil's question—the latter's worldly candles are then the source of the former's reference to the *lume*. For the *Fourth Eclogue*, Statius followed the same exegetical procedure that he had employed to interpret in a moral vein those verses from the *Aeneid* that disclosed to him the virtue of moderation, and for the second time in this canto, Dante presents a translated and slightly modified version of Virgil's text. Virgil may have composed the *Fourth Eclogue* to celebrate the birth of a son to the Roman consul Gaius Asinius Pollio. The verses

> *Magnus ab integro saeclorum nascitur ordo.*
> *Iam redit et Virgo, redeunt Saturnia regna;*
> *iam nova progenies caelo demittitur alto.*

> The great line of the centuries begins anew.
> Now the Virgin returns, the reign of Saturn returns; now
> a new progeny descends from heaven on high.

                                        (5–7)

become in the *Purgatorio:*

> *Secol si rinova;*
> *torna giustizia e primo tempo umano,*
> *e progenïe scende da ciel nova.*

> The ages are renewed;
>   justice and man's first time on earth return;
> from Heaven a new prodigy descends.

                                        (70–72)

The interpretative paraphrase—*giustizia* for *Virgo* and *primo tempo umano* for *Saturnia regna*—demonstrates that Dante fashioned Statius's reading of this passage to conform to the generally accepted allegorical interpretation of the Virgilian verses. According to the providential view of history, the birth of Christ would usher in the new age, and justice would be restored. Since the time of Constantine, the *Eclogue* was interpreted allegorically as a prophecy of Christ's coming, and thus Virgil, as a prophet, took his place in the long line of Old Testament prophets—Isaiah, Habakkuk, and so on—in the mystery plays and in the iconography of medieval Europe. The combined effect of Virgil's tutelage on Statius is wonderfully presented in the verse that both summarizes and celebrates—"per te poeta fui, per te cristiano" ("Through you I was a poet and, through you, / a Christian," 73). Statius could offer no higher praise to his mentor, and, conversely, no greater irony could be imagined, given Virgil's personal situation. Statius's tribute to Virgil is also Dante's acknowledgment of his own great debt to the Roman poet, from whom he learned his poetic craft.

Statius Elaborates

Employing the figurative language of the rhetorician (on St. Jerome's authority Dante conflated Statius the classical poet with Lucius Statius Ursulus, a first-century rhetorician from Toulouse) and the imagery of the artist, Statius says that he will elaborate on what he has just said by "coloring" it in and proceeds to describe his conversion within its larger historical context:

> Disseminated by the messengers
> of the eternal kingdom, the true faith
> by then had penetrated all the world,
>   and the new preachers preached in such accord
> with what you'd said (and I have just repeated),
> that I was drawn into frequenting them.
>   Then they appeared to me to be so saintly
> that, when Domitian persecuted them,
> my own laments accompanied their grief;
>   and while I could—as long as I had life—
> I helped them, and their honest practices
> made me disdainful of all other sects.
>   Before—within my poem—I'd led the Greeks
> unto the streams of Thebes, I was baptized;
> but out of fear, I was a secret Christian
>   and, for a long time, showed myself as pagan;
> for this halfheartedness, for more than four
> centuries, I circled the fourth circle.

(76–93)

Dante has his character Statius openly declare his reluctance to embrace Christianity, a reluctance that also resulted in his being guilty of spiritual lukewarmness (*tepidezza*, 92), for which he spent, according the Dante's chronology, some four hundred years on the terrace of sloth. The connection between poetry and Christianity so incisively demonstrated earlier is reiterated and enhanced when Statius indicates that his baptism occurred at a precise point in his poetic narrative—just before the Greeks arrived at the Theban rivers (*Thebaid* VII: 424–425). While some critics take Statius's words in a more general sense to mean that he had received baptism before beginning the *Thebaid*, others, including some fourteenth-century commentators, view this as a precise reference to that moment in Book VII. The natural association of rivers, water, and baptism would provide an artistic and poetic reason to favor the latter interpretation.

Critics have long debated the historicity of Statius's conversion to Christianity in an attempt to discover possible sources for Dante's account. Is Dante's biography of Statius pure fiction, dictated by literary exigencies? Given Statius's noted admiration for Virgil, was the former's salvation via the latter conceived by Dante? Or did some evidence suggest to Dante that Statius was indeed a Christian? To be sure, we possess some accounts of pagans who were converted to Christianity through a reading of Virgil's *Fourth Eclogue:* for example, Secundianus, Marcellianus, and Verianus. Some critics base their views on evidence internal to the *Thebaid*. In the fifteenth century Poliziano suggested that Dante understood Tiresias's mysterious invocation to the "triplicis mundi summum, quem scire nefastum" ("the high lord of the triple world, who may not be known," *Thebaid* IV, 516) as a reference to the Christian God. Others (Lewis) have argued that the *Thebaid* contains enough Christian or apparently Christian traits to have allowed Dante to consider its author a Christian. David Baumble, for example, sees the epic poem as a "forerunner" of the *Comedy,* as "shadowing forth the same kind of pilgrimage of the spirit" (65). On the other hand, through an investigation of external evidence—medieval glosses and allegorical interpretations of the *Thebaid*—Giorgio Padoan argues for Theseus as a *figura Christi* and declares that the last part was written by a Christian *ancorché chiuso* (443).

Some marginal glosses in medieval manuscripts suggest that the *Thebaid* was consistently read and interpreted in a Christian vein. The pseudo-Fulgentian allegorization *(Super Thebaiden)* interprets Thebes as the human soul that has been liberated from the tyranny of pride (Creon) by the coming of divine good (Theseus). According to the commentator, Theseus's name derives from *Theos suus,* that is, God Himself. In the *Comedy* Dante alludes to Theseus in precisely this manner, stressing the Christological overtones in his presentation, and the early commentator Guido da Pisa notes this association. Theseus's descent to the underworld with his friend Pirithous to take Proserpina is, on the surface at least, the typological counterpart to Christ's Harrowing of Hell (*Inf.* IX, 54). Because of his defeat of the drunken and riotous centaurs (*Purg.* XXIV, 121–123) and his dispatching of the Minotaur (*Inf.* XII, 16–21), Theseus was generally interpreted allegorically as the one who established order in a corrupt and degenerate society, the one who secured the triumph of law and civilization in barbarous lands. That Dante may have known these allegorizations and drawn on them for his characterization of Statius is not inconceivable.

Tragic Irony and a Lapse

In a final reference to Virgil's role in his conversion Statius again employs typical exegetical language: the lifting of the allegorical lid or veil to reveal the truth (94). Passing then to a discussion of their mutual friends and acquaintances, Statius, following the pattern of conversations between Dante and souls, wants to know the fate of certain people. Where are, for example, the dramatic poets Terence, Caecilius, Plautus, and Lucius Varius? The prominent *ubi sunt* theme adds a note of melancholy to the episode, which stands in sharp contrast to the jubilant note of triumph that heralded Statius's release from Purgatory. At the same time, this bittersweet note underscores the tragic irony of these two classical poets who were so similar historically and literarily but not spiritually. Statius's question in the form of a command—"tell me if they are damned, and in what quarter" ("Dimmi se son dannati, e in qual vico," 99)—contains, of course, its own answer, as the coda discloses—*e in qual vico*. That these souls are damned is beyond question; much more crucial, it seems, is their location in Hell. Virgil's reply takes the form of an epic catalog, which complements the list of inhabitants of Limbo (*Inf.* IV, 121–144). While some critics have suggested that this second list represents those authors with a prehumanistic bent who were not known to Dante at the time he was writing the episode in *Inferno* IV, others have spoken of the two catalogs as demonstrating the total range of Dante's knowledge of classical figures. Virgil's account abounds in references to the nature, source, and rewards of poetry—to the muses and the poetic nourishment they provide, to Parnassus, and to the laurel crown:

> "All these and Persius, I, and many others,"
> my guide replied, "are with that Greek to whom
> the Muses gave their gifts in greatest measure.
> Our place is the blind prison, its first circle;
> and there we often talk about the mountain
> where those who were our nurses always dwell.
> Euripides is with us, Antiphon,
> Simonides, and Agathon, as well
> as many other Greeks who once wore laurel
> upon their brow."
>
> (100–109)

The intensity of these verses is heightened by the constant contrast between the present state of these souls—damned in Limbo—and their honorable earthly existence. So acutely does Virgil describe their suspended state in Limbo that these verses could be interpreted as his defense, his attempt to justify on an earthly plane his poetic craft and beliefs. Although recognizing that this is insufficient for salvation, he realizes, at the same time, that this is all he has, and the memory of what was and the knowledge of what could have been constitute the torment of those souls in Limbo. After mentioning Persius, Homer (the only one whose name is repeated here from the earlier catalog), Euripides, and others, Virgil speaks specifically of eight characters—all women—who should be of particular interest to Statius since they appear in the latter's poetry, both in the *Thebaid* and in the *Achilleid:*

> "And there—of your own people—
> one sees Antigone, Deiphyle,
> Ismene, sad still, Argia as she was.
>   There one can see the woman who showed Langia,
> and there, Tiresias' daughter; there is Thetis;
> and with her sisters, there, Deidamia."
>
> (109–114)

The reference to the "daughter of Tiresias"—Manto—and her place in Limbo has been a major interpretive crux since the fourteenth century, for it appears to contradict Dante's earlier presentation of her among the diviners in Inferno xx. If such is the case, then it is the only instance of the Poet's "nodding" in the *Comedy.*

Some critics have tried to explain this apparent lapsus by arguing that because the more extended treatment of Manto occurs in *Inferno,* the episode in *Purgatorio,* with its much briefer reference, was composed earlier, a conjecture with no basis in fact. Others have suggested that a scribal error is to blame for the contradiction and have proposed emending the passage in various ways, all of which pose serious paleographical problems. In an attempt to resolve the discrepancy, the early commentator Benvenuto da Imola proposed that the phrase "nel primo cinghio del carcere cieco" ("Our place is the blind prison; its first circle," 103) should be understood as referring both specifically to Limbo and more generally to all of Hell, an untenable view from the double perspective of syntax and context. Working on the assumption that Dante could not make such a glaring mistake, Richard Kay has proposed that there must be two Mantos in the poem. His examination of classical authors discloses a distinction between the historical Manto (of the *Aeneid* and *Metamorphoses*), who is relegated to *Inferno* xx, and the fictional literary figure of Manto (of the *Thebaid*), who is in Limbo. Along somewhat similar lines, Robert Hollander, following the lead provided by Boccaccio in

De Mulieribus Claris, proposes that the impious Manto—Virgil's creature—is in *Inferno* XX and pious Manto, the filial virgin of the *Thebaid,* is in Limbo. Hollander explains that the attraction of this "intentional self-contradiction" is that "its context is grounded in the paradox of the salvation of Statius and damnation of Virgil" (211–212).

The Strange Tree

Reaching the sixth terrace between ten and eleven o'clock in the morning, the three wayfarers begin to move to the right in a counterclockwise direction, the two classical poets in front followed by Dante, who is avidly listening to their conversation for the poetic instruction it gives him:

> Those two were in the lead; I walked alone,
> behind them, listening to their colloquy
> which taught me much concerning poetry.
>
> (128–129)

At a certain point, however, this pleasant conversation stops, for they have come to a strange tree whose delectable fruit attracts them but whose unnatural shape signifies prohibition:

> and even as a fir-tree tapers upward
> from branch to branch, that tree there tapered downward,
> so as—I think—to ward off any climber.
>
> (133–135)

A clear liquid cascades down the cliff and flows over its branches: "Bright running water fell from the high rock / and spread itself upon the leaves above" (137–138). In addition to specific function in the purgation process on this terrace, the *liquor chiaro* ("bright . . . water") serves to remind the reader of the earlier metaphorical allusion to the waters of Parnassus: "You were the first to send me / to drink within Parnassus' caves" (64–65), whence Statius first drew his poetic inspiration. Both streams are seen as salutary, but on different levels, the second acting as a Christian corrective to the first.

When Virgil and Statius approach the tree, a voice utters a warning: "This food shall be denied to you" (141) and then proceeds to recite examples of temperance:

> "Mary's care was for the marriage-
> feast's being seemly and complete, not for
> her mouth (which now would intercede for you).
> And when they drank, of old, the Roman women
> were satisfied with water; and young Daniel,

through his disdain of food, acquired wisdom.
   The first age was as fair as gold: when hungry,
men found the taste of acorns good; when thirsty,
they found that every little stream was nectar.
   When he was in the wilderness, the Baptist
had fed on nothing more than honey, locusts:
for this he was made great, as glorious
   as, in the Gospel, is made plain to you."

(142–154)

Following the pattern established for such rituals, Dante presents first an example of virtue from the life of Mary—the wedding feast at Cana (John 2:1–3)—and then from classical antiquity—the Roman women's reputed abstinence from wine. The final two verses of the canto, "for this he was made great, as glorious / as, in the Gospel, is made plain to you" (153–154), which allude to the greatness of the Baptist as presented—or better revealed—in the Gospel (Luke 1:15; 7:28), reiterate the leitmotif of Canto XXII: the interpretation of texts. The wayfarers—and we the readers of the *Comedy*—are invited to meditate on the story of the Baptist as presented in the Gospel and on its meaning as disclosed through scriptural exegesis. Just as Statius was able to arrive at a morally and spiritually satisfactory interpretation of Virgil's text and, consequently, to achieve salvation, so are we asked to apply similar interpretive methods to Holy Scripture.

The contrast between pagan and Christian, between earthly poetry and divine poetry, and between material and spiritual nourishment is also a constant in this canto and establishes a context that foreshadows subsequent episodes in the *Commedia,* the most important of which is the account of Eden, the recapturing of primal innocence, the regaining of justice and the true Golden Age of man.

Echoes of the Baptist

Just as Virgil preceded Statius and was the one who, albeit unknowingly, guided him to the Christian faith, so too was John the Baptist the forerunner of Christ, and the one who baptized him in the river Jordan. The analogy is powerful, for Statius enters the poem accompanied by numerous Christological references and, as a Christ figure, anticipates in some ways Beatrice. As we remarked at the beginning of this essay, this is a canto of celebration and triumph, and this episode appropriately concludes with the reference to the much-heralded glory of John the Baptist. By stating that the greatness of the Baptist will be revealed (*aperto,* 154) in the Gospel, Dante seems to suggest that the sort of exegesis applied by Statius to Virgil's text is valid but perhaps secondary in importance to the interpretation of Holy Scripture. If we consider the entire verse in Matthew, the allusion here assumes even greater importance: "Amen dico vobis, non surrexit inter natos mulierum maior Ioanne Baptista: qui autem minor est in regno caelorum, maior est illo" ("Amen I say to you, there hath not risen among them that are born of women a greater than John the Baptist: yet he that is the lesser in the kingdom of heaven is greater than he," II:II). In his proclamation of the new age (the *regno caelorum*), in which even the lesser *(minor)* is greater than the Baptist *(maior est illo),* Jesus does not intend so much to diminish John but rather to declare the glory of the Christian era. The subordinate position of John the Baptist as described in Matthew is recalled here so as to parallel and complement the same sort of ordering between Virgil and Statius, and it was, of course, the former who proclaimed the coming of the new age *(ordo)* in the *Fourth Eclogue,* the new age in which he would ironically have no part.

The pattern of subordination, of the complementary relationship between inferior and superior, runs throughout this episode. However, the deference paid to Virgil by Statius at the end of Canto XXI eventually comes full circle, as we see the inversion, sub specie aeternitatis, of their positions: Statius destined for salvation, Virgil consigned to eternal exile in Limbo. The example of John the Baptist, who spent two years in Limbo before he was lifted up to glory as a consequence of Christ's Harrowing of Hell, serves to further the sense of pathos and the tragic irony of Virgil's position. The bittersweet celebration of the ancient world that reverberates in Virgil's account to Statius of their mutual friends in Limbo and the purely earthly triumph of Virgil yield then, as yield they must, to the unconditioned celebration of Christ in His triumphal advent, foretold dimly in the *Fourth Eclogue,* recognized and celebrated by John the Baptist, and believed in and embraced by Statius. The engaging drama of Statius's conversion and his very presence in Purgatory attest to the mysterious workings of Divine Providence and provide ample evidence, as it were, of the supreme power of faith and, more specifically, of the transcendent power of poetry.

BIBLIOGRAPHICAL NOTES

As for most cantos in the *Divine Comedy* there is no lack of scholarship on Canto XXII, although, given the nature of the episode, some scholars consider Cantos XXI and XXII together. Numerous commentators on the *Comedy*—medieval (Jacopo della Lana, Pietro di Dante, Ottimo, Benvenuto da Imola, Francesco da Buti) and modern (Grandgent, Sapegno, Gmelin, Singleton, Bosco-Reggio) alike have also provided valuable interpretive accounts of this canto. For some well-balanced general readings of Canto XXII, see the following: Alfredo Galletti, "Il canto XXII del *Purgatorio,"* in *Letture scelte sulla Divina Commedia,* ed. Giovanni Getto (Florence: Sansoni, 1970), 437–455; Aulo Greco, "Canto XXII," in *Lectura Dantis Scaligera: Purgatorio* (Florence: Le Monnier, 1971), 831–61); Fausto Montanari, *Il canto XXII del "Purgatorio"* (Turin: Società Editrice Internazionale, 1965); Giovanni Cecchetti, "'Per te poeta fui, per te cristiano'" (*Purg.* XXII, 73), *Pacific Coast Philology* 16 (1981): 25–32; and J. H. Whitfield, "Dante and Statius: *Purgatorio* XXI–XXII," in *Dante Soundings: Eight Literary and Historical Essays,* ed. David Nolan (Dublin: Irish Academic Press, 1981), 113–129. Some of the commentaries mentioned in the text are the following: Charles S. Singleton: Dante Alighieri, *The Divine Comedy, Purgatorio: 2 Commentary* (Princeton: Princeton University Press, 1973); Natalino Sapegno: Dante Alighieri, *La Divina Commedia,* 3 vols.

(Florence: La Nuova Italia, 1985); and the *Commento di Francesco da Buti sopra la Divina Commedia di Dante*, 3 vols., ed. Crescentino Giannini (Pisa: Fratelli Nistri, 1858–1862).

Good overviews of the figure of Statius are provided by E. Sacchi ("Dante e Stazio," *Giornale dantesco* 8 [1900]: 449–465), Giorgio Brugnoli ("Stazio in Dante," *Cultura neolatina* 29 [1969]: 117–125), and Ettore Paratore ("Stazio," *Enciclopedia dantesca*, 6 vols. [Rome, 1970–1978]). The connections with Juvenal are discussed by Edward Moore (*Studies in Dante, First Series: Scripture and Classical Authors in Dante*, ed. Colin Hardie [Oxford: Clarendon Press, 1896, 1969], 255–258) and Ettore Paratore ("Giovenale," *Enciclopedia dantesca*). Describing the relationship between Virgil and Statius, Teodolinda Barolini (*Dante's Poets: Textuality and Truth in the "Comedy"* [Princeton: Princeton University Press, 1984], 256–269) notes especially pertinent parallels between *Inferno* IV and *Purgatorio* XXII. Robert Hollander (*Il Virgilio dantesco: Tragedia nella "Commedia"* [Florence: Olschki, 1983]) provides a full presentation of the "tragedy" of Virgil in the *Comedy*. For a general study of Statius in the political context of the *Divine Comedy*, see Christopher Kleinhenz, "Dante, Statius, and Virgil: An Unusual Trinity" (*Lectura Dantis Newberryana*, ed. Paolo Cherchi and Antonio C. Mastrobuono [Evanston: Northwestern University Press, 1988], 37–55).

Since this canto presents no fewer than three major interpretive cruxes, much scholarship has been directed at their resolution. For a good overview of the various positions vis-à-vis the problem of interpreting the Italianized version of Virgil's lines *"Quid non mortalia pectora cogis,/auri sacra fames!"* (*Aeneid* III: 56–57), see Felicina Groppi (Dante traduttore [Rome: Herder, 1962], 163–168), Francesco D'Ovidio ("D'un famoso errore ermeneutico di Dante su un passo dell'*Eneide* e non di ciò solamente," *Studi danteschi* 7 [1923]: 57–82; also in *L'ultimo volume dantesco*, Opere di Francesco D'Ovidio, V [Rome: Casa Editrice A.D.E., 1926], 175–200), Alessandro Niccoli ("Sacro," *Enciclopedia dantesca*), Luigi Blasucci ("Reggere," *Enciclopedia dantesca*), Paolo Nicosia ("Come Stazio, per Dante, abbia potuto apprendere da Virgilio che anche la prodigalità è peccato (*Purg.* XXII, 40–41)," *Alla ricerca della coerenza: Saggi di esegèsi dantesca* [Messina-Florence: D'Anna, 1967], 241–266), Charles Singleton (*Purgatory Commentary*, 521–524), and Paolo Baldan ("Stazio e le possibili 'vere ragion che son nascose" della sua conversione (*Purg.* XXII, 40–41), *Lettere italiane* 38 [1986]: 149–165).

Many of the arguments were made and lines of division drawn even among the early commentators. While Jacopo della Lana believed that Virgil's verses were directed solely against prodigality, Pietro di Dante and Francesco da Buti interpreted them as being directed at both avarice and prodigality. Buti recognized the possibility that Dante may have transformed Virgil's verses into a counsel to follow moderation. Some modern studies interpreting these verses as an exhortation to moderation include Carmine Jannaco ("I canti XXII e XXIII del *Purgatorio*," *Lettere italiane* 9 [1957]: 329–341) and H. D. Austin ("*Aurea Justitia*: A Note on *Purgatorio* XXII, 40 f.," *Modern Language Notes* 48 [1933]: 327–330). Following along this general line, R. A. Shoaf ("'Auri sacra fames' and the Age of Gold (*Purg.* XXII, 40–41 and 148–150)," *Dante Studies* 96 [1978]: 195–199) proposes that "sacra fame de l'oro" be read as a "mistranslation" on the authority of St. Augustine (*De Doctrina Christiana* II, 40–42). In several studies—"Latinismi virgiliani nella *Divina Commedia*" (*Cultura e scuola* 20, [1981]: 79–86), "L'incontro di Stazio e Virgilio" (*Cultura e scuola* 4 [1965]: 566–571) and "Per una semantica dei virgilianismi" (*Lingua nostra* 11 [1950]: 81–85)—Alessandro Ronconi argues against the notion that Dante has misunderstood Virgil's verses; rather, Ronconi posits that Dante has transformed their pagan meaning into a Christian one.

On the allegorical interpretations of Virgil's *Fourth Eclogue*, see Domenico Comparetti, *Virgilio nel Medio Evo* (2 vols., nuova edizione di Giorgio Pasquali [Florence: La Nuova Italia, 1937], I:118–127) and Pierre Courcelle, "Les exégèses chrétiennes de la quatrième Églogue," *Revue des études anciennes* 59 (1957): 294–319. For the iconography, see Emile Mâle, *Religious Art in France, Thirteenth Century: A Study in Mediaeval Iconography and Its Sources of Inspiration*, tr. Dora Nussey (1913; repr. as *The Gothic Image: Religious Art in France of the Thirteenth Century* [New York: Harper and Row, 1958]), 152–170.

For the general question of Statius's conversion to Christianity, see the following: Michele Scherillo ("Il cristianesimo di Stazio secondo Dante," *Atene e Roma* 5 [1902]: 497–506) and the criticism leveled at these views by Giuseppe Albini ("Se e come la THEBAIS ispirasse a Dante di fare

Stazio cristiano," *Atene e Roma* 5 [1902]: 561–567); the two articles by Carlo Landi: "Sulla leggenda del cristianesimo di Stazio" (*Atti e memorie della Reale Accademia di scienze lettere ed arti in Padova,* n.s. 29 [1913]: 231–266) and "Intorno a Stazio nel Medio Evo e nel purgatorio dantesco" (*Atti e memorie della Reale Accademia di scienze lettere ed arti in Padova,* n.s. 37 [1921]: 201–232); L. A. MacKay ("Statius in Purgatory," *Classica et Mediaevalia* 26 [1965]: 293–305); H. David Baumble, III ("Dante's Status," *Cithara* 15 [1975]: 59–67); C. S. Lewis ("Dante's Status," *Medium Aevum* 25 [1956]: 133–139); Winthrop Wetherbee (*"Poeta che mi guidi:* Dante, Lucan, and Virgil," *Canons,* ed. Robert von Hallberg [Chicago: University of Chicago Press, 1984], 131–148); and Scevola Mariotti ("Il cristianesimo di Stazio in Dante secondo il Poliziao," *Letteratura e critica: Studi in onore di Natalino Sapegno,* ed. Walter Binni et al. [Rome: Bulzoni, 1975], 2:149–161). For a specific discussion of Poliziano's comments on Dante's presentation of Statius and Statius's Christianity, see Manlio Pastore Stocchi ("Il cristianesimo di Stazio (*Purg.* XXII) e un'ipotesi del Poliziano," *Miscellanea di studi offerta a Armando Balduino e Bianca Bianchi per le loro nozze* [Padua: Seminario di Filologia Moderna dell'Università, 1962], 41–45), and Scevola Mariotti (see above). For the importance of Giovanni Colonna's "Vita Statii" in his *Liber de viris illustribus,* see Giorgio Brugnoli, "Statius Christianus" (*Italianistica* 17 [1988]: 9–17).

For the medieval allegorizations of the *Thebaid* and their possible influence on Dante, see Giorgio Padoan, "Il mito di Teseo e il cristianesimo di Stazio" (*Lettere italiane* 11 [1959]: 432–457). An English translation of the *Super Thebaiden* is given in *Fulgentius the Mythographer,* trans. Leslie George Whitbread (Columbus: Ohio State University Press, 1971).

For an overview of the ambiguous location of Manto, see the following studies, each of which proposes a different solution: Giorgio Padoan ("Manto," *Enciclopedia dantesca*); Richard Kay ("Dante's Double Damnation of Manto," *Res Publica Litterarum* 1 [1978]: 113–128); and Robert Hollander ("The Tragedy of Divination in *Inferno* XX," Studies in Dante [Ravenna: Longo, 1980], 131–218, esp. 205–215). In his commentary on the poem (*La Divina Commedia nuovamente commentata,* 8th ed. [Milan: Società Anonima Editrice Dante Alighieri, 1935]), Francesco Torraca proposed the emended reading for v. 113: "Evvi la figlia di Nereo, Teti," a reading that also garnered the support of E. G. Parodi in a review of the Scartazzini-Vandelli edition of the *Commedia* (*Bullettino della Società Dantesca Italiana,* n.s. 23 [1916], 46–48). In "Nuova interpretazione d'un tormentato verso del *Purgatorio* in relazione col Limbo" (*Giornale dantesco* 35 [1934]: 139–142), Gioacchino Maruffi proposed that the verse be emended to read: "Evvi la figlia di Titonio e Teti," thus referring to Penthesilea. Padoan ("Manto") suggested the emendation: "Evvi la figlia di Chirone, Teti."

Paul Renucci (*Dante disciple et juge du monde gréco-latin* [Clermont-Ferrand: G. De Bussac, 1954], 329–337) offers a curious but generally untenable proposal concerning the relationship between this episode and Limbo.

The symbolic nature of the tree on the sixth terrace is treated by Alherto Del Monte, "Forese" (*Cultura e scuola* 4 [1967]: 572–589). On the tree as a palm and its consequent moral significance, see Thomas D. Hill, "Dante's Palm: *Purgatorio* XXII: 130–135" (*Modern Language Notes,* 82 [1967]: 103–105). On the particular significance of the reference to Daniel among the *exempla* of temperance, see Christopher Kleinhenz, "Food for Thought: *Purgatorio* XXII, 146–147" (*Dante Studies* 95 [1977]: 69–79).

CANTO XXIII

Reading Literary and Ethical Choices

RINALDINA RUSSELL

Soon after Dante and his two guides enter the terrace of the gluttons (Cantos XXII–XXIV), they come across a tree laden with appetizing fruit and sprinkled with fresh water, a tree whose branches widen as they reach higher into the sky. Later on, just before the travelers exit from the terrace, they will encounter another such tree. The gluttons run around this cornice and purge themselves of their sin by suffering the pangs of hunger and thirst, made sharper by the sight of fruit and water. The moral meaning of the trees, that is, the equation of gluttony to covetousness and therefore to injustice, is made explicit by Dante at least twice. Descending from the first tree, a voice admonishes: "This food shall be denied to you" (XXII, 141), a reference to God's injunction to Adam and Eve not to eat from the Tree of Knowledge. At the second tree, the voice declares: "There is a tree above from which Eve ate, / and from that tree above, this plant was raised" (XXIV, 116–117). That is the plant Dante will see in the Earthly Paradise, acknowledged by commentators to be the Tree of Divine Justice. As Canto XXIII opens, Dante is peeping with childlike inquisitiveness through the branches of the first tree to see where the voice is coming from. In a fatherly manner, Virgil urges him to walk on. This apparently insignificant, if charming, incident, serves a precise expressive function: it not only reminds us that Dante is journeying up the mountain and that his encounter with his old friend Forese occurs on the way to greater visions and knowledge, but it also suggests a mood of friendly and trusting human exchange.

Stylistic Registers, Compositional Patterns

Dante creates this impression by employing a plain, colloquial manner of address. According to medieval definitions of "style," this is the "medium" or moderate style, the linguistic and stylistic register, in fact, that is recognized to prevail in *Purgatorio,* since it is as best suited to the climate of human trust and of redress and the soothing of once injured human relationships. It is the conversational style that two friends would use when meeting up and inquiring about each other, as Dante and Forese do, and about relatives and friends. At mid-canto, when Forese explains why he is already in Purgatory and how his wife, Nella, has interceded for him with her devout prayers, his lines become crowded with possessives, a nickname, and a cluster of diminutive endings, thus reaching down to a "lower" style, to a more intimate, familial type of discourse. Later, at the close of the canto, when it is Dante's turn to satisfy his friend's curiosity and to recount his journey through Purgatory, the language again becomes plain, as the use of personal names and the direct indication of place and time would have immediately indicated to the medieval student of rhetoric.

This medium stylistic register is first interrupted early in the canto. As a throng of spirits approaches, Dante notices and is shocked by their hollow eyes and skeletal bodies. The language here reaches a high expressionistic level, a reprise, in fact, of the harshly incisive, metaphorically realistic style used in the depiction of infernal perversion and deformity. Forese, too, bears the purgatorial imprint of the sin he indulged in on earth and is recognizable only by his voice. Throughout this section, which includes Forese's explanation of the penance meted out here, words like *faccia* (face), *buccia* (skin), *becco* (beak), *squama* (scurf), and *scabbia* (scabs) are also indirect reminders of the verbal violence characterizing the scurrilous and abusive sonnets Forese and Dante exchanged in life, in compliance with a fairly common literary fashion and genre. The realistic style register is scattered with an even more noticeable cluster of rhetorical figures characteristic of the "high" style. We have a series of erudite similes in the description of the spirits (25–33). A complex periphrasis encases a rare antithesis describing the penitents' joyous assent to their remedial pain (73–74). Further, metaphors such as "Questa favilla tutta mi raccese/mia conoscenza" ("This spark rekindled in me everything/I knew" 46–47), "Però mi dì . . . che si vi sfoglia" ("But tell me . . . what has unleaved/you so" 58–59), and "m'ha condotto/a ber lo dolce assenzo d'i martìri" ("has guided me / to drink the sweet wormwood of torments" 86–87) are all striking images of the type encountered in high-style lyric poetry, in which they signify the gnawing passion of love, the lover's painful ecstasy. A second shift in stylistic register occurs suddenly, as we shall see, in the second half of the canto. Here Forese, after remembering with indulgent affection his wife's loyalty and devotion, abruptly launches into a violent harangue against contemporary Florentine women, quickly surging into the grand style of biblical prophecy.

Since the first *lectura* of Canto XXIII, critics have tried to harmonize the shifts in stylistic register and explain what they saw as the discordant tonalities of alternating forgiveness and anger. Laboring under Benedetto Croce's theory of interpretation, which separated poetry, conceived as lyrical weltanschauung, from the doctrinal and allegorical as well as from the rhetorical aspects of the poem, the first "readers" strove to identify the specific psychological category, in their emotional responses, that might unify the various segments. Thanks to these "readers," the beauty of the canto was unveiled. The Forese episode was perceived as the most autobiographical one in the *Divine Comedy:* the tender reunion of two friends reconciled in eternity after an injurious estrangement in life; a song, indeed, to friendship and to what friendship makes possible; the recollection of youth, of past mistakes, of wrongs committed and received, against the background, ever so present here, of beloved, and detested, Florence. It was seen as fitting that this should happen during an encounter with a member of the Donati family, the family to which Dante's wife, Gemma, belonged and the cause of so many joys and sorrows for Dante: Forese's brother, Corso, was at the head of the political party that drove Dante into exile.

The *tenzone,* still considered by most scholars a dramatic antecedent of the purgatorial episode, was known to fourteenth-century readers, as the quotation from one of its sonnets by the *Anonimo fiorentino* attests. The interpretation of its implied presence in this canto shifted from a biographical to a literary one after Gianfranco Contini published his essay on Dante as the character-poet in the *Divine Comedy.* Forese's considerate handling of his friend and of his wife, Nella, whom Dante had treated disrespectfully in the *tenzone,* was no longer seen exclusively as the denunciation of morally degrading and spiritually aberrant way of life; rather, it was interpreted mainly to mean the literary rejection of the *tenzone* style, a genre that, as seen by Contini, stood for virtuosity in the gratuitously injurious and the obscene— for a verbal aggression not corrected, not subsumed into the synthesis and the encyclopedia of styles that is the *Divine Comedy.*

A more recent approach to Canto XXIII is one that views it in connection with a larger pattern of values and the protagonist's ascent toward a revelation of the cosmic order. Alberto Del Monte was the first to read it entirely as part of an integrated episode, extending to Canto XXIV, whose sections can all be grouped under the common theme of justice. The sense of righteousness at work here would refer to Dante's personal situation and would lead him to retract the insults hurled at Nella in the *tenzone;* to assert, in the following canto, his own poetic primacy; and subsequently to represent Corso as an offender destined for damnation. In contrast, we have the approach of Vittorio Russo, whose view of the *Divine Comedy* as the archetype of a genre yet to come, the bourgeois novel, allows him to integrate the Forese character into the meaningful general pattern of the poem. Narrative techniques, such as allusions and identifications, thematic anticipations and recapitulations, are

detected as signs pointing to the pilgrim's progress toward upcoming revelations and toward his imminent self-definition as a "tragic" poet of morality.
Further, the linguistic and stylistic echoes of the *tenzone* in Forese's speech indicate this character's specific function: to reject the realistic satirical mode of
the *tenzone* sonnets and to usher in the appearance of Bonagiunta in Canto
XXIV, considered the climax of the whole episode.

A Militant View of Womanhood

In my reading of the canto, I would underline an observation made by
Teodolinda Barolini in her recent study of Dante's poets: the heroes of the
terrace of the gluttons are women. Indeed, because the main themes are
carried by female figures, I would also point out the change that Dante's figurative use of women has undergone since the time of the "sweet new
style" of praise.

The *donne gentili* who moved in that vague locality that is Florence in the
Vita Nuova, who were subservient to the *gentilissima* and received from her a
reflected loftiness of mind and heart, were described as ethereal confidants
partaking of the emotional and literary crises of the young men around
them. They were women who, with their teasing and sympathetic questioning, functioned as catalysts in the process of poetic creation. They were the
"ladies who have intellect of love." Whenever we find *donne gentili*, Contini
tells us, we are to read in the notion of nobility to women, as per the definition of love and the noble heart expounded by Guido Guinizzelli in his song
"Al cor gentil," which Dante endorsed in the sonnet "Amore e 'l cor gentil
sono una cosa" ("Love and the noble heart are the same thing") and clearly
extended to women in the last line: "E simil face in donna omo valente"
("Similarly a woman is effected by a worthy man"). In the *Comedy,* the word
gentile is applied to a woman once; in that instance it refers, in all probability,
to the Virgin ("In Heaven there's a gentle lady, "*Inf.* II, 94). Men, however, are
still described by that qualifier: Virgil is *gentil* ("The gentle sage," *Inf.* VII, 3);
so is Dante's friend, "Noble Judge Nino" (*Purg.* VIII, 53). The equation of nobility and love, a fundamental tenet of Dante's theorization of love poetry,
no longer pertains; it was renounced by him on his conversion to ethical poetry and substituted by a notion of nobility understood as a compound of
intellectual and moral qualities. In "Doglia mi reca," a song probably destined to be included in the *Convivio* and already cited in *De vulgari eloquentia*
as an example of Italian songs of rectitude, Dante discusses the ethical condition of men and women and specifies that beauty pertains to women, and
nobility to men. More important to our discussion of Canto XXIII, women
are severely cautioned not to offer their beauty to unworthy men, for if they
were to love ignoble men, theirs would not be love but bestial appetite.

The correspondence between these women of bestial appetite and their
unworthy men is the same as that which connects the immodest Florentine

women of Canto XXIII, who exhibit themselves wantonly in the city streets, with the men repeatedly upbraided in the poem, men who are maddened by pride, greed, and envy and whose political leader, Corso Donati, is chastised in Canto XXIV. These men and women live in a very circumstantiated Florence, crowded with people made rich by sudden gains and by corruption; a city, in reality, burgeoning with manufacturing, commerce, and banking, about to flower with the glorious, if licentious, bloom of Renaissance art. To the contemporary Florence of the *Divine Comedy,* the poet contrasts a utopian town of virtuous men and modest women, like Cacciaguida and the chaste Gualdrada Berti of old. The idealized Nella belongs in this utopia, along with those "good" and "beautiful" widows, daughters, and sisters remembered in the *Purgatorio,* who are loyal to their loved ones and pray for them: Alagia Fieschi—"she in herself is good" says her father in Canto XIX, 143; Costanza of Aragon, "mia bella figlia . . . mia buona Costanza," as she is described by Manfred (III, 115 and 143); Piccarda Donati, of whom her brother Forese declares, "I know not whether she / was greater in her goodness or her beauty" (XXIV, 13–14). Nella is remembered with a note of almost commiserating sympathy by her husband, as the slightly disparaging suffix - *ella,* in *vedovella mia,* implies. Nella, who in the *tenzone* unwittingly figures as an unattended sexually dissatisfied woman, now is viewed as a tenderly loved, devoted spouse, in contrast to Nino Visconti's disloyal wife, whose new marriage and quick political choice Dante brands as female sexual wantonness:

> Through her, one understands so easily
> how brief, in woman, is love's fire—when not
> rekindled frequently by eye or touch.
>
> (VIII, 76–78)

Of the many women inhabiting Dante's afterlife world of justice, only six, beside Beatrice, could actually be visualized by the author in a contemporary, or almost contemporary, setting. They are Francesca da Rimini, Pia de' Tolomei, Sapia de' Provenzani, Costanza d'Altavilla, and Cunizza da Romano. Their allegorical function traces a parabolic curve that is emblematic of the poet's literary and moral growth and that shows the extent of his militant view of womanhood: from the eternal torments of Francesca, who succumbed to Guinizzelli's ambiguous, self-legitimatizing concept of love, to the paradisiacal splendors of a notorious aristocratic lady, albeit mistress of a celebrated poet of rectitude, Cunizza, who shares God's glory with a militant woman of biblical times, Rahab.

"Because the women of Zion hold themselves high and walk with necks outstretched and wanton glances . . . the Lord will strip the hair from their foreheads. In that day the Lord will take away all finery: anklets, discs, crescents, pendants, bangles, coronets, headbands . . . and flowing veils"

(Is. 3, 16–23). This passage, evoked by Forese's rebuke of Florentine women, is an example of that biblical invective and prophecy that was continued by the Apostles and the Fathers of the Church, and was labeled by St. Gregory the Great as "wrath of the just." Some of the most vehement instances are found in the writings of Tertullian, who, in *De cultu feminarum*, contemptuously described the extravagances of female fashions, and who, in an instruction booklet to his wife, *Ad uxorem*, urges her not to remarry after his death. Moral invective and admonishing prophecy were the new literary commonplaces that Christianity contributed to oratory, as new principles and techniques brought about the transformation of a long-lived classical genre.

The Latin polemical oration was called *controversia* and implied praise and blame, *laus* and *vituperatio*. In the fourth century A.D., it became known as "invective." Christian invectives in most cases renounced personal attacks and vituperative language; however, they retained the harsh reprehension and condemnation of the classical genre, a view that was strengthened by the examples of the biblical prophets, thus turning into threats and obscure prophecies. Dante's *tenzone* with Forese is a vernacular genre closer to the classical type of *controversia* in that it brims with verbal abuse, derisive expletives, and defamatory accusations thrown at the adversary with the intention of destroying his reputation. Modern scholars have illustrated the verbal abuse of the *tenzone* genre at work in the disputes and the blistering exchanges that occur among the damned of *Inferno*. The evil use of the word seems to me best illustrated by Vanni Fucci's frame of mind and by his defiant declaration: "E detto l'ho perché doler ti debbia" ("And I have told you this to make you grieve," *Inf.* XXIV, 151). Language used with malice or with the intention to hurt others is, for Dante, the most grievous example of the will turned to *malo obietto* (evil end), outwardly exemplified by the physically and morally distorted condition of those who are in Hell.

Forese's speech in Canto XXIII is an example of the power of the word put to a good end. His speech runs the gamut from praise to condemnation and prophecy. It reflects the principles of sacred oratory and follows the rhetorical guidelines of the medieval Arts of Poetry. Geoffrey of Vinsauf considers praise and blame, invective and prophecy, as a means of amplifying a topic, and offers them as examples of description, apostrophe, exclamation, comparison, *subiectio* (self-answer), and *dubitatio* (*Poetria Nova*, 220–460). Replying to Dante's question, Forese gives at first a direct answer: "It is my Nella who / . . . has freed me / from circles underneath this circle" (85, 89–90). The amplification begins with a descriptive *laudatio*: "My gentle widow, whom I love most dearly" (91). A *comparatio* follows:

> "For even the Barbagia of Sardinia
> is far more modest in its women than
> is that Barbagia where I left her."
>
> (94–96)

Then comes an *apostrophatio* tied to a *subiectio*, both introducing the first part of the prophecy:

> "O
> sweet brother, what would you have had me say?
> A future time's already visible
> to me—"
>
> (96–99)

The second part of the prophecy is ushered in by a first *dubitatio*, concerning human ignorance of future events:

> "But if those shameless ones had certain knowledge
> of what swift Heaven's readying for them,
> then they would have mouths open now to howl."
>
> (106–108)

And by a second one about the penitents' capacity for prophecy:

> "for if our foresight here does not deceive me
> they will be sad before the cheeks of those
> whom lullabies can now appease grow beards."
>
> (109–111)

The Dialectics of Praise and Blame

When Dante turned from love to ethical poetry, he was heir to two illustrious traditions: the classical one, which asserted the rightful power of the word as a tool of government; and the Christian one, which believed in the possibility, by persuasion, of turning humanity from evil to good. Brunetto Latini taught Dante the Roman tradition of oratory: "Et Tuilles dist que la plus haute science de cité governer si est la rectorique . . . car se parleure ne fust cités ne soit, ne nus establissemens de justice ne de humaine compagnie" ("Tullius says that the highest science of governing a city is rhetoric . . . for, without speech, there would be no city, nor establishment of justice, nor human companionship," *Li livres dou Trésor*, III, 1–2). St. Augustine provided him with the Christian principles of oratory and with the rationale for the mixture of styles needed in the *Comedy*. In the fourth book of *On Christian Doctrine*, notwithstanding remonstrances to the contrary, St. Augustine gives ample indication of what he considers necessary and appropriate rhetorical techniques. The Christian writer of sermons—he explains throughout—is to set his work in one of the three styles but to vary it appropriately according to his needs. The plain style is to be used when one wants to teach, and the moderate, which can also be suave and ornamented, is to be applied when one wishes to entertain and hold the reader's attention; but when one needs to alert men to a great evil and move them to action, suavity of diction and plainness of speech are not sufficient, and the author will turn to the heights of eloquence and, by reproaching and rebuking, will use the style capable of changing men's behavior. To provide an example of moderate or "medium" style, St. Augustine quotes St. Cyprian's praise of virginity and St. Ambrose's description of the virgin's correct demeanor and attire. Among the examples of the "grand" or "high" style, we find Cyprian's condemnation of the women who "color, or discolor, their features with paint." His harangue climaxes with a prophecy: "With brazen audacity and sacrilegious contempt you dye your hair; as an evil omen of the future, your hair already presages flames." St. Augustine goes on: "It is sufficiently apparent, I think, that women are vehemently urged by this eloquence not to adulterate their appearance with rouge and to be shameful and fearful. Thus we recognize that the style is neither subdued nor moderate, but altogether grand" (De doctrina christiana, IV, 17–50).

Purgatory is a religious symbol of the human ascent toward perfection: that is, toward the full development of the intellectual and moral virtues bestowed on man by God, which alone guarantees the attainment of social justice. The mountain is guarded on its shores by Cato, the classical champion of political freedom and moral integrity; it is crowned, in the Garden of Eden, by an allegorical pageant dramatizing the history of humanity and the correct relationship between Church and Empire. Forese's appearance in Purgatory is appropriately set before the scene of historical redemption and after Marco Lombardo's and Virgil's discourses on the responsibility of man, free will, and the nature of love. As a purveyor of truth, still bearing the visible and audible signs of his earthly transgressions, Forese, the old antagonist of the *tenzone,* becomes the voice of redress, of castigation of sin. He signifies the will's reorientation from greed and aggression to social responsibility and the pursuit of orderly justice; at the same time, he indicates the embrace of a poetic mode that subsumes both blame and praise and makes use of them in an all-encompassing variety of styles.

In the frame of the whole episode, the short conversation with Bonagiunta in Canto XXIV appears to be not the climax, but the timely realignment into an updated context of yet another of Dante's past poetic experiences. Retrospectively, and in all purgatorial humility, the protagonist-poet recognizes his youthful apprenticeship of love poetry to have been, yes, addressed to the Good, but in virtue of an obedient, almost unwitting, submission to the dictates of Love. This is because Dante, in my view, has not repudiated the *tenzone* style in favor of the "style of praise"; rather, he has redirected them both. The theory and practice of verbal aggression have been rejected; the power of the word, as a means of correction and redress, whatever the styles suited to that function, is reconfirmed and the role of the poet redefined.

"Love is the seed in you of every virtue / and of all acts deserving punishment," explained Virgil in Canto XVII, 104–105. "L'uomo è degno di loda e di vituperio solo in quelle cose che sono in sua podestà di fare o di non fare" ("Man is worthy of praise and of blame only in those matters that are in his power of doing or of not doing"), the poet had stated in *Convivio* III, 4, 6. As a consequence, praise and blame have become key elements in the *Comedy*. They are the stylistic correlative of the dialectical opposition between a utopian vision of humanity and the consideration of contemporary society; they lend force to the many moral and political invectives scattered throughout the poem, from Hell to Paradise. The dialectics of praise and blame also mediates the passage from one section to the other of Canto XXIII. It explains the sudden changes in tone, stylistic register, and direction of discourse: from the harsh, realistic description of the gluttons to the plain and tender manner of Forese's recollection of Nella; from the violent rebuke of the self-indulging Florentine women to the low-key, nostalgic address used by the two reconciled friends. In this perspective, the pictorial symbolism of the terrace is integrated with what happens in it. The trees, after whose fruits and liquid refreshment the penitents hunger and thirst, signify the opposite of what greedy and aggressive people strive for on earth; they symbolize, as we have seen, the knowledge of good and evil and give hope of the solace that only Divine Justice can bring.

BIBLIOGRAPHICAL NOTES

The following are the most useful modern *lecture* of Canto XXIII, along with studies partly or totally concerned with the Forese episode: Vittorio Capetti, "I Canti di Forese (XXIII–XXIV *Purg.*)," in *L'anima e l'arte di Dante* (Livorno: Giusti, 1907), 307–337; Ciro Trabalza, *Il Canto XXIII del Purgatorio: Lectura Dantis* (Florence: Sansoni, 1909), repr. in *Letture dantesche*, ed. G. Getto (Florence: Sansoni, 1970), 2:457–478; Giovanni Antonio Venturi, "Il Canto XXIII del *Purgatorio*," *Giornale dantesco* 8, no. 1 (1910): 1–12; Luigi Fassò, *Il Canto XXIII del Purgatorio letto da L. F. nella Casa in Dante in Roma* (Florence: Sansoni, 1922); Carmine Jannaco, "I Canti XII e XXIII del *Purgatorio*," *Lettere italiane* 9, no. 4 (1957): 329–341; Gianfranco Contini, "Dante come personaggio poeta della *Commedia*," *L'approdo letterario* 4, no. 1 (1958): 19–46; repr. in *Un'idea di Dante* (Turin: Einaudi, 1976), 33–62; Aleardo Sacchetto, *Il Canto XXIII del Purgatorio: Lectura Dantis Romana* (Torino: SEI, 1962); Umberto Bosco, "Il Canto XXIII del *Purgatorio*" (1963), in *Lectura Dantis Scaligera. Purgatorio* (Florence: Le Monnier, 1971), 865–885; Alberto Del Monte, "Forese," *Cultura e scuola*, 13–14 (1965): 572–589; Salvatore Accardo, "Canto XXIII del *Purgatorio*," *Alighieri* 11, no. 2 (1970): 25–28; repr. in *Capitoli danteschi* (Rome: Baldacci, 1976), 85–101; Adolfo Jenni, "Il Canto XXIII del *Purgatorio*," in *Nuove letture dantesche* (Florence: Le Monnier, 1972), 5:1–31; Vittorio Russo, "*Purgatorio* XXIII: Forese, o la maschera del discorso," *MLN* 94 (1979): 113–136; Piero Cudini, "La tenzone tra Dante e Forese e la 'Commedia' (*Inf.* XXX, *Purg.* XIII–XXIV), *Giornale storico della letteratura italiana*" 159, no. 505 (1982): 1–25; Teodolinda Barolini, *Dante's Poets: Textuality and Truth in the Comedy* (Princeton, NJ: Princeton University Press, 1984); Mario Marti, "Il passato al filtro del presente" (*Purg.* XXIII), *Studi su Dante* (Galatina: Congedo, 1984), 135–152; Antonietta Bufano, "Forese Donati nel Canto XXXIII del 'Purgatorio': La forza dell'amicizia," *Italianista* 25, no. 2–3 (1986): 219–237; and Vittorio Sermonti, *Il Purgatorio di Dante,* con la supervisione di Gianfranco Contini (Milan: Rizzoli, 1990). Anthony K. Cassell, in "'Mostrando con le poppe il petto'" (*Purg.* XXIII, 102), *Dante Studies* 96 (1978): 75–81, and Robert E. Kaske, in "Dante's *Purgatorio* XXXII and XXXIII: a Survey of Christian History," *University of Toronto Quarterly* 43 (1974): 193–214, deal with specific questions mentioned in my essay.

In "Una proposta per Forese: Dante e il 'memorar presente'," *Rassegna della letteratura italiana* 94, no. 8 (1990): 5–20, Gennaro Savarese places Dante's friendship with Forese in a *Vita Nuova* context, which implies the literary experience of the *tenzone* as "jocose" poetry but from which all direct reference to it, and to Forese's and Dante's sinful ways, is excised as inappropriate to Forese's ontological character. For the attribution of the *tenzone* to Dante and Forese, which is contested by Antonio Lanza, as it was by Witte, Fraticelli, and Guerri, cf. Eugenio Chiarini, "Tenzone con Forese," in *Enciclopedia dantesca,* 6 vols. (Rome, 1970–1978), and Barolini, *Dante's Poets,* 48–49. For the placement of the *tenzone* genre in the thirteenth-century literary tradition and within the realistic register of the *Divine Comedy,* see Franco Suitner, "Dante e la poesia satirica del suo tempo," *Letture classensi* vol. 12 (Ravenna: Longo, 1983); Franco Manca, "Dante e la poesia realistico-borghese," *Canadian Journal of Italian Studies* 8 (1985): 32–45; and Rinaldina Russell, "Oratoria sacra e i tre gradi dello stile nella *Divina Commedia,*" *Forum Italicum* 21, no. 2 (1987): 197–205.

Of primary importance to any consideration of Dante's poetics, rhetoric, and style are: August Buch, "Gli studi sulla poetica e sulla retorica di Dante e del suo tempo," in *Atti del Congresso internazionale di studi danteschi* (Florence: Sansoni, 1965), 249–278; Erich Auerbach, "Sermo humilis," *Literary Language and its Public in Late Latin Antiquity and in the Middle Ages,* trans. Ralph Manheim, Bollinger Series 74 (New York: Random House, 1965), 25–66; Ignazio Baldelli, *Dante e i poeti fiorentini del Duecento* (Florence: Le Monnier, 1968) and "Lingua e stile delle opere in volgare di Dante," *Enciclopedia dantesca, Appendice,* 55–112; K. Foster and P. Boyde, *Dante's Lyric Poetry,* 2 vols. (Oxford: Clarendon Press, 1967); Patrick Boyde, *Dante's Style in His Lyric Poetry* (New York: Cambridge University Press, 1971); and Pier Giorgio Ricci, "La tradizione dell'invettiva tra il Medioevo e l'Umanesimo," *Lettere italiane* 26, no. 4 (1974): 405–414.

My readings and quotations of ancient texts are from these editions: *The New English Bible with Apocrypha* (Oxford University Press, Cambridge University Press, 1970); St. Augustine, *On Christian Doctrine,* trans. and introd. D. W. Robertson Jr. (Indianapolis-New York: Bobbs-Merril, 1958); Edmond Faral, *Les Arts Poétiques du xiie et du xiiie siècle* (Paris: Honoré Champion, 1958); Geoffrey of Vinsauf, *Documentum de modo et arte dictandi et versificandi,* trans. and introd. Roger P. Parr (Milwaukee, WI: Marquette University Press, 1968) and "The New Poetics," trans. Jane Baltzell Kopp, in *Three Medieval Rhetorical Arts,* ed. James J. Murphy (Berkeley and Los Angeles: University of California Press, 1971), 27–108; and Brunetto Latini, *Li livres dou Trésor,* ed. Francis J. Carmody (Berkeley and Los Angeles: University of California Press, 1948).

Finally, for the symbolic treatment of women in Dante see Maria Zanella, *L'idealità femminile nella Commedia di Dante* (Florence: Tipografia Galileiana, 1915); Giovanna Abete, *La donna in Dante,* Leopardi, Manzoni (Rome: Azienda Beneventana Tipografia Editoriale, 1956); Marianne Shapiro, *Woman Earthly and Divine* (Lexington, KY: University Press of Kentucky, 1975); Joan M. Ferrante, *Woman as Image in Medieval Literature from the Twelfth Century to Dante* (1975; repr., Durham, NC: Labyrinth Press, 1985); and Victoria Kirkham, "A Canon of Women in Dante's *Commedia,*" in *Annali d'Italianistica, Women's Voices in Italian Literature,* ed. Rebecca West and Dino S. Cervigni, vol. 7 (Chapel Hill: University of North Carolina Press, 1989), 16–41.

CANTO XXIV

Of Poetry and Politics

LINO PERTILE

Canto XXIV of *Purgatorio* is one of the few cantos of the *Comedy* that, though formally complete in itself, does not form a complete narrative unit. The account of Dante's visit to the terrace of the gluttonous begins at Canto XXII, 115, and ends with the last line of Canto XXIV. From Canto XXIII, 37, to Canto XXIV, 99, the focus is on Dante's encounter with his Florentine friend Forese Donati. This episode is in turn interrupted by Dante's exchange with the poet Bonagiunta da Lucca (XXIV, 34–63). As a result of this complex structure, Canto XXIV can only be interpreted with reference to the greater narrative unit of which it is an integral part.

At the beginning of Canto XXIV, Dante, Virgil, and Statius are briskly walking up the terrace, Dante talking all the while with Forese, with the other penitents looking on.

> Our talking did not slow our pace, our pace
> not slow our talking; but conversing, we
> moved quickly, like a boat a fair wind drives.
>
> (1–3)

This theme of moving along the terrace, now slower and now faster, with new characters now joining and now leaving Dante and his two companions, will musically and visually punctuate the whole canto, though here it serves mainly to smooth over the transition between Canto XXIII and Canto XXIV. Continuing his dialogue with Forese, Dante the character tells him something about Statius that was not included in the preceding canto. There, after naming and pointing to Virgil, Dante had explained that his other companion (i.e., Statius, whom he does not identify by name) was "the shade for whom, /just now, your kingdom caused its every slope /to tremble as it freed him from itself" (XXIII, 131–33), and at that point the canto had come to a close. Now, "continuing *his* telling," Dante adds that this un-named shade "is more slow in his ascent /than he would be had he not met the other" (8–9)—an addition that, while not being much of an eye-opener for Forese, at least tells the reader that Statius's love for Virgil is so great that he is willing to stay in Purgatory beyond his due.

This explanation of Statius's unusual slowness belongs, in narrative terms, to the matter of Canto XXIII, a canto that, being shorter than the average (it numbers only 133 lines), had plenty of space for it. The poet deliberately chooses to break the natural continuity of the narrative and to place it here at the beginning of a new canto, which, with its 154 lines, is seven tercets longer than Canto XXIII. It is impossible to know for sure why Dante did this. What can be said is that this uneven division reflects, and draws attention to, the struc-tural complexity of the greater narrative unit. It is also artistically very effec-tive, since it binds together the action while separating the narrative into two discrete units. Moreover, with its veiled reference to Statius's love for Virgil, it sets the pilgrim's next question to Forese—the question about Piccarda—in an intimate and affectionate context. In fact, the matter of Canto XXIV begins here, and it can be broadly divided into two sections: the first (10–100) falling within the scope of the Forese episode, and the second dealing with the remainder of Dante's visit to the sixth terrace. Thus, the two sections bring successive clo-sures to two narrative lines set out one within the other. In the following pages I will focus mainly on the first section.

The arrangement of this section is so sophisticated that the reader might not perceive the art or the problems concealed beneath the smooth flow of the verse. The story can be easily summarized. Forese briefly speaks of his sister, and then he identifies some of his companions (10–33). One of these, the poet Bonagiunta da Lucca, converses directly with Dante (34–63). Then the focus returns, and stays, on the dialogue between Dante and Forese un-til the latter leaves the stage (64–100). Looked at it in greater detail, the first segment of this section (10–63) appears to be organized around three repeti-tions of the adversative conjunction *ma—Ma dimmi* ("But tell me," 10), *Ma come fa* ("But just as he," 34), *Ma dì* ("But tell me," 49)—each signaling a sharp turning point in the narrative register.

A Preview of Piccarda

"*Ma dimmi, se tu sai, dov'è Piccarda*" ("But tell me, if you can: where is Piccarda?" 10). In its simplicity, Dante's question underlines the intimate and friendly tone of the entire conversation. Piccarda had died in obscure circumstances a few years before her brother Forese, so it is only natural for Dante to enquire after her. Dante also has another purpose in mind, which will presently become clear. Meanwhile, however, the reader must listen to Forese's gentle reply:

> "My sister—and I know not whether she
> was greater in her goodness or her beauty—
> on high Olympus is in triumph; she
> rejoices in her crown already."
>
> (13–15)

Forese had already sung the praises of his "gentle widow" Nella ("la Nella mia," XXIII, 87; "la vedovella mia," XXIII, 92). Now, his syllables echoing the sound of those praises (*Nella, vedovella*), he tells us of his sister, "La mia sorella, che tra *bella* e buona (13)." There is no reaction from the pilgrim, and the reason is that, since Dante intends to make Piccarda the protagonist of the Heaven of the Moon in *Paradiso* III, any comment now would diminish the future impact of that episode. However, it should be noted that our canto's rhyming scheme *tarda-Piccarda-riguarda* (8, 10, 12) will resonate in Canto III of *Paradiso* in inverted order: *riguarda-Piccarda tarda* (III, 47, 49, 51), as will, though perhaps in a contrasting way, Piccarda's self-introduction not as Forese's "sorella," but as a former "vergine sorella" (a virgin sister, a nun) whom death has made more, not less, "bella":

> Within the world I was a nun, a virgin;
> and if your mind attends and recollects,
> my greater beauty here will not conceal me,
> and you will recognize me as Piccarda,
> who, placed here with the other blessed ones,
> am blessed within the slowest of the spheres.
>
> (*Par.* III, 46–51)

Bonagiunta: The Gentucca Prophecy

Coming back to our canto, Forese addresses the second part of Dante's question by identifying some of the other penitents, beginning with "Bonagiunta,/Bonagiunta da Lucca" (19–20) and Pope Martin IV, who, rather than caring for the holy bride he held in his arms (i.e., the Church), he preferred to gorge himself on eels marinated in wine. Forese goes on to mention some other egregious gluttons, but Dante's attention is already elsewhere.

"Ma come fa chi guarda e poi s'apprezza" ("But just as he who looks and then esteems," 34). This simile describes how, having allowed his eyes to stray a little, the pilgrim literally turns them back to "him of Lucca" (35), the first shade Forese had pointed at. The conjunction *ma* works like a sudden jolt that opens a third narrative line, an episode within the episode of Forese. At first Bonagiunta murmurs something that Dante is unable to grasp, but then his words become clear. Bonagiunta prophesies that a woman named Gentucca, still a young girl in the current year, 1300, will give Dante reason to appreciate the much maligned city of Lucca, the Tuscan city that Dante himself had slandered in *Inferno* XXI, 41–42. This prophecy looks somewhat out of place here, for the context does not seem to justify it, although Lucca is Bonagiunta's hometown. The most likely explanation is that Dante, having stayed in Lucca, probably as a guest of Gentucca's family, uses Bonagiunta to make a public recantation of what he had said about Lucca in the episode of the barrators. Be that as it may, Bonagiunta seems very eager to move on to a more pressing concern. His *ma,* the third in the series, implies: "Enough of this, let's talk about something really interesting now." The curious thing, as we shall see, is that this new topic of conversation is contextually even less justified than Bonagiunta's prophecy, for it is neither about gluttony nor about purgation. It is about poetry— Dante's poetry.

Bonagiunta and the New Poetry

"Ma dí s'i' veggio qui colui che fore / trasse le nove rime" ("But tell me if the man I see here / is he who brought the new rhymes forth," 49): Bonagiunta's question to Dante signals the beginning of a fifteen-line exchange (49–63), on which a major chapter in the history of Italian literature rests, a chapter, now canonical, that bears the title of "dolce stil nuovo" (sweet new style).

> But tell me if the man whom I see here
> is he who brought the new rhymes forth, beginning:
> *'Ladies who have intelligence of love.'"*
>   I answered: "I am one who, when Love breathes
> in me, takes note; what he, within, dictates.
> I, in that way, without, would speak and shape."
>   "O brother, now I see," he said, "the knot
> that kept the Notary, Guittone, and me
> short of the sweet new manner that I hear.
>   I clearly see how your pens follow closely
> behind him who dictates, and certainly
> that did not happen with our pens; and he
>   who sets himself to ferreting profoundly
> can find no other difference between
> the two styles." He fell still, contentedly.

(49–63)

Critics of the nineteenth century, starting with Francesco De Sanctis, took Bonagiunta's use of the phrase "dolce stil nuovo" as evidence for the existence of a "school of the sweet new style"—a school of poets sharing the same or similar poetics, including Guido Guinizzelli as its precursor and Guido Cavalcanti, Dante Alighieri, Cino da Pistoia, Lapo Gianni, Gianni Alfani, and Dino Frescobaldi as its practitioners. Although eventually this notion was questioned and restricted or discredited (Gorni 1989, 28–30), it is still common to write about the sweet new style as a concept and a style of poetry that was practiced at least by Dante and Cino da Pistoia. Partly as a result of this enduring habit, and partly as the inevitable consequence of Dante's very ambiguous text, the episode of Bonagiunta remains one of the most controversial of the entire *Comedy*.

Bonagiunta Orbicciani (1220?–1296?) was a notary and a major poet from Lucca. He is credited with introducing into Tuscany the love poetry of the Sicilian court. There is no evidence that Dante ever met him. In the *De vulgari eloquentia* (I, xiii), Dante, in fact, dismisses his writing as "municipal." Nothing else is certain about Bonagiunta, nothing in particular about the habits that consigned him to Dante's terrace of gluttony. Writing in the 1370s, Benvenuto da Imola mentions Bonagiunta's weakness for wine, but it could well be a commentator's invention, based on the *Comedy*. What perhaps gave Bonagiunta notoriety was his attack, in the 1260s, on the poetic style of his contemporary Guido Guinizzelli (1225?–1276), whom Dante, when he meets him on the terrace of the lustful, will describe as his "father" and "[father] of the others—those, *his* betters / who ever used *sweet*, gracious rhymes of love" (*Purg.* XXVI, 97–99: my italics): in short, an early practitioner of the new poetry. Particularly well-known, judging by the abundance of manuscripts in which it is found, was Bonagiunta's sonnet beginning "Voi ch'avete mutata la mainera," in which he censured as conceited, bookish, and abstruse the *canzone* that begins "Al cor gentile rempaira sempre amore," Guinizzelli's major, albeit isolated, contribution to the new poetry. In his turn Guinizzelli had rebutted with the sonnet "Omo ch'è saggio non corre leggero." It is worth pointing out that, in keeping with the second line of "Al cor gentile" ("come l'ausello in selva a la verdura": "as a bird to the greenery of the forest"), bird imagery was a central theme in the exchange.

When they meet on the terrace of the gluttonous, Bonagiunta recognizes Dante so readily as to be immediately able to predict his future. Therefore his question ("But tell me if the man I see here," 49) is meant to express amazement rather than puzzlement: "Are you *really* the one "who brought the new rhymes forth, beginning: / '*Ladies who have intelligence of love*'" (49–51)? As a pivotal lyric in the *Vita nuova* and in Dante's poetic development, and as the manifesto of his poetry of praise, "Donne ch'avete" is well chosen—after all, it is Dante himself who does the choosing! But what are we to make of Bonagiunta's amazement? And what is the meaning of the

metaphor "brought" (50), with its echo of the last line of "Voi ch'avete mutata la mainera," in which Bonagiunta had denounced Guinizzelli's attempt
"traier canson per forsa di scrittura," that is, forcibly to beat poetry out of
books, if not out of Scripture?

There are also some troubling chronological problems. Dante probably
wrote "Donne ch'avete" around 1289–1290 and included it in the *Vita nuova*
four or five years later, when Bonagiunta was an old man, if not already
dead, as some believe (Pasquini, 649), and his dispute with Guinizzelli was a
thing of the past. Did the real Bonagiunta ever read or hear "Donne ch'avete"
? We do not know. Furthermore, though the action of the *Comedy* is set in
the year 1300, the writing of *Purgatorio* XXIV can be dated to about twelve to
fourteen years later, that is, almost fifty years after the Bonagiunta-Guinizzelli
controversy. Thus Dante's revisiting of it cannot be motivated by the topi-
cality of the issues but, rather, by the poet's desire both to write the history
of those issues and to draw attention to his own role in settling, if not su-
perseding, them.

The trouble is that Dante's answer seems as indirect as Bonagiunta's
question. Instead of confirming his identity, as the question would require,
Dante proclaims that he is just one—that is, he is not the first, nor is he the
only one—who, when Love breathes in him, takes note and then produces
words according to how they are dictated within him by Love (52–54). The
first implication, a humble one, is that Dante Alighieri is not the *author* of
his *nove rime*, merely the *writer;* that is, Love is the "dictator," and Dante is
merely Love's scribe. The second implication, a bold one, is that Dante has
the poetic ability to match with his own words the voice he hears within
him. Indeed, he contrasts Bonagiunta's *fore trasse* with his own *ditta dentro*
(54), thus suggesting that, far from being contrived and abstruse, the new
poetry is completely faithful to its internal source of inspiration.

Bonagiunta seems stunned by this declaration. Now I see, he says, the
knot that held us older poets back on this side (*di qua,* 57) of the sweet new
style I hear, just as the knot on the falconer's leash holds back the falcon, pre-
venting it from flying high and free after what it desires: such is, I believe, the
semantic implication of the metaphor of the knot in this context (Pertile
1994). Now I see what is new about the poetry that you and your colleagues
write today: your wings fly close behind the lure; that is, your pens adhere
strictly to Love's dictation—something we never did. Bonagiunta's acknowledgment of Dante's superiority could not be more abject. In his *De vulgari
eloquentia,* Dante had cautioned uninspired poets against "laying hands on
the noblest topics, those that should be sung in the highest style": "Let them
lay such presumption aside; and if nature or their own incompetence has
made them geese, let them not try to emulate the starseeking eagle" (II, iv,
11; trans. S. Botterill). Here Bonagiunta acknowledges his former presumption: he believed himself to be an eagle, now he sees that he was no more
than a goose.

But he is in good company. Among poets older than Dante, Bonagiunta includes by name the Sicilian Jacopo da Lentini, known as the Notary, who died in 1250; and Guittone d'Arezzo, who was fifteen years younger than Bonagiunta and died in Florence in 1294. Neither was a personal friend of Bonagiunta. His discourse, therefore, seems to have historical rather than personal scope, for it covers by implication the entire tradition of Italian poetry prior to Dante, from the "Sicilian school," embodied in the Notary, to the "Sicilian-Tuscan" poets who followed it, represented by Bonagiunta and Guittone.

The mention of the Notary is particularly interesting, since it helps us define the focus of Bonagiunta's exchange with Dante. Having died in 1250, fifteen years before Dante's birth, and several more before the Guinizzelli-Bonagiunta controversy, the Notary could not have had any notion of the "sweet new style." Therefore Dante could not, through Bonagiunta, blame him for failing to be a *stilnovista*—to do so would have been anachronistic. At stake is something at once more general and more fundamental: in Dante's view, the Notary failed to express himself as an inspired poet. Indeed, the inability to fly or write close to the one who "dictates" (53), which means harmonizing form and content, is the "knot" (55), or fault, Bonagiunta admits to have shared with Guittone and the Notary; it is also what separates the old poetry from the new.

If we step outside the fiction, we see that Dante makes the dead Bonagiunta do something he never did while alive, namely, concede that the new love poetry was, and is, more authentic (because it is directly authored by Love) and more accomplished (because it is faithful to the style of the dictator) than any love poetry written before in Italian. What Dante does not do is authorize the notion of a "school of the sweet new style" or even of a "sweet new style" as something distinct from the "new poetry" (*nove rime*, 50) or the "new style" (*stil novo*, 57), which he and other like-minded Tuscan poets and friends practiced for a time, each in his own way.

Dante and the New Poetry

The description of Dante's own poetic practice raises a question that is more troublesome than the question it purports to answer: Who or what is the Love that breathes in Dante and his friends and dictates the poetry they write? Is it the god of Love, as in Francesca's speech, or is it the Christian God, or even, as some would have it, the Holy Spirit (Hollander 1980, 82, and Hollander 1999)? In other words, is Dante referring to a traditional and secular kind of inspiration, however spiritual, refined, and ennobling, as in the passage from the *De vulgari eloquentia* quoted above, or is he claiming a religious experience that is radically new for secular poets?

Dante's words echo a text that used to be listed among Saint Bernard's works and was later attributed to Richard of St. Victor (d. 1173, a theologian and mystic who will appear in the Heaven of the Sun, *Par.* x, 131–132). It has finally been identified as coming from the *Epistola ad Severinum de charitate* written by a Brother Ives, a friar, probably a follower of Saint Bernard:

> What man can speak of love who does not know love, who does not feel the power of love? Of other subjects there is abundant matter in books; but of this one, it is either entirely within or it is nowhere, for it does not transpose the secrets of its sweetness from the outside to the inside, but it transmits it from the inside out. *Only he can speak worthily of love who, as his heart dictates within, sets forth his words without.*

This is a mystical text whose subject is the love of the Creator rather than the love of creatures. The idea is hardly unique. In the *De laudibus Beatae Mariae Virginis*, a widely read work attributed to Saint Albert the Great but in fact compiled in Rouen around 1245 by a Richard of St. Laurent, the following explanation is given of the much quoted Psalm 45:2 ("lingua mea calamus scribae velociter scribentis," "my tongue is the pen of a fast scribe"):

> *Sicut enim calamus non scribit quod vult, sed quod scribens vult: sic et ipsa ea verba proferebat, quae Spiritus Sanctus in corde ejus scribebat et ei dictabat.*
>
> Just as the pen does not write what it wants to write, but what the writer wants, so she [the Virgin Mary] said words which the Holy Spirit had written into her heart and dictated to her.
>
> (Book IV, cap. 31, § 14, ed. A. Borgnet, vol. 36, 262)

The context is Mary's reply at the Annunciation "Quomodo fiet istud, quoniam virum non cognosco?" (How can this be, since I have no relations with a man? Luke 1:34:), a passage that, interestingly enough, Dante will quote in part in the next canto as a supreme example of chastity (*Purg.* XXV, 128).

However, the notion of *Amor* as *dictator* is familiar in the classics, too. For example, Ovid writes "Tu amor mihi dictasti iuvenalia prima" (You love dictated my first youthful things), and "mea carmina / purpureus quae mihi dictat Amor" (my poems, which purple Love dictates to me). Indeed, the notion is so common that it appears in one of the inscriptions discovered at Pompei: "scribenti mi dictat Amor mostratque Cupido" (Love dictates to me, and Cupid shows all that I write) (Favati, 133). Either way, intertextuality can be deceptive, and, though the words may be the same, we cannot assume that Dante intends to invest them with the meanings they have in their source. Ultimately, either the religious or the secular answer is possible (as well as several in between): our choice will depend on what we assume to be Dante's intentions.

Other questions contribute to the ambiguity of the whole passage. How are we to understand Dante's use of the present tense ("*I am* one who, when Love / breathes in me, *takes note*") in relation to Bonagiunta's past definite (are you the one who, ten years ago, *"brought* the new rhymes forth")? More crucially, how does the character Dante's description of his poetical practice *in the present of the narrative* (1300) relate to the poetry Dante wrote *before* and is writing now *in the present of the narration (ca.* 1312)?

Answering Bonagiunta's question, Dante seems to be saying that he wrote "Donne ch'avete" because he is the poet—"one who when Love breathes/in me, takes note" (52–53)—thus suggesting that nothing has changed since then and that there is continuity in his poetic career. In his turn, Bonagiunta sticks precisely to his temporal *décalage:*

> *"Now I see . . .* the knot
> that kept [*then,* when we were alive] . . . me
> short of the sweet manner that I hear;
>   I clearly see how your pens follow closely [*sen vanno*]
> behind the one who dictates, and certainly
> that did not happen [*non avvenne*] with our pens."
>
>   55–60

Thus Bonagiunta seems to imply that the new poetry exists ("the sweet new manner that I hear," 57) and has existed for many years, at least since "Donne ch'avete," but that he had failed to realize what made it different and superior. Now Dante's account of how it is born reveals that secret and satisfies Bonagiunta's curiosity.

However, when is *now?* Is it the year 1300, or twelve years later? Or do we take the pilgrim's present tense to be a timeless present referring to both times, as though Dante's poetics never changed—with the crucial implication that Dante is now, as he is writing Canto XXIV, writing in the style of "Donne ch'avete"?

Dante, Forese, and Bonagiunta

In Canto XXIII Forese asks Dante twice to explain how he can be here in Purgatory while he is still living. At first Dante avoids the subject (52–54). It is only when Forese asks him a second time (112–114) that he replies:

> "If you should call
> to mind what you have been with me and I
> with you, remembering now will still be heavy.
>   He who precedes me turned me from that life [*quella vita*]
> some days ago."
>
>   (XXIII, 115–119)

This statement acknowledges two facts: first, Dante and Forese shared a life of moral dissipation until Forese died (July 28, 1296); second, Dante continued

with "that life" (118) until he was rescued from the "dark forest" (*Inf.* I, 3)—
which now appears to be an allegory of "that life"—*l'altr'ier,* literally "the
other day" but more precisely of five days previous, Good Friday 1300. The
information that Dante deliberately conveys to his reader at this point, and
that will be fully confirmed by Beatrice at *Purgatorio* XXX, 124–141, is that the
poet's life in the 1290s was corrupt and sinful; it was a period of grievous
straying (*traviamento,* as it is traditionally known in Italian). Thus, within a
few lines, the character Dante presents himself both as a *stilnovista,* directly
inspired by Love, and a mortal sinner. However, how can *stilnovismo* coexist
with moral degradation? Is there a way to make sense of this contradiction?

Accepting the authenticity of the *tenzone* with Forese—an exchange of six
sonnets, three of which are purported to be by Dante and three by Forese—
the prevailing critical view explains Dante's *traviamento* in poetic and philosophical, rather than moral, terms. Dante's reply to Forese in Canto XXIII,
115–119, would then be a recantation of the *tenzone* and of all the misguided
experimentation with poetry and philosophy the *tenzone* would come to
stand for, including the *Convivio:* a recantation, therefore, that belongs not to
the fictional year 1300 but to the years of the *Comedy.* Further evidence for this
interpretation is found in the Bonagiunta exchange. Here the "sweet new
manner" is viewed as the antithesis of the *tenzone,* and its recovery, as al-
legedly signaled at Canto XXIV, 52–54, the condition sine qua non for escaping
the "selva oscura" and writing the *Comedy.* Thus Bonagiunta's mention of the
sweet new style is invoked to prove the authenticity of Dante's *tenzone* with
Forese, and Dante's condemnation of the *tenzone* is taken as evidence of the
religious nature of the new style. Indeed, the two dialogues, the one with
Forese and the other with Bonagiunta, are said to be placed deliberately side
by side as poison and antidote (Bosco, 391), sin and redemption, failure and
triumph (Barolini, 48).

This symmetry looks compelling, but is it really in the text, or is it forced
in there by some wishful thinking of ours, supported by Dante's manipulation of chronology (Barolini, 94)? I suggest that, if we follow this seductive
symmetry, Dante's two statements, to Forese (concerning his straying in the
1290s) and to Bonagiunta (concerning the nature of his poetic practice in the
same period), become incompatible on chronological and logical grounds.
Indeed, we have seen that the new style, as symbolized by "Donne ch'avete"
and the poetry of praise, is an attainment and a conscious discovery dating
back to the years between the deaths of Beatrice and Forese (1290–1296).
These are the years of the *Vita nuova* (1292–1295) but also the years to which
Dante's *traviamento* and his *tenzone* with Forese are ascribed on the evidence
of Canto XXIII. However, Dante cannot at the same time reject to Forese his
life in the 1290s, and praise to Bonagiunta his poetry of the same period, to
the point of claiming divine inspiration for it. The two statements blatantly
contradict each other. It is said that Dante begins the dolce stil nuovo with
"Donne ch'avete," abandons it after completing the *Vita nuova,* and takes it

up again fifteen to twenty years later, in the *Comedy* (Hollander 1999, 274). Of course, it is easy to accommodate Dante's *traviamento* and the *tenzone* within this time line. Unfortunately, there is no evidence to back it up.

We could accept that, in his effort to edit his past, Dante occasionally contradicts himself. However, does he *really* do so? Let us take note that there is a substantive difference between the two dialogues. The dialogue with Forese is not about poetry; there is no allusion in it to poetical or literary activity of any sort. Instead, what is at stake in it is "that life" in Florence, prior to the year 1300, the way of life for which Forese is atoning now, and about which, having been saved from it while in extremis so recently, Dante is still utterly ashamed (see *Purg.* XXXI, 1–90). But Dante's corruption, explicitly stigmatized in the dialogue with Forese, is also Florence's corruption; "that life" is also, as Forese will shortly make clear, symptomatic of contemporary Florence's condition.

Conversely, the exchange with Bonagiunta is about poetry, and there is, on Dante's part, no hint of moral recantation or shame in it. Bonagiunta's presence on the terrace of gluttony is nowhere justified or accounted for in moral terms. Nor is it based on some special connection between Bonagiunta and Forese. In fact, although Bonagiunta may have died the same year as Forese (1296), Dante does not even bother to explain his prodigiously fast climb to the second highest terrace, as he does in Forese's case. To be sure, if he is in Purgatory now, Bonagiunta must have repented of some sin or other before he died. But evidently this could not have been the sin of bad poetry, for only now and only through the words of a living man does Bonagiunta come to realize what was wrong with his style.

Dante's Bonagiunta is a character with no significant life of his own. He only functions as Dante's mouthpiece on matters of poetics. Through him, Dante will tell us something about his own future (his experience as a refugee in Lucca), and also, above all, something about his own poetic past: the last word on the *vexata quaestio* of the new poetry and his own position in it. None of this concerns Forese. Bonagiunta appears here not because of Forese but, rather, to acknowledge the new poets, Guinizzelli in particular. Before praising, on the terrace of lust, the new poets' "sweet, gracious rhymes of love" (*Purg.* XXVI, 99), Dante deals with Guinizzelli's most notorious opponent, Bonagiunta, the only poet stranded among the gluttonous and one of the rare characters in the poem totally lacking in exemplary depth.

It follows that Dante's recantation to Forese is meant to be exclusively moral. Indeed, if behind it there truly was a *tenzone*, Dante keeps very quiet about it. We do not need to believe uncritically all that Dante states in the poem, but it is one thing not to believe him and another to make him say something that he does not say. Thus, we cannot take Canto XXIII as acknowledging the existence of the *tenzone*, let alone demonstrating its authenticity. Nor in turn can we base our interpretation of the Bonagiunta episode in XXIV on the existence of the *tenzone*. The dialogue with Bonagiunta is a vindication of the value and novelty of Dante's lyric poetry, despite his lifestyle in the 1290s. It is also a nice way for Dante to pay homage to his old fellow poets and friends while suggesting between the lines that the poetry he is writing now (i.e., the *Comedy*) surpasses anything he and they ever wrote. After all, is not Guido Guinizzelli, the "father" (26–97) of all the new poets, burning away in the fire of the seventh terrace for having, not unlike Francesca, followed his instinct as a beast?

Forese and Florence

The controversial part of the exchange between Dante and Bonagiunta takes place over five tercets, two of which are occupied by Bonagiunta's question and Dante's reply. The following three tercets dramatize Bonagiunta's posthumous discovery of the new poetry and his final contentment and silence. As though his faults had been poetic rather than moral, his sufferings now seem all but over. His silence works as a sign for the next change of register. In contrast to the three adversative conjunctions, *ma*, highlighted above, here two parallel similes suggest the opposite but perfectly balanced movements of Forese and Bonagiunta as they respectively move on and off the stage. It is a seamless, musical transition in which Dante's mastery, his inspired control of the medium, just now acknowledged by Bonagiunta, quietly shines through every line and every word. Here is how Bonagiunta and his cohort, having regrouped, form a long line like cranes (the falcons' favorite quarry) and resume their quick pace:

> Even as birds that winter on the Nile
> at times will slow and form a flock in air,
> then speed their flight and form a file, so all
>   the people who were there moved much more swiftly,
> turning away their faces, hurrying
> their pace because of leanness and desire.
>
> (64–69)

And here is how, letting his companions run ahead of him, Forese slows down, recovers his breath, and rejoins Dante:

> And just as he who's tired of running lets
> his comrades go ahead and slows his steps
> until he's eased the panting of his chest,
>   so did Forese let the holy flock
> pass by and move, behind, with me, saying:
> "How long before I shall see you again?"
>
> (70–75)

His question to Dante, "How long before I shall see you again?" gives rise to the last segment of the encounter. This natural and, apparently, innocent question contributes significantly to the deceptive air of ordinariness that pervades the Forese episode. Dante's answer seems equally innocent: he can't tell, of course, when his time will come, but he cannot wait to get back, the sooner the better, for he has grown weary of Florence, so corrupt has the city become, so close to ruin (76–81).

At this point, as Forese quietly speaks, we realize that what seemed ordinary and innocent was in fact a preparation of the ground for one of the most nightmarish visions of the whole poem:

> "Do not be vexed," he said, "for I can see
> the guiltiest of all dragged by a beast's
> tail to the valley where no sin is purged.
> At every step the beast moves faster, always
> gaining momentum, till it smashes him
> and leaves his body squalidly undone.
>
> (82–87)

A man is dragged by the tail of a horse toward the valley of Hell; the diabolical beast moves faster at every step, until it smashes the body and leaves it "undone." We have to go back to *Inferno* to find comparable horrors: the black bitches eager and swift as greyhounds pursuing the naked bodies of the spendthrifts through the forest of the suicides and tearing them to bits (*Inf.* XIII, 109–129); the lean and keen and practiced hounds hunting the whelps and tearing their flanks in the dream of Count Ugolino (*Inf.* XXXIII, 28–36). A similarly hallucinatory violence flashes, not by chance, in Forese's previous prediction, where he envisions the Florentine women with mouths wide open, ready to howl at the punishment that divine justice is readying for them (*Purg.* XXIII, 106–108). The two visions differ in that the first concerns the women of Florence in general, while the second is about one man in particular, unmentioned by name but identifiable as Corso Donati, brother of Forese and Piccarda, violent leader of the Black Guelfs and Dante's bitter enemy, who was killed in 1308 in circumstances not unlike those predicted by Forese—a fictional prediction, of course, of an event that, by the time Dante predicted it, had already taken place. Thus, in the same family, we have a saintly nun, a reformed glutton, and a bloodthirsty fiend; in the same family, Hell, Purgatory, and Paradise; Dante's dearest friends and his cruelest foe.

The Donati family, a branch of which Dante had married into in 1285, turns out to be a microcosm of the tensions, the divisions, and the bloody conflicts tearing apart the city of Florence around the year 1300, and it is to make this point that Dante devotes a tercet to Piccarda here. It should not be overlooked that, in a culture in which family ties were sacred (see the episode of Geri del Bello, *Inf.* XXIX, 1–39), it is Forese who, astonishingly, condemns his own brother to such a macabre and vile end; and it is Forese who sides *against* his brother to comfort his friend Dante and endorse the correctness of Dante's political and moral stance. This is nothing less than scandalous. Indeed, it is the stuff of Hell, and Forese's character displays a latitude of sentiments (warm friendship for Dante; tender love and respect for his own widow, Nella; hatred and revulsion for the corrupt Florentine women; joyful admiration for his sister Piccarda; intransigent contempt for his brother Corso) that can be matched only by a few of the other inhabitants of Dante's underworld, and perhaps by no one better than Brunetto Latini. Florence is the driving impulse behind both episodes, and their target too. Dante uses Forese to express his indignation against his political opponents, just as he uses Bonagiunta to stigmatize the inferiority of his poetical adversaries. Thus Dante the writer places Dante the character at the receiving end of seemingly objective data concerning the two driving forces behind his life: poetry and politics. Through Bonagiunta he vindicates the superiority of his poetic practice; through Forese he vindicates the correctness and goodness of his moral and political stance.

Now that he has completed his task, he can let Forese go. Forese's exit matches his reentry to the stage a few moments earlier. First, Forese slows down just as someone tired of running ("trottare," literally, trotting) lets his companions run on ahead, while he, walking, eases the heaving of his chest. Now, taking longer strides, Forese leaves Dante behind with Virgil and Statius, "just as a horseman sometimes gallops out, / leaving behind his troop of riders" (94–95). Finally, he disappears ahead of them (100). Here the Forese episode ends, and Dante returns us to the wider terrace and its crowds of penitents.

The second section of Canto XXIV describes the pilgrims as they approach and pass a great tree similar to the one encountered coming onto the terrace (*Purg.* XXII, 130–138): as they approach, they see a crowd of souls gesticulating beneath it and then moving away (100–112). A voice from the tree tells them to pass but to keep their distance; then it recites ancient examples of gluttony punished (113–129). A little farther ahead, a dazzling angel suddenly addresses the pilgrims, showing them where to climb up to the next terrace (130–144). This angel then erases the sixth *P* from Dante's brow, singing another of the beatitudes. His words bring the canto, and the narrative of the sixth terrace, to a close (145–154).

BIBLIOGRAPHY

The scholarly controversies over the dolce stil novo have produced, and continue to produce, a vast bibliography. For an excellent, up-to-date synthesis see:

Barański, Zygmunt G. "Dolce stil novo." In *The Dante Encyclopedia*, ed. R. Lansing. New York and London: Garland, 2000, 308–311.

Among the most recent and important contributions, see:

Barański, Zygmunt G. " ' 'nfiata Labbia' and 'Dolce Stil Novo': A Note on Dante, Ethics, and the Technical Vocabulary of Literature." In *Sotto il segno di Dante. Scritti in onore di Francesco Mazzoni*, ed. L. Coglievina and D. De Robertis. Florence: Le Lettere, 1998, 17–35.

Barolini, Teodolinda. *Dante's Poets. Textuality and Truth in the* Comedy. Princeton NJ: Princeton University Press, 1984, 40–57 and 85–123.

Bosco, Umberto, ed., *La divina commedia. Purgatorio,* a cura di U. Bosco and G. Reggio. Florence: Le Monnier, 1979, 386–394.

Favati, Guido. *Inchiesta sul dolce stil nuovo.* Florence: Le Monnier, 1975.

Giunta, Claudio. *La poesia italiana nell'età di Dante. La linea Bonagiunta-Guinizzelli.* Bologna: Il Mulino, 1998.

Gorni, Guglielmo. *Il nodo della lingua e il Verbo d'Amore. Studi su Dante e altri duecentisti.* Florence: Olschki, 1981.

———. "Paralipomeni a Lippo." *Studi di filologia italiana* 47 (1989): 11–30; now also in his *Dante prima della* Commedia. Florence: Cadmo, 2001, 59–79.

Hollander, Robert. "Dante Theologus-Poeta." In Id., *Studies in Dante* (Ravenna: Longo, 1980), 39–89.

———. "Dante's 'dolce stil novo' and the Comedy." In *Dante. Mito e poesia. Atti del Secondo seminario dantesco internazionale (Monte Verità, Ascona, 23–27 giugno 1997),* ed. M. Picone and T. Crivelli. Florence: Cesati, 1999, 263–281.

Marti, Mario. "Stil nuovo." In *Enciclopedia dantesca,* 6 vols. Rome, 1970–1978.

Pasquini, Emilio. "Il 'dolce stil novo.'" In *Storia della letteratura italiana,* ed. E. Malato. Rome: Salerno Editrice, 1995, 1:649–721.

Pertile, Lino. "Dante's *Comedy* Beyond the 'Stilnovo.'" *Lectura Dantis* 13 (1993): 47–77.

———. "Il nodo di Bonagiunta, le penne di Dante e il Dolce Stil Novo." *Lettere italiane* 46 (1994): 44–75.

Rossi, Luciano. "Il *nodo* di Bonagiunta e le *penne* degli stilnovisti. Ancora sul XXIV del *Purgatorio.* In *Fictio Poetica. Studi italiani e ispanici in onore di Georges Güntert,* ed. K. Maier-Troxler and C. Maeder. Florence: Cesati, 1998, 27–52.

Squarotti, Giovanni Barberi. *Selvaggia dilettanza: la caccia nella letteratura italiana dalle origini a Marino.* Venice: Marsilio, 2000, 141–156.

The authenticity of the so-called *tenzone* with Forese has been challenged several times. See:

Cursietti, Mauro. *La falsa tenzone di Dante con Forese Donati.* Anzio: De Rubeis, 1995.

Lanza, Antonio. "A norma di filologia: ancora a proposito della cosiddetta 'Tenzone tra Dante e Forese,'" *L'Alighieri* 10 (1997): 43–54.

Stefanini, Ruggero. "'Tenzone' sí, e 'tenzone' no." *Lectura Dantis* 18–19 (1996): 111–124.

In favor of authenticity, see:

Alfie, Fabian. "For Want of a Nail: The Guerri-Lanza-Cursietti Argument Regarding the *Tenzone.*" *Dante Studies* 116 (1998): 41–159.

CANTO XXV

Statius's Marvelous Connection of Things

RONALD MARTINEZ

Canto XXV of the *Purgatorio,* largely taken for granted in the late fourteenth century and during the Renaissance, had, in the modern period, become a kind of curiosity: a part of the poem thought of as bound to outdated cosmologies and esthetics. But since the pathfinding studies of Bruno Nardi, the canto has begun to receive wider and more sympathetic attention. Beyond its illumination of doctrinal and intellectual issues of critical importance to Dante's cultural milieu—which, as Vittorio Russo has shown, mirror the passage of intellectual vigor from Parisian Scholasticism to the bourgeois, "scientific" culture of Bologna, Florence, and Padua—Canto XXV has come under scrutiny for its close links to the discussions of poetry in the cantos surrounding it. More recently still, the passages in Canto XXV have interested students of scientific and cosmological lore as keys to the intellectual rigor of Dante's imagination. I shall sketch each of these aspects in the following pages, suggesting, at the same time, an approach to reading the canto as a whole, with an inevitable emphasis on Statius's discussion of human generation and the nature of fictitious bodies in Dante's otherworld.

The Process of Human Generation

The bulk of Canto XXV (31–108) is dedicated to Statius's answer to the pilgrim's question regarding how the gluttons in Cantos XXIII–XXIV, given that they have no need of food, can become lean. To answer the question, Statius returns to first principles and describes the entire process of human generation. The explanatory summary given follows the embryology and pneumatology of Albertus Magnus, which, as Nardi has shown, dominates Dante's thinking on the subject of human generation. Perfect blood, a residue from the several digestions and purifications of food (in the stomach, liver, veins, and members), is purified again in the heart and becomes semen. Because it is derived from blood that nourishes the whole body and from the vital spirit centered in the heart, semen has the power to fashion an offspring that resembles its father. After descending to the testicles and from there into the womb of the mother, the semen, whose formative power derives not only from the heart of the male but also from the powers of the physical elements composing it, as well as from the power of the heavens, coagulates and vivifies the mother's blood. Dante does not mention the latter two powers in Statius's account, but they are mentioned in the parallel account in the *Convivio* IV.21, 4–5, and remain implicit in Canto XXV. The formative power of the semen then produces from the coagulate the vegetative soul that exists potentially in the seed. But the coming into existence of the vegetative soul does not conclude the work of the formative power; it is, in Dante's words, only on the way *(in via)* and not perfect. The process exemplifies the Aristotelian account of a change in substances as a passage from potency to act: the mother's blood provides the passive matter for the formative virtue in the semen and is thus in potency to the act of existence of the vegetative soul; the vegetative soul in turn is in potency to the animal soul produced by the formative virtue from the seed, and this animal soul incorporates the powers of the vegetative soul—nutrition, growth, reproduction—as well as exercising its own powers of selective appetite and locomotion.

When the formative virtue, which for Dante *becomes* the vegetative and subsequently the animal soul, rather than simply functioning as an agent in the process, as in the account of Albertus Magnus, has completed its articulation of the physical organs through which the inner and outer senses operate, God turns to the work of Nature. The development of the embryo has thus far been conducted strictly according to the processes of natural generation; God now directly inspires the embryo with a newly created soul. Because it is endowed with intellect, this new soul is self-conscious and immortal. At this point Dante registers his disagreement with the view attributed to Averroes Ibn Rushd, the great commentator on Aristotle, that the possible intellect, the faculty by which man understands, is not ontologically one with the individual. In Dante's view, which follows both Albertus Magnus and Thomas Aquinas here, the rational soul draws into itself the powers of the sensitive soul (including those of the negative) and acts as the form of the physical body, which provides organs for the function of all the powers of the soul, save understanding itself. Although the inspiration of the rational soul is a superaddition to the work of Nature, it is implicit that the goal of the whole generative process—the rational creature—is in a sense intended from the very beginning, because the work of Nature is itself originally intended by the First Mover.

At death the human soul, which, like its intellectual faculty, is separable, departs the body. The powers that work through bodily organs—sight, smell, imagination, and so on—suspend their operations but persist virtually. Upon the descent of the soul to its appointed site in Hell or Purgatory, the formative virtue—continuously in existence since its production from the blood of the father—reconstitutes in the air surrounding it the figure of the original physical body, complete with organs for the powers of the soul. It is this body, Statius explains, that expresses visible emotion to the pilgrim as he goes through the otherworld, and it is the existence of this body that explains how the dead can diet and become thin. As the fleshly body, when deprived of food, becomes lean, so the aerial bodies, which include a nutritive power, become emaciated when subjected to the hunger provoked by the tree of Canto XXIII. Thus, although the aerial bodies have no need of food, their bodies visibly express the hunger they feel in their beings. Fernando Figurelli and other readers note that Statius's explanation does not quite suffice to explain how the bodies of the gluttons diminish in corpulence: since the dead take in no substance, under what rule of consistency can they appear to lose it? We can answer Figurelli by saying, along with John Freccero, that if Dante wishes to represent the soul or its affections, he can only do it through the representation of a body: that the bodies of the gluttons "represent" hunger is nearly to say that the best metaphor for physical hunger is the emaciated body. The poem's expressive need here overrides the technical difficulty Figurelli raises; or, to put it another way, the poem's expressive need decrees a juncture between the affections and the body that is part of its specific poetics.

Evaluating Dante's Milieu

In an important series of articles, Bruno Nardi scrutinized the doctrines of human generation available to Dante in the late thirteenth century. Nardi sifted through the competing accounts guided, in part, by the criterion that a good explanation had to satisfy in the thirteenth century itself. First, such an explanation had to safeguard the unity of the soul and the person, for in Aristotle's authoritative account the soul and body are uniquely coapt and naturally united to each other; their union, as Thomas Aquinas puts it, makes a substance that, though composite, is "one in reason." Second, a good explanation had to preserve for Nature a major role in generation, lest she appear—in violation of another fundamental Aristotelian principle—to exist and act in vain. Finally, a good explanation had to satisfy the explicit dogma of both Aristotle and the Bible that the immortal part of the soul is introduced in the animal soul from without.

Nardi's evaluation of the numerous positions current in Dante's milieu led him to conclude that Dante's views in the *Convivio* and the *Purgatorio* are closest, if not identical, to those of Albertus Magnus in his *De natura et origine animae* (in which Nardi chiefly distinguishes the presentation of generation as a metamorphosis during which the creature passes without discontinuity of essence through vegetative and animal stages). As Nardi emphasizes with a certain satisfaction, Thomas Aquinas on several occasions denounced such an account of continuous generation as heretical and anti-Aristotelian. Aquinas, who was strict in his definition of form as having an essence like that of a geometric figure, would allow no gradual metamorphosis in the developing embryo. In Aquinas's view, a distinct soul, as different from the prior soul as one number or one geometric figure is from another, is generated and corrupted at each stage of development.

Nardi's insistence on the differences between Aquinas and Dante has been criticized, most recently by Patrick Boyde, as overstated and essentially irrelevant. The distinctions, however, may well be crucial to understanding not only Dante's account of generation but also his thinking on the related concept of the possible intellect as apparently formulated by Averroes. In the terms of the medieval debates on the possible intellect, Averroes seemed to argue that it was unsuitable for an immaterial substance like the intellect to be embodied, for this would make it a material form and therefore corruptible—a conclusion that contradicted Aristotle. Thus the only correct interpretation of Aristotle's words in the *De anima* regarding the intellectual part of man was that it not only entered man from without but was in fact ontologically separate. Not the intellect itself, but phantasms, the images used by the intellect in perception, inhered in man, making possible a sporadic continuity of the individual with the unitary possible intellect. In Averroes's most famous analogy, the intellect is like the sun, a unified source; its connection to the thinking processes of individuals may be compared to the light of the sun falling on, and hence divided among, several objects. It follows from this view that the death of the individual breaks his link to the unitary intellect. Since only the intellect is immortal, the individual has no share in immortal life. As the critics of Albertus Magnus and Thomas Aquinas insist, to accept the view attributed to Averroes means abandoning not only the promise of personal immortality but also free will, a power of the immortal soul. Along with free will go also the system of reward and punishment fundamental to Christian morality and eschatology. By the same logic, the justification for Dante's poem, which depicts the consequences of moral choice in this life, disappears. Beyond this fundamental point, however, the arguments against Averroes offered by Albertus and Thomas are crucial to our reading of Canto XXV.

The Guiding Principle

In elucidating the most problematic assertion in Aristotle's discussion of the soul—that the intellect alone is separable and divine (*De anima* III.5)—both

Aquinas and his teacher insist that man is singular in creation in having a separable immortal soul that takes the form of a material body. Both Scholastics illustrated this principle through recourse to the Platonic definition of the World-Soul as the boundary or horizon of spirit and matter. In Dante's own works, the notion surfaces explicitly in the *Monarchia* (III.15, 3–6), where it is part of the argument for the two goals, earthly and heavenly, of the human race.

A chapter of Aquinas's *Summa contra gentiles* (II.68, 6) is typical. Aquinas quotes the pseudo-Dionysus, stating that the beginnings of higher states are connected to the ends of the lower, so that there is a "marvelous connection of things." The principle is illustrated, Aquinas goes on to say, by the existence of oysters, which hold the middle ground between plant and animal life—a detail Dante may have appropriated for Statius's reference to the mollusk, the *spungo marino* ("sea-sponge," 56) that holds the boundary of vegetative and animal life. Explicit recourse to the figure of the astronomical horizon is even more marked in Albertus's works, where it forms a main premise of his answer to the Averroists and is also cited in both the *De animalibus* and the *De natura et origine animae*. Albertus insists on the "marvelous connection of things" because of his own emphasis on the work of Nature as being always informed and guided by the First Mover, God; indeed, that "the work of nature is the work of the intellect" has been identified as a persistent refrain in his writing.

In Statius's discourse, the hinge of the whole generative process is the moment when Nature's work, guided by the secondary causes of the stars and planets, meets the breath of God as he infuses the new soul. Thus, for Dante, too, a human being is fashioned at the horizon where the work of Nature joins the work of God or, in the formulation of the fourteenth-century commentator Benvenuto da Imola, where the cycles of God's creative Word working through and independent of Nature are joined. Hence Albertus Magnus's distinction, quoted by Nardi, that although the Intellect is said to be infused in the embryo by a first mover extrinsic to matter, the first mover is not for that a wholly extrinsic agent. God is more intimate to his creation than any other natural principle, and nothing can act unless moved and informed by him. Creation and generation are the hemispheres of a vast cycle embracing Nature and Grace.

The horizon of rising matter and descending spirit is, in fact, the guiding principle of Statius's entire discourse in Canto XXV, which describes a series of informative acts in which the relation of active to passive reiterates, in several contexts, the figure of the boundary, or horizon. At the beginning of generation, the formative virtue coagulates the passive blood in the womb; at the end of the process God gives the embryo a rational soul and "breathes into it new spirit" (72). Beyond the grave, the formative virtue stamps the surrounding air with the complex of powers inhering in the soul. Nor are these the only acts of information in the canto: Statius's teaching of the pilgrim itself recalls, as we will see, Statius's study of Virgil's fourth *Eclogue*. In the act of understanding as described by Aristotle, the agent intellect informs the possible intellect, just as matter is moved to act by the agency of celestial forms. These several pieces of information focus on the moment when the rational soul draws into itself the animal soul. For Giovanni Busnelli, it is a moment that echoes, with the word *tirare* ("to draw," 73), a passage in Aquinas describing how the Godhead draws human nature to itself. Nardi objects that such a parallel implies that divine and human natures, like the rational and animal souls, form a single substance and thus leads to the Eutychian heresy. Nardi suggests that *tirare* is a metaphorical term drawn from the nutritive function of the vegetative soul, thus bringing Statius's discourse full circle by returning to the digestive figures of its beginning. It can be added that Dante's own philosophical use of *tirare* in the *Paradiso* refers to how the angels in their hierarchies both draw and are drawn: "Tutti tirati sono e tutti tirano" ("All are drawn and draw," *Par.* XXVIII, 129). In a more general sense, then, *tirare* is consonant with the universal tendency for higher-ranked powers to draw lower-ranked powers into themselves: for the universe to return, turned by the tropism of love, to its origin.

Continuities

The tradition of a "marvelous connection of things" informs Dante's emphasis, throughout Canto XXV, on continuities, verbal and cosmic: in the role of Statius, who as a disciple of Virgil and a Christian convert, mediates classical and Christian worlds; in the order of Purgatory, where the discourse on generation mediates the gluttons and the lustful, just as, in Aristotle's teleological biology, nourishment is for the sake of sexual reproduction. Statius's discourse consequently begins with metaphors of drinking and dining (perfect blood is like "leavings that are taken from the table," 39), and the canto ends by mentioning the regimen imposed on the lustful, harking back to the dieting gluttons (*con tai pasti,* with "this the nourishment," 138). The entire process of nutrition and generation, directed from the outset toward the production of a human being, is a model of continuous movement toward form, which Charles Singleton has taught us to understand as the logical model for the journey up the mountain of Purgatory.

In several respects, the continuity of generation is exemplified in the language of the passage itself, which enacts as well as describes the continuous action of the *virtù informativa*. The tightly constructed logical and syntactic order of Statius's speech has been often remarked on: Gilson, Russo, and Figurelli all note that the formative virtue, whether acting in blood, semen, or posthumously, is repeatedly the logical subject. Russo's analysis of rhetorical devices such as alliteration (e.g. *spirito / spira*, "breathes / spirit," 72) and acoustic patterns in the text, show to what extent the language exhibits the *aspro* (harsh) style Dante reserved for difficult topics. But the same figures are evidence of a tightly knit linguistic continuity that places Dante within the tradition of magisterial *canzoni* written by Guinizelli and Cavalcanti. Verbal framing, another feature of *canzone*-structure, also helps to unify Statius's discourse: the echo of *geme* ("drips," 44), the action of the semen fertilizing the womb, and the winesap flowing from grapes in Statius's simile for the fusion of immortal and mortal souls, suggest the parallel between the initial and final stages of generation. The wounds (*piage*, "doubts," 30) of the pilgrim's ignorance about the emaciation of the gluttons finds its pendant in the wound of lust—"the final wound of all" (139)—to be healed on the next terrace. Most significant is the recurrence of *vedutta* ("sight"), referring first to the *veduta etterna* (31), the godlike prospect that Statius promises to open for the pilgrim, and subsequently to the visual power (*veduta,* 102) that is the final perfection of the reconstituted aerial body. This link between godlike insight and the highest bodily sense, whose perception of light is repeatedly cited by the Scholastics to illustrate how the immaterial mind, sometimes called the speculative intellect, understands, reiterates the continuity of spirit and organic power that is the point of the whole discourse.

One aspect of the formal organization of the passage is crucial: its perfect symmetry in respect to its principal moment, the infusion of the soul. God turns to the embryo in the thirteenth of Statius's twenty-five tercets. Two tercets before, the separation of intellect and personality claimed by Averroes is signified by a verse break: *Disgiunto/da l'anima* ("separating from . . . /the soul," 64–65). Four tercets beyond we find not *disgiunto,* but *giunto* ("combined," 77) at the beginning of the line describing the fusion of sunlight and sap in wine as an expression of the union of animal and intellectual powers in the soul of each human being. We shall see later how this nexus of junction and disjunction is itself reiterated in the difference of understanding that separates Statius and Virgil.

It has become a refrain of analysis that Statius's speech bears a direct relation to the possibility of the fiction of the *Comedy*: without the aerial bodies (to be called "fictive bodies" in Canto XXVI, 12) what the poem represents would be literally invisible. This reflexive dimension of the passage, and its impact on questions of Dante's poetics, has been touched on in some of the most suggestive analyses of Canto XXV. Robert Durling calls attention to the parallel between the soul, clothed with an aerial body, and the formation of speech, in which the soul imposes the form of words on moving air. Thus the aerial bodies are the vehicles by which souls express emotions visibly, in parallel to speech as the audible expression of thought. In support of Durling's view, we can note that Statius's account centers on the moment when the soul becomes a *fante* ("speaking/being," 61–62) and concludes when he has explained how the souls express themselves with words: *Quindi parliamo* ("This airy body lets us speak," 103). This includes, necessarily, the speech he has just given the pilgrim. Drawing the link between the afflatus granted the poet and the infusion of the soul by God, John Freccero argues that the discourse on embryology is covertly a discourse on poetics, guided by the systematic analogy between the act of writing and procreation and thus immediately related to the birth of the pilgrim's "sweet new style" described in Canto XXIV. Giuseppe Mazzotta, too, has drawn attention to the importance of Augustine's account of the threefold soul in making the connection between the soul's triplicity of powers in Canto XXV—living, feeling, and reflecting on itself (75)—and the pilgrim's inspiration by Love, the third person of the Trinity, in the same passage of Canto XXIV. The analogy of verbal artifice and generation rests, as Freccero notes, on the Aristotelian view that art imitates Nature. But Dante's account of generation, drawing on artisanal metaphors used everywhere by Scholastics to describe Nature's work, illustrates the converse principle as well. For Albert Magnus and Thomas Aquinas, the formative virtue of the father in the semen is like the art of the sculptor exercised through his chisel. Thus, in another significant suture, the central line of Statius's discourse is the precise textual site in which God contemplates the "art in Nature" (71). Canto XXV is remarkable for its richness of variation on the verb *fare,* "to make" or "to do," and this is where, implicitly, Dante's own shaping art stakes its claim to imitate the work of God.

In the context of the Averroist controversy raised at the center of Statius's discourse, a concern with self-reference is highly pointed. Both Thomas and Albertus appeal to the self-evidence that we think as an existential, if not logical, argument against Averroes's notion that an external intellect thinks through us. Even the pilgrim's listening to Statius is tacitly a rebuttal of Averroistic premises. For as Aquinas argued, the Averroist position, by allowing contact with the unitary intellect only through the phantasm, could not adequately explain how a man understands. Conversely, Statius's instruction of the pilgrim through a return to first principles recalls Aquinas's attack on the Averroist position that teaching occurs because teacher and pupil share an identical understanding. The teacher, rather than transmitting his knowledge to a student, excites the natural disposition of the mind to learn, just as a doctor stimulates the body's natural tendency to health. In fact, the recurrence in the canto of the figures of teacher and healer in Statius, who cures the pilgrim's ignorance with wisdom, itself echoes the Scholastic debate over the possible intellect.

Statius

A focus for the concerns aired thus far—continuity of being, man as horizon, reflexivity, and the act of the poet—is the choice of Statius as the pilgrim's teacher. Since the time of the Old Commentators, it has been received wisdom that Statius is chosen because as a Christian imitator of Virgil he ideally mediates pagan and Christian civilization. Subsequent commentaries have in the main reiterated this view. A highly suggestive exception is Winthrop Wetherbee's identification of an "embryonic" sense of divine *virtù* in Statius's account of the death of Menoeceus in Book X of the *Thebaid*. But Statius also participates in the movement toward form both in terms of his embryological account and in terms of his place in the *Purgatorio* itself. Statius is the one soul Dante meets who completes his purgation, bringing to perfection his own rebirth in the spirit and fulfilling the purpose, or telos, of the mountain. Just as Canto XXV concerns generation and, implicitly, birth (there is a reference to the pregnant Callisto at the end of the canto, 130–132), Statius's purgation earlier in the *Purgatario* proceeds like a gestation and delivery: he rises to the *Gloria in excelsis Deo* that accompanied the birth of Christ (XX, 136), while the prodigal and avaricious in general, from among whom Statius rises to meet the pilgrim, cry out as "a woman would outcry in labor pains" (XX, 21).

But Statius's relation to the metaphor of gestation is still fuller and more specific. We know from his words in Canto XXII that Virgil's fourth *Eclogue,* prophesying the birth of a divine child and the return of an age of gold, was decisive in his conversion. What is more, Statius's conversion by the *Eclogue* reenacted in his spiritual life the descent from heaven announced in Virgil's text: "From Heaven a new progeny descends" (XXII, 72). Thus, when Statius comes to his discourse in Canto XXV, God's completion of Nature's work is presented as itself an act of reading, so that the central moment of the discourse on generation mirrors the act of reading that led to Statius's conversion. This anthropomorphic image of God is the exemplar for Statius's discernment of the Incarnation in Virgil's *Eclogue*. In embryological terms, the text of Virgil, whom Statius earlier referred to as mother and nurse (XXI, 98), furnishes the passive material of the inspiration by God the Father with the meaning of the Word. Statius not only exemplifies the analogy between the inspiration of the poet and the inspiration of the embryo, he is, so to speak, the incarnation of that analogy.

Statius's reading of Virgil's words, so as to draw from them, paradigmatically, the thread of continuity uniting pagan and Christian civilization, again reiterates the topic of continuity that characterizes the canto. It also resonates with the plight of Virgil, who had conceded in Canto VI, 42, that the prayers of the pagan world were separate, *disgiunto,* from God. Here, in Canto XXV, Virgil's participation in this separation is recalled in his inadequate answers to the pilgrim's initial question. The comparisons of the aerial bodies first to Meleager, who perished when the brand that magically contained his life was burned, and then to a mirror image moving with the body producing it, are unsatisfactory precisely because they are fragmentary. The mirror simile accounts for the aerial bodies as mimetic representations of the soul, and Meleager's brand represents the separability of the vital principle from the physical body. But even taken together, the examples do not account for the conjunction of the separated soul and the eventual aerial representation. Statius's final similes, comparing the aerial body to flames and solar spectra, although still metaphorical in character, rest on the explanation from first principles he has provided for the pilgrim: they illustrate a doctrine that has been firmly grasped by the pilgrim's understanding. Ironically, Statius's similes recall Virgil's examples: the fiery death of Meleager, the optical image flitting in a mirror. What in Virgil is fragmented is, in Statius's discourse, sufficient and unified because it derives from that "light upon the *how* that you have asked" (36).

But Statius's words, though transcending Virgil, are also conspicuously mediatory, an exemplar of how the Christian experience incorporates and renews pagan culture by rewriting it. If Virgil's role emphasizes his disjunction from the verbal order of prayer and grace, Dante compensates by making Virgil's text the model of the genealogical account Statius gives. As commentators note, the conclusion of Statius's speech, alluding to the cosmological discourse of Anchises in *Aeneid* VI, corrects the Stoic-Platonic notion of the body—as the cause of the passions—with the Christian view that desire and fear are motions of the soul. At the same time, Statius's account of how human beings reproduce and die to immortality, following a hermeneutic tradition, is both a correction and a transformation of the great cycle of human reincarnation that is the subject of Anchises' full discourse. Fulfilling his role as mediator, as horizon of pagan and Christian worlds, Statius rewrites Virgil's pagan lore in Christian terms and founds the continuity of ancient Rome and Christendom that is itself one of the bases of Dante's historical vision and his poetics. It might be added here that Statius's creative, indeed, inspired reading of Virgil's *Eclogue* is a model of the ideal continuity, in Dante's hermeneutics, of the first intellect and the reader's act of interpreting, even re-creating, the text. Contemporary readers of the poem may wish to substitute a system of signs and rules of combination, a langue, for the ultimate signified, the God-term, in Dante's poem. Ironically, in doing so, they appear to posit a kind of intellect separate from the existential individual and so reenact, in the terms of Aquinas's pun, the error of Averroes.

BIBLIOGRAPHICAL NOTES

Giovanni Busnelli's *Cosmogonia e antropogenesi secondo Dante Alighieri et le sue fonti* (Rome: La civiltà cattolica, 1922), and *L'origine dell'anima razionale secondo Dante e Alberto Magno* (Rome: La civiltà cattolica, 1929), have been superseded by the several accounts by Bruno Nardi: see "Sull'origine dell'anima umana," in *Dante e la cultura medievale* (Bari and Laterza, 1949), 260–283; "La formazione dell'anima umana secondo Dante," in *Studi di filosofia medievale* (Rome, 1960), 9–68; and "Il canto XXV del Purgatorio," in *Letture dantesche*, ed. G. Getto (Florence, 1964), 1175–1191. Also important is Vittorio Russo, "A proposito del canto XXV del Purgatorio," in *Esperienze e/di letture dantesche (tra il 1966 e il 1970)* (Naples, 1971). Among the several *lecturae dantis*, F. Figurelli, "Il canto XXV del Purgatorio," in *Nuove letture dantesche*, vol. 5 (Florence, 1972), stands out. Articles and treatments in English include: F. Fergusson, *Dante's Drama of the Mind* (Princeton, NJ, 1953), 143–150; E. Gilson, "Dante's Notion of a Shade: Purgatorio XXV," *Medieval Studies*

29 (1967): 124–142; Robert M. Durling, "Deceit and Digestion in the Belly of Hell," in *Allegory and Representation: Selected Papers from the English Institute, 1979–80* edited, and with a preface, by Stephen J. Greenblatt, n.s. no. 5 (Baltimore: Johns Hopkins University Press, 1981), 61–93; Giuseppe Mazzotta, "Literary History," in *Dante, Poet of the Desert* (Princeton, NJ, 1980), 193–226 (esp. 211–216); John Freccero, "Manfred's Wounds and the Poetics of the Purgatorio, in *The Poetics of Conversion* (Cambridge, MA: Harvard University Press, 1986), 195–208 and Winthrop Wetherbee, "'Per te poeta fui, per te cristiano': Dante, Statius, and the Narrator of Chaucer's Troilus," in *Vernacular Poetics of the Middle Ages,* ed. Lois Ebin (Kalamazoo, MI, 1984), 153–176.

CANTO XXVI

The Fires of Lust and Poetry

PRUE SHAW

No canto of the *Comedy* has compelled the imagination of twentieth-century English-speaking poets more powerfully than Canto XXVI of the *Purgatorio*. When T. S. Eliot added his famous dedication to the second English edition of *The Waste Land,* echoing line 117 ("miglior fabbro") of our canto and making it an obligatory point of reference for any literate English reader, he not only paid his friend and fellow poet Ezra Pound an exquisite compliment, he also completed what, in hindsight, seems a necessary trajectory. The closing line of Canto XXVI ("Poi s'ascose nel foco che li affina"; "Then, in the fire that refines, he hid," 148) had from the earliest drafts of the final section been one of the "fragments I have shored against my ruins" with which *The Waste Land* closes; with the new dedication the whole poem comes to be inscribed, as it were, between lines 116–118 of Canto XXVI:

> he was a better
> artisan of the mother tongue, surpassing
> all those who wrote their poems of love or prose.

Creating meaning by making explicit reference or implicit allusion to other texts is a large part of Eliot's method, and not only in *The Waste Land.* By citing Dante he places himself, as a poet and as a Christian, in relation both to his contemporaries and to his predecessors, to the culture of his own age and the literary heritage of the past. And this, of course, is precisely what Dante himself is doing in Canto XXVI, which exploits the resources and techniques of intertextuality—the many ways in which one literary text echoes, or is inescapably linked to, other texts—to create a density and richness of meaning and poetic effect that make this one of the great cantos of the *Comedy*.

The immediate connotations of Eliot's dedication to Pound—poetic distinction, poetic indebtedness, the generous acknowledgment of another's superiority—are very much at the fore of our canto. But in Dante the situation is both more complex and simpler: more complex in the scale and the scope of the literary relationships involved; simpler in that it is embedded in a narrative in which poets themselves are among the principal dramatis personae, and the narrative line can make explicit much that in Eliot remains allusive, even elusive. In Eliot, only the "familiar compound ghost" of *Four Quartets* is, possibly, a poet—some have recognized in him the figure of Yeats, others of Mallarmé. In Canto XXVI, Dante the protagonist is a poet. He is accompanied by two other poets, Virgil and Statius, the supreme masters of the classical school: the one is a pagan, the other, according to Dante's fiction, a secret convert to Christianity. They meet two further poets, Guido Guinizzelli and Arnaut Daniel, in Dante's eyes the supreme masters of vernacular literature in its two principal linguistic variants, Italian and Provençal. Two more poets are mentioned, Guittone d'Arezzo (124) and "the man from Limoges" (120), Giraut de Bornelh, both of whom, in Dante's mature estimation, enjoyed falsely inflated reputations. Two further groups of poets are alluded to, those whom Arnaut Daniel surpasses (119) and those who, along with Dante, think of Guinizzelli as their poetic mentor, or, in Dante's more emotionally charged word, as father (97). At least four of the poets who are physically present are also textually present—their poetry is consciously echoed or alluded to in Dante's text; and there are echoes and allusions to the work of yet other poets who are not present in the narrative.

Points of Reference

So Canto XXVI is preeminently a canto about poetry. The closing lines, which so haunted Eliot, form a natural climax, not just to the canto itself, as they superbly do, and not just to the story of the journey up the mountain—these are the last sinners Dante is to talk to before emerging into the Earthly Paradise—but to one of the central thematic strands that has revealed itself over the length of the poem so far: the theme of Dante's relationship to the poetic tradition that preceded him, both his immediate vernacular precursors and his more distant classical forerunners. To appreciate the full force of Canto XXVI, we must not lose sight of the crucial points of reference in the working out of this wider theme: the scene in which Dante is welcomed by the great poets of antiquity as one of their number (*Inf.* IV); the two episodes in which Guinizzelli has already been quoted or named (*Inf.* V and *Purg.* XI); the encounter with the father of the other Guido, who learns that for all

Cavalcanti's *altezza d'ingegno,* intellectual or ideological error has made him unfit to be Dante's companion (*Inf.* X).

Then we have the cluster of encounters with poets as Dante nears the top of Mount Purgatory: first Statius, who becomes a traveling companion, and whose conversation with Virgil is listened to with professional interest by an attentive Dante, who follows in their footsteps literally and metaphorically; then Forese, implicated in some shaming episode in a shared past; then Bonagiunta, eager to discuss with Dante exactly what distinguishes the new vernacular poetic manner from the old.

Finally, before Dante arrives at the terrace of the lustful, the long climb between the terraces has provided an opportunity for Statius to enlighten him on the nature of the shadow bodies of the souls, human conception and embryonic development, and the moment at which the fetus ceases to be merely animal and becomes human. The word used is *fante,* "child"—but etymologically the word means a "speaker," a creature with the gift of reason for whom speech is the necessary medium of communication. Statius's account, apparently a digression, is a vital piece in the pattern, adding to what Dante has learned from Virgil about love in the central doctrinal cantos of *Purgatorio,* and showing, if only by implication, that the proper end of copulation is procreation and not mere sensual gratification.

For if Canto XXVI is a canto about poetry, it is also a canto about lust, human sexuality, the proper ordering of sexual appetite, and the loss of humanity that ensues when passion is not bridled by the controlling force of reason. While the second half of the canto is dominated by the figures of the two poets and their eloquence, the first half is filled with two groups of souls (the heterosexual lustful and the homosexuals, as Dante learns to identify them) and is dominated by the compelling and disturbing image of Pasiphae, who took on animal form in order to satisfy her lust—the only explicit image of the sexual act the canto offers us, and offers twice.

Finding Balance

In a canto concerned with what bodies do, we find an insistence on Dante's own physicality ("they're here with me, / together with their blood and with their bones," 56–57); just as in a canto where the notion of literary composition as craftsmanship is central we find Dante-character referring with unusual precision to the tools of the poet's trade (*carte,* 64, the pages of the manuscript which are *vergati,* or ruled, and thus written on in lines with *incostri,* "inks," 114) and Dante-poet displaying a notable stylistic resourcefulness. We find, too, an abundance of animal images—more than in any other canto of the *Purgatorio,* as well as an overriding interest in language, speech, communication.

Canto XXVI brings into balance images of man when he is less than human, merely a body satisfying instinctual animal drives, and man when he is supremely human, exercising the gift of speech in its noblest form, poetry. Lust is represented by poets in Purgatory and by a reader of poetry (Francesca) in Hell: the connection with literature seems inescapable. The choice of poets to represent lust here leads us away from intertextuality, literature as a self-referential activity, a closed system, and back to the relationship between literature and life, the reality of human experience from which it is born, which it reflects, and which in its turn it influences—a relationship that for Dante was perhaps marginally less problematical than it is for us. In any event, a stay on this *girone* could almost be regarded as an occupational hazard for a poet of Dante's time: love was a mandatory theme for all poets who aspired to distinction, and it is the relationship between the erotic impulse—however sublimated, rarefied, or intellectualized—and lust that our canto calls into question.

At the end of Canto XXV we are already on the last terrace of the mountain, where the lustful are punished in fire. The fire is unleashed from the mountain wall with some force, engulfing the whole of the flat surface where the souls are walking. At the very edge, the flames are deflected upward by a wind blowing from below, which creates a path on the extreme outer rim; but the path is so narrow that the poets must walk in single file, as they will do throughout Canto XXVI, with Virgil leading, Statius following, and Dante bringing up the rear. The situation is dangerous, requiring concentration and effort to avoid being burnt by the fire on the one hand or falling off the cliff edge on the other. Dante feels more threatened than he has by any other form of punishment on the mountain. His acute fear is coupled with unusually insistent warnings from Virgil about the need both for alertness and for a willingness to let himself be guided—already once at the end of Canto XXV as they emerge on to the terrace, and again, repeatedly (*spesso,* 2), at the beginning of our canto. Whether or not we accept Boccaccio's perhaps suspect testimony that Dante himself was guilty of lust ("my limbs—mature or green—have not been left / within the world beyond; they're here with me," 55–56), the text itself emphasizes his vulnerability; and, uniquely for the punishments in Purgatory, he will himself briefly share the condition of the sinners, for he must pass through the fire in order to emerge from this last circle to the Earthly Paradise.

Indeed, throughout the canto we are aware of fire as a distinct and separate medium in which the souls move and operate. They are as meticulously careful not to come out of the flames, since Dante is not to get burnt (15). As they move away from the foreground they blur and fade from view altogether, like a fish going down through water to the bottom (135)—a simile deservedly famous for its economy and precision, the verbal equivalent of a cinematic dissolve. The distinctiveness of the visual effects created by fire provides the starting point of the encounter with the shades, an elegant variation on the theme of the amazement caused by Dante's condition as living man visiting the afterlife.

Suspension of Time

As the canto opens, the sun is low in the western sky, which turns pale in the late afternoon of Dante's third day on the mountain; the pilgrim's shadow falls, not on the ground, but laterally, onto the flames; where it falls, the flame appears redder, more glowing (*più rovente*, 7). This visual clue catches the attention of a group of shades; they first murmur among themselves, then move toward Dante and question him. But Dante's attention has been caught by the arrival of a second group of souls moving in the opposite direction from the first group. The two groups now intermingle, exchange rapid kisses, call out examples of lust, and then move off. The first group again draws closer to Dante, and he, before articulating his own intense curiosity about the seemingly anomalous behavior of the second group—they are moving around the mountain in a direction unprecedented in his experience of the other terraces—nonetheless satisfies the curiosity of the first group, matching the exquisite courtesy of his interlocutor, and only then asks his own question: Who are these two groups? The original speaker reveals that they are the homosexuals and the heterosexual lustful.

This first half of the canto is remarkable for a number of reasons: the intricate patterning of the narrative; the concentration of similes, which are often marked by the use of rare or unique rhymes; the contrasting presentation of homosexuals and heterosexuals.

The narrative interweaves curiosity and satisfaction, eagerness and hesitation, speech and silence, animated activity and long pauses. The interlude separating the shade's question from Dante's answer is all movement and animation, a penitential imperative that takes precedence over the satisfaction of merely contingent curiosity. It provides a striking example of Dante's *tecnica ad incastro*, the "embedding" technique by which one episode interrupts or is inserted into another. But the interlude, if not dramatically unprecedented in the poem, is grammatically so. Normally Dante preserves a distinction between the past tense of narrative, reserved for Dante-character, and the present tense of writing the poem, reserved for Dante-poet (used in invocations to the Muses, comments on the difficulty of his theme, asides to the reader, and so on, and in similes referring to constants of human experience that lie outside the temporal sequence of the narrative). Occasionally, in moments of great drama or tension, he slips into the historic present for narrative, but rarely for more than three lines. Here, exceptionally, he sustains the narrative present for twenty-one lines, so that the interlude is grammatically demarcated from the surrounding action that it interrupts. The effect created, with extraordinary vividness and immediacy, is of a suspension of time, as we witness a recurring ritual of penance, which for these souls is a part of their purgatorial routine. We revert to the normal past tense of narrative only at lines 53–54, *incominciai* ("I/began"), when Dante picks up the thread of his conversation with the soul.

Of Ants and Cranes

Remarkable also in this first half of the canto is the high incidence of similes, the ants (34–35), the cranes (43–45), and the mountaineer (67–69). The ants and the cranes to which the thronging souls are likened as they first come together and then separate are creatures of impeccable literary pedigree. (The chiastic disposition of the comparisons within the intermezzo is striking: "l'una gente sen va, l'altra sen vene"; "one group moves with—the other opposite—us," 46). Ants had been used by Virgil in a famous extended simile in the *Aeneid* (IV, 402–407)—his *nigrum agmen* becomes Dante's *schiera bruna*. Cranes also had been used by Virgil in a brief simile in the *Aeneid* (X, 264–266), and then by Statius, at much greater length and consciously echoing Virgil, in the *Thebaid* (V, 11–16). But in Virgil and Statius the people had been warriors; here they are saved souls, one of the most active groups we meet on the mountain and those most clearly behaving in a specifically Christian way. They greet each other with the kiss of chastity and charity recommended by St. Paul (Romans 16:16), which stands in unmistakable *contrapasso* relationship to the lingering, lascivious kisses of lust. It is the exchanging of kisses between individuals within the group that is likened by Dante, with an almost instantaneous shift of focus from long-shot to close-up, to the gesture of ants who rub their muzzles together. The final line of the simile is strictly gratuitous, adding nothing in visual terms but conveying very relevant notions of solidarity, helpfulness, community spirit—and doing so in the very Dantesque form of conjecture about whether the gestures of the ants are a form of nonverbal communication.

Dante's intense speculative interest in language had led him in the *De vulgari eloquentia* to examine the case of talking animals—an apparent exception to the rule that speech defines man alone—and to dismiss it as illusory. Here he considers the possibility of nonverbal communication, a notion already found in Pliny, who uses the words *conlocutio* (conversation) and *percontatio* (enquiring)—Dante's *spiar*—in his description of ants in the *Natural History*, but no commentator to my knowledge has identified a source for the description of the movement by which the ants appear to communicate. This, we must suppose, like so much else of the physical detail in the canto—the effect of shadow on flame, the blurring of outline as an object sinks through water—came from direct observation: a perfect example of how Dante can effortlessly and magically combine the very literary and the utterly everyday to produce an image of uniquely Dantesque stamp. The impression of intense originality is reinforced on this occasion by the knowledge that *s'ammusa* is a Dantesque coinage, one of a number of examples in our canto where lexical inventiveness seems to have been stimulated by the pressure of figurative utterance.

The image of the ants has been universally admired, the reaction one of delighted recognition at the freshness and accuracy of its observation of the natural world. Up to this point in the *Comedy* birds (cranes, storks, starlings, doves) have been captured with this same exactness and delicacy. The simile of the cranes at lines 43–45 is therefore disconcerting: it describes what never occurs in nature, two flocks of cranes flying in opposite directions, one heading north, one south. The description starts as if it were naturalistic. Only at the beginning of the second line with the dislocating past subjunctive *volasser* does it become clear that it is a hypothetical situation. The third line seems consciously to counter the reader's mounting perplexity: one group would be shunning the cold, the other the heat. Some critics are frankly disappointed with Dante for what they see as a falling away from his usual impeccable standards of descriptive realism. Manfredi Porena, for example, comments that the simile is so absurd that Dante would have done better to "rinunciare alle gru"—to do without the cranes. But there are several reasons why Dante might have been reluctant to *rinunciare alle gru*.

The lustful in *Inferno* V had been likened to cranes, and to find them here reinforces the web of connections between these two cantos, which for so many reasons form a pair. Both Virgil's and Statius's cranes had been flying to named geographical destinations in the north: that Dante mentions the Riphaean Mountains—located vaguely by mediaeval cartographers somewhere in the extreme north of Europe—suggests that the Virgilian model, and its elaboration in Statius, were uppermost in his mind.

Pasiphae

Most important, as has often been noted, the image is functional on another level altogether. It is the only way that Dante signals to us, obliquely, that there is something odd or deviant in the way the second group of souls is going around the mountain. The laws of nature are broken in the simile describing those who broke the natural law, just as their punishment includes a symbolic element of "unnaturalness" in the direction in which they move. Homosexuality is for Dante a sin against nature—so much seems clear from the *Inferno*, where the homosexuals are in a different circle and indeed a different section of Hell from the heterosexual lustful, whose sin is merely one of incontinence or excess. But nowhere here does he state that explicitly. Indeed, the notion of an infraction of the natural order seems more pertinent to the heterosexuals than to the homosexuals, since the example they shout out, an example of bestiality, is much more clamorously a violation of that order.

The heterosexuals and the homosexuals are distinguished only by the direction in which they move around the mountain and the examples of lust they call out as they go. But whereas the homosexuals call out simply "Sodom and Gomorrah," the biblical archetype that requires and receives no further elucidation, the heterosexuals call out not just the name of Pasiphae (the mythological queen of Crete who coupled with a bull and gave birth to the Minotaur), but the story of her infatuation, telescoped into its single, significant moment, the brutal, dehumanized sexual act: the monstrous coupling of human being and animal. Again, Dante's question about the identity of the groups elicits in the case of the homosexuals only a second classic, but anecdotally oblique, instance of the practice. They sinned in the way that caused Caesar to be called "queen," a reference to his reputed relationship with the king of Bithynia. There is no definition of their sin, no description of their activities, and anonymity reigns. No such reticence inhibits the statements about the heterosexuals. (In dramatic terms the greater degree of explicitness reads as self-recrimination, for it is a heterosexual speaking, but the choice of emphasis is, as always, Dante's.) These sinners failed to observe human law (83), pursuing their appetites like beasts (84), hence they call out the name of the woman "che s'imbestiò ne le 'mbestiate schegge" ("who, in / the bestial planks, became herself a beast," 87). The original exemplum is repeated periphrastically in a line that is surely one of the most remarkable in the poem.

Dante's choice of Pasiphae as sole representative of heterosexual lust is shocking and is meant to shock. What makes her case so much more disturbing than conventional images of sexual excess such as promiscuity is the perverse ingenuity required to act out her lust. She had a cow fashioned out of timbers—the *schegge* of line 87; the deluded bull mated with the cow, thus mating also with the woman concealed inside it. Bestiality is the extreme case, the end of the spectrum of physical desire unrestrained by "human law." In the *Convivio* Dante had said that the man who abandons reason and lives only by the senses lives not as a man but as an animal: Pasiphae's story literally and emblematically enacts this moral truth. The explosive harshness of the consonantal clusters of line 87 suggests both the violence of the transgression enacted against the natural order and the urgency of the speaker's moral revulsion: sexual and moral energy fuse with verbal energy, for *imbestiare* is yet another Dantesque coinage. The reflexive verb implies not just that Pasiphae "became an animal" but that she "made an animal of herself," that she "turned herself into an animal." Where modern moralists might locate the offence in the denial of the sexual partner's humanity, the treating of another person as an object, Dante's exemplum invites us to see lust as self-injury, a willfully and wantonly self-inflicted loss of humanity and human dignity.

Struck Dumb

The extraordinarily vivid simile describing the reaction of the souls to the revelation that Dante is alive—like the mountain dweller who comes to the city and gazes dumbstruck at what he finds, they fall silent in astonishment—appears to have no literary source. Benvenuto tells us that Dante drew the image from his own experience of people from the hills coming to Florence. Again there is a high degree of lexical inventiveness: *s'inurba* and *ammuta* are both Dantesque coinages. If it is difficult to tease out the full implications of the curious inverse symmetry between vehicle and tenor of the simile (Dante, a city dweller, is visiting the inhabitants of a mountain; it is not the visitor who registers amazement, but the visited), its function in the broader pattern of the narrative is clear. It offers a powerful image of inarticulacy in a context notable for its concern with speech and degrees of skill in its use. In the *De vulgari eloquentia* Dante had dismissed the language of mountainous regions—*montaninas loquelas*—as uncouth. The linguistic resources of this mountain dweller are so limited that he is speechless—he could almost be added to the bestiary, along with the ants, cranes, and fish. The image adds another piece to the patterning of speech and silence through the canto, setting off not only the eloquence of the soul who will now answer Dante's question but also, perhaps more significant, the quality of Dante's silence when, only a few lines further on, he too will be unable to speak—a silence of a different order entirely.

Dante falls silent when the shade, who has until now acted as spokesman for the group, abandons the collective plural and begins to speak for himself alone. This he does at line 90, declining to name his companions, for time is pressing, but identifying himself: "Son Guido Guinizzelli" ("I am Guido Guinizzelli").

Dante's silence at this news reflects not the unedifying astonishment of the *montanaro,* but complex and conflicting feelings—it conveys an intense inwardness of experience. The simile he uses now (94) is not descriptive and realistic, but literary and allusive. There is an almost palpable sense that we are approaching an emotional climax. The episode to which the simile alludes is recounted by Statius at the end of Book Five of the *Thebaid,* which opens with the cranes. The sons of Hypsipyle come upon their mother unexpectedly as she is about to be put to death for having inadvertently allowed Lycurgus's baby son, entrusted to her care, to be killed by a snake. They rush forward, embrace her, and pull her to safety. By not detailing the circumstances in which the mother and sons found themselves, by not naming them or discursively elaborating on their reactions, Dante gains a notable compression and resonance.

On learning the identity of the man he has been talking to, Dante feels the same surge of emotions as the sons of Hypsipyle (shock, delight, devotion, dismay); but unlike them he does not act. A second switch to the narrative present, arrestingly in midline and very briefly, marks this moment of stasis, the failure to respond physically to the emotional climax. The failure to embrace Guinizzelli in the flames not only stands in counterpoint to the earlier scene, where the shades do rush forward and embrace each other in the flames—as Dante himself will do in the afterlife, we may suppose—but also becomes the latest element in the series of embraces or failures to embrace marking out the action of *Purgatorio* (Casella and Dante, Sordello and Virgil, Statius and Virgil). Dante's affection extends not just to the man and his poems but to the very ink with which he wrote (*caro* in lines 111 and 114): all the tenderness and warmth in the canto are here.

Guinizzelli (with Guittone and Giraut)

But for all Dante's feelings of affection and gratitude, Guinizzelli cannot draw him into the fire, let alone lead him out the other side. There is a long pause as the two walk along in parallel, Dante gazing at Guinizzelli, unable to express the filial feelings that Dante-poet articulates for us at line 97. When Dante-character does manage to speak, voicing his admiration for Guinizzelli's poems, he will address the older poet in the deferential *voi* form, which Guinizzelli's use of *tu* implicitly and tactfully corrects, as does the appellation *frate,* echoing Virgil to Statius at a similar moment of recognition and high emotion.

It is unremarkable that Guinizzelli should deflect Dante's compliment by pointing to a better artist—Oderisi had done just this in Canto XI. Like the illuminator, Guinizzelli has transcended all pride in his own earthly achievement. What has made some critics uneasy is the animus with which he elaborates the point. He is still, it seems, deeply involved in literary matters and now becomes curiously exercised on the question of true value and false reputation. The figure he points to in the flames, as yet unnamed, was better than all the others, even though fools persist in overvaluing the man from Limoges (the periphrasis is dismissive, yet paradoxically confirms Giraut's fame: he does not even need to be named to be identified). In Italy the same thing happened with Guittone. The repetition of the word *ver,* the emphatic alliteration of lines 121 and 126, the biblical ring of line 126: all convey the vehemence of his belief in the objective nature of literary value and achievement, which is not a matter of opinion or whim, of taste or fashion. The asperity of this attack on the fools who get it wrong, surprising in a soul who is supposedly beyond earthly rivalries, is doubly amazing in the light of the parallel episode in Canto XI, where Oderisi's disclaimer is followed by an impassioned denunciation of the vanity of earthly fame.

Literary polemic erupts into the afterlife as Dante, through Guinizzelli, imposes his own pattern of meaning on recent literary history. The double denigration of Giraut and Guittone serves his purpose in two ways: it adds further detail and emphasis to the picture of the history of vernacular poetry that began to emerge in Canto XXIV (and in so doing corrects and amplifies the *De vulgari eloquentia,* his first systematic attempt to map out the terrain of vernacular literature); and more important, it introduces the *miglior fabbro* (whose identity Dante-character must surely suspect) as the figure for whom Guinizzelli feels the kind of admiration that Dante feels for Guinizzelli. The poetic perspective lengthens and broadens, temporally and geographically, as we are carried back to the Occitan tradition from which Italian lyric poetry is derived and which the closing lines of the canto so memorably celebrate.

Dante evidently changed his mind about the man from Limoges, for reasons we can only guess at and that bear directly on his revised estimate of the stature of Arnaut Daniel. In the *De vulgari* Giraut had ranked higher than Arnaut, by clear implication if not by explicit comparison, in accordance with the received opinion, which proclaimed him to be the finest of all the troubadours. The treatise's judgment on Guittone is, however, confirmed. There Dante had used the damning word *plebescere*, "to write in a plebeian or commonplace manner," or to lack precisely the stylistic refinement he admired in Guinizzelli—the key adjective *dolce* ("sweet") of *Purgatorio* XXIV is twice repeated here at lines 99 and 112. Dante's fierce consistency in his harshly negative assessment of Guittone is matched by the unfailing constancy of his admiration for Guinizzelli.

But Guinizzelli himself had admired Guittone early in his career, addressing him as *caro padre meo* in a poem that acknowledged his role as literary mentor. Dante's *padre mio*, the possessive *mio* made more emphatic by the enjambment, is intended as a corrective to Guinizzelli's sonnet, the point being underlined by the deliberate echoing of the rare rhyme *imbarche-marche* from that same poem. The purgatorial encounter in effect rewrites the record, polemically asserting the true line of poetic succession. Although there is an implicit acknowledgment of human fallibility—Guinizzelli had been wrong about Guittone, as Dante had been wrong about Giraut—Guinizzelli now speaks with authority from a world beyond the human, putting the seal on a radical and definitive realignment of poetic reputations. To suggest, as some critics do, that the celebration of Arnaut is Guinizzelli's tribute, not necessarily or not fully endorsed by Dante, is to ignore the authority that the biblical echoes confer on his words. It is ultimately as unsatisfactory as the view (now generally abandoned) that grudgingly limits the sense of *miglior fabbro* to the acknowledgment of a merely technical brilliance.

The Celebration of Arnaut

Arnaut is presented as the supreme master of vernacular literature who surpassed all other writers, whether of verse or prose. (The reference to *prose di romanzi* in line 118 is now widely accepted in this sense.) His influence on Dante, already acknowledged in the *De vulgari* as profoundly important, must in retrospect have come to seem decisive. He had provided the indispensable model or exemplar for Dante's stylistic apprenticeship in the *aspro* ("harsh") register, whose immediate fruit was the *rime petrose*, but without which, in the longer view, the lower cantos of Hell could not have been conceived or written. The experience of writing the *Inferno* itself lies between the *De vulgari* and Canto XXVI and is perhaps sufficient to account for the revaluation of Arnaut.

When Arnaut himself at last addresses Dante, in courteous response to the pilgrim's eager solicitation, he speaks Provençal. The narrative convention that all souls, even foreigners, speak Italian is, on this one occasion and to brilliant dramatic effect, abandoned. (Pluto and the giants in Hell had spoken gibberish, and Pope Adrian in Purgatory had spoken Latin, each for a single line, but there has been nothing to prepare us for a sustained passage in a foreign language.) Everything in the canto has led to this moment, to Arnaut's unexpected speaking in his own tongue. As we analyze the marvelous complications of the canto, we should not lose sight of the dramatic simplicity that underlies the complication or, at any rate, that emerges from it.

The effortless switch into Provençal, in addition to its simple surprise value and its poetic effectiveness in surrounding the figure of Arnaut in an aura of remoteness and isolation, reinforces the notion of the modern vernacular tradition as a continuum, geographical and temporal, set off from the literary heritage of antiquity. It seals the new linguistic and stylistic ideal of the *Comedy,* which abandons the theoretical position of the *De vulgari,* substituting for a rigorous selectivity a willingness to exploit all the expressive possibilities of human speech.

Arnaut's Address

Dante, in this ultimate act of homage to a waning poetic tradition, has Arnaut speak words that are representative—a distillation of the essence of troubadour lyric, as it were—and yet also personal. His lines are on one level a skillful mosaic of poetic fragments from his own poems and those of others: *Tan m'abellis* is the incipit, already cited in the *De vulgari,* of a poem by Folchetto di Marsiglia (the only poet Dante is to meet in Paradise, the one love poet who transcended the profane); there is a tissue of reminiscences of poems by Lanfranc Cigala and Guillem de Berguedà; and there are other generic echoes of Provençal poetry. "Ieu sui Arnaut" is a self-citation from Arnaut's most famous poem, quoted in the *vida* ("signing" his poems by naming himself was a habit, attested in fourteen of his eighteen extant compositions); here it is linked with the very Dantesque theme of weeping while speaking. The themes of joy and suffering in love, and the vocabulary associated with them, are generically troubadour rather than distinctively Arnaldian, as has rightly been emphasized; yet the words here do stand in counterpoint to Arnaut's own poetry. *Joi* is almost a leitmotif in his poems, where it is characteristically associated with the lady's favor, sometimes even more explicitly with her bedchamber; her aloofness causes suffering; value belongs to her or (less frequently) to the poet or his words. Everything is recognizable here, yet everything has taken on an opposite significance. Arnaut's poems give a powerful sense of time as a dimension of human life, with the poet experiencing and expressing his passion in relation to the natural cycle of the seasons, in a physical world full of material objects. Here in Purgatory time has been reduced to its essence: Arnaut, a ghostly figure in an insubstantial medium, is poised between past and future, folly and joy. *Folor,* like

Petrarch's *vaneggiar,* encompasses biography and literature, the experience and the poetry that grew out of it: the folly of obsession with an earthly love, the folly of turning his poetic talents to the celebration of such a love.

But there is no talk of poetry. Where Bonagiunta was still absorbed in his own practice as a poet, and his shortcomings, where Guinizzellli brushed aside references to his own distinction yet was still concerned with setting the literary record straight, Arnaut has transcended literature both as a topic for discussion and as a pretext for display. The most striking of all the ways in which his words here in Purgatory contrast with his own poetry is the directness, the lack of artifice with which he expresses himself. He had been a poet whose dazzling technical virtuosity was inseparable from the difficulty, the obscurity, of his poems, as the *vida* testifies. The only ambiguity is in his final line, 147, which can mean, as it has usually been glossed from Benvenuto on, "remember my suffering and pray for me"; it can also mean "remember my suffering and act on it, take heed, learn your lesson." These are the last words Dante hears from any soul in Purgatory. Their ambiguity perfectly encapsulates the double aspect of his relationship to the penitent shades on the mountain, just as Arnaut's whole speech—Dante's leave-taking from sinful humanity—reminds us (in the rhyme words *folor-valor-dolor*) of the three constants of the purgatorial experience: human folly; God's goodness, which offers the possibility of redemption; and the suffering through which that redemption is achieved.

Harmony Restored

But if Arnaut's words invite us to look back, they also compel us to look forward. In the protective custody of Virgil and Statius—indeed, he is now sandwiched between them—and with their active and solicitous encouragement, Dante must pass through the fire, and in spite of his terror, he will emerge unscathed on the other side. Virgil and Statius, and the mention of Beatrice's name, bring him through; and after the ordeal the three poets will settle down to pass their third night on the mountain: Dante like the goat and Virgil and Statius like the shepherds, an image of perfect harmony restored between the animal and human worlds. Guinizzelli and Arnaut, the revered vernacular masters, must be left behind, trapped in the fire, the penitential reality that has replaced the poetic metaphor for passion. The fire refines the poets as they had once refined the language: the artisan image of purifying and tempering a resistant medium, implicit in the verb *affina,* as it had been implicit in the noun *fabbro,* but now transposed from the artistic endeavor to the spiritual one, becomes the haunting image with which the canto closes.

BIBLIOGRAPHICAL NOTES

Readings of the canto (all entitled "Il canto XXVI del *Purgatorio*" unless otherwise specified) include those by F. Torraca (Florence, 1900) (reprinted in *Nuovi studi danteschi* [Naples, 1921], and again, with cuts, in *Letture dantesche,* ed. G. Getto [Florence, 1964]); V. Crescini, "Tra i pentiti dell'amore," *Rivista d'Italia* 15, no. 2 (1912): 177–195; A. Sacchetto (Florence, 1931); A. Roncaglia, in *Nuova Lectura Dantis* (Milan, 1951); L. Pietrobono (Rome, 1956); F. Gabrieli, in *Lectura Dantis Romana* (Turin, 1963); B. Porcelli, in *Letture del Purgatorio* (Milan, 1965); A. Monteverdi, in *Lectura Dantis Scaligera* (Florence, 1965); R. Koffler, "The Last Wound: *Purgatorio* XXVI," *Italian Quarterly* 12 (1968): 27–43; G. Toja, in *Nuove letture dantesche*, vol. 5 (Florence, 1972); G. Folena, "Il canto di Guido Guinizzelli," *Giornale storico della letteratura italiana* 154 (1977): 491–508; M. Marti, "Il XXVI del *Purgatorio* come omaggio d'arte: Guinizzelli e Daniello nel cammino poetico di Dante," in *L'Albero*, fasc. 29, no. 60 (1978): 5–26 (reprinted as "Il canto XXVI del *Purgatorio*" in *Purgatorio: Letture degli anni 1976–79* [Rome, 1981], 601–625).

T. S. Eliot's obsession with the closing lines of the canto—he had already given the title *Ara Vos Prec* to a volume of verse published in 1919, while *sovegna vos* will become line 11 of *Ash Wednesday IV*, and the "familiar compound ghost" of *Four Quartets* will speak of the "refining fire"—is further documented in T. S. Eliot, *The Waste Land, a Facsimile and Transcript of the Original Drafts, including the annotations of Ezra Pound*, edited by Valerie Eliot (London, 1971), 100–101; and in Peter Ackroyd, *T. S. Eliot* (London, 1984), 179. Critical studies of the *Comedy* that emphasize the element of Dante's confrontation with his own poetic past include G. Contini's seminal essay "Dante come personaggio-poeta della *Commedia*," in *Un'Idea di Dante* (Turin, 1970); and T. Barolini, *Dante's Poets: Textuality and Truth in the Comedy* (Princeton, 1984). On Dante's literary judgments as those of a "militant" critic, see P. V. Mengaldo, "Critica militante e storiografia letteraria," in the introduction to his edition of the *De vulgari eloquentia* (Padua, 1968), lxxviii–cii; and M. Marti, "Gli umori del critico militante," in *Con Dante fra i Poeti del suo tempo*, 2d ed. (Lecce, 1971), 69–121.

On echoes of Guinizzelli's poetry in Canto XXVI and their significance in our understanding of the canto see E. H. Wilkins, "Guinizzelli Praised and Corrected," in *The Invention of the Sonnet* (Rome, 1959); G. Folena, *op. cit.*; G. Gorni, "Guido Guinizzelli e la nuova 'mainera,'" in *Per Guido Guinizzelli* (Padua, 1980), 37–52; on echoes of Arnaut Daniel and other Provençal poets, see G. Contini's introduction to the Toja edition of Arnaut Daniel cited below; R. M. Ruggieri, "Tradizione e originalità nel lessico "cavalleresco" di Dante: Dante e i trovatori provenzali," in *L'umanesimo cavalleresco italiano da Dante al Pulci* (Rome, 1962), 67–83 (esp. 80–83); M. Braccini, "Paralipomeni al 'Personaggio-Poeta' (*Purgatorio* XXVI, 140–147)," in *Testi e Interpretazioni: Studi del seminario di filologia romanza dell'università di Firenze* (Milan-Naples, 1978), 169–256; N. B. Smith, "Arnaut Daniel in the *Purgatorio*: Dante's Ambivalence Towards Provençal," *Dante Studies* 98 (1980): 99–109; and in particular M. Perugi's "Arnaut Daniel in Dante," *Studi danteschi* 51 (1978): 59–150, which reassesses Dante's debt to Arnaut over his whole poetic career. The textual tradition of Arnaut's speech, from the earliest surviving manuscripts of the poem, shows that the language that was accessible to Dante's generation was less so to copyists only a generation or two later: textual variants are unusually frequent in this passage. The lines will be familiar to many readers, as they were to Eliot, in a form that differs at two points from the version here reproduced: *condus* (leads) instead of *guida* ("guides") at line 146, *jorn* ("day") instead of *joi* ("joy") at line 144—but *joi* would seem to be a deliberate echo of Arnaut's poetry, the replication of *jausenn . . . joi* recalling the same wordplay in his *sestina*. (Mandelbaum prints *joi* but translates "day.") A particular difficulty is that the word *escalina* exists neither in Provençal nor in Italian: this has been a focus in recent years for scholarly dissatisfaction with the received text, and there have been several attempts to suggest alternative readings for line 146, all of which start from the assumption that *escalina* is a corruption of *calina* ("heat"). (That the *escalina* proved such a potent image for Eliot may make English readers reluctant to accept any radical emendation of the line.) Less controversial is Contini's elegant suggestion that instead of the traditional reading of line 144 "lo joi qu'esper, denan" ("the joy I hope for, in front of me") we read "lo joi qu'es per denan" ("with joy; I see the hoped-for day draw near"). This removes a syntactic awkwardness and (I would add) fits the context better, for Dante himself has reminded us (54) that all these souls have the certainty of peace, the sure knowledge that it awaits them.

On the textual problems posed by Arnaut's speech, see G. Petrocchi, ed., Dante Alighieri, *La Commedia secondo l'antica vulgata*, vol. 3 (Verona, 1967), 456–458; G. Folena, *op.cit.*; M. Perugi, *op.cit.*; G. Contini, note in *Studi danteschi* 51 (1978), 150; M. Braccini, *op.cit.*, esp. "Appendice I: Sul testo dei vv. 140–147." The proposals for line 146 of Folena, Perugi and Braccini are respectively: "qu·us guida al som ses freg e ses calina"—"which guides you to the summit [which is] without cold and without heat"; "que vus guida ses dol e ses chalina"—"which guides you without pain and without heat"; "que·us guida al som ses dol e ses calina"—"which guides you to the summit, without pain and without heat." (Folena's interpretation, accepted by Marti, takes the second half of the line to refer to the Earthly Paradise; Perugi and Braccini take it to refer to Dante the living man.) Editions of the texts of the vernacular poets who appear in Canto XXVI include the indispensable *Poeti del Duecento*, ed. G. Contini (Milan-Naples, 1960); Arnaut Daniel, *Canzoni*, ed. G. Toja (Florence, 1960); Le canzoni di Arnaut Daniel, ed. M. Perugi (Milan-Naples, 1978); G. Folena, *Vulgares eloquentes: Vite e poesie dei trovatori di Dante* (Padua, 1961).

An exemplary brief account of Dante's literary relationships with Guinizzelli and Guittone is offered in the *Enciclopedia dantesca*, 6. vols (Rome, 1970–1978) entries by M. Marti under their respective names. A bibliography covering every aspect of the history of critical response to Dante's celebration of Arnaut is provided in Toja 1960, 389–390, and in the Perugi article in *Studi danteschi* cited above, 150–152. On Dante and Giraut see M. Picone, "Giraut de Bornelh nella prospettiva di Dante," *Vox Romanica* 39 (1980): 22–43; on Guinizzelli as "father" to the dolce stil novo, see G. Favati, *Inchiesta sul Dolce Stil Novo* (Firenze, 1975), 138–148; M. Marti, 1978; G. Gorni, *op. cit.* On the poet as artisan or craftsman *(fabbro)*, who shapes and molds a difficult medium, the canonical references are to *Convivio*, I, xi, 11–3, and to two of Daniel's poems (II, 12–4 and X, 1–4 in Toja 1960, 195 and 271–272); see also M. Braccini, *op. cit.*, esp. "Appendice VIII: 'fabbro del parlar materno,' " 250–256; on the barrier of fire, see G. Contini, "Alcuni appunti su *Purgatorio* XXVII," in *Un'Idea di Dante* (Einaudi, 1970), 171–190; on languages other than Italian in the *Comedy* see M. Braccini, *op. cit.*.

On Dante's stylistic resourcefulness in this canto, and the use of rare and difficult rhymes (-*ife*, -*altro*, -*urgo*, -*urba* and -*erghi* are all rhymes found only once in the more than 14,000 lines of the poem), see the *lecturae* of A. Roncaglia, A. Monteverdi, G. Folena, and M. Marti. M. Bowra, in "Dante and Arnaut Daniel," *Speculum* XXVII (1952): 459–474, incautiously asserted that Arnaut's "characteristic phrases" are "picked up and turned to a special purpose" in *Purgatorio* XXVI, 140–147, and has been repeatedly taken to task for doing so. The placing of Guinizzelli among the lustful (always seen as more problematical than that of Arnaut) hardly requires us to assume that Guinizzelli left "ideal lyrics, but beastly memories" (Crescini 1912, 191). Modern critics assume that "Guido's lust, like Arnaut's, had in effect verbal (i.e. textual) origins" (Folena 1977, 497), and point to lines in the poem "Chi vedesse a Lucia" (Contini 1960, vol. 2, 479): "Ah, Prender lei a forza, ultra su' grato / e bagiarli la bocca e 'l bel visaggio / e li occhi suoi, ch'èn due fiamme de foco!/Ma pentomi" "Ah, to take her by force, against her will, and kiss her mouth and her fair face and her eyes, which are two fiery flames. But I repent." Ezra Pound seems to have been the first to connect line 142 *Ieu sui Arnaut* with Daniel's canzone X, 43 (Toja 1960, 274) in the essay entitled "Il miglior fabbro" in *The Spirit of Romance* (London, 1910), 30–31.

CANTO XXVII

At the Threshold of Freedom

GLAUCO CAMBON

When Mario Sansone stated that Canto XXVII functions as a narrative pause between two climactic sequences (the rise through the three richly populated last cornices of the purgatorial mountain and the meeting with Matilda and Beatrice in the Terrestrial Paradise), he certainly did not mean to reduce Canto XXVII to merely a link lacking a poetical strength of its own. In fact, Sansone has added that the pauselike quality or narrative suspension following the poignant voice of Arnaut Daniel in the refining fire and foreshadowing the apparition of Matilda in the place of perennial springtime is counterpointed by an "ascending development," a rise of pitch from realistic depiction to ecstatic dreaminess to the "sacred solemnity" of the "investiture scene."

The sensitive Neapolitan critic, heir to the De Sanctis-Croce tradition, also feels the need to qualify this neat description of the canto's overall design by remarking that such structural elements should not be confused with the issue of poetry per se, as if poetry were just incidental to the design (Croce's view) rather than intrinsic to it. One doesn't even need the doctrinal firmness of a Singleton to realize that the specific intensity of Virgil's voice would be lost if it did not culminate the canto and, with it, the whole narrative line of Dante's apprenticeship and emancipation. The same "ascending line" or tonal heightening Sansone descries in this canto had marked the previous one, which Arnaut Daniel memorably capped with his not-so-foreign utterance. Or we could go back all the way to Pia's violin solo raising the epic orchestration of Canto V to pure lyrical pitch; it would be inconceivable *before* the tumultuous manly voices of Jacopo and Buon-conte. Placement gives song its proper space of resonance; poetry actual-izes design.

No critic has commented more eloquently than Ulrich Leo on the dra-matic significance of Virgil's liminal figure as it achieves itself at the end of Canto XXVII with functional rhetoric and later on, in Canto XXX, with the si-lence of a disappearance in which his poetical voice still reverberates. The attentive reader will certainly overhear the intense silence of Virgil's immi-nent departure in his final words to his pupil and ward. In a way, Canto XXVII is the "crowning and mitring" of Virgil even more than of Dante's pilgrim persona. One may hesitate between Leo's definition of Dante's Virgil as the tragic figure of the essential humanist who is totally severed from the realm of Grace and can only bestow an illusory accolade on his disciple, and Domenico Consoli's vindication of Virgil as a complex savant poet who is both conscious of his limits and somehow in touch with what operates be-yond. In either case we can agree that he is the most intriguing poetical char-acter in the entire *Comedy*, whether we look at his typological dimension or at the dramatic embodiment he receives in the poem's verbal texture. There is even one respect in which he symbolically functions beyond the allegori-cal framework allotted by the *Comedy*'s intentional design, though by no means in contrast with it. For Virgil, vis-à-vis Dante, represents not just the enlightening action of reason and classical culture but also the perennial drama of education, individually and collectively speaking. Individually, Vir-gil is the father figure who must lead his disciple until the latter must leave him behind; collectively, he is the personification of a culture that serves as a basis for a new one, just as historically happened to the Greco-Roman and Hebrew cultures with regard to the Christian one. The paradox by which the fulfillment of the teacher lies in his being superseded by the pupil makes a Moses out of Virgil, since he guides Dante to the threshold of a Promised Land that will remain forever denied to him.

Setting the Stage

Apart from these anthropological and historical implications, what happens between Dante and Virgil in Canto XXVII suffices to fill the "narrative pause" with unique poignancy. From the start the "suspension" is suspenseful:

> Just as, there where its Maker shed His blood,
> the sun shed its first rays, and Ebro lay
> beneath high Libra, and the ninth hour's rays
>   were scorching Ganges' waves; so here, the sun
> stood at the point of day's departure when
> God's angel—happy—showed himself to us.

(1–6)

A cosmic perspective is established, like a meditative resonance to set the stage for further dramatic developments. Within the canto itself, this resilient pattern works like an overture: it prefigures the larger movement that will bring to a close the pilgrim's experience of the last cornice by taking him through the fire barrier toward the midst of the canto (49–57) and into the serene apparition of Leah in the last of *Purgatorio*'s three dreams (94–108). This apparition in turn leads to the verdant edge of the Terrestrial Paradise as the appropriate setting for Virgil's conferral of independent status on his beloved charge.

No better climax could have been devised for the canto (and for Virgil's posthumous career as Dante's reeducator); yet this memorable conclusion is also the beginning of that decisive new sequence (Cantos XXVII–XXXIII) that will see the pilgrim through the crucial experience of apocalypse, penance, and vatic initiation at the hands of imperious Beatrice. Virgil points beyond himself; so does the whole canto; so did its initial syntactical unit, the "overture" mentioned above. For indeed, the two opening tercets climaxing in the angel's appearance prelude more events than are contained within Canto XXVII, if we pay attention to the recurrence of that key verb *apparire* in close connection first with lovely Matilda (XXVIII, 37–42) and then with Beatrice herself (XXX, 22–33). In the latter case it is also the verb's positioning toward the end of a rich syntactical conglomerate, and not just its lexical identity, that reminds us of Canto XXVII's beginning; the more so as a detailed simile makes a sunrise of Beatrice's appearance, symmetrically offsetting the sunset context of the angel's appearance in Canto XXVII.

"I Seem to See Her Eyes Already"

The foreshadowing of Matilda's and Beatrice's intervention in Dante's pilgrim progress compounds the more pointed annunciation entailed by his dream of Leah. The explicit, repeated references that Virgil makes to Beatrice's arrival tide his uncertain pupil over the last ordeal. The suspense is itself climactic, whether in the painful crossing of the purifying fire (which, as sublimated Eros, will reappear in the red color of Beatrice's gown when she shows herself at XXX), or in the prophetic dream, in the restful awakening, and in Virgil's loving words:

> Among them, you can rest or walk until
> the coming of the glad and lovely eyes—
> those eyes that, weeping, sent me to your side.
>
> (136–138)

Earlier, to conquer the frightened pilgrim's fear at the fire barrier he had finally had to resort to Beatrice's magic name: ("Now see, son: this/wall stands between you and your Beatrice," 35–36); and to sustain his disciple

during the ordeal itself, he had followed up that surefire formula with a ped-
agogic white lie, "I seem to see her eyes already" (54).

For Virgil as well as for Dante the pilgrim character, presentiment of
Beatrice is also recall. In approaching her near the green summit of the
hard-won mountain, Dante is looking forward to his past, to the decisive
event of his remote youth, or *vita nova,* just as Virgil remembers her eyes
and her voice (*Inf.* II, 70–72):

> For I am Beatrice who send you on;
> I come from where I most long to return;
> Love prompted me, that Love which makes me speak.

The love that moved her moves him, and never more so than now, when he
must perform the last momentous office of his ritual task before leaving the
emancipated disciple to his own devices. For both of them, though in different ways, love is now prophetic memory; and the canto itself accordingly
looks backward and forward at the same time, in simultaneous recapitulation and expectancy. When Dante still hesitates to enter the fire after hearing from his master "the name that's always flowering / within my mind"
(42–43), Virgil cajoles him "as one smiles at a child fruit has beguiled" (45)
and then breaks the lingering hesitancy by striding ahead into the flames
(46): "Then he, ahead of me, entered the fire." Only the force of example,
added to the spell of the name that means everything to Dante, can achieve
the result that persuasive reasoning had failed to elicit (20–32). Not accidentally, that verbal form *si mise* echoes the one in *Inferno* III, 21: "Mi miso dentro
a le segrete cose," since the specific situation symmetrically mirrors the earlier one.

The Father Teacher

There at Hell's gate, Virgil, after urging Dante to dispose of cowardice, took
him by the hand into the moaning darkness; here at the forbidding fire that
fills and limits the last cornice, marking both the exit from Purgatory and
the access to Eden, Virgil again has to use all his resources of eloquence,
wisdom, and determination to take his disciple over a crucial threshold, the
last one where his help will be needed. This happens because in both cases
Dante understandably falters, but the second time he does so even more
seriously, for he regresses into childish fear and waywardness and thereby
causes Virgil to resume the full authority that the trip through the unfamiliar purgatorial terrain and Dante's dawning independence had eroded. In
this way, for a moment the two pilgrims of the Beyond are cast back into
their strong original bond and mutual role just when they are about to part
forever. This amounts to a stroke of genius on the part of Dante as creator
of the mythic twosome. Especially because in returning them momentarily

to their initial situation he has avoided a mechanical repetition of that beginning; he has added a subtly differentiating touch. At the start of their descent into the netherworld, Virgil had taken the bewildered Dante by the hand and gently but firmly drawn him along. At the conclusion of their shared journey, Virgil brings Dante beyond the last threshold by simply preceding him to set an example that encourages emancipation even while urging imitation, as the teacher of freedom he has been all along. From this gesture to the final speech, "libero, dritto e sano è tuo arbitrio" ("your will is free, erect and whole," 140), is a logical step.

The pattern of verbal recall, which animates much of *Purgatorio,* in Canto XXVII finds analogical validation in Virgil's words to Dante at lines 21–24:

> Remember,
> remember! If I guided you to safety
> even upon the back of Geryon,
> then now, closer to God, what shall I do?

Virgil tells his perplexed pupil to remember everything he has done for him and thereby to take heart. It is as if Virgil wanted to bequeath a full image of himself to the adoptive son he'll never see again, just while he urges that son to go on beyond himself, to Beatrice, who will supersede the putative father bound back for Limbo. He thus summarizes himself for Dante in the very act of pointing beyond himself, and if Dante the character still balks, Dante the poet responds to the prayerlike command and extends it to us readers. We must indeed *remember* the traveled road that is the Virgil part of the poem if we want to make full sense of its momentous present station and progress further. We must draw on the internal memory of the poem.

Recapitulation

We shall then see more clearly how this canto, far from amounting to a mere interlude, rehearses from the purgatorial vantage point the poem's itinerary, from bewilderment to enlightenment. At the end of Canto XXVII that quest is proclaimed successful by none other than Virgil himself: "your will is free, erect and whole" (140), and again it is the recurrence of a pivotal word (*libero-libertà*) that affords us a sharp "backward glance o'er travelled roads" and a commensurate appreciation of the moral as well as physical distance covered. This particular modifier (or its cognate noun and verb) emerges for the first time on the open horizon of *Purgatorio,* not before; it will reemerge in *Paradiso,* notably at XXXI, 85, when Dante, in taking provisional leave of Beatrice, gives her credit for his achievement of final and total freedom and in so doing echoes some of Virgil's parting words to him. Virgil's final speech at the end of Canto XXVII deftly anticipates the analogous scene of Dante's leave-taking from Beatrice on high. Recapitulation propels the poem into *Paradiso,* just as the forward movement of *Purgatorio* resiliently banks on filtered memories of *Inferno.*

Within the resilient progression of Canto XXVII, Dante's sudden relapse into paralyzing fear before the necessary ordeal swings the pendulum back almost to a state that was supposedly left far behind: the fearful bewilderment at Hell's gate. In one stroke, this recoil widens the narrative space available for the canto in progress; elicits the richly modulated display of Virgil's revealing, pragmatic eloquence; and adds dramatic suspense to a development we might otherwise take too much for granted: Dante's gradual attainment of freedom. For although words like *libero, libertà,* and *liberare* have constellated *Purgatorio*'s diction since that first dawn on the beach, freedom itself does not come easily to Dante, who must earn it through constant endeavor. Statius's "my free will for a better threshold" (*Purg.* XXI, 69) is not yet for him; and surprisingly, the hardest obstacle to the qualified freedom available on the edge of Eden at Virgil's hands comes up at the end of the purgatorial climb, to complicate somewhat the stated law of the place by virtue of which the higher one mounts, the lighter and nimbler one gets. Certainly the way to liberation, the straightening and healing of the will, has been anything but straight. It pays to notice the strategic lexical occurrence, just after Dante's crossing of the fire barrier and before his idyllic allegorical dream and Virgil's crowning pronouncement: "The path we took climbed *straight* / within the rock" (63–64). The rocky pathway into Purgatory's first cornice (*Purg.* X, 7–12) was not straight but zigzagging and had to be painfully negotiated. The equally rocky and steep path symmetrically leading out of the fire-girt last cornice and into what I'd like to call ante-Eden follows a straight course and lets the fire-tempered and sleep-refreshed pilgrim run through, in sprightly rebound from his recent stiffening, as if he had sprouted wings:

> My will on will to climb above was such
> that at each step I took I felt the force
> within my wings was growing for the flight.
>
> (121–123)

In keeping with the system of symbolic correspondence in the Dantean cosmos, matter mirrors spirit, nature portrays soul, and the word can act as a hinge between object and mind. Many lexical, semantic, and iconic lines of force converge in Virgil's conclusive declaration of independence for his pupil; among which, we might add, one should consider the thematics of will (interwoven with the idea of freedom) that Statius had formulated in Canto XXI, 61–69, and that now comes to a head with the breezy passage quoted above and its subsequent resolution on the moral level, as uttered by Virgil. But in our eagerness to trace these dynamic innervations of poetical language we should not lose sight of another aspect too often ignored by Dantists: verbal playfulness.

A Better Mountain Climber

A good example comes from the tercet quoted above, where the emphatic repetition of the word *voler* (will) in the first line, reinforced by the alliterating rhyme word *venne* (came), projects its phonic and semantic charge into *volo* (flight) in the third line, a pun worthy of Chaucer, Shakespeare, and Donne at their mischievous best. If the medieval rhetoric acknowledged this figure of speech mainly as ornament, the use Dante makes of it here is semantically structural rather than just ornamental. Placing a world like *volo* in culminant position vis-à-vis the preparatory chain *voler . . . voler . . . venne* makes sound form dramatize the causal link between effort of the will and achieved liberation—the very point Statius had earlier made in Canto XXI, the lesson Virgil had constantly reiterated in his pragmatic pedagogy, the idea so unforgettably translated into image at Canto X, 124–125: for the whole *Purgatorio* keeps stating or suggesting that it is really up to us human "caterpillars" to evolve into "angelic butterflies." The entire verbal operation is leavened by a joyous liberty that impels the poet to play sleight of hand with words, a formal counterpart of the liberating joy experienced by the pilgrim character in his triumph over the recent obstacle. Paronomasia is a reinvention of language, in the teeth of formal constraints.

Wordplay brightens the canto's texture, and not just in the guise of *bisticcio*, the rhetorical game that caught the eye of philologist Contini. There is a playful recurrence of the word *pome* (apple) from line 45, where simile provides the context for the real apple with which wayward children are to be lured into compliance, to line 115, where Virgil talks of a metaphorical apple, the earthly happiness attainable in the terrestrial Paradise. Both simile and metaphor are smilingly aimed at a childlike Dante; the well-meant lure becomes truthful promise, and it is noteworthy that both the vehicle and the context of the metaphor should arouse thought of the forbidden fruit. More conspicuous, the elaborate pastoral simile unfolding from line 76 to line 87 to depict the three travelers' preparation for a good sleep after the crossing of the fire barrier likens Virgil and Statius to shepherds and Dante to a goat. Very few commentators (Stambler and Colì) have noticed the peculiarity of such a comparison, while Pazzaglia explains it with the uplifting symbolism that some medieval bestiaries ascribe to the goat. Without discrediting that explanation, I nevertheless feel that the image is richer. The evangelical sheep would have been more plausible than the suspect goat in this context, at a point when Dante the pilgrim has finally overcome the trial by fire and purified himself of his spiritual dross. But the goat, as an observant Dante well knew, is less gregarious and more independent than its tame cousin. It is friskier, harder to manage, and a better mountain climber; therefore it fits Dante's humorous self-characterization at this point as the sheep could not. Let us not forget that here he is not part of a flock, that he has done much mountain climbing, and that he has occasionally (as in this last phase of the purgatorial climb) given a hard time to his teacher and guide. The comic component of the simile is emphasized by the play on *ruminare* (ruminate), a verb that first describes the goat's literal digestion process (76) and then, metaphorically, the pilgrim's tired brooding on the verge of sleep (91).

Just as it was with the punning linkage of *volo* to *voler,* a joyful verbal inventiveness is at work here, and it is of a piece with the amused detachment with which Dante the poet looks back on the youthful awkwardness of his autobiographical persona. That smile, compounded by wistfulness, is objectified in Virgil's patient insistence toward the balking disciple, who at a decisive moment proved to be goatish: "But I was stubborn, set against my conscience" (33). It did not escape Ulrich Leo's alert sensibility, and it should help us to descry the tonal richness of Dante's craft, which includes humor along with pathos.

BIBLIOGRAPHY

Colì, Piero. "Purgatorio XXVII," in *Dante Commentaries,* ed. David Nolan, 99–113. Dublin: Irish Academic Press, 1977.

Consoli, Domenico. *Significato del Virgilio Dantesco.* Florence: Le Monnier, 1967. Id. id., "Virgilio." In *Enciclopedia dantesca,* 6 vols. Rome, 1970–1978.

Contini, Gianfranco. "Alcuni appunti su 'Purgatorio' XXVII." In *Varianti e altra linguistica,* 459–476. Turin: Einaudi, 1970. Besides stressing the rhetorical element of wordplay, Contini points out Dante's resort to archaistic lexicon, his coinage of *antelucani,* and refutes the interpretation of *corono e mitrio* as a symbolic reference to Empire and Church. In so doing, Contini brings historical linguistic evidence to confirm the opinion of Orsini-Darbi (*La Divina Comedia: Purgatorio*), con i cosenti di T. Cassini/S. A. Darbi ed. Francesco Mazzoni, 628 (Florence: Sansoni, 1973) e di Natalino Sapegno, ed., *La Divina Commedia* (Milan-Naples: Ricciardi, 1957), 708n.

Croce, Benedetto. *La poesia di Dante.* Bari: Laterza, 1921.

———. *The poetry of Dante.* Trans. Douglas Ainslie. 1922. Reprint, Mamaroneck, NY: Appel, 1971.

Hollander, Robert. *Allegory in Dante's Commedia.* Princeton: Princeton University Press, 1969. For a more aesthetically oriented vindication of the poem's structure and doctrinal background, see Irma Brandeis, *The Ladder of Vision* (Garden City, NY: Doubleday 1961). Also see (with regard to *Purgatorio*) Francis Fergusson, *Dante's Drama of the Mind: A Modern Reading of the Purgatorio* (Princeton: Princeton University Press, 1953).

Leo, Ulrich. "Il canto XXVII del Purgatorio." In *Letture dantesche,* ed. Giovanni Getto, 1213–1233. Florence: Sansoni, 1964.

Passaglia, Mario. "Il Canto XXVII del Purgatorio." In *Nuove letture dantesche,* vol. 5, 1972.

Porcelli, Bruno. "The Recapitulating Bent of Canto XXVII Has Been Noticed by Bruno Porcelli" In *Studi sulla Divina Commedia,* ch. 5, 85–94. Bologna: Casa editrice Pàtron, 1970.

Sansone, Mario. Il canto XXVII del *Purgatorio."* In *Letture e studi danteschi,* 165–184. Bari: De Donate, 1975.

Singleton, Charles. *Dante's Commedia: Elements of Structure.* Cambridge, MA: Harvard University Press, 1957.

———. *Journey to Beatrice.* Cambridge, MA: Harvard University Press, 1958.

Stambler, Bernard. *Dante's Other World—The Purgatorio as Guide to the Divine Comedy.* New York: New York University Press, 1957, 232.

Toynbee, Arnold. *A Study of History.* Oxford: Oxford University Press, 1934–1961.

CANTO XXVIII

Watching Matilda

VICTORIA KIRKHAM

Certified fit to travel alone by Virgil at the close of Canto XXVII, Dante strolls eagerly into the Garden of Eden. This shady forest atop Mount Purgatory is the setting for his meeting with a stunningly beautiful maiden who appears all alone, laughing and singing, on the other side of a two-pronged rivulet. As she gathers flowers to weave a garland, she reminds him of Persephone; her glance recalls Venus, luminescent with love for Adonis. Dante, longing to step across the narrow stream, compares himself to Leander grounded on the shore of the Hellespont by storm-swollen breakers, just where once Xerxes had traversed that same strait. The lady, whose name will be revealed as Matilda by Beatrice only in the closing moments of Canto XXXIII (119), addresses Dante and his walking mates, Virgil and Statius, to explain why she laughs in this place chosen as human nature's first nest (78). Then, answering Dante's questions, she recounts how God gave it to man in earnest, or as a pledge of eternal life, but man, for his "fault" (94), dwelt here only briefly. To prevent nature from warring against man, the mount soars above earthly climatic variations. Here grow all manner of plants, including some not found in the inhabited world. They propagate spontaneously when struck by an airstream whose source is the whirling motion of the Prime Mover and whose music hums low in the pine boughs. No physical cycle of vaporization and rainfall waters the stream. Like the wind, it flows from above, from a spiritual source in the fixed fount of God. Lethe, one branch of the rivulet, takes away the memory of sin. The other, Eunoe, restores memory of all good deeds. Matilda concludes her lesson with a corollary (136): the ancients on Parnassus may have dreamt of this place of innocence, perpetual spring, and fertility when they wrote poetry of the Golden Age: "Here, mankind's root was innocent; and here / was every fruit and never-ending spring" (142–143). Her remembrance prompts Dante to look over his shoulder at Virgil and Statius, who have listened to her last "final corollary" (147) with a smile. The canto ends as Dante turns his face again to *la bella donna* (148). In subsequent cantos she will pull him through Lethe and immerse him in Eunoè. Final stages in his purification, these bathings ready him for the procession in which, as a passenger on a griffin-drawn chariot, Beatrice will make her epiphany.

Close to seven centuries of commentaries have thrown into relief predictable features of Canto XXVIII. Prominent among these features is the landscape, a pastoral oasis vivid in the minds of later artists from Boccaccio to Poliziano and Botticelli, to Lord Byron and Gabriele D'Annunzio. Dante's *divina foresta* (2) differs enough from the biblical description of Eden that, as he enters at dawn of his fourth day on Purgatory, he does not realize where he is until Matilda tells him. How much does the poet's conception of the place follow tradition, and where does it deviate? Where are Enoch and Elijah, Adam and Eve? Why only two rivers instead of four? Why represent the Garden as a wood?

Expositors also pay their due to the canto's geographic, historical, and mythological allusions. Dante's landscape, where breezes play bass notes with force (18) as accompaniment to the little birds' high-pitched song, is like the pine forest on dunes at Classe, near Ravenna, a real place that the exiled poet knew. But its prevailing sirocco comes less from the southeast than out of a book, Virgil's *Aeneid* I. The first simile in the canto reminds us of the tempest unleashed, at Juno's instigation, on the Trojan fleet by Aeolus, king of the winds, a disaster that beaches Aeneas at Dido's new Carthage and launches Virgil's epic. Ovid's *Metamorphoses* and *Heroides* contribute three themes to the canto. First is Matilda's similitude to the flower maid Persephone, daughter of Ceres, whose abduction by Pluto into Hades ended the Golden Age of perpetual spring and caused seasonal variation to enter the world (*Metamorphoses* V, 385–571). Second is Matilda's likeness in beauty to Venus, who was accidentally pricked by one of her son's arrows and stricken with obsessive passion for Adonis (*Metamorphoses* X, 525–532).

Third is Dante's temporary kinship with Leander. As he holds back on the bank of the rivulet that separates him from Matilda, he realizes the frustration Leander must have felt when turbulent waves stopped him from swimming across the Hellespont for a night of love with Hero on the opposite shore (*Heroides* XVII–XVIII). Surprisingly, Dante then conflates Ovid's pathetic tale of Hero and Leander with that of a bellicose intruder from history, Xerxes. Orosius and Lucan told how he, too, crossed the Dardanelles, not for romance but for conquest, moving his huge invading army on a pontoon bridge. Routed at Salamis by Themistocles, the Persian general was reduced to ignominious retreat in a tiny fishing boat. Although this reference to the haughty Xerxes seems at odds with the Ovidian sexual allusions, it completes a symmetry in Canto XXVIII. Two feminine comparisons for Matilda (Persephone and Venus) are balanced by two masculine analogies for Dante (Leander and Xerxes). Loss is the theme common to all these myths, aptly remembered in the Earthly Paradise. Finally, Matilda's comparison of Eden with the Golden Age allows us to hear two ancient Parnassians in a perfect duet. Virgil, poet of the *Bucolics,* gives background harmony to an aria cited from Ovid's *Metamorphoses* I.

As glossing goes, our own century has seen a shift in emphasis, away from old-fashioned coverage that touched all the bases. Increasingly, one particular subject usurps all the others as an area of focus, a perfect example of the tendency Leo Steinberg has put into an aphorism: "the interpretative tradition feeds on itself, with minimal interference from the object interpreted." Now, I don't mean to suggest that the *Lectura Dantis* as a critical form has declined and mutated into a freakish beast, self-sustaining and self-perpetuating, headed away on a mad tangent from the poetry that originally set it in motion. But I do think that this lectural genre we continue to practice since Boccaccio inaugurated it in 1373 has produced some narcissistic off-shoots. One of them is the body of writing that in the last hundred years or so has swelled around Matilda. *Dantismo,* ready to accommodate, has awarded single-minded scholars of Matilda their own special label, a coinage of Francesco D'Ovidio: they are the *Mateldisti.* Even though early commentators all understood who she was—and were satisfied—in modern times doubts and disputes have arisen. Who is Matilda? Does she have a historical identity, like Dante's other guides Virgil, Cato, Statius, Beatrice, Bernard? If so, is her existence part of Dante's personal life, in the way that we suppose was true of Beatrice, or was she someone he knew as a literary figure, as was the case for all the others, from Virgil to Bernard? Could she be purely symbolic? And if so, why does she have such an odd name? Why, for that matter, do we have to wait so long to learn it, six cantos from the time she appears until Beatrice names her, a greater time lapse than for any other character to the *Divine Comedy?* And whether or not she is historical, what role does she play in the allegory of the *Comedy?* These are questions to which I shall return, my hope being not to feed the monster but to help it.

Repetition as Rhetorical Figure

The 148 verses of Canto XXVIII divide neatly into two halves. The first, Dante's description of the *divina foresta* and of Matilda, ends with line 75. Matilda's welcoming message to the newcomers, "You are new here" (77), opens part two, in which, after identifying her mountaintop as Eden, she teaches its supernatural climatology and botany, a scientific lesson rounded off by her thoughts on what intimations of Christian immortality may have inspired the poets of pagan antiquity.

Just as the narrative promotes her from damsel in a landscape to Matilda the Scholastic preceptor, so does Dante's language shift. First the canto is lyrical; later it is doctrinal. Doctrine, the intellectual defogging *(disnebbiar)* Dante receives from Matilda, devolves into a technical vocabulary cast in difficult syntax. This scientific register, which Niccolò Tommaseo found unbefitting a female spokesperson, contrasts with the simpler transparent linguistic medium that carries the canto to its midpoint. There Dante appropriates the style of the vernacular love lyric. His encounter with Matilda, amorous apparition in a spring landscape, repeats the stock motif of the *pastorella*, a poetic type that had been passed down from the troubadours to the Tuscans. Portraying Matilda as a Primavera figure, Dante points to Guido Cavalcanti's mistress of poesy, Giovanna-Prima Verrà, and he affectionately cites his friend Guido's *pastorella*, "In un boschetto trova' pasturella." With lexicon he recurs to the Siculo-Tuscan poets, whose typical forms echo in diphthongs of Latinate and Provençal origin: "lo suol che d'ogne parte *auliva*" in "un'*aura* dolce" made melodious by singing *augelletti* (6–7, 14). In words like *dolce* and *riso* we hear regulation bisyllables from the vocabulary of the *Siciliani* and dolce stil nuovo, and another favorite trio finds stronger places in rhyme position: *fiore-amore-core* (41–45). Diminutives are frequent: *augelletti, fiumicello, donna soletta, fioretti, novella [fede]*. To intensify this musicality, Dante composes a fugue of sounds that link the first two *terzine*: ("Vago già di cercar," "sanza più aspettar") that elsewhere suggest internal rhyme ("disvia / per maraviglia") and that play deftly as paronomasia and polyptoton, even in Matilda's didactics: "All of the atmosphere revolves / within a circle" (103–104).

Duplications are striking, beginning with the rhythm of Dante's gait, which is *lento lento* (5). The adverbial doubling, which makes the meaning emphatic, has the strength of a superlative *lentissimo*. It asks us to think by contrast of the haste enjoined on Dante in his ascent of the mountain, voiced in Cato's rebuke down at the shore when a herd of souls paused, seduced by the sweetness of Casella's song, "Che è ciò, spiriti lenti?" ("What have we here, you laggard spirits"? *Purg.* II, 120). In other echoic couplings birds sing, *di ramo in ramo* (19); pure water of the rivulet flows in the shadows, *bruna bruna* (31); Matilda sings and gathers, *fior da fiore* (41); she walks *piede innanzi piede* (54). Dante varies the device when he puts repetition to service in *rima equivoca* or *rime riche* with homonyms of *mai: l'ombra . . . che mai / raggiar non lascia sole* and then as the noun *i freschi mai* (32, 36). Reiteration is concentrated in the first half of the canto, with one exception later, when the same phrase initiates two successive verses. It is the formidable anaphora referring to the "fault" that caused man to fall and lose Eden:

> Man's *fault* made brief his stay here; and man's *fault*
> made him exchange frank laughter and sweet sport
> for lamentation and for anxiousness.
>
> (94–96; my italics)

Why is repetition as a rhetorical figure so conspicuous in this canto? In one respect, Dante tropes Cavalcanti's *pastorella* about his pliant shepherdess, "che *sola sola* per lo bosco gia." In another, these reverberations help convey the dreamy atmosphere of the poet's experience in Eden, its hypnotic qualities and beauty, at once real and surreal. But the dualities are more than literary tribute and oneiric sound. They have thematic validity in their twofold landscape, a garden bisected by two rivers:

> To one side, it is Lethe; on the other,
> Eunoe; neither stream is efficacious
> unless the other's waters have been tasted."
>
> (130–132)

The two rivers themselves enter a larger pattern of dualism, stamped into the poem in other ways. Just before Virgil's dismissal, Dante had awakened in Canto XXVII from his third night and prophetic dream on Purgatory, a vision of Leah and Rachel. Symbolically these two Old Testament women personify the active and contemplative lives, and commentators have always recognized how as a duo they anticipate, respectively, Matilda and Beatrice. Beatrice in turn will ride in the processional chariot pulled by the griffin, the bipartite creature formed of eagle and lion that symbolizes Christ in his divine and human natures.

Eden is itself ambivalent terrain, a sort of split land of double possibilities—before the Fall and after, then and now, innocence and temptation. Even more to the point, I think, the Earthly Paradise is exactly what the two-ness of its name indicates, both earth and paradise. It is a composite, literally an oxymoron, a God-made paradox. The highest peak on the earth, nearly touching the moon, it is the vestibule of Celestial Paradise, the pad for a lightninglike launch into Heaven. It partakes of both the natural and the supernatural, the corporeal and the spiritual. And now we see that the two halves of the canto are not just passively or arbitrarily contiguous. Rather, they constitute a logical sequence: from the idyllic landscape to its miraculous hidden mechanics, from the physical to the metaphysical. In that progression are encapsulated the dynamics of Dante's whole journey.

The "Perfect" Number

Why does Dante reach Eden in Canto XXVIII, and on the seventh day of his journey (counting from Maundy Thursday in Hell and adding the three days and nights he spends in Purgatory, starting Easter Sunday morning)? His entry into Eden and the canto begin simultaneously, not an unplanned coincidence. Moreover, Canto XXVIII evidently enjoyed a privileged status in Dante's thinking. It was, for example, in chapter 28 of the *Vita Nuova* that Beatrice died. Among all the women of the *Comedy,* tallied in my own census,

Matilda, mirabile dictu, turns up in Canto XXVIII as the twenty-eighth. We can approach these riddles through the Pythagoreans, who recognized the lunar month number 28 as perfect because it is the sum of its factors $(28 = 1 + 2 + 4 + 7 + 14)$. Their idea doubtless resulted from the rarity of such numbers, there being only seven between 1 and 40,000,000. (The series is 6: 28: 496: 8,128: 130,816: 2,096,128: 33,550,336.) Inherited by the Church Fathers, this system was converted to Christian purposes. Thus Bede corroborates the perfection of 28 as the product of its divisors 7 and 4. In 7 he understands the Sabbath, the day of God's rest and hence eternity, which we reach via the four Gospels, the four Evangelists, and the four cardinal virtues. Actually, 28 can be equated symbolically with 7 in its meaning of eternity, insofar as 28 is the sum of the first seven numbers $(28 = 1 + 2 + 3 + 4 + 5 + 6 + 7)$.

Of course, Dante reserves his final vision of the Godhead for a nightless eighth day in Paradise, applying the formula articulated by Augustine, who reckoned the transition from 7 to 8 as our passage from the hebdomad of the created world to heavenly salvation, from mortal life to New Life. Dante's placement of Eden in Canto XXVIII (a canto with 148 verses) and his meeting there with the twenty-eighth woman of the Comedy, while turning on 7 $(7 \times 4 = 28)$, also announce the fulfilling 8 to come. In 28 the poet has found a perfect number for Eden, that Garden at once material and eternal. Numerology here tends to confirm that he knew the Navigatio Sancti Brendani Abbatis, an anonymous tenth-century travelogue to the Otherworld probably composed in Ireland. This widely read Voyage of St. Brendan, of which more than 120 manuscripts survive, describes how the saint and his companions sail until they discover Paradise, an island in mid-ocean. Bisected by a river that living humans are forbidden to cross, it is bathed in endless daylight and brightened by trees constantly bearing fruit. Brendan and his men reach the blessed isle in the last chapter of the tale, number 28, after a seven-year journey of four parts each, hence an odyssey with twenty-eight fixed points.

The Divine Forest

Dante's Earth-Heaven is terrain much more complex, a field of tension. One line of narrative force draws us up and ahead in the poem; another pulls us down and back. The Latinate language spoken by Matilda in her lecture is a prelude of Paradiso, the canticle of abstract, philosophical discourse. At the same time, with Canto XXVIII we return to the beginning of the Divine Comedy, to Inferno I. Once again the wayfarer enters a springscape furnished with a mountain and forest as the sun is rising. But now Dante is on the summit, not ruining in a valley below. The air is sweet, not harsh and bitter; pleasantly shaded, not wild and dark. When he awoke lost in the dark wood, Dante could not say how he had wandered in: "I cannot clearly say how

I had entered" (*Inf.* I, 10); in Eden, he walks contentedly so far along that he can't see where he entered:

> I'd gone so far
> into the ancient forest that I could
> no longer see where I had made my entry"
>
> (22–24)

There his way was blocked by wild animals, but here he is stopped by a stream (25). Each place is the scene of a sudden apparition. In *Inferno* Virgil appears before Dante's eyes: "Before my eyes there suddenly appeared /one who seemed faint because of the long silence" (*Inf.* I, 62–63; in Eden it is Matilda: "I saw a solitary woman."

> (34–40)

She warms herself in "rays of love" (44), which must remind us of those beneficent rays of the planet that leads on the straight path rising over the mountain in *Inferno* I, 16–18:

> I . . . saw its shoulders clothed
> already by the rays of that same planet
> which serves to lead men straight along all roads.

By poetic association, Matilda becomes a loving source of enlightenment.

Thus the forest of entrapment in Hell that was the labyrinth of this world finds its redeeming counterpart in the divine forest (2) with breeze, birdsong, and brightly colored flowers. In the system of the *Comedy*, each wood illuminates the other. *Inferno* I depicts a moral landscape with no literal model on earth. Unlike the forest at Lake Avernus, where Aeneas enters the Underworld, Dante's dark valley, his anti-Eden, is nowhere. Eden, by contrast, has a specific geographic location. It is at the center of the hemisphere of water, at the antipodes of Jerusalem, and it rises in solid symmetry to the conical concavity of Hell. While drawing on a rich medieval tradition for his Earthly Paradise—a locale separated from the inhabited world, sometimes by an expanse of water, land so high it almost touches the sphere of the moon—Dante crafts his own cosmography bound and unified by textual topology.

The forest of Eden was judged by Ruskin to be "the sweetest passage of wood description which exists in literature." Many other readers have admired Dante's depiction of nature here because it is the most natural place in the whole *Comedy*. Paradise is immaterial, pure spirit, Hell is the poetic realm of *adynata,* the natural world inside out, upside down, a zoo of horrifying monsters. In Earthly Paradise nature is neither warped and twisted, as it is in Hell, nor virtual and abstract, as it is in Paradise. Here is a happy medium with changeless conditions in an ideal, vernal balance. Although man fell out of this nest, it is not a place of sadness. Matilda does not mourn; on the contrary, she praises the Creator. Her laughter displays the joy in her soul.

To put it simply, here is the happiest place possible on the earth. How could Dante convey that extreme *gaudium* without such dazzling devices and grandiose effect as the gems and gold in Ezechiel's vision of the promised land, a festive throng of the saved, music *in chorale?* There is not very much here: a forest, songbirds, a breeze, grass, red and yellow flowers, a bifurcating streamlet, one smiling maiden. This enviable economy of means is deceptive in its simplicity. The minimal landscape and its single inhabitant all carry maximal allusive value. What seems most natural is, in fact, most symbolic.

Each detail resonates with multiple meanings. A mountain summit is sacred because it brings man close to God, as when Moses received the Law on Sinai, or when Christ dwelt in the Mount of Olives, preached a Sermon on the Mount, and suffered Crucifixion on Golgotha. For the Anonymous Florentine, the mountain means that the farther the soul is from sin, the closer it is to reason and the Creator; mountain climbing is the path to self-knowledge; attaining the peak signifies the moral perfection of man in this life. Early commentators held that the trees, like the flowers and birds, are virtues that spread their seeds over the earth, that is, sow the impulse to good in human hearts. Flowering and fruit bearing, they are fair signs of spring, rebirth, and fertility. While the forest labyrinth stands for this world, from Augustine through Aquinas the Garden was envisioned as a shady grove linked both with the Fall and with the wooden Cross of redemption. Whoever held in memory Ambrose's *Hexameron* (v, 36) would know that the reason birds sing at dawn is to praise the Creator and remind us to praise the Lord by chanting Psalms.

If the stream, three feet wide but an impassable barrier for Dante, is a separator between time and eternity, the breeze he feels against his forehead complements those angels' wings that had brushed his *fronte* on each terrace in the ascent and confirms invisibly the erasure of his sins. It is a soft, low, steady air current, not wind as we know it—unpredictable, gusting, turbulent. Easterly in one of its vectors, it blows from the direction of God and signifies rational restraint and temperance, as opposed to impulse and unleashed passions. Taken overall, the Garden is a *locus amoenus* and a majestic *lento* that marvelously combines ingredients from nature, the Bible, medieval legend, and classical myth. In allegory it may be a symbol of just government, and it is certainly emblematic of harmony in the soul. According to what Dante wrote in his *De monarchia* III, v, 7, the Earthly Paradise signifies virtue in operation, which is to say, happiness.

Who Is She?

And Matilda? Dorothy Sayers expostulated for many readers when she wondered with some irritation who the blazes Matilda is. Alas, Dante does not oblige us. He dispenses with the usual courtesies and proceeds directly to voice his puzzlement at the wind and water, circulating in apparent contradiction to what Statius had taught him about unchanging weather conditions above the mountain gate (*Purg.* XXI, 40–57). If Dante recognizes her, why does he not introduce her? If she is a stranger to him, why not inquire about her credentials before talking about the weather? Since she is all alone, no one else can perform the formalities. Of course, she could perfectly well name herself, as do many others, like Pia and Piccarda. Can Dante possibly have forgotten our curiosity as readers? Why does the poet not pronounce her name, at least for our benefit?

Some commentators have suggested that Dante withholds her name to challenge us, to make us think *what*, not *who*, she is and to sublimate the woman into a symbol. But there are two problems with this. First, it would mean that Matilda differs from Dante's other guides, being the only one without a prior historical existence. Virgil is Reason, but Virgil is also Virgil; Cato is Freedom, but Cato is also Cato of Utica. Second, if Eden's lone resident is purely symbolic, why is she eventually christened Matilda? Why is she not granted a more obvious and euphonious sign of personification, say, Grazia or Letizia?

To be consistent with the other characters in Dante's *Comedy*, this lady must have two identities, one historical or literal, the other symbolic or moral. By consensus in the commentary tradition, from its origins to the end of the nineteenth century, she is the Countess Matilda of Canossa (d. 1115), a powerful noble faithful to the Church who ruled generously from her Tuscan stronghold. Although Boccaccio's public readings never extended beyond *Inferno* XVII, we know that he agreed with his learned colleagues because he anticipates his *lectura* on Canto XXVIII in a discussion of Guelfs and Ghibellines prompted by the Farinata episode. But this identification was broken as our century began when it was called into question by D'Ovidio, who could not see in such a *soave giovinetta* the fierce old warrior dame of Tuscany. Thereafter the Countess of Tuscany fell out of fashion as Matelda's historical counterpart. Attilio Momigliano, bothered by the gap between the maid's beauty and her flat, philosophical speech, could hardly have been more blunt: "Whoever thinks that Matilda is Matilda of Canossa has a mind surrounded by cold shadows. It is laughable."

But if not the Countess of Tuscany, then whom do we have here in such a privileged role? She could be a friend of Beatrice (recall that she will lead Dante to Beatrice and that it is Beatrice who names her), perhaps any one of several ladies from the *Vita nuova*. Or she could be a thirteenth-century German mystic, two of whom have been nominated: Mechtild of Magdeburg and Mechtild of Hackeborn. The latter was D'Ovidio's substitute, and he has found some thoughtful followers, including the Dominican sister Mary Jeremy Finnegan. What, however, would Dante's enticing young girl, a picture of springtime, have in common with a German woman who mortified the flesh in her cloistered cell? Parallels between Dante's scene and Mechtild of Hackeborn's *Liber specialis gratiae* are too fragmentary and generic to clinch the matter: in one vision she sees herself on a mountain for forty days and nights; it has seven levels and seven fountains; first is the fountain of humility, which washes the soul of pride; other fountains above cleanse ire, envy, disobedience, avarice, carnality, and sloth. Even more implausible than these Northern nuns are assorted remaining alternatives: Eve, assuming that Cato plays Adam and Dante is "Adamesque" (but Adam appears in *Paradiso* XXVI and Eve, denied a speaking part, enacts the Eve-Ave palindrome as she sits below Mary in the celestial rose); Leah, regardless of the fact that Leah has already just appeared as herself in the preceding canto; Mary Magdalene; Matilda, virgin daughter of the German Emperor Henry I (in the first half of the tenth century), Dante's mother, Bella; and Dante's wife, Gemma.

Uncertainties being what they are about her literal existence, it goes without saying that Matilda's status as an allegorical figure is far more bemused. But again, the befuddlement is ours as moderns, for consensus united the older commentators, who called her the Active Life and connected her with Leah, making Matilda-Leah complement Rachel-Beatrice as the Contemplative Life. Outside that, she has been forced into a whole wardrobe of symbolic costumes, some sensible enough but others oddly colored, ill-fitting, or downright outlandish. Thus Matilda has been named Earthly Happiness before the Fall, Earthly Happiness in the Natural State, Perfect and Happy Human Nature, Innocence, Natural Innocence, Primitive Innocence of Humanity, Return to Primitive Innocence, Perfect Purification, Astrea or Original Justice, the New Eve, Christian Doctrine, Doctrine of Holy Church (either read by studious men of letters or understood and learned by the unlettered from public preaching), Love of the Church, Practical Theology, The Priesthood, Working Charity, the Catholic Life, Mysticism, Path to Paradise, Contemplation (in the transition from the fifth to the sixth degree), the Soul of Paradise, a Cherub with a Flaming Sword, Provisional Happiness, Grace, Prevenient or Cooperant Grace, Habit of Good Choice, Monarchic Principle, Philosophy reconciled with Theology, Docility, Art Born of Learning, Imagination, She Who Glorifies God's Wisdom, Wisdom, and, simply, Woman.

Exposed to such a parade of personalities, no wonder most readers nowadays confess to feeling at an impasse. The time has come to cut loose from this masquerade that marches dizzily with the critics in lengthening file. If we double back to Dante, *his* Matilda need not elude us. Precursor to Beatrice, she who "comes before" is by gender feminine, and by rank she holds the summit of a hierarchy. Like old Cato at the mountain base, she cleanses and has presided since before Christ as Genius or Guardian Spirit of her place. Her name (spelled Mathelda sometimes), scrutinized and dissected, contains letters that give the anagram "Ad Letham," appropriate for one who leads "to the Lethe." Etymologically, Mat(h)elda seems to be cognate with the Greek root "math" (learning) and so could mean Love of Wisdom. Buti, whose information may have come from John of Salisbury's *Policraticon* or Uccione's *Derivations*, explained Matilda as *mathesim laudans*, that is, *lodante la divinazione* or *scienza di Dio* (praising prophecy of God's wisdom). And knowledgeable she is, so primed with scientific erudition that Peter Dronke has called her the "resident physicist" of a Christian Eden.

In view of her gender, her placement at the peak, her "mathematical" name, and her lecture, she must symbolize Wisdom. Scripture and Dante's *Convivio* offer plentiful support for this identification, proposed by Luigi Pietrobono, accepted by Mario Casella, and persuasively buttressed by Peter Armour. Matilda bears an uncanny resemblance to her biblical ancestress, hymned in the Wisdom of Solomon: "He who rises early to seek her will have no difficulty. . . . She goes about seeking those worthy of her, and she graciously appears to them in their paths . . . The beginning of Wisdom is the most sincere desire for instruction" (6:14–17). When Matilda appears beauteous with love in the Garden, we recognize her resemblance to Filosofia from the *Convivio*, whose face showed forth the pleasures of Paradise.

Matilda, I find then, is *ad litteram* the Countess of Tuscany and *spiritualiter* Wisdom. If the former died after an active life at an advanced age, the latter is firstborn and eldest of all God's creatures: "The Lord created me at the beginning of his work, the first of his acts of old. Ages ago I was set up, at the first, before the beginning of the earth" (Proverbs 8:22–23). Yet she appears young to Dante. We can suppose the countess has risen in youth, as souls will, according to Thomas Aquinas, who puts our ideal, resurrected age at around thirty. And for Dante's portrait of Sapientia, no more in allegory than theology would an old woman be suitable. So he has conceived a *puella-senex*, maidenly in body and mature in spirit, comely precisely because she is wise. She who was with Him at the Creation and delighted in it lives on joyfully in the *Comedy* in endless juvenescence.

Literal (Erotica) vs. Allegorical (Platonic) Love

Ten times Dante refers to Matilda in the *Comedy*, but only once is she named. To Beatrice, who utters "Dante," the sole occurrence of his being named (*Purg.* XXX, 55), will go the honor of one time declaring "Matilda" (*Purg.* XXXIII, 119). Every culture ritualizes naming—who can bestow a name, when a name can be spoken or written, or when it must be withheld and kept in silence, as the name of God sometimes is. Always attuned to symbolism in nomenclature, medieval poets kept the process under tight control, witnessed by the fraught moment of the narrator's self-naming in the *Comedy*. Thus if Dante delays naming Matilda, it is not because her name is simply unimportant, as Momigliano opined. On the contrary, Dante wants to heighten her stature, so he deliberately postpones the revelation and saves it for a solemn hapax legomenon. By building our curiosity and keeping us in suspense, he creates a mystery around her name, and when we finally hear it, we must understand that Beatrice intones it not by accident. What entitles her to disclose Matilda's identity? Although the historical Beatrice (d. 1290) could not have known the Countess Matilda, there is nonetheless a logic of homonymy to unite them. Armour has pointed out in a wonderful aperçu that Matilda of Tuscany was the daughter of a Beatrice. Thus as her mother, Beatrice named her Matilda. Dante's Beatrice "names" Matilda in the *Comedy.* The two ladies gravitate into another alliance on allegorical ground. There Beatrice is familiar with Matilda and her habits, as we can infer from the *tu*-form command to dip and revive Dante in Eunoè, the task she is wont to perform for all souls who pass through the Garden: "Lead him to it and, *as you're used to doing,* / revive the power that is faint in him" (*Purg.* XXXIII, 128–129; my italics). At the spiritual level of meaning in the *Comedy,* to sum up in schematic terms, we can say that Virgil-Reason leads Dante to Matilda-Wisdom, who will bring him face-to-face with Beatrice-Revelation.

The return to Eden is the attainment of wisdom. But it is nothing like a dry cerebral conquest. Matilda has, using Dronke's phrase, "spellbinding physical seductiveness," a magnetism also felt by Charles Singleton, who rightly understood how Dance is attracted to her sexually. (Momigliano would have frowned; Matilda, he maintained, was an emblem of purity in a forest that is merely a state of mind.) Yet Dante is explicit. She radiates love, like Venus at her most intensely amorous at the onset of her obsession with Adonis:

> I do not think a light so bright had shone
> beneath the lids of Venus when her son
> pierced her in extraordinary fashion.
>
> (64–66)

As much as Matilda, Canto XXVIII is thoroughly sensual and Venerean. But by now in the journey, erotic love at the literal level implies Platonic love in allegory; sensuality transmutes to spirituality. In Canto XXVII a dream of "Cytherea" (94) anticipates the power of Venus over Canto XXVIII, where Ravenna's pine grove, apart from its autobiographical resonance, is a forest of seed-hung conifers sacred to Venus. Blooming branches, "newly-flowered boughs" (36), allude to May First, the feast of Venus. Pluto, smitten by Cupid's arrow, snatched Persephone at the behest of Venus on the Sicilian plain beneath Eryx, the city famous for its temple to Venus. Persephone ate a pomegranate, seed-filled fruit of fertility; Cupid's arrow scratched his own mother, in whom Adonis obliterated all thought of anything else; Leander risked his life, and would eventually drown, swimming to meet Hero, a priestess of Venus. The magically fertile plain of Eden, Matilda explains, is "full of every seed" (119). This canto appeals felicitously to every one of our five senses with its "painted" flowers (sight), birdsong (hearing), fragrance (smell), breeze (touch). and even though Dante does not eat or drink, he is exposed to both recollection and anticipation of gustatory delight, the most exquisite imaginable, from the Golden Age of "fruit" and "nectar," and still to come from Eunoe, all other tastes surpassing ("their savor is above all other sweetness," 133). Yet, as we have seen, the canto's language and imagery, taken from vernacular love lyric, cede in the second part to *terzine* paced for Scholastic disquisition. While Dante cites the *pastorella,* his sylvan scene, unlike Cavalcanti's, does not culminate with seduction. Being in Eden, he and Matilda behave. His Matilda, a miraculous paradox, is both Venerean and virginal.

A Moderate, Tempered Breeze

In closing, I return to the first simile in the canto. Little songbirds warble greeting to the morning and to their Father's world; the branches of their tree accompany them with a continuous wind-blown bass line, technically called "burden":

> For to the leaves, with song, birds welcomed those
> first hours of the morning joyously,
> and leaves supplied the burden to their rhymes—
>   just like the wind that sounds from branch to branch
> along the shore of Classe, through the pines
> when Aeolus has set Sirocco loose.
>
> (16–21)

What creates this *basso continuo* in the pine boughs is a breeze sweet and steady that originates at the remote fringe of the cosmos in the *primum mobile,* generated as that Ninth Heaven whirls within its orbital radius all the lower planetary spheres. Likened to sirocco, a wind that blows from the southeast, this is a gentle, warm air current. Dante want us to contrast it with the gelid drafts that spirate from below, at the center of the universe, from Dis locked frozen in the pit of Hell.

Dante's similes, heightened rhetoric that signals intensified meaning, are stylistic embellishments significant both for their content and their placement. We all well understand now, especially thanks to studies of Singleton and John Freccero, how powerful the first epic simile of the *Comedy* is. It functions proleptically. The sinner's near death as if by drowning in a shipwreck points ahead to Ulysses' failed navigation and sinking ship, the negative counterpart to providentially authorized missions by Aeneas and by Dante. What is the significance of the first simile in Canto XXVIII? How does it illuminate the poem on a larger scale?

With his mention of Aeolus, Dante nods to Virgil and the storm unleashed on Aeneas's fleet as it sailed from Troy to Carthage. It should go without saying that Dante adduces Virgil in the mantle of allegory that commentators from Servius onward tailored to his verses. Already Servius on *Aeneid* I, 57, says that Virgil has Aeolus tame the passions of the winds to show that the vices of nature can be mitigated. Starting with Fulgentius, in the tradition that reads the first six books of the *Aeneid* as an allegory of human life from birth to maturity, the winds are fleshly libido. Thus the so-called Bernard Silvestris (twelfth century) who follows and expands on Fulgentius, says Aeolus symbolizes birth, when the human spirit leaves its celestial home and takes on the burdens of fleshly libido, represented by the release of the winds.

Petrarch, in both the *Secretum* and his *Seniles* (IV, 5), understands the tempest in *Aeneid* I as an allegory of human passions, and so does Boccaccio, who dedicates an entire chapter to Aeolus in his mythographic encyclopedia, *Genealogia deorum gentilium*. Dante himself exploits this well-defined cultural framework in the first simile of the *Comedy*. Comparing the wayfarer to a man who almost perished in a storm at sea, he alludes to the *fluctus concupiscentiae*, or tumults of passions, that have threatened to swallow the pilgrim. Naturally, Dante's early commentators saw how, by the dawning day he reaches the Earthly Paradise, his problem has been corrected. There reason dominates sensuality. For Buti, the Earthly Paradise is, in allegory, the state of innocence; for the Anonymous Florentine, there are no storms in the Earthly Paradise to signify allegorically that in the state of innocence there are no bodily passions and hence no sin; Buti and Landino agree that "whoever has raised himself from the earth, that is, from cognition of earthly things, and has made sensuality obey reason and unified himself so that the flesh does not fight the spirit, has a tranquil spirit free from winds of appetite, from waters of sadness, and from every perturbation." For Benvenuto, Eden represents the happy state of perfect virtue, remote from climatic alterations because not subject to the passions.

Contrary to the *bufera infernal* of *Inferno* V, the storm that relentlessly buffets Francesca, Paolo, and all "Dido's troop" on winds of passions, the breeze in Eden is moderate, tempered. It is small, we could say, as the waters are diminutive—only three steps across. For Dante it might as well be a gulf as wide as the Dardanelles or the Red Sea. He keeps his place, restrains himself, holds back in humility—unlike prideful Xerxes and unlike Ulysses, who had in hubris flown madly over the ocean and transgressed the pillars of Hercules. Wind and waters are symbols of the passions, their tumult and storms here tamed. In fact, the Garden as a whole is of relatively diminished dimensions: contrast the wild beasts of *Inferno* I with the "little birds" of *Purgatorio* (XXVIII, 14). Dante's pilgrim has traveled a great moral distance. As Emerson Brown has noticed, there is indeed an undercurrent of sensuality here, but each of Dante's Ovidian similes, if fully read, hints at loss while focusing on the moment before the loss: Proserpina *before* Pluto abducted her; Venus, whose beauty is augmented by her love for Adonis, *before* her grief at his bloody death; Leander facing the Hellespont *before* his fatal plunge into the storm-tossed waters, an emblem of his own indomitable passions. Dante and Matilda together belong to this innocence: she because she has never been corrupted, he because he has been purged and verges on recovering the primal innocence that she personifies. Thus stylistic economy of means in Canto XXVIII is a poetic simplicity that complements the small proportions of the things depicted. This downsizing reflects what the pilgrim has achieved morally to this point in his journey, the capacity to contain his passions and restrain himself. Virgil as Reason has led him to Wisdom. Crowned and mitred, Dante is his own king: he rules himself.

At the end of the canto, Dante calls us back from the Scholastic lesson on meteorology to Virgil and Statius. Matilda, anticipating that her smile might strike them as discordant in this place of the Fall, had addressed all three newcomers early in the canto:

> "You are new here and may—because I smile
> . . . wonder, perplexed, unable to detect
> the cause"
>
> (76–79)

But immediately after, she directs her words just to Dante, who stands in front of them, "And you, who have stepped forward" (82). Virgil and Statius, still with him here in the Garden, are nonetheless fading into the background. As it happens, neither will speak again in the poem. Present but silent, no longer leading (or at Dante's side), now they take position behind him. Dante, who had thrilled to trail along after Homer, Horace, Ovid, Lucan, and Virgil as he walked through the first circle of Hell, now, above the brightest terrace of Purgatory, stands alone, at the forefront. He precedes and overshadows Statius, and Virgil. He, Dante, is first. For a moment he allows us to glimpse Parnassus, to see in our memory's eye the ancient poets assembled and dreaming there in an image that would inspire Raphael. After all the theologizing, the lecture on the nature of Eden with its erudite sources in Isidore of Seville, Peter Lornbard, Albertus Magnus, Thomas Aquinas, and Alanus of Lille—we return, as we trust always in Dante's *Comedy,* to poetry.

BIBLIOGRAPHY

Below are some of the studies and commentaries that I have consulted in preparing this *lectura:*

Anderson, William. *Dante the Maker.* London: Routledge and Kegan Paul, 1980.

Armour, Peter. "*Purgatorio* XXVIII." In *Dante Commentaries. Eight Studies of the "Divine Comedy,"* ed. David Nolan. Dublin: Irish Academic Press, 1977, 115–141. Idem. "Matelda in Eden: The Teacher and the Apple." *Italian Studies* 34 (1979): 2–27. Idem. *Dante's Griffin and the History of the World: A Study of the Earthly Paradise.* Oxford: Clarendon Press, 1989.

Barolini, Teodolinda. *Dante's Poets. Textuality and Truth in the "Comedy."* Princeton: Princeton University Press, 1984.

Biagi, Guido et al. *"La Divina Commedia" nella figurazione artistica a nel secolare commento,* vol. 2. Turin: UTET, 1931.

Bindoni, Giuseppe. "Matelda." In *Indagini critiche sulla "Divina Commedia."* Milan: Società Editrice Dante Alighieri, 1918, 601–619.

Boccaccio, Giovanni. *Genealogia deorum gentilium libri,* ed. Vincenzo Romano. Bari: Laterza, 1951.

Idem. Esposizioni supra la "Comedia" di Dante, ed. Giorgio Padoan. Milan: Mondadori, 1965.

Bode, W. H., ed. *Scriptores rerum mythicarurn latini tres Romae nuper reperti.* Celle: E. H. C. Schulze, 1834.

Bosco, Umberto. "Il canto XXVIII del *Purgatorio.*" *Nuove Letture Dantesche,* vol. 5. Florence: Le Monnier, 1972, 131–147.

Boyde, Patrick. *Dante Philomythes and Philosopher. Man and the Cosmos.* Cambridge: Cambridge University Press, 1981.

Brown, Emerson Jr. "Proserpina, Matelda, and the Pilgrim." *Dante Studies* 89 (1971): 33–48.

Busnelli, Giovanni. *La concezione del "Purgatorio" dantesco.* Rome: Civiltà Cattolica, 1906.

Caccia, Ettore. "Il mito di Matelda." *Letture Classensi* 2 (1969): 171–217.

Carroll, John S. *Prisoners of Hope. An Exposition of Dante's "Purgatorio."* 1906. Reprint, Port Washington, NY: Kennikat Press, 1971.

Cazzato, Carmelo. *Una nuova proposta sulla questione della "Matelda."* Città di Castello: S. Lapi, 1900.

Chiorboli, Enzo. *L'aspettazione e l'apparizione di Beatrice nel Paradiso Terrestre. Purgatorio XXVIII–XXX.* Ferrara: Taddei, 1921.

Conigliani, Emma Boghen. *Il Canto XXVIII del "Purgatorio."* Brescia: Pavoni, 1902.

Di Pino, Guido. "Il Canto XXVIII del *Purgatorio.*" *Letture Classensi* 2 (1969): 219–241.

D'Ovidio, Francesco. *Nuovi studi danteschi: Il "Purgatorio" e il suo preludio.* Milan: Hoepli, 1906.

Dronke, Peter. "Dante's Earthly Paradise: Towards an Interpretation of Purgatorio XXVIII." *Romanische Forschungen* 82, no. 4 (1970): 467–487.

Enciclopedia dantesca, 6. vols. Rome, 1970–1978, s.v. "arra," "Leandro," "Matelda," "Proserpina," "Serse."

Fairchild, Hoxie Neale. "Matelda: A Study in Multiple Allegory." *Romantic Review* 16 (1925): 136–164.

Fanfani, Pietro, ed. *Commento alla "Divina Commedia" d'anonimo fiorentino del secolo XIV.* Bologna: Romagnoli, 1868.

Federzoni, Giovanni. *L'entrata di Dante nel Paradiso Terrestre.* Bologna: Zanichelli, 1890.

Finnegan, Mary Jeremy. *The Women of Helfta: Scholars and Mystics.* Athens: University of Georgia Press, 1991.

Flamini, Francesco. *Il significato e il fine della "Divina Commedia."* Leghorn: Giusti, 1916.

Freccero, John. "The Firm Foot on a Journey without a Guide. In *Dante, The Poetics of Conversion,* ed. Rachel Jacoff. Cambridge, MA: Harvard University Press, 1986, 29–54.

Fulgentius. *Mythologiae.* In *Fulgentius the Mythographer,* ed. Leslie George Whitbread. Columbus: Ohio State University, 1971.

Gilbert, Allan H. "Dante's Hundred Cantos." In *American Critical Essays on the "Divine Comedy,"* ed. Robert J. Clements. New York: New York University, 1967, 17–25.

Gmelin, Hermann, trans. and comm. *Die göttliche Komödie.* Stuttgart: E. Klett, 1949.

Goudet, Jacques. "Une nommée Matelda." *Revue des Études Italiennes,* n.s., 1 (1954): 20–60.

Graf, Arturo. "*Purgatorio* Canto XXVIII," in *Letture dantesche,* ed. Giovanni Getto (Florence: Sansoni, 1964), 1235–1256.

Hawkins, Peter S. "Transfiguring the Text: Ovid, Scripture and the Dynamics of Allusion," *Stanford Italian Review* 5, no. 2 (1985): 115–139.

Hollander, Robert. *Allegory in Dante's "Commedia"* (Princeton: Princeton University Press, 1969), esp. ch. 4, "The Women of *Purgatorio.*"

Isidore of Seville. *Etymologie,* ed. W. M. Lindsay. Oxford: Clarendon Press, 1911.

Jones, Julian Ward, and Elizabeth Frances Jones. *The Commentary on the First Six Books of the "Aeneid" of Virgil Commonly Attributed to Bernardus Silvestris Silvestris.* Lincoln: University of Nebraska Press, 1977.

Kallendorf, Craig. *In Praise of Aeneas: Virgil and Epideictic Rhetoric in the Early Italian Renaissance.* Hanover: University Press of New England, 1989.

Kirkham, Victoria. "A Canon of Women in Dante's *Commedia.*" *Annali d'Italianistica* 7 (1989): 16–41.

Lansing, Richard H. *From Image to Idea. Study of the Simile in Dante's "Commedia."* Ravenna: Longo, 1977.

MacQueen, John. *Numerology Theory and Outline History of a Literary Mode.* Edinburgh: University of Edinburgh, 1985.

Mandalari, Mario. *Matelda. Purgatorio* XXVIII. Rome: Palotta, 1892.

Meyer, Heinz. *Die Zahlenallegorese im Mittelalter. Methode und Begrauch.* Munich: Fink, 1975.

Momigliano, Attilio, comm. *La Divina Commedia,* 2d ed. Florence: Sansoni, 1950.

Moore, Edward. " Matelda," in *Studies in Dante,* 3d ser. Oxford: Clarendon Press, 1903, 210–216.

Nardi, Bruno. "Intorno al sito del *Purgatorio* e al mito dantesco dell'Eden." *Giornale Dantesco* 25, no. 4 (1922): 289–300.

Nardi, Tilde, "Il Canto XXVIII del *Purgatorio*" In *Lectura Dantis Romana,* no. 66. Turin: SEI, 1963.

Panzacchi, Enrico. "Nella 'divina foresta,'" *Nuova Antologia;* ser. 4, 114 (Nov.-Dec. 1904): 13–22.

Parker, Mark. "Lectura Dantis: *Inferno* XXVIII." *Lectura Dantis* 3 (fall 1988): 41–49.

Parodi, E. G. "Intorno alle fonti dantesche e a Matelda." In *Poesia e storia nella "Divina Commedia."* Naples, 1920, 313–363.

Pattarini, Marcello. *Il paesaggio del Paradiso Terrestre nel* XXVIII *canto del "Purgatorio" di Dante.* Bologna: Palmaverde, 1962.

Perez, Paolo. *I sette cerchi del "Purgatorio" di Dante,* 3d ed. Milan: L. F. Cogliati, 1896.

Pietrobono, Luigi. *Dal centro al cerchio. La struttura morale della "Divina Commedia."* Turin: SEI, 1956. *Idem.,* ed. and comet. *La "Divina Commedia" di Dante Alighieri,* 4th ed. Turin: SEI, 1959.

Poggioli, Renato. "Dante *Poco Tempo Silvano:* On a 'Pastoral Oasis' in the *Commedia.*" *Dante Studies* 80 (1962): 1–20.

Quaglio, Antonio Enzo. *Il canto* XXVIII *del "Purgatorio."* Florence: Le Monnier, 1966.

Rava, Luigi, "La pineta di Ravenna." *Nuova Antologia,* ser. 4, 70 (1897): 247–272.

Ronzoni, Domenico. "Perché nella *Divina Commedia* c'è il Paradiso Terrestre." *Giornale Dantesco* 21 (1913): 258–263.

Rossetti, Gabriele. *Comento analitico al "Purgatorio" di Dante Alighieri,* ed. Pompeo Giannantonio. Florence: Olschki, 1967.

Ruskin, John. "Modern Painters." In *The Complete Works of John Ruskin,* ed. E. T. Cook and Alexander Wedderburn. London: George Allen, 1915, 5:248–281.

Saly, John, "Matelda's Poetics." *Italian Culture* 9 (1991): 55–62.

Santi, Antonio. "Chi sia veramente Matelda." *Giornale Dantesco* 21 (1913): 173–180.

Santoro, Domenico. "Matelda." *Giornale Dantesco* 125, reviewed in *Bulletino delta Società Dantesca,* n.s., 12 (1905): 42–43.

Sapegno, Natalino, ed. and comm., *La Divina Commedia.* Florence: La Nuova Italia, 1957.

Sayers, Dorothy L. *Introductory Papers on Dante.* London: Methuen, 1954.

Scartazzini, G. A., comm. *La Divina Commedia.* Milan: Hoepli, 1899.

Schiavo, Giuseppe. *Tra la selva sacra.* Florence: F. Lumachi, 1903.

Shapiro, Marianne. *Woman Earthly and Divine in the Comedy of Dante.* Lexington: Kentucky University Press, 1975.

Singleton, Charles S. "Su la fiumana ove 'l mar non ha vanto." *Romantic Review* 39, no. 4 (1948): 269–277. *Idem.* "Journey to Beatrice." *Dante Studies,* vol. 2 (1958. Reprint, Cambridge: Harvard University Press, 1967). *Idem,* tr. and comm., *The Divine Comedy,* 6 vols. (Princeton, Princeton University Press, 1970–1975).

Stambler, Bernard. *Dante's Other World.* New York: New York University Press, 1957.

Steinberg, Leo, "Michelangelo's Last Judgment as Merciful Heresy." *Art in America*, (Nov.–Dec. 1975): 48–63.

Thilo, G., and H. Hagen, ed. *Servii grammatici qui feruntur in Vergilii carmina commentarii*, vol. 1. Leipzig: Teubner, 1881.

Tommaseo, Niccolò. See Biagi.

Torraca, Francesco, comm. *La Divina Commedia*. Rome: Società Editrice Dante Alighieri, 1905.

Vernon, William Warren. *Readings on the "Purgatorio" of Dante*. Chiefly based on the *Commentary* of Benvenuto of Imola; 3d ed. rev. London: Methuen, 1907.

Vossler, Karl. *Mediaeval Culture: An Introduction to Dante and his Times*, vol. 2. 1929. Reprint, New York: Ungar, 1958.

Wlassics, Tibor, ed. *Dante's Divine Comedy: Introductory Readings*, vol. 1. "Inferno," supplement to *Lectura Dantis* 6 (1990).

CANTO XXIX

Dante's Processional Vision

PETER ARMOUR

To the modern reader this canto might seem at first to be of a somewhat remote and antiquarian interest with, at best, a certain formal and old-fashioned poetic beauty. Coming immediately after the richly textured account of humankind's lost paradise on earth and of the beautiful lady who explains it to Dante, Canto XXIX introduces a series of symbols from which the reader is required to deduce a corresponding series of "other meanings." It would appear, therefore, to belong to that outmoded form, the allegory, and indeed virtually all commentators agree that it is an allegorical presentation of the history of the Redemption up to the coming of Christ and the foundation of his Church. The procession of seven candlesticks, twenty-four elders, four animals, and a griffin drawing a chariot escorted by seven ladies and followed by seven men may be broadly outlined. With the guidance and illumination of the seven Gifts of the Holy Ghost, the divine plan for humankind's salvation evolved and was revealed through the twenty-four books of the Old Testament. At the time described in the four Gospels, Christ, with two natures like the griffin, brought his Church into the world accompanied by the three Theological and four Cardinal Virtues and succeeded by the remaining books of the New Testament, classified as seven. The scene is a combination of historical pageant and *sacra rappresentazione,* or symbolic religious drama, which in visual terms may recall the stylized processions of Byzantine and medieval art, along with illustrations of the Apocalypse. It may also be visualized in terms of the processions, religious or secular, of Dante's own day and was in fact reconstructed, with some variations, over two and a half centuries later as a Corpus Christi Day parade in Modena. As a triumphal procession it both takes up an ancient Roman celebration and anticipates the allegorical triumph of Renaissance literature and art. Even so, for many readers, it probably remains a rather abstract and artificial creation, a coded sequence of symbols to which tradition has attached what is, generally speaking, a single more or less clear and straightforward explanation.

Dante, however, did not find this part of his poem easy either to invent or to express in poetic form. Just before describing the details of the procession, he interrupts his narrative with a fervent appeal to the Muses, and especially to Urania, the Muse of astronomy and thus of heavenly themes, to help him to "put in verses things hard to conceive" (42). As on the previous occasions when Dante has employed this classical literary device (*Inf.* II, 7–9 and XXXII, 1–12; *Purg.* I, 7–12), the invocation indicates his increased awareness, at this particular point, of the conceptual and technical difficulties of his enterprise: his task of matching the great but limited resources of poetic language to his ever more elevated themes, his continual search for the higher "art" required by his more sublime subject matter (*Purg.* IX, 70–72). In effect, he is here marking out what is to follow as a great challenge both to his intellect and to his poetic powers, a challenge so great that he turns to imagined external powers. He justifies his plea for their assistance on the sufferings he has undergone in their service, the grueling effort he has devoted to his massive project, the price he has paid in hunger, cold, and lack of sleep in order to create the "sacred poem" that made him "grow thin over many years" (*Par.* XXV, 1–3). In this way he also challenges his reader to investigate, interpret, and admire the daunting intellectual and poetic complexity of the concluding scenes of his *Purgatorio*.

Somewhat surprisingly, what immediately follows this invocation is a group of symbols that are not Dante's own, for, although he adds to and embellishes them, initially they were borrowed from the Book of Revelation. The seven candelabra, the twenty-four elders, and the four beasts all appear in one of St John's visions of heaven (Rev. 1:12–13, 20; 4:4–11; the last have an antecedent in the prophecy of Ezekiel 1:4 ff.). Dante alludes directly to these biblical sources in the second interruption of the narrative in this canto, the address to the reader in lines 97–105. Here he invokes the constraints that his great project places on his expression of it; having no space in his rhymes for further details, he orders his reader to consult the dramatic account of the whirlwind from the North, the cloud and fire in which Ezekiel saw the four animals, each with four faces—of a man, a lion, an ox, and an eagle—their appearance as of glowing bronze, of burning coals, of lamps (Ez. 1:4–6, 7, 10, 13). The obedient reader must therefore supply additional visual and symbolic elements from this source, but with one exception. Whereas in Ezekiel the animals each had four wings, in St John they had six, and in this respect Dante's vision corresponded with St John's. So Dante acknowledges his borrowings, emphasizes that his principal model was the Book of Revelation, and places his own poetry in the same tradition. Canto XXIX—in itself and as a prelude to the cantos that follow, particularly Canto XXXII—is Dante's own prophetic vision and version of the apocalypse. Having established this, Dante in fact abandons these sources, for the last section of the canto consists to all intents and purposes of his own inventions and additions.

The two addresses, to the Muses and to the reader, divide the canto into three parts. The first (1–36) acts as a transitional passage between the themes of the previous canto and new and astonishing events that begin with light and music. In the second (43–96) Dante openly switches from the imagery of the Garden of Eden, based on Genesis, the first book of the Bible, to an episode constructed principally on symbols taken from the last. Finally he develops his own symbols for the central features and the rearguard of the procession and builds the scene toward its climax—the thunderclap that brings all to a halt (106–154). The scene is, however, not yet complete; the chariot, directly opposite Dante, is still empty. The true culmination and meaning of the procession is not revealed until the next canto, when Beatrice appears.

Variations on the Wonderful

The opening lines of Canto XXIX contain allusions to the three main literary traditions—thirteenth-century love poetry, the Bible, and the classics—which Dante has brought together in his presentation of the earthly Paradise and the beautiful lady who is later called Matilda. The description of her singing like an enamored woman is reminiscent of a ballad by Guido Cavalcanti and evokes, at a new and higher level, the themes of love and women's beauty seen among the natural beauties of springtime. Her song, in Latin, "Blessed are those whose sins are covered up" (3), is taken from one of the Psalms and alludes to the fact that, the effects of the seven sins having been purged away, it is in the earthly Paradise that the souls, and Dante himself, find innocence again and oblivion of their sins in the Lethe. Dante's use of classical imagery continues with the comparison of Matilda to forest nymphs of the light and of the shadows.

On opposite sides of the river, they walk upstream until it turns, and Dante is facing east. Then, with Matilda's instructions to him to look and listen, the visual, auditory, and psychological experiences of the canto begin. The sudden flash, like lightning but persisting and growing brighter, arouses Dante's astonished curiosity. The melody makes him rebuke the disobedience of Eve, for its sweetness measures humanity's tragic loss of its earthly Paradise. It summons up in Dante's mind the entirely hypothetical ideal of an alternative history of a human race without sin and of a Dante born to live among the ineffable delights of the original garden of temporal and spiritual happiness on earth. Meanwhile the light has come to seem like fire and the music to be distinguishable as singing. Thus is established the sense of a progressive revelation characteristic of the whole episode.

The narrative resumes, after the appeal to the Muses, with further stages in this gradual unfolding of something unexpected and wonderful. What at a distance looked like seven golden trees come to be seen, as the space between them and Dante decreases and as his reason is able to order the various sense impressions correctly, as seven lit candlesticks, and the syllables of the singing become audible as *Hosanna*. Dante and Virgil are equally amazed. In the simile of the newlywed brides is expressed the even slower calm and solemn pace of this procession, and Dante's total absorption is conveyed by Matilda's reprimand, telling him to look not just at the lights but at what follows. After seeing the white-robed figures across the shining water, in which he himself is reflected, Dante stops in order to see better all that is to come (72).

At this point, Dante introduces a feature not found in St John's account of the seven candelabra—the extraordinary, indeed miraculous, pennants of light that "paint" the air and form a "handsome sky" over the rest of the procession. In another variation from his source, the twenty-four elders are not crowned with gold but garlanded with lilies and are singing a different song, a modification and expansion of the phrase "Blessed art thou among women," applied in the Old Testament to Judith and in the New Testament to Mary, the mother of Christ (Judith 13:23; Luke 1:28, 42). Replacing the word "women" with "the daughters of Adam," they praise a lady's eternal beauties, and it seems natural to assume that their greeting includes Matilda, the only lady present. Hence, if she is taken to be Dante's version of the biblical lady Wisdom, the elders' song extols the eternal beauties of God's wisdom on earth, which permeates the history of all holy women to Mary, the new Eve. To the last of his borrowed symbols, the four animals, Dante gives garlands of green leaves; each animal has six wings, as in St. John, and these are "full of eyes," like Argus. Again diverging from his sources, Dante restricts the detail of the eyes to the wings alone, and this, along with the fact that he alludes to the eyes of Argus as inanimate, might indicate that the reference is not directly to the mythical guardian of Io but to the peacock's tail in which his eyes were placed. The eyes in these wings are as those of a peacock, but alive.

In this central section of the canto, Dante departs from the Book of Revelation, not only in these details but also in some major ways. St John's vision was sudden: "I saw ... / and immediately I was there in spirit" (Rev. 1:12; 4:1–2); and what he saw was a static scene of seven lights, twenty-four elders seated, and four animals surrounding the throne of God and the Lamb. Dante, however, introduces these symbols into a procession that comes slowly into his sight; next, it approaches through the trees and over the grass and flowers of the beautiful garden (17, 35, 43–45, 88–90), for Dante witnesses all this not in the heavenly, but in the earthly, Paradise.

The Triumphal Chariot

As has already been noted, the remainder of the procession consists of Dante's additions. Indeed, the central feature and focus of Dante's apocalypse marks such a striking departure from St. John's that it is a challenge to the reader to seek new meanings in what Dante now presents. The throne and the Lamb in Revelation are replaced in Dante's version by a chariot drawn by a griffin. This beast was traditionally described as a fierce and rapacious flying quadruped, with the head, wings, and foreparts of an eagle and the rest of a lion. Dante's griffin, however, is a peaceful draught animal whose wings pass between the bands of light without harming them. This is not the wild animal that classical and medieval writers reported as living in Scythia or the East, but a miraculously transformed creature that is part of the extraordinary design unfolding before Dante's eyes.

The two-wheeled chariot may indirectly recall Ezekiel's complicated vision of wheels (Ez. 1:15–21; 10:2, 6, 9–19) or the wheeled throne of God (Dan. 7:9), but directly it is presented as a symbol taken not from the Bible but from classical history. It is a triumphal chariot and thus introduces a completely new definition of the whole procession as a Roman triumph. Dante may not have known all the details of the triumphal processions of ancient Rome, with the standards and soldiers, the prisoners, booty, and sacrificial animals, and the *triumphator* in his horse-drawn chariot. One possible source of information was the Arch of Titus in Rome, which depicts the booty taken from Jerusalem, including the seven-branched candlestick, and which was known in the Middle Ages as the Arch of the Seven Lamps. Since Dante's seven candlesticks look like trees from a distance, they are probably to be visualized as separate; nevertheless, their symbolism may obviously be linked with that of the Jewish menorah. Perhaps Dante constructed this triumph not so much with the Roman model in mind but rather its medieval descendant. Thus, the seven pennants of light, the *ostendali,* act as processional banners, or *gonfaloni,* and the chariot is a *carroccio,* the war chariot or, more generally, the ceremonial vehicle of the medieval Italian city-state. Dante's procession, though obviously peaceful, is in a sense also military, a "glorious army," the "troops *(milizia)* of the celestial kingdom" (*Purg.* XXXII, 16–17, 22).

This chariot is described as more handsome than those used in ancient Rome for the triumphs of one of the greatest generals, Scipio Africanus, or of the greatest emperor, Augustus, and more handsome even than the chariot of the Sun, which Phaëthon drove astray (115–120). Here Dante alludes first to exceptional heroes and events in the glorious history of ancient Rome, and second to the mythical age of gods and demigods. This double comparison, introduced by the word "not," elevates this chariot and this triumph above those ever known or even conceivable on earth, above even the heaven of the Sun. This chariot could never be badly guided, or threaten the earth, or earn God's just punishment. This triumph is above history and is ultimately providential and supernatural, devised beyond the Sun, in the highest heaven where God is. It is the triumph, as the next canto will reveal, of Beatrice.

The seven dancing ladies who escort the chariot directly derive not from the Bible or the classics but from the tradition of allegorical personification, which stems from both. The colors of the three by the right wheel and the leader's three eyes help to define their meaning as the Virtues. This is confirmed by their later words: they are both nymphs and stars and are thus linked with the two constellations seen by Dante on his arrival and on his first night in Purgatory (*Purg.* I, 23–7; VIII, 88–93; XXXI, 106; see also *Par.*, XX, 127–129).

Of the seven men who form the rearguard of the procession, the first two are dramatically contrasted: one looks like a healer of men, nature's dearest creature; the other, who bears a bright, sharp sword and strikes fear into Dante, seems to have the opposite intent, that is, to kill, wound, or punish. The next four are described merely as "of humble aspect." The last, an old man, is a sharp-featured sleepwalker. Although Dante sees them, they do not pass before him, for it is when the chariot is opposite him that the procession halts.

Natural and Supernatural

This strange symbolic revelation, which unfolds so slowly and mysteriously and ends suddenly and with a sense of expectation, is not presented by Dante as a marvelous illusion or dream or inner vision but as an external, perceived event, both seen and heard. Under this aspect, it is natural and real but at the same time more than real: it pertains to man's original home and lost ideal, the earthly Paradise. The elevated and idealized naturalism of Dante's description of the garden is, in fact, continued in his narrative of the procession. Light is a particularly important component and image of comparison, with the references to lightning, fire, the full moon, and so on.

To this Dante adds a great range of color symbolism: the gold of the candlesticks; the otherworldly whiteness of the elders' robes; the pennants of light with the colors of the rainbow or the lunar halo; the garlands of lilies and green leaves; perhaps the peacock eyes of the animals' wings; the gold, white, and red of the griffin; the three ladies of more-than-fiery red, emerald green, and the white of fresh snow; the purple robes of the other four; and the garlands of red flowers that, from a distance, look like flames. All these are to be visualized across the illuminated river and against the greenery and multicolored flowers of the garden (34–35, 67–72, 88–90).

Numerical patterns add further complexity: the hundred paces shared by Dante and Matilda at the beginning; the procession of seven, of twenty-four arranged as twelve pairs, of four; a chariot with two wheels, with groups of three to the right and four to the left; and a final seven divided as a pair, then four, then one. The ten paces' distance over which the bands of light spread provide the intriguing mathematical relationship of 10/7, which is made more complicated still by the further division of these bands into the pattern 3/1/3 by the griffin's two wings. The slow progress of the procession as a whole is animated by the controlled dancing of the lady Virtues, of whom the three alternate both their leader and their pace. To the music in this canto—Matilda's love-filled song, the "sweet melody" that becomes audible as *Hosanna,* the singing of the *Benedicta*—a totally different sound, the thunderclap, acts as a final sudden contrast. With these details and effects Dante enriches his version of the apocalypse in *terza rima* and suggests an intricate scheme of meanings for the reader to decode. Not every detail, however, conveys an obvious meaning; some, such as the words of the songs, the colors, the division of the seven lights, the four ladies' purple robes, are perhaps evocative and mystifying rather than strictly allegorical.

All these elements—light and color, music, measured movement, and perfect spatial order—act as ideal, though still earthly, adumbrations of the imagery and themes of the *Paradiso*. Indeed, in this respect, the procession is not merely natural but also supernatural. Dante at times explicitly elevates his description toward the world above: the moving candlesticks that paint the air are a miracle; they shine more brightly than the full moon at midnight; the elders' robes are supernaturally white: the chariot surpasses those of earthly Rome, and even that of the Sun. This raising of the episode toward the marvelous and otherworldly is emphasized by the descriptions of Dante's reactions, which punctuate the earlier part of the narrative: his puzzlement and sense of loss of "ineffable delights," his suspense and joyful expectation, his and Virgil's amazement, his rapt concentration, and his desire to see everything better. At the interpretative level too, it becomes clear that the procession is exceptional and supernatural, for none of its components is "real" in the sense in which this term may generally be applied to Dante's fictional representation of the afterlife, that is, in the context of the souls of the dead and their eternal fate. In the whole procession only Beatrice, who has not yet appeared, is the soul of a real person.

The procession, like the later scenes in Canto XXXII, is presented by Dante as both an objectively real event in the poem and as a revelatory vision. The resulting combination of naturalistic clarity and mysterious unreality has recently led to its being defined as a "phantasmagoria" and even, by association, as "surreal." As regards the former term, Dante is indeed constructing a series of imagined forms, but they must not be seen as illusory phantasms but rather as meaningful things and beings, perhaps even as examples of objective correlatives. As regards the latter, Dante is not attempting to express a heightened experience of reality through images taken from the subconscious or the world of dreams but is, as a poet, consciously exploiting and elaborating on a powerful and challenging written text, a text that describes a divine revelation made to St. John and that, both as experience and as text, came from God himself. At the highest point on earth, the threshold to the heavenly Paradise, Dante witnesses a similar event, or series of events, to be revealed in his own book. What he sees may be defined as surreal in the sense that it belongs to the area between, and is even a fusion of, the natural and the supernatural, the real and the ideal, the earthly and the heavenly. It is a divine design or plan revealed on earth to the living Dante in visible and audible forms. In creating this design for this section of his narrative, Dante the poet found himself working with things difficult both to conceive and to put into verse (42), devising and fashioning into poetry the fiction of a Johannine revelation of heavenly mysteries made to him and to be communicated by him to his readers for them also to ponder and unravel.

Interpretations

As has already been noted, Dante's apocalypse is not, like St. John's, the sight of a static scene in heaven but of a slowly unfolding procession on earth. The most obvious conclusion for the reader to draw is that it represents a historical process evolving in stages through time, and this is the basis for interpreting it as an allegory of sacred history, of God's plan for humanity from after the Fall to the establishment of Christianity. This, the accepted explanation, outlined above, refers exclusively to the past. Without rejecting it, however, the reader may feel tempted to seek alternative concepts and patterns in Dante's design. After all, St. John himself allots two meanings to the seven candelabra, as the seven churches of Asia and as the seven spirits of God (Rev. 1:20; 4:5); and in Dante they may, at least indirectly, allude to the sevenfold process of purification, for the seven Gifts of the Holy Ghost were sometimes linked with the seven Virtues and seven of the Beatitudes as counterforces against and remedies for the Seven Deadly Sins. The ten paces over which the lights spread have been interpreted as the Ten Commandments, and the lights themselves or the seven bands as the Sacraments. This last suggestion, however, introduces an anachronism into the historical scheme, for the sacraments did not precede or accompany the Old Testament but only came into existence through Christ.

St. John's twenty-four elders, who also recall the pattern of David's reorganization of Judaism (I Chron. 24–27), were usually interpreted in Dante's time as Old Testament patriarchs or saints, or twelve patriarchs and the twelve apostles. Thus they represented the fulfillment of the whole history of the Redemption in heaven. To identify them as the books of the Old Testament requires acceptance of St. Jerome's calculations that the Old Law consisted of twenty-two books (five by Moses, eight of prophets, and nine hagiographies), to which some added Ruth and Lamentations. This list, however, raises the most acute questions concerning the authentic biblical canon, from which St. Jerome explicitly excludes the Wisdom of Solomon,

Ecclesiasticus, Judith, Tobias, and Machabees, as well as the Shepherd of Hermas.

Of Dante's earliest readers known to us, the fourteenth-century commentators, both Jacopo della Lana and the poet's son Pietro provide different lists in their attempts to match the canonical books of the Old Testament to the symbol of the twenty-four elders. In any event, the elders cannot stand for real people, the authors of the books, for then Moses would appear five times, Jeremiah twice, and—for St. Jerome and Pietro Alighieri—Solomon three times. Thus they are taken to be personifications of the actual books. This, then, requires that the four winged animals, although traditionally symbols of the Evangelists, that is, the authors, must here also stand for the books. In curious contrast, however, the central animal, the griffin, is virtually always identified as Christ, neither a book nor an abstract personification but the supremely real person of God made man. Its golden aquiline parts, with their immensely tall wings, are taken to allude to Christ's precious and sublime divinity, its white and red parts to his flesh-and-blood humanity, or his purity and charity. This interpretation rests mainly on a later image (*Purg.* XXXI, 81), and it is not entirely clear in Canto XXIX exactly how the griffin is supposed to "represent" Christ, whether Dante is supposed to be seeing Christ in person disguised or solely as some symbolic expression. In any case, he pays no particular attention to the griffin here, and in the procession it is not the draught animal but the *triumphatrix* herself, Beatrice, who will stand in for Christ.

This last point raises a further ambiguity. If Beatrice, who is yet to come, is the representative of Christ, then the chariot cannot here symbolize the Church, which did not exist before the coming of Christ. In fact, one of the early commentators, Francesco da Buti, spotted the historical inconsistency in interpreting the chariot, from the first moment of its appearance, as the Church. For him it is the Synagogue, which was changed into the Church, that is, the Jewish religion that preceded and was fulfilled in the Church, and the thunderclap marks the moment of this transformation. Although this does not remove the anachronism of a Church preexisting and prepared for Christ, Buti's more dynamic and therefore more logical approach to analyzing an evolving historical process does suggest an interesting possibility: that in Canto XXIX the chariot stands for something that is not yet the Church but the potential Church. Thus it could stand not just for the Jewish Synagogue but for the human race as a whole at that moment in history when the divine and the human came together in God's plan and Christ, both God and man, was born.

It becomes equivalent to the metaphor of a ship that Dante had used elsewhere as an image of human society perfected at the time of the Emperor Augustus, and indeed the chariot is later compared to or described as a ship (*Convivio* IV. v. 8; *Purg.* XXX, 58–61; XXXII, 116–117, 129). In this context, though purely as an optional extra, one might consider a theory mentioned by Benvenuto da Imola, that the chariot's two wheels represent the Jews and the Gentiles. Thus it would come to express in even closer detail Dante's known beliefs concerning pre-Christian history when, to redeem the human race from Adam's sin, God prepared the world for the coming of his Son not only through the Jews in Palestine but also through the Romans in Italy (*Convivio* IV. v. 9). Borne along its true course upon the civilizations of Jerusalem and Rome, superior to the manmade chariots of pagan earthly Rome, and impossible to lead astray as was the Sun's, this chariot is the world community at the culmination of God's plan for the Redemption, by which it was to become, ideally, the universal Christian Church.

By the chariot's right wheel, which may thus be associated with the Jewish religion, dance the three Theological Virtues for which it prepared—white Faith, green Hope, and red Charity. The three colors are also those of the garlands and of Beatrice's veil, mantle, and robe in the next canto. As elsewhere in Dante (*Purg.* I, 37–39; VII, 34–36), the four Cardinal Virtues by the other wheel may be related to pagan civilization before Christ's coming; their leader, Prudence, has three eyes for the consideration of the past, the present, and the future.

The remainder of the procession consists of more "book-people," though in contrast with the earlier twenty-four these seem to have taken on rather closer connections with their authors: there is a doctor, like St. Luke, and a sword bearer, who recalls St. Paul; the seven Catholic Epistles are grouped as four because they had four authors: the old sleepwalker evokes St. John experiencing the apocalyptic visions that he wrote down in his old age. Again they cannot be the actual authors, for then, taken with the four animals, St. Luke would appear twice and St. John three times. Surprisingly perhaps, the fourteenth-century commentators offer a wide variety of identifications here, and only one of these scholars, Buti, gives the list that is accepted today.

The Divine Design

Other interpretations of the details of Dante's procession have been suggested through the ages: the lights as seven parts of the Church, as the sacraments, as the seven orders of the clergy; the two wheels as the two Testaments (although this would duplicate the symbolism of the book creatures), as the Active and Contemplative Life, as the Franciscan and Dominican orders (see *Par.* XII, 106–111); and so on. There is a way in which some of these alternatives may, if one wishes, be reintegrated into a multiple or parallel reading of Dante's scheme. It is, after all, rather strange that Dante should be so astonished to see enacted before him a past historical process about which every Christian already knew. It must therefore be remembered that he presents himself as a living man who witnesses this revelation in the year 1300; when Matilda tells him to pay full attention to it (15, 61–63), this means it is important. The ideal divine design that is being revealed is also a message to the present, to the world of Dante's readers.

Thus one can construct a parallel reading in which the seven Gifts, and perhaps now the sacraments too, along with the Scriptures, the divine and human griffin, and the Virtues, usher in the ideal world community of the present, that is, the Church reformed and perfected, in which will appear she who in 1300 is the personal representative of Christ for Dante: Beatrice. Moreover, this ideal, not realized in the corrupt world and corrupted Church of that centenary year, stands both as an inspiration for reform in the immediate future and as the promise of its certain realization one day: Christ will come again to establish his perfect rule during the millennium on earth and then, after the final Judgment, will take his Church to triumph eternally with him in heaven. Dante's procession, constructed as it is on St. John's vision of the end of the world, is a triumph; its troops are not merely those of the Church Militant on earth but of the "celestial kingdom" (*Purg.* XXXII, 22). The most obvious level on which to interpret Dante's apocalypse is, in fact, the millenarian and eschatological, when God's plan will be completed and the Church fulfilled forever as the Church Triumphant. Beatrice, who is to come from heaven to judge Dante, represents Christ not only at his First but also at his Second Coming.

These levels of reference are not alternatives but ultimately one and the same. While preserving some of the ambiguities and choices regarding details, they provide a simultaneous and interlocking reading in a scheme of threefold allegory that broadly reflects the technique of biblical interpretation proposed in the Epistle to Cangrande. Here, because of an event described in the Old Testament (humankind's loss of the Garden of Eden), God prepared the world for Christ's coming, thus revealing his program for the salvation of living Christians and promising eternal life for the Church of the saved. So, in a single scheme of difficult concepts and challenging images, through his own prophetic vision of these strange surreal or super-real processioners, Dante conceived and put into verse God's entire plan for the history of the descendants of Adam and Eve: as it was revealed once at a perfect moment in the past; as a model for the contemporary Christian world; and as it will be, once more perfected, in the future and forever.

BIBLIOGRAPHICAL NOTES

The main lines of interpretation of this canto, with many alternative suggestions concerning details, were laid down by the early commentators: Jacopo della Lana (ed. L. Scarabelli, Bologna, 1866, vol. 2, 344–358); the Ottimo (Pisa, 1828, vol. 2, 510–523); Pietro di Dante (ed. V. Nannucci, Florence, 1845, 502–509); Benvenuto da Imola (Florence, 1887, vol. 4, 182–203); Francesco da Buti (ed. C. Giannini, Pisa, 1860, vol. 2, 697–723); the Anonimo (ed. P. Fanfani, Bologna, 1868, vol. 2, 468–482); see also the *Chiose sopra Dante* (Florence, 1846, 479– 489) and the commentaries of Landino (Florence, 1481) and Vellutello (Venice, 1544). St. Jerome's listing of the books of the Old Testament is in his Prologue to the Book of Kings (the *"Prologus galeatus"*) (*Patrologia latina*, vol. XXVIII, columns 593–604). The description of the procession in Modena on May 21, 1583 is in A.

D'Ancona, *Origini del teatro italiano* (2d ed., Turin, 1891, vol. 1, 361–363). Dante's apocalyptic imagery and technique in *Purgatorio* XXIX and XXXII–XXXIII have been investigated by, among others: G. A. Scartazzini, "Dante's Vision im irdischen Paradiese und die biblische Apokalyptic," *Jahrbuch der deutschen Dante-Gesellschaft* 2 (1869): 99–150; G. Ghirardini, "Della visione di Dante nel Paradiso terrestre," *Il Propugnatore* 10 (1877): pt. 2, 193–227, and 11 (1878): pt. 1, 27–76; E. Moore, "The Apocalyptic Vision," in *Studies in Dante: Third Series* (Oxford, 1903), 178–220; G. Salvadori, *La mirabile visione nel paradiso terrestre di Dante* (Turin, 1915); L. Tondelli, "La grande visione allegorica che chiude il *Purgatorio*," in *Il libro delle figure dell'abate Giochino da Fiore*, 2d ed. (Turin, 1953), 1: 275–304; and P. Dronke, "The Phantasmagoria in the Earthly Paradise," in *Dante and Medieval Latin Traditions* (Cambridge, 1986), 55–81.

Readings of Canto XXIX itself include: D. Fransconi, "Alcune riflessioni sull'allegoria del Canto XXIX del *Purgatorio*," in *Studi vari sulla "Divina Commedia"* (Florence, 1887), 241–263; L. Rocca (Lectura Dantis, Florence, 1904) and "La processione simbolica del canto XXIX del *Purgatorio*," in *Dai tempi antichi ai tempi moderni* (Milan, 1904), 143–151; W. W. Vernon in *Readings on the "Purgatorio" of Dante*, 3d ed. (London, 1907), 2:465–500; L. Pietrobono (Lectura Dantis, Florence, 1910); N. Zingarelli, "La processione nell'Eden dantesco," in *Miscellanea di studi in onore di Attilio Hortis* (Trieste, 1910), 363–369; G. Mazzoni, "Sulla processione mistica nel Paradiso terrestre di Dante," in *Mélanges . . . offerts à Henri Hauvette* (Paris, 1934), 89–90, and in *Almae luces malae cruces* (Bologna, 1941), 285–287; U. Bosco in *Tre letture dantesche* (Rome, 1942), 51–75, and a revised version (Nuova Lectura Dantis, Rome, 1951), and in G. Getto, ed., *Letture dantesche: Purgatorio* (Florence, 1958), 585–602, and in *Dante vicino* (Caltanissetta-Rome, 1966), 274–296; G. Mariani (*Lectura Dantis Siciliana*, Trapani, 1956) and in *La vita sospesa* (Naples, 1978, 33–49); C. S. Singleton, "The Pattern at the Center," in *Dante Studies I: "Commedia": Elements of Structure* (Cambridge, MA, 1957), 45–60; G. di Pino, "Presagi di linguaggio paradisiaco nei canti XXVIII e XXIX del *Purgatorio*," *Humanitas* 13 (1958): 521–532, and in *Studi di lingua poetica* (Florence, 1961), 30–47; C. Hardie, "Beatrice's Chariot in Dante's Earthly Paradise," *Deutsches Dante-Jahrbuch* 39 (1961): 137–172, and "The Symbol of the Gryphon in *Purgatorio* XXIX, 108 and following Cantos," in *Centenary Essays on Dante* (Oxford, 1965), 103–131; C. Filosa (*Lectura Dantis Romana*, Turin, 1963); A. Ciotti, "Processione mistica," in the *Enciclopedia dantesca*, 6 vols. (Rome, 1970–1978); E. N. Girardi in *Lectura Dantis Scaligera: Purgatorio* (Florence, 1971), 1067–1101, and in *Studi su Dante* (Brescia, 1980), 89–113; P. Brezzi in *Nuove letture dantesche*, vol. 5 (Florence, 1972), 149–165; D. Bertocchi, "Segni e simboli in *Purgatorio* XXIX," in *Psicoanalisi e strutturalismo di fronte a Dante* (Florence, 1972), 2:251–267; P. Dronke, "The Procession in Dante's *Purgatorio*," *Deutsches Dante-Jahrbuch* 53–54 (1978–1979): 18–45, and in K. Foster and P. Boyde, eds., *Cambridge Readings in Dante's "Comedy"* (Cambridge, 1981), 114–137; A. Vallone, "La processione del XXIX *Purgatorio* e il medievalismo di Dante," *Deutsches Dante-Jahrbuch* 55–56 (1980–1981): 50–68, and in S. Zennara, ed., *Purgatorio: Letture degli anni 1976–79* (Rome, 1981), 675–694; E. Travi, "Il Paradiso in terra della Chiesa militante," *L'Alighieri* 22, no. 2 (1981): 31–45. A Eucharistic interpretation of the procession was proposed by L. Andrews Fisher, *The Mystic Vision in the Grail Legend and in the "Divine Comedy"* (New York, 1917), 100–116, by H. Flanders Dunbar, *Symbolism in Medieval Thought and its Consummation in the "Divine Comedy"* (New Haven, 1929), 314–321, and by D. L. Sayers, *Purgatory* (Penguin, 1955), 302–306.

Among recent critics, both Colin Hardie and Peter Dronke put forward interpretations of the griffin and the chariot that are radically different from the traditional one and are more "internal" or psychological; the former sets them within the context of Dante's own double nature and his poetry for Beatrice, and the latter sees them as images of aspects of Dante's soul. The allegorical scheme described in the Epistle to Cangrande (once no. X, now no. XIII of Dante's Epistles) interprets a literal event from the Old Testament (the Exodus) at three levels: with reference to the Redemption by Christ; as consequently an image of moral conversion for Christians in life; and finally as the passage of the saved soul after death to eternal life.

CANTO XXX

At the Summit of Purgatory

RACHEL JACOFF

Canto XXX is commonly regarded as the structural and emotional center of the *Comedy*, its kernel or nucleus. Preceded by sixty-three and followed by thirty-six cantos, it even has a symbolic centrality in the poem's trinitarian numerology. Here Dante is at last reunited with Beatrice after his "ten-year thirst" (*Purg.* XXXII, 2–3) in a sequence that also unites the *Comedy* with the *Vita Nuova*, Dante's present with his poetic past. His guide up till this moment, Virgil, disappears from the poem in between the very lines in which Beatrice is presented. The style of the canto is deliberately elevated—rich in Latinisms, complex syntactical constructions, extended similes, citations, and allusions. At the same time, it contains some of the rawest emotion we see in the poem, as a tearful Dante comes face-to-face with his past, and with the regret and shame that such a confrontation forces on him. This intensely personal episode constitutes the first half of Beatrice's two-part indictment of Dante; in Canto XXXI she will complete the indictment by telling Dante how he ought to have behaved after her death. In between her two long speeches, Dante himself will confess his own failure in a single *terzina* (XXXI, 34–36). Cantos XXX and XXXI deal, then, primarily with Dante's own salvation history, while Cantos XXIX, XXXII, and XXXIII frame such concerns within the universal and public dimensions of salvation. The highly stylized allegorical procession, which leads up to Canto XXX, represents a book within a book: Scripture portrayed as a processional of its component texts. The complex allegorical dumb show, which concludes the sequence, offers a capsule history of the Church. In between comes Dante's own moment of truth in which his identities as both emblematic Everyman and as unique historical and poetic personage are powerfully fused.

Dante's Signature

This particular fusion is part of the larger pattern of the canto—the extraordinary interlacing of polarities operative throughout the *Comedy* as a whole. The heightened syncretism of the canto forces us to place it in relation to a series of other texts, including other parts of the *Comedy;* Dante recapitulates and rewrites his own earlier work as well as Scripture and, among others, that of Virgil, Boethius, and Ovid. Paradoxically, this extreme dependence on the language of others is coordinate with Dante's overt assumption of authorial particularity. This is, after all, Dante's signature canto, the only place in the whole poem where he is named.

Names, in fact, are of the essence in Canto xxx. Virgil's name is given five times in the space of ten lines, including its threefold repetition in the moment of Dante's awareness of his disappearance. Beatrice gives her own name with a threefold repetition of the adverb *ben* in the central line of the whole canto: "Guardaci ben! Ben son, ben son Beatrice" ("Look here! For I am Beatrice, I am!" 73). And her first word in this powerful recognition scene is "Dante" (55). Dante explains the presence of his name in an aside, "che di necessità qui si registra" ("Which, of necessity, I transcribe here" 63) that has reminded most commentators of the passage at the opening of the *Convivio* where he adduces the rhetoricians' authority for saying that one must not name oneself except out of necessity. The two reasons he describes are either to excuse oneself from false accusation (as Boethius had done in the *Consolation of Philosophy*) or to give witness (as Augustine did in the *Confessions*). But commentators have not noticed that the circumstances here, at least in one respect, are an inversion of those allowable in the *Convivio*. For Dante's name is given precisely at the moment of accusation rather than in the service of self-exculpation. To fulfill the second condition (bearing witness), Dante, in fact, must assume the burden of guilt as the condition of his actual historical specificity.

The placing of Dante's name between that of Virgil and Beatrice implies the second function of its occurrence. Since Dante is named exactly when his poetic father is superseded, the movement from Virgil to Beatrice coincides with Dante's own coming of age poetically. Throughout these final cantos of the *Purgatorio,* Dante prepares to announce the daring endeavor of the *Paradiso,* where he sets sail, guided by Beatrice, on waters that have never been sailed before. By making his name her first word, Beatrice, calls Dante into existence at this crucial juncture, just as her very being had called him into the possibility of salvation, both in the *Vita Nuova* and in *Inferno* ii, texts alluded to specifically in this canto.

Beatrice Reappears

The linkages between the *Vita Nuova* and the *Comedy* are nowhere more visible than in this canto, where even the title of the earlier work makes its way into the text (115); as Umberto Bosco and Giovanni Reggio remark, Canto XXX is "the *explicit* of the *Vita Nuova*," its completion and reinscription in Dante's culminating work. Charles Singleton argued powerfully for the necessity of "holding the *Vita Nuova* and the *Comedy* together and reading the story which they together tell." Singleton's argument stresses the analogical representation of Beatrice as Christ in both works, paying close attention to the specific liturgical language associated with her death in the first work and with her reappearance in this one:

> In the *Vita Nuova,* at the center of the *Vita Nuova,* Beatrice is seen to depart this life, uplifted in the company of a host of angels, in a cloud, and the cry that accompanies her is Hosanna. At the center of the *Divine Comedy,* Beatrice comes, Beatrice returns, in the company of a host of angels, in a cloud of glory, and in a company whose first cry is again *Hosanna. (Dante Studies* 1, 57)

Whereas Beatrice's death and ascension in the *Vita Nuova* resemble Christ's, in Canto XXX it is her appearance, her second coming, that resembles both Christ's advent and his second coming as judge. All the signs (the liturgical language, the simile of the rising sun, Beatrice's role as judge), as Singleton insisted, point to the analogy. Traditional readings assumed that Beatrice is an allegorical personification of Scripture, Revelation, or Theology; certain aspects of the presentation of Beatrice (such as the color symbolism that connects her with the three theological virtues) seem to point to such allegoresis. But Singleton's emphasis on the Christological significance of the details associated with her appearance accounts more adequately for the nature of the figuration in this scene. Even in Singleton's reading, however, no one meaning exhausts the complexity of that figuration; as a *figura Christi,* Beatrice is also a figure of Wisdom and of Sanctifying Grace. Furthermore, references to the narrative of the *Vita Nuova* also assure a continuity with Dante's earliest experiences of Beatrice's human nature, her real presence as it is posited in that book. His trembling before her reminds us of comparable visceral reactions to her presence in the *Vita Nuova* (II, 4; XI, 3; XIV, 4; XXIV, 1), while Beatrice herself speaks of her role in his early life in terms familiar from the earlier work. The lines in which Dante anticipates her appearance are rich with a sense of then and now, of what he felt for her as a young boy and a young man, and what returns to him now, years later, with full power in her presence.

Reversing Narcissus

While Dante's reactions to the wonder of that presence are congruent with his responses in the *Vita Nuova*, this canto also recalls episodes from the earlier work in order to dramatize differences from it. For example, Dante's inability to weep at Beatrice's first reproach resembles his situation after her death. In the *Vita Nuova*, Dante needs the compassion of another woman, the *donna gentile*, to unlock his self-pity: "when unhappy people see the compassion of others towards them, they are more speedily moved to weep, as though having pity for themselves" (XXXV). The implicit narcissism of this situation gets him into trouble there, leading him to a temporary betrayal of Beatrice in his fascination with the *donna pietosa*. Here, the compassion of the angels functions comparably to allow Dante to dissolve into tears and sighs, but Dante is not allowed to dilate on such emotion and turn it into a form of self-regard; this time he is forced to take a hard look at his flaws. As Kevin Brownlee and R. A. Shoaf have both shown, Dante becomes an anti-Narcissus in this canto (76–78). His glance into the reflecting surface of the river that separates him from Beatrice (a river described as a *fonte* ["clear stream"] to underscore the allusion to Narcissus) presents him with an image of himself, but one that he turns away from in shame: "tanta vergogna mi gravò la fronte" ("such shame weighed on my brow," 78). The threat of compassion as a form of complicity was dramatized earlier in Dante's responses to other sinners: in his encounter with Francesca, Dante's compassion mimes her passion, leading him to "fall" in imitation of her fall. In Canto XXX, however, Dante's potentially narcissistic gesture gives way to a pained self-awareness that opens the way for change. While Ovid's Narcissus melts away into nonexistence, Dante, reversing the type, melts into tears of contrition that are the first stage in his return to life. His tears and sighs constitute, as Phillip Berk says, an "inner baptism" of water and spirit, a necessary prelude to his subsequent immersion in Lethe:

> My lowered eyes caught sight of the clear stream,
> but when I saw myself reflected there,
> such shame weighed on my brow, my eyes drew back
>   and toward the grass; just as a mother seems
> harsh to her child, so did she seem to me—
> how bitter is the savor of stern pity!
>
> (76–81)

In this lachrymose canto, we are also reminded, by Beatrice's pointed response to Dante's tears at Virgil's disappearance, of Virgil's brusque criticism of Dante's tears at the sight of the distorted human forms of the diviners in *Inferno* XX. The threefold repetition of *piangere*, which rhetorically balances the threefold repetition of Virgil's name in the preceding lines, focuses the question of just what is worth crying over. Dante must indeed weep, as the canto's concluding lines insist, but he must weep for his sins and he must do so ultimately to get beyond even that much self-preoccupation. Beatrice's urging of Dante not to weep for Virgil is reminiscent of Lady Philosophy's response to Boethius's fruitless tears in the opening scene of the *Consolation of Philosophy* (I, ii). And Dante's futile weeping for Virgil rather than for his own sins has rightly reminded several critics of Augustine's retrospective critique of his own weeping for Dido rather than for himself: "What can be more pitiful than an unhappy wretch unaware of his own sorry state, bewailing the fate of Dido, who died for love of Aeneas, yet shedding no tears for himself as he dies for want of loving You?" (*Confessions*, I, 13). The tears that are valorized in Canto XXX are not those shed by Dante for Virgil, which lead nowhere, but rather those he sheds for his sins and those Beatrice sheds for him, tears that were instrumental in his rescue. At the canto's conclusion, Beatrice links the necessity of his tears of remorse to those she shed for him earlier, tears we first heard of in *Inferno* II and that are recalled twice (XXVII, 136–138 and XXX, 139–141) at the top of the mountain of Purgatory.

> For this I visited the gateway of
> the dead; to him who guided him above
> my prayers were offered even as I wept.
>   The deep design of God would have been broken
> if Lethe had been crossed and he had drunk
> such waters but had not discharged the debt
>   of penitence that's paid when tears are shed.
>
> (139–145)

The Double Plot

The double plot of Virgil's disappearance and Beatrice's appearance is accomplished through a tour de force of intertextuality. Dante opens this allusive sequence on a note of expectation sounded by one of the Old Testament elders, presumably Solomon, who sings the line from Canticles (4.8) "Veni, sponsa da Libano," a line whose allegorical implications were already established by medieval exegetical traditions, which read the bride as the Church or, as seems more fitting here, as Wisdom (cf. *Convivio* II, 14). The preparation of Beatrice's entrance into the poem reads almost like a stage direction or liturgical cue, for Dante specifies that the line from Canticles is sung three times (as it is in the original), and is then responded to antiphonally. Next the angels sing *Benedictus qui venis,* the opening words of the line from Psalm 117, which was sung at Christ's entry into Jerusalem (Mark 11) and which is sung in the liturgy immediately before the consecration of the host. "Blessed is he who comes in the name of the Lord" thus serves three textual functions, apart from Dante's use of it: in the Psalms, where it fittingly is part of a festal procession; in the Gospel, where it precedes Christ's entry; and in liturgy, where it precedes his presence in the Eucharist. Dante adapts the line by shifting the verb from third person to second, but he retains the masculine adjective *benedictus;* while this led earlier commentators to think that the angels could not be addressing Beatrice, Singleton argued that it was precisely the gender incongruity that underscored the Christology of Dante's presentation of Beatrice. (The ambiguity of reference in this line resembles that of the greeting in the previous canto (55–57), which some commentators have read as heralding Mary and others as Beatrice).

Dante rhymes the Latin of the Vulgate with the Latin of Virgil's *Aeneid,* as the angels sing "Date, oh, manibus lilia plenis" (21), strewing flowers, which form a nimbus around Beatrice. The shock effect of this astonishing pairing of Virgil and Scripture is usually mitigated by reference to Dante's syncretisim (Sapegno) or by describing the quotation of Virgil as homage (Bosco-Reggio). Andreoli (1856) comments with delightful innocence, "E veramente non si può che saper grado a questi Angeli di Dio, di prendere il buono e il bello ovunque si trovi" ("And truly one must hand it to these angels of God for taking the good and the beautiful wherever it can be found"). All the traditional responses to this citation ignore its original context, treating the line as if it is merely a stylistic token; it is, however, that context which determines the function of the citation. The line is drawn from the climax of Anchises' catalog of future Roman heroes at the close of Book VI of the *Aeneid.* Anchises concludes with the presentation of Marcellus, Augustus's nephew, who ought to have been the greatest hero, were it not for his early and tragic death; he is described as "a youth of wondrous beauty and brilliant in arms" whose "noble presence" is surrounded by black night. This youth, the great "hope of his forefathers," a figure of the highest virtues, is nonetheless a figure of ultimate pathos. In the face of that ineluctable reality, Anchises can only make a vain gesture of mourning, "manibus date lilia plenis":

> With full hands, give me lilies; let me scatter
> these purple flowers, with these gifts at least,
> be generous to my descendant's spirit,
> complete this service, although it be useless.
> (*Aen.* VI, 883–886)

The contrast between the context of the line in the *Aeneid* and that in Canto XXX could hardly be greater, and that contrast becomes an invitation to meditate on the differences between the two texts and the two worldviews that subtend them. While Virgil mourns the defeat of hope and faith (both words are part of the description of Marcellus) by the stark finality of death, Dante transforms Anchises' gesture into a joyous greeting, a sign of the triumph of hope and faith (and love) over death. Both Marcellus and Beatrice died before their promise was fulfilled, but Beatrice's promise continues on after death. She speaks of her death not as an end, but as a threshold, a change of life ("As soon as I, upon the threshold of / my second age, had changed my life" 124–125). The insistence on the Resurrection in the lines immediately preceding the Virgilian citation (13–15) is absolutely strategic, for it is the hope and, for Dante, the fact of the Resurrection that authorizes the transfiguration of the Virgilian lilies of mourning into the lilies of welcome. There is a perfect gloss on the key word *inani* (the word describing the uselessness of Anchises' gesture) in a comparable context in I Corinthians 15:12–14, where St. Paul uses the same word repeatedly to describe what the scenario would be if Christ had not risen from the dead: "If Christ be not risen, then is our preaching vain, and your faith is also vain."

Virgil's Loss

The second Virgilian allusion in this sequence comes as Dante experiences the powerful effect of Beatrice's presence; he turns to Virgil to announce this effect in a translation of the line with which Dido tells her sister Anna that she "feels the marks of the ancient flame" (*Aen.* IV, 23). In that very scene, Dido defines her new love for Aeneas as a betrayal of her old love, Sichaeus, her dead husband; and both Virgil (IV, 551) and Dante think of her as one who "betrayed the ashes of Sychaeus" (*Inf.* V, 62). Dido's experience of the ancient flame becomes literal, since the passion she feels will lead to her suicidal funeral pyre. This passion, which leads to death, is the very opposite of Dante's love for Beatrice, a love that redeems him from spiritual death. Dante's fidelity to Beatrice was interrupted, as this canto reminds us, but ultimately it becomes the defining loyalty of his life; Dante feels the marks of the *antica fiamma* for his *antico amor* so that the continuity of his love for Beatrice takes precedence over any intervening apostasies of affection.

As Dante prepares to speak to Virgil in words that translate Virgil's own text, he turns to Virgil exactly as he had just done in Canto XXIX (55–57), where the two exchanged their last glance, only to discover that Virgil is already gone. This is one of the most brilliant moments in the poem: rather than stage an elaborate farewell to his *dolcissimo patre,* Dante makes the reader experience the shock of Virgil's loss even as he himself does. Nor do the Virgilian resonances of the scene end with Virgil's actual disappearance; Virgil is kept before us even as his presence is occluded. Dante's lament at Virgil's loss is itself another Virgilian recall, an allusion to the fourth book of the *Georgics,* as Bernadino Daniello, Edward Moore, and several recent critics have shown. In the fourth *Georgic,* Orpheus nearly conquers death by the power of his song, but his backward glance loses Eurydice irrevocably. He remains inconsolable and is torn to pieces by the Thracian women in revenge for his disinterest in them. Even after death, his severed head rolling down the Hebrus River continues to mourn for Eurydice. Though more grotesque than Anchises' speech and strewing of flowers, this is an equally vain performance. The threefold repetition of Eurydice's name by the severed head of Orpheus is a futile, if pathetic, reiteration of loss:

> the bare voice and death-cold tongue,
> with fleeting breath, called Eurydice—ah, hapless
> Eurydice! "Eurydice" the banks re-echoed,
> all adown the stream.
>
> (*Georgic*, IV, 525–527)

As with the preceding Virgilian echoes, a comparison with the original context makes us aware of the gap between the two texts. While Virgil's text reveals the inability of poetry to conquer death and loss, Dante is, in this scene, about to be reunited with his own Eurydice. Like Orpheus, he has braved the passage to the Other World in search of his love, but, unlike Orpheus, he is allowed, indeed encouraged, to look at his beloved. The "bare voice and death-cold tongue" of Orpheus must be set against the *revestita voce* ("new-clothed voices," 15), the reclad voices of the blessed in whose context Dante will ultimately rejoin his beloved. But this allusion can point in a contrary direction at the same time, suggesting similarity as well as difference. For it is Virgil who becomes a figure like Eurydice, and the pathos of her loss adheres to him; he, too, was almost out of the world of shades, but he, too, must return to it. The adjective *dolcissimo,* which Dante attributes to Virgil, reminds us that in his first lament for his wife Orpheus addressed her as *dulcis coniunx* (405). Insofar as Dante mourns Virgil with the repetition of his name, he becomes like Orpheus in the fourth *Georgic,* a figure of futility.

This allusion is further complicated by the fact that it also points to another text in which the same moment of the fourth *Georgic* is recalled. At the end of the narrative conclusion of Statius's *Thebaid,* the young male virgin warrior Parthenopaeus is mourned by both sides in the up to now relentless fratricidal conflict that is the subject of the poem. This Arcadian figure represents the undifferentiated prehistory of Roman civil history, which Statius, like Virgil himself, reads as essentially a history of unending civil war. The threefold repetition of *Arcada* (the Arcadian) as the poem's closing act of communal mourning transforms Orpheus's private lament for his beloved into a public dirge for the one figure in Statius's poem that both sides are able to mourn. Dante's familiarity with the end of the *Thebaid* is well-known; it is likely that he would have thought of the way Statius adapted Orpheus's lament as he was doing so himself. Statius is, of course, present in Canto XXX as a character. Furthermore, the whole sequence, which runs from line 44 to 48, brings to mind another "Statian" episode. The rhyme scheme here (*mamma-dramma-fiamma*) picks up the rhyme scheme of Canto XXI, 95–99, where Dante has Statius articulate the *Comedy*'s most explicit tribute to the *Aeneid:*

> I speak of the *Aeneid;* when I wrote
> verse, it was mother to me, it was nurse;
> my work, without it, would not weigh an ounce.

Dante brings this tribute into the farewell to Virgil by incorporating its rhyme scheme. And one might say that the passage also serves as a farewell to Statius; even though Statius remains with Dante until the end of the *Purgatorio,* there are no further narrative allusions to the *Thebaid* in the *Comedy.* Statius's "poetic" presence disappears alongside Virgil himself.

The Admiral Simile

The progress from citation, to translation, to allusion that we have been tracing constitutes, as John Freccero was the first to note, a fade-out or effacement of Virgil's voice as he is leaving the text as character. Although these three instances of Virgilian allusion are the key ones, there are other instances of Virgilian diction throughout this scene. For example, Dante's periphrasis for Eden ("even all our ancient mother lost," 52) recalls an important scene in *Aeneid* III where Apollo's oracle urges Aeneas to "seek out your ancient mother" (*antiquam exquirite matre* [III, 96]). In the *Aeneid,* this call to return to an Edenic origin is a (misinterpreted) mandate to seek out Italy, from whence the founder of Troy had originally come. But Dante is *actually* in Eden, which is the origin of the *whole* human race. Furthermore, the superlative *dolcissimo patre,* which forms part of Dante's lament for Virgil, is, as Teodolinda Barolini points out, the only time the superlative is used for him; Michael Putnam connects the unique instance of the superlative with Aeneas's comparable tribute to Anchises *(optime patre)* at the moment of the latter's death in his suggestive reading of Virgil as an Anchises figure. The Latinizing *matre* and *patre,* used only one other time in the *Comedy (Inferno* XIX), rhyme with *atre,* a word used strategically, as we have seen in Anchises' introductory description of Marcellus.

And it is likely that the extended simile in which Beatrice is compared to an admiral is also partially Virgilian in provenance. For many modern readers the comparison of Beatrice to an *ammiraglio* is bizarre, although it was much admired by the early commentators and is praised by several modern critics, in particular, Edoardo Sanguineti. The simile describes Beatrice as "quasi ammiraglio che in poppa e in prora / viene a veder la gente che ministra / per li altri legni, e a ven far l'incora" ("Just like an admiral who goes to stern / and prow to see the officers who guide / the other ships, encouraging their tasks" [58–60]). The word *poppa* recalls the *Aeneid,* where its Latin form is used in a crucial phrase: "stans celsa in puppi" ("standing on the lofty stern"). It is used once for each of the poem's key male figures at the moment when he takes control of his destiny: Anchises (III, 527), Aeneas (X, 261), and Augustus (VIII, 680). By making Beatrice his admiral, Dante reveals his very un-Virgilian sense of the proper and positive possibilities of female guidance, suggesting an implicit critique of the Aeneid's patriarchal ethos exactly as Virgil is replaced by Beatrice.

The admiral simile is part of a whole pattern of gender reversals that are crucial in this canto. First we have the masculine adjective *benedictus* used for Beatrice. Then we have a sequence of Virgilian allusions, each of which reverses the original gender attribution: a line describing Marcellus is used for Beatrice, Dido's feelings are articulated by Dante, Eurydice's loss is a figure of Virgil's disappearance. Dante turns to Virgil as a child turns to a mother ("quasi fantolin che corre alla mamma") and finds Virgil gone (43–49). His long anticipated beloved arrives and is like an admiral. The gender reversals are dizzying and kaleidoscopic; they unsettle the reader, suggesting both the importance of conventional gender attributions—and their ultimate irrelevance.

A Veiling and a Revelation

Another way in which Dante unsettles the reader is by simultaneously arousing and defeating our expectations. We have been led all along to imagine the reunion with Beatrice as joyous. Virgil leads Dante on with its promise (*Purg.* VI, 47–48, and XXVII, 136), envisioning a happy and smiling Beatrice. As Christopher Ryan has shown, this is a sign of Virgil's limited understanding of what is at stake in Dante's journey. Nonetheless, in dramatic terms, it takes the reader by surprise as well as Dante. Beatrice's severity in the canto is underscored by the way she talks about Dante rather than to him. Her longest speech (103–145) credits Dante with remarkable propensities, gifts of nature and of grace, but accuses him of betraying such gifts in his turning from her to another. The Boethian critique of false images of good and the indeterminate nature of Dante's betrayal—are we to think that he loved another woman or that he followed an incorrect path intellectually, substituting philosophy for theology?—will be reiterated and expanded in Canto XXXI.

Even though Beatrice's arrival at the top of the mountain of Purgatory is a climactic event, the climax also contains a series of deferrals. As the *Vita Nuova* should have taught us to expect, Beatrice's presence is simultaneously a veiling and a revelation. Dante defers until the end of the following canto the unveiling of Beatrice's face; here she appears veiled by the cloud of flowers strewn by the angels and by an actual veil. Dante reacts to her presence just as he had in the *Vita Nuova*, but that presence, at least throughout this canto, maintains the doubleness of disclosure and a hiddenness with which it was associated in the earlier work. Beatrice's veiling becomes a figure of Dante's own clouded vision: she is unveiled only after Dante's immersion in Lethe, after he is no longer clouded by sin. These terms are implicit in the language of Canto XXX's opening lines, where Dante describes the sinless perfection of the Empyrean by invoking the "first heaven's Seven Stars . . . / . . . that are / not veiled except when sin beclouds our vision" (1–3). And it is precisely in the "first heaven," that "heaven of pure light, / light filled with love," that Dante will take leave of Beatrice in the parallel canto, *Paradiso* XXX (38–39). The anguish he experiences in *Purgatorio* XXX, the memory of his earlier betrayal of Beatrice, her just severity—all will be forgotten and subsumed by his summation of her significance in his life, and in his poetry:

> From that first day when, in this life, I saw
> her face, until I had this vision, no
> thing ever cut the sequence of my song,
> but now I must desist from this pursuit,
> in verses, of her loveliness, just as
> each artist who has reached his limit must.

(Par. XXX, 28–33)

BIBLIOGRAPHY

Auerbach, Erich. "Figurative Texts Illustrating Certain Passages of Dante's *Commedia*." *Speculum* 21 (1946): 474–89.

Ball, Robert. "Theological Semantics: Virgil's *Pietas* and Dante's *Pietà*." *Stanford Italian Review* 2 (1981): 59–79.

Barolini, Teodolinda. *Dante's Poets: Textuality and Truth in the "Commedia."* Princeton: Princeton University Press, 1984.

Benvenuti de Rambaldis de Imola. *Comentum super Dantis Aldigherij Comoediam.* Ed. J. P. Lacaita. 5 vols. Florence: Barbera, 1887.

Berk, Philip P. "Shadows on the Mount of Purgatory." *Dante Studies* 97 (1979): 47–63.

Biagi, Guido. *La Divina Commedia nella figurazione artistica e nel secolare commento.* Turin: Unione Tipografico-Editrice Torinese, 1924.

Bosco, Umberto, and Giovanni Reggio, eds. *La Divina Commedia*, vol. 2. Florence: Le Monnier, 1979.

Brownlee, Kevin. "Dante and Narcissus (*Purg.* XXX, 76–99)." *Dante Studies* 96 (1978): 201–206.

Chiarini, Eugenio. "Il Canto XXX del *Purgatorio*." In *Lectura Dantis Scaligera*. Florence: Le Monnier, 1965.

Curtius, Ernst Robert. "Mention of the Author's Name in Medieval Literature." In *European Literature in the Latin Middle Ages*. Trans. Willard R. Trask. New York: Harper and Row, 1963, 515–518.

Freccero, John. "Adam's Stand," *Purg.* XXX, 82–84. *Romance Notes* 2 (spring 1961): 1–4.

———. "Manfred's Wounds and the Poetics of the *Purgatorio*." In *Dante: The Poetics of Conversion*. Ed. Rachel Jacoff. Cambridge, MA: Harvard University Press, 1986, 195–208.

Grandgent, C. H., ed. *La Divina Commedia*. Rev. by C. S. Singleton. Cambridge, MA: Harvard University Press, 1972.

Hollander, Robert. "Dante's Use of the Fiftieth Psalm (A Note on *Purg.* XXX, 84)." In *Studies in Dante*. Ravenna: Longo, 1980, 107–113.

Jacoff, Rachel, and Jeffrey Schnapp. *Virgil in Dante: Studies in the Poetry of Allusion.* Stanford: Stanford University Press, 1991.

Mazzotta, Giuseppe. *Dante, Poet of the Desert*. Princeton: Princeton University Press, 1979.

Moore, Edward. *Studies in Dante, First Series*. 1917. Reprint, New York: Haskell House, 1968.

Putnam, Michael. "Virgil's Inferno," in *Virgil in Dante, op. cit.*, pp. 94–112.

Romagnoli, Sergio. "Il Canto XXX del *Purgatorio.*" *Nuove letture dantesche* 5. Florence: Le Monnier, 1972.

Ryan, Christopher J. "Virgil's Wisdom in the *Divine Comedy.*" *Medievalia et Humanistica* 11 (1982): 1–38.

Sanguineti, Edoardo. "Il Canto xxx del *Purgatorio.*" *Letture dantesche*, vol. 2. Ed. Giovanni Getto. Sansoni: Florence, 1964, 605–623.

Shoaf, R. A. *Dante, Chaucer and the Currency of the Word: Money Images, and Reference in Late Medieval Poetry*. Norman, Oklahoma: Pilgrim Books, 1983.

Singleton, Charles S. *Dante Studies 1. Commedia: Elements of Structure*. Cambridge, MA: Harvard University Press, 1957.

———. *Dante Studies 2. Journey to Beatrice*. Cambridge, MA; Harvard University Press, 1958.

CANTO XXXI
Dante's Repentance

EMILIO PASQUINI

Translated by Charles Ross

However much Canto XXXI forms a solid continuation of the one preceding it, only here does Dante render a full account of himself, even if his confession is directed at Beatrice, who draws it out after she turns directly toward him. It has been preceded by her condemnation of his past behavior that she mediates by addressing the angels around her chariot, as Dante listens from across the stream of Lethe (XXX, 103), and by her ironic, sarcastic comments (XXX, 55–57 and 73–75), with which she nonetheless implicates herself.

The canto is divided into four parts: first (1–63), Beatrice's attack on Dante, to which he responds with sighs and a brief confession (34–36); second (64–90), Dante's faint from remorse once Beatrice invites him to regard her new beauty, during which he recalls his love for her when he was young; third (91–117), Matilda's immersion of Dante in Lethe once he recovers and his dedication to the cardinal virtues; fourth (118–145), Beatrice's unveiling of her face, after the intercession of the theological virtues and the ecstasy of her devoted Dante. Other divisions are possible, however, such as between lines 75 and 76, which divides the continuation of Beatrice's disappointment in Dante from her ritual contemplation of Christ and Dante's repentance. A third section might be said to start at line 146, where Dante sees mirrored in Beatrice the metamorphosis of the griffin, which shines forth from her divine features.

The lineaments of the canto give rise to several symbolic and liturgical elements that the oldest commentators tried to explicate. Nineteenth-century Romantic and aesthetic critics stressed the sentimental and emotive aspects of this scene of accusation and repentance, going so far as almost to forget the allegory. Whereas they undoubtedly explained the drama of expiation, they obscured the figural reality of Beatrice and Dante, despite the ritual framework the canto creates. One might also mention the infinite series of speculations on the nature of Dante's crisis in his youth. Better to turn to the scene in the *Vita Nuova* following the death of Beatrice, where Dante expresses his love for the "pietosa" lady and his remorse for yielding to his will to live. Also relevant are his poems about a "green young girl" (*pargoletta*, *Purg.* XXXI, 58) and references to Dante's degradation that appear in his *tenzone* with Forese Donati. In short, Dante's struggle (*traviamento*) is multiple, both moral but also intellectual and religious. Equally persuasive are critics like Francesco Mazzoni who believed that Dante yielded to a spiritual adventure, as witnessed by the poems on the *loda*.

Whatever the case may be, the palinode celebrated here forms a refutation not of rationality so much as of intellectual pride. It climaxes a movement that starts in Canto XXVI, when Guinizzelli affirms the art of Dante as poet and continues in Canto XXVII with the moral investiture of Virgil. Canto XXVIII, with the entrance into the forest of the Terrestrial Paradise (a symbol of natural felicity, according to *Monarchia* III, xvi), signals the recovery of original genius coincident with the conversation of Dante the man. The result is a personal but also exemplary catharsis, the goal of that spiritual liberty invoked during the encounter with Cato, which in turn softens the hesitations and misdirections of the regeneration of all humankind. This is the concept behind the "sacred representation" that encompasses Cantos XXIX–XXXIII, including a series of visionary spectacles that relate the story of humanity and the "society of the faithful," as seen from a perspective that is Italian and ecumenical, temporal and eternal, nondenominational and Christian.

The Triumph of Beatrice

In its connections with the previous canto, Canto XXXI serves the primary function of concluding Dante's private history, his sentimental and ideological autobiography. But at the same time, the first section of Canto XXX (1–33) and the final part of Canto XXXI (91–145) combine with the sacral-symbolic sequence of the procession to form the neural ganglion where the private events of the soul—after the slavery of sin has managed to attain moral freedom, and the providential history of humanity, which after traumatic crises arrives at a horizon of hope and total renewal—converge in the personality of the poet, whose message takes an intermediary place between heaven and earth.

Although common enough in the *Comedy*, even the exordium *ex abrupto* (where Beatrice directly questions Dante) contributes to a continuation of the tone and material of the previous canto. This canto continues (at least in the first section) the "triumph" of Beatrice. She is a sacral figure, almost

Christological with regard to her solemn entrance into the heavenly Jerusalem and the fullness of her function as a judge. No longer indirect, her colloquy now becomes adversarial. Her accusations no longer result in humiliating silences but in painful admissions and bitter tears. Dante's response to her final harangue is no longer anxious but full of repentance. The rhythm of his confession is exactly that of a ritual liturgy. The "contrition of the heart" (13, 88) and "confession of the ears" (34) will be followed by the "satisfaction of works" (91). These phases correspond to the three steps of the threshold to Purgatory that Dante climbed during his ritual entrance to the second realm (IX, 14). The narrow opening and the ritual of the humble rush and dew in Canto I are now replaced by the oblation of penitence and the forgetting brought about by Lethe.

But this accumulation of ritual elements is surmounted, at least for modern readers, by the passionate declaration of love uttered by Beatrice. First she speaks of her own beauty (49–54), although her words are laced with a melancholy sense of the fallenness of all earthly things ("the lovely limbs in which / I was enclosed—limbs scattered now in dust," 51–52). These words truly breathe the feeling the author promised he would express at the end of *Vita Nuova*. The "beauty" (50) of Beatrice is the highest possible worldly beauty (52), yet it transforms into the supreme beauty of God, or better, what Mazzoni called a "reflective representation of the divine," the "decor creaturarum" (beauty of creation) that is "simulacrum Dei" (the image of God). This topos was largely disseminated during the Middle Ages: that is, Celestial Beauty ("godly / beauty," *Par.* XXVII, 95) is anagogically present in Creation, according to Hugo of St. Vicor (*In Hier.* II), for example.

Pointed Words

In general Dante employs a discursive style at the beginning of Canto XXXI and an elevated tone at the end without, however, losing any of the metaphoric energy of the opening. As usual he softens the more complex literary features and points of ideological tension. Here the result is an intense dramatization of the interior life that draws on a military and civil vocabulary: "her speech's point . . . its edge had seemed too sharp" (2–3); "was spent" (8); "what chains were strung, what ditches dug" (25); "to promenade before" (30); "charge" (40); "the whet- / stone turns and blunts our blade's own cutting edge" (41–42); "the tears you sowed" (46); "when the first / arrow of things deceptive struck you" (54–55); "weighed down your wings" (59); "the poison in her argument" (75). And so even the thrust of the similes, apparently domestic, arches toward what will be called the "objective correlative": a "crossbow" for spiritual tension (16), a "fledgling bird" for prudence (60), the roots of an oak tree for hesitation (70).

And there is more. An interplay of rhyme and the very timbre of two tercets (7–12) carry another echo from Dante's system of rhythms and sounds.

On the threshold of consciousness there reoccurs a pause that underlines Dante's troubled state after the revelation of Francesca, emphasized by the same rhyme words, though in a different order (*spense, che pense, offense,* compared to *spense, offense, che pense* in *Inf.* V) and the same intonation (i.e., the interrogative after *pense*). Watching Dante react to Francesca's story of sinful love, Virgil asks Dante "What are you thinking?" (*Inf.* V, 111).

Here it is Beatrice who poses the question as she seeks an open confession from one who must burn away his own excesses and prepare himself for penitence. These are two parallel moments of moral crisis for the poet-character that differ from his autobiography of victimhood. Francesca's story revives the risks of a sentimental education too ready to intermingle life and literature, while Beatrice's accusations resurrect memories of the crucial stages of Dante's troubled past. There remains that fact that Beatrice herself is directly involved in that drama, so much so that an ingenuous reader—that is, one who overlooks the inconsistencies of Beatrice's spiritual appearance—might have the impression of a female flirt (like Petrarch's Laura in the *Triumph of Death*) or even of a jealous woman (discernable in her ironic reference to the *pargoletta*). One might add the self-irony of 74–75 (namely, "the poison in her argument"), and the ambiguous play on the term *barba*: an allusion both to the chin (according to the semantics of northern Italian dialects) but also to the mature age of the weary pilgrim. Along with the word *scola* ("gondola," 96) from Venice and Ravenna, one feels the atmosphere of the Po Valley that pervades this canto. But in the wake of the metaphoricity of "to promenade before them" (30), it is necessary to recall (with Mazzoni) that Dante's troubles cannot be reduced to the terms of an erotic or sentimental susceptibility, nor the accusations of Beatrice to the psychology of a jealous woman. The issue, rather, is the overemphasis on the temporal rather than the eternal (as confirmed by Canto XXX, 130–132): that "cupiditas" (desire) for "mere appearances" (34) instead of the steadiness of will that leads to God.

The dialogue of the first section of the canto gives way to the narrative and descriptive elements of the second. But these are prepared for by the last part (76–90), from the moment in which the angels give way to an expectant pause, as they cease to strew their flowers. Here, in that space of silence and isolation, Beatrice remains absorbed in contemplation of the griffin (79–84), almost forgetting her rebukes, as if transferred to a secret distance. Before this enigmatic figure of light, Dante remains immobile and amazed. Then as his lady transfigures herself, he feels pangs of remorse until he faints (85–90). At this point the state of Dante's soul is sealed in mystery by the echo between La Pia—"salsi colui che 'nnanellata pria" (*Purg.* V, 135)—and Beatrice: "salsi colei che la ragion me porse" ("is known to her who was the cause of that," 90). This genuine faint and reawakening foreshadow a mystical death in sin and spiritual rebirth, as well as recalling the protagonist's other moments of ascetic catharsis, such as the close of Cantos III and V of the *Inferno*.

A Second Beauty

Once signaled and then interrupted, the rhythm of the sacred mystery spreads through the following scene (92–102), which is dominated by the shade of Matilda, who now has also become a liturgical figure, full of hieratic majesty. She immerses the poet in the waters of Lethe and then guides him toward the far shore, where she embraces him. The ritual of purification echoes a biblical baptism in the Jordan. Appropriate too is the suggestion that comes from the penitential psalm intoned by the angels, in which David asks pardon for the sin he has committed with Bathsheba. This ritual, with its intense intertextuality (comparable to Dante's own regretful situation), merges into the first encounter with the cardinal Virtues, who sing and invite the pilgrim to contemplate Beatrice, standing nearby. Then they guide him, dancing, to the griffin (103–114), recalling a passage in the *Monarchia* that connects the virtues to the Terrestrial Paradise (XXX, XVI: 7). The eyes of the griffin may figure the transmutation of the Word that can reflect others and remain equal to itself. There is an analogy but not an identification between Beatrice and Christ that creates a certain, far-off vision of the Empyrean. Undoubtedly this image veils some kind of particular, indirect knowledge of the divine, as Dante suggests when he addresses the reader (124), but the most prevalent feature is Dante's immediate fascination with the play of lights and mirrors (115–126). The ritual is completed by the intervention of the theological Virtues that dance in rhythm to their song. Their *angelico caribo* ("to their chant, they danced," 132) is at once a sacred and popular metaphor. They implore a final concession from Beatrice to her faithful lover, that he may experience her unveiled face, which already shines with the full splendor of Paradise (127–138).

On the allegorical level the transition from the four nymph-stars to the more profound, theological handmaidens *(ancelle)* is plain enough. The nymphs inhabit the Adamic forest and are therefore the same as the four stars "not seen before except by the first people" *(Purg.* I, 24). The theological virtues are those representing the eternal life of beatitude, which finds fruition in gazing on the face of God. Man's virtue may not ascend so far unless aided by divine illumination, which is the meaning of the celestial paradise *(Monarchia* III, IV: 7). The ineffable emotionality of this long-awaited moment of transition is emphasized by the extraordinary final sequence (139–145): an invocation of the "second beauty" of his lady which—uniquely in the poem—turns the close of the canto into a rapid interrogative. The usual interpretation of "second beauty" contrasts it with the "first beauty" of Beatrice's eyes. The *Convivium* (III,VIII: 9, 11 and XV: 2) celebrates both her eyes and mouth, as does the canzone "Donne ch'avete" (one of many connections between the *Vita Nuova* and Cantos XXX and XXXI, including the technical term *fedele* in line 134 of Canto XXXI). Mazzoni, however, glosses "second beauty" as the second appearance of Beatrice that radiates from her like a reflected light. One may compare the "splendor" of line 139 with *Convivium* III, XIV: 5–6 and the "Eternal Loveliness" of *Paradiso* XVIII, 16, where divine beauty shines from the veiled face of the lady, a radiant mirror of the light of God. The interrogative that ends this section declares the insufficiency of any expression to capture the divine, one of the great theses of the *Paradiso*.

But that suspended and final question reflects the artistry that governs the entire second part of the canto. One may note the number of pleonasms (83–84, *vincer . . . vincer*, which is picked up in 89, *vinto*) and repetitions (93, *Tiemmi, tiemmi;* 119, *li occhi a li occhi;* 133, *Volgi . . . volgi*); the expressiveness of the metaphors (85, the *nettle* of remorse; 116, the *emeralds* of the eyes; 117, the *shafts* of Love; 128, the *food* of divine contemplation; 132, the *angelic dance* of the theological Virtues; 140–141, *Parnassus's shade [and] fountain*, for the ardors of inspired poetry) and similes (96, *light as a gondola;* 118, *more than flames;* 121, *Just like the sun within a mirror*). Set against the stylized ritual of the close of the *Purgatory* that culminates in Dante's immersion in Lethe, this stylistic system creates a strangely luminous and musical effect. And everything converges (in the wake of one of the most significant appeals to the reader in the poem) in the great central motif of the rapport between Beatrice and the griffin. It reoccurs in verses 79 and 118, first as an abstract and static contemplation, then as a dynamic flickering in her eyes, indicating the two, continually intertwining, natures of Christ. The transformation of the apparently immobile griffin is a metaphorical vision that relates to *Paradiso* XXXIII, 114, where even the phrasing is similar: "si trasmutava" and "si travagliava."

But it is true that the entire confrontation (118–123), which hinges on the simile of the mirror, forbids an "analogical" perception of the divine on the part of Dante, who sees things not as they are but through a glass darkly. In other words, as Mazzoni says, "the humanity and divinity of Christ are brought together by the mirroring eyes of Beatrice in the symbolic and metaphorical image of the 'two-formed animal,'" referring to *Purgatorio* XXXII, 96. Mazzoni rightly extends Dante's knowledge of the analogical mirror to the mirroring angels and ranks of the blessed, on the basis of *Paradiso* XVIII, 2, and XXIX, 144.

The Secret Biography

In reality, the continuum of the poem's allegorical structure underlies the entire complex of these final cantos, which are tied together by what used to be called "poetry." We are not talking about little riddles that may be solved by literal or even nonliteral explanations or that require a hermeneutic at odds with the actual lyricism of the poem. Rather, one must keep in mind the double dimension of the events and the personalities, literal as well as figural and typological. In Canto XXXI the autobiographical elements are individual and typical, or rather, activated by both poles, which lend each other strength. Beatrice remains Madonna Bice Portinari without ever ceasing to be revealed Truth. Dante's personal drama, whose resolution is the theme of Cantos XXX and XXXI, attains a profound sense of contiguity with the "triumph" of Beatrice and the historical and the providential "sacred representation" that is the heart of the entire procession. Dante is authorized as a prophet and given the moral authority to rescue Christian society.

On the other hand, the story also concludes the secret biography of the poet, who is here freed from the anxiety and paralysis of his own contradictions. The line "you stare too fixedly" (XXXII, 9) affirms an irrevocable gap, although Bosco also detects a warning not to proceed too far into theological speculations, precisely because Beatrice combines both terrestrial and sacred dimensions. We must also bear in mind Giorgio Petrocchi's observation that Dante here reprises and reinterprets the *Vita Nuova,* which he wrote twenty years earlier, by replaying events in a universal key. Dante's former love reappears on this stage as a sacred representation. The poet recuperates the Stilnovo (with Beatrice at the center) by conjoining her role as salvific figure (almost Christlike) with parts of his own persona. The newfound peace of Dante the man is thereby reworked into an exemplary figure that no longer retains any vestige of the private, while bearing a message to "profit that world which / lives badly" (XXXII, 103). From this base Dante can rise to the level of an apocalyptic prophet in Cantos XXXII and XXXIII, as the *Purgatorio* touches on its most disturbing aspiration from the anxious vantage point of a transforming vision.

BIBLIOGRAPHICAL NOTES

Comprehensive studies of the canto include E. Moore, "The Reproaches of Beatrice," in *Studies in Dante* 3 (Oxford, 1896 and 1903), 221–252 (particularly for the Boethian themes in the initial encounter); Charles S. Singleton, *Advent of Beatrice* (Cambridge, MA, 1954) and "Rivers Nymphs and Stars," in *Journey to Beatrice* (Cambridge, MA, 1958); O. Hardie, "Beatrice's Chariot in Dante's Earthly Paradise," *Deutsches Dante-Jahrbuch* 39 (1961): 137–172; F. Mazzoni, "Il Canto XXXI del Purgatorio," in *Lectura Dantis Scaligera* (Florence, 1965); and G. Petrocchi, "Il Canto XXXI del Purgatorio," in *Nuove letture dantsche* vol. 5 (Florence, 1972): 189–206.

CANTO XXXII
The Parallel Histories

H. WAYNE STOREY

Canto XXXII depends heavily on the effect of its incipit, an opening verse that almost seamlessly links this canto to the preceding one in which Beatrice makes her dramatic appearance, on a much more profound level, to the experience of world and Church history in Dante's own keenly developed sense of political and moral poetics.

On the poetic stage of the six cantos that conclude the *Purgatorio* (XXVIII–XXXIII), the double spectacle of world order and Dante's personal-poetic drama unfolds in the symbolic state of innocence unique to Earthly Paradise. In the narrative trajectory of these six cantos, Dante's personal story of moral and poetic inspiration, concentrated in the figure of Beatrice (*Purg.* XXX–XXXI), alternates with the spiritual-political history of humankind and the Church (*Purg.* XXVIII–XXIX, XXXII–XXXIII). Canto XXXII represents a link between the two histories, moving from the purely personal reference to the "ten-/year thirst" (2–3), the time between Beatrice's death and the fictional date of Dante's extraordinary journey into the afterlife), to the appearance of the universally recognized symbol of the meretrix of the Apocalypse ("securely seated there, ungirt, a whore," 149). Beatrice herself attests to this fusion of the personal and the universal when she declares Dante's ultimate mission as witness, scribe, and prophet of the mystery of human history and of the corruption of the Church ("to profit that world which / lives badly, watch the chariot steadfastly / and . . . transcribe / what you have seen," 103–106).[1] This sense of transition, of essential linkage, is concentrated and announced in the opening of Canto XXXII, in which Dante's gaze is still intensely fixed on the vision of Beatrice's true, or second, beauty unveiled at the close of Canto XXXI.

The syntactic structure of the first verse, inimitable in translation, the reinforcing adverb *(Tanto)* and imperfect tense *(erano)* convey the intensity of the preceding canto's closing activity of rapturously staring into Beatrice's blinding splendor: "Tant'eran li occhi miei fissi e attenti" ("My eyes were so insistent, so intent," 1). The fixity of Dante's stare, indifferent even to the extraordinary presence of all else around him in Earthly Paradise (4–5),[2] is reiterated and remarked on in line 9 by the nymphs, introduced in Canto XXXI, as too intense *(Troppo fiso)*. But the effect does not end there. As he slowly regains his vision to turn his eyes to the exceptional, symbolic events about to occur in the next portion of the canto, Dante returns to the intensity of Beatrice's beauty in an uncommon gloss of "lesser" *(al poco)* in the preceding verse: "e dico 'al poco' per rispetto al molto / sensibile onde a forza mi rimossi" ("that is, lesser than / the mighty force that made my eyes retreat," 14–15).

Neither the recall nor the technique is casual. The prolonged transition between the personal and the universal fixes Beatrice's extraordinary significance at the center of both soon to be inseparable trajectories. The impenetrable meaning of the mystery of Beatrice that forces the suspension of the *Vita Nova,* equally recalled in Canto XXX (22–39) and XXXII (2), is about to become one of the principal motivating forces of the rest of the *Divine Comedy,* as Beatrice is central to the scenes of the symbolic chariot and then is seated beneath the renewed tree of life.

The renewed movement of the mystical procession toward Adam's tree and the griffin, as well as the violent transformations of the chariot, are the topics of centuries of interpretations. Much of this erudition is based on the methodological formula by which characters and objects in Purgatory's Earthly Paradise represent theological personages and historical events, suggesting that Dante's role is to disguise significant universal events with a codified symbolism. The problem with this system of interpretation, as Peter Armour demonstrated in the case of the griffin, is that a shift in symbolic register changes the entire symbolic system.[3] Additionally, these corresponding symbols tend to be the object of scholarly inheritances whereby the griffin is usually associated with Christ because the long commentary tradition suggests such a reading.

The Spiritual Franciscans

If there is an overarching theoretical orientation that conditions the symbolism not only of Canto XXXII but also, for example, of *Inferno* XIX and other political and moral works by Dante, even on the level of the biblical citations in his *Epistles* and *Vita Nova,*[4] it is the extraordinary influence of the various tenets of the Spiritual Franciscans, in essence diverse groups of Franciscans dedicated to the reform of a Church they believed corrupted by worldly wealth and political power. Pivotal episodes and characters through-out the *Comedy,* from the presence of Pope Celestine V (*Inf.* III) and what one senses is the imminent arrival in Hell of Boniface VIII to St. Peter's vehe-ment invective in *Paradiso* XXVII against the corruption of the papacy, reflect Dante's concurrence with fundamental historical and theoretical tenets of the Spirituals, not in advocacy of the movement's eventually declared hereti-cal and disruptive politics but in accord with their critiques and proposed re-forms of the papacy's, and the Church's, spirituality.[5] And while this influence has come to be recognized more and more, thanks to the research of reli-gious historians such as Marjorie Reeves and Raoul Manselli, much of how we read Canto XXXII depends on the long-inherited critical tradition particu-larly affected, for example, by Michele Barbi's insistence that Dante shared none of the Spirituals' views.[6] As we shall see, the interpretive risk has al-ways rested in the assignment of Dante's knowledge of texts from which he might have drawn the intricate system of symbols found in Cantos XXIX, XXXII, and XXXIII.

The most probable systematic source not only for the symbols of Canto XXXII but also for Dante's views of world order and moral reform is the Spiritual Franciscans. There is little doubt that their moral reform of the Church based on a renewed ecclesiastic poverty and spiritual—rather than worldly—interests rings true in Dante's criticism of Church corruption due, in large part, to what Dante and his contemporaries believed was Constan-tine's historical "donation" of temporal power to the pope.[7] Much of the Spirituals' theoretical underpinnings rely on interpretative glosses, written by Joachim of Fiore (1135–1202), of prophetic books of the Bible, such as Revelations and Isaiah.[8] In his eyewitness chronicle mostly of the second and third quarters of the thirteenth century, Salimbene de Adam notes the circulation of large collections of Joachim's biblical commentaries, espe-cially among reform-minded Franciscans in Paris.[9] Joachim's interpretation of Apocalypse, for example, as a history of the Church and the eras of hu-manity and the ages of the Holy Spirit garnered extraordinary readership among those who sought a systematic explanation and platform for reform. Perhaps even more representative of the intensity, and interpretative diffi-culty at this distance, of Joachim's reception among the Spirituals is what has come to be known as the Pseudo-Joachimite commentary on Jeremiah, the so-called *Super Hieremiam.*[10] The widespread circulation of this commen-tary in distinctively different lengths and versions suggests that the small core of this commentary was, in fact, written by Joachim and that major sec-tions were then added by reforming Franciscans.[11] But modern notions of authenticity and authorship did not apply to Dante's culture. Given Dante's affinity for Jeremiah and the Lamentations, it is difficult to imagine that if he had access to this commentary he did not read it. As we shall see, the crucial structuring elements of this canto suggest that Dante knew and made use of the religio-political stance of the *Super Hieremiam.* We know, for example, that Dante would have had access also to the commentaries of the Spiritual Franciscan Peter John Olivi, who notably authored two commentaries that would have served Dante well, the *Super Lamentationes Ieremiae* and the *Lectura super Apocalipsim,* and who taught at the Franciscan Church of the Holy Cross (Santa Croce) in Florence from 1287–1289. And while the ex libris of Dante's library remains an elusive mark, the poet's intellectual and moral dedication to commentaries on the prophetic books is borne out in many passages of his works. Given the controversy surrounding the Spirituals from the 1240s until beyond Dante's death and the reformational parallels in Dante's political and moral attitudes, it is likely that the poet had significant encounters with these Franciscan principles not only as formal texts and informal discussions but even, given the cultural penetration of their theories, with thirteenth- and fourteenth-century illumination cycles, especially of the Apocalypse.

Essential to Joachim's, the Spirituals' and Dante's reforming views are the notions of history and prophecy spelled out and guaranteed by parallel symbolic representations in the Old and New Testaments. Joachim's systematic interpretation of Apocalypse, for example, attempts to calculate with a certain precision (1220–1240) the end of the age of man according to the coordination of the histories of the Old and New Testaments. However, what remains of Joachim's historically based predictions in the Spiritual commentary tradition is the Bible's, and especially Apocalypse's, prophetic condemnations of a future corrupt Church as a foundation for their reforming principles. Especially in the *Super Hieremiam,* the interpolating Spirituals converted Joachim's historical prophecies into "a simplistic and literalist typological interpretation of scripture as referring directly to mid-thirteenth century events" and founded "a fierce polemic against the wealth and worldliness of the church hierarchy."[12] The *Super Hieremiam*'s prophecy of the creation of two orders, quickly associated by the Spirituals with the Franciscans and the Domenicans, to lead the Church back to its true path will be echoed in *Paradiso* XI (31–36) and XXII (44), where we also will find the prophetic Joachim (*Par.* XII, 139–141).[13] The commentary's harsh criticism of the Church's cardinals (depicted as "grabbers") will be linked at the close of *Paradiso* IX (133–138) to another of the *Super Hieremiam*'s reproaches: the study of Church law and the Decretals at the expense of the Gospels.[14] Consequently, we find a shift in the nature of the symbol itself in the Spiritual tradition, a shift that is fundamental to understanding the tenor of the symbolism in the cantos of *Inferno* XIX, the Earthly Paradise where—as we shall see—symbolism becomes a vehicle not for conventional Augustinian representations of the apocalyptic but rather for suggestive historical interpretations that would lead the reader to contemplate the necessity of ecclesiastic reform in a world gone astray.

Pugatorio XXXII's return to the previously halted divine procession (*Purg.* XXIX) is caused by the renewed movement of the "glorious army" (16–27), a reincorporation of the larger motif of the world's necessary redemption coming after the cantos devoted to Dante's symbolic personal atonement (*Purg.* XXX–XXXI). Matilda, Dante, and Statius are now in movement with the procession, following the right wheel of the triumphal chariot as it makes its way through the deserted forest of Earthly Paradise. Here, where original innocence and harmony were created, the contrast of Eve's sin is recalled (32) and, once the procession has come to another halt and Beatrice has descended from the chariot, the name of Adam is murmured by all.[15] On the most literal level, this intoning recalls the origins of humanity in its brief and ultimately tragic innocence, in need of the redemption offered by Christ. However, we find ourselves also at the origins, the essential step, of Joachim's "key metaphor of the universal 'psalter' whose 'tenth string' was broken in Adam, and needs to be mended."[16]

Adam's name reminds us of the fall and the promise of a return to the harmonious state of creation, to be partially fulfilled also by the two new orders (Franciscans and Dominicans) prophesied by Joachim and reiterated by the Spirituals. The dense symbolism that follows both reenacts and prophesies the history—rather than the moral lesson—of that redemption but always in terms of the mystical that stimulates associations rather than fixing them.[17] On the other hand, many of the symbols themselves were well-known to readers of thirteenth- and early fourteenth-century illustrated manuscripts of the Apocalypse and even to common folk who contemplated fresco cycles of the Apocalypse in their parish churches.[18] Dante's poetic reusing of these symbols risks, as critics have demonstrated, wildly varying interpretations based on numerous medieval and ancient allegorical keys.[19] But we should remember that Dante's adaptation of this symbolism was probably not designed to enter into theological debate. Instead, as he does in so many other passages of the *Divine Comedy,* Dante uses symbols well-known to his medieval audience as a support structure for his own poetic and moral goals. As the poet himself reminds us in this canto, he is the imperfect scribe and informant of this episode, described very much in artistic rather than religious terms.[20] His poetic and moral mission is, as we noted above, "to profit the world which / lives badly . . . [and] transcribe / what [he] has seen" (*Purg.* XXXII, 103–104, 105–106).

A Constellation of Symbols

The first important symbol of the canto is the Tree of Knowledge of Good and Evil, which has been stripped of its leaves and flowers, and around which the procession has drawn. Dante's own interpretation of the tree as divine justice in Canto XXXIII (70–72) tells only part of the story, as the poet himself justifies the condensed explanations of the *cantica*'s final canto. The tree is part of an extended symbolic act of obedience, at once tragic and reassuring, that marks the expulsion of humankind from this place of harmony. This act includes humanity's redemption by the "Roman Christ": "Thus is / the seed of every righteous man preserved," (47–48), whose act of rejoining humanity and the Church (chariot) to the tree pays tribute to that Obedience (right from wrong) and renews the promise of paradise (the tree's flowers and leaves).

The griffin, the symbolic agent of this renewal, presents us with a problem. As Armour demonstrated, in medieval symbology this mythical animal— a combination of eagle and lion—usually serves as a negative sign and is never associated with a dual-natured Christ. It could well be that Dante intends to shock his medieval public with this *animal binato* ("two-natured animal," 47) and *biforme fera* ("two-form animal," 96), linking an usually negative hybridism with the divine and human qualities of Christ.[21] Armour suggests that the griffin symbolizes Rome as the "custodian and executor of earthly justice" and that it "stands for the dual jurisdiction of Tiberius . . . when Christ was crucified and the entire human race redeemed from Adam's sin. For Dante, the legitimacy of the Roman Empire was confirmed by Christ the Redeemer's submission to it both at his birth and at his death."[22] The subtlety of Armour's reading changes Dante's description of the tree's renewed flowers from empirical to metaphorical, revealing in lines 59 and 60 the hues of Christ's redemptive blood. Armour's solution also resolves the larger narrative problem imposed by the long intervening descriptions and related metaphors involving Dante's charmed sleep and his awakening (64–81). During Dante's sleep, the griffin and the procession have "climbed / on high" (89–90), leaving only Beatrice, the chariot tied to the tree, and the seven nymphs (or virtues). Despite this departure, the narrative thread continues, now focused on the tree ("the boughs that were renewed," 86) and the chariot; its guardian, Beatrice; and another Rome, where Dante will live eternally and where Christ is Roman (100–102). This second, eternal Rome, where Christ is Roman, coordinates the symbols of the other two Romes: the imperial Rome, rightful guarantor of the *Res Publica Christiana,* we saw in the dual-natured griffin and the second Rome, which we see at the close of the canto, the papal curia of Rome.

This constellation of symbolic Romes figured heavily in Dante's critique of the moral corruption that had left the world upside down, a demonstration launched in *Inferno* XIX, where curial Rome is represented by some of the most recent popes (such as Nicholas III) and where Boniface VIII and Clement V are expected. Even more important, however, is the cause of this moral disorder, the corrupting influence of wealth, first transferred to the *Curia* in the *Donation of Constantine,* a document particularly suspect among the Spirituals, for whom the metaphor of Lady Poverty as a woman and potential bride, abandoned for over a thousand years between Christ and San Francesco, is reiterated in *Paradiso* XI, 63–66:

> He wed her; day by day he loved her more.
> She was bereft of her first husband; scorned,

> obscure, for some eleven hundred years,
> until that sun came, she had had no suitor.

The parallel associations—on the one hand—of San Francesco as the inheritor of Christ's message of a spirituality founded on poverty and the prophesied third Adam, according to Joachim's general prediction and then the Spirituals' specific claims (Dante's "sun," 66) and—on the other—of Lady Poverty and the mother Church's mission of poverty and necessary refusal of worldly wealth, inherent in the *Donatio,* become the implied antidote offered by various luminaries in Dante's Paradise to the apocalyptic civil and moral deprivation caused by the Church's abandonment of poverty and spirituality.[23] While this system of moral reform runs throughout Dante's *Comedy,* the textual frame that extends from the keys of St. Peter in *Inferno* XIX (91–92 and 101) to St. Peter's vehement invective against the corrupt papacy in *Paradiso* XXVII represents a return to the founding moral principles of humanity and Christianity in Christ, Peter, and San Francesco.[24] The papacy's moral depravity affects not only the ecclesiastical ("From here on high one sees rapacious wolves / clothed in the cloaks of shepherds," *Par.* XXVII, 55–56) but also world order itself ("your avarice afflicts the world," *Inf.* XIX, 104).

The image of Beatrice, now seated alone on the ground ("She sat alone upon the simple ground," 94) recalls Dante's beloved incipit of the Lamentations of Jeremiah and foreshadows the unpredictable tribulations of moral humanity and its Church that the poet will witness in the concluding part of the canto. The key terms, *sola sedea* ("she sat alone") and *terra* (ground or earth), signal what will become the foundations of Dante's witnessing of the Apocalyptic prophecy of humanity's state of moral confusion at the hands of a curial Rome so dissipated by wealth's corruption that Rome herself, as he will argue in his letter to the Italian Cardinals on the topic of the transfer of the papacy to Avignon, sits alone like a widow.[25] This is the same "Rome" that the Middle Ages associated with Babylon: its corrupt curia is the meretrix of the Apocalypse, whose victim is spiritual Rome, the *ecclesia spiritualis.*

Of course, the "simple ground" (94) on which Beatrice sits at the root of the tree is hardly simple. It is, rather, the ground from which all humankind has been exiled. And even after humanity's redemption, its moral path is tormented by the corrupt. Here in the symbolic nest of innocence, the significance of place and space, now uninhabited except—from what we can tell—by Matilda and the unique appearance of the procession and Beatrice, accentuates exile, redemption, and reform.[26] The simple ground contrasts with the promise of the true ground, the true city of Rome, and to the metaphorical earth from which the dragon will emerge (130–131).[27] The medieval sense of exile from one's homeland enriches the promise of redemption and Paradise (celestial Rome), forever denied in the deserted Earthly Paradise.[28] Humankind's exile from the original happiness of Eden intensifies not only the importance of Christ's redemptive act and San Francesco's spiritual mission to return humanity to its promised state of material and spiritual harmony but also Dante's role as both literal and metaphorical pilgrim, witness, and scribe of divine vision and prophecy. The canto's initial insistence, in that unusual incipit, on a fusion between Dante's personal journey of confession and revelation (*Purg.* XXX–XXXI)and the universal revelations (*Purg.* XXIX, XXXII–XXXIII) he attests bears dramatic fruit. Dante must gather all this experience of exile and promise, personal and universal, and report it as a good copyist, faithful to the text of the experience, on behalf of world order.

The Predators

The canto's concluding scene, which Beatrice directs Dante to watch and report in writing (103–105), amounts to an apocalyptic vision. This divine prophecy—seemingly performed for Dante—reveals the destruction of those institutions whose disobedient disregard and disdain for moral rectitude and human happiness, as Dante conceived them, throw humanity into chaos. The symbols are so common in the Middle Ages that their roles here seem expansive rather than limiting: the eagle ("bird of Jove," 112 and 125), the fox lacking all "honest nourishment" (119–120), the wasplike dragon of the Apocalypse (131), the chariot that changes its nature. Medieval symbolism is so diverse and extensive that identification of a precise source or an explicit significance may depend on the symbolic system that Dante intended to use.[29] The case of the fox, for example, is particularly problematic since, in some traditions, its symbolic fate is often mixed with that of the wolf. In learned discussions of allegory and symbolism, such as the Bishop Ambrose's *Expositio super Lucam,* which Dante would have known, heretics are especially associated with the fox.[30] Saint Peter's admonition (*Par.* XVII, 55–56) regarding religious leaders who are "rapacious wolves" echoes not only Old and New Testament passages (Genesis 49:27), Isaiah 11:6), Jeremiah 5:6, Matthew 7:15) but also contemporary descriptions, such as Salimbene's in his *Chronicle* (I, 275) of predatory wolves that were feared in the Middle Ages for their commonly believed in attacks on human beings. Dante reprises this popular belief in the wolf on Canto XXXII, 120, with the same formulations he used in Inferno I, 97–99. Even those symbols that are exclusively biblical, such as the seven-headed dragon of Apocalypse 12:3 or the Babylonian whore of Apocalypse 17:3 ("I saw a woman sit upon a scarlet coloured beast, . . . having seven heads and ten horns"), depend not only on historically divergent interpretations (divided roughly between the Augustinian and the Joachimite readings) but also, given their extraordinarily visual dynamic, on contemporary visual representations of the Apocalypse.[31]

When Dante declares that the transfigured chariot turned seven-headed beast is like no monster ever seen (147), his vision recalls similar visions of

Isaiah, Daniel, and John. As do the symbols in the Apocalypse, Dante's symbols lead suggestively to the meditation of redemption, exile, and the history of humankind. But we should keep in mind that unlike the Apocalypse, these critical cantos in the Earthly Paradise are not the final book of Dante's vision but an integrated part of his poetic message of reform. The final scene of this canto symbolically depicts the recent transfer of the papacy to Avignon, as well as its submissiveness to the French state. Therefore, Dante's apocalyptic borrowings suggest, like their Franciscan counterparts, a fulfillment of prophecies as a call to conscience, an attitude we see reflected in Beatrice's charge ("to profit that world which / lives badly," 103–104).

Velocity

If there is one element that characterizes John's dream on the Isle of Patmos to which Dante is especially attentive in the apocalyptic scene he is charged to transcribe, it is the sense of movement and transformation. The final scene of the canto unfolds with a velocity we have not seen since *Inferno* XXV. The action occurs in rapid strikes that seem to tear and contort simultaneously. The eagle (bird of Jove) first swoops—and later "plunges" (124)—down through the tree faster than lightning (109–114), rending its new foliage and twisting the chariot, tied to the tree, with the velocity and power of its descent (115–117). The fox "leaps" into the chariot and is repelled "as quick / as . . . its bones permitted" (118–123). What remains of the damaged chariot, the pole shaft and the wheels, is re-covered by the eagle's plumes in less time than it takes to yawn (136–141). Immediately after this transformation, the wrecked chariot sprouts seven heads, three with two horns and four with but a single horn (142–147). The scene slows only in its final phase of the giant and the whore (148–160).

Dante's poetic emphasis on the timing of these symbolic acts of transformation is not casual. Especially as understood by the Spiritual Franciscans, the critical elements of Joachim's interpretative system of the parallel histories, the *concordiae* of the Old and New Testaments, depends on timing. Dante's syntactic insistence on the dynamic of velocity and timeliness reiterates also the rapid destructiveness depicted in often dramatic illustrations of the Apocalypse, especially in a thirteenth-century illuminated New Testament, to which Dante, a privileged guest of Cangrande della Scala, would have had access at the Chapter Library in Verona.[32] And while Dante's depiction of the whore of Babylon seems to reflect the visual dynamic of the *meretrix* he found possibly among the *chartae* of this New Testament, his sense of the visual impact and movement of such illustrations gives his descriptions a vivid urgency that goes beyond dry Scholastic symbolism. Dante knew that if his call for reform was to be effective, his images would had to live and move on the page.

According to Dante's symbolic orientation in the *Comedy* and in his *Epistles* V and VI, as well as the vision of Ezechiel, the "bird of Jove," the "aquila in auro terribilis" (*Ep.* VI, 12), points to political authority, in this case probably—as traditionally glossed—the first persecutions of the Church and the *Res Publica Christiana* at the hands of Imperial Rome (first to the third century). The fox that leaps into the chariot, and is immediately repulsed by Beatrice, seems also to represent Dante's use of a conventional symbol for heresy and its "squalid sins" (121); its poor nourishment arises from heresy's lack of just and rigorous moral justification. But it is the second descent of the Imperial Eagle, Rome in its Christian vestige, that sets the stage for the final apocalyptical images of the canto. It seems to mean, with the eagle's feathers covering the chariot, that the symbolic transport of humanity (the *navicella,* we presume, of the Church) must now carry the weight of worldly and political concerns: "O my small bark, your freight is wickedness!" (129). Dante adds that the eagle's plumes were "perhaps / offered with sound and kind intent" (137–138). The implication is that good intentions do not always produce good results, a rationale that reflects not only Dante's attitudes but also those of many jurists and moralists of his day regarding the Donation of Constantine that covered, like the eagle's plumes, the Church with the weight of worldly wealth and power.

This critical moment in the Church's history and in the history of human happiness has profound ramifications in the symbolic actions that follow. While the dragon who skewers the bottom of the chariot has been interpreted variously as debilitating schisms that have harmed the Church, even the syntax of the verses that follow the second descent of the eagle seem to clarify the message: the dragon is able to rend the chariot (Church and humanity) weakened by the Donation of Constantine. Numerous challenges of faith by diverse schismatic sects arose against the spiritual authority of the Church after the Church was vested with mundane authority. In lines 142–147, this transformation of the chariot and the Church ("the saintly instrument") assumes its final form as an apocalyptic beast, less as a biblical symbol than as a hideous monster, divided within itself, deformed and weakened. Such a gross perversion of the image of spiritual harmony and authority seems now remote from the fusion of Lady Poverty and the mother Church envisaged in Dante's Franciscan conception of redemption.

The Whore of Babylon

The righteous authority first presented in the procession of Canto XXIX is supplanted by the image of the whore of Babylon, seated securely atop the devastated chariot now transformed into the hideous monster contaminated by worldly power.[33] She is the emblem of perversion and the antithesis of spiritual integrity. She has fornicated with the kings of the earth. She is the symbol of impurity, the mother of abomination, drunk on the blood of the witnesses of Christ (Apocalypse 17:5–6), and the sign of base desire and lust. Here again, as Domenico Consoli points out, her symbolic role varies according to the interpretative system. For Richard of Saint Victor she represents individual moral and religious crisis. For Joachim of Fiore, she is the *ecclesia malignantium,* the spiritually bereft Church. But for Peter John Olivi, the Spiritual who taught at Santa Croce in Florence, the Apocalyptic prophecy of the whore of Babylon predicts the *clerus carnalis,* the Church of worldly concerns, the exact opposite of the *ecclesia spiritualis,* the reformed Church revitalized in Christ's and San Francesco's dedication to Lady Poverty and spirituality.[34] This is almost the same symbol of perverted power we saw in *Inferno* XIX, 106–111, where Dante expressly identifies her apocalyptic role and the Evangelist's authorship.[35]

The specificity of the *Inferno's* recall of the corrupt papal curia of Boniface VIII can probably be extended here to include the additional prophecy of the papacy's exile from its rightful place in Rome to Avignon under Clement V. The canto adds details: the loosened hair (149) and lascivious eyelashes (150) might easily have come from the manuscript of the New Testament in the Chapter Library (*charta,* 166r) to reinforce the debased and promiscuous nature of this antispiritual figure, whose paucity of faithfulness is apparent in the lascivious kisses she shares with her giant ("and they—again, again—embraced each other," 153) while turning "wandering, wanton eyes" on Dante (154).[36]

We have already seen giants in the *Comedy,* usually noted for their size, the terror they strike, and their utility in Dantean transport.[37] But the principal characteristic of the giant of Canto XXXII is ferocious jealousy and possessiveness. Stepping outside his apocalyptic vocabulary of symbols, for there is no giant in the Apocalypse, Dante forces us to interpret not only the giant but also the whore in light of his contemporary politics. The powerful and possessive giant that violently controls not only the Babylonian whore (*puttana,* 160) but also the chariot turned monster on which she is seated (*nova belva,* 160) leads us only to think of the French control of the papal curia at the end of Boniface VIII's reign (concluding in the disgrace of the violent attack against Boniface at Anagni in 1303) and the transfer of the Papal See and the curia to Avignon under Clement V. The scene's overt violence and crude sexuality underscore the unnatural squalor of this relationship between political and religious authority:

> that ferocious amador
> beat her from head to foot; then, swollen with
> suspicion, fierce with anger, he untied
> the chariot-made-monster, dragging it
> into the wood, so that I could not see
> either the whore or the strange chariot-beast.
>
> (155–160)

The Scribe as Witness

The most tragic moment of this vulgar scene occurs when the giant unties the beast from the tree, undoing both humanity's obedience to divine truth and Christ's redemptive act. The implication of this final revelation of prophecy in Dante's here and now is that redemption is again required to right this state of affairs ("to profit that world which lives badly," 103–104). Like San Francesco, one must obey Christ's principles (*Par.* XI, 64–66, 107). The spiritual Church that can renew the balance between worldly and religious authority and lead humanity to spiritual happiness must be restored.

The final scene's curious involvement of Dante himself, the scribe witnessing this revelation of prophecy, has gone rather unnoted.[38] However, it is because the whore turns her roving and wanton attention to Dante that the jealous giant unleashes his violent anger: "but *because* she turned her wandering, wanton eye / to me, the ferocious lover / beat her from head to toe" (my italics and adaptation of Mandelbaum's translation, 154–156). It hardly makes sense that Dante would have conceived of himself as the cause of France's abuse of the Papal State. Moreover, the poet's inclusion in the scene seems to disrupt the allegory. Yet it is hard not to contextualize Dante's own harsh stance on the Avignon exile of the papacy in *Epistle* XI, written no later than 1314—and probably in Verona—to the Italian cardinals.[39] We can extrapolate little from the concubine's lascivious glance at Dante, but the giant's reaction to another possible suitor, a public voice of moral conservatism and papal reform that could distract—or even persuade—the object of his jealous attention, seems clear.[40] His suspicion and anger (157) are turned not just toward the meretricious curia but also toward those who criticized the move as a perversion of the papal mission.[41]

That the giant wanders off dragging the fruits of Constantine's gift into the forest reminds us of the linguistic and thematic proximities that connect Dante's initial ascent toward happiness in *Inferno* I and the bucolic forest he finally reaches in Earthly Paradise. In this place of innocence where humankind briefly knew perfect happiness, however, God has created a prophetic representation—and with a divine soundtrack (128–129)—of the reasons for humankind's unhappiness: a history of human error (the fall), redemption, and corruption, and an implicit call to humankind and its Church for spiritual reform. Thus it is that Canto XXXII—from its unusual incipit to its final revealed prophecy—connects Dante's personal confession in Cantos XXX–XXXI to the universal truth of history and the principal institutions (Church and Empire) designated by God to guarantee world order and spiritual happiness.

NOTES

1. Dante's mission of revealing this state of affairs will be reiterated by St. Peter in *Paradiso* XXVII, 64–66.

2. Echoes of Guido Cavalcanti's poetic style and vocabulary find their way into many of the verses of Earthly Paradise, certainly from *Purgatorio* XXVII to XXXII, including here in v. 3 ("li altri sensi m'eran tutti spenti"), where we hear Dante's proximity to the phenomenology of Cavalcanti's *spiriti* and *spiritelli* ("senses" or "sensations"), often in imbalance owing to the experience of intense love. See, for example, Cavalcanti's "E dico che' miei spiriti son morti" in the single-strophe *canzone* "Poi che di doglia cor conven ch'i' porti" (XI, 5 in *Guido Cavalcanti, Rime*, ed. Letterio Cassata [Anzio: De Rubeis, 1993]) or Cavalcanti's self-ironic investigation of the term itself in "Pegli occhi fere un spirito sottile," especially v. 4 ("e fa ogn'altro spiritel earliest works, including the *Vita Nova* (see his sonnet "Spesse fiate vegnonmi all mente," 6–7, "sì che la vita quasi m'abandona; campami un spirto vivo solamente" in *Dante Alighieri, Vita Nova*, ed. Guglielmo Gorni [Turin: Einaudi, 1996, 84]).

3. See Peter Armour, *Dante's Griffin and the History of the World* (Oxford: Clarendon, 1989), and, in a more compact version, his *Lectura Dantis* "Purgatory XXXII," in *Dante's Divine Comedy: Introductory Readings II: "Purgatorio"* (Supplement of *Lectura Dantis Virginiana*, 12), ed. Tibor Wlassics (Charlottesville: University of Virginia Press, 1993), 476–90. Armour's alternative view of the symbol's actual significance is noteworthy most of all for its methodological implications. See, however, Pertile's additional historical evidence in his *La puttana e il gigante: dal "Cantico dei cantici" al Paradiso terrestre di Dante* (Ravenna: Longo, 1998). I am indebted to Alessandro Vettori for the typescript of a forthcoming article on Matilda, whom he proposes as a symbol of harmony.

4. I refer particularly to the incipit of the Lamentations of Jeremiah ("Quomodo sedet sola," discussed below), which serves as the opening of Dante's *Epistle* XI and as the interruptive—rather than epigraphic—announcement of Beatrice's death in the *Vita Nova*. See my "Di libello in libro: problemi materiali nella poetica di Monte Andrea e Dante," in *Da Guido Guinizzelli a Dante. Nuove prospettive sulla lirica del Duecento,* ed. Furio Brugnolo (Padua: Poligrafo, 2004), 271–290.

5. Dante's insertion of Celestine V in the Ante-Inferno, among those whose lack of commitment deserves not even the condemnation of Hell, is anything but casual. Viewed by many Spirituals as the simple *pastor angelicus*—promised in earlier prophecies—who would have fostered a new age of poverty and spiritual renewal in the Church, Celestine's support for the creation of a separate order of Spirituals, the "Poor Hermits of Celestine" (discussed by Arsenio Frugoni in his "Dai 'Pauperes Eremite Domini Celestini' ai 'Fraticelli de paupere vita,'" *Celestiniana* [Rome: Istituto storico per il Medio Evo, 1954], 125–167), finds its antithesis immediately after Celestine's renunciation of the papacy in the election of Boniface VIII, who revoked the permission of Celestine's poor hermits and sought to reimpose the powers of the worldly Church. St. Peter's specifically severe condemnation of the pope (*Par.* XXVII, 22–27) is clearly aimed at Boniface VIII, the traditional foe of the Spirituals. The second part of Peter's rebuke contrasts the sacrifices of true spiritual martyrs of the Church with the Church's corruption and fomenting of civil strife for its own gain (*Par.* XXVII, 40–63), echoing again the guileful effects of the Church's wealth, the Spirituals' principal tenet. For the history of the Spirituals, see David Burr, *The Spiritual Franciscans: From Protest to Persecution in the Century after Saint Francis* (University Park: University of Pennsylvania Press, 2001).

6. For our purposes here Marjorie Reeves's principal contributions are her *Influence of Prophecy in the Later Middle Ages: A Study in Joachimism* (Oxford: Claredon, 1969); "The Originality and Influence of Joachim of Fiore," *Traditio* 36 (1980): 269–316, and her collaborative studies with Beatrice Hirsch-Reich (*The Figurae of Joachim of Fiore* [Oxford: Clarendon, 1972]) and with Warwick Gould (*Joachim of Fiore and the Myth of the Eternal Evangel in the Nineteenth Century* [Oxford: Clarendon, 1987]). Of Raoul Manselli's numerous studies on the commentary tradition and spiritual culture of the Franciscans in the thirteenth and early fourteenth centuries, we recall here only his main works: *La "Lectura super Apocalipsim" di Pietro di Giovanni Olivi* (Rome: Istituto storico italiano per il Medio Evo, 1955); "Dante e l'*Ecclesia Spiritualis*," in *Dante e Roma* (Florence: Le Monnier, 1965), 115–135; and "Firenze nel Trecento: Santa Croce e la cultura francescana," *Clio* 9, no. 32 (1973): 5–42. To summarize, Barbi believed that Dante's interpretation of the symbolism of the Apocalypse came from a direct reading of the biblical text, essentially uninfluenced by

biblical commentary (see principally Barbi's articles "Il gioachimismo francescano e il Veltro" and "L'apocalisse dantesca," *Studi danteschi* 18 (1934): 209–211 and *Studi danteschi* 22 (1938): 195–197, respectively, as well as his *Problemi fondamentali per un nuovo commento della Divina Commedia* (Florence: Sansoni, 1956), 134–139. Barbi's view was also partially founded on Bonaventure's apparent repudiation of the Spirituals in *Paradiso* XII, 124, a reference to the Spiritual leanings of Ubertino da Casale's leadership of the Franciscans. But the passage in *Paradiso* XII, 109–126 reflects the Franciscan Bonaventure's complaint about the philosophical divisions in the order. As Salimbene de Adam tells us (*Cronica*, ed. Giuseppe Scalia. vol. 2 [Bari: Laterza, 1966], 332–334, 659–665), the Spirituals were not a univocal and organized group but consisted of many factions of reform-minded Franciscans. It is especially noteworthy that immediately after his observations on the straying of many Franciscans from the order's original path (away from poverty), Bonaventure, himself raised on Spiritual teachings, cites the wise theologians of the Church who are with him in the Heaven of the Sun, including the textual foundation of the Spirituals' reform philosophy, Joachim of Fiore, in a clear reference to the Calabrian monk's historical prophecies ("e lucemi da lato / il calavrese abate Gioacchino, / di spirito profetico dotato" [. . . at my side / shines the Calabrian Abbot Joachim, / who had the gift of the prophetic spirit; *Par.* XII, 139–141]). Felice Tocco's early *lectura dantis* of 1902, "Il canto XXXII del *Purgatorio*" (now in *Letture dantesche*, ed. Giovanni Getto, 3rd ed. [Florence: Sansoni, 1313–1330]) proposed a Spiritual interpretation as well, publishing in an appendix Peter John Olivi's then unedited commentary on Apocalypse 17 (from the Laurentian codex Conventi soppressi 397 in Florence). Noting that Dante might not have met Olivi during his brief stay in Florence, Tocco suggests the influence of, rather than a direct reliance on, Olivi's commentary on the *Divine Comedy*. Domenico Consoli's study of the canto ("Il canto XXXII del *Purgatorio*," in *Nuove letture dantesche*, vol. 5 (Florence: Le Monnier, 1972), 207–234) and Raoul Manselli's essay on a related canto ("*Paradiso* XII," in *Nuove letture dantesche*, vol. 6 [Florence: Le Monnier, 1973], 107–28) develop significantly this Spiritual-Franciscan reading. Also of note is Ronald Herzman's work on the presence of apocalyptic literature in Dante, of which we note here his "Dante and the Apocalypse," in *The Apocalypse in the Middle Ages*, ed. Richard Emmerson and Bernard McGinn (Ithaca, NY: Cornell University Press, 1992), 398–413. For alternative interpretative orientations, see Giovanni Fallani, "Il canto XXXII del "*Purgatorio*," in *Lectura Dantis Scaligera* (Florence: Le Monnier, 1965); Vittorio Rossi, *Il canto XXXIII del "Purgatorio"* (originally delivered at the Casa di Dante in Rome, 1921) (Turin: Societá editrice internazionale, 1965); Colin Hardie, "The Symbol of the Gryphon in *Purgatorio* XXIX, 108 and following Cantos," in *Centenary Essays on Dante, by members of the Oxford Dante Society* (Oxford: Clarendon Press, 1965), 103–131; and Lino Pertile, *La puttana, cit.*, 1998.

7. For a general orientation to the political issues and arguments regarding the principles and documentation of the Donation of Constantine, by which the converted emperor would have ceded to Pope Sylvester a ritualistic and worldly control over the Empire, see Bruno Nardi, "La 'Donatio Constantini' e Dante," in *Nel mondo di Dante* (Rome: Edizioni di Storia e Letteratura, 1944), 109–159; as well as Francesco Mazzoni's introductory essay, "Teoresi e prassi in Dante politico," in *Dante Alighieri: Monarchia e Epistole politiche* (Turin: ERI, 1966), ix–cxi. See also Joan Ferrante's *Political Vision of the Divine Comedy* (Princeton: Princeton University Press, 1984). Taking much of his argument from jurists of his own day, who were usually unfavorable to what they contended would have been the illegal depletion of the Empire's juridical power in Constantine's grant to Sylvester, already considered by many a document of questionable authenticity, Dante tackles the Donation from a moral-political and logical perspective in Book III, 10, of his treatise on the Monarchy *(Monarchia)*, written notably—according to P. G. Ricci—in Verona in 1317 (and in Bruno Nardi's view in 1308 [see Pasquini, "Dante e la sua prima fortuna, *cit.*, 609]). *Inferno* XIX, 115–117, represents the moral-poetic essence of Dante's attitude toward the insidious effects, rather than the motives or authenticity, of conceding worldly power and wealth to the papacy: "Ah, Constantine, what wickedness was born—/ and not from your conversion—from the dower / that you bestowed upon the first rich father!"

8. For an introduction to the historical figure and context of Joachim of Fiore, see Bernard McGinn, *The Calabrian Abbot* (New York: McMillan, 1985); Marjorie Reeves's *Joachim of Fiore and*

the Prophetic Future: A Medieval Study in Historcial Thinking (Stroud, UK: Sutton Publishing, 1999); and Stephen Wessley's *Joachim of Fiore and Monastic Reform* (New York: Lang, 1990). Of more interest here, however, is the system of Joachim's biblical exegesis in numerous authentic and partially authentic biblical commentaries, including his *Expositio in Apocalypsim,* his *Psalterium decem chordarum,* the *Liber Concordiae,* and probably the *Liber figurarum,* and its subsequent development and interpretation by mendicant orders, especially by Franciscans, such as Peter John Olivi and Matthew of Acquasparta. For synthetic treatments of Joachim's prophetic system and essential bibliography, see Morton W. Bloomfield's essays "Joachim of Flora: A Critical Survey of His Canon, Teachings, Sources, Biography, and Influence," *Traditio* 13 (1957): 249–311; and "Recent Scholarship on Joachim of Fiore and his Influence," in *Prophecy and Millenarianism: Essays in Honor of Marjorie Reeves* (Essex: Burnt Hill, 1980), 23–52; Delno West and Sandra Zimdars-Swartz, *Joachim of Fiore: A Study in Spiritual Perception and History* (Bloomington: Indiana University Press, 1983); and. E. Randolph Daniel, "Joachim of Fiore: Patterns of History in the Apocalypse," in *The Apocalypse in the Middle Ages,* ed. Richard Emmerson and Bernard McGinn (Ithaca, NY: Cornell University Press, 1992), 72–88. In the same volume, see also David Burr's introductory study to Franciscan and Dominican interpretations of the Apocalypse, "Mendicant Readings of the Apocalypse," 89–102.

9. Discussing Hugh of Digne's Joachimite leanings, Salimbene notes that Hugh had in his possession the complete works of Joachim in a deluxe script ("omnes libros abbatis Ioachim *de grossa littera* habebat" [*Cronica, cit.,* I, 339; my italics]) and that multiple copies of his opus were often coveted, and even hidden, by Franciscans ("omnes libros suos a Iachim editos in conventu Pisano sub custodia collocaverat" [*Cronica, cit.,* I, 339]).

10. As Marjorie Reeves has noted, in the Middle Ages the *Super Hieremiam* was usually associated with Joachim of Fiore (*Influence of Prophecy, cit.,* 76). Salimbene certainly believed as well that the *Super Hieremiam* was authentically Joachim's ("Habebant enim Expositionem Ioachim super Ieremiam et multos alios libros" [*Cronica, cit.,* i, 340]). For a study of the versions and growth of the *Super Hieremiam* from Joachim's brief commentary to the integration of Franciscan embellishments and addenda, see Robert Moynihan's "The Development of the 'Pseudo-Joachim' Commentary 'Super Hieremiam': New Manuscript Evidence," *Mélanges de l'Ecole française de Rome, Moyen Age* 98 (1986): 109–142. Moynihan's demonstration of the three strata of Joachimite commentary and subsequent Franciscan gloss in the manuscript tradition of the *Super Hieremiam* is especially useful in illustrating a common occurrence in the medieval transmission of texts whereby subsequent glosses are incorporated into the body of the original work, rendering virtually invisible the distinction between the original author's primary text and generations of additional notes and commentary.

11. Moynihan, *Development, cit.:* 109–110.

12. Moynihan, *Development, cit.:* 114.

13. It is worth noting both the historical context and the risk that Dante ran in citing Joachim's prophetic nature in *Paradiso* XII. Joachim's principal ideas on the Trinity were condemned at the Fourth Laterine Council of 1215 (see Manselli, "Spiritualismo," *cit.,* 167). His theories elaborated in the form of commentary by Gerard of Borgo San Donnino, in the latter's so-called *Eternal Gospel,* were censured along with Gerard's "little book" in 1254. Olivi's *Lectura super Apocalipsim,* written around 1297 and founded on a critique of many of Joachim's historical interpretations of the final book of the Bible, was posthumously condemned, and in the last years of Dante's life and well into the 1320s the Spirituals were deemed heretical (see David Burr's *Olivi's Peaceable Kingdom* [Philadelphia: University of Pennsylvania Press, 1993]). Nevertheless, many of Joachim's interpretations survived even among Franciscans well aware of the overly zealous Joachimite tendencies of others, especially his reading of Apocalypse 7:2, as a prophecy of San Francesco's role as the second Christ ("Angelus ascendens ab ortu solis, habens signum Dei vivi"), a view vehemently shared, for example, by Bonaventura.

14. See Manselli, "Spiritualismo," *cit.,* 172; and Manselli, "Dante e l'*Ecclesia Spiritualis,*" 120.

15. In *Monarchia* II, xi, 1, Dante follows Paul's assessment of the sin as Adam's ("peccatum Ade").

16. Moynihan, "Development," *cit.*, 116. The nine unbroken strings are the nine choirs of angels; see also Daniel, "Joachim of Fiore," *cit.*, 78–83.

17. For discussions of the traditional currents of commentary of the Apocalypse, see E. Ann Matter, "The Apocalypse in Early Medieval Exegesis," in *The Apocalypse in the Middle Ages*, ed. Richard Emmerson and Bernard McGinn (Ithaca, NY: Cornell University Press, 1992), 38–50; and, in brief, Raoul Manselli's "Apocalisse," in *Enciclopedia dantesca*, 6 vols. (Rome, 1970–1978).

18. Typical of the frescos of the Apocalypse is the cycle found, for example, in the baptistery in Padua.

19. The extensive bibliography on this symbolism in Dante constitutes a study and essay unto itself. Two diverse kinds of treatment of Dantean symbology have been, for example, Robert Kaske's encyclopedic approach in his *Medieval Christian Literary Imagery: A Guide to Interpretation* (Toronto-Buffalo: University of Toronto Press, 1988) and Pertile's more restricted orientation according to the poet's application of a limited range of symbols through the filter of a given biblical book (in his *La puttana e il gigante, cit.*, 1998, the whore and the giant through Dante's reading of the Song of Songs).

20. In several places in this canto, Dante does not understand what he sees and hears. He falls asleep and is distracted by Beatrice's presence ("I do not know if she said more than that,/because, by now, I had in sight one who/excluded all things other from my view" [*Purg.* XXXII, 91–93]). The canto is particularly marked by the extended metaphor of the painter painting from a model to describe his own act of falling asleep (*Purg.* XXXII, 64–69).

21. Cf. the hybridism of the snakes and thieves in *Inferno* XXV.

22. Armour, *Purgatorio* XXXII, 479.

23. The structure of Dante's thought is spelled out in *Monarchia* III, iii, 7, identifying Peter's, rather than Christ's, importance in the founding of the Mother Church ("Summus nanque Pontifex, domini nostri Iesu Cristi vicarius et Petri successor, cui non quicquid Cristo sed quicquid Petro debemus, zelo fortasse clavium necnon alii gregum cristianorum pastores, et alii quos credo zelo solo *matris Ecclesie* promoveri . . ." [my italics]).

24. Both uses of the symbolic keys contrast sharply to Dante's repeated invective against the ability of gold and silver to corrupt the moral mission of the Church.

25. Dante's *Epistle* XI poignantly opens with the first verse of the Lamentations of Jeremiah ("Quomodo sola sedet civitas plena populo! facta est quasi vidua domina gentium" [How alone sits the city once filled with people! she who ruled the people has become like a widow]). The letter's development of Dante's theories of *cupiditas* as the mother of impiety and injustice ("semper impietatis et iniquitatis est genitrix" [*Ep.* XI, 7]) embraces the principles of the Spirituals and incorporates his own economic plight in exile ("quoniam divitie mecum non sunt. Non ergo divitiarum, sed gratia Dei sum id quod sum" [*Ep.* XI, 5; "since I am without wealth; thus it is that not because of riches but by the grace of God that I am what I am"]). All citations of Dante's letters are from Ermenegildo Pistelli's edition in *Opere di Dante* (Florence: Societá Dantesca Italiana, 1921).

26. Dante's development of the definition of human happiness, lemmatically identified, as we shall see, first as *beatitudo* and in a second instance as *felicitas*, occurs most notably in the final chapter of Book III of the *Monarchia,* in which worldly happiness is constituted in relation to Earthly Paradise, and eternal happiness to Paradise proper ("Duos igitur fines providentia . . . homini proposuit intendendos: beatitudinem scilicet huius vite, que in operatione proprie virtutis consistit et per et per terrestrem paradisum figuratur; et beatitudinem vite ecterne, . . . que per paradisum celestem intelligi datur" [*Mon.* III, xv, 7]). The second instance brings us to the heart of Dante's moral code in which human happiness is vested in the well-defined, dual—but separate—roles and realms of the pope and the emperor: "Propter quod opus fuit homini duplici directivo secundum duplicem finem: scilicet summo Pontifice, qui secundum revelata humanum genus perduceret ad vitam ecternam, et Imperatore, qui secundum philosophica documenta genus humanum ad temporalem felicitatem dirigeret" (*Mon.* III, xv, 10). All citations from Dante's *Monarchia* are from Bruno Nardi's edition reprinted in *Dante Alighieri Opere minori,* vol. 3, bk. 1 (Milan-Naples: Ricciardi, 1996).

27. For the importance of the medieval notions of place and space, see Paul Zumthor's *La mesure du monde: représentation de l'espace au Moyen Age* (Paris: Ed. du Seuil, 1993); as well as Eugenio Ragú's entry "Terra" in the *Enciclopedia dantesca*.

28. Dante explains the profound significance of humanity's exile from Earthly Paradise in *Monarchia* III, iv, 14, in terms of humankind's absolute need for spiritual and worldly guidance and government as a condition entirely dependent on his loss of innocence: "si homo stetisset in statu innocentie in quo a Deo factus est, talibus directivis non indiguisset."

29. Even in the context of his own description of the four symbolic animals of the Evangelists in the procession in *Purgatorio* XXIX, 97–105, Dante moves declaredly between the representational systems of Ezechiel and John (Apocalypse).

30. See Ambrosius, *Expositio Evangelii secundum Lucam* (Turnhout: Brepols [Corpus Christianorum Series Latin, 14], 1957), 225. However, here again we find a certain historical confusion between the fox and the wolf. See Ortalli's reference to the fifth-century Eucherius of Leon's sententious "lupus diabolus vel haeretici" (*Lupi, cit.,* 84).

31. For the typologies and diffusion of pictorial representations of Apocalypse in the Middle Ages, see Peter K. Klein's "Introduction: The Apocalypse in Medieval Art," in *The Apocalypse in the Middle Ages*, ed. Richard Emmerson and Bernard McGinn (Ithaca, NY: Cornell University Press, 1992), 159–199, especially the sections on the "Apocalypse in Book Illumination" (171–196) and on the "Influence of Exegesis" (168–171).

32. For decades the dates of Dante's sojourn in Verona varied according to the acceptance of Dante's authorship of the "Treatise on Water and Earth" (*Quaestio de aqua et terra*), the subject of years of debate and bibliography, now convincingly resolved by Pasquini, "Dante e la sua prima fortuna," *cit.,* 605–609. In the late nineteenth century, when the debate was hotter, Corrado Ricci (*L'ultimo rifugio di Dante,* 3rd ed. [1891; repr., Ravenna: Longo, 1965]) argued against the authenticity of the *Quaestio* and in favor of 1317, rather than 1320, as the year when Dante moved from Verona to Ravenna. Dante's stay in Verona probably began in 1313. The manuscript of the New Testament in question belongs today to the Vatican Library, Latino 39, but was from the mid-thirteenth century until well after Dante's death in the possession of the Chapter Library in Verona. The illumination program for the Apocalypse is particularly noteworthy for its extensive development of the transformations in John's vision. For a placement of this manuscript among the "families" or typologies of Apocalyptic illustration and for a bibliography on illustrated manuscripts of the Apocalypse, see Richard K. Emmerson and Suzanne Lewis, "Census and Bibliography of Medieval Manuscripts Containing Apocalypse Illustrations, ca. 800–1500," parts 1 and 2 respectively, *Traditio* 40 (1984): 337–379; and 41 (1985): 367–409.

33. This scene of the Babylonian whore seated on the beast is depicted in the Veronese New Testament, *charta* 166r, the subject of a study now in preparation.

34. See Consoli, "Canto XXXII," *cit.,* 228; and Manselli, "Dante e l'*Ecclesia Spiritualis*," *cit.,* 125.

35. "You, shepherds, the Evangelist had noticed/when he saw her who sits upon the waters/and realized she fornicates with kings,/she who was born with seven heads and had / the power and support of the ten horns, as long as virtue was her husband's pleasure" (*Inf.* XIX, 106–111). It is worth noting here that Dante's earlier version of the monstrous, seven-headed beast in *Inferno* XIX is the whore of Apocalypse 17:2 fused with the beast on which she sits ("vidi mulierem sedentem super bestiam . . . habentem capita septem, et cornua decem" [Apoc. 17:3]). Dante's invective delivered to the corrupt popes (the shepherds of v. 106) suggests the beast's symbolism of the Antichrist common in some medieval glosses (see Daniel, "Joachim of Fiore," *cit.,* 83).

36. Pertile's proposal (*Puttana, cit.,* 214–217) for a sacrilegious and parodic use of the incipit of the Song of Songs ("Osculetur me osculo oris sui") concentrated in v. 153's "basciavansi insieme," which as Pertile reminds us recalls the whoring (*puttaneggiar*) of the meretrix of Bablyon in *Inferno* XIX, 106–108 ("cum qua fornicati sunt reges terrae" [Apoc. 17:2]), assesses the ironic sexual passion quickly converted into a violent beating. I would note, however, that the insistent syntactic combination of the reflexive verb (*basciavansi*) and the seemingly redundant adverb (*insieme*), followed by the reiterative *alcuna volta* (variously translated as "again and again" and "repeatedly"), underscore the squalid obscenity of the union between the Church and the

French monarchy and ironically recall Adam and Eve's discovery of sin in Genesis. But as we shall see, there is a distinct motive for the scene's shift from overt lust to violence.

37. See *Inferno* XXXI, 34–145. Approaching the City of Dis, in *Inferno* XXXI, 20, Dante believes he sees the towers of a city but is corrected by Virgil ("I'd have you know that they are not towers, but giants" [*Inf.* XXXI, 31]). As we recall, the giant Anteus conveys Dante and his guide into the ninth circle of Hell (*Inf.* XXXI, 139–145).

38. Cf., however, Consoli's stylistic observations in "Canto XXXII," *cit.*, 230.

39. See Pasquini, "Dante e la sua prima fortuna," *cit.*, 609.

40. See, for example, *Inferno* XIX, 100–105 ("And were it not that I am still prevented / by reverence for those exalted keys / that you held within the happy life / I'd utter words much heavier than these, / because your avarice afflicts the world / it tramples on the good, lifts up the wicked") and *Ep.* XI, 9: "Iam garrulus factus sum: vos me coegistis. Pudeat ergo tam ab infra, non de celo ut absolvat, argui vel moneri" (Now I have become the harsh censor in rebuking you, [but] you have left me no choice. Shame on you, that you should have to be accused and admonished by one so lowly as myself and not by heaven so that you can be absolved).

41. It is after the papacy's transfer to Avignon that the Spirituals, severe critics of this additional indicator of papal degeneration, become more and more the focus of curial investigations and repudiations of their heretical positions, resulting in the condemnation and posthumous excommunication of many Spiritual Franciscans between 1315 and 1330 (see Burr, *Olivi's Peaceable Kingdom, cit.*, 231–247).

CANTO XXXIII

Beatrice's Prophecy, Matilda's Name, and the Pilgrim's Renewal

DINO S. CERVIGNI

Closely connected with the allegorical scene described at the end of Canto XXXII, and consequently, also with Cantos XXX–XXXI, Canto XXXIII begins with the seven ladies' sad proclamation of the chariot's destruction (1–6). It then continues with Beatrice's prediction of an ultimate redemption (7–102) and concludes with Dante the Pilgrim's total transformation and renewal through the waters of the second Edenic river, Eunoe (103–145). Furthermore, in the last part of Canto XXXIII, Beatrice first instructs the lady whom Dante the Pilgrim encountered on entering the Earthly Paradise to complete the role assigned to her and then reveals her name, Matilda. Beatrice's proclamation of the future coming of a redeemer is prophetic and apocalyptic. By contrast, the Pilgrim's individual transformation takes place at a specific moment of his journey, shortly after Beatrice's prophecy. His renewal marks the conclusion of his purgatorial experience, linking it directly with his imminent ascent to Paradise. Beatrice's prophecy confirms, on the one hand, the presence of evil forces in human history, and, on the other, God's ultimate victory, as is shortly afterward evidenced by the Pilgrim's total transformation (91–99).

Immediately after the seven ladies' announcement at the canto's beginning, Beatrice's prophecy of a future redemption brings to completion the sacred drama enacted for the sake of Dante the Pilgrim. Preceded by the appearance of Matilda, who describes the structure of the Earthly Paradise (XXVIII), the allegorical pageantry (XXIX) culminates in the manifestation of Beatrice, who calls Dante by name and rebukes him harshly (XXX). Becoming fully aware of his past transgressions and verbally acknowledging them,

Dante the Pilgrim is purified of his past failings through the waters of the first Edenic river, Lethe, which deletes the memory of his past sins (XXXI). Thus purified, he witnesses the unraveling of the past and future history of humankind and the Church, represented, respectively, by the tree and the chariot (XXXII). The conclusion of this personal and historical drama occurs in the last canto of the second *cantica* with Beatrice's prophecy and Dante's inner renewal.

An Inherent Mysteriousness

Canto XXXIII dramatically opens with the alternate chanting of Psalm 78 by the two groups of the seven ladies (1–3), who thus comment on the sad vicissitudes of the Church symbolically reenacted in front of the Pilgrim (XXXII, 106–160).[1] Applied to the Church's past history and present condition as it symbolically unfolds in front of Dante the Pilgrim, the psalm proclaims the profanation of God's Temple, that is, the Church, by the hands of God's enemies (1–5). The psalm then invokes divine mercy on behalf of God's people (6–10a), concluding with an imprecation against their enemies (10b–12) and with a renewed statement of the people's steadfastness in praising God (13). Tears accompany the seven ladies' psalmody (1–3), which is followed intently by Beatrice, who, in her outward countenance of sorrow, resembles Mary standing at the foot of the cross (4–6). The Church's destruction and Christ's death are, therefore, the backdrop against which the Canto's opening is set.

After the ladies have concluded their song and become silent, Beatrice's outward aspect quickly turns a fiery color, because of her rage at the Church's corruption but also because of her desire for the Church's renewal.[2] Consequently, Beatrice, appropriating the prophetic words Christ pronounced shortly before his death and resurrection (John. 16:16) and addressing the seven ladies, announces her disappearance after a short time and her new appearance after another short while.[3] Biblical commentators interpret these words of Christ from John's Gospel as a prophecy of his imminent death and resurrection. In the biblical story, Christ's words remained obscure to his apostles even after Christ, who understood their desire to question him, did not answer their questions directly but went on to encourage them to keep faith in him (John 16:16–33). In fact, both biblical texts—Psalm 78 and John 16—are rather indeterminate, while the Gospel passage, which is shrouded in mystery, is understood fully by the apostles only after Christ's death, resurrection, and the Holy Spirit's descent (John 16:13). Consequently, the critics' attempt to ascribe a precise historical meaning to the two Dantean appropriations of the Bible (1, 10–12) cannot but fail in seeking to uncover their inherent mysteriousness. Unquestionably, the two biblical texts are employed as a commentary on the sad vicissitudes of the Church, symbolically represented by the chariot in the last part of Canto

XXXII, and also as a statement of the Church's future transformation consequent on a divine intervention.

The Condemnation

The mysteriousness hovering over the beginning of the canto is further emphasized by the ritualistic procession that Beatrice initiates immediately after she first speaks (15–17). The pageantry's procession described in Cantos
XXIX–XXXI moved first from east to west (XXIX, 10–12) and then from west to
east (XXXII, 15–17). By contrast, here the text offers no clues as to the direction
of Beatrice's brief ambling, the arguably symbolic meaning of her nine steps
(16–17), or the arrangement of the procession, in which Beatrice has the
seven ladies precede her and Dante, while Matilda and Statius follow her.[4]
The nine-step procession, nevertheless, creates a ritualistic and formal backdrop to the following scene, during which Beatrice, addressing Dante standing in front of her, prophesies. The brief verbal exchange between Beatrice
and the Pilgrim (19–29)—she inviting her disciple to inquire, and he pro-
claiming her full knowledge of his needs—further enhances Beatrice's
prophecy immediately afterward (30–78).

After urging her disciple to free himself of all fear and shame and to ask
freely and clearly (31–33), Beatrice makes an announcement preparatory to
her prophecy:

> Know that the vessel which the serpent broke
> was and is not; but he whose fault it is
> may rest assured—God's vengeance fears no hindrance.
>
> (34–36)

Referring to the chariot, which symbolizes the Church and was first broken by the dragon, then transformed into a monster, and finally dragged into
the forest by the giant (130–160), Beatrice forcefully states that the Church
was but no longer is. Thus, in a powerful condemnation of the present condition of the Church, she anticipates St. Peter's proclamation that his papal
seat on earth is presently vacant (Par. XXVII, 22–30).[7] Nevertheless, God's puni-
tive justice—Beatrice adds—will prevail (35–36), as St. Peter will also proclaim
in heaven (Par. XXVII, 61–63). Continuing to speak authoritatively, she adds
that, just as the Holy See will not remain vacant indefinitely, so the Empire
(symbolically represented by the eagle) will not always be without an heir:

> The eagle that has left its plumes within
> the chariot, which then became a monster
> and then a prey, will not forever be
> without an heir
>
> (37–39)

Beatrice's Prophecy

Thus, after condemning the corrupt condition of the Church and the vacancy of the emperor's seat, Beatrice makes her prophecy:

> for I can plainly see,
> and thus I tell it: stars already close
> at hand, which can't be blocked or checked, will bring
> a time in which, dispatched by God, a Five
> Hundred and Ten and Five will slay the whore
> together with the giant who sins with her.
>
> (40–45)

Like all the saints in heaven, who see the future in God, Beatrice is also empowered to know things to come with certainty. Thus she is now ready to foretell the future with assured knowledge. Her prophecy is nevertheless shrouded in mystery, according to the visionary and apocalyptic style characteristic of the vicissitudes of the Church, described at the end of the previous canto.

Countless readings have been proposed for Beatrice's enigma: the *cinque cento diece e cinque,* the Five Hundred and Ten and Five, in Roman numerals *DXV,* and thus, slightly anagrammatized, *DVX* or *dux,* leader, in Latin. Virtually all attempts to identify this divinely sent messenger can be grouped around three major readings: 1) The *DVX* is a religious leader (the so-called Guelf position): Christ, a pope (*Domini Christi Vicarius*), another religious leader, or, for some, Dante himself (*Dante Christi Vertagus* [= *Veltro,* the hound of *Inf.* I, 101]); 2) the *DVX* is a secular leader (the Ghibelline position): Henry VII, Cangrande della Scala, Uguccione della Faggiola, or another secular leader, who will help the Church return to its original mission; 3) finally, the *cinquecento diece e cinque* does not symbolize a person but a year or an epoch: the year 1315, which marks the five hundred and fifteenth anniversary of Charlemagne's crowning as emperor in Rome; or a renewed age, according to the prophecies of Joachim of Fiore; or another indeterminate epoch.[5]

The impossibility of finding a clear solution for this crux does not thwart understanding the nucleus of Beatrice's prophecy: someone sent by God will slay the whore and the giant, who, as Dante saw at the end of Canto XXXII, profaned and enslaved the chariot, that is, the Church. In brief, Beatrice predicts a time when the Church, through an intermediary sent by God, will be able to overcome all corrupting forces and thus return to its original purity. The vagueness of Beatrice's language not only fits its visionary and apocalyptic mode, but it also protects the Dantean text from ever failing to hit its mark, whatever it might be, while still emphasizing its main aim: namely, the Church's regeneration through a divine intervention.

Although Beatrice is aware that her prophecy is obscure, and consequently that Dante's intellect is unable to understand her words (46–48), she predicts that future events will solve the *enigma forte* ("this obstinate enigma," 50). She then urges Dante to take note of what he hears and to make it known to all those "who live the life that is a race to death" (52–54): a proclamation of the mission earlier entrusted to Dante by Beatrice herself in Canto XXXII, 103–105 and later reiterated by Cacciaguida in *Paradiso* XVII, 124–142.[6] Beatrice further enjoins Dante to bear in mind how the tree, which is holy to God and grows toward heaven in a manner inverse to that of earthly trees, was twice despoiled: an offense that she views as a blasphemy to God (55–78). Finally, aware once again that her words exceed Dante's present capacity of understanding, Beatrice urges him to keep her speaking, "se non scritto, almen dipinto," "if not inscribed, at least outlined" (77).

Overwhelmed by the words he has just heard and desirous to please Beatrice, Dante immediately answers that her words are as firmly etched in his mind as a seal is impressed in wax (79–81). And yet he cannot but express his dismay at her words' loftiness, which leaves his understanding struggling to comprehend them (82–84). Beatrice's rejoinder further confounds her interlocutor: his failure to understand her words proves the insufficiency of the doctrine he has pursued and of the distance of the human ways from the divine ways (85–90).[7] Commenting on Dante's forgetfulness of having strayed from her (91–93), she adds smilingly (94–99) that his oblivion is further proof of having gone awry and a confirmation that he has just drunk from the waters of the river Lethe (91–96). She concludes by saying that from that moment on her words will be as clear as befits his limited understanding (100–102).

Fullness of Light

The second part of Canto XXXIII (103–145: less than one third of the whole canto) leads to the culmination of the entire purgatorial journey, that is, the Pilgrim's total transformation. Once again the reader sees at work some of the most salient elements and most important characters of *Purgatorio*: Beatrice, who once again appears in her function as a nomenclator and as such calls Matilda by name; Matilda, who fulfills her assigned role by taking the Pilgrim and Statius to the river Eunoe; Statius, who as a converted pagan and a redeemed Christian, holds the promise of salvation, purification, and final glorification for all believers; the river Eunoe, which brings about Dante's final renewal; and finally the arboreal metaphors, through which the Poet portrays the Pilgrim's new condition.

Lines 103–105 indicate the time of day—noon, with its fullness of light—at which Beatrice's prophecy has just taken place and at which Dante is about to complete his inner transformation, thus becoming ready to ascend to heaven with Beatrice. The same time of day, with a reference to the sun's position, is again indicated in *Paradise* I, 43–48, just before the heavenly ascent begins. The Pilgrim, therefore, who has begun the first phase of his journey, his descent into Hell, toward dusk (*Inf.* II, 1–3), now completes his purification and renewal, and will shortly ascend into heaven, when the sun is at its brightest. In fact, according to what we read in the *Convivio,* "No object of sense in the whole universe is more worthy of becoming the symbol of God than the sun" (*CV* 3:12.7), which in the poem time and again symbolizes divine guidance (*Purg.* XIII, 16–21; 22:61). Accordingly, Dante the Pilgrim enters the Earthly Paradise early in the morning (XXVIII, 3), at about the same time when Adam was created in Eden (*Par.* XXVI, 139–142). The Pilgrim also completes his purification and prepares to ascend to heaven at the approximate time when Adam was expelled from Eden (*Par.* XXVI, 141–42). The Pilgrim's ascent is also patterned after that of Christ who, according to Dante, died at noon (*Inf.* XXI, 112–114; *Convivio* 4:23.10–11) and, according to some ancient beliefs (Guéranger, *Paschal Time,* vol. 3:152), also ascended into heaven at noon.

Shortly after Beatrice speaks, the seven ladies stop at the edge of the forest, in front of a spring from which a stream issues forth that immediately divides into two rivers (106–114). Having finally learned how to inquire, Dante asks, addressing Beatrice:

> "O light, o glory of the human race,
> what water is this, flowing from one source
> and then becoming distant from itself?"
>
> (115–117)[8]

Calling her by name, Beatrice defers the answer to Matilda (118–119), who is here called for the first and only time and who answers that she has already instructed Dante about the Earthly Paradise and thus about the function of the two rivers (120–123). Excusing Dante's oblivion, Beatrice suggests that the Pilgrim's forgetfulness might have been caused by some greater care overwhelming his memory.

Matilda's Task

In calling almost nonchalantly the "fair lady, Matilda," by name, Beatrice has created an arguably insolvable crux. However, the critics' inability to identify Matilda with any historical person and her name's mysteriousness should not foil the reader's proper understanding of her function, which the Pilgrim has come to know and experience since he first caught a glimpse of her (*Purg.* XXVIII, 40). Matilda's function, in fact, becomes clear to Dante and to the reader when she finally carries out her last task aimed at purifying Dante and Statius, in accordance with Beatrice's urging:

> But see Eunoe as it flows from there:
> lead him to it and, as you're used to doing,
> revive the power that is faint in him.
>
> (127–129)

Matilda's usual and principal task, therefore, is to take the souls through the river Lethe, as she does for the Pilgrim, but arguably also for Statius (*Purg.* XXXI, 91–96), and then to lead the souls to the river Eunoe, as she does for both wayfarers (127–135). In addressing her, Beatrice states that Matilda performs this twofold but inseparable (*Purg.* XXVIII, 131–132) task not for a limited time but, rather, *habitually* ("'as you're used to doing,'" 128), and thus, arguably, for as long as Mount Purgatory has been accessible to the souls after Christ's Redemption. If one interprets Beatrice's words "come tu se' usa" ("as you're used to doing") in light of this suggestion, any attempt to identify Matilda with such historical figures as Matilda of Canossa (1046–1115) or the German nuns Mathilde of Hackenborn and Mathilde of Magdeburg must be shelved. If Matilda has been performing her twofold task since the time of Christ's Redemption, she is by necessity the soul who first ascended Mount Purgatory and first drank from the waters of the two Edenic rivers. Arguably, therefore, the first soul ever to be purified now carries out for Dante and Statius the task she was assigned to perform for all the souls who climb Mount Purgatory and reach the Earthly Paradise.

According to this suggestion, therefore, Matilda has a name because Dante the Poet does not present her as a symbol but rather as a real person. Her historical identity remains nevertheless shrouded in mystery so as not to deflect the readers' attention from what she stands for in the poem's Earthly Paradise. In all she does and says since the Pilgrim first sees her (*Purg.* XXVIII), she evinces the essential characteristics of both the active and the contemplative life, which are necessary for the soul's salvation. She thus represents the virtues of Leah and Rachel, as well as those of Martha and Mary, according to the Fathers' interpretation of the two Old Testament and New Testament figures and Dante's reading (*Purg.* XXVII, 94–108; *Convivio* 4:17.10). Since Matilda has attained Mount Purgatory after Christ's Redemption, she cannot portray prelapsarian innocence, which was lost once and for all by Adam and Eve (*Purg.* XXVIII, 94–96; 142; XXXII, 31–32; *Par.* XXVI, 139–142). Rather, she personifies regained innocence; namely, the innocence that, after being lost, can only be reacquired through Christ according to a measure that far exceeds the original innocence lost forever by humankind's primogenitors (Rom. 5:18–21).[9]

The Rivers Transform

As the purgatorial drama quickly comes to a close, for the last time in this *cantica* Dante the poet addresses the reader:

> If, reader, I had ampler space in which
> to write, I'd sing—though incompletely—that
> sweet draught for which my thirst was limitless;

> but since all of the pages pre-disposed
> for this, the second canticle, are full,
> the curb of art will not let me continue.
>
> (136–141)

In this *cantica* the reader is first addressed directly in Canto VIII, 19–21, when Dante the Poet challenges him to comprehend the truth by piercing through the story's veil. Here, through the rhetorical figure of *praeteritio* (or passing over), Dante the Poet emphasizes the transforming power of the river's water by avowing the impossibility of describing its sweetness, namely, the river's supernatural and transforming effects. At the same time, by attributing his failure to a material and artistic cause (space limitation and art's constraint, respectively), Dante the Poet implicitly proclaims having fully discharged the mission Beatrice had entrusted to Dante the Pilgrim: announcing Beatrice's words to the living (52–54; 76–78).

Having thus carried out through his poetry—no matter how limited—his mission as a prophet, Dante the Poet can finally describe the newly achieved transformation of the Pilgrim:

> From that most holy wave I now returned
> to Beatrice; remade, as new trees are
> renewed when they bring forth new boughs, I was
> pure and prepared to climb unto the stars.
>
> (142–145)

A wholly Dantean creation, the river Eunoe completes the transformation of the first Edenic river, Lethe, just as Matilda has explained (*Purg.* XXVIII, 127–129). Accordingly, after the Lethean waters have deleted the memory of all past sins, Eunoe fulfills the soul's renewal by bringing back to memory all good deeds, reviving the soul's faint *virtù* (129), and thus re-creating the creature anew. Thus remade, the Pilgrim's soul is likened to new trees being renewed after a harsh winter with the coming of spring (142–145).

The function of the two rivers can best be understood by keeping in mind some theological considerations. Theology attributes to the sacrament of Penance simultaneous effects enacted on the penitent's soul: namely, the destruction of sin, the infusion of grace, and the revival of the soul's virtues and merits. Dante's poetry renders the sacrament's concomitant effects by means of two poetically distinct but closely interrelated moments: the first river deletes the soul's sinfulness, while the second brings back to life the good that the soul previously owned and later lost because of sin. The effects of the two rivers on the soul are ultimately likened to a new creation; namely, the death of the old creature consequent upon the birth of the new creature.

Forgetfulness

Since Eunoe returns to the soul the memory of the lost good, the text im-plies that the soul has previously lost that good: namely, all the good deeds and virtues previously practiced before turning away from God. The Bible describes such a loss by means of a metaphor. When the creatures forget God by sinning, God forgets them and their past good deeds and virtues, which thus become, as it were, dead (Ezek. 33:13). Furthermore, by forget-ting God, the creatures are also condemned not only to oblivion but also to death (Ezek. 18:24). In contrast, when the creatures repent and do penance for their sins, God will forget the sinners' past injustices (Ezek. 18:21–23). Dante renders poetically this biblical and theological notion by means of the ritual enacted by the souls through the river Lethe, which causes them to forget their sinfulness, just as God forgets their injustices when they repent. When the souls repent, however, what happens to the past good deeds and virtues that died when they sinned? Because of God's mercy, they are brought back to life when the soul drinks from the waters of the second Edenic river, Eunoe. In brief, what scholastic theology attributes to the sacrament of Penance—the simultaneous destruction of sin, infusion of grace, and revival of the soul's virtues and merits—Dante's *Purgatorio* ren-ders in two poetically distinct but closely interrelated moments: Lethe deletes the soul's sinfulness, while Eunoe gives back to the soul the good the soul had previously owned and then lost because of sin. Consequently, Dante the Pilgrim, after reenacting the twofold ritual of drinking from the two Edenic rivers, is made anew and becomes, as it were, a new creature.

Dante's Earthly Paradise, therefore, not only restates poetically the pres-ence of evil in the history of humankind, as evidenced in the apocalyptic scene described in the second half of Canto XXXII and Beatrice's prophecy in Canto XXXIII. More important, it also proclaims that salvation, by overcoming evil, reenacts an even greater form of creation (Rom. 5:18–21; Ricoeur, 227). Accordingly, the outcome of the battle that God, the just one, will carry out against evil at the end of time is already announced and guaranteed in the sal-vation, purification, and re-creation of Dante and Statius. Thus the meaning of the silent presence of Statius in the Earthly Paradise becomes clear. A mys-teriously converted and saved pagan who has now completed his purgatorial journey and is ready to ascend to heaven, Statius is the silent guarantor that God's privilege bestowed on the Pilgrim will remain efficacious (as far as God is concerned) in bringing about Dante's, and humankind's, eternal salvation.

Springtime of Renewal

Thus, on the mountaintop, after drinking the water first of the river Lethe (*Purg.* XXXI, 91–96) and then of the river Eunoe, the Pilgrim is made anew, in a clear reference to God's creation of humankind. Dante's renewal constitutes

a spiritual creation. He has, in fact, reacquired not just the original innocence, which Adam and Eve lost forever for themselves and all their descendants, but a renewed condition of grace, which exceeds humankind's
original state, since Dante, like all Christians, attains it through Christ's Redemption (Rom. 5:12–21). Dante the Pilgrim has thus totally overcome the
condition of neither death nor life into which he plunged in Hell's nether-
most pit when he saw Lucifer (*Inf.* XXXIV, 22–27).

Dante the Poet renders the Pilgrim's transformation and re-creation
through arboreal metaphors of springtime renewal. Thus at the end of the
cantica these metaphors (143–144) explain and bring to closure the function
of the reed with which the Pilgrim was girt at the beginning of his purgatorial journey (*Purg.* I, 94–95; 100–105; 133–136). As the symbol of humility,
penance, and renewal, the reed, which is reborn as it is cut, fully discloses its
spiritual meaning when Dante's transformation is described through the
metaphor of the renewed tree.

Unquestionably, the character's sloughing off of the old man and his consequent renewal mark a true ending and signal a true beginning in the story,
respectively. Thus the last four lines of Canto XXXIII constitute a closure,
since the old man of *Inferno* I, 1–3, no longer exists and has been completely
transformed and renewed. At the same time *Purgatorio's* ending marks a
new commencement, since the Pilgrim, thus renewed and remade, is now
ready to begin another journey. To narrate such a voyage of the character's
renewed existence and extraordinary experience in the *Comedy's* final *cantica, Paradise,* the poet is once again challenged to mold an equally transformed and renewed poetry (*Par.* I, 1–36).

NOTES

1. The canto's opening in Latin is a quotation of a biblical text, which constitutes the only
biblical beginning in the second *cantica* and, indeed, in the whole *Comedy* (but see also *Inf.*
XXXIV, 1 and *Par.* VII, 1–3). This Psalm is numbered 78 in the Septuagint and the Vulgate and 79
in the Hebrew Bible. Psalm 78 was written at a time when Jerusalem was in ruins and the
Temple was profaned. In Church liturgy, this Psalm is recited at matins of Friday and during
times of war; it also constitutes the prayer of the just, primarily martyrs (*La Sainte Bible* 321n,
ed. Pirot).

2. In changing the color of her face, Beatrice anticipates the discoloring of St. Peter's face as
he readies to proclaim his papal seat to be empty (*Par.* XXVII, 19–21).

3. Using Christ's words, Beatrice most likely announces not a specific event—the papal seat's
transfer to Avignon and its return to Rome shortly afterward, as some critics suggest—but rather
the Church's moral decadence and the firm conviction of its renewal. Beatrice's words, therefore, are echoed in St. Peter's proclamation of his seat being empty (*Par.* XXVII, 19–27) and of an
imminent divine intervention (*Par.* XXVII, 40–66, especially 61–63).

4. Dante's style imitates the enigmatic indication of a person through numbers as exemplified in a biblical passage often quoted: "Qui habet intellectum, computet numerum bestiae. Numerus enin hominis est: et numerus eius sexcenti sexaginta sex" 'Let any one who understands
calculate the number of the beast. In fact the number of the man is six-hundred sixty-six' [vari-
ant: 616] (Rev. 13:18). In both Greek and Latin, according to gematry, each letter of the alphabet
has a numeric value, which produces the following readings: 666 = Caesar-Nero (according to

the letters' value in Hebrew); 616=Caesar-Christ (according to the letters' value in Greek) (*La Sainte Bible . . . de Jérusalem* 1631n. a; also *La Sainte Bible,* ed. Pirot, vol. 12:635n).

The Calabrese monk Joachim of Fiore (ca. 1135–1202), a biblical commentator and a philosopher of history, was highly influential in the later Middle Ages. He argued that, after the age of the Father (Old Testament) and of the Son (New Testament until about 1260), a new age was to begin, that of the Holy Spirit, to be characterized by love, perfection, and freedom. Dante places Joachim in the heaven of the Sun, among the theologians, and has St. Bonaventure proclaim him to be endowed with prophetic spirit (*Par.* XII, 140–141).

5. For a summary description of all these readings see *Enciclopedia dantesca;* further bibliography can be found in *La divina commedia,* ed. Mazzoni; for a reading of the *Cinque cento diece e cinque* as a figure of the cross, and thus of Christ, see Mastrobuono; on the DVX as Christ see Kaske. Further proposals, variations of previous readings, keep appearing (Dozon, 593–595).

6. Commentators point out the biblical echo in Beatrice's words: Revelation 1:11: "Quod vides, scribe in libro" ("What you see, write in the book"); also in Revelation 1:19; 21:5. Dante's mission to recount what he hears and sees is reiterated also by St. Peter, who arguably announces a secular savior of the Church (*Par.* XXVII, 61–63).

7. Most Trecento and Quattrocento commentaries propose that the spring from which the two Dantean rivers of the Earthly Paradise originate symbolize God or divine grace (Buti 2:822–823; Lana 284; Benvenuto 4:179; Landino; etc.), as the text itself suggests (*Purg.* XXVIII, 121–126).

8. The rivers of the Dantean Eden originate from one source, in full accord with the biblical text, which says: "One river sprang forth" (Gen. 2:10). The difference in the number of rivers (four in the Bible, and two in Dante) springing from that one source can be explained by a different exegesis of the biblical text; namely, that the division into four rivers took place outside the Earthly Paradise, as Lombardi, Andreoli, and then Nardi argued, in agreement with some Fathers and biblical exegetes (Cervigni, "The Eunoé" 61–63).

9. The reed, which serves a specific function in the Pilgrim's purgatorial journey (*Purg.* I, 94–105; 130–136) and then assumes a purely spiritual role at the end of the cantica, contrasts with the cord, which (unbeknownst to the reader) girds the Pilgrim throughout his descent of Upper and Middle Hell and then ambiguously disappears in the abyss of Malebolge (*Inf.* XVI, 106–136).

BIBLIOGRAPHY

Alighieri, Dante. *La divina commedia di Dante Alighieri col comento di Raffaele Andreoli.* 2d rev. ed. Naples: Stamperia Nazionale, 1863.

———. *La divina commedia di Dante Alighieri nuovamente comentata, spiegata e difesa da F. B. L[ombardi], M.C.* 3 vols. Rome: A. Fulgoni, 1791.

———. *La divina commedia. Purgatorio.* Com. T. Casini, S. A. Barbi, and A. Momigliano. Ed. Francesco Mazzoni. Florence: Sansoni, 1977.

Angela da Foligno. *Il libro della beata Angela da Foligno.* Ed. Ludger Their and Abele Calufetti. Spicilegium Bonaventurianum 25. Grottaferrata, Rome: Editiones Collegii S. Bonaventurae ad Claras Aquas, 1985.

Benvenuto. *Benevenuti de Rambaldis de Imola comentum super Dantis Aldigherij Comoediam, nunc primum integre in lucem editum sumptibus Guilielmi Warren Vernon, curante Iacopo Philippo Lacaita.* 5 vols. Florence: Barbèra, 1887.

Buti. *Commento di Francesco da Buti sopra la Divina Commedia di Dante Alighieri pubblicato per cura di Crescentino Giannini.* 3 vols. Pisa: Nistri, 1858–1862.

Cervigni, Dino S. "Beatrice's Act of Naming." *Lectura Dantis: A Forum for Dante Research and Interpretation* 8 (spring 1991): 85–99.

———. "Dante's Lucifer: The Denial of the Word." *Lectura Dantis: A Forum for Dante Research and Interpretation* 3 (1988): 51–62.

———. "The Eunoè or the Recovery of the Lost Good." In *Lectura Dantis Newberriana.* Ed. Paolo Cherchi and Antonio C. Mastrobuono. Evanston: Northwestern University Press, 1990. 2:175–198.

————. "The Muted Self-Referentiality of Dante's Lucifer." *Dante Studies* 107 (1989): 45–74.

Dozon, Marthe. *Mythe et symbole dans la Divine Comédie.* Biblioteca dell'Archivum Romanicum, ser. 1, vol. 233. Florence: Olschki, 1991.

Forti, Fiorenzo. "Matelda." *Enciclopedia dantesca,* 6 vols. Rome, 1970–1978.

Guéranger, Prosper. *The Liturgical Year.* Trans. of L'Année liturgique. 15 vols. London: Burns Oates and Washbourne, 1921–1927.

Kaske, R. E. "Dante's 'DVX' and 'Veltro.'" *Traditio* 17 (1961): 185–264.

Lana. *Comedia di Dante degli Allagherii col commento di Jacopo di Giovanni dalla Lana bolognese a cura di Luciano Scarabelli.* Milan: C. Moretti, 1885.

Landino. *Dante con l'espositioni di Christoforo Landino et d'Alessandro Vellutello. Sopra la sua Commedia dell'Inferno, del Purgatorio, e del Paradiso, con tavole, argomenti, e allegorie; e riformato, riveduto, e ridotto alla sua vera lettura, per Francesco Sansovino fiorentino.* Venice: Gio. Battista e Gio. Bernardo Sessa, 1596.

Mastrobuono, Antonio C. "Purgatorio XXXIII." In *Dante's Divine Comedy: Introductory Readings,* vol. 2. Purgatorio. Lectura Dantis: A Forum for Dante Research and Interpretation 12, supplement (1993): 491–500.

Mazzamuto, Pietro. "Cinquecento diece e cinque." In *Enciclopedia dantesca.*

Nardi, Bruno. "Intorno al sito del 'Purgatorio' e al mito dantesco dell'Eden." *Il giornale dantesco* 25 (1922): 289–300.

Pertile, Lino. *Il gigante e la puttana.* Ravenna: Longo, 1998.

Ricoeur, Paul. *The Symbolism of Evil.* Trans. Emerson Buchanan. Boston: Beacon Press, 1967.

La Sainte Bible. Texte latin et traduction française d'après les textes originaux avec un commentaire exégétique et théologique. Ed. Louis Pirot. 12 vols. Paris: Letouzey et Ané, 1937–1938.

La Sainte Bible. Traduite en français sous la direction de l'école biblique de Jérusalem. Paris: Les Éditions du Cerf, 1956.

Singleton, Charles S. *Journey to Beatrice.* Baltimore: Johns Hopkins University Press, 1958.

CONTRIBUTORS

Peter Armour died in June 2002 at the age of sixty-one. A graduate of Manchester University in England, he taught at the University of Leicester and at London's Bedford College and subsequently at Royal Holloway. An editor at the periodical *Italian Studies,* he was also one of its most active reviewers, especially of new books on Dante and Michelangelo. His articles on Dante are too numerous to mention. His books include *The Door of Purgatory: A Study of Multiple Symbolism in Dante's Purgatory* (1983) and *Dante's Griffin and the History of the World: A Study of the Earthly Paradise (Purgatorio, Cantos XXIX–XXXIII)* (1989).

Glauco Cambon taught at the University of Michigan, at Indiana University, at Rutgers University, and at the University of Connecticut, where his papers are kept. He died in North Windham, Connecticut, at the age of sixty-seven, in March 1988. A translator and a comparatist, he published an acclaimed Italian translation of William Faulkner's *Absalom, Absalom!* in 1954. Educated in Italy, Cambon published many books in English, including *The Inclusive Flame: Studies in Modern American Poetry* (1963), *Luigi Pirandello: A Collection of Critical Essays* (1967), and *Dante's Craft: Studies in Style and Language* (1969). Several of his books were published by the Princeton University Press: *Foscolo, Poet of Exile* (1980), *Eugenio Montale's Poetry: A Dream in Reason's Presence* (1982), and *Michelangelo's Poetry: Fury of Form* (1985). He coedited volumes 114 and 128 of the *Dictionary of Literary Biography: Twentieth-Century Italian Poets, First Series* (1992) and *Second Series* (1993). He was commemorated in the homage volume edited by

Joseph Francese, *The Craft and the Fury: Essays in Memory of Glauco Cambon* (2000).

Jo Ann Cavallo, Associate Professor of Italian at Columbia University, is the author of Boiardo's *Orlando Innamorato: An Ethics of Desire* (1993) and *The Romance Epics of Boiardo, Ariosto, and Tasso: From Public Duty to Private Pleasure* (2004) and is coeditor of *Fortune and Romance: Boiardo in America* (1998).

Dino S. Cervigni is Professor of Romance Languages and Comparative Literature at the University of North Carolina at Chapel Hill. His main interests are the Middle Ages and the Renaissance. Cervigni has written about Dante, Petrarch, mystical writings, and autobiography. The founder and editor of the annual monograph *Annali d'italianistica* and the series *Studi e Testi*, he has edited more than thirty volumes. A National Endowment for the Humanities fellowship recipient, Cervigni has served as president of the American Association for Italian Studies (AAIS) for two terms.

Hermann Gmelin (1900–1958) has been called "the most significant Dante scholar of twentieth-century Germany" (Robert Durling). He was the author of *Dante Alighieri: die Goettliche Komoedie* (1954–1957), a three-volume commentary on Dante. He was also the author of *Die Französische Zyklenroman de Gegewart, 1900–1945* (1950).

Robert Hollander, Professor Emeritus at Princeton University, is the author of numerous books and articles on Dante and Boccaccio. He and his wife, Jean, are finishing their translation of *Paradiso,* which will join their translations of the first two cantiche (2000 and 2003). In 1988 Hollander was awarded the Gold Medal of the City of Florence; in 1997 he was made an Honorary Citizen of Certaldo. He continues to direct the Dartmouth Dante Project and the Princeton Dante Project.

Rachel Jacoff is the Margaret Deffenbaugh and LeRoy Carlson Chair in Comparative Literature and Italian Studies at Wellesley College. She is the editor of the *Cambridge Companion to Dante* (1993) and coeditor of *The Poets' Dante and The Poetry of Allusion: Virgil and Ovid in Dante's "Commedia"* (1991). Jacoff is also the author of numerous articles on Dante.

János Kelemen was born in Kassa, Hungary, in 1943. In 1984 he became full professor of philosophy at the University ELTE in Budapest; in 1986 he became head of the Department of Philosophy there. From 1990 to 1995 Kelemen was director of the Hungarian Academy in Rome, and from 1995 to 1997 he was head of the Department of Italian literature of the University of Szeged, Hungary. Kelemen is the author of more than fifteen books, published in Hungary and Italy, on different philosophical problems and Italian literary history (such as linguistic philosophy, G. A. Moore, Benedetto Croce, and Dante). In 1994 he was elected a corresponding member of the Hungarian Academy of Sciences.

Victoria Kirkham is Professor of Romance Languages at the University of Pennsylvania. She is the co-author of *Diana's Hunt, Caccia di Diana:*

Boccaccio's First Fiction (1991) and the author of *The Sign of Reason in Boccaccio's Fiction* (1993) and of *Fabulous Vernacular: Boccaccio's Filocolo and the Art of Medieval Fiction*, which won the Modern Language Association of America's Aldo and Jeanne Scaglione Publication Award for a Manuscript in Italian Literary Studies for the year 2000; and *Laura Battiferra and Her Literary Circle* (2006). She has written articles on *The Divine Comedy*, Boccaccio, Italian cinema, and the poet Laura Battiferra degli Ammannati (1523–1589). Kirkham is the winner of a Guggenheim Fellowship (2005–2006) for her book in progress, *Creative Partners: The Marriage of Laura Battiferra and Bartolomeo Ammannati*.

Robin Kirkpatrick is Professor of Italian and English Literatures at Cambridge University. He has published three books on Dante, along with two on the Renaissance, and has recently completed a verse translation of the *Commedia*, the first volume of which, with commentaries, appeared in 2006. His poetry includes *Prologues and Palinodes* (2000).

Christopher Kleinhenz is the Carol Mason Kirk Professor of Italian at the University of Wisconsin-Madison, where he recently received the Chancellor's Award for Excellence in Teaching and the Hilldale Award in Arts and Humanities. He has served as President of the American Association of Teachers of Italian, the American Boccaccio Association, and the Medieval Association of the Midwest and as editor of *Dante Studies*. His publications include *The Early Italian Sonnet: The First Century (1220–1321)* (1991) and *Medieval Italy: An Encyclopedia* (2004), as well as a translation of *The Fiore and the Detto d'Amore* (2000).

Ronald L. Martinez is Professor of Italian Studies at Brown University. In addition to Dante and Trecento studies, he has teaching and research interests in Italian Renaissance cultural history. He is currently completing, in collaboration with Robert M. Durling, an edition with translation and commentary of Dante's *Paradiso*.

Marilyn Migiel is Professor of Romance Studies at Cornell University and the author of *A Rhetoric of the "Decameron"* (2003), winner of the MLA's Howard Marraro Prize for outstanding scholarship in Italian, and of *Gender and Genealogy in Tasso's 'Gerusalemme Liberata'* (1993). Migiel is coeditor, with Juliana Schiesari, of *Refiguring Woman: Perspectives on Gender and the Italian Renaissance* (1991). Her current research focuses on ethical questions in the *Decameron*.

Vincent Moleta left his position as Professor of Italian and set up his own Institute at Fontecolombo in 2000, after twenty-seven years at the University of Western Australia. Among his numerous publications he is most noted for *Guinizzelli in Dante* (1980), *Gloriosa donna de la mente: A Commentary on the Vita Nuova* (1994), and *Umberto Saba, Poetry and Prose* (2004).

Anthony Oldcorn was born in the North of England and emigrated to the United States in his early twenties, after graduating from Oxford. He holds advanced degrees from the University of Virginia and Harvard and has taught at several East Coast colleges and universities, most recently, for thirty-odd years, at Brown, where he was chair of Italian Studies. Oldcorn is currently teaching in Italy.

Emilio Pasquini was born in Padua in 1935. Since 1975 he has been full professor of Italian literature in the Faculty of Literature and Philosophy at the University of Bologna. In 1986 he became President of the Commission on Language Texts. A philologist and an expert, above all, on the first three centuries of Italian literature as well as on the nineteenth century, he has over 250 publications to his name, among which are especially noteworthy his critical edition of the *Rime* of Saviozzo (1965), his edition of Leopardi's *Appuntie e recordi* (2000), his commentary on Dante's *Divine Comedy* (1982–1986), as well as on the Ricordi (Memoirs) of Guicciardini, and these three volumes: *Le botteghe della poesia* (1991), *Ottocento letterario* (2001), and *Dante e le figure del vero* (2001).

Lino Pertile, Carl A. Pescosolido Professor of Romance Languages and Literatures at Harvard, is the coeditor, with Peter Brand, of *The Cambridge History of Italian Literature* (rev. ed., 1999). He recently published *La puttana e il gigante. Dal Cantico dei Cantici al Paradiso Terrestre di Dante* (1998) and *La punta del disio. Semantica del desiderio nella Commedia* (2005).

Maurizio Perugi, a student of Gianfranco Contini, is currently Professor of Romance Philology at the University of Geneva. His publications include critical editions of the *Sermo of Ramon Muntaner* (1975), of the poetical works of Arnaut Daniel (1978), and of the anonymous Vie de Saint Alexis (2000). His *Trovatori a Valchiusa. Un frammento della cultura provenzale di Petrarca* (1985) concerns the Provençal element in Petrarch's verse, while the essays collected in his *Saggi di lingusitica trobadorica* (1995) confront problems of linguistic exegesis in the works of the major troubadour poets. Perugi is also the author of a seminal commentary on the selected poetry and prose of the nineteenth-century poet Giovanni Pascoli (1980).

Enzo Quaglio is one of the leading interpreters of early Italian literature. An accomplished philologist and textual editor as well as a perceptive critic, he edited Boccaccio's minor works for Vittore Branca's standard *Tutte le opera de Giovanni Boccaccio* (1964). In the same year he updated the classic Busnelli and Vanelli edition of Dante's *Convivio* for Le Monnier of Florence. Quaglio is a scholar's scholar, and the bulk of his publications has appeared in specialized journals. His critical studies on Boccaccio, *Scienza e mito nel Boccaccio* (1967), and on Petrarch, *Al di la' di Francesco e di Laura* (1973), are, however, indispensable. He collaborated with Emilio Pasquini and Nicolo' Moneo on the two volumes of the *Letteratura Italiana Laterza* dealing with the thirteenth century: *Il Duecento: dalle origini a Dante* (1970–1980) and, subsequently, with Emilio Pasquini on a three-volume commentary to the three canticles of Dante's *Commedia* (1988).

Ricardo J. Quinones is Professor Emeritus of Literature at Claremont McKenna College in California. A former director of the Gould Center for Humanistic Studies, Quinones received his doctorate from Harvard in 1963. His publications include *The Renaissance Discovery of Time* (1972), *Dante Alighieri* (repr., 1998), *Mapping Literary Modernism: Time and Development* (1985), *The Changes of Cain: Violence and the Lost Brother in Cain and Abel Literature* (1991), and *Foundation Sacrifice in Dante's "Commedia"* (1994).

Ezio Raimondi, at eighty-two, is the dean of Italian literary critics. Emeritus Professor at the University of Bologna, he is also President of the Instituto dei beni Culturali for the Emilia-Romagna region. Raimondi is frequently invited to some of the most prestigious American universities (Johns Hopkins, the CUNY Graduate Center, UC Berkeley, and UCLA), and his critical output, informed by a firsthand acquaintance with the latest developments in literary theory in English, French, and German, is as acute as it is prolific: it includes more than forty books dealing with philology, textual criticism, and literary history and theory from Dante to the twentieth century. His major reflections and insights have been conveniently anthologized by Andrea Battistini in three volumes, under the title *I sentieri del lettore:* 1. *Da Dante a Tasso,* 2. *Dal Seicento all'Ottocento,* and 3. *Il Novecento: storia e teoria della letteratura* (1993–1994).

Rinaldina Russell is Professor of European Languages and Literatures Emerita at the City University of New York, Queens College. She has contributed articles, entries, and reviews to encyclopedias and to academic journals in Italy and the United States. She is also the author of two books on medieval and Renaissance poetry: *Tre versanti della poesia stilnovistica* (1973) and *Generi poetici medievali* (1982). Among her more recent works are *Sister Maria Celeste's Letters to Her Father, Galileo* (2001) and the translation of Margherita Sarrocchi's *Scanderbeide* (2006).

Arielle Saiber, Associate Professor of Italian at Bowdoin College, is the author of *Giordano Bruno and the Geometry of Language* (2005) and coeditor of *Images of Quattrocento Florence: Selected Writings in Literature, History, and Art* (2000). She has published articles on Renaissance literature and mathematics, on genre theory, and on Dante. She is currently writing on Dante in contemporary culture, and working on a way to visualize Dante's cosmos through an interactive, digital model.

John A. Scott is Professor Emeritus of Italian and Honorary Senior Research Fellow at the University of Western Australia. The author of books and numerous articles on Dante, Petrarch, the Italian Renaissance, Leopardi, and Baudelaire, he is a Fellow of the Australian Academy of the Humanities and has taught at leading universities in the United States, Britain, Canada, and Australia. He is also an Honorary Life Member of the Dante Society of America.

Prue Shaw (James) is Reader Emerita in Italian at University College, London. Her edited translation with commentary of Dante's *De Monarchia* was published by Cambridge University Press in 1995.

Charles Ross is Professor of English and Chair of the Comparative Literature Program at Purdue University. A former Fulbright Scholar in Italy and winner of a National Endowment for the Humanities Grant for his translation of Boiardo's *Orlando Innamorato* (1989), he is the author of *Vladimir Nabokov: Life, Work, and Criticism* (1985), *The Custom of the Castle from Malory to Macbeth* (1997), *Elizabethan Literature and the Law of Fraudulent Conveyance: Sidney, Spenser, Shakespeare* (2003), and a verse translation of Statius's *Thebaid* (2004). His literary articles include studies of Virgil, Ariosto, and Milton. Ross is one of the editors of the *California Lectura Dantis*.

Aldo Scaglione is Professor Emeritus of Italian at New York University. His specialties are medieval and Renaissance literature and the history of linguistic theories in Italy and France. Scaglione published an edition of Boiardo's *Orlando Innamorato* (1951). His books include studies of Ariosto and Petrarch as well as *Nature and Love in the Late Middle Ages* (1963) and *Knights at Court: Courtliness, Chivalry, and Courtesy from Ottonian Germany to the Italian Renaissance* (1991). He and his wife, Jeanne, are the sponsors of several prestigious book prizes awarded by the Modern Language Association.

Maria Picchio Simonelli studied Romance Philology at the University of Florence with eminent Dante scholar Mario Casella. After establishing the graduate program in Italian at Boston College, she returned to Italy to teach at the Instituto Universitario Orientale in Naples. Her publications include editions of Dante's *Convivio* (1966) and of the collected poems of Provençal poet Bernart de Venzac (1974). She was honored by a *Festschrift,* edited by Pietro Frassica: *Studi di filologia e letteratura italiana in onore de Maria Picchio Simonelli* (1993). In 1900 she organized and edited the proceedings of the symposium *Beatrice nell'opera di Dante e nella memoria europea, 1290–1900* (1994).

Janet Levarie Smarr is Professor of Theater History and Italian Studies at the University of California, San Diego. She received her doctorate in comparative literature from Princeton University in 1975 and taught in that field for many years at the University of Illinois in Urbana-Champaign. Her books include *Italian Renaissance Tales* (1983), winner of "best translation of classical texts" award from American Association of Italian Studies; *Boccaccio and Fiammetta: The Narrator as Lover* (1986); *Boccaccio's Eclogues* (1987); and *Joining the Conversation: Renaissance Dialogues by Women* (2005); plus many articles on Italian literature of the fourteenth to sixteenth centuries. Essays on Dante include "Celestial Patterns and Symmetries in the *Vita Nuova*" (1980); "Poets of Love and Exile," (1991); and "Boccaccio Pastorale tra Dante e Petrarca" (2002).

H. Wayne Storey, Professor of Italian and Director of the Medieval Studies Institute at Indiana University, is editor of *Textual Cultures,* author of *Transcription and Visual Poetics in the Early Italian Lyric* (1993), and coeditor of *Dante for the New Millennium* (2003) and the Antenore facsimile edition and commentary of Petrarch's personal copy of the *Rerum vulgarium fragmenta* (2003–2004).

Sara Sturm-Maddox is Professor Emerita of French and Italian Studies at the University of Massachusetts, Amherst. A former member of the Council of the Dante Society of America, she has published numerous books and essays on topics in medieval and Renaissance literature and culture, including Dante and Petrarch.

Massimo Verdicchio is Professor of Italian and Comparative Literature at the University of Alberta, Canada. He is completing a book on the *Paradiso*.

Albert Wingell is Professor Emeritus of Philosophy at the University of Toronto. He has published articles on Dante and reviewed important philosophical studies of Dante's texts.

INDEX

Adam: expulsion from Eden, 383; name of, 364; in Paradise, 233; regaining of innocence, 384; sin of, 338; tree of, 361

Adrian V, Pope, 174, 211; avarice of, 207, 212, 214; Dante's homage to, 229; self-abnegation of, 218; solitude of, 208; use of Latin, 299

Aeneas: address to Venus, 227; failed embraces of, 16; guidance by Apollo, 139; shield of, 97; tour of future site of Rome, 224. *See also* Virgil, *Aeneid*

Ahasuerus (Old Testament), revenge of, 185

Alanus de Insulis, *Contra Acediam*, 198

Albertus Magnus: on the cuckoo, 114; embryology of, 278; influence on Dante, 280; pneumatology of, 278; on rational soul, 278. Works: *De laudibus Beatae Mariae Virginis*, 269; *De natura et origine animae*, 280

Aldobrandesco, Omberto, 105; in Canto XI, 107–8; death of, 107; pride of, 108; request for intercession, 108

Alighieri, Piero di Dante: on allegorical procession, 337; on charity, 134; on dietary proscriptions, 172; on *Fourth Eclogue*, 250

Allegory, nature of, 239. *See also* Procession, allegorical

Ambrose, Bishop: *Expositio super Lucam*, 367; *Hexameron*, 318; *Te lucis ante*, 68, 74, 75–76; on virginity, 259

Anchises, 286; death of, 349; enumeration of spirits, 70–71, 346–47

Angels: in Book of Revelation, 229–30; in Canto II, 14–15; in Canto VIII, 76–77; of Canto IX, 85, 92–93; of Canto XII, 124–26; in Canto XV, 151, 155–58, 161; in Canto XIX, 206; in Canto XXII, 237; in Canto XXIV, 275; in Canto XXVII, 305; in Canto XXXI, 356; in *Convivio*, 132; at gates of Dis, 204; at gates of Purgatory, 92–93; mirroring, 358; Sordello on, 77; translation of light, 157, 158

Anger: in Canto XVII, 179–82; classical writers on, 168; definitions of, 181–82; evil, 182; folly of, 167–69; pseudo-Bonaventure on, 168; righteous, 168, 186; terrace of, 151; without justice, 182

Anjou, House of: corruption of, 216; Dante's attitude toward, 221; depredations in France, 216; greed of, 213, 214

Anonymous Florentine: on Belacqua, 39; on Earthly Paradise, 318, 324; on prayer to the sun, 130–31; on steps of Purgatory, 90

Text:	10.75 / 12 Dante
Display:	Castellar
Compositor:	BVC
Binder:	Maple-Vail